HYPOTHESES *about* MARY

The Vittorio Messori Series
edited by Aurelio Porfiri

Hypotheses about Jesus

A Wager on Death

VITTORIO MESSORI

HYPOTHESES *about* MARY

Facts, Clues, Enigmas

The Vittorio Messori Series
edited by Aurelio Porfiri

SOPHIA INSTITUTE PRESS
Manchester, New Hampshire

Cover by LUCAS Art & Design, Jenison, MI

Cover image: *Icon of the Virgin Mary, Tanguirea from a Romanian Monastery* (Alamy 342820457); *County in Romania* (Shutterstock 1621064386)

Sophia Institute Press
Box 5284, Manchester, NH 03108
1-800-888-9344
www.SophiaInstitute.com

Sophia Institute Press is a registered trademark of Sophia Institute.

paperback ISBN 979-8-88911-010-1

ebook ISBN 979-8-88911-011-8

Library of Congress Control Number: application in progress

First printing

"Publie ma gloire!"

Mary to Estelle Faguette,
the visionary of Pellevoisin, 1876

Contents

Foreword
(New Italian Edition)

This book, published in 2005, has seen many reprints and numerous translations throughout the world. Now it has been released in an enlarged edition with the addition of thirteen new chapters to the original fifty. In the introductory pages of the original edition (pages which I did not modify in the least, as they seemed still capable of explaining my intentions for these "hypotheses"), I had already foreseen an expansion. I wrote, "I consider this book unfinished, as requested by its Protagonist. Therefore, I do not exclude the possibility of adding other chapters in future editions. In the pages that follow, I repeat the perception not only of theologians but also (and this is what really matters) of saints: de Maria numquam satis, *one can never say enough about Mary."*

These new chapters add other tiles to the inexhaustible mosaic of her who prophesied, "All generations will call me blessed." Despite its limits, this book seeks to offer its contribution to the fulfillment of this prophecy which, century after century, has always been realized, and which will continue to be realized generation after generation, until the end of history and the return of the Son.

May the paper of these pages be transformed into the flesh of life in faith, in active devotion, in reconciling consolation: this is my hope, this is my wish for every reader.

V. M.

Post Scriptum:

From the first chapters, Lourdes is very present throughout this book. These are glimpses into the research that has accompanied me for many years and which found its first organic arrangement in 2012, when I published Bernadette Did Not

Deceive Us. *This volume ought to be followed up by another that would complete everything the historian can say, insofar as possible, about those mysterious and luminous events that began in 1858 in the Grotto of Massabielle.*

I mention that book for readers who, stimulated by the following pages, might want to go deeper into the origins of the most famous and most visited pilgrimage site of the Catholic Church.

HYPOTHESES *about* MARY

INTRODUCTION

Mary, the Great Misunderstood

Aurelio Porfiri

In recent decades, within the Catholic Church, we have witnessed a certain unease regarding devotion to the Virgin Mary — as though belief in the Mother of the Lord were no longer suitable for "mature" Catholics. Yet our Faith tells us that this is a serious mistake, since the Virgin Mary is not an obstacle to Jesus but rather the way leading us to Him: *ad Iesum per Mariam,* "to Jesus through Mary."

We must acknowledge that a Protestant influence on Catholic thought has unfortunately led many to oppose the Mother of Jesus, making devotion to her something one might almost feel embarrassed about. This is quite strange, if you think about it, considering that the very people so often evoked by certain liturgists remain strongly attached to Marian devotion. "*De Maria numquam satis,*" says St. Bernard: we can never say enough about Mary. How many books have been written about her, how many paintings created, how many pieces of music composed? I believe the number is beyond counting.

That is why I think it is so important to read carefully a book like *Hypotheses about Mary,* a book whose very title calls to mind the most famous work by Vittorio Messori, *Hypotheses about Jesus.*

This book holds special meaning for me because it was precisely through this text that I met Vittorio Messori in person for the first time, after having been a devoted reader of his for decades. Our meeting took place in the beautiful Roman church of Sant'Andrea delle Fratte (site of a significant Marian apparition) during the official launch of *Hypotheses about Mary* by the Ares publishing house. From that first encounter, a wonderful friendship was born — one that continues to this day. It is fitting to say that our friendship began under the auspices of the Mother of Jesus. Over the years, it has blossomed further, even leading to a few collaborative efforts. This has been a great honor for me, given that Messori is one of the writers who has most influenced my intellectual and spiritual formation.

Vittorio Messori's role was significant in the challenging postconciliar period. He was among those who strove to keep Peter's barque afloat during a stormy season. Indeed, he was able to do so in his capacity as a layman and journalist, yet his influence extended palpably to many within the clergy as well. We recall in particular his rapport with two popes: he interviewed St. John Paul II in 1994, yielding the famous work *Crossing the Threshold of Hope*, and he interviewed Benedict XVI in 1985, when he was still Cardinal Joseph Ratzinger, for a book that caused quite a stir: *The Ratzinger Report*. In speaking with me from time to time, Messori has confided some of his memories, telling me of his great esteem for these figures — a sentiment they evidently reciprocated.

Knowing him and his profound Marian devotion, I believe *Hypotheses about Mary* is one of his dearest works. It is the fruit of many years of research, and, in reading it, you will discover countless details that will enrich your understanding of the Blessed Virgin Mary and her place in the plan of salvation.

I believe Vittorio Messori could easily adopt as his own the words of St. Alphonsus Maria de' Liguori from *The Glories of Mary*:

> My most beloved Redeemer and Lord Jesus Christ, I, your miserable servant, know how much you delight in those who seek to glorify your Most Holy Mother, whom you so love and whom you so desire to see loved and honored by all. That is why I decided to bring forth this book, which speaks of her glories. I therefore do not know to whom I could more suitably recommend it than to you, who take such care in ensuring the glory of your Mother. I thus dedicate and commend it to you. Accept this little offering of love that I have for you and for your beloved Mother. Protect it by showering upon all who read it the light of trust and flames of love for this Immaculate Virgin, in whom you have placed the hope and refuge of all the redeemed. In return for my poor effort, grant me, I

> beg you, that love for Mary which, through my small work, I desired to see enkindled in all who will read it. To you also, my sweetest Lady and my Mother Mary, I turn. You know well that next to Jesus I have placed all my hope for eternal salvation in you; for I acknowledge that everything good in me — my conversion, my calling to leave the world, and every other grace I have received from God — has been granted through you.

I believe there are no more fitting words than these to encourage everyone to read this work — a reading that will take some time but is sure to bring forth many spiritual fruits.

INTRODUCTION: (NEW ITALIAN EDITION)
A Mother Who Defends Her Son

Gaude, Maria Virgo:
Cunctas haereses
Sola interemisti
In universe mundo

Antiphon for the Feast
of the Annunciation, Eighth Century

All that has been collected in this book is the result of the review, updating, and completion of what I published, month after month, in the journal *Jesus* from 1995 to 2000, in a column that I called "Marian Diary."

This was not an attempt at recycling things tied to extemporaneity or to journalistic improvisation. This is not a random hodgepodge but the result of an intentional and premeditated project, whatever its merits might be.

Allow me to be more precise. At the end of 1978, two years after the unforeseen and amazing impact provoked by my first book, *Hypotheses about Jesus*, I left *La Stampa* in Turin, where I had been working for years on the cultural insert. I confess that it was with some regret that I quit that newspaper, the place where I had made my professional debut, and left the city so dear to me. But I had no other choice.

In fact, I felt the need to continue my reflections, my research, and my writing on religious themes, Christian ones in particular. Time and energy were being robbed from me by the demands of quite different topics, those I had to face every day for the newspaper of which I was an editor. It was no longer possible for me to neglect studying a book on biblical exegesis or ecclesial history or the exchange of ideas with a good theologian (and they do still exist . . .) to listen to the platitudes of an Alberto Moravia[1] and his peers in one more interview; or to spend hours in the newsroom typesetting material concerning an insipid "culture" that presented itself moreover, with all its intolerance, as the only true one. And all along, the drastic Gospel injunction ran through my head: "the blind leading the blind."

The personal need to deal with the real Problem, the one whose light illuminates all others, met with the pressing request of a crowd of readers, not only Italian, asking me to continue my research. How could I waste my life at the service of questions so often ephemeral and irrelevant like the ones in the "cultural section" of the secular media?

The solution to my distress was offered to me by the Pauline Periodicals Group, which was programming a religious monthly under the most demanding of names: *Jesus*. I accepted the proposal to participate in its creation and launch, and from the first edition, under the title "Dialogues with Jesus," I published encounters with interlocutors from around the world who might have something meaningful to say about the gospel, both in affirming it and in denying it. This commitment lasted for years, and its results flowed into a book: *Investigations into Christianity*. Those "dialogues," which I carried out with passion (I was finally free of the sensation of wasting time), proved not to be entirely vacuous, seeing that the book is still in print.

After having tested in the field the reasons for and difficulties with the gospel in the contemporary world, interrogating people of every creed and incredulity, I perceived the need to return to investigating the foundations using the foundational texts of the Faith. To return, I say, because "The Case for Christ," the column that started appearing in *Jesus* in 1988, was the continuation of the work begun with *Hypotheses about Jesus*. From the investigative work of digging word by word into the Easter narratives, two books were born: *He Suffered under Pontius Pilate?* and *They Say He Is Risen*.

Once again, the generous attention of readers was not lacking. Was it due to a lack of anything better, seeing the desert of Catholic culture? This

1 The pseudonym of Alberto Pincherle (1907–1990), an Italian novelist.

suspicion is well founded, although it did not prevent me from persevering in continuing my work.

After seven years of work on the historicity of the narratives of the Paschal Mystery, in 1995 a new column began: "Marian Notebook." I chose the pages of the monthly magazine for this project because I found that the method of publishing "by installments" was advantageous for the books deriving from it. In fact, it allows more time for the elaboration of the text, it subjects writings to the prior judgment of readers (always open-minded in their observations and criticism) and it allows a meditated review at the moment of collection into a unified volume, after the material had been deposited, so to speak.

From the Son to the Mother, therefore. The term "notebook" indicates all that has characterized this work. A series of reflections, in-depth analyses, experiences, quotes, small and large discoveries, written down in a little notebook carried everywhere: to the library, on journeys, to church. Everything centered on the mystery of the Woman of Nazareth.

In these pages I have explored not only theology, but also history, exegesis, apparitions, literature, shrines, and devotion. Pages that are meant to be "colorful," at times surprising, where reflection on dogma is accompanied by anecdotes, historical investigation by current events—and where, if necessary, polemical barbs and mordant comments are not avoided: always well-motivated and never beyond the pale, and in the awareness that not all opinions are worthy of respect. There are opinions that are not to be respected but to be rejected, and if necessary, to be contradicted. Whereas the people who express them, and of whom we are not the judge, are indeed to be respected. Christian tolerance is for people, not for their ideas, dutifully exposed to debate and if necessary to refutation. The well-known distinction between a person's error and the erroneous person holds true.

This duty to disagree applies always and only, one must understand, on the terrain of free debate, far from all nostalgia for censure or worse, for coercion, which have nothing to do with the freedom to believe or not to believe, which God desires to safeguard at all costs.

This is a matter that concerns the vivacity of the journalist, but accompanied by the obligation of rigor and precision which is required of the scholar. To toil like a diligent professor and to write like an expert journalist is an acceptable working motto. As with all my preceding books, I have not used footnotes, but the reader knows by now that there is nothing to fear: behind every affirmation and all information there is a carefully sifted bibliography and secure sources, and research carried out over the course of decades. Popularizing a theme does not always mean being approximate.

Naturally, the personal character of this work has left its mark abundantly: for example, my attraction to Lourdes and affection for Bernadette are evident, given that the waters of the Gave de Pau[2] seem to flow everywhere. But I repeat, this is not a treatise; these pages are the revelations of a personal diary. And the Grotto of the Pyrenees is worthy (for the reasons we all know and for others that I shall attempt to point out) of a position of significance, almost a test case of the nature and the style of the Virgin.

But why was this book needed in the first place? Why these years of work, travel, and reading on the "*Madonna*," as the people of God call her? Among the many letters I received after the publication of the first book back in distant 1976, there were some from readers who, saying they were satisfied with it, exhorted me to write another, to concentrate on "hypotheses of Mary." I confess that such a proposal seemed extravagant at the time.

Like all "converts" (I employ this demanding word with hesitation, and in any case with humility), the light of my encounter with Christ had blinded me, preventing me from seeing anything else. In fact, in that book, born of the sudden discovery of a faith I had rejected above all because I had ignored it, Mary was not treated at all. She was not even mentioned. The Mother, as has been observed and as I experienced myself, is discovered *later*, when one has entered into intimacy with the Son, and this allows one to enter "into her home." One realizes then that this discreet presence is in fact essential, that it is not an extra, an accessory that can be added or not, a devotion to be tolerated in bigoted old people, that she is not the "diversion" that prevents you from concentrating only on Jesus. On the contrary!

Through the incursions by which these chapters progress, I would like to show what I experienced: without the root of flesh which is that Woman, the entire mystery of the Incarnation ends up losing its indispensable materiality

[2] Editor's Note: A river that runs through southwestern France, including Lourdes.

and becomes evanescent spiritualism, sermonizing moralism, or worse, dangerous ideology. "Mariology" is not "the tumor of Catholicism" as certain Protestant professors still hold today, but the logical and organic development of gospel postulates. It is not an illegitimate excrescence of Christology, but rather one of its fundamental chapters, without which one of the supports to its stability would be lacking. According to the ancient liturgical proclamation we shall quote numerous times in these pages (and which history has always confirmed), Mary is "the destroyer of every heresy." Her maternal function of protecting her Son continues, and will continue until the Parousia.

I will not insist further, given that so much will be said on these affirmations in the following pages. There is a chapter (the twentieth) where, with the help of the teaching of Benedict XVI, I cite some of the possible answers to the questions: "But why should we concern ourselves with Mary? Why should we continue to give her the place that Tradition has granted her by means of an in-depth analysis that has lasted twenty centuries, which constitutes a scandal for some and which is instead a treasure for which Catholicism ought to be grateful and jealous?"

François Mauriac, an "adult and critical" Catholic (as the hendiadys of today would have it) and certainly not a clerical Catholic, wrote, "We must not distance ourselves from Our Lady for the sake of drawing near to those who have rejected and relegated her to the corner. We must give her back to them, showing them the treasure they have lost. There is a fraternal charity in ecumenism that should be practiced also, and perhaps above all, in regard to Mary and her veneration. It is a duty to share one's wealth and not stoop to the indigence of others."

Yet another meaningful quote comes from John Henry Newman, the great Anglican theologian who knocked on the door of the Church of Pius IX and then became a cardinal. Holding Newman back for so long from taking this step was also, if not above all, what the Reformed communities born in the sixteenth century call "Mariolatry." But, as a good English empiricist, it was precisely his experience that led the Anglican theologian to reflect, "If we take a look at Europe, we find that those who have stopped worshipping the Divine Son and have moved on to a mundane humanism, are not the people who are distinguished for their Marian devotion, but precisely those that have rejected this devotion. Zeal for the glory of the Son has been extinguished wherever this was no longer joined with ardor for the exaltation of the Mother. Catholics, unjustly accused of worshipping a creature instead of the Creator, still worship Him. While their accusers who had presumed to be worshipping God with greater purity and fidelity to Scripture, have ceased to worship Him."

And so, what has guided me along the paths of "Mariology" is not a devotion that is an end in itself. It is my anxiety for the situation of faith in Christ threatened (as always, but perhaps more today than ever) by errors, deviations, and pollutions for which the Mother has the decisive remedies, available by simply preserving and reiterating the place that is her due.

I shall stop here because, as I have said, I do not want to anticipate what will be said in reflections to be developed over some fifty stages. These are not few, but they could have been many more as well, if it had not been necessary to come to an end, provisional as it may be. If, as has been said, "a book cannot be concluded, only interrupted," how much more so for this one that treats such a subject! During the years of its publication in *Jesus*, I had confirmation every month of the inexhaustibility of this theme that might seem circumscribed, negligible, based entirely on a few words from Scripture. And yet, my problem was never one of penury but rather of abundance, the embarrassment of having to choose which theme to dedicate the installment to, so many were the possibilities and the accumulated material.

For this reason as well, I consider these "hypotheses" an unfinished book, as its Protagonist demands. Therefore, I do not exclude the possibility of adding other chapters in coming editions. I repeat more than once in the following pages the affirmation of theologians but also (and this is what really matters) of saints: *de Maria numquam satis*, one can never say enough about Mary.

Even without extensions, this volume already has conspicuous dimensions. But the reader should not be startled by this. Precisely because it sprang from monthly installments, every chapter (except for a few exceptions when a topic required a two-part treatment) can be read separately. The reader can pick a starting point almost at random. Some repetition has been left insofar as it was necessary for situating and comprehending the topic of that chapter.

Among the various challenges I have set for myself is that of seeking to demonstrate that it is possible to love, venerate, and praise the Virgin Mary as she is worthy to be (to the unfathomable depths) without falling into a certain *kitsch* style. By this I mean the soothing tones, the inflected voice, the choirs of children, the flower bouquets, the languor, the saccharine fervor, the appeals to sentimentalism which are the contrary of sentiment. This latter is necessary when speaking of the Mother. But it is appropriate also not to fall into a syrupy treacle which, my personal experience tells me, distances rather than attracts those who are outside the circle of such devotionalism.

Every temperament, charism, and sensibility ought to be respected, and even fostered. The more the Church is "catholic," the more it is variegated and hospitable to every human expression, insofar as it lies within the confines of the Creed. No one stands more in solidarity than do I with the proverbial old lady and her rosary, or is so enamored of this simple, solid faith of the pilgrim people with whom I associate myself. The world of the "*fioretti*" and the "inspired elevations" of preachers and perhaps even writers is quite welcome, whose best intentions are not to be questioned and whose style can be profitable to some.

But in the name of that same "catholicity" there must also be room for a devotion that is both convinced and virile, profound and allergic to all rhetoric. A devotion founded on meditation of the mystery of that Steadfast Woman who intoned the *Magnificat,* which certainly was not the hymn of some exhausted devotionalism. The Steadfast Woman who at Cana knew how to say with serene determination (and this is, if we think about it, the synthesis of her role, the heart of her mission, what she herself repeats at every one of her apparitions): "Do whatever he tells you."

CHAPTER 1

LOURDES: FALSIFIERS AT WORK

IN 1820, A PRINTER named Giuseppe Pomba founded a publishing house in Turin which, in 1854, was to take the name "*Unione tipografica editrice torinese*" or UTET. This publisher has survived down to our days with undeniable prestige thanks to its catalogue of high-level works, despite the threat posed by the relentless march of the Internet to all publishers, especially in the scientific sector.

The same precision and completeness were to characterize the volume released for the first time in 1979 in large format (later reprinted and updated numerous times) under the title *Universal Chronology*. Its thirteen hundred dense pages line up more than thirty-five thousand charts that, beginning with the Paleozoic era and ending in our own days, order year by year all the events relevant to human history on every continent. "Events" should be understood here in a broad sense: not only politics, wars, battles, alliances, but also scientific inventions, literary works, social events, even curiosities and significant anecdotes. In fact, it displays an extravagant thoroughness, without consideration of effort or means.

Despite this stated ambition to register every aspect of the human adventure, it is particularly significant that, for 1858, this *Universal Chronology* opens by recalling the assassination attempt by Felice Orsini on Napoleon III and then continues for many columns, registering even the posthumous publication of a novel by the Armenian writer Khachatur Abovian, but is silent about what happened that same year on the eleventh of February.

Indeed, as confirmed in the meticulous analytical index, among the thirty-five thousand charts of this work it was not considered opportune to include one event in particular, however small, that marked the beginning of a unique religious adventure, which would not remain exclusive to an intimate circle of devotees but would involve (as it continues to do so today) tens of millions of people from around the world. The editors of the *Chronology* did not forget that 1858 was the year in which Francesco De Sanctis wrote the essay entitled *Schopenhauer and Leopardi* and that William Thompson Kelvin invented the mirror galvanometer, while the treaty between China and Russia granted to the latter the left bank of the Amur River. Reminding their readers of these events and many others, they did not consider relevant that one Bernadette Soubirous bore witness to having been the protagonist of "something" that would have as one of its effects the transforming of an until then insignificant town at the foot of the Pyrenees into the most frequented destination in France and perhaps in all Europe, with over fifty thousand hotel beds.

But the same distraction can be found when one peruses, for example, the dense columns dedicated to 1917, where one learns among other things that in this year Canada instituted obligatory military service, that the excommunicate priest Alfred Loisy published his work *Religion*, that the New Jazz Age was born in Chicago with the advent of the Dixieland Style, and so on. But not the least mention, not even this time, to what began in that 1917 on May 13, in the remote Portuguese village known as Fatima.

Yet, here too, ignoring the religious dimension and limiting oneself to mere social, demographic, and economic reflexes, one can certainly not say that the "encounter" of which the three shepherds were witnesses was irrelevant. But not the least mention of Fatima, while a full page was given to the comedian Raffaele Viviani, who in 1917 debuted at the Theater Umberto in Naples with the sketch *'O vico*.

Are we to be scandalized by such "lacunae" of information? Despite appearances, this would not seem appropriate. No, it is not justified to indulge in scrutinizing hidden motives, suspecting bias, or censuring as anti-Catholic the zealous editors in this prestigious collaboration on Italian publishing's most complete *Chronology*.

These editors suffer from neither bias nor hostility, but are simply unknowing hostages of the deformation that has characterized for centuries now the outlook of an intellectual world for which only politics, economics, and culture (understood in a limited secular sense) have relevance and the right to the attention of realistic and serious people. From a similar perspective, religious realities that are not mixed with politics or not subjected to socioeconomic analysis are irrelevant; they are considered an expression of an anachronistic subculture not worth registering. Even less so if those "religious realities" concern something vapid, clumsy, ill-advised, or politically incorrect, such as a presumed "Marian apparition"! Merely recording something of this sort — a matter that belongs to a dimension not suitable to an adult, educated person — would disqualify a work from being esteemed as academically rigorous.

Who is this hysterical girl known to devotees as Bernadette? Who are these poor Portuguese shepherd children named Lucia, Jacinta, Francisco? Who do they think they are to presume a place next to the illustrious names of those who have "made history," *real* history? What role could they ever have had in events for these devotees (religious bigots, no doubt) that would merit inclusion in the chronology of culture, politics, and economics?

As concerns Lourdes, for example, the "serious" historian will study the political relationships that those presumedly prodigious events affected, in particular between the world of French Catholicism and the ecclesiastical strategy of Louis Bonaparte, proclaimed "Emperor of the French" six years earlier. Or the scholar will investigate the phenomena of popular religiosity among the "subordinate classes" of the mid-nineteenth century in southwestern France.

This is how it is usually done. This is not what we shall do. This notebook is guided by a certainty that is regarded as absurd by what the New Testament calls "the wisdom of the world." Namely, the certainty that, despite all appearances, history and especially the history "that counts" takes place and is incarnated in personalities that are irrelevant for those who do not acknowledge the perspective of faith. Guiding us, therefore, is the certainty that a secure way for understanding both the little chronicle belonging to each of us and the great history of all humanity is found in overturning the usual tables of value and reflecting on the mystery of the Mother of Him who thanked the Father, because what really matters "is hidden from the wise and learned" while "it is revealed to the little ones," to those who are ignorant according to the world.

We are among those who stubbornly suspect that the destiny of the world is decided, mysteriously, much more where people pray than where people govern, command, do business, and study; that history therefore is made by the proverbial anonymous old ladies who run their rosary beads through their fingers, more than by the great ones in politics, economy, and culture in their palaces, offices, and academies.

At any rate, if this were not the case, where would we find that "scandal," where would we find that "folly" that characterizes the gospel, according to one who understood these matters, a certain Paul? If this were not the case, what would the Christian paradox be? Where would its foolishness be, in the eyes of those to whom the profound vision of faith was not given and to whom believers have the duty, with humility and respect, to propose the proper perspective? What type of believers would they be if they were not convinced that in 1870, the destiny of the world passed through places like the infirmary in Nevers, where Sr. Marie-Bernarde (Soubirous, in the world) completed her martyrdom of chronic illness, rather than places like the Chancellery of Berlin, where Otto von Bismarck celebrated his political and military triumphs?

And so, let us begin our journey of discovery, or rediscovery, of the Marian mystery precisely from that year 1858, in which the most important event was not the Plombières Agreement between Napoleon II and Cavour, as "positive" historians might think, but was (to use the words of Pope John, who was a tender and tenacious devotee) "the sudden opening wide of a window onto Heaven from a grotto."

Those who know the history of those apparitions and the extraordinary consequences they have had for a multitude of souls whom only God knows, and for the entire Church, have the duty of vigilance that this unexpected and unhoped-for gift be protected from every suspicion. "Lourdes needs only the truth," the great bishop of Tarbes, Pierre-Marie Théas, replied in 1954, paternally and insistently, to those who considered imprudent the publication of all the documents by the young historian René Laurentin, whom he had asked to establish with scientific precision what had really happened. This truth can and must counter those who have sought every means, even fraudulent propaganda, to insinuate doubt about the genuineness of all that happened on the banks of the Gave de Pau.

Thus, we would like to begin by considering a false document. It is worthwhile because those lines were not limited to provoking dismay among believers and enthusiasm among skeptics during the early years of the 1900s, when they were produced and published. As we ourselves have been able to verify, the perplexity (to use a euphemism) sown by this fictional work has continued to spread and reemerges in our own days as well. The denunciation of the forgery, with unassailable confutation, seems to be confined to old (and by now forgotten), nearly inaccessible Catholic publications of that period. Thus, it often happens even today that one runs into newspapers and books which, with the pedantry of the *demi-savants,* smile at the gullible who still do not realize that "the supposed apparitions of Lourdes were known beforehand, expected, prepared and organized."

The above-quoted words are verbatim those of Jean de Bonnefon, an anti-Catholic polemicist who, in 1906, published a 280-page pamphlet in Paris under the unequivocal title *Lourdes et ses tenanciers*: literally, "Lourdes and Its Innkeepers," where the reference to "innkeepers" in the French implied "houses of ill-repute." This reference was not random, as the closure of the apparition shrine was requested not only in the name of science and the fight against speculation to the harm of the unwary, but also in the cause of hygiene. Impelled by the political and cultural elite of the French Third Republic carrying out an unrelenting fight against the Church, those were the years in which the army dragged the Carthusians, declared suppressed, out of the Great Chartreuse, which was confiscated by the state. The estate of Lourdes as well was taken from religious who had been chased away, and so the book had a vast resonance and corresponding popularity. Moreover, it was widely recognized that Bonnefon was not an amateur but rather an insidious polemicist: thus, the forgeries and the fictional works were mixed with authentic documents from the archives. And so, the book had a "scientific" appearance that left many impressed, even Catholics, who had been targeted already on the literary level in the sensational novel by Zola, *Lourdes,* which came out in 1894. At any rate, precisely because it was inserted into a work full of references to archives and sources, it derived (and perhaps still does today) the insidious nature of the document that interests us now, in which (as Bonnefon wrote) "it is enough to prove without appeal" that the facts in the Pyrenees had already been foreseen by the authorities, being the fruit of a machination hatched by priests.

The pamphleteer published a letter signed by Pierre-Claude Falconnet, the general prosecutor at the Tribunal of Pau, which had jurisdiction over the territory of Lourdes. Those who know the history of the apparitions will recognize the rigid and hostile role that Falconnet played in the turbulent initial period.

On December 28, 1857, forty-five days before February 11, 1858, the date of the first apparition, the general prosecutor Falconnet had written to his subordinate, the imperial prosecutor at the Tribunal of Lourdes, Vital Dutour, the letter published for the first time by Jean de Bonnefon in 1906 and which we translate here verbatim.

> DISTRICT ATTORNEY'S OFFICE OF THE IMPERIAL COURT OF PAU
>
> Sir imperial district attorney, I have been informed of the manifestations simulating [*affectants*] a supernatural character and feigning a miraculous appearance, being prepared for the end of the year. I beg you to be vigilant that these events be carefully overseen. I need to know the details in order to ascertain under which articles of the penal Code they can be prosecuted. I fear you have little on which to rely in the local civil or religious administration, in your support. Our duty is to do what is necessary to avoid the repetition of scandals similar to that in La Salette: since the religious motive [*ressort*] hides a political motive.
>
> Best wishes …
> The district attorney,
> Signed, Falconnet.

It suffices to skim through similar passages to be startled: if authentic, this is a devastating document that tears the edifying veil of Lourdes, revealing a swarm of dark deceits. And Bernadette, she who would be solemnly enrolled by the Church into its canon of saints, suddenly appears either to be an accomplice in a stunningly successful fraud or the poor unsuspecting instrument of a cynical conspiracy.

The uproar caused at the time by the publication of this letter is therefore understandable. But to concern ourselves with it today is not a matter of erudite archaeology, indulging in the curiosity of reevoking a question from the *Belle Époque* that has been closed forever. The "Forgery of Bonnefon," as historians of all stripes (even non-Catholics) have been calling it for some time now, seems to have had a tenacious persistence: it emerges here and there and is still quoted, without ever citing its confutations. We know that what is often lacking to the Catholic world of our day is historical memory.

We affirm, therefore, that it is opportune to return to the search for the reasons that expose this fictional work: Lourdes is much too serious, although it is obviously not dogma. It has been too close and too deeply involved in the faith of the people of God for some time now that we should tolerate shadows of the faintest doubt. Experience shows that, in similar cases, even the least crevice in trust in the veracity of the facts can have ruinous consequences. At stake here is a canonization ("infallible" according to theologians), a proper in the liturgical office (*lex orandi, lex credenda* ...), an encyclical (of Pius XII, in 1957), and an infinite number of other events and words at every ecclesiastical level. From Pius IX to John Paul II, all the popes without exception have "committed" the entire Church without hesitation to the supernatural reality of Lourdes. It is even more perilous to forget the reasons that led to the rejection of forgeries, still at work, that seek to obscure the light that was lit in that grotto.

Let us investigate, then. Bonnefon's work was a forgery not only because, when challenged to produce the original or to indicate the archive from which it might have been taken, the scholar confessed he could not do so. He had written that the letter was "a definite testimonial," which proved "without appeal" that the "apparition" had been foreseen and was thus the fruit of dark machinations. But when required to demonstrate that this "testimony" was truly "certain," as he stated, he simply replied that a copy of the text had been supplied to him by a vague "intermediary." Thus, while nearly all the other documents of his book are given the precise indication of the archive or source from which they were taken, the explosive letter of the district attorney of Pau to his subordinate in Lourdes refers only to itself, asking to be considered authentic (introducing moreover a new element into such a controversial topic!) without the least confirmation.

This is obviously so contrary to the methods of historiography that it justifies the words of Georges Bertrin, author of the weighty *Histoire critiques des évènements de Lourdes,* which tore to pieces ("without appeal") the pseudo service note of Falconnet: "Similar documents, presented without any reference, are absolutely lacking in authority: historical criticism considers them as inexistent; there is not a tribunal in the world that, in the most modest of cases, would accept to give it the least credence."

Bertrin added,

> If this presumed letter were authentic, it would have been published long ago. It has been half a century [Bertrin wrote in 1908] that the friends and adversaries of Lourdes have been rummaging through the archives. Yet no one had quoted this document. After fifty years of research, a writer not even from this region, who has only passed through here, had the strange good fortune of discovering in the dossier what no one else had discovered up to that point! At any rate, if this is truly how matters unfolded, on what other occasion than this would it have been indispensable to arm oneself with all the precautions to be beyond reproof? And on the other hand, such a document is presented without the least guarantees demanded: the historian tells us neither where he found it, nor where it is, nor where it can be consulted if, as is fitting, one wants to verify it.

But there is more. Not only had no scholar before Bonnefon's *pamphlétaire* ever produced this letter, but not one of the contemporary figures in the case made any reference to it — not even the sender or the recipient.

René Laurentin, as we mentioned, is the preeminent expert on Lourdes, having dedicated a lifetime of research to it, which flowed into seven large volumes of *Documents authentiques*, into the six volumes of *Histoire des apparitions*, and into a myriad of other works, all dedicated to those events and to their protagonists, beginning with Bernadette. Laurentin, writing sixty years after his colleagues who immediately clashed with Bonnefon, is equally severe: "We can be sure that the document attributed to the district attorney is, beyond a shadow of a doubt, a forgery."

Laurentin also pointed out, of course, the lack of any indication of the place where the original letter had been found, and synthesized thus the aspect to which we alluded above: "The letter cannot be authentic also because it contradicts everything we know with certainty about the events of Lourdes; because it is an element of incoherence in a whole in which everything fits together." In fact,

> on numerous occasions, the district attorney Falconnet, proud opponent of the truth of the apparitions, reprimands his substitute in Lourdes, Vital Dutour, whom he accused of negligence. If Falconnet had truly sent him some weeks earlier the "service note" that Bonnefon attributes to him, Dutour, as scrupulous as a

> man could be, would have been more capable of accounting for the apparitions: and he would have done so, naturally, making reference to the precise and explicit warning so recently received from his hierarchical superior. If he had not done so, he would have merited the rebuke of not having taken into consideration the warning he received from the authority to whom he owed obedience.

Furthermore (still quoting Laurentin), "If Falconnet had known of a conspiracy like the one he denounces in the document bearing his signature, he would have immediately informed his superiors in Paris." We know with certainty that this did not happen, and we know this thanks to a document that the forger Bonnefon shows he ignores. We have the text of the report that Falconnet wrote at the beginning of January 1858, giving an account to the Ministry of Justice about the situation in the Departments of the Pyrenees over the last six months of 1857 — that is, precisely the period in which the magistrate would have received news of a conspiracy in Lourdes. Yet not only is there not one mention of this in the lengthy semiannual report to Paris, but Falconnet even summarizes the situation in the territory under his competency: "Public peace has never been so complete, nor authority more respected. We begin the year under happy auspices." It is impossible to suppose that a magistrate of this stature and enjoying this level of esteem from his government would alarm his subordinate and at the same time fail to warn his immediate superior, the severe Minister of Justice of the semi-dictatorial government of Napoleon III.

But there is still more, and it concerns precisely the contacts between the district attorney and the minister. Writing to the latter in another report on April 20 (the penultimate apparition, the seventeenth, had taken place on the seventh of that month, and the affair had by this time involved the entire region and was reaching Paris), Falconnet himself said, "This is not a situation similar to that of Rosa Tamisier, who had organized a miracle. Here, the little girl is hallucinating but straightforward, sincere [*loyale*]. She saw or believed she saw."

Because this letter was published by Bonnefon as well, Bertrin is right in commenting:

> Our author did not realize that, in this manner, he gave the lie astonishingly to the presumed "service note" of Falconnet. And from whom? From Falconnet himself, who had first announced that the story of the apparitions had been prepared in the shadows. But then he announced to the minister that he believed the exact opposite: as distinct from other cases, the affair had not been organized; Marie-Bernarde Soubirous can be deceived, but she acts in good faith!

Of the presumed expectation of pseudo-miraculous manifestations there is not the least trace, not even in the minutes of the many, persuasive, often violent interrogations to which not only Bernadette but also her parents, relatives, and friends were subjected.

Let us read once more in this regard the author of the *Histoire des évènements*, Georges Bertrin:

> Consider Dominique Jacomet, the police commissioner of Lourdes, capable and zealous, who had declared war on what he called "the superstition." If the district attorney Dutour had truly received the order from his superior to be on guard against events prepared by hidden hands, he would have immediately warned the police commissioner, charging him to be vigilant. Yet, Jacomet always ignored this supposed conspiracy. For confirmation of this, we need only turn to the long interrogation to which he subjected Bernadette.

In fact, taking up Bertrin's narrative again, on that dramatic occasion (it was Sunday, February 21, the day of the sixth apparition), the terrible police chief

> sought to intimidate the girl, not backing down in the least. He told her he would have the gendarme arrest her. When the miller Soubirous came to get his daughter, he ordered him to prohibit her from visiting the grotto, threatening both with prison if they failed to obey. And when the occasion would be more favorable, when the moment of revealing the fraud and closing the case with a single word had come, resting on the weight of an official letter that revealed how the comedy had been prepared in order to abuse popular credulity, the commissioner said nothing, absolutely nothing, of the supposed warning of the higher judicial authority. He did not make the least allusion to it. Evidently, he ignored it. But if he too were to ignore it, the first one who would have been informed by

> the district attorney of Lourdes, the conclusion is certain: that the warning never existed.

Furthermore, Bertrin insists, "the height of the falsehood is that the addressee himself, the one who is said to have received the letter, the imperial district attorney, Monsieur Dutour, even ignores the document. Never does he mention it, not even on the occasion in which it would have been impossible for him to keep silent about it, had it ever existed."

Nor can any trace of it be found anywhere else: not in newspapers or private letters, nor in private conversations; not even in the controversies that arose immediately afterward. Nothing before 1906, when Jean de Bonnefon came out with his surprise, announcing the "proof without appeal" of the fraud of the century. In reality, it is certain that he himself was the one seeking to deceive, out of his biased spirit, if he was the one who created the forgery.

At this point, the case should be quite clear, and we could interrupt our examination of it, having exhumed from the old papers long forgotten by Catholics themselves more than sufficient elements for clearing the playing field of any doubts about the pseudo-revelations of Jean de Bonnefon.

Yet, we cannot resist the temptation to continue. An examination of the fictional letter of Pierre-Claude Falconnet turns up a number of pearls which, while confirming that this is the work of a counterfeiter, show that he was not able to escape the fate prophesied by the popular proverb: "The devil teaches us his tricks but not how to hide them."

CHAPTER 2

The Mishaps of the Apocryphal Work

As announced at the end of the preceding chapter, we shall now complete the list of reasons that lead us to condemn as a forgery the letter that the district attorney of Pau wrote to his subordinate in Lourdes at the end of 1857. The letter, published only in 1906, asserts that "the apparitions in the grotto were nothing more than a successful machination for exploiting public credulity."

The quoted expression is taken from a recent publication which (unfortunately not the only case) continues to take seriously the fictional letter whose echoes can be heard even in our day. It is still possible to hear discussion of a "decisive document." Exposing it, without leaving the least doubt in the reader's mind, is important also for reasons listed in a study in the *Revue pratique d'apologétique,* a long-running publication in France begun in the early 1800s and which is still an important journal. Its annual collections are a mine of rigorous news (the biggest names of European Catholic intellectual circles collaborated in it) and surprising above all to Catholics who are afraid of investigating too deeply into the reasons for the Faith. Faith is a gift of God indeed, a mystery that demands a "wager," that obliges us to trust. But it still remains "reasonable": Are not the faculties of the human intellect also a gift that is right and proper to use to the best of our ability? Next to the *credo ut intelligam* ("I believe in order to understand"), which highlights the gratuitous aspect of divine revelation that culminates in Christ, Catholic tradition has always firmly placed the *intelligo ut credam* ("I understand in order to believe"), which refers to the rational aspect of faith.

Thus, the *Revue* praised above wrote,

> If the letter published by Jean de Bonnefon were authentic, the consequences might extend well beyond the events of Lourdes. In fact, de Bonnefon wanted not only to prove that those apparitions had been prepared. Given that it was the clergy, as he insinuates, who organized the fraud, the intention was to show that "priests" in general are capable of having recourse always and everywhere to any sort of swindle and deceit, for the sake of their ideas or personal interest.

If the clergy had spun a web to trap the gullible back in 1858 in the Pyrenees, why would they not do so in other places, on other occasions, in other circumstances? Are not shrines, beginning with Lourdes, the places where they siphon money out of the faithful and fill the minds of the simple and unwary with legends and myths?

Behind this fictional work we are examining, there lies the intention to cast suspicion on the entire ecclesial attitude toward supernatural manifestations — a suspicion that is the more necessary to polemicists, the more the historical reality testifies to the contrary. The facts of Lourdes were imposed upon the Church: she was not the one to impose them. Everyone knows the attitude assumed by Bernadette's parish priest, Fr. Dominique Peyramale, at the start of the extraordinary adventure. This man with "a heart of gold but thick-skinned, diffident if not hostile to popular credulity" can be accused of anything but an equivocal complicity with the tales of the little Soubirous.

Although everyone knows this, very few know about the letter which Gustave Rouland, the Minister of Religious Affairs in the government of Napoleon III, wrote to his colleague the Minister of Justice on May 20, 1858. Four months after the first apparition, Rouland observed that the clergy (not only in Tarbes, the diocese where the events took place, but also throughout France, seeing that word had already reached Paris) there reigned *une grande defiance,* great diffidence toward what was being said about the events in Lourdes.

The generous and fiery Louis Veuillot, loved and hated, exalted and vilified layman and chief editor at *L'Univers,* the most influential Catholic daily of the time, and the apple of Pius IX's eye, already in July of 1858 met with Bernadette, struck by the perfume of the gospel that accompanied her and thus persuaded by the radical genuineness of her testimony ("She's an ignorant girl. But she's better than me!" he exclaimed immediately after interrogating her). So Veuillot had to wager the full weight of his enormous prestige in the Church of the time, in a series of articles disseminated in brochures as well, to win over that "grande defiance" that reigned especially among the clergy and which persisted at least until the official recognition by the bishop, Bertrand-Sévère Laurence. When the apparitions were referred to him, Bishop Laurence refused to believe them. He responded flatly to those saying that it was not the duty of the Church to go looking for "proofs"; on the contrary, it was the duty of the "beautiful lady" to provide them. As the pressure from the faithful increased, by now convinced, the bishop waited nearly six months before nominating a commission, which then proceeded to take its time. The decision came only after four more years.

This is nothing new. It has always been this way, as recent cases of rumors of apparitions demonstrate, and as is generally true of "supernatural" events. Every time, popular fervor clashes against reservation it results in slowdowns, silence, or exhortations to prudence (if not to skepticism) by the clergy. We must not be scandalized by this: on the contrary, it is good and just that this is the case. Essential to ecclesial dynamics is the balancing of weights and counterweights: in the Church, the gift of charisms, ever present throughout its life, must be controlled and ordered by the institution. The visionary and the canonist, the prophet and the curial official, the enthusiast and the realist, the shepherdess and the bishop are not irreconcilable personalities, but rather complementary. Each role must exist, and each must be carried out to avoid allowing the Church to become, on one side, an anarchical community of visionaries, fanatics, and real or presumed charismatics; or on the other side, a sort of multinational, a corporation of liturgical services held together by the dryness of canon law and the Realpolitik of clerical functionaries.

If Bernadette is a gift, her diffident parish priest is no less a gift, as is her impassible bishop, and the pragmatic monsignors of the curia, both diocesan and Vatican, who examined the credibility of the facts. That the important truth about the grotto might be established, it was indispensable (as in every case of this sort) that the immediate fervor and enthusiasm of the crowds of faithful should be sifted through the sieve and disciplined by churchmen who would reconcile availability with acceptance of the Unforeseen and, if necessary, of the Mystery, with detached, objective, and fitting prudence. "Test everything; hold fast what is good" is one of Paul's exhortations we should never forget; without omitting, however, the words that immediately precede them: "Do not quench the Spirit, do not despise prophesying" (1 Thess. 5:19–21).

Returning now to the pseudo-document published by Bonnefon, we can see better now (in the light of this axiom of history which expects those exercising authority in the Church not to excite the credulity of the faithful but, on the contrary, to oversee it and, if necessary, suppress it) how unconvincing the forgery was. Above all, because it even mistook the sender and the recipient of the letter. In fact, the document bears witness to an implausible confusion of powers. Georges Bertrin commented, "To intervene in this way, before any violation of the law and in order to maintain order, is the task of the police, not that of the judiciary. Even more so when it is a matter of the highest degree of the district attorney's office or a court of appeals regarding a matter of a province, suspected or expected based on a number of rumors."

In the end, the counterfeiter did not respect the rules that regulated, in the France of that time (and still today as well, as in all Western nations), relations among governmental institutions. The one who ought to have written such a letter, if anyone, was the prefect (the representative of executive power in the department and guarantor of public order), placing his subordinate *in loco*, the police commissioner, on guard. But to attribute that "service note" (which had an official and not private character, one must remember) to the general prosecutor is to ignore what the task of the public ministry was at the time: to request that the judge apply the law, but only when it has already been violated. This enormous oversight was quite peculiar and reveals that the document was constructed by a fraudster — one who seemingly displayed unbelievable naivete, unacceptable in a forger.

One must ask the meaning behind such a self-inflicted wound, too obvious to be involuntary. Among the various hypotheses, one seems most convincing: as the historians of Lourdes (René Laurentin most forcefully among them and with great precision) have denounced, the archives of the public offices that had anything to do with the case in Lourdes were "purged" of the documents most embarrassing to the functionaries who were protagonists in the events, some even removed entirely in order to hide their responsibility, or at least their errors and naivete. And so the hypothesis runs: it is probable that it was opportune to our counterfeiter to attribute his invention to one office rather than another, so as better to justify the lack of precise references with which, as we saw, the document was published. And so, knowing the situation of the archival assets, he attributed the alarm over a presumed conspiracy to an office that would not have had jurisdiction in the matter but from which most of the files had been removed, thus rendering more credible at least the sudden appearance of an official letter fifty years after it had been written. But the same stratagem led to the document's a priori inadmissibility due to the confusion of powers.

At the end of the previous chapter, we announced some improbable elements within the very content of the letter, some of the "pearls" that escaped the counterfeiter and would not have been easily identifiable to those who are not adept in the times and events. Pearls, nonetheless, that lead us to think instinctively (as we said) of the popular saying which has been found to be a constant in human experience: "The devil teaches us his tricks but not how to hide them." Let's examine these pearls, then. They are not necessary for relegating this document definitively to the limbo of the fiction shelf, but as in every self-respecting mystery novel, is not the greatest pleasure for the investigator, and thus for the reader, that of sleuthing out and discovering the subtle and hidden clues?

To begin with, the letter ends with a bureaucratic *Veuillez agréer* (Best wishes), which precedes the *signé* (signed), Falconnet. Well, the *Revue pratique d'apologétique* published (in the June number of 1908) the testimony of Jules Cauvière, well-known law professor at the *Institut Catholique* in Paris after many years spent in the courts serving precisely as a district attorney. Professor Cauvière, based on his personal experience and therefore with perfect knowledge of bureaucratic usage, wrote, "In the period of which we are speaking, especially in the judicial system, there was a rigid respect for protocol and never (I say never) would a district attorney have ended a service letter with the formula *Veuillez agréer*. Falconnet, giving his orders to his deputy in Lourdes, ought to have written (and certainly would have written, rigid as he was in respect for the formal norms, if it had been his letter) a *Recévez,* 'Receive.' The nuance cannot be missed by any functionary of the judicial order." Effectively, while "Best wishes" was a sort of courteous invitation used by the hierarchy of the state with their peers, “Receive” sounded like a sort of order and was therefore reserved to dependents. These formulas of bureaucratic courtesy were even codified in service manuals with a precision that did not admit exceptions.

Should we go further? Shall we push our entertainment to the extreme? Are we tempted not only to win but to rout the foe, regarding this counterfeit and its insidious appearance, which disturbed so many yet is so fragile to critical analysis? Let us abandon then the letter and turn to the rest of Bonnefon's book, *Lourdes et ses tenanciers,* wherein the letter was published.

Several lines below the presumed note of the district attorney of Pau, the historian and polemicist writes verbatim, “Falconnet, for the occasion of the New Year's reception, renewed his recommendations of vigilance to the imperial procurator in Lourdes.” Yet, because the “innkeepers” of Lourdes (to use the contemptuous expression of their adversary) were not the kind who would remain passive in the face of dishonest attacks, they produced an unassailable extract from a newspaper. This was from the official gazette of the Region of Pau, the *Mémorial des Pyrénées,* which, on December 31, 1857, published the following headline: “The District Attorney, impeded by family concerns, will not be able to receive on January first.”

Thus, on that New Year's Day of 1858, the reception did not take place during which, according to the information produced by the polemicist Bonnefon, the high-ranking magistrate would have renewed “his recommendations to vigilance to the imperial procurator in Lourdes”! Bonnefon literally invented an event which did not take place, not suspecting he would be so unfortunate as to set his tale precisely on that New Year's Day on which, due to causes beyond their control, they were forced to interrupt the usual exchanges of official greetings in the halls of the district attorney's office. An invention exposed by two providential lines of a newspaper.

Someone correctly observed, “In the end, is it not highly flattering for Lourdes that, to deny the truth, one was forced to stoop to performing the unworthy trade of counterfeiter?” And yet: despite being entirely persuaded of the need to oppose with the arms of the facts these attempts to twist the truth, we cannot withhold some reflections on this situation.

If we look to the past, around that grotto an actual “war of religion” raged for nearly a century, often without pulling punches. Opposing the fervent devotion of believers was the reaction of those who could see only (having recourse even to the fabrication of forgeries) fanaticism, illusions, and even fraud. Jean de Bonnefon was certainly not an isolated agent. Before and after him, incredulity (but also religious passion, as in the case of Protestants, bitter enemies who considered these to be "blasphemous manifestations of Mariolatry") made use of every literary genre: from the novel to the medical review, from the historical study to the propaganda pamphlet. They made use of everything, if only to oppose a "fact" that was more distasteful than all others. Consider just two aspects of this unpleasantness: During the century of scientific triumph, how could one tolerate a place of "miracles"? And during the century in which the war against the papacy raged more fiercely than ever, how could one put up with a "Virgin Mary" who brought the ratification from Heaven itself of a dogma, the Immaculate Conception, so recently proclaimed by a pope as despised as Pius IX?

Those who are familiar with the limitless bibliography of Lourdes, for and against, works of "friends" and of "enemies," know well how these events recall the Gospel passage in their having become an outrageous "sign of contradiction."

And yet, for several decades now, the white-hot passions seem to have cooled. In fact, the attentive observer will notice some peculiar facts. Examples are everywhere. Stretching out my hand, I find here on my desk that volume of 1,700 pages which, with several million copies sold over a few decades, is the most widespread reference book in Italy. I am speaking of the little yet dense *Universal Encyclopedia* of Garzanti Editions. The entry "Lourdes" offers but a few lines, among which we read, "the place of the apparitions of the Virgin Mary to Bernadette Soubirous (1858)." One notices what is not said: "believed" or "presumed apparitions." The prodigious fact, the supernatural mystery, seems to be a given for this manual whose absolute secular identity is well known.

From this paperback, we progress to the many-volume, unabridged *European Encyclopedia* by the same editor. The entry receives nearly an entire column, wherein it is stated that the little town has been "known throughout the world as a pilgrimage destination ever since, in 1858, Bernadette Soubirous received eighteen apparitions of the Virgin Mary who appeared to her as the Immaculate Conception." Here, too, not that the little girl "seems to have had" or is “said to have had,” but rather an explicit affirmation: “received eighteen apparitions of the Virgin Mary.”

We shall leave aside the many pages we have gathered from other more authoritative and popular (not only in Italy) contemporary encyclopedias in our study of the topic which interests us here. It suffices to confirm that the situation is the same: one finds everywhere a surprising elimination of the conditional, of the doubtful tones, of the rigorous skepticism that prevailed until just a few decades ago. What has happened and what is happening? Has the agnostic culture expressed in those sources of information converted to Catholicism, and even to Marian devotion?

This cannot be truthfully said. And so, what has happened? What is the reason for those precise and categorical statements on the reality of the facts, once judged as unacceptable when present in Catholic publications? These are some of the questions I shall seek to answer in the next chapter.

CHAPTER 3

Rediscovering Wonder

There are gospel truths, not at all secondary, which we tend to forget and repress today more than ever. One of these uncomfortable realities which we would all gladly do without was reiterated by Jesus himself. It is the dramatic question he addresses to disciples of all times in the form of a warning: "Do you think I have come to give peace on earth? No, I tell you, but rather division." A "division" so profound that it will not stop even in the face of the most tenacious bonds, those of blood: "For henceforth in one house there will be five divided, three against two and two against three; they will be divided, father against son and son against father, mother against daughter and daughter against her mother, mother-in-law against her daughter-in-law and daughter-in-law against her mother-in-law" (Luke 12:51–53). As the parallel passage in the Gospel of Matthew repeats, the Son of Man has "not come to bring peace, but a sword"; he appeared in order to "set against" (Matt. 10:34).

Of course, he brings with him the gift of peace as well, but *his* peace, not that which we men struggle, always in vain, to construct. The Gospel of John gives us Jesus' solemn and intimate farewell to his disciples, "Peace I leave with you; my peace I give to you; not as the world gives do I give to you" (14:27).

Thus, according to the prophecy of old Simeon, the child brought to the temple for the purification by Mary and Joseph is destined to be in eternity a sign of contradiction (Luke 2:34). The same fate awaits all those who choose to be faithful to him, because "A disciple is not above his teacher, nor a servant above his master" (Matt. 10:24).

This is an important premise, because this Gospel dynamic concerns Mary as well; in fact, it concerns her first among all in the Church and in a most special way, given her relation to the Son. The sugary tone of some Marian devotion is therefore not only an attack on good taste but also on the dramatic dimension of the gospel. It is immersed in an unrealism, deluded by the facile justification of a good intention to "draw everyone to our Heavenly Mother."

"Division," "contradiction," "scandal," cannot be lacking, even around her; and neither are they lacking at Lourdes, the enigma we are continuing to investigate and reflect upon here. In the preceding chapter, we alluded to an authentic, all-out "religious war."

Let us be clear: the believer has no right to complain (in fact, he has reason to rejoice) at the violent opposition unleashed from the very beginning and carried out for a century around that grotto of miracles, as the polemicists sarcastically defined it. Such reactions constitute, according to the perspective of faith, the counterproof that those events are coherent with the evangelical dimension. Wherever everyone agrees, the suspicion that Christ is far distant arises immediately. In the words of an ancient Father of the Church: "The One who loves all will be saved, but the one who wants to be loved by all will not be saved."

But besides the confirmation of its Christian character, this opposition to the "fact" of Lourdes has offered us an occasion for important analysis. From the beginning, from the brutal and continually repeated interrogations to which Bernadette was subjected, threatening her even with prison, to the furious polemical rants against the truth of the miraculous events, believers have been obliged to take the defensive. This had many repercussions in terms of efforts to establish the reality of the facts — not only the foundational ones of which the visionary was the protagonist but also successive events tied to pilgrimage, which the Lady herself requested on March 2: "Go and tell the priests that the faithful should come here in procession and that a chapel should be built."

Thus, for example, Lourdes is the only religious site in the world where a structure like the celebrated *Bureau de constatations médicales* (Bureau of Medical Findings, reorganized and expanded in 1947 with the name *Bureau médical de Notre Dame de Lourdes*) has been established, and only because this scientific agency was required as a response to repeated aggression toward and mockery of the many cases of "humanly inexplicable" healings. The archives of the bureau bear witness to efforts that are as vast as they are precious to the believer who, in Lourdes, does not want to be suspected of being a superstitious and gullible victim of speculation.

At any rate, the work of those physicians and historians is influenced by the fact that Lourdes and its protagonists have become a "sign of contradiction," a force of division. Thus, in the light of faith, the opposition has played a providential role. This gives us one further reason for loving them and for avoiding all acrimony toward them, while vindicating the rights of a truth which, for believers, is comprehensible only within a religious perspective, though founded on demonstrable facts.

In the previous two stages of our notebook, we saw how there was no hesitation even to the point of publishing false documents to try to remove the mystery that hovers tenaciously around the cavern of the *Gave* (a generic noun indicating a "mountain torrent," in the dialect used in the Pyrenees) called *Pau*.

Adding to the falsifications of historians and of Bonnefon there are also those of intellectuals. For this purpose, we reproduce a page that denounces the most famous of the literary falsifications: that of Émile Zola, the son of a man from Veneto who became the leader of positivism in the French novelistic tradition. With his spectacular incursion into the Dreyfus Case in favor of the captain condemned for espionage (his famous article "*J'Accuse*," which cost him a one-year sentence from which he escaped by fleeing abroad) and with other such initiatives, this "progressive" was at the origin of the modern, disturbing figure of the "committed intellectual," the cultured figure seeking to play a part in political life, wanting to be master of life and esteemed well beyond his bookish competence. The writer would replace the priest; sociopolitical pamphlets would be the new form of encyclicals or pastoral letters; the new dogmas of the secular Culture (with a capital C!) would supersede those of the Church. Some might suspect, despite everything and given the results, that this was not a great progress....

We return now to the page we said we would like to reproduce, which we take from the dossier titled *One Hundred Years of Miracles in Lourdes*, published in 1958 (a century after the apparitions) by Michel Agnellet, a very well-known writer in France and entirely beyond suspicion, given that he himself, in the preface to the book, reminds us that he wrote it, after a long investigation into the archives and at the site, "with all the skepticism and caution that an atheistic education and the medical discipline have inculcated in our mind."

We give voice then to the agnostic though impartial Agnellet, knowing we could not have said it better:

> On the morning of August 20, 1892, the "White Train" entered the station at Lourdes. It was the train of desperation and of hope, the train of pilgrims, mostly suffering from late-stage illnesses.... Among them, two women dying of tuberculosis united their ardent prayer unknowingly: Marie Lebranchu and Marie Lemarchand. In one carriage of the same convoy, an illustrious man, a great writer: Émile Zola. The two women had gone to Lourdes with a last hope. The man went there in search of "documents," concrete proof to construct a work he had hoped would be decisive for Lourdes, where his heart's desire was to expose the impostor of the grotto. Faith would certainly provide what the two women had gone looking for in Lourdes: healing. But Zola's bad faith would grant him only the material to put together a dreadful book, unworthy of him. So unworthy that his admirers and many authors who, after his death, considered his works, often pass over it in scrupulous silence.

At this point, in order to avoid misunderstanding, Michel Agnellet hastens to point out, "We want our readers to understand that it is not our intention to 'defame' Zola.... We cannot be, nor are we Zola's enemy. But we cannot understand how such a learned man, coming to the source of the inexplicable healings, could have deformed the truth to such an extent that, when later attacked by those whom he had vilified, he never dared to respond or contradict them."

The French essayist continues,

> For Émile Zola had the rare good fortune, which I did not have during these two years of investigations, of witnessing at least two miraculous cures. And not only did he deny them, but he gave two versions so absurd and so odious that when he realized this later, he did not hesitate to go looking for one of the women who had been miraculously cured but who, in his book, had died. He went to her asking that she move to Belgium, that she disappear from Paris where, according to his book, she had died; and he thus attempted to bend the living truth for the sake of his truth—Zola, the great writer!

We shall return in a later part of this book to those two Maries, healed in reality and consigned to death by the acclaimed *maître-à-penser* of the "freethinkers," of the "strong spirits." But we would also like to dwell for a moment on Zola to show that his book, though consciously stained by falsehood due to its positivist bias ("Miracles cannot exist," he wrote), in terms of its literary quality is not as "dreadful" as Agnellet judged it to be. Few works better convey the flavor of that authentically Catholic epic which was the pilgrimage to Lourdes in the years in which being Catholic meant being banned from politics and culture. And it is easy to understand how a novel as factious and tendentious as this one, where the facts are denied and distorted if they do not fit into the a priori atheistic framework, was to carry out a providential role.

In 1895, one year after the triumphant publication of *Lourdes,* an article in the *Civiltà Cattolica* bore the title "The Fruit of Zola's Calumnies." It explained how the number of pilgrimages had almost doubled: believers hastened to offer "reparations" while the incredulous and agnostic went with their curiosity aroused by the pages of the celebrated writer. The anonymous editor of the Jesuit journal wrote, "New and unusual visitors have arrived here, correspondents of newspapers, men who had never encountered such a place. Many, arriving incredulous and derisive, won over by the evidence of the prodigies taking place there right before them, go away penitent and converted." The *Civiltà Cattolica* concluded, in the style typical of an epoch that loved to juxtapose one polemic with another, "As Satan serves, to his great spite, to glorify God in the world, so too the Masonic sect, with its Zola, serves to increase the honor and praise of Her who keeps Satan vanquished under her feet."

Yes, perhaps greater charity was in order in the awareness of the beneficial role carried out, as instruments certainly unaware, by Zola and by many other adversaries of these realities. They were sometimes moved by motives not ignoble: in the author of *Lourdes* there is compassion for the suffering, made keen by concern that they might be deceived by an illusion; and Bernadette, although seen as a dreamer, is kept far from any suspicion of fraud. She is not an accomplice, but a victim before whom one must bow. And who else but God can penetrate the heart of Zola who, from Lourdes, sent a disease-wracked friend a bottle of water from the fountain, saying, "*On ne sait jamais*" (You never know)?

We return to our story. For the moment, we seek only to reinforce how fierce was the "Battle of the Pyrenees." The forgery of documents, recourse to nonfiction and to literature as blunt weapons, are unpleasant aspects that characterize every war. And this was truly that, at least for a century.

If Michel Agnellet wrote the things we have just reported at the end of a century of apparitions, in that same 1958 a married couple, both of them physicians with materialistic leanings (like Zola), Sumy and Thérèse Valot, were still capable of writing a treatise under the significant title *Lourdes and the Therapeutic Illusion*, the content of which could be summarized as an old script: "Every time science takes a step forward, miracles take a step backward." Following the century-old script once more, the punctual and as usual highly documented Catholic response was swift in coming, entrusted to Fr. André Deroo who published *Lourdes, City of Miracles or Market of Illusions?*

But the two opposing pamphlets were among the last in the long series. Toward the end of the 1950s, the "struggle for Lourdes" began to calm slowly, and it seems today to have become a distant and somewhat embarrassing memory. And here we connect directly with what we observed at the end of the preceding chapter: even the entries of secular encyclopedias seem to take for granted the truth of the apparitions to Bernadette, endorsing implicitly the extraordinary and prodigious facts that followed them and whose demolition had been the task of the parents, grandparents, and great-grandparents of their editors. Even among Protestants (with the exception of the polemical installments that characterize almost exclusively the "Reform gone haywire," the new sects), new direct attacks are no longer recorded on this presumed "Mariolatry superstition." And it would be difficult to find someone who might dare to express in public the brutal definition given Lourdes by perhaps the greatest of Protestant theologians of the twentieth century, Karl Barth: "That grotto is the place where the true nature of Catholic Mariology appears most evidently: a blight of authentic Christology."

What happened? we asked earlier. Has there been a sort of general conversion to Marian devotion? Why, after having caused so much scandal and uproar, does Lourdes no longer seem to pose a problem, not even among traditional adversaries?

In attempting a response, one must take note of the obvious mutation in the cultural climate. The ingenuous presumption of nineteenth-century science of being capable of dissolving every hint of mystery in the world has given way, if not to humility, at least to greater prudence. Not even among the most radical secularists is there anyone willing today to recite, without an ironic smirk, verses like those written by Giosuè Carducci in 1863, a significant date because just a year after the recognition by the bishop of Tarbes of the truth of the apparitions to Bernadette. These verses, exemplary as a mirror of that period, are taken from the *Hymn to Satan*; namely, to Progress, Science, and Reason, which were destined to vanquish the obscurantism of the "Jehovah of the priests" and are symbolized by "a beautiful and horrible Monster." Satan is portrayed, in fact, as nothing less than the latest invention of the age, the steam locomotive.

It is likely that the laborious discovery of greater ecumenical respect explains the termination of the controversy, at least in part, of the historical Protestant churches, while sects such as the Jehovah's Witnesses are now furiously in action.

There is, therefore, a positive aspect in the "silence" that has fallen upon Lourdes, and thus on the immense reservoir of the inexplicable, the enigmatic, and the mysterious that surrounds it and that no longer sows division.

But the reality, every reality, is by its very nature ambiguous: the luminous aspect always exists with the obscure aspect. So, it is appropriate to reflect on provocative observations like those of Julien Green, the French-American writer: "The most the devil can do is to give to mystery a normal appearance." In fact, we recalled that "division" and "scandal" are essential in all that is truly evangelical. In the Christian perspective, would Lourdes still be the gift that it represented to the faith of many generations if it no longer "divided" or no longer "scandalized"? It would go against all logic if it were to be brought within the canons of "normality."

What comes to mind is one of the constants identified by those who reflect on the twenty centuries of Christian history. It is that the strategy of the world to neutralize the Church can follow either of two directions, according to the circumstances and the times: attempt to destroy it or attempt to assimilate it. In the twentieth century alone, did not the East try to destroy the Faith for decades? And in the West, was there not an attempt (today more than ever) to assimilate it, giving it in Green's words, "a common appearance," reducing it to a soothing ethical manual of what is politically correct?

Lourdes (along with many other Catholic realities of this type) is entirely incapable of being assimilated into a project that tries to convince the Church to belittle itself into a sort of agency with the hobby of "religion," dedicated only to peace, ecology, democracy, and the prevalent morality of the moment. Lourdes, if believers are right, is a tear in the veil opened suddenly on Another World; it is the truth entrusted not to professors and experts but to the illiterate; it is Heaven itself that ratifies the dogmas of a pope, considered "obscurantist" and "reactionary," like Pius IX; it is ridiculed Catholic Mariology that finds full confirmation; it is the blind who regain their sight, the cancer-ridden who are cured, the paralytic who walks. Lourdes is (and cannot be otherwise) the scandal, division, negation of the common sense imposed by the new conformity. It has not ceased to carry out its role of provocation; nor could it ever.

Is it thus the case that after decades of attempts at "destruction," opponents have passed to the phase of "assimilation," no longer confronting the problems it causes and the questions it raises but relegating it to a twilight zone for surviving devotees, they too soon become "adult Christians," "open and enlightened believers"?

These do not seem unfounded questions. On the contrary, it seems that the good-natured satisfaction with the less polemical climate must be accompanied by restlessness (according to the Catholic logic of "both-and"), if the meritorious repression of the controversy is in fact accompanied by the repression of the problem.

The problem also consists, we must recall, in events that the Church can certainly not disavow, because she solemnly guarantees them: the "miracles," the "prodigies," the "inexplicable."

We must remain calm. I am not so naïve as to attempt to recover the apologetical and somewhat triumphalist "miracle doctrine" of yesteryear. Quoting oneself can be ridiculous, but also convenient. Allow me to fall into a bit of laziness and reproduce what I wrote several years ago in an article (which later became a book, *Thinking about History*, 1992) dedicated to Lourdes:

> The miracles: emphasizing almost exclusively the physical ones, believers have often conformed themselves to the rationalistic mentality of those who see only the body. But to heal this, one only needs a good doctor or perhaps a guru or a shaman. It is in healing the soul and the heart that the true miracle lies and for this one needs the God of the Bible. "For which is easier to say, 'Your sins are forgiven,' or to say, 'Rise and walk'?" (Mt 9:5) The former is the more difficult. But let us not forget then that, according to statistics,

> Lourdes is the place in the world where more confessions are heard and where more absolutions are dispensed. It is this secret and daily power capable of bending the hearts of men that are often harder than steel, more tightly shut and pricklier than a hedgehog, wherein lies the true, great Miracle of the grotto. Priest friends who have had the fortune of confessing there have witnessed to me their amazement at this wonder that happens so often. A "hidden" prodigy, for sure: but that is how the Gospel works, whose protagonist breaks history in two, and yet leaves nearly no trace of himself in the annals of history. Lourdes shows its conformity to the Gospel in being an impressive but at the same time hidden reality.

Let it be clear, then: I am well aware that on the banks of the Pau as well, "Physical miracles are only rare signs and, in the end, less important than the spiritual wonders which are greater and are repeated daily."

Truly, we all believe it now. But the temptation to swing with the pendulum, the law of "action and reaction," must not push us to the opposite extreme: the past search for "physical miracles" at all costs must not lead us to reducing it all to mere "spiritualism." Let us not forget that the verse from Matthew quoted above is followed immediately by another: "He then said to the paralytic[,] 'Rise, take up your bed and go home' " (Matt. 9:6).

Physical healing is a tangible sign and proof of spiritual healing: both are essential, not to be overlooked, and both are part of the divine strategy.

Sixty-five times the Church has committed herself, declaring a cure "miraculous" and attesting that it "was obtained through the intercession of the Blessed Virgin Mary venerated as Our Lady of Lourdes."[3]

It is interesting to mention, by way of example, the initial part of the most recent official declaration of healing, the one signed by Msgr. Luigi Bommarito, archbishop of Catania, on June 28, 1989. The text, posted also in Lourdes in its official form, as is the practice, reads as follows: "After having been informed of the reports of the Medical Commission and the canonical diocesan report, designated for studying the healing of Delizia Cirolli of Paternò, I recognize this healing as 'scientifically inexplicable' given the

[3] Editor's Note: Archbishop Malcolm McMahon of Liverpool in England has approved the healing of a British World War I soldier as the seventy-first miracle of Lourdes on December 8, 2024.

conditions in which it was produced and maintained, and as Archbishop of Catania, I declare its miraculous character."

The bishop's declaration continues: "This healing is added to all the others carried out over the past 130 years in Lourdes, a privileged place of prayer and faith, through the maternal intercession of Mary, Mother of Jesus, the Son of God." After other considerations, Msgr. Bommarito concluded in this manner: "This healing is a sign that God gives to his Church for its faith and its conversion. It lies to each of the faithful to receive this gift and express it in life."

He is not sparing, as one can see, with his acknowledgments.

But those who are surprised by the scarcity of the number of cases recognized ecclesiastically (only 65, in more than 130 years) ignore a fundamental distinction: namely, between healings and miracles. Between 1858 and 1914, the former registered 4,445. Reports of "scientifically inexplicable healings" recognized as such after the successive and severe degrees of scientific scrutiny are, according to the archive of the *Bureau médical*, many thousands. There have been many more who did not leave a complete file for whatever reason, perhaps simply the desire of many of the healed not to undergo the complex series of tests — often lasting for years, given that the absence of remission of disease is essential.

Various other reasons create conditions that lead just a small number of the dossiers of verified "healings" to be transmitted to the dioceses of those receiving the healing (impeccable on the scientific level, entrusted to the doctors of the bureau and then, in a second round, to those of the *Comité Médical International*). If this occurs, another long and complex procedure begins. The examination of the episcopal commission is medical as well as religious, at length reaching the eventual declaration regarding the "miraculous character" made by the ordinary, as in the case in Catania. This has occurred, as mentioned, sixty-five times: in each of them (we use the words of Dr. Alphonse Olivieri, president of the bureau from 1959 to 1971), "The Church officially recognizes the supernatural character in a healing."

The number of "miracles" is therefore significantly lower than the reality of what actually happens and continues to happen there, but it is still such as to confirm abundantly the scandalous character (to human reason) which Lourdes necessarily has had and which ought to be maintained. Or, as it seems today, rediscovered. This is not a matter for discussion or confrontation with arguments that are more or less efficacious and dialectic, with theories to counter other theories. Lourdes (and this is its important aspect for the faith of us poor "Christians on the street" who, like the father of the epileptic boy, can shout, "I believe; help my unbelief!" Mark 9:24) "is a fact, or rather a block of facts, against which every philosophical or theoretical consideration crashes." Thus Alexis Carrel, the Nobel Prize winner for medicine, converted precisely because he directly witnessed a healing.

A block of facts which, furthermore, has not been relegated to the archives but which continues to be enriched. In the words of Msgr. Théas in 1958: "We do not celebrate one hundred years of distance from the apparitions concluded forever and relegated to history. We attest, rather, that for one hundred years, an active and unceasing *presence* manifests itself here."

Even if in these postconciliar decades, one notices the reticence of some bishops in carrying on the work of the dossier furnished by the bureau to the stage of recognizing the "supernatural character" of the miracles, the healings have not stopped in the least and every year new ones are declared. The proper emphasis placed on Lourdes over these years as a "clinic of souls" has not invalidated a mysterious reality: that it continues to be a "clinic of the body" as well, a place of physical healing.

It is this enigma which we would like to probe in the following chapter: even if the terrain in which we must execute the "core sample" seems well known (thank God, the publications have not been lacking), we hope to say something that is, if not new, at least singular.

Does not the gospel to which the Grotto of Massabielle is so intimately connected need to rediscover in every generation the wonder of an unexpected gift?

CHAPTER 4

The Peasant of Monferrato

In the chronological list of the sixty-five healings of Lourdes which the Church, in the person of the bishop of the healed person's diocese officially recognizing the "supernatural character," the fifty-first place is held by an Italian: Evasio Ganora, a peasant from Casale Monferrato. In 1949, when he was thirty-six years old, he was stricken by a terrible illness, malignant lymphogranulomatosis, known as Hodgkin's disease. For months, the unfortunate man, father of five children despite his young age, went from hospital to laboratory to a specialist to medical consultants, often famous university professors. No one, obviously, could have foreseen that in this way a medical dossier was being created that would allow for the irrefutable assertion of the miraculous event that was about to occur.

In fact, when all the treatments, both chemical and physical, permitted by the science of the time turned out to be of no use, the specialists following Ganora's case emitted a terrible, unanimous verdict: death was incumbent within a matter of weeks or, at the most, a few months.

When he learned of the imminent departure of a train organized by Opera Federativa Trasporto Ammalati a Lourdes, one of the worthy organizations for the transport of the sick to Lourdes, the dying man asked if he could participate. The doctors gave him permission, convinced there was nothing more to lose: at the very least, the stress of the journey would shorten the suffering of a path whose tragic destination, now so close, was marked out. Lying on a stretcher, with a high fever that had not left him for some time, the unfortunate man reached Lourdes the evening of June 1, 1950. The next day he was brought to the pools.

During the immersions he felt "struck by an electrical shock, like burning hot electrical current running through his entire body"; thus ran his testimony. It was an "immediate and radical" healing, as established by the college of doctors in the long series of tests which, according to protocol, he underwent after the extraordinary event of that June 2. It suffices to say that Ganora, who had arrived on a stretcher, returned from the pools walking to the hospital where he had been admitted on arrival.

The visit carried out immediately (by the same doctor who had examined him upon arrival and who thus knew well his previous condition) established that the fever had disappeared; that the enlargement of the lymphatic ganglion was gone; that his spleen and liver, swollen due to the disease to an amazing extent, had resumed their normal dimensions. That same evening, the former patient began to eat once more in the abundant manner which was his custom before his infirmity. The following morning (after a long and peaceful night's rest), he climbed the hill above the grotto with the others and followed the stations of the *Via Crucis*. The day after that, he joined the *brancardiers*, the stretcher bearers: he now led the other unfortunates to the pools where just two days before he himself had been transported in his moribund condition.

Later, returning to Casale de Monferrato, he took up once again his strenuous work as a peasant farmer.

It is a classic case of what can happen in Lourdes. Classic as well was the itinerary of visits over the following years of the *Bureau médical* to verify that the healing was maintained and that there were no relapses. In 1954, after yet another visit to Lourdes in the presence of some twenty doctors (any health-care worker — of any nationality, belief, or ideology — who wishes to do so can participate in these sessions, and each can present his point of view), the bureau decided to pass the case on to the higher level, the court of appeals for the cases that make it past the first, severe judgment — namely the *Comité médical international*, which met in Paris in 1955.

The specialists (all university professionals chosen for their competence in their specialization and not according to their religious faith) had at their disposal the results of the examinations carried out on the patient before the healing, allowing them to confirm, although there was no need, given the number and the thoroughness of the visits and exams, the diagnosis of "malignant lymphogranulomatosis of the Hodgkin's type."

It must be observed how this experience shows that the doubts, objections, and controversy surrounding these "medically inexplicable" cases almost always focus not on the fact that the person was found healthy, but that he must not have been ill before the mysterious "intervention." The old rationalism always grabs hold of the pretext of an erroneous diagnosis to negate the obvious in a person who, when examined, turns out to be in good health.

We shall produce here some of the interesting phrases from the final report of the committee, signed unanimously by the twenty-five physicians present on February 22, 1955:

> Four years and four months after the declared healing, Mr. Evasio Ganora displays a normal state and not one relapse of his disease has been verified. We are correct in declaring that this evolution diverges profoundly from that which medical experience would allow to be ascribed to Hodgkin's Disease. We physicians signing this document have not been able to identify other examples of a similar evolution of this disease.

The specialists concluded: "We affirm that the Ganora case presents all the traits that would authorize the *Comité médical international* to propose an inexplicable healing to the ecclesiastical authorities. We dare to add that this Committee is seldom concerned with facts as unusual as those we have just reported."

Thus, the entire dossier was transmitted immediately afterward to the diocesan authorities in Casale. The commission created by the bishop nominated another made up of doctors as well, according to the practice. More visits, analyses, and verifications were made. Meanwhile, theologians and canon lawyers went to work, too. This shows the complexity and duration of the process, which requires three degrees of judgment with all the interrogations and the visits they entail, leading many of those who receive inexplicable healing to thank Heaven privately without presenting themselves to the bureau. This fear of "bureaucratic" complications, instinctual especially among the popular classes (from which, statistically, the majority of those healed at Lourdes come), contributes to rendering the official numbers much lower than the actual number of cases healed.

Returning to our narrative, on May 31, 1955, Msgr. Giuseppe Angrisani, then bishop of the Diocese of Monferrato, whose patron is St. Evasio (the baptismal patron of the protagonist of this case), promulgated the short document that follows: "We judge and declare that the healing of Evasio Ganora, occurring in Lourdes on June 2, 1950, is miraculous and must be attributed to the special intervention of the Blessed Virgin Immaculate, Mother of God."

If we have chosen to examine close up the case of this peasant farmer from Piedmont, it is not only because the international committee considered the event particularly eloquent, given the gravity of the disease, the character of the healing as "immediate, radical, and enduring," and the abundance and thoroughness of the medical dossier. Yes, of course: a textbook case, as is said, both for the circumstances of the event as for the forms and the degrees of the scientific scrutiny which allow us to see the work of the mystery that hovers over the Gave de Pau and the methods used to carry out the verification, at least insofar as it is allowed to man. For these reasons, but not only these, we have spoken of this; it is also due to the disturbing sequence of subsequent events that adds enigma to enigma in Ganora's story.

The centenary of the first apparition, February 11, 1958, was drawing near. Under the energetic impulse of Pierre-Marie Théas, the bishop of Tarbes and Lourdes (the latter jurisdiction having been added in 1912, a further confirmation of the importance the Church gave to the events originating in that grotto, leading her to change the millenary ecclesial nomenclature: Tarbes is one of the oldest dioceses in France), impressive celebrations were being prepared. Among other things, work was being carried out to add to the three superimposed churches a large underground basilica named after St. Pius X, as vast as Notre Dame in Paris and slightly less capacious than St. Peter's in Rome, capable of holding more than the entire fixed population of the city of Lourdes.

It was consecrated on March 25, 1958, by a cardinal whose imminent, extraordinary destiny no one could have foreseen: seven months later, the Patriarch of Venice Angelo Roncalli, the personal delegate of Pius XII and always intensely devoted to Lourdes, was elected pope, taking the name John XXIII.

We also point out in passing that no one could have foreseen how the extraordinary Marian triumph of that year 1958 marked the apex, and with it, the decline, the beginning of the end, of a historical phase of the Church that had lasted more than three centuries, since the early decades of the 1600s. As René Laurentin said,

> Pius XII defined the dogma of the Assumption of Mary in 1950. The celebrations of this solemn act were prolonged into the Marian year 1954, during which the centenary of another "modern" dogma was celebrated, that of the Immaculate Conception. Then came the magnificent centenary of Lourdes in 1958. The pontificate of Pius XII, who died that same year, thus marked the apogee of the "Marian movement" that began shortly after the Council of Trent. Certain discourses, certain books in 1958, advocated the growth of new ascensions and new conquests for the dogma and devotion surrounding the Mother of God. In reality, precisely from that moment a shift could be noticed which produced an ebb tide.

After the Second Vatican Council (first announced by Pope Roncalli just ten months after the consecration he had performed for the new basilica in the Pyrenees, in the midst of an impressive host of bishops and archbishops, a crowd of overflowing and enthusiastic faithful, convinced that this veneration of the Virgin would only continue to expand in the future), there began what some called "a Marian winter." In a very short time, certain theological settings passed from age-old fervor to a sort of frost or, at least, chilled reserve that would show signs of warming only with the arrival of a pope who placed in his coat of arms an *M* and the motto of consecration to the Virgin: *Totus tuus*.

We shall return to this. For the moment, we need to continue with the case of Ganora. It was naturally understood that the miraculously cured peasant from Casale Monferrato would leave his fields in 1958 to give his testimony in Lourdes of the mystery of maternal love confirmed in that place through such extraordinary events. Even that anonymous farmer would be a central figure, and rightly so, of the imminent centenary celebration. His was only the fifty-first case of an officially recognized miracle in the century that passed with the "gust of wind" with which it started. And the vast majority of the other cases concerned people who were by then deceased, given the long interruption of ecclesiastical recognitions due to the outbreak of the First World War in 1914 and then to another series of causes.

But instead of the celebration there was drama. Just a few days before the start of the centenary year, at the end of December 1957, Ganora was as always at work in his fields in his customary excellent health. A sudden jolt knocked him off the tractor he was driving, he fell to the ground, and the wheels rolled over him, crushing his chest and leaving him dead. He was not even forty-four years old, survived by his five children, some still young and more than ever in need of him.

Yes, it was also for this reason that we chose his case: healed, certainly, and in an "inexplicable" manner for science; "miraculously" according to the Church. But returned to health and to life only for seven years, after which his life was once again requested of him — and in a bloody, dramatic way — though still young, still decades from the average life expectancy in the contemporary Western world. The intervention of Heaven and the mobilization of terrestrial science, and all this only for a short dilation, a brief postponement which seemed to aggravate the pain of his family, trusting that things would take a turn for the better after such a sign of divine benevolence. Just two years had passed since the bishop's declaration in his favor, recognizing "a special intervention of the Blessed Virgin Immaculate, Mother of God."

There is no answer, obviously, to the many questions that crowd our minds. None, if not in returning to meditate on the word of God pronounced by the prophet ("Neither are your ways my ways," Isa. 55:8) or the cry of the apostle Paul, "How unsearchable are his judgments and how inscrutable his ways! 'For who has known the mind of the Lord?' " Rom. 11:33–34). At any rate, no one can ignore that not only Ganora but everyone who has received bodily healing at Lourdes has died or will die, even if due to sicknesses different from those for which they sought out the intercession of Mary.

If the case of our peasant farmer strikes us in particular, all the others obey the law of life as well, which does not concede "happy endings," since a grave awaits everyone at the end of a more or less lengthy (though always provisional) sojourn among the living. "And they lived happily ever after" is the ending of fairytales, not of true stories. The latter have the propensity that Pascal cruelly summarized, "as beautiful as the comedy was, sooner or later a few shovelfuls of dirt on the face, and it is over."

This is an obvious reflection, perhaps with a mundane appearance. Yet, it allows one to clarify the Catholic perspective in the face of a nonetheless impressive dossier of "physical" healings which have not stopped occurring in the foothills of the Pyrenees since 1858. The believer knows that what the gospel promises everyone is a radical and definitive "healing" of the body, yes, but only when it rises again to eternal life.

Christianity is the only religion that announces not only the salvation of the soul, the survival of the "spirit," but also the resurrection of the flesh. It too is destined, though mysteriously transfigured, to live in eternity. It was also to show this that the risen Jesus, the model and anticipation of the resurrection of every man, asked for food to eat, as he sat once more at table with the disciples.

Except for particular cases (and those taking place at Lourdes are among those), cases that only have value as "signs," as indications of the future reality, the Christian has not been promised these partial, temporary healings, provisional at any rate, from the evils that threaten our flesh. Bodily *health* (*salus*) has not been guaranteed the believer, but rather the *salvation* of the whole person.

For this reason, in places like Lourdes, where faith is forcefully confirmed and reaffirmed, everyone is "healed," even those millions and millions of pilgrims (the vast majority) who do not receive cures for their physical sufferings. Many are healed, in the sense that they return home aware that, beyond the possible though rare miracle, there is a decisive and definitive medicine distributed to everyone in faith. And this medicine is the "scandal" of that resurrection in which the flesh will be healed forever; it is the confident expectation of that "new world" in which there will be no more clinics, hospitals, sanatoriums, or care homes. Neither will there be pools in which stretchers are lowered and fountains bubbling with the waters of the Pyrenees.

Christ said to Pascal in the pinnacle of mysticism known as the *Le Mystère de Jésus* fragment, "Doctors will not heal you, because in the end you too shall die. But I make things heal truly, because I render the body immortal. Suffer now the chains and the slavery of the body. For now, I free you only from the chains of the spirit."

What has been said here can be an attempt at answering those (and they have never been lacking nor will they be) who say they are more scandalized than edified by Lourdes and, in general, by that type of "miracle." They ask why such a "biased" and (in the end) "unjust" God privileges the invocation of just a few of the suffering while seeming to ignore that of the great majority.

Would this not be a good reason for rejecting such a divinity or at least his intervention in the events, though apparently inexplicable, that take place there?

This is a question, however, that seems to disturb only those who judge from the outside, without being involved in the concrete, vital experience of the sick and suffering. Among those who are closest to the latter, whether those accompanying the pilgrimages or voluntary nurses, family members, or priests, there is no sense of frustration at not having received a miraculous cure, nor envy of those who have, nor revolt against Our "undemocratic" Lady who seems to intercede only for some.

If disappointment were to accompany those returning from Lourdes still on a stretcher or in a wheelchair or at any rate sick as they had gone there, how can one explain the unanimous desire to return there which is the constant experience uniting all? Why the consolation, gratitude, and perhaps even joy despite the tribulation that characterizes the masses of those not spared?

Because to each and all, we repeat, grace has been given, discovering in that privileged place (or rediscovering with renewed strength) that what binds man to death, more than physical infirmity, is in St. Paul's words moral sickness, sin. Discovering or rediscovering, we repeat, that in the Christian vision what matters is not so much health, always provisional and precarious, as salvation. It is that which will place us forever beyond the dark threats that harass all of our days.

Here we find perhaps the intimations of a possible response to another question: Why does Our Lady appear at all? Why, at Lourdes (as at Rue du Bac in Paris, La Salette, Pontmain, Beauraing, or Fatima, just to mention those of the last century and a half approved by the Church), did not Jesus show himself, or one of the canonized saints appear? It is according to theology as meditated by the mystics to the Catholic creed, "the Immaculate Mother of God, the ever Virgin Mary, at the end of her earthly life, was assumed to the glory of heaven in soul and body." Thus speak the words of the dogma of the Assumption, defined and proclaimed by Pius XII in 1950, though its content has been believed in from the times of the Church Fathers in both the East and the West (the feast of the Dormition, which is in essence the Assumption of the Virgin Mother, is probably the oldest Marian feast that unites the universal Church).

Having carried in her womb the One who said, "I am the resurrection and the life" (John 11:25), Mary followed her Son into His eternal destiny before every other human being. She is the one who has preceded all of us, who has already been welcomed into eternity in "soul and body." So, if she is the one who appears to mortals, it is also to remind us that what she is already we too shall be. We see the sign and the seal in her very person of the salvation that gives us real health (*salus*): the vision of the body of Mary already "saved" is the guarantee that everyone's body shall also be saved.

Here too, the Catholic system shows us a coherence that appears more obvious as one goes more deeply into it: a system in which *tout se tient*; and in this harmony as well, so often unknown to the superficial onlooker, the believer sees the trademark of truth.

But are these all not merely theoretical discussions? Perhaps contaminated by the usual devotional rhetoric? We understand these suspicions, far as we are from the irritating, unrealistic, triumphalist devotionalism (something quite different from worthy devotion) that seemed incapable of perceiving the full scope of the human condition with all its suffering. To such suspicions there is no other response but to refer to concrete reality, to the direct experience of the crowds in Lourdes. These throngs of faithful are composed of normal people who know little of theology, and today know even less of the catechism. But they perceive, they "feel" with that which the learned call the *sensus fidei*, this sort of instinct of the baptized which has been fundamental in the increased flow of pilgrims to shrines, especially Marian ones, even throughout the "winter" years mentioned above.

As we continue our soundings in that unique place, we arrive at other questions asked so often by so many, if not by each one of us. As seen in the photographs of that period, until the drastic clean-up job (carried out as well for the centenary year) to restore the site to its primitive, austere nudity, from the ceiling of the Grotto of Lourdes hung clusters of canes, crutches, bags, and other orthopedic instruments. These poignant ex-votos were left as a grateful testimony by those who had been liberated of their physical ailments.

A pamphlet, written by a Protestant and recently reprinted, opens with a quote from Félix Michaud as a general motto for the booklet: "No believer would be so naïve as to solicit the intervention of the Virgin Mary that an amputated leg might grow back. A miracle of this sort has never been ascertained; and yet, it would be decisive!"

Also recently, on the front page of *La Stampa*, the daily out of Turin, in a comment on the presumed "Marian prodigies" spreading like a plague in the early months of 1995, an esteemed op-ed writer and jack-of-all-trades quoted the words of one of his professors: "I will believe in miracles when I see an arm or a leg grow back: we have all too many paralytics who walk again and crying statues of the Virgin Mary. But not one cripple with a hand or a foot that grew back. I ask the devoted, then: Why?"

Why, then? Since it has been asked too many times, this question must not be dismissed. Why? This is what we shall examine in the next chapter.

CHAPTER 5

Crutches and Wooden Legs

August Vallet, a famous doctor and investigator into the enigma of the Pyrenees, said, "Medicine knows almost no disease that has not found an inexplicable and well-attested cure in Lourdes."

Yes, but what about amputated legs? Severed arms? Limbs reduced to stumps by congenital deformities or illnesses or traumatic accidents? "Under the grotto there are many crutches, but no wooden leg." So commented Émile Zola, and with him, many others before and after. Why at Lourdes, a doctor asked, has there never been registered "the regrowth of an amputated leg, a never-seen wonder that would be decisive?" As promised, we now shall seek, from the perspective of faith as well as of history, a possible response.

First of all, leaving behind Lourdes for a moment and looking at the whole of Catholic history, it is not true that an official ecclesial verification of a "miraculous fact" obtained through the intercession of Our Lady has not been verified concerning a limb that has grown back.

At least once (to our knowledge; we cannot exclude other cases therefore) that recognition was given by the archbishop of Zaragoza, and in a particularly solemn form, after a trial worthy of modern critical methods. In fact, on April 27, 1941, the bishop of that Spanish city (so dear to the Iberian peoples and also to those in Latin America for the great shrine of the *Virgen del Pilar*) issued an official decree in Latin whose final lines run thus:

> All having been examined, we utter, pronounce, and declare that Miguel-Juan Pellicer, inhabitant of Calanda, with whom the present trial is concerned, has miraculously recovered his right leg which had been amputated. This restitution cannot be attributed to

> nature, but has been performed in an admirable and miraculous manner (*mirabiliter et miraculose*) and must be registered as a miracle, given the fact that herein contribute all that, according to law, is requisite in an authentic prodigy. Thus, it is by miracle that we recognize the present event and we authorize it; thus we have spoken.

One would be wrong to shake one's head, thinking this was a sort of delirium or superstitious illusion to be set in the framework of "Spanish fanaticism of the seventeenth century."

One would be mistaken because few events in history have been verified with the precision and the certainty of that which was known as the *Gran Milagro de Calanda*: a leg amputated under the knee and, in one night, regrown. Or better, "re-implanted," given the attestation that the lower parts of the leg in question and the foot, both buried in the cemetery of the hospital in Zaragoza almost three years before the miracle, were reattached to the stump of the young Miguel-Juan Pellicer.

It is truly peculiar that this was nearly lost to historical memory, even in the Church, a wonder that was irrefutably verified with all possible guarantees. Even I, as an investigator into these matters, learned of this news quite late through the dossier published in 1959 and reprinted in 1977 (after thorough investigations in the archives and at the site) by Fr. André Deroo, a historian and apologist well known in all things concerning Lourdes. He was investigating this matter because of the tight bonds between the great shrine of the *Virgen del Pilar* (through whose intercession the young man of Calanda was the beneficiary of this amazing miracle) and the equally great, though much younger, shrine in the Pyrenees. Based on the investigations of Fr. Deroo, and after repeated reconnoitering in Spain, I had to surrender to the evidence: taking seriously the truth of the events did not mean falling in line with the credulous, the naïve, or the deluded. I sought to document this in a book (*The Miracle*) whose widespread popularity and numerous translations into various languages brought about the renewal of pilgrimage to the remote Calanda.

But leaving Aragon, we remain in the department of the Hautes-Pyrénées, noticing that here as well, it is not true that a limb has never grown back. Or at least, its "foundational" part or "frame": the bone.

On the contrary, one of the most attested cases, and one of the most famous and rightly so of the sixty-five healings officially recognized as "miraculous," concerns precisely such an event. We are referring to Peter van Rudder, a gardener for the Viscounts Du Bus in Jabbeke (in the Belgian region of western Flanders), who, on February 16, 1867, had his left leg crushed just below the knee during a fall from a tree. The doctors verified the complete fracture of both bones, the tibia and the fibula: the two trunks were separated by a "void" of three centimeters through which a hand could easily pass — thus, the loss of six centimeters of bone altogether. The large fragments pierced the skin, provoking not only atrocious pain but also horrible, gangrenous wounds. The calvary of this poor man lasted eight years, during which the useless medical visits and therapies carried out by the best specialists in Belgium built up an impressive dossier of documentation that was obviously important for the following judgment.

Among the physicians who encountered Peter, and who would later give his testimony, there was the famous professor Thiriart, the personal surgeon of the Belgian Royal House, who could only advise the amputation of the limb. The patient obstinately refused this mutilation: his already well-rooted devotion to the Virgin Mary was greatly strengthened when news of the events in Lourdes began to reach his village, whose official recognition had preceded his accident by only five years. His doctors, relatives, and friends insisted on having the amputation, but the gardener replied with unshakeable faith: sooner or later, the Immaculate Conception who appeared to the little Bernadette would take care of it.

On April 7, 1875, the crippled man, accompanied by his wife, dragged himself on his crutches to the closest railway station. It took him more than two hours to walk the two kilometers. He changed the dressings while seated on a bench at the station: random passersby that morning testified that the necrotic extremities of the broken bones poked out of the gangrenous flesh. An attendant even intervened in an effort to prohibit him from traveling. He was hoisted onto a train car heading to Ghent, where he took the horse-drawn omnibus for Oostakker amid the protests and the disgust of the driver and the other passengers: the floor of the vehicle was immediately soiled by the smelly pus leaking from his wound, which would not stop despite the fresh dressing. Finally, he reached the destination he had longed to visit for years but which had been out of reach for him: in Oostakker, an exact reproduction of the grotto of the Pyrenees had been built and pilgrimage had immediately begun, attracting the devoted from all over Flanders.

We now follow the narration of one of the official reports:

> As he arrived before the reproduction of the statue of the Virgin exposed in Lourdes, van Rudder implored (as he would later declare) forgiveness for his sins and the grace of being able to return to work to earn a living for his family. Immediately, he felt passing through his body what he defined as "a sort of revolution." Not aware yet of what had happened to him, he dropped his crutches, made way among the pilgrims and threw himself on his knees (an act unthinkable for him up to that point) before the Immaculate. Only as he heard his wife's shouts did he realize he had been instantly and completely cured.

The first medical report, written by two general practitioners who had known his case for years, read, "The leg and the foot, quite swollen, have suddenly resumed their normal volume, such that the cotton and dressings fell off on their own. The two gangrenous wounds appear healed over. Above all, the fractured tibia and fibula are reconnected, despite the distance that separated them. The welding is complete such that the two legs are once more the same length."

Astonished, the Viscount Albérich Du Bus, a well-known senator of a sectarian anticlerical political party, converted upon seeing his gardener return healed from the pilgrimage; and the same occurred for several of the doctors who had previously examined him.

Thus, over six centimeters of bone grew back, appearing suddenly out of nowhere; or better, by mystery. It was certainly less spectacular than half a leg reattached during the night, as happened to the man devoted to the *Virgen del Pilar*. But whereas in Spain it was a matter of a "suture," however incredible it might be, and the "recovery" of flesh that had been buried for years, in Oostakker there was evidently a sort of creation of matter ex nihilo, as can be witnessed in the photographic documentation still on display in the *Bureau médical* in Lourdes. In fact, for the twenty-three years he had left to live, in full health and once more at work as a gardener, until a bout of pneumonia led to his death, van Rudder was followed by Belgian and French physicians who confirmed unanimously the inexplicable nature of his case.

In 1958, the secular medical expert Michel Agnellet quoted above wrote,

> "Impossible." That is the only word that can define this case. There is no other healing that is more impossible, more unthinkable than that of a double fracture complicated by gangrenous wounds and executed spontaneously in the space of a few seconds. Physiology requires weeks (using today's technology), at times months of immobility, therapies, and antiseptics to heal such a serious, profound, extensive wound involving the skeleton, muscles, and connective and epithelial tissues.

This is not even to mention the regrowth of the two pieces of bone to full length, growth equivalent to some twenty typed lines in a book. According to Agnellet, there was but one conclusion: "The instantaneous healing of Peter van Rudder was dictated with all the violence of an unassailable fact."

A "violence" (and at the same time a surprising delicateness) confirmed later by the autopsy. In 1898, after the death of the seventy-five-year-old gardener, his body was examined by a team led by the same doctor who had followed his case from the moment of his fracture. The historian of Lourdes, Georges Bertrin, comments, "The photos of the legs of the deceased, freed of flesh, clearly display that the left leg witnessed a miraculous cure, because the two bones are as long as those of the right leg. But at the same time, those images bear witness to the accident, with quite visible signs of the double fracture." So, for Georges Bertrin, "the invisible Surgeon who intervened where human doctors were impotent, operated with admirable art. But also, the prodigious Hand left traces that remain as clear proof of the 'operation.'"

This case registers another extraordinary detail we must notice, however. The healing, in fact, was so conspicuous and incontrovertible that the civil authorities, notables, and fellow citizens of van Rudder desired to write and sign a unanimous declaration that would serve as a further testimony, "to future memory." That truly remarkable document (an entire town gave testimony, as had happened in Calanda as well) says,

> We the undersigned citizens of Jabbeke declare that the leg of Peter Jakob van Rudder, born and residing here, fifty-two years old, was so broken by the fall from a tree that, after having exhausted the possibilities of surgery, the stricken man was abandoned and declared uncurable by the doctors and considered such by those who knew him. We, undersigned citizens, give testimony concurrently

> that van Rudder invoked Our Lady of Lourdes, venerated in Oostakker, and returned home the same day entirely healed and without crutches, such that he was immediately able to resume every type of work as before his accident. We declare and give testimony that this healing, immediate and admirable, took place on April 7, 1875.

Among the signatures was that of the viscount, immediately converted as we said to fervent devotion to Our Lady of Lourdes, to the scandal of his fellow senators in the party aligned with the most anticlerical Freemasons. It was a change of life that made news even in political circles and which represents a significant confirmation of the unassailability of the case.

It should not be marveled at, therefore, that Peter van Rudder is found at number twenty-four on the list (a merely chronological list, of course) of the sixty-five "miracles" recognized by the Church. Before proceeding to the official recognition, the Church waited for his death, to allow for a visual inspection by means of a necroscopic examination to see what had really happened to his leg. Thus proceeded confirmation with the usual caution (despite whatever some might say), even in the face of one of the most obvious, verified, and famous miracles. As we saw from the notable difference between the great number of declared "healings" and the limited number of "miracles" recognized as such by the privileged person's local bishop, what characterizes Lourdes is certainly not the superficial enthusiasm that could be suspected of naivete, but if anything a prudence that in certain periods (like in recent decades) seems to slip into "minimalism" according to some, an excess of caution.

The ideal, obviously, would be a balance between methodical doubt and openness to the mystery. At any rate, between these two options, that of prudence seems preferable to us. The truth of the Event of the Pyrenees of 1858 is too important, in the perspective of faith, not to be supported by a complexity of facts (first of which, the miracles) sifted scrupulously to avoid eventual refutations that, even if partial, would be ruinous for the entire edifice.

One must not forget that the early stages of Lourdes risked being damaged by the less than critical enthusiasm ("*une ardeur parfois hâtive*," an ardor at times precipitous, as Laurentin defines it) of Pierre-Romain Dozous, the only physician that personally witnessed the apparitions and the first to be professionally interested in the healings. Skeptical about Bernadette (and religiously agnostic), on April 7 Dozous was present at the seventeenth apparition, without removing his hat (arousing the protest of the other thousand people present), faithful to his attitude of mockery toward "the foolishly devoted" and toward that *drôlette*, that little buffoon of a girl.

Just a few steps away, however, he saw for ten long minutes the flame of the candle pass through Bernadette's fingers, too heavy to be carried; she rested it then on the ground, keeping it steady by holding the lighted wick. Verifying to his amazement that the visionary's hand had not suffered the least damage, Dr. Dozous converted on the spot and transformed into a vociferous, passionate, often intolerant and imprudent apostle of the truth of the facts, to the point of recognizing "prodigious cures" where there were none and proclaiming nonexistent "miraculous qualities" in the chemical composition of the waters bubbling from the spring. His intemperance permitted many critics to indulge in irony, sarcasm, doubts, and objections against the truth of Lourdes that Dozous wanted to demonstrate with excessive ease, without sufficient consideration, ending up damaging the good cause to which he had vowed himself so generously and in good faith.

And so, it is better that the prudence of the old religious leaders in Lourdes not be lost, those leaders who quickly distanced themselves from that doctor and continued to keep their distance from him.

We return now to Peter, the miraculously healed gardener of Jabbeke.

The case of the Belgian is above all a response to the denigrating line "There are many crutches, but no wooden legs," seeing that van Rudder left only his crutches under the pseudo-grotto of Oostakker; but he was able to do so because several cubic centimeters of his leg were inexplicably "restored" to him, after first the trauma and then the gangrene had destroyed them. But it is truly a "wooden leg," at least metaphorically, that he hung as an ex-voto: it was this artificial prosthesis that the doctors unanimously wished to substitute for his useless, maimed, decomposing limb, which would have been left a stump.

From Flanders too comes an answer to another classic objection: "Excited by the journey, religious emotion, prayers, songs, processions, rivers of incense, psychic powers that are emitted from every fervent crowd: this was the cocktail that unleashed the energies, still poorly known, but which sooner or later science would fully clarify, that led to those nervous events that superstition or religious credulity take for miracles."

This is "*le souffle guérisseur*," the "healing breath" of which Zola spoke and with him all his emulators, even today, perhaps seeking refuge behind the term "parapsychology," which sounds good but in reality means little or nothing and at any rate explains nothing.

And so, as far as one should be cautious regarding nature's ability as yet unknown (the enigma of man is much richer and deeper than "scientific" naivete thinks), one can however with all serenity exclude the possibility of ever arriving at identifying the psychic (or "parapsychological") causes of the immediate scarring over of profound, festering wounds and, above all, of the instantaneous growth of bone tissue.

Such a mysterious "creation" occurred, moreover, much more recently in another case, that of an Italian, Vittorio Micheli. An Alpine trooper from Trentino, Micheli was twenty-two in 1962 when he was stricken by a sarcoma of the left hip bone that soon led to the nearly complete destruction of the iliac bone. The bone was re-formed after Micheli was transported by stretcher, given the gravity of his condition, to Lourdes at the end of May in 1963. After thirteen years of the usual series of examinations, analyses, and checkups, on May 26, 1976, Archbishop Alessandro Gottardi of Trent signed the official declaration that recalled above all how all the committees had verified "the inexplicable and perfect reconstruction of the iliac bone." This was, in the final analysis, nothing other than a variation on the request for a "leg that grows back."

The closure of the document seems quite significant and worthy of attention: "In the face of such an extraordinary event, tied in an intimate way with the religious context of Lourdes, we must admit that there are sufficient elements for recognizing a special intervention of the power of God, Creator and Father. Through a similar intervention is manifested, beyond the sign of divine mercy towards suffering man, the reality of the intercession of the Immaculate Virgin."

There is no need to continue gleaning through the dossier to find other events that would only confirm the two we have chosen to point out. What has been said is sufficient to show that what is impossible par excellence has found its place in the annals of Lourdes.

And yet, why deny it? There might remain deep down almost a sense of dissatisfaction, a desire for "something more." Certainly, in the case of the Flemish man, in the case of the Italian from Trent, in other cases one could recall, bones were reconstituted, flesh reappeared, the unthinkable wonder of the re-creation of matter has been verified by science itself; and with such guarantees that denial, after having seen the documentation, might inevitably run the risk of appearing dishonest.

Yet, what we might desire is something even more "spectacular," if such an expression were permissible in these matters. Certainly, Peter van Rudder threw down his crutches, the dressings fell off the wounds healed in an instant, and he set off walking again. Just as Vittorio Micheli stepped off the stretcher (although in a much more gradual and less violent way), with his iliac bone reconstructed *ex novo*. It is certainly stunning, but the effect of the miraculous intervention on the bone material and on the flesh appeared in its entirety only to the experts, to the doctors taking the X-rays, doing the examinations, or perhaps the autopsies.

What we believers would like as well, and what many skeptics certainly desire, is the maimed who, immersed in the pool, reemerges immediately with his arm grown back. It is the man or the woman with just one leg, or perhaps neither, who during Eucharistic Benediction in the afternoon on the embankment (the moment in which the greatest number of healings has been verified) throws into the air the blankets covering him or her on a wheelchair and starts running.

This is the "decisive miracle," mentioned in the early lines of this chapter, that is so often demanded.

Decisive in the sense of compelling even the most skeptical to believe? In the sense of convincing everyone of the truth of Lourdes and therefore of the entire Catholic "system" to which the apparitions are tightly knit?

Well, at the cost of scandalizing some, we do not hesitate to say that such "miracle shows" would not aid the cause of faith. On the contrary, they would be fatal, stripping Lourdes of one of the most obvious signs of conformity to the gospel.

The reasons? We shall see in the next chapter.

CHAPTER 6

FREE TO ACCEPT OR REFUSE

ALL AGREE, THEN, THAT at Lourdes even legs can grow back; even bones can develop anew. And in an obvious way: according to the medical analyses, certainly. But also to those who are not doctors, but can see with their own eyes that what was immobile, inert, or agonizing moves and lives once again.

Yet even this seems insufficient to satisfy the requests of the skeptics (and perhaps the unexpressed desire of believers, as I said) for a "decisive prodigy," for a "miracle so unassailable that it could convince everyone." For example, if one by one those descending into the pool without an arm or a leg were to reemerge with their limbs instantly grown back.

The doctor and positivist Agostino Gemelli (who later converted and became a Franciscan) was right in his 1912 observation on Lourdes: "There is nothing so unscientific, so intimately philosophical (in the sense of a 'philosophy of misbelief') than such requests. The scientist has no need to see a leg or an eye grow back. For him, the reproduction of just one microscopic cell is enough. The phenomenon, for the scientist, does not vary substantially, but only quantitatively."

Yes, the future founder of the Catholic University of Milan was right. Neither were we wrong in writing the lines we shall repeat here to give fitting help to the reader's memory: "At the cost of scandalizing some, we do not hesitate to say that such 'miracle shows' would not aid the cause of faith. On the contrary, they would be fatal, stripping Lourdes of one of the most obvious signs of conformity to the gospel."

In fact, precisely therein lies what is "different" about the Christian God from every other: the fact that He proposes faith to men (which is, at the same time, experience *and* hope, use of reason *and* adherence to revelation, also in that which transcends reason); that He does not impose adhesion to something obvious (in which one must "believe" necessarily, demanding it be verified, at the risk of irrationality). As long as earthly life lasts "we see in a mirror dimly"; only "then," when the veil beyond the door of death shall be torn, shall we see "face to face," in the words of St. Paul (1 Cor. 13:12).

Yes, indeed. This is a speech — which can never be repeated too often, as a warning to the apologetics of a former time which, with its presumption to demonstrate too much, seemed not to support the Faith but to jeopardize it, stripping it of its proper character — a speech about a God who "has chosen to give sufficient light to those who want to believe and sufficient darkness to those who do not want to believe." About a God who seems to play hide-and-seek with mankind: "If he were to reveal himself completely, there would be no merit in believing in Him; if He were not to reveal himself completely, there would be no faith." Thus, Blaise Pascal was led to admit that, because experience shows us always and everywhere this mysterious strategy of God, "every religion that fails to state as a first premise that God is hidden cannot be true."

A Christianity that seeks to transform the revealed truth in Jesus Christ into an undeniable fact to be accepted willingly or not cannot be "true." Instead, Christianity demands a faith that must preserve its character of secure adhesion *and* of "wager," of certainty *and* of "risk," of necessity *and* of "freedom."

The final word is freedom, and it helps us see the plan of a God "who has placed in every truth a semblance of its contrary, so that it might be possible to believe in Him but also to doubt Him." Only a God who proposes Himself through signs, clues, tracks, fingerprints, and who does not impose Himself, appearing in His dazzling glory, can establish with His creatures a free relationship rather than a necessary dependence.

At any rate, we can say here too, "*tout se tient*"; everything has a profound coherence. If the Christian God is "Love," as the apostle John says, is it possible to return that love in kind if not in freedom, gratuitously, voluntarily, in the *chiaroscuro* — the lights and shadows — of faith? And again: "You are my friends.... No longer do I call you servants ... but I have called you friends" (John 15:14–15). Can love or friendship exist, by chance, where one imposes himself on the other?

We must not forget that the monotheism that affirms the undeniable evidence of God (to the point of refusing to recognize atheism or even doubt and goes so far as to punish, perhaps even with death, those who hesitate) calls itself *Islam*, which means "submission," and its faithful *Muslims*, "the subjugated."

Christian freedom stands before a God who proposes the Son as a "friend" to men. But it is freedom also in the sense identified by Jean Guitton: "For Christians, God is necessarily discreet. He has given an appearance of probability in the doubts that clothe His existence. He has wrapped Himself in shadows to render faith more passionate and, without a doubt, to have the right to forgive our refusal. The contrary solution to faith should always preserve its credible truth claim so as to leave entirely free the action of His mercy."

This is why, in this sense as well, Lourdes is fully in line with the gospel. Through the intercession of Mary, the Christian God privileges this corner of the world, where He intervenes not only in souls but in bodies as well, in matter, in an entirely inexplicable manner. "Miracles" occur there, signs of divine power, and sufficiently numerous and obvious to confirm believers in their faith, to reinvigorate the uncertain and spur on the tepid, to lead those who have strayed far to accept the encounter with the gospel.

But this light that radiates from the grotto, though sufficient to illuminate, is not so bright as to blind. The indispensable possibility of doubting — "the truth claim of a contrary solution" as Guitton says — is safeguarded here too. In this way, it is safeguarding man's freedom to refuse the encounter, and at the same time guaranteeing God's freedom to forgive that refusal.

Therefore, the incredulous who expect from Lourdes (and from all that is tied to the Faith) the "undeniable miracle," the famous leg that grows back instantly, do not in the least suspect that, if that fails to happen in a spectacular manner as if performed by a magician, it is due to mercy. It is as if God, in some way, were limiting his power so as to limit the responsibility of those who deny it.

Yes, responsibility. Because the suspicion of Georges Bertrin is well founded, that specialist of the wonders in the grotto quoted above: "Someone would always find some excuse. They would say: 'It is true that, under certain still-undefined conditions, nature could make a limb grow back, like it does for the tails of lizards or the legs of shrimp or some species of grasshoppers. Science will explain this too, one day.' They would shake their heads and ask for some other performance and thus unto infinity." In this way, however, their "guilt" would truly be increased according to Paul: "For although they knew God they did not honor him as God or give thanks to him, but they became futile in their thinking and their senseless minds were darkened" (Rom. 1:21).

A warning, however: here too the saying seems to hold which states that there is no rule without at least one exception. In this case, the exception of the reimplanted leg took place in 1640 in the case of the beggar of Calanda. If I did not want to succumb to the truth of that case, if I multiplied my efforts, it was precisely because here the Christian God seemed to step out of his usual chiaroscuro. But because (as I explained in the many pages of my book dedicated to that *Gran Milagro*) the documentation is so rich that it renders unassailable the truth of the event, I was left only with acceptance of and respect for the mystery. I observe, moreover, that the Author of that anomalous wonder, obtained through the name of the Virgin invoked in Zaragoza, seems to have wanted to leave it in the corner, as if not allowing the fullness of its splendor to shine, so that it would not go beyond merely local notoriety. Consider the fact that my book, which came out in 1998, was the first in 358 years to be published in Italy on a case that even many specialists had ignored or about which they had only little and generic information. In Spain also, as the echoes of the Spanish translation display, many knew nothing about it or had forgotten it, at least outside of Aragon. It was thus an incomparable but also discreet miracle, as if wanting to convince of its truth those who discover and investigate it; but which, at the same time, would not want to place humanity's back against the wall.

At any rate, the God of the Gospels seems to insist on his choice of playing a sort of hide and seek. It is the choice according to which the prodigy par excellence, on which all the others are based — the resurrection of Jesus — came about in the dark of night.

We speak of the Risen One who even refused to say a word before Herod Antipas, "who had hoped to see him perform a miracle"; who did not respond to the desperate cry of the one crucified next to him, "Are you not the Christ? Save yourself and us too!"; who refused to pray to the Father to send in his defense "more than twelve legions of angels." The Risen One who came out of the tomb without witnesses, in darkness, is not going to display his triumph to his enemies, but shows himself only to his friends. And in such a way that even at the Ascension into Heaven, the moment he left the disciples definitively, "he presented himself alive after his passion by many proofs, appearing to them during forty days," as stated in the Acts of the Apostles (1:3). "But some doubted": Matthew (28:17) was forced to recognize this with such an embarrassing phrase (for those who have an "Islamic" conception of God) that some ancient copyists felt the need to alter the text, replacing it with, "Those who had doubted." "Had," but no longer, because all were now certain not only of his messiahship but also of the divinity of the Crucified One. . . .

But that's not how it was. This enigmatic strategy of the proposal pushes to such extremes, refusing any imposition. He wants us to be "friends who freely accept the encounter," therefore, and not "servants forced to prostrate themselves before the master."

Could the strategy in Lourdes have been any different? No, it seems to us that it could not have; above all, if one is aware that the acceptance of the truth of the facts of that grotto is not marginal in the least but reaches into the heart of faith. It cannot follow laws other than those that support the entire structure of belief.

Believing that Lourdes is "true" necessarily means believing as true the entire Christian, Catholic system: theology, Christology (with its integral part, Mariology), ecclesiology, liturgy. . . . The whole Magisterium of the Church finds confirmation here, whether explicit or implicit. It might be theologically tenable (at least in theory, though some theologians doubt it with good reason) that one could be a good Catholic while denying the "truth" of Lourdes. This despite the unanimous and resolute acceptance not only by the people of God but by the entire hierarchy, from the approbation in 1862 by the bishop of Tarbes down to the passionate pilgrimages of John Paul II who returned there on his last trip abroad (his very last journey was to another Marian shrine, Loreto), pronouncing the words that did not go unobserved, "Here I am at the end of my pilgrimage." This great pope wanted to give right in front of the grotto the farewell to his inexhaustible apostolate on the paths of the world.

It might be that the perspective of faith of the believer could handle hypothetically the refusal of the authenticity of what St. Bernadette reported. But one cannot recognize Lourdes as "true" without accepting the exacting logic, and without seeing oneself as Catholic, or even entirely faithful to orthodox teaching, considering the Virgin's confirmation of the dogma proclaimed four years earlier by Pius XII, which affirmed the primacy of eternal life over life in this *lacrimarum vallis*: "I cannot promise to make you happy in this world, but only in the next"; and that exhortation to Bernadette: "Go and tell the priests that the faithful should come here in procession and that a chapel should be built here," recognizing the authority of the clergy and the legitimacy of the Roman liturgy.

Even in Lourdes, so bound to the heart of the Faith, there could not be lacking "sufficient light to believe," but also the bit of "shadow" that in some way allows for denial — or at least offers a pretext that might safeguard the appearance of the credibility of refusing. It is a probability, however small, that reserves for man the freedom to refuse and for God that of forgiving. It was necessary, more than ever, here, where the face of God in Christ is presented in the image of mercy par excellence, the Mother.

A quite singular fact has been noticed: in the six months (from February to July of 1858) during which the cycle of apparitions occurred, in the vast juridical district to which Lourdes belongs, not one crime was registered and no one was imprisoned. A truce without precedent, never witnessed before or after, not only there under the Pyrenees but in no other region in France. It was as if to reiterate that this was a "season of mercy"; Mary showed herself to bring peace in hearts and, in this way, among men.

Returning to our assumption: the Marian function in the divine plan is to intercede with the Son for the salvation of her brothers and sisters in humanity. Could Lourdes possibly be, then, the cause of perdition for those who have obstinately decided to refuse? No, it could not without rejecting its indelible gospel imprint.

Let us consider once more the case of Peter van Rudder, which we treated in the previous chapter. We chose his case for good reason, being one of the most astounding: an instant healing (with the regrowth, moreover, of six centimeters of bone), among the most attested and stunning.

As I write, I have before me a book printed in 1912 by the Catholic *Libreria Editrice Fiorentina* (Florence Bookstore Publisher): on its cover, there is an image drawn from the unmistakable art nouveau, in which the Angel of Truth (the Catholic one, not the Masonic one), holding in one hand a Eucharistic monstrance and in the other a sword, and behind her the spires of the basilicas beside the grotto in Lourdes, triumphs over figures with satanic sneers that obviously represent the demons of Deception, Evil, and Atheism. The title of the book reads, *How the Adversaries of Lourdes Respond*. The author was prestigious: already famous at the time and destined to become even more so later as founder and rector for life of the Catholic University of the Sacred Heart.

Fr. Agostino Gemelli, who as a young and brilliant physician worked for the socialist movement and for scientific positivism, proudly polemical toward all religion, was granted the grace of an amazing conversion that led him to become a Franciscan. In January of 1912, "Doctor Friar Agostino" accepted the challenge offered him by his old subversive companions and was the protagonist (one against all) in a memorable, uproarious public challenge in the headquarters of the Milan Healthcare Workers Association, an organization of anticlerical doctors, atheists, agnostics, and political extremists. Very well prepared, relying on his prestige as a scholar of medicine recognized abroad, a polemicist, a fine orator, an expert in the methods and limits of his colleagues who had also been his companions in the struggle against "clerical obscurantism," Fr. Gemelli stirred up a hornet's nest, and even risked being beaten physically. In the end, a sort of jury made up of editors of independent newspapers gave him the victory in that clash in which the facts presented by the religious friar countered the theories of the deniers.

The association that had challenged him (whose organizer was Paolo Pini, the renowned psychiatrist and apostle of "medical socialism" whose name was given to an insane asylum in Milan) did not give up. It even denounced Gemelli "for serious and repeated falsifications of the truth," requesting the professional order to issue a letter of condemnation "for the deplorable example of subjugation of science for partisan aims." They countered the positivist-turned-friar (who had written a widely read brochure titled *The Battle against Lourdes*, which reproduced the stenographer's text of the debate he had won) with another publication: *The Miracles of Lourdes and Doctor Gemelli before the Milan Healthcare Workers Association*.

It was a concise confutation with a scientific appearance, conducted by doctors seeking to disparage another doctor, Gemelli. The latter, of sanguine temperament, would not suffer this in silence and published his *How the Adversaries of Lourdes Respond*, which we mentioned above.

The sole subject of the friar-scientist's challenge (or at least the main subject), the theme on which his arguments in favor of the miracle centered, was precisely the healing of van Rudder. This case seems so evident as to be unassailable by any criticism, as we have verified by our treatment, however brief. Yet even here some gaps were found: agnostics and atheists added other insidious and seemingly authentic medical difficulties to the crude objections which Fr. Gemelli had already shot down. It seems that whoever reads with an objective spirit both this booklet of the Franciscan and his response to his colleagues' attacks cannot but conclude in favor of the truly miraculous character of the instantaneous and definitive healing of the Flemish gardener. But at the same time, we harbor the suspicion that some doubt might arise in those who read only the arguments of the "freethinkers." Well, it must be confirmed: this possibility of hesitating, even of denying, not only does not compromise the truthfulness of the mystery of Lourdes (and of the Christian mystery in general) but reiterates and reinforces it.

Remaining in the context of those signs of the divine which are the Marian apparitions, the pretext to deny seems safeguarded even in that "overflowing explosion of the Supernatural in a world imprisoned by matter" (Paul Claudel) which is Fatima. No other "Maryophany" (characterized in general by great discretion) had ever displayed such an apparatus of mysterious signs perceptible to everyone: the lightning that preceded the apparitions; the sound of thunder that accompanied the end of some of them; the dimming of the sun's light to the point of being able to distinguish the moon and the stars at midday and provoking a fall in the temperature; the white cloud that surrounded the visionaries and the tree in which Our Lady alighted; the columns of smoke, "as if angels were swinging invisible thuribles"; the luminous globe that seemed to bring the Lady there and back on September 13 (when a downpour of white petals, or perhaps snowflakes, occurred). Above all, on October 13, 1917, during the sixth and last apparition, the great wonder called the "dance of the sun" took place, which, according to an expert on the matter, Joaquin-Maria Alonso, "by common witness consisted of two elements: a vertiginous rotational movement of the star that took on all the colors of the rainbow, projecting them in every direction on the crowd, and then a translational movement toward the earth in three successive movements."

As is known, the event, extraordinary and amazing, destined to certify the truth of the apparition, had been pre-announced for that day three months before, during the third vision on July 13, and promised by the Lady two other times. Thus, the daily newspaper in Lisbon had spoken of it for some time, attracting to the Cova da Iria at least fifty thousand pilgrims, or simple curiosity seekers, among whom were many unbelievers. Along with other authorities, there was even the minister (a self-declared Freemason) of National Education, at the time strongly anticlerical. Along with many other news correspondents, there was Avelino de Almeida, the editor-in-chief of *O Seculo*, the daily of the liberal Portuguese bourgeoisie, skeptical and mocking toward all that had happened in Fatima. With his three famous articles, accompanied by photos of the frightened crowd staring into the sky, de Almeida ruined his career among his unbelieving readers. Yet, he was only doing his duty as a reporter: to testify to a fact as inexplicable as it was objective, which he himself had witnessed.

The verifications of the truth of that phenomenon, which lasted more than ten minutes, are innumerable; it would seem impossible to deny it, keeping in mind that it had been foretold numerous times, and precisely for the day on which it occurred. Nor should it be underemphasized that, at the shout of Lucia ("Look at the sun!"), one hundred thousand eyes fixed on the sun and continued to do so for more than ten minutes. Despite the fact that the clouds had almost entirely burned off and the sun shone unfiltered (it was midday and in October it is still vigorous on the Portuguese moors), no one complained about damage to their eyesight. This too is inexplicable, especially in light of other examples: recently in Italy, in the Marche, a presumed visionary prophesied a miracle of the sun; hundreds of people believed him and many had to be treated for damage to their vision.

Here too, at the Cova da Iria . . . Yes indeed, here too there seem to be discordant elements: first, the fact that not one astronomical observatory around the world (not even the one in Lisbon) noticed anything unusual on that day. In this case as well, God seems to "limit Himself": fifty thousand people witnessed a stunning phenomenon of cosmic agitation (there were some who fainted, some who panicked, some who began to flee; there were loud cries when the sun seemed to fall on the crowd three times), but this did not leave one trace on scientific instruments. If that had happened, every chance for the possibility to deny it, or at least to doubt it, would have been removed. The crushing force of the scientific document registered by objectively impassible machines would have removed all room for faith and for its pertinacious "risk." Significant in this regard were the words of Professor Federigo Oom, the well-known astronomer and director of the observatory at the University of Lisbon, interviewed by *O Seculo* just a few days later: "If it had been a real cosmic phenomenon, we would have registered it. But we did not perceive anything, and so. . . ." And so, light for faith and shadow for hesitation remain.

Thus, some spoke of a natural atmospheric phenomenon: the air was saturated with humidity due to the rains that had fallen abundantly, the sky was furrowed with clouds that frequently lowered—a refraction, an optical illusion, that's all. This was the reassuring thesis with which the unbelieving education minister sought to extract himself from embarrassment. Or one was able to take refuge in the hypothesis of a collective hallucination, however unlikely that might be, as psychiatry has long shown that there can only be individual hallucinations.

Based on some dissonant voices among the crowd of eyewitnesses, some arrived at a paradox. While, in fact, the Voltairean editor-in-chief of *O Seculo* pushed for the recognition of the miracle (or at least the mystery, the inexplicable), the Catholic newspaper *A Ordem* published the article of a renowned exponent of the believing laity who, while confirming the facts ("The sun was wrapped in colors that were changing, then it began to spin, then it seemed to leap out of the sky and fall to the earth, generating great heat"), proposed a natural explanation, considering only the fact that it had been foretold to be prodigious. He believed in the truth of Fatima, but not (or not only) of that "wonder" which, in his view, could not convince everyone.

There was even an illustrious Belgian Jesuit, Edoard Dhanis, who became rector of the Gregorian University in 1963, who while also recognizing as authentic the "Maryophany" of Fatima, clung to elements like those we have just mentioned as he concluded, "The favorable signs in the apparitions are not decisive; one can contradict them with unfavorable signs."

Important words, it seems, in the perspective of the Christian God: "Reasons for believing, reasons for doubting."

Among the great Catholic writers of the twentieth century, many cite Giovanni Papini, the *maudit*, the blasphemer who, converted in a fashion similar to that of Gemelli, ended up on his knees and wrote *The History of Christ* that scandalized secularists as much as it impassioned believers. Well, in Papini's posthumous *Diary*, one reads under the date July 19, 1944, "They make me read the book of a Jesuit (Fonseca) on the apparitions of Fatima. The Virgin seems to have descended six times from heaven to speak to three Portuguese children.... These stories, even if in good faith, are more adapted to inspire doubt than faith. And they harm the Church, even if the plebeians like them and they procure lucre for the inhabitants of that place."

Now, despite certain disturbing questions about his Christianity (in which there seems to be lacking a comprehension of the Marian aspect), it is not for us to judge the faith of Papini. The courage with which he faced the long, terrible illness that led to his death in 1956 testifies in his favor, nonetheless. A man of faith, therefore, despite it all. And the book on Fatima that he read is the classic one by the Jesuit Luigi Gonzaga da Fonseca, professor at the Pontifical Biblical Institute — not the usual devotional booklet but a serious, informative work. Of course, I have it in my personal library as well. Yet, here are the results: If the Catholic (and apologist for the Church) Papini reacts this way, how can one blame nonbelievers who doubt? Does all this not confirm the plan, the chiaroscuro plan of the Christian God?

We, naturally, are on the side of the bishop of Leiria, on the side of the Portuguese episcopate, with the Holy See and the popes (it is superfluous even to recall what Fatima meant for John Paul II and the assassination attempt on his life, on May 13); we are on the side of the *sensus fidei* of millions of devoted believers who fill with their inspiring faith the *Rainha do Portugal,* the immense field before the shrine.

But if we are on the side of all those, and without hesitation or doubts, it is precisely because even in Fatima the strategy of the *Deus absconditus* (the God who wants to be sought) seems to be enacted: propose, not impose; illuminate, not blind; allow to see, yes, but alongside shadows and enigmas.

At Lourdes a similar strategy has been enacted (as we have seen) in the healings that have occurred ever since the first day; but it seems particularly evident in the beginning, marked by a discretion compared to which the visibility of Fatima represents an exception.

In the next chapter we shall continue with these reflections.

CHAPTER 7

THE STRATEGY OF THE VIRGIN

AS I SAID, "EVEN in Fatima the strategy of the *Deus absconditus* seems to be employed: propose, not impose; illuminate, not blind; allow to see, yes, but alongside shadows and enigmas. At Lourdes a similar strategy is being enacted (as we have seen) in the healings that have occurred ever since the first day; but it seems particularly evident in the beginning, marked by a discretion compared to which the visibility of Fatima represents an exception."

We continue from this point our reflections of the Christian God who proposes and does not impose, always leaving a margin of penumbra that allows for refusal, saves man's freedom, and preserves for God the right to forgive. Let us observe, then, how the colossal constructions in the citadel in the Pyrenees, which millions of the faithful have transformed into the most important pilgrimage site in the world, rest on a very fragile base, almost inconsistent for what Paul calls "the wisdom of the wise," those whom God confounds. Everything, in fact, rests on what just one witness has told us, to whom no human tribunal would have given their trust.

Let us not forget that only from a radically evangelical perspective can signs of credibility be revealed, those which for the "world" and to "good sense" are, on the contrary, reasons for insurmountable incredulity. Only the perspective indicated by Christ, revolutionary in the proper sense (from *revolve*: overturn, capsize, invert) can make us believe in the incredible. In other words, that God decided to entrust His message to this adolescent who lacked everything. It is not edifying rhetoric, but reality: her condition was equal to the biblical "poor of Yahweh."

Social status, culture, wealth, even health: the opposite of all this could be found in Marie-Bernarde Soubirous, called Bernadette, a fourteen-year-old (but with the maturity of a ten-year-old, according to the doctors who examined her, not yet a woman, due to insufficient nourishment) asthmatic, suffering from a stomach ailment, closed in the silence of a timid and introverted youth, illiterate and considered by several of her relatives incapable of learning anything, uneducated in religious matters as well, to the point of ignorance of the mystery of the Trinity, the daughter of the most miserable family in the city, residing in the cell of the municipal jail that had been emptied because it was considered too unhealthy even for the inmates, with a father who was not only a failure and with a reputation (though unfair) of being a do-nothing and a heavy drinker, with prison time in his past for suspected theft: released after nine days, he did not pursue the accusation's being so inconsistent and failed to proceed to a verdict, thus leaving an infamous suspicion upon him.

We must realize that, in all this, only the eyes of faith can detect a mysterious conformity to the gospel and therefore the stigmata of the truth. Only acceptance of an overturned perspective with respect to the "eyes of the flesh" can make resonate the Magnificat intoned by the One to whom Bernadette Soubirous gave witness: "He has regarded the low estate of his handmaiden. . . .; he has scattered the proud in the imagination of their hearts, he has put down the mighty from their thrones, and exalted those of low degree; he has filled the hungry with good things, and the rich he has sent empty away" (Luke 1:48, 51–53).

Therefore, the awareness of the "scandal and the folly" (to human good sense) of taking seriously the words of such a visionary might be useful for keeping far from any surprise (which caused indignation for some old apologists) in the face of the refusal of the truth of Lourdes by so many. How can one accept the credibility of those events from their very beginning, if one remains on a purely human plane, indifferent to the gospel dimension? Is it not through the choice of intermediaries who are objectively quite unreliable that God safeguards His discretion, His penumbra?

Let us not forget that in the beginning, even that priest of firm and sincere faith, the parish priest Fr. Peyramale, remained diffident (to use a euphemism) before the sickly, ignorant girl from such a miserable family, surrounded by less than edifying voices. Moreover, the first meeting between the parish priest of Lourdes and his insignificant little lamb (before then unknown to him) took place in the presence of two of Bernadette's aunts, Basile and Bernarde—a presence that certainly was not conducive to increasing the credibility, even the "moral" credibility, of the girl, given that both of these relatives had been chased out of the Daughters of Mary by Peyramale himself when they were found to be pregnant before getting married. In fact, here is the conclusion shouted by the terrifying priest before the women: "It is a disgrace to have such a family that brings disorder to the town." Then, addressing the "sinful" aunts after having menaced with his look the supposed visionary (who later said she tried to "make herself little, little like a grain of millet"), he commanded, "Close her up in the house and don't let her out anymore!"

Only with time would the hierarchy of gospel values make headway among the clergy, until arriving, four years later, at the words by which the bishop of Tarbes recognized the supernatural character of the apparitions: "Once more, the instrument of which the Omnipotent makes use to communicate His mercy is that which is weakest in the world." But here, the bishop placed himself in a perspective incomprehensible outside of faith: How can one be indignant with those who are enclosed in merely human categories and shake their heads incredulously? Faith can understand even the disturbing episode of that bishop who threw himself down on his knees before the little girl as she peeled potatoes for the convent of the nuns, asking for her blessing. Faith understands, but the "reason" of the world, left to itself, condemns or is awestruck.

As historical research has shown, the view that Bernadette was persecuted by the civil authorities, from the prefect to the mayor, from the judges to the police commissioner, considering those authorities to have been animated by an anticlerical or even anti-Christian spirit, is mostly unfounded and thus unjust. It is like a script from an old, edifying film, where on one side there are the good guys who believe and pray, and on the other the bad guys who mock and persecute. That was not the case: those men were, at least formally, good Catholics; all of them were at least practicing and died (without exception) in a religiously edifying manner. They carried out their duties as zealous functionaries, which was providential and has provided us a dossier of indispensable information and correspondence. Which brings to mind the saying of an ancient Church Father according to whom "the long doubt of Thomas was more useful than the immediate faith of the Magdalen."

If at times those authorities pushed their severity beyond what was required, it was not only for love of the constituted and legal order, not only for their human concern for their careers, but above all because role and formation did not allow them, though believers, to place themselves in harmony with the gospel folly. Therefore, seeing the low quality of the girl's social extraction, they could not think otherwise than of a hallucination or a fraud, a scam on the part of her ravenous relatives. Those who examine the documents collected by René Laurentin in his monumental dossier find that those functionaries of the Second Empire (which in those years, moreover, was passing through a "Catholic" phase, with a renewed understanding between Throne and Altar: Napoleon III needed the political support of the faithful) declared themselves defenders of "divine dignity," refusing to believe that the Omnipotent in Heaven would make use of an intermediary of such illiterate misery, of that insignificant figurine wrapped in her rags and in her patched mantle only four and a half feet tall. The very last in stature as well: the "smallest" girl, not only socially but physically, in all Lourdes. And matters did not change with age: in the convent in Nevers, where novices and sisters, in the liturgy, on their walks, in processions, were arranged by height, she was always the first in line, the "little one" in all senses, the confidante of the Immaculate.

Further justifying the behavior of the authorities (confirming once more that the status of faith is chiaroscuro, a "for" that is always opposed by an "against"), one often forgets that after the last public apparition to Bernadette, from April to July in Lourdes and in many of the neighboring valleys, there was an outbreak of an "epidemic of visionaries." Dozens of people (children as well as adults, women and men) stated they too had had visions, falling into ecstasy, announcing "secrets," often finding a trusting audience, perhaps even among the clergy. But not the bishop, who intervened on July 8, energetically denouncing the abuses and finally bringing them to a halt.

This confused period is often passed over in embarrassed silence. But wrongly so: in fact, precisely this chaotic situation can help us understand why the authorities decided to block off the grotto with a fence, and why they threatened with imprisonment "whoever might declare they have had supernatural visions." But above all, such an "epidemic" offers further confirmation of the power of the truth of the message entrusted to Bernadette, who succeeded in triumphing over those dangerous imitations. They too can be counted among the "contrary" reasons that always accompany the walk of faith. Was not Émile Zola's thesis (and that of all those like him) about hallucinations being the basis of the great pilgrimage to the grotto reinforced by these scenes abounding in ecstasies and pseudo-mystical trances?

René Laurentin attempted to reflect on his decades-long experience as a collector of every document and every historical crumb regarding the events that began in 1858. He spent himself trying to reach a broader vision of the enormous puzzle he had assembled, to distill "the meaning of Lourdes."

Sens de Lourdes (The meaning of Lourdes) was the title he gave the booklet whose preface by Bishop Pierre-Marie Théas offered these exacting words: "Nothing has been written that is as beautiful or luminous as these few but very dense pages that truly reveal the mystery of Massabielle, its value as an evangelical sign, its place in the life of the Church."

Let us draw from this work, then, words with the authority of the expert and the *sensus fidei* of an obedient priest, words which seem opportune for reiterating and confirming all we have said to this point. The quotation is noticeably lengthy, but entirely justified. We have no intention of saying at all costs something new here, but when necessary, of collecting the best of what has already been said and merits being repeated. Those who write about these matters, so near to the gospel mystery, should imitate the "householder who brings out of his treasure what is new and what is old" (Matt. 13:52).

Here is the reflection of Fr. Laurentin:

> This surprising fact must be emphasized: only Bernadette saw the apparitions. She was the only one to witness the Virgin Mary, visible and audible to her, invisible and inaudible to the others.... But why would Mary make an appeal to such testimony? Why did she not reveal herself to the twenty thousand people gathered there on March 4, rather than secretly and only to a girl lost in that crowd? Why should a message with a worldwide significance pass through this channel so feeble and disproportionate? Well, Mary did nothing other than place herself in a more general divine disposition, whose meaning we must discover.

The "meaning" is this, as Laurentin recalls: "God's tactic, when he wanted to reveal Himself to the world, was not that of making a big show before the masses, but that of choosing a person, or a little group of people, to whom He entrusted the task of transmitting his word." So it was from the very beginning with Abraham, then with the prophets of the Old Testament. Finally, "the incarnate Word Himself, leaving the world without having converted it, tasked a group of twelve witnesses to take to the nations the knowledge of Salvation."

Here then is the question (continuing to quote our Mariologist):

> Why does the omnipotent word of the Master of the world pass through paths so limited and often so fragile? Because such a design reveals the delicacy of God toward man. He created him free; he does not want to force his freedom; he does not impose himself through duress (in the style of earthly dictators) but proposes His Word with the humble means properly fitted to our scale. He acts among humanity not by means of exterior violence, seductions of terror which are the weapons of the Antichrist, but from within, making use of people whom no greatness "according to the flesh" can distinguish from others. In effect, God proposes himself to humanity in a human way.

As can be seen, this is the discourse of the chiaroscuro, of the "hidden God," that we are attempting to present here.

Returning now to our topic, Laurentin observes that "the Virgin of Lourdes enters into this same general disposition established by God. Entirely dependent on Christ, steeped in His aims and methods, Mary transmits her message in the same manner, the most humbly human: by means, namely, of a poor little girl, illiterate, sickly, despised, so that the work of Heaven might pass entirely through an earthly channel, through the free action of a human creature."

Here we have an authoritative confirmation, one of the many possible, on the path which has already placed before us a question: Why does "the Miracle" not happen at Lourdes, the one with a capital *M*, the one capable of cornering everyone, of convincing even the most skeptical, of bringing about the triumph of the Truth in which the devout believe?

It is the same reason, as we have already observed, for which, after the Resurrection and before the Ascension, Jesus made no spectacular appearances but appeared to his disciples and to them only "for forty days, speaking of the kingdom of God." It is their turn to be the instruments for the construction of that kingdom, founded on faith, whose evidence is given *in interiore hominis*[4] by grace; not by external, spectacular, undeniable, and therefore "violent" proofs that would oblige everyone to believe. This type of reflection enables us to understand how far from the Marian "strategy" (which is simply that of the Christian God) were the religious of whom Zola spoke in his novel. The episode is not the fruit of fantasy: during the French national pilgrimage of 1894 in which the writer took part as a skeptical and distressed observer on the famous White Train (bearing the "gravely ill"), there was a man who died. The director of the pilgrimage, a friar with great fervor and heroic commitment in the service of the suffering but also not known for his great discernment, in the atmosphere of general religious excitement proposed a sort of dramatic challenge. From the height of the pulpit rising next to the grotto, he posed the dramatic question: "Might God have wanted this man to die to show to the world His omnipotence?" Getting the pilgrims to pray in the most intense manner possible, he cried: "It depends on you whether an amazing miracle shall stun the world!" As the cadaver was lowered into the pool of the waters of healing (a macabre scene wherein Zola was able to display all his extraordinary art as a realist), the crowd was incited to let forth a cry of invocation: "Lord, may Your voice be raised to convert the earth! Say but one word and the whole world shall celebrate Your name!"

Naturally, the miracle of resurrection did not occur. God knows better than men what is appropriate to His glory. Among the consequences of that "attempt to violate Heaven" (as Zola said), beyond the obvious disappointment of the pilgrims there was the delicious pretext given to the writer to confirm his prejudice of "Catholic fanaticism" to the point of delirium.

Let it be clear: for too many centuries, too many believers have sought to reduce to the "reasonable" (and perhaps today to the "politically correct") the disturbing role of disciple indicated by Jesus at the moment He bid His disciples farewell. It is a description provided by the Gospels that has very little to do with the pale common sense of too many contemporary Christians, timorous above all to "believe too much." "And these signs will accompany those who believe: in my name they will cast out demons; they will speak in new tongues; they will pick up serpents, and if they drink any deadly thing, it will not hurt them; they

[4] Editor's Note: "Inside the person"; a reference to a line from St. Augustine: *In interiore hominis habitat veritas* (Inside men lives the truth).

will lay their hands on the sick, and they will recover" (Mark 16:17–18). It seems that for many the assurances and examples throughout the New Testament have remained a dead letter, such as that in the Letter of James: "The prayer of faith will save the sick man, and the Lord will raise him up," because "the prayer of a righteous man has great power in its effects" (James 5:15–16).

Yet, rediscovering, as one should hope, the amazing strength of faith that might "move mountains" (see Matt. 21:21) (if it could really overcome all hesitation) does not imply the right to demand proof and undeniable confirmation out of a desire more to "confound skeptics" than to show compassion to the suffering.

As Laurentin says, "Apparitions and miracles are *exceptional signs*: they do not fall under the guarantee of the promise 'ask, and it will be given you' (Matt. 7:7). Christ clearly demonstrated that similar signs, not necessary for salvation, would not be given, at least not ordinarily. Thus, he refused to give the Pharisees a sign from Heaven." As the experience of more than 130 years of pilgrimages and tens of millions of the faithful confirm, "the divine concession of the Marvelous is the exception, even in Lourdes, and is out of our control: when some, through an error excusable only by their sincere fervor, sought to violate Heaven to obtain a miracle, Heaven denied it." And denied it, we believe, to safeguard the "penumbra" of a God who loves discretion. His ways are not our ways (see Isa. 55:8), although we would appreciate evidence and irrefutable proof. The divine way is other: "For now we see in a mirror dimly," and only after having crossed the threshold of this world shall we see "face to face" (1 Cor. 13:12). There, *verification*. Here, the *wager*.

But was the little, modest "miracle," the "guarantee" of the supernatural, not denied to the human instrument of the apparitions, Bernadette, which her parish priest Fr. Peyramale had asked of her?

Laurentin gives his philological reconstruction of the evening of March 3, 1858, in the following way. "Bernadette called at the rectory: 'Reverend Father, the Lady still wants the chapel.' 'Did you ask her name?' 'Yes, but she would only smile.' 'She is making fun of you.' But at this point, it came into Fr. Peyramale's mind to ask for a sign. In Guadalupe in Mexico, in the sixteenth century, the Virgin made the mountainside bloom with flowers in the heart of winter. 'Well, if the Lady really wants her chapel, she must tell her name and make roses blossom in the grotto.' "

The following day, after the apparition, "Fr. Peyramale: 'So, what did the Lady tell you?' Bernadette: 'I asked her what her name was. She smiled. I asked her to make a rose garden bloom. She smiled again. But she still wants the chapel.' "

No miracle show, then. This greatly disappointed even people formed in a spirituality not in the least prosaic, such as Mother Marie-Thérèse Vauzou, novice master in Nevers, who remained a skeptic almost to the end (although she died invoking Our Lady of Lourdes), precisely because, as she repeated, "Despite it all, the rose garden did not blossom!"

So too, as apologists more enthusiastic than critical imprudently held, the discovery of the famous wellspring on February 25 was not a miracle. We read here the text of the visionary's testimony, reconstructed from historical sources: "*The Lady* told me: 'Go to drink at the fountain and wash yourself.' Not seeing any water, I went to the *gave*. But she made a gesture with her finger to go under the rock. I found some water, like mud. So little that I was hard pressed to collect some in the palm of my hand. Three times I threw it down because it was so dirty. The fourth time I succeeded."

Well, as was shown from the interrogations of others (peasants, fishermen, goat herders, and pig herders) who frequented Massabielle "before," water had always been there in that grotto so close to the river and located under a crag rich in springs. Bernadette's hands did not make water flow from a dry terrain, as certain old and edifying texts say, from a spring that had not been there; it was already there, although until then it had not been noticed. Furthermore, the analyses established that the water is chemically pure, but similar to all the other mountain springs, without particular chemical traits that might render it "mysterious." Here too, as is known, indiscreet apologetics has indulged itself. In the words of the marvelous evangelical wisdom of Bernadette ("She knows nothing, but understands everything," her parish priest said of her), "It's not the water that can cure you. It's your faith. The water is only a sign."

The "wonder" is quite discreet, as is its habit: the little girl knew nothing of the presence of a spring, as demonstrated by her first reaction to go to the river to seek the water, and then her turning toward the grotto, ending up crawling on her knees and elbows to reach the point that had been indicated "by the finger" of the Lady—a spot she had not known about. A surprise: when work began to create the canalization, it was found that the little hole excavated by Bernadette's hands was exactly where the water was seeking an opening to come out. It was a detail worthy of a hydraulic engineer. A skeptic would call it a chance discovery.

As regards its "quality," if there is a mystery here, it too is well hidden, in dimensions accessible only in the depths. If, in the chemical analyses performed by normal laboratories, that water appeared normal, yet according to the radiesthesists, it had a unique trait: it would "not die"; in other words, it preserved over time its magnetic field. But as René Laurentin, who also heard these claims, warns, we are on risky ground here, and caution and prudence are necessary.

Are we not once more in the chiaroscuro that always surrounds and envelops all that truly belongs to the gospel?

CHAPTER 8

Europe and the Woman of Revelation

I PROMISED AS WE began this study that I would try to respect its notebook character: hence, a variety of topics, rather than the rigidity of a treatise that runs the risk of stagnation.

Therefore, after several chapters dedicated to reflecting on the meaning and the "style" of the Marian apparitions, giving the events of Lourdes pride of place as a cornerstone to build on, this time I would like to take the liberty of making an anomalous incursion.

Remaining all the while on Marian terrain that can be considered narrow and limited only by those who do not know it. On the contrary: the truth of the old Catholic adage I have already quoted ("*de Maria, numquam satis*," one can never say enough about Mary) is confirmed as well by the excessive amount of material I have at hand, after years of reading, experience, and reflection. And so, the problem, for me, is certainly not penury, with the subsequent question, "What can we talk about this time?" But on the contrary, it is abundance, as I ask myself, "What should I give precedence to?"

Given that a choice must be made, we shall begin with a curiosity (allowing that such a term has meaning in these matters) tied to the apparitions in a discreet, almost hidden way, as is the style of the Lady we are contemplating. Or shall we say, the mysterious series of apparitions which in Paris seems to have set off a sort of "Marian epiphany in various acts" (as it has been called) and whose stage was nineteenth-century France. Obviously, we are speaking about the year 1830 and the place Rue du Bac,[5] with its celebrated "Miraculous Medal." The successive stages of the mysterious "epiphany" were La Salette (1846), Lourdes (1858), and Pontmain (1871). The "supernatural character" of all these episodes was recognized by ecclesiastical authorities, as was the fifth "act" that took place in 1876 in Pellevoisin: a washer woman of that locality along the Loire, working in the Castle of La Rochefoucauld, was instantaneously and completely cured from her agonizing acute peritonitis. Mary, who would appear to her fifteen times as the "Mother of Mercy," confirmed her strategy in the words "I chose the little and the weak for my glory." Pilgrimages were carried out to the place for many years, even in the absence of formal recognition — an important criterion but not the only one. The primary criterion is that of the Gospels: the tree will be judged by the quality of its fruit.

We shall return to what took place in Paris in 1830, as it deserves. Not by chance did a philosopher such as Jean Guitton (one of the last cultivators of this "theology of history" which seems lacking in the Catholicism of our day) choose precisely this series of events for the profound meditation to which he dedicated a famous book.

For our purposes here, we shall limit ourselves to a summary outline. On various occasions in July and November of 1830, Mary appeared, conversing with and even allowing herself to be touched by (a unique case, I believe) a novice of the Daughters of Charity (the Vincentian Sisters) in the chapel of their Parisian motherhouse. The young girl was named Catherine Labouré. She was beatified in 1935 (two years after the canonization of Bernadette Soubirous) and was enlisted in the ranks of the saints in 1947. Her body, buried in the same chapel of the apparitions in Rue du Bac, is the subject of one of the most impressive (and discreet) pilgrimages in Europe; it seems nearly two million visitors flock here every year from every part of the world. And all this under the noses of many Parisians who pass by without even knowing why this cosmopolitan and silent crowd files into an apparently anonymous courtyard, at the back of which they might glimpse a chapel surrounded by other buildings.

It is a hiding place that fits the Marian style we have come to know, and it extends to the visionary as well, and in a dramatic way. For forty-six years, the

5 Editor's Note: The name of the Paris street on which is located the Chapel of the Miraculous Medal, where St. Catherine Labouré received her apparitions.

woman privileged by the celestial encounter served the poor and the sick ("our masters," she called them) in the hospices of the order, not only with great humility but also in absolute silence. During her lifetime, no one but her superiors (and only very few of them) ever knew of the favors that had been granted her: and even her sisters who treated her as ignorant, if not as a fool, were stunned (and a few scandalized) when after her death, they learned that Our Lady had privileged that little peasant girl who, in silence, carried out the heaviest and most unpleasant chores. "An example, as in Bernadette's case, of a silent, hidden sanctity," wrote René Laurentin. Here too we are in line with the "hidden" wonder. As recalled in the last chapter of the biography of St. Catherine, "When her corpse was exhumed, the hands that had touched the Virgin Mary and the eyes that had seen her appeared extraordinarily well-preserved."

It is poignant to recall that in 1858, twenty-eight years after her mystical experience, when Labouré learned of the events in Lourdes and was given some information about the Lady, she exclaimed immediately, "*C'est la même*!" She is the Same! — that is, as the Lady who appeared to her. It came to be known after her death that she had prayed to the Virgin Mary that she might "wish to show herself elsewhere," given the difficulty she had in communicating the truth of what had happened in Rue du Bac. Thus, after this peasant girl from Burgundy, it was the turn of a shepherdess of the Pyrenees, perhaps because of the former's humble request?

Mysteries of God, naturally. The perspective of faith is not unjustified, however, which sees a sort of intentional chain linking the "Maryophanies" of the nineteenth century, among which that revealed to St. Labouré was the first (with the preamble, which we shall discuss, at the end of the eighteenth century in the "*Madonne animate*," or animated statues of Our Lady, in Rome and elsewhere). For this reason as well, it is unique and significant for the believer that precisely the apparition in the heart of Paris, in those first decades of the nineteenth century to a nun unknown to the world, had etched a mark into the daily life of our contemporaries — a mark that is both profound and reticent, under the eyes of all yet ignored by most.

On November 27 of that year 1830, Mary showed herself with rays coming out of her hands and the terrestrial globe under her feet to the Vincentian novice. Around her head was a crown of twelve stars and, written in an oval, the words: "*O Marie, conçue sans péché, priez pour nous qui avons recours à vous*" (Oh Mary, conceived without sin, pray for us who have recourse to thee). In this inscription there was already the precise reference of Lourdes to the Immaculate Conception that explains more clearly the exclamation of the future saint: "She is the same!" Just as St. Maximilian Kolbe understood so well, noting that the words that were only *written* in 1830 were the anticipation of the words *spoken* in 1858: "I am the Immaculate Conception." Which is, as Fr. Kolbe says, "a definition by means of her very essence."

Returning to the description of the medal that arose from these apparitions, in the lower part are two hearts: that of Jesus, wrapped in a crown of thorns; and that of Mary, pierced with a sword, in conformity with the prophecy of Simeon (Luke 2:35). When the novice's confessor, as well as the superior of the Sisters of Charity (the only two who knew of the visions, both agreeing to keep silent about them: they would not speak even to the archbishop of Paris, who authorized the medallion), went to an engraver to prepare it to be minted, the artist was at a loss due to the tiny dimensions he had to work with in arranging the twelve stars around Mary's head. Therefore, that highly symbolic element ("A great portent appeared in heaven, a woman clothed with the sun, with the moon under her feet, and on her head a crown of twelve stars," Rev. 12:1) was placed on the backside surrounding the *M*, the cross, and the two hearts. This is how it appears on the millions of "Miraculous Medals" disseminated throughout the world and which still today are distributed in innumerable copies, in bags filled by the sisters of Sr. Catherine from a little office next to the chapel in Rue du Bac.

Bernadette as well, on that fated February 11 of the first apparition, was wearing one around her neck, tied by a thread, because her misery could not afford a necklace. Yet another sign of a bond as direct as it is enigmatic between Paris of 1830 and Lourdes of 1858. The little girl had, in the pocket of her patched apron, her only other treasure: her "two-penny rosary" with coarse wooden beads, a gift from her family bought at the Shrine of Bétharram.[6] Thus, the only two things she had on, other than the clean, threadbare clothes, were two signs of Marian devotion.

[6] Editor's Note: About nine miles from Lourdes, a pilgrimage destination since the Middle Ages. According to legend, at this location the Virgin Mary rescued a young girl from drowning in the Gave de Pau.

Returning to what I said, in May of 1949, at the European Council in Strasbourg, an organization was instituted, at that time lacking all effective political power and tasked only with "laying the foundations for the constitution of a European federation," as stated in the acts of its foundation. The following year, in 1950 that is, that council announced a contest of ideas, open to all artists, for a flag of the future united Europe. An Alsatian designer, at the time quite young, Arène Heitz, entered a sketch in which twelve white stars were spread in a circle on a blue background. As was to be revealed later, the idea was not random: devoted to the Virgin Mary, Heitz recited the Rosary daily. When he learned of the European contest and decided to participate, he had been reading the history of St. Catherine Labouré and, stimulated by her story, decided to obtain for himself and for his wife a Miraculous Medal, which until that time he had never heard of. The stars in his design, then, had come from there: and from there, directly from the book of Revelation and the "Woman dressed in the sun" with a crown on her head. As for the blue background, it was the traditional color of the Virgin (as we shall see later).

Of the 101 sketches from around the world, "inexplicably," as Heitz himself said (who entered the contest without great hope, almost as if to respond to an impulse given him by the discovery of the medal), the European Council chose his. One should note that the head of the commission responsible for the choice was a Jew, Paul M. G. Lévy, director of the Press and Information Service of the council. There was no hidden play of confessional motivations, despite the fact that the three great "founding fathers" of Europe were practicing Catholics and leaders of their respective Christian Democrat parties: the German Konrad Adenauer, the Italian Alcide De Gasperi, and the Frenchman Robert Schuman.

Furthermore, confirming the peculiarity of the decision, there were not twelve nations in the council at that time, although Heitz did place twelve stars on his proposed flag. In fact, in the face of criticism, the designer had to reply that the twelve represented "a symbol of fullness" (as it represents in the Old Testament as well: there were twelve sons of Jacob, as well as twelve tribes of Israel; and for this reason Jesus wanted twelve to be the number of his apostles, to signify that the Church is the "new chosen people").

Having adopted this symbolic perspective, when the number of member states of Europe exceeded twelve, European authorities officially established that the number of stars on the flag was to be considered immutable.

Among the other "cases" there was this: the blue flag with the circle of twelve white stars was officially adopted in 1955. That day was the eighth of December, the feast of the Immaculate Conception of Mary. Yet that time as well, they were not religious reasons that led to the choice of the date; instead, it was set according to an entirely political calendar. So thought the Eurocrats, at least, whose members seem truly to be instruments unaware of a plan that transcends them. In fact, the believer cannot fail to think, in the face of this strange affair, of the apparently senseless announcement that resounds in the Magnificat intoned by the obscure and humble Virgin of Nazareth: "Henceforth all generations will call me blessed" (Luke 1:48).

To cite but a few examples of what this unwitting choice by the European Council has meant in the daily life of all: obeying a directive, the license plates of all vehicles in Europe have been standardized to one model in which the initials of the country are inserted onto the blue flag with the twelve stars. Thus, the "sign of the Immaculate," the "symbol of the Woman of Revelation," marks in some way every street of Europe on which for centuries Mary has been proclaimed queen by those devoted to her. And is not the starry crown on the blue field displayed next to the colors of the local national flag on the façade of public buildings in every country of the Union?

These are only two examples, but all of this unites the glory, the fulfillment of the prophecy of the Magnificat, with discretion. How many among the hundreds of millions of European drivers are aware they are taking for a ride, on the front and back bumpers of their vehicles, an enigmatic though precise reference to the Virgin Mary? And how many know the origins of the flag when they see it waving above ministries, schools, hospitals, or police stations?

Along these lines, one could point out that, if united Europe has the "Marian" white and blue, these are also the colors chosen for the United Nations flag. Here, that symbol of universality which the Mother of God incarnates expands from Europe to the far reaches of the earth.

But those are also the colors of the pennant of the State of Israel. Whitney Smith, director of the Flag Research Center, the world leader in "vessilology" (the science of flags), states,

> On July 21, 1891, during the consecration of the Jewish House of Boston, the American "Israeli Educational Society" unfurled for the first time a flag inspired by the *tallis*, the prayer scarf used by Jews. In 1897, the United States delegate at the Basilea conference of the World Zionist Organization, Isaac Harris, submitted the flag for the approval of those present. In 1948, the insignia was adopted by the new State of Israel.

"White with blue stripes" — the Jewish flag — and a white garment with a blue sash was the dress of the Lady who appeared to Bernadette (always dressed this way, all eighteen times, and this fact scandalized some of the good ladies of Lourdes at the time).

But also the Virgin who lingered so long and so often in the chapel of the novitiate in Rue du Bac with St. Labouré wore garments that were "dawn white" with a "silvery-blue" mantle (to use the very words of the visionary). In the perspective of faith, would suspicion truly be inappropriate? Could it be mere chance, the identity of colors (and of forms: white crossed by a blue stripe) between the garment of the "Daughter of Zion," of the Jewish girl in whose body the messianic promise of Israel was fulfilled, and the insignia assumed by her people, the people from whom she came and to which she will always belong, despite everything?

But if for the United Nations or the State of Israel it is permissible (for those not open to the mystery of symbols) to think of a fortuitous coincidence, this was not the case for the flag that flies over Rome from its highest hill.

Here is another curious story. As we know, in 1870 the House of Savoy took possession of Rome and chose as their royal palace the Quirinale, which had previously belonged to the popes. With the inglorious flight of the dynasty, first in 1943 and then definitively in 1946, the presidents of the Republic were installed in the palace made glorious by the hands of Gian Lorenzo Bernini and Carlo Maderno. When they are present, on the highest turret, next to the Italian national flag, flutters a blue flag. This is the "president's pennant," the insignia of the head of state.

That flag is all that remains of an explicit testimony of Marian devotion. One must return to the fourteenth century, when the Duke of Savoy, Amadeus VI, called the Green Count, established the official insignia of his little state: a square banner of blue silk with an eagle in the center. The choice of color, as documents attest, was decided by the duke himself as a reference to the Virgin Mary to whom he was deeply devoted. In fact, a few years earlier he had created the Supreme Order of the Most Holy Annunciation. From that time, the color "Marian celeste" remained the characteristic of the Savoys. A trace of this can be found in the blue sash worn across the chest by officers of the Italian army on certain occasions of honor. There is also a vestige (also ignored) testified in the blue of the jerseys the Italian national soccer teams wear, as in those of the other athletic representatives of the nation. The color of the jerseys was chosen at the beginning of the twentieth century in honor of the Savoy Dynasty, although they had chosen it in a distant century in honor of the Virgin Mary.

As long as the "true" Savoy reigned, it was considered an unthinkable sacrilege to abandon the old blue flag, with its precise religious symbolism. The break was the work of Carlo Alberto, from the collateral branch of the Carignano family. In 1848, given that the intervention against Austria in Lombardy was in difficulty, the new king renounced article 77 of the Statues which he had granted just two months earlier and which stipulated: "The State shall preserve the flag, and the blue cockade is the only national one." Catholics saw in the "revolutionary" tricolor flag (whose origin is found in the Napoleonic invasion) the sign of tyranny, and for this reason as well they resisted the repudiation of a flag that recalled the ancient devotion of the dynasty to the Virgin Mary. Believers considered the abandonment of a symbol that recalled maternal protection an ominous sign. And in fact, less than one hundred years later, the Savoy were sent into exile. But history has its treacheries. More than a century and a half after 1848, after many events and upheavals, the ancient "cloth of the Madonna" flutters once more, and over the highest point in the city, over the Rome "captured" in 1870 by the Savoy waving their Jacobin tricolor. The presence of that blue banner is charged with meaning in the city that is home to the one in whom faith sees the Vicar of the Son of Mary.

And if one were to ask why precisely white and blue would be "felt" by believers as Marian colors (many centuries before the apparitions in Paris and Lourdes), the first response would be elementary: white, for purity; blue, for the sky (appropriately, *celeste* is another word in Italian for sky blue). Elementary, because this response, true as it might be, only touches the profundity of the enigma that has always bound the religious man to colors. Recall Mary's stone is sapphire blue which, according to the book of Revelation (21:19), supports the foundations of the walls of the New Jerusalem. As canto 23 of his *Paradise* illustrates, "the sapphire beautiful / which gives the clearest heaven its sapphire hue" is to Dante the image of the Virgin Mary.

It is in the depths of humanity, often unconscious, that the veneration of Mary sets its roots so deep as to reach beyond the Judeo-Christian confines, the yearning for the sacred among creatures of every time and nation.

CHAPTER 9

The Emperor Who Was Jealous of the Assumption

I do not regret having adopted in the preceding chapter a formula a bit tangential and fragmentary rather than compact: one topic per chapter. I do not repent and will do the same on other occasions. I am convinced that the vastness of the Marian discussion is so great that it requires a sort of mosaic technique, drawing together various tiles that never exhaust a theme that has its roots in God Himself.

In any case, jumping here and there while continuing to circle around Mary and the extraordinary "case" it represents for the Faith allows us to avoid the pedantry of the manuals and to keep the reader vigilant (perhaps). Here again, I shall collect another tile of the Marian mosaic.

Devotion to Mary is indisputably tied, for the people of God, to the "graces" obtained by her intercession: the spiritual prodigies, certainly, but also the physical ones — the healing of the body, above all. Well, the current declassing of miracles on the part of some theological schools as if they had no importance in the Christian system and ought even to be repressed as a mark of "alienation" or of a faith "not yet adult" must come to terms with the entire New Testament, beginning with the Gospels, full of wonders that are anything but accidental. It must also come to terms with the entire Tradition, beginning at the very origins of the Church.

In fact, the very first apologist of whom we have information is St. "Quadratus." We use quotation marks because that is the translation of the name which sounds in Greek like *Kodràtos*. Our information about him comes to us from the main historian of primitive Christianity, Eusebius, the bishop of Caesarea. At the beginning of the fourth century, Eusebius wrote in his famous *Ecclesiastical History* (based on original documents, still extant at that time), "After Trajan, Hadrian received the empire (117–138). Kodràtos addressed and submitted a discourse to this monarch that he had composed in defense of our religion because malevolent people had attempted to harass our own. This book can still be found among many of the brothers, and we have it, too."

At this point, Eusebius gives us the nucleus of Kodràtos's defense, his main argument, quoting verbatim the following words taken from the work of his fellow writer: "The works of our Savior were continuously visible because they were true. Those whom he healed, whom he resurrected from death, were not only seen when they were healed and raised, but were continually present, not only while the Savior lived on earth, but also after his departure, for a considerable time, such that some of them have survived to our day."

This is the only fragment we have of the first apologia of Christianity, written by a believer particularly prestigious and widely followed, seeing that even Eusebius defined him a "disciple of the Apostles." Well, is it not significant that precisely the "physical" wonders ("those whom He healed and those whom He raised from death...") were immediately chosen as the main reason for the gospel's credibility? Are those who, in the healing miracles in Lourdes and in every other Marian shrine (the modern equivalents of the miracles narrated in the Gospels), see signs that reveal and confirm the truth of faith in Christ really that far from authentic faith (as some demythologizing theologians would have it)? Does not one like St. Quadratus, the progenitor of a line of defenders of the gospel, remind us of the continual urgency of apologetics and point to the strongest of arguments that we can leverage?

In these pages, we have already placed the reader on guard against a type of materialism within Christianity that chases after physical proof alone, the intervention on the body. Thus, despite the best of intentions, one yields to the same partiality of those whom one seeks to contradict, the materialists for whom only "health" (*salus*) exists and not "salvation."

As concerns Lourdes, the most important part of the miracle that occurs is certainly that which one "does not see," that which is "beyond verification" by experts because it takes place in the depths of the soul, with the greatest of all miracles: repentance, the forgiveness requested and obtained, conversion.

In the face of certain excesses or deviations among the wealth of important and often moving popular Marian devotions, some rightly observe, "We run the risk of asking Mary too many 'graces' and too little 'Grace.'" Too many requests for intercession on issues, however urgent and important, that concern only our earthly life and not the eternal. We all forget, too often, the words pronounced by Mary to her darling, to the little one chosen for the encounters in the grotto: "I do not promise to make you happy in this life, but only in the next." This is true and must be continually remembered.

But this does not necessary disqualify the bureau doctors like those of the Pau. Kodràtos teaches, and with him, all apologists from the beginning of the Faith, who have never been lacking in the Church. The healing of the body is not, in the Christian vision, the priority, but it is nonetheless always a sign of the healing of the heart, and thus not to be overlooked.

We continue to revolve around the particular preoccupation of the present moment for what is called an "adult faith." This is truly peculiar, given that, in the gospel perspective, it is a contradiction in terms: Is it not written that "becoming like little children" is the indispensable condition for entering into the kingdom of Heaven? And is it not written that only "to the little ones" will the secrets of the kingdom be revealed? The more we are "adults," then, the more we risk not understanding what really counts.

Continuing with such considerations, we discussed in the previous chapter the object of the most widespread Marian devotion in the world (besides, of course, the Rosary, which is a separate case). This is the Miraculous Medal, from which the twelve stars on the European flag are derived, as we have said. It seems that over a century and a half of dissemination, as discreet as it has been massive, over a billion of these images have been stamped. This phenomenon flies in the face of those who consider it "devotional kitsch" to be renounced in the name of a supposedly "pure" faith — but in reality callous, because it would be entirely theoretical, without the least attention to the religious needs of concrete human beings.

Those advocates of a disincarnated Christianity reduced to a heady ideology detest even the waste of lighting candles in shrines on the part of the faithful. We recall that the "intellectuals" (a character fortunately unknown until the eighteenth-century Enlightenment) call themselves that because they wish to use only the intellect, expelling all the rest, the complicated part that adds so much richness to the person. We are also intellect, reason, brain. *Also*, but thank God, not *only* …

We do well here to proceed to the foundations of the Faith. For example, in the Gospel of John: "As he said this, he spat on the ground and made clay of the spittle and anointed the man's eyes with the clay, saying to him, 'Go, wash in the pool of Siloam' " (9:6–7). Or we can take another look at the first Gospel, in the chronological sense, that of Mark: "And taking [the deaf man] aside from the multitude privately, he put his fingers into his ears, and he spat and touched his tongue" (7:33). Farther along, in the same Gospel of Mark: "And he took the blind man by the hand, and led him out of the village; and when he had spit on his eyes and laid hands upon him, he asked him, 'Do you see anything?' " (8:23).

Saliva, mud, fingers in ears and on eyes: if Christ himself (although he did not need to do so to exercise his miraculous power) wanted to use such signs, how can one condemn the Christian who has recourse to "icons" such as medals, candles, images, statues? Is not all Christianity a system of signs, beginning with the Incarnation itself?

The most ancient of the Marian feasts is that which the entire Church still celebrates on August 15. "Entire" in the full sense, given that the feast is common to the Eastern Rites, to the Greek-Slavs and the so-called "Orthodox," who even dedicate the first half of the month to prepare for it and the second half to thanksgiving for it, confirming the exalted place that it reserves for the *Theotokos*. Indicated for centuries as the "Dormition of the Blessed Virgin," the celebration received even more solemn sanction through the most recent of dogmas proclaimed by a pope: that of Mary's Assumption into Heaven body and soul, proclaimed in 1950. Defining this dogma, Pius XII was simply giving solemn definition to a truth the faithful had always believed: the "necessity" that the Woman who gave flesh to the very Son of God must have escaped the corruption of the flesh.

Not only is the antiquity of this liturgical celebration extraordinary, but also the fixedness of the date. It was not established on that mid-August day in order to Christianize the pagan celebration of the *Feriae Augusti*, the feasts in honor of the emperor (as is often heard); these were celebrated on the first, not the fifteenth of the month. In fact, according to the monumental (five volumes) and meticulous *Etymological Dictionary* by Cortelazzo-Zolli, only in the early 1900s with the term "*Ferragosto*" did one begin to refer to the same day on which the Church celebrates the Assumption of Mary. Before that time, so close to our own, *Ferragosto* indicated the first or (in some regions) the tenth of the month, when the masters gave a bonus to servants and employees, allowing them to enjoy a richer meal than usual, outdoors, to enjoy the summer and in lieu of vacations, which were unknown at the time.

Nothing about the Christianization of a pagan festivity, then, even though the prospect does not scandalize us in the least. Those scandalized are only the ones who forget the word of Jesus, "I have not come to abolish [the law and the prophets] but to fulfill them" (Matt. 5:17). The gospel is not some sort of meteorite that crashes down on humanity's concept of the sacred, that destroys everything or at least devastates it, to set up camp on the ruins. The Incarnation of the Word is respectful of history and its rhythms: it completes, it does not destroy. This is a fundamental law of Christianity that is true for each aspect of it, including and above all that which concerns the Blessed Virgin. The controversy raised first by Protestants, then by rationalists, against the most profound and eternal archetypes of *homo religiosus* that resonate naturally in the Catholic veneration of Mary is a controversy that leaves unimpressed whoever remembers the evangelical constant of the Incarnation as we mentioned. On the contrary, that myopic polemic confirms those who are devoted, aware of the value of the veneration of the Mother of God and the importance of her role, for in it live the most intimate aspirations of humanity throughout the ages.

This discussion is too important to race through hurriedly and summarily. Here we have merely mentioned it. There will be time and space to return to the topic adequately. Here we only give a first warning: do not come to us recalling, with a triumphant air, the "Great Mothers" of the Assyrians, Babylonians, Egyptians, Phoenicians, and even of the Aztecs and Mayans. Do not do so, because we know everything there is to know about these: these figures not only fail to place in doubt the Marian presence in the churches of the West and the Christian East but reinforces its value.

Returning to August 15, the reasons for the choice of that date for the celebration plunge not into pagan Rome (recent historians of liturgy and spirituality assure us), but rather into ancient, early Christian Jerusalem. There, on that day, in Constantinian times was carried out a Marian celebration in the church on the Mount of Olives, which tradition has indicated as the place of the *Dormitio Mariae,* though not without debate among archaeologists.

Many centuries later, an event occurred that, although no one suspected it, would change the history of Europe. On August 15, 1769, a child was born in Ajaccio, Corsica, and was given the completely unusual name "Napolione" (as the baptismal certificate reads). When that fateful child grew and became the scourge we know, he found it embarrassing for himself and his courtiers that his birthday should coincide with the most popular Marian feast in France. Furthermore, his embarrassment was heightened by the fact that on the recurrence of the Assumption was celebrated the "Vow of Louis XIII." He was the king who, on August 15 of 1637, had issued a solemn, official decree which placed the entire nation under the explicit protection of Mary.

Could the man who wanted to become the progenitor of a new dynasty (not royal, but imperial) tolerate such an affront — an affront which would obscure the remembrance of those kings of France whose last representative had just been guillotined and who in Napoleon's eyes was guilty of being "too Catholic," of having even given saints and blessed to the Church? Furthermore, it was not in the least pleasant that, on the very birthday of the despot, the Magnificat was solemnly intoned, wherein such embarrassing words resound for the "great of the earth." Beginning with "He has cast down the mighty from their thrones" and ending in "he has scattered the proud." No, this could not continue: August 15 must be purged of such an awkward connection.

Thus, with the complicity of several sycophant bishops (and that of the weak pontifical legate in Paris), they began searching in the ancient liturgical lists and discovered that in Rome the Church once celebrated the martyrdom of a group of Christians: Saturninus, Germanus, Celestine, and *Neopoli*. Having made this discovery, philologists were paid to come up with a "scientific" demonstration of how, beginning with the name *Neopoli,* through a series of unlikely phonetic modifications, one arrived at pronouncing *Napoleo,* the name of the saint of whom nothing has ever been known. The following step was of course an official decree (on February 19, 1806) which imposed the substitution in France and throughout the empire of the celebration of the Assumption with that in honor of the unheard-of "St. Napoleon." A double feast for the state: not only the birthday but also the feast day of the parvenu who believed he could bend to his will even the liturgical calendar and uproot from the heart of the people their devotion to the Mother of God.

In Rome, the courageous Cardinal Michele di Pietro (who would find himself in prison for having opposed the emperor) drafted, upon the order of Pope Pius VII, an energetic memorial of protest and condemnation, in which he declared it "inadmissible that the civil power would substitute the veneration of the Virgin Mary Assumed into Heaven with that of a saint nowhere to be found, with an intolerable interference of the temporal in the spiritual." But the tyrannical character of the regime prevented the publication of the document. In confirmation of that character, a few years later, the pope was taken into custody by the French and dragged as a prisoner first to Savona and then to Fontainebleau.

Naturally, the end of Bonaparte also marked the end of the veneration of the "saint" fashioned in his image. And the people once subservient to the despot could now return to celebrate, in mid-August, their Blessed Virgin. In France, they were able to return to the ancient and beloved devotion also thanks to the remarkable fact recalled by a historian of hagiography, Gérard Mathon: "The veneration of this 'St. Napoleon' that arose more out of the intrigues of his flatterers than out of history, produced a surprising and unexpected benefit: it served to maintain as an obligatory feast the 15th of August, which otherwise would have been suppressed as were so many others in the articles added to the Concordat of 1801."

Thus, another example of those mysterious tricks of time upon which those who investigate the hidden yet tenacious presence of Mary in the world so often stumble, with emotion and surprise. The powerful were not only thrown down from their resplendent thrones, but wanting to dethrone her who had intoned the Magnificat, ended up entrenching the veneration even more deeply. Still today, after so many decades and events, all France closes down for vacation every August 15, because the festive character of that day had been reiterated by an emperor who sought to promote his own eternal glory — an "eternity" that lasted a mere eight years from the decree signed on August 15 dedicated to "St. Napoleon" to the abdication in March of 1814. The imperial birthday is now remembered only by a few specialist historians, while for the Assumption, despite everything, much of the West continues to shut down — de-Christianized, perhaps, but not to the point of renouncing several tenacious Marian signs in its calendar.

We must add, in this regard, something that is more than a mere curiosity; something that seems to indicate an opportune task for the Lady who, we recall once more, intoned, "He has scattered the proud in the imagination of their hearts, he has put down the mighty from their thrones, and exalted those of low degree." The task, namely, of exorcising the solemn remembrance of the great of the earth, often those who were tyrants.

In fact, if Napoleon was born on the feast of the Assumption, the first apparition of Lourdes took place on the day which would become Adolf Hitler's patronal feast. It has always surprised me that no one has ever noticed it, as far as I know: February 11 is the liturgical celebration of St. Adolph, the name given to the future Führer at the baptismal font in Braunau am Inn. Even more incredible is that he was one of the few ancient Germanic saints, bishop of Osnabrück. Thus, Germany had celebrated the date for centuries, as it did in 1858, the year in which the events in Lourdes began.

Those who so desire can attribute this to "chance."

CHAPTER 10

A True Culture

According to specialists, a complete list of the written works dedicated to Mary, throughout all history and in every language, would be practically impossible due to the exorbitant amount of material. At any rate, it seems certain that this bibliography would exceed two hundred thousand titles. Whatever the exact number, one fact is certain: no person in the history of the entire world has had such homage of words paid to them. This limitless bibliography, without any possible comparison, is one of the aspects of this mysterious realization of prophecy that Luke attributes to Mary: "Henceforth all generations will call me blessed."

Yet, a seemingly bewildering fact must be acknowledged: the "world," at least the Western world of the past two centuries, has banished the better part of this immense Christian literature to the limbo of subculture, to the ghetto of devotion that does not interest academic Culture, the only culture with the right to a capital *C*, a right to full citizenship in the domain of intellectuals. This is a general reality in the religious realm that seems to intensify in the specific sector of Marian output: it is ignored through a mixture of indifference, disdain, and compassion.

To see this, it suffices to examine the particularly significant indicators of the actual market found in the catalogues of antiquarian booksellers, where one discovers that the volumes dedicated to the Virgin Mary are offered at some of the lowest prices, unless they are ancient books with beautiful plates or interesting bindings. But the price, in these cases, is due to these editorial characteristics. When the book has nothing else to offer than its religious content (whether devotional or theological), it is offered at a clearance price.

Rubbish, then, of no interest to a man of "true" culture. The latter, if interested in Mary, is so for the sake of ethnological or sociological investigations on places of worship, pilgrimages and their social composition, the historical origins of certain devotions, and other similar questions. Or one makes elaborate show of one's erudition to display the true origins of Marian veneration in the context of ancient, pre-Christian cults. Or psychoanalytic readings are ventured on the "profound needs," on the "unconscious impulses," that might explain that sort of "Catholic pathology" which is devotion to the Virgin Mary. All this is carried out with the apparatus of scientific appearance that excludes, obviously, every hypothesis entailing even the least involvement of the specialized authors of those studies, the only ones with the right to speak on these matters.

Thus, it seems that the Virgin Mary "does not make culture," that the tens or even hundreds of thousands of books dedicated to her never existed, or have value only to circulate in the devotional ghetto. But if the situation in the Marian field reaches its extreme here, it extends as well to all the rest of the immense Christian output, all that is written by believers for believers. A subculture, precisely. Useless stacks of paper that no one would ever cite in their bibliographies.

Is there anything to regret? Many believers are convinced so. Some of them reach the point of suspecting a sort of conspiracy of agnostic secularism or rational materialism which leads to the repression of Catholic realities. Other believers, especially today, risk a type of cultural inferiority complex from this "secular" refusal to take seriously the general religious literary production (and that on Mary in particular).

It seems there is here a fundamental misunderstanding that must be clarified. It is important to do so to understand how one often approaches the Christian dimension in an erroneous way which ends up distorting it. In essence: what truly is of interest to the Faith is the "culture of sanctity," which has little if anything to do with the culture that despises the "products of devotion."

This story comes from afar. Beginning in the eighteenth century, the Enlightenment proposed one objective above all: substitute religion with politics and culture. The latter was understood in a restrictive, academic sense.

Culture would become a religion in its own right, with professors (and intellectuals in general) as its new priesthood.

The use of the terms *cattedra* (tenured chair) and *cattedratico* (university professor) is significant: they were previously exclusive to the place where the bishop taught, from which the word *cathedral* derives. Now the magisterium passed to professors. *Devotion* was substituted with *erudition*; the *seminary* with the *university college*; the *breviary* with the *manual*; the *Summa Theologica* with the encyclopedia of sciences and techniques which became the instrument the Enlightened set to work on.

From such a perspective would necessarily derive the downgrading of all religious literature and the expulsion into subcultural limbo the genre considered "devotional." Namely, the genre that was directed toward believers and which moved in the realm of faith, which has nothing to do with the kind of erudition and human wisdom to which God is not even a hypothesis to be taken into consideration. And, in any case, "has nothing to do with" freethinking and the actions of men who have left childhood and the darkness of the sacrificial ages they were refusing, fighting, and defaming.

Certainly, one must recognize that, among the nearly two hundred thousand Marian books, there have been many that (as René Laurentin, who is beyond suspicion, says) are "marked by a disturbing mediocrity"; there are perhaps too many that show how "good will, good intentions, and good sentiments often are not enough."

It is true that good writing and literary genius are not always positive traits, in the perspective of faith, given that "heresy has always had its brilliant writers: from Pelagians to Jansenists, to the Reformers down to Modernists; not to mention atheists and agnostics who have had at their service excellent pens" (G. K. Chesterton).

Having recalled this, we nevertheless confess that the believer is the first to feel embarrassment when, in certain aspects of Marian devotion, the religious spirit seems to tie itself to kitsch, bad taste, saccharine sentimentalism. This has nothing to do with authentic "sentiment," the sentiment that moved Pascal to say that the Christian God is a God who is "*sensible au coeur*" even more than "*sensible à la raison.*" And for this "sensibility to the heart" the Marian aspect at its very best is certainly not irrelevant.

But while denouncing or rejecting what can be improved or even censured, the believer knows that, in whatever is authentic to it, religious products, including devotional works, are the expression of true culture. All of this instructs, consoles, saves, for only this is capable of drawing upon the truth about God and therefore about man. Intimidated by the violence (so often disguised as tolerance) of the "wise according to the world," we too seldom meditate on the consequences of these upsetting words (in the truly etymological sense of "overturning") transmitted by Matthew and Luke.

It is significant that those words that belittle worldly wisdom are both in the Gospel of Matthew, addressed to the Jews, and also in that of Luke, addressed to Hellenistic gentiles, as if to communicate to both traditions the new "cultural parameters," the new criteria for distinguishing between those "who know" and those who "do not know." "In that same hour he rejoiced in the Holy Spirit and said, 'I thank thee, Father, Lord of heaven and earth, that thou hast hidden these things from the wise and understanding and revealed them to babes; yea, Father, for such was thy gracious will' " (Luke 10:21).

It is in this logic that Bernadette Soubirous was chosen to be a true "wise one," who knows much more about what truly counts than the entire academic corps of Europe. It was to her that the "things" of the good news were revealed, while they were hidden from the "learned and the wise," from the intellectuals, the priests of the new cultural religion. Not to deny their merits and potential, except when it comes to consoling, saving, making known the profound Truth that lies behind the chaotic mass of partial truths.

This discussion is true not only of Bernadette, whom we take here as an example. When has the Church ever placed diplomas, degrees, or academic culture among the conditions for recognizing the sanctity of one of the baptized? Is this not the same Church that (in 1970, by the "intellectual" and "learned" Paul VI) proclaimed as one of its Doctors a woman, Catherine of Siena, who could read only poorly, and only toward the end of her life learned how to write?

Even with their inevitable dross, the two hundred thousand books on Mary are to be situated and evaluated in this dimension. Why should we be amazed or scandalized then if they are ignored and despised as "subculture" by those who believe they know better but in reality cannot see beyond their own library, containing all the words of all the sciences? All, that is, except those of the *Scientia salutis*, the science of salvation, as Christian tradition defines faith.

In the end, all this is already found in the Magnificat. The "proud" and the "mighty" whom the God of the Annunciation "scattered" and "overturned" are not to be understood only in the political or economic sense, as is often thought today. Capitalists and politicians are not the only two human categories that run the risk of incarnating the anti-gospel. In a certain type of culture (to which some Catholics pay excessive attention, if not deference) it is easy to find "arrogance" resting on the "might" which the intellectual, the man of academia, enjoys in our society, to the point of an amusing idolatry of the media toward whoever has the title of Nobel Prize winner.

Should we, then, radically overturn the dominant attitude and renounce books of culture "according to the world" and only preserve the books of devotions, edification, and spirituality? Certainly not. What is needed is to rediscover the law that regulates Catholicism, which is not the *aut-aut* (either-or) but, on the contrary, the *et-et* (both-and), the union of contraries, of synthesis and harmony between what seems contradictory. Therefore, not religion *or* science, but one *and* the other; not devotion *or* reason, but devotion *and* reason; not university culture *or* the catechism, but the former *and* the latter; and so forth.

As concerns Mary, who said that the study of the manuals and the texts of secular culture should deprive us of the nourishment drawn from devotion, from the booklets on meditation or the books on spirituality? Who says that the dutiful frequenting of places where the "wisdom of the world" is elaborated and explicated would be unreconcilable with reciting the Rosary or with pilgrimage to a shrine? Examples are not lacking in the history of sanctity in the past two centuries of men and women who have lived fruitfully this synthesis. Even among the learned and renowned professors there are rich lists of blessed and saints in recent decades. And it is through taking inspiration from these examples that we can rediscover the need for, and the dignity and the nobility of, the innumerable pages written by believers in meditation on her whom the centuries and the peoples have "called blessed."

We have spoken of the immense mass of writings on Mary, writings that should foster and deepen our knowledge of her, the theological privileges, the veneration and devotion. Naturally, we must not forget that next to this directly religious production (so marginalized if not disregarded) lies that of the "classics" of literature.

The most celebrated examples come to mind immediately: from the sublime thirty-third canto of Dante's *Paradiso* to Petrarch's canzone "*Vergine bella, che di sol vestita*" (Beautiful Virgin, dressed in the sun) to Alessandro Manzoni's *The Name of Mary*. Let us not forget that this Lady found a breach even in unsuspecting hearts: How many remember, for example, the case of the author of the *Hymn to Satan*, the terrible Freemason and anticlerical author of the blasphemous invective against the "Semitic numen," namely, against Jesus himself ("Crucified martyr you crucify men, / you who pollute the ethereal with sadness"). Yes, Giosuè Carducci, acclaimed as the Seer from Italy by the nineteenth-century "legalists," who wanted to uproot Catholicism from the Italian people and send into exile the papacy that he now considered a pathetic, moribund institution, though still poisonous. Well, in one of his final poetic compositions, the old lion, who had been for so long not only anticlerical but downright anti-Christian, nostalgic for cheerful paganism, finally surrendered to the grandeur of the Mother, the "Semitic numen" against whom he had inveighed. Thus, he gave us those last quatrains of *La chiesa di Polenta* (The church of Polenta), which are perhaps among the most beautiful writings on the emotions aroused by the sound of the evening *Ave Maria* ("a sweet will to cry / the soul invades").

Setting off on this path, one finds surprises at every turn. Very few, for example, would be able to guess the author of the verses that begin with "O Queen of the Angels, O Mary, / that adorns the heavens with your glad resemblance." The quote is from the *Rhymes* of Giovanni Boccaccio, a master of something quite different from religious devotion, at least in the imagination of those who see in literature only the reductive synthesis of scholastic manuals.[7]

If we move from literature to the figurative arts, the discussion is utterly predictable. Too well known now is the series of absolute masterpieces given to us by the greatest masters of painting and sculpture, representing the Immaculate, or the Annunciation, or the Mother and Child, or the Sorrowful, or

[7] Editor's Note: Boccaccio was a Renaissance Italian author known best for his *Decameron*, a set of stories that often satirize Catholic officials and practices.

the Assumption. All too well known and in the end (we hazard our opinion at the risk of scandalizing some) perhaps less meaningful than other witnesses of homage and Marian devotion. In fact, most of those figurative masterpieces were executed on commission: and the buyers, as we know, were for many centuries religious entities that suggested subjects, among which Mary obviously took second place only to her Son.

And was it perhaps due to this somewhat "mercenary" feeling, this suspicion of a lack of spontaneity, that the mysterious instinct of the people gave rise to a phenomenon as curious as it is rare? One hardly notices, in fact, that the veneration of Christian peoples has crystallized not around the masterpieces of the great artists, but around images that are often anonymous, lacking in true artistic value. They have prayed before humble, modest, apparently insignificant paintings and statues — that is, in the style of the one portrayed. The splendors of art are in museums, for profane pilgrims, for tourists, or for the erudite or aesthetical consideration of scholars and connoisseurs.

Those paintings, those illustrious statues, are illuminated by the flashes of cameras. Candles, on the other hand, shine before the "daubs" such as those so often appearing in churches and shrines — not admired for their aesthetic value, ignored by critics, yet venerated and loved for what they say to the hearts of the faithful.

One of the most exemplary cases is that of Rome. Everywhere here the artistic glory of the most beautiful and renowned Madonnas of the world radiates from inside imposing, famous temples. Yet, the devotion of the Romans seems to be concentrated for the past two centuries on an anonymous, discolored fresco displayed inside the inchoate architecture of a shrine on the remote periphery of the city, a shrine called *Divino Amore* (Divine Love).

The surprise is accentuated as one discovers that the "miracle" that drew the crowds of faithful out of the city that is the seat of the Vicar of Christ himself and that boasts of much greater treasures than this insignificant image: an anonymous passerby was threatened by the dogs of some shepherds and, having invoked the Virgin Mary, was not bitten by them. What prodigy could this possibly be, compared to the marvelous miracles attributed to other images in Rome? Yet, here, and not elsewhere, the instinct of faith has called Romans for some years now to perform a pilgrimage on foot, during the night of every first Saturday, without any organization or formality but driven only by love for that poor image in the Roman countryside. This offers further confirmation of the spontaneous character, truly "popular," of Marian devotion, sustained by the fervor of the people and not created artificially by the clergy.

This fact is not isolated. Spain would not be Spain ("The Land of Mary par excellence," as its inhabitants define it) without its millenary, passionate fidelity to the *Virgen del Pilar* in Zaragoza. In the immense shrine on the banks of the Ebro, the flags of all the nations that speak Spanish are flown: she is, in fact, Our Lady of all Hispanidad, where Pilar is a very common name among women. But the famous *Virgen*, the image in the heart of millions of devotees, is a statuette made of wood (and a bit unshapely, one must admit), thirty-eight centimeters tall, less than two hands' width, on top of a column lacking in adornment or any artistic touch. The masterpieces can be found in the Prado in Madrid and in the other great museums, venerated by tourists; the "true" pilgrims, on the other hand, prostrate themselves before this quite small, modest, and for this reason beloved image.

And what about that other Madonna, decisive for the history of a people, on the hilltop of Jasna Gora? Does it have any artistic splendor? Or might a fervent Pole find "beautiful" the black, battered icon in Czestochowa?

Examples could be multiplied, but this would only confirm the surprising fact: no human creature has had at her service this many illustrious paintbrushes or chisels, yet the works of those greatest of masters, while honored, are rarely venerated. The faithful gather in prayer, at times after long and strenuous pilgrimages, around other images. Is this by chance or is it one of those intuitions of faith we have mentioned — namely, the feeling that humility and modesty are always united in Mary beside her royal glory?

At the end of the nineteenth century, a French writer from Holland, Joris-Karl Huysmans, abandoned the atheistic naturalism he had espoused up to that time, following the path of his friend and teacher Émile Zola, and passed over to a full-fledged Catholicism, which led him to retreat to a monastery.

When he went to Lourdes, the convert Huysmans was religiously edified but also aesthetically horrified by the "unbearable ugliness" (as he called it) he seemed to notice in everything that surrounded worship in the grotto. But in general, the whole world of Marian devotion seemed to him marked by a lack of beauty, to the point of offering a hypothesis of his own: that mediocrity, that artistic dearth, was the devil's assault on the biblical Woman who had crushed his head. The devil of bad taste had tried to avenge himself on the beauty of Mary, and on the Truth she symbolizes.

This is a colorful thesis, but one that does not seem to hit the mark. In fact, more appropriate is to locate this within the logic of the Magnificat once more. The "world" that is condemned in those verses is often capable of good taste, fine artistic education, and elegance. It is the world of the culture that satisfies the aesthetic sense, but that does not give what really counts, the meaning for living and dying.

Looking at a map, one notices that not many kilometers separate Lourdes from Arcachon on the plain of Guascogna. There, for four years from 1910 to 1914, in a villa among the dunes and the pine groves beside the Atlantic, lived Gabriele D'Annunzio. The legendary *princeps elegantiarum* (elegant aristocrat) thus dwelt, not far then from the rags of Bernadette, and not far from the architectural pastiche of the three superimposed basilicas, from the mediocre statue by Fabisch, a modest sculptor who gave his worst there, or from the plebeian tastes of the crowds of pilgrims. This offers a crushing comparison to Lourdes, from a human point of view. But is it not the opposite when seen from the point of view of faith? Are the words that console and save to be found in those theatrical dramas in elegant Old French, written by the sex-crazed aesthete in Arcachon? Or are they found in the rough dialect of the Pyrenees, heard and transmitted by the illiterate shepherdess?

CHAPTER 11

Apparitions: Instructions for Use

The largest secular publisher in Italy, Mondadori, recently published an important initiative, the most extensive, in-depth, meticulous study of "religiosity in Italy." Carried out by the Catholic University of Milan, "with the encouragement and support of the Italian Episcopal Conference," as the rector of the university writes in the preface, the study involved a vast, statistically representative cross-section of the entire Italian population from eighteen to seventy-four years of age. It employed specifically trained researchers, who went to the homes of those interviewed (agreed upon beforehand by letter): 4,500 Italians in 166 cities responding to the 340 variables that would compose the complete panorama of attitudes toward religion.

As far as our reflections are concerned, we understand the interest of sociologists (it is their trade), but as believers interested above all in the apostolate, we hesitate to give too much importance to such initiatives. Often, these only confirm what is already known — deduced and intuited by those who live with a lucid and affectionate awareness in the midst of our fellow human beings. The evangelization of the world (from the enthusiastic beginnings witnessed in the Acts of the Apostles to the missionary heroism of many centuries) was not preceded or accompanied by sociologists, cultural anthropologists, or even by any other professor or "expert." And not because they were not in fashion at that time, but because the proclamation of the gospel corresponds to laws and purposes that have little to do with "market research," "opinion polls," or the graphics and diagrams by which specialists earn their living.

The only "experience" that the Church has used (often with extraordinary effectiveness, the more so when entrusted with the power of the kerygma and its ability to breach the heart of men) was recalled by a pope attentive like few others to the demands of the modern apostolate. Paul VI, in his discourse to the United Nations General Assembly in the same period in which the Second Vatican Council was concluding (autumn of 1965), defined Christians as "experts in humanity." And precisely this extraordinary experience in that which truly counts risks being jeopardized (overturning expectations: it is the old curse of unintended consequences) by theoretical "programming" by ecclesiastics, a certain abstract "pastoral planning" elaborated by Church leaders based on survey results and socio psychological activism.

Despite it all, alongside many predictable confirmations of what an attentive pastor already knows from living next to his contemporaries, scrutinizing hearts and minds, initiatives like that of the Catholic University and the Italian Bishops' Conference can offer reasons for reflection and even surprises at times.

Among such reasons for reflection, there is one that concerns in a particular way the themes on which this notebook is focused. Concrete points for the apostolate can be drawn from these.

In fact, the fifty-third point of the questionnaire to which the 4,500 people in the cross-section were subjected (a mixed group, one must recall, composed not only of believers) asked the following question: "What do you think about the apparitions of the Virgin Mary that supposedly took place in Lourdes and Fatima?" Well, we discover that 55.7 percent of those questioned had no doubts and chose the most affirmative response that read: "They are signs of the presence of God in the midst of men." Another 29.4 percent opted for the response, "I am uncertain, I don't know how to answer this." Thus, 85 percent of Italians (if the survey is reliable, as the sociologists and bishops who endorsed it swear it is) are either sure of the truth of Fatima and Lourdes, or take an agnostic position, ready to be convinced if one were to explain how things actually took place. In any case, they declare they are ready to go from uncertainty to assent, and do not deny the possibility that in those two places God manifested Himself. They only say they do not know enough about it.

The results of the survey are even more probative if to that already significant 85 percent one were to add the 3.9 percent that chose the response, "It does not matter to me." And this is the case probably because no one in the Church or in general among believers has ever tried to arouse their interest by demonstrating not only the fascination but also the significance of those two extraordinary events for all people.

Examining these results, one must not think these are attitudes of "residual fideism" or "pockets of superstition gradually being overcome" that might involve women, in particular those who are emotive, older, from rural and economically depressed areas. When one looks at the detailed analysis, one finds that, filtered by sex, men represent a weighty 47.4 percent of the people convinced without hesitation of Lourdes and Fatima.

Filtering by age, one finds even more interesting discoveries: the "convinced" are more numerous (52.2 percent) among the very young (the 18–21 cohort) than among the young (the 22–29 cohort) at 47.9 percent. But credence in the apparitions rises immediately among the 30- to 49-year-olds to the same percentage (52.2) as those who are around 20 years old. A further rise is found in the following age group, arriving at its high point (67.1) among the over-75-year-olds. There is overall a substantial equilibrium, therefore, that sees the same percentage "trusting" in Lourdes and Fatima in both the 20-year-olds and the 50-year-olds.

We turn now to the third variable, that tied to geographical area. We discover that those in Piedmont, Lombardy, and Liguria (thus, the inhabitants of the areas most economically and culturally developed in Italy) give affirmative answers to the Marian apparitions only to a slightly lesser extent than Sicilians or Sardinians. In fact, the percentage of those saying yes to the enigma of Lourdes and Fatima is 56.1 percent on the Islands and 51.9 in the Northwest. The advantage of the Islands is even less pronounced with respect to Central Italy, where the "convinced" rise to 52.6 percent. The most convinced of all are the regions of the South, where a good 67.6 percent of the population has no doubts: Mary has truly appeared in their opinion.

In any case, the most significant data are this: from the Alps to the Mediterranean isles, the majority of Italians being asked responded affirmatively that the Virgin Mary has given us an authentic "sign of the presence of God in the midst of men" in the Pyrenees and in northern Portugal. Only in the

Northeast did the percentage go below the absolute majority, 47.9 percent (50 percent was exceeded in every other zone of the country). The data might surprise us, given that Veneto and Trentino Alto-Adige are part of that area, regions considered traditionally religious, although times are changing even in those parts. But the average was lowered by taking into account Friuli-Venezia-Giulia, a more problematic zone (take, for example, Trieste, the historical crucible of various faiths and incredulities), and above all, the anticlerical Romagna and the skeptical and at times mocking Emilia. More than unbelief, a sort of "human respect" reigns here, which induces one to deny in public (in this case, before the interviewer of the survey) what one professes within. I observed this with the affectionate solidarity of one who was born in that area and can speak with knowledge of the facts.

At any rate, a further, definitive confirmation of the attitude of faith of the Italians toward Lourdes and Fatima (with all that those two names signify and carry with them) comes from the percentages found from the two possible negative responses to the question.

Naturally, we must remember that the survey involved a sample of the population of the country, and not specifically of Catholics, or even practicing Catholics. This helps us to evaluate better the following data. In fact, only 1.8 percent of those interrogated chose the response "They are inventions of priests." Even fewer than one woman among one hundred (0.9 percent) opted for this hypothesis. As for the age groups, including males and females indiscriminately, the two groups ranging from 22 to 49 registered only 1.6 percent who are suspicious of clerical mischief. Even more importantly, the highest percentage of those who fear the "deception of priests" is registered neither among the very young nor the young but among the elderly from 65 to 74. Contrary once more to popular conceptions, those in the Islands (2 percent) and in Central Italy (2.2 percent) are more diffident, while in the Northwest and Northeast they registered a modest 1.7 percent.

More elevated, on the other hand (though they are marginal numbers in the end), are the percentages of those who chose the other negative possibility: "Lourdes and Fatima are popular inventions, hallucinations or suggestions." Altogether, this collected a total of 9.3 percent. But here too, there was no abyss between the shrewd, adult rationalists in the North and the backward, superstitious people in the South. Between the skeptical Northwest (11.3) and the Islands (8.1) there is a difference of little more than three percentage points.

Such Marian feats lead to even deeper reflection when compared to other items from the same inquiry concerning the very foundations of the Creed. In fact, if 55.7 percent of Italians of every faith and lack of faith say they are certain of the truth of the two most famous and attested apparitions of the Virgin Mary, yet only 27.5 percent responded, “I believe deeply,” to the affirmation proposed to them: “Every man will rise again at the end of time”; and only 36.5 percent gave the same positive response to the phrase “An immortal soul exists in man.” But the disturbing percentages could be multiplied at will: only 34.8 percent respond, “I believe deeply,” to “the Catholic Church is an organization desired by and assisted by God”; 41.5 percent to, “I think that after death there is another life”; and even a miserable 27.5 percent to, “I believe that every man will rise again at the end of time”; finally, 49 percent to, “I am convinced that the Word of God is revealed in the Holy Scriptures.”

Gleaning through the concrete religious attitudes, cues for reflection — or dismay — can be bundled together. For example, only a slight 7 percent opted for the response “Follow the indications of religious authorities” to the question “What should a person who believes in God do?” (As a warning to us scribes, “Catholic” journalists and writers, there were only an insignificant 2.6 percent of Italians persuaded that a believer ought to “read religious publications ...”)

All this and much more could be drawn from such a sophisticated and extensive study, but it must be seen against the background of the results of a particularly revealing question: “Whom do you address more often in your prayers?” Well, of the 4,500 in the survey group, a good 46.8 percent responded “to the Virgin Mary.” But only 38.2 percent “to Christ.” The percentage concerning Mary was passed only by the 57.2 percent who address God Himself. Here too, the data were not prejudiced by higher numbers in certain age groups or place of residence: only three percentage points separate a 22-year-old from a 49-year-old in privileging Marian prayer; and fewer than five percentage points divide a citizen in the Northeast from one in the South. We see here a homogeneity found in few other cases. Throughout all Italy, the response “I turn in prayer above all to the Virgin Mary” has few fluctuations: from a minimum of 43.6 percent in Central Italy (followed by another minimum of 44 percent in the Islands, a further denial of preconceived notions) to a maximum of 52.1 percent in the South.

But the Northeast opted for Mary to a nearly equally massive degree: 47.4 percent. Thus, not even the privileged place Mary continues to have in the religious universe of the people (fortunately, the "common," "anonymous" people that have nothing to do with certain pastoral theories) is the legacy of an underdevelopment that is being overcome. The new generations of the regions on the cutting edge look to the Virgin Mary, despite everything, to the same degree as previous generations. Certain attempts to displace or downsize her notwithstanding, Mary continues to live in the hearts of youth as well ("instinctively" it almost seems, given the scarce help offered by current catechesis). Could turning to her in prayer in a privileged way be an unequivocal sign of her tenacious life?

If we were now to offer a "pastoral" suggestion (insofar as a similar gesture behooves a layman — but does not the duty of the apostolate fall to each of the baptized?), the indications seem quite clear. Mary and the places of her apparitions represent extraordinary opportunities for faith, today more than ever. The reason for this persistent efficacy is found in the fact that in those places the gospel is reproposed not as an abstract system of beliefs and moral directions but as an encounter. The "theory" becomes concrete experience there. For the visionaries, certainly; but also for the pilgrims who find there emotion and awe in their contact with the sacred.

For some time now, we have been exponents of a somewhat disturbing opinion: that the afflictions of the Church in recent decades are caused above all by a crisis of the ecclesial institutions seeking a new order after the Second Vatican Council. Behind that institutional crisis, there is in fact a crisis of faith, as confirmed moreover by the results of the survey we have examined. If that is the case, why not take advantage of the extraordinary trust the faithful (including youth) have in the truth of places like Fatima and Lourdes? Why not begin there with a re-evangelization that we might call "deductive": from the reality of those events to the truth of faith they presuppose and confirm?

In Lourdes, do not the words of the Virgin Mary to Bernadette ("I cannot promise to make you happy in this life, but only in the next") confirm the hope of eternal life which is among the least accepted truths today or of which there is the most uncertainty, as this survey confirms? Likewise, the definition the Lady gave herself ("I am the Immaculate Conception"), reiterating the dogma defined by the pope just four years prior: Is it not perhaps the clear confirmation of a Church aided by God and authorized to speak in His name?

Continuing on this line: Is not the command "pray to God for sinners" an expression of at least three truths? Namely, that there is a merciful God who can be reached by prayer; the communion of saints is a reality in which each can intercede for others; and the existence of the negativity of sin. These concepts were repeated even in the triple "Penance!" and by the invitation "Go and kiss the ground, as penance for the conversion of sinners."

And when the Immaculate exhorts, "Go and tell the priests to come here in procession and to build here a chapel," is this not repeating the truth of the Church: the legitimacy and the privileged prerogatives of the clergy, the necessity and the opportunity of liturgical worship and, in general, of manifestations of public devotion?

The deniers of Lourdes, at times even Christians, have often ironized about this Lady who troubled herself to come down from Heaven to come and say to an ignorant girl just "a few, prosaic words." In reality, one could demonstrate (and some have) that in those "few and prosaic" expressions lies an entire Christian catechesis. From those brief phrases all the main truths of the Faith are confirmed, and not the simply Christian faith but that which is entirely Catholic.

Well then: if nearly 56 percent of Italians (not of believers, but of all Italians!) do not hesitate to assent to the response that Lourdes and Fatima "are signs of the presence of God in the midst of men"; and if nearly 30 percent are uncertain but ready to be convinced; if all this corresponds to an actual reality, as the bishops themselves admit, why not take advantage of it? Is it not for this reason that such surveys are carried out? Why not, in other words, begin precisely with that rock on the banks of the Pau (and the discussion is true of Fatima as well) to begin the re-evangelization that we called "deductive"? It is a question of logic, before which we need to place our interlocutor: Are you convinced of the truth of those encounters between earth and Heaven? If yes, be coherent and accept the consequences that can be derived from them.

It must not be forgotten that trusting in the truth of Lourdes necessarily means believing even in the truthfulness of its witness, the only one of that event. Thus, as logic imposes here too, even the life of Bernadette, from that fateful February in 1858 until her death, is included in the possible catechesis, in the "deductive" re-evangelization (this argument can be true for Fatima as well, where two visionaries have already been beatified and the same destiny seems to await Lucia who died shortly after that glorification of her companions).

Remaining with the shepherdess of the Pyrenees: Mary herself chose her, promised her eternal salvation, revealed to her three secrets and a prayer (also secret) to help her, comfort her and nourish her in her spiritual life toward the announced paradise. Those who believe in the truth of Lourdes cannot fail to consider as a genuinely evangelical example the life choices of this girl over whom Mary herself promised to keep vigil.

When the Church enrolls one of her sons or daughters in the "canon," the list of saints, it commits her to affirming solemnly that that man or woman is surely saved, living in eternal joy with God. But the canonization of Bernadette Soubirous is unique: in this case, in fact, the Church attested that the promise of salvation and eternal joy made to this girl by Mary ("happy ... in the next life") has come about; that this young woman was followed and helped from on high so that she would be able to realize the conditions for that salvation. Bernadette did, in other words, that which other saints have done. But doing so, she carried out an explicit, divine project for her. Thus, the path to sanctity as the Church teaches it is the "right" one; it has been sanctioned by God Himself with the choices and behaviors He inspired in the former shepherdess whom the Virgin Mary announced was destined to eternal happiness.

In this light, one sees the pastoral importance assumed by the decision of Bernadette to become a nun. Today especially, given the radical objections the religious life must face, or the ferment in the Church in recent years for modern ways of living out that vocation. Bernadette was "pushed" by Mary herself to become a nun and, therefore, to obtain eternal life through obedience to the rules (judged today by many as intolerable, anachronistic, inhumane even) of an *ancien-régime* congregation, of traditional Catholicity. To become a nun with the Sisters of Charity of Nevers was not, obviously, "her" decision: such a choice, though respecting her freedom, was inspired, was driven forward by Someone — a Someone who approved that type of vocation, that search for "Christian perfection" that passes, for one so called, through the threefold path the Church has always proposed: chastity, poverty, and obedience. Are consequences not to be derived from this about the judgment to be given to this heavily contested life of religious in convents and monasteries?

Given that our pastors consider sociological surveys like this one we have examined here as useful ecclesial strategies, let them draw the conclusions. The trust in the "Marian apparitions" which persists so tenaciously in a society apparently secularized is a bulwark to stand on and make use of.

In light of this, it seems that there is no need to consider, as a sort of blasphemous deviation to be corrected in the name of who-knows-what "adult" faith, the discovery that there are more people who turn to Mary in prayer than to Jesus. Tradition has always known that if there is no Son without the Mother, neither can there be a Mother without the Son. Where she is, He is there, too. There is no "illicit competition," it seems, nor "abuse" to correct. Was it not the dying Christ who said to John at the foot of the cross, representing all humanity, "Behold, your mother" (John 19:27)?

CHAPTER 12

The Times of Heaven

The following is not our conviction alone: it is shared by many contemporary historians. The conviction, namely, that modernity, the epoch in which we are still immersed (although many speak of a passage that has already taken place into the postmodern period), did not begin with some battle or some treaty. The "new age" began, it seems, one morning between summer and autumn, in a port city on the western coast of England. Indeed, in Liverpool, toward midday on September 15, 1830, as the first train in history began regular public service for passengers and goods. Five years earlier, a line was opened on the eastern coast, but those forty-three kilometers of track between the river port of Stockton and the coal mines of Darlington were not employed for regular service, as is essential for public railway service, but only for the transport of fuel. On that September day of 1830 in Liverpool, just a few hours after its departure, the train reached Manchester (according to the printed schedule, the first in history), some fifty kilometers away. Although the average speed was twenty-one kilometers per hour, the maximum exceeded forty-seven kilometers per hour, the highest land speed ever obtained by human beings, besides some horse races. George Stephenson was right, then, to christen the steam engine he had designed and constructed to pull the cars "The Rocket."

From those puffs of steam that day, the world was changed, and radically, for better or worse. This is not the place for writing a sort of socioeconomic treatise on the problem. On the profit side, it suffices to remember that industry and commerce which would in just a few decades revolutionize the world would not have been imaginable without the locomotive. The merit of having liberated at least Europe and America of the nightmare of periodic famines must also be attributed to the railway, which assured the rapid exchange of goods from one country to another. And then tourism, personal encounters, correspondence, and so forth — all this would characterize the world for more than a century (before the arrival of mass individual motorization; but this too, reaching saturation, is making room for the train once more, whose future is looking bright again), beginning with that departure in 1830 from the station in Liverpool.

On the side of losses, the rapid increase in violent warfare was facilitated by trains, from the first true "total war" in history, and by far the bloodiest, that between 1914 and 1918. For those four-plus terrible years, only the thousands of trains that ran the lines day and night to and from the front enabled the replacement of troops and the supplying of millions of combatants. But from the very beginning, from the first days of the slaughter, mass mobilization on a previously unimaginable scale was possible only because all Europe was wrapped in a network of railways.

But why are we speaking of trains in a "Marian notebook"? What does Our Lady have to do with railways? It might be the case that she has much to do with them. It might be, in the mysterious plan of God, that 1830 had a significance that is not in the least accidental.

In fact, just a few months after the entrance into history of that "object" never before seen, the train convoy drawn by a steam engine on iron wheels, Mary herself had asked a young novice of the Vincentian Daughters of Charity to become an instrument for bringing into history another "object." Much smaller and much less sensational than a steam locomotive, certainly. On the contrary, it was subdued and almost hidden, but rich in profound significance and mysterious power to the eyes of faith and disseminated throughout the entire world in an incalculable number of copies. We have already spoken of this, but it is important here to return to it. If the first scheduled train journey took place on September 15, on November 27 of that same year, in the motherhouse of the Vincentians in the Parisian Rue du Bac, as we know, Catherine Labouré saw the Virgin Mary standing on a globe, while from her open hands rays emanated. All around her, the visionary could read the words "O Mary conceived without sin, pray for us who have recourse to thee." Then the scene seemed to change, and Catherine noticed the letter *M* with a cross on top of it, and below, the hearts of Jesus and Mary, and she heard the Virgin herself saying, "Have a medal coined on this model!"

This was, as we know, the origin of the Miraculous Medal. One of the most renowned contemporary Mariologists, Stefano De Fiores, observes, "This medal is not a simple material mini-object; it is a sign, something that points beyond itself." Among the many possible readings, continues De Fiores, there is that of a "figure of divine protection: the medal can be seen, in the oval form desired by the Virgin Mary herself, as a reduction to minimum proportions of the shield of defense used by soldiers."

Could this be the profound, hidden reason for the chronological coincidence between the train constructed by Stephenson and the medal "commissioned" of Sr. Catherine? Did Heaven want to supply believers with a sort of antidote, a protection, at the very moment in which modernity with its opportunities and its risks to the Faith emerged? Did He want to give Christians that "shield of defense" of which De Fiores the Mariologist spoke?

Due respect for the mystery of God does not impede us from reflecting on His movements. To be sure, even in His choice of timing He can hide an important sign of his care for humanity.

We must also not forget that the French monarchy, the symbol and pillar of the *Ancien Régime,* bade farewell to history precisely in 1830 and not in 1793 when Louis XVI climbed the gallows. In fact, once Napoleon disappeared from the political scene, there was a fifteen-year period of restoration, such that the last Bourbon king of France, Charles X, was dethroned in 1830 by a revolution that, in Louis Philippe of Orleans, established a sui generis monarchy. It was no longer based on a divine-right king, God's secular arm, consecrated by priests with sacred oils. Louis Philippe was the "bourgeois king," brought to power by the bourgeois merchant and industrial class. A king who had even participated in the revolutionary armies and whose father, a Freemason Grand Master, was among the "regicides," the deputies who voted to put Louis XVI to the guillotine. A king who would immediately open negotiations with the English to transfer the remains of Napoleon to Paris and have them enter the capital with solemn ceremonies. A king who wanted to show how the sacred monarchy was definitively terminated, assuming the title not of "King of France" but "of the French," understood as citizens and no longer subjects. He abolished the white Bourbon flag with the lilies and returned to the revolutionary tricolor which would never again be abandoned, confirming that something definitive had occurred.

Thus, for historians, 1789 had its fulfillment and assumed its definitive form precisely in 1830, when the bourgeois who had begun and managed the Great Revolution reached power and would not concede it again. It was there in the year of the Miraculous Medal that contemporary history began, with the end, among other things, of the Holy Alliance (inspired by Christianity in all three of its confessions: Catholic, Protestant, and Orthodox), which had attempted, despite ambiguity and political cynicism, to stem the tide of revolution in the name of tradition, the sacred, and God.

Significant, in summary, is the observation of the unlikely Proudhon,[8] that prophet of socialism, anarchism, and voluntaristic atheism ("Even if God existed, we should not recognize him"): "The philosophy and the revolution of the 18th century notwithstanding, Catholicism kept itself firm and received the first decisive shock — I am speaking of the masses — in 1830."

It is nevertheless certain that the beginning of the contemporary period, symbolized by the first-ever steam-powered journey between the two English cities and by the end of the *Ancien Régime*, was also the start of a series of apparitions that spanned the rest of the 1800s and persisted into the 1900s.

As noted by the historian Yves Chiron, who recently investigated these themes (in a work appropriately open to the enigma but also rigorously academic), in 1830 there began an entirely new period in this genre of mysterious events because "that in Rue du Bac was the first Marian apparition that had an echo and an influence on world events." And it was, he continues, "the beginning of a series that, through many stages, reaches all the way to Betania in Venezuela, where apparitions began in 1976 and received the approval of ecclesiastical authorities in 1987."

The beginning of modern times, therefore, was also the beginning of a series of celestial interventions (as they are considered by the Church itself), with the delivery by Mary to her children of a sign that summarizes the whole of Faith and is also a peaceful weapon destined to defend that Faith from the attacks raging against it.

8 Editor's Note: Pierre-Joseph Proudhon (1809–1865) was a prominent French intellectual and anarchist.

Was this the secret of the divine choice of times anticipated, almost forewarned, in those "Eyes of Mary" in Italy in 1796, to which I, with Rino Cammilleri, dedicated a book?[9]

We limit ourselves to advancing a hypothesis. The same could be done, at any rate, for the times of the other stages that followed Rue du Bac.

If, in Paris, Christians seemed to receive a "shield" for use in future battles, in La Salette there was the dramatic reference to the existence of God, to His majesty, to the obligation to respect His law. For this reason, she was "*la Vierge qui pleure*," the Virgin who cried, as Léon Bloy called her. The year 1846, when this apparition took place in the French Alps near Grenoble, was when Ludwig Feuerbach published his *The Essence of Religion* that completed and radicalized the attack, unprecedented to that point, put forward by *The Essence of Christianity*. God is only "alienation," the illusory and harmful projection into heaven of human needs, he asserted. God is like a vampire that sucks the blood out of humanity, a myth that must be dissolved once and for all. The famous play on words that this disciple of the Hegelian left used to synthesize the perspective of radical materialism ran thus: *Der Mensch ist was er isst* ("Man is what he eats"). Marxist atheism, which would lead to the longest, bloodiest, and most systematic persecution of religion in human history, sinks its roots into the thought of Feuerbach, who reached his point of arrival with the work published in the same year as La Salette.

Then, in January of 1862, the bishop of Tarbes, at the end of a long investigation he initiated and directed, issued the famous decree in which he declared that "the Immaculate Virgin Mary has truly appeared to Bernadette Soubirous in the Grotto of Massabielle." In that same year, Ernest Renan, the former seminarian become rationalist, held his inaugural lecture amid tumult at the *Collège de France*, contending that Jesus was "an incomparable man," but only a man, whom the faith of His disciples had falsely divinized. And the following year, Renan came out with his *Life of Jesus*, which became the most famous bestseller of the agnostic and atheistic nineteenth century and which, thanks to its persuasive style and erudite writing, had devastating effects on

9 Editor's Note: *Gli occhi de Maria* [Mary's Eyes], published in 2001, describes a series of miraculous animations of the eyes of Marian images in Italy during the invasion by Napoleon's forces.

the faith of the great masses and on the new bourgeoisie, who found in it confirmation of their anticlerical skepticism.

Curious, and perhaps symbolic, is the fact that in 1858, while the apparitions were taking place, secular and anticlerical France remembered with solemn celebrations the hundredth anniversary of Maximilien Robespierre's birth, the one who had sought to replace worship of Jesus Christ with that of the goddess of Reason. And just one year later, Charles Darwin published *The Origin of Species*, which (perhaps beyond the intentions of the author: *sed habent sua fata libelli*, "but books have their own destiny") is at the root of much atheism, not only scientific but also political and ideological, given that without Darwinism, neither Marxist-Leninism nor National Socialism would have become what they did.

If we wish to consider Fatima (in this our all-too-summary excursus, to which so much could be added), is it not fitting to recall how those events took place in the year 1917, in which Lenin came to power in Russia? This connection is too well known to belabor further.

But much less well known is the fact that Beauraing and Banneux (both in Belgium) were the settings of the last two apparitions approved by the Church, before that long silence was broken in 1987 regarding the events in Venezuela we mentioned. Well, both Beauraing and Banneux took place in 1933, and in January precisely, in perfect synchronicity with the rise to power of Adolf Hitler. We shall speak of this at length in one of the coming chapters.

This type of reading is at any rate entirely coherent with the function that the Church discerns in such phenomena. The apparitions, in other words, add nothing to revelation, but are an entirely gratuitous aid which divine mercy concedes to men to strengthen their faith. A new response to the pathetic cry that resounds in the Gospel: "I believe; help my unbelief!" (Mark 9:24).

The age that opens in 1830 (and even earlier, with the Jacobin invasion of Rome in 1796) is that in which unbelief has most threatened Christians. It is therefore legitimate to think that every stage in this attack on faith can be tied to a spiritual antidote constituted by the manifestation of the mysterious heavenly reality. To resist the massive impact of modern ideologies, of the "isms" of persuasive appearance and disastrous effects, was there not a need for that extraordinary assistance consisting in the visible intervention of the Mother in history, with her cycle of apparitions that accompany the stages of Christianity's *Via Crucis*?

But if, at it seems, there is a message to be discerned and received in the choice of these years in which the Marian apparitions have been taking place, is there not a significance in their "internal" timing as well? We shall try to clarify this: When those mysterious phenomena are not contained in a single episode (as at La Salette, for example, where it all took place in half an hour on the afternoon of September 19 — a Saturday, moreover), when the apparitions are staggered over time, will the cycle that they form be by chance? Or is the believer invited to reflect, to seek to glimpse any hidden riches, possible confirmations of truth (even in the chiaroscuro that always characterizes the Faith) of that gift of the celestial epiphanies, especially the Marian ones?

Among the most highly studied cases in discerning the hidden structure are the eighteen apparitions of Lourdes. We owe to René Laurentin the best synthesis of this matter. Already back in 1954, at the beginning of his monumental work of collecting the documentation on the events of the grotto, Laurentin went so far as to say in a session at the International Marian Conference in Rome (later written down in an invaluable but now unavailable booklet): "One can see a meticulous order in the apparitions in Lourdes, in which a concerted plan seems to appear. The eighteen encounters of the Virgin with Bernadette took place in a harmonious pattern, where certain striking symmetries immediately present themselves."

The French scholar dutifully recalls the reverence fitting to the mystery, about which we cannot presume to understand everything, and in the face of which we must avoid interpretative stretches that might lead down imaginary paths. To respect Lourdes fully (as with every other event of its kind), one must avoid a certain type of rationalism that aims to render everything transparent and explain everything, as well as a type of esoterism that posits everywhere obscure meanings hidden from the "non-initiated."

Having said this, it is also true that, when arranged in a framework, the group of eighteen apparitions in the grotto presents two at the beginning (on the eleventh and the fourteenth of February) and two at the end (on the seventh of April and the sixteenth of July), characterized by their being silent and sudden. In these two extremities of the cycle, the Virgin Mary did not give Bernadette an appointment, nor did she address her; she only smiled. The first two apparitions were to make contact and the last two a farewell, "until we meet again in the next life."

If we consider the first (that of February 11) and the last (on July 16), we notice that "the apparitions end just as they began: at the beginning and at the end, the water of the river flows between the visionary and the Virgin Mary." In fact, the first time, Bernadette stood on the other side of the canal that deviated from the Gave, not daring to wet her feet, in obedience to her mother. The last time, however, access to the grotto had been prohibited by the police and the entrance barred off by a palisade. Thus, the visionary encountered "the Lady" for the last time standing in the meadow beyond the waterway (she later testified, "I saw neither the wooden boards nor the river. I seemed to be in the grotto like the other times. I only saw the Holy Virgin: she had never been so beautiful").

The central grouping stands as if held between two initial columns and two final columns sharing their harmony. Laurentin comments,

> These fourteen apparitions are the development of the message. The first and the last of this fundamental block — February 18 and March 25 — are sudden (Bernadette was summoned by an interior appeal) and contain the first and last words of the Virgin: her opening words and her closing words. On February 18 it was the convocation ("*Would you have the grace to come here for fifteen days?*"); on March 25 it was the conclusion ("*I am the Immaculate Conception*"). Between these two apparitions that open and close are situated the harmonious number of twelve apparitions spread over two weeks. It is here that the pedagogy of Lourdes is developed in three cadenced progressions: prayer, penance, pilgrimage.

There seems to be a predetermined order, then, behind the seeming randomness perceived by an inattentive reader of the chronology of events.

Causes for reflection increase, Laurentin continues, when we discover that

> all the most important apparitions took place on Thursdays: the initial one, February 11; the first and the last of the fifteen; the central apparition on February 25 (during which the spring was discovered: it separates the two halves of the cycle); the revelation of the Lady's name on March 25. Does this fact correspond to a plan, and are we being given a further sign? I am inclined to think that this coincidence is to be added to the dossier of the affinities between

> Lourdes and the Eucharist, whose institution, as every Christian knows, took place precisely on Thursday.

While repeating the need to exercise great prudence in a study which, if pushed too far, could lead us off course, other important considerations might be made. For example: all of the "penitential" apparitions are situated in the season of Lent. In particular, few have noticed that it was on precisely the Thursday after Ash Wednesday that the Virgin said to Bernadette, "I cannot promise to make you happy in this life, but only in the next." Furthermore, it was on the Sunday of Quadragesima (the first Sunday of Lent) that she said for the first time, "Pray to God for sinners." The next day, the Monday of the first week of Lent, she inflicted maternally on the visionary, for the first time, the salutary penance of her absence. It was Wednesday of the same week of Lent in which the exhortation resounds: "Penance! Penance! Penance!" It was a Friday of Lent, an eminently penitential day, on which the second absence occurred, which caused Bernadette much suffering (we recall what she said later in Nevers, "The grotto was my heaven on earth").

On the contrary (thus confirming that it was not by chance), Laurentin observes, "during the apparition of Easter week, April 7, there was only joy." Neither did the Mariologist overlook another observation which is cause for much reflection:

> The first apparitions took place on days without any particular liturgical significance (not even on a Saturday: from Thursday, February 11, they skipped to Sunday the fourteenth). It was as if the Virgin Mary wanted to avoid any sign that might give away her identity; as if she wanted to arouse curiosity. She revealed her face without revealing her name. The final and crucial revelation on March 25, when she solemnly declares to be "the Immaculate Conception," and the epilogue on July 16, are both situated on two important Marian feasts: the Annunciation and Our Lady of Carmel.

The profound opportuneness of the coincidence with the recurrence of the Annunciation is evident to any who reflect on this. It was on that day that the unknown Virgin of Nazareth entered into human history; but she did so because, *ab aeterno*, it was in God's plan. Conceived without sin to be made an instrument for the Incarnation of the Word. There was an "Annunciation" precisely because there had been an "Immaculate Conception."

Neither is the fact insignificant that the farewell coincided with the recurrence of Carmel that is tied to a "scapular" similar in some ways to the Miraculous Medal: both are instruments of protection, tangible signs of divine solicitude for man.

We conclude with two other considerations. First, the discovery of the internal coherence in the cycle of the eighteen apparitions reinforces their credibility, as is evident. In the light of Lourdes, those who have suspected a fraudulent plan or expressions of the hysteria of an adolescent, fostered by popular credulity, must take into account this harmony, convincing because it is hidden, concealed, discoverable only by those who not only reflect on it but also have familiarity with religious realities. One discovers, moreover, an unsuspected density to the message, even in the few words of the apparition alone: those words assume a much more complete meaning, they give an unimaginable resonance, when placed in the framework of the liturgical seasons and the rhythms of their succession.

Second, if there is any foundation to the reading we have tried to give here, Lourdes reiterates and reinforces its value as a validation of Catholic truths. We have already mentioned the confirmation from Heaven of a dogmatic definition given by the pope — the relationship, that is, between the truth of faith proclaimed by Pius IX in 1854 and the announcement on March 25, 1858: "I am the Immaculate Conception." To this we must add the fact that the cycle of apparitions was arranged within the liturgical cycle of the Church: Lent, Easter, Thursdays, the Marian feasts. God Himself seems to accept and respect the breadth which Catholicism has given to Marian veneration that accompanies the passage of time.

So, it is not a stretch on the part of apologetics but the verification of an objective fact: the "calendar of Our Lady" at Lourdes follows the rhythms of the Catholic calendar. And it does so by choosing a year unlike any other: that of an extraordinary Jubilee. One reads with emotion the initial words of the decree of Bishop Laurence of Tarbes: "Public prayers are requested and a plenary indulgence, in the form of a Jubilee, is granted in our diocese.... This indulgence can be obtained until December 31, 1858."

The document was dated January 20, 1858. It arrived in Lourdes the next day. Just twenty days later the wind would blow in the meadow next to the Gave. In those days, as we recalled, secular France was beginning the political and cultural ceremonies for a quite different jubilee: the hundredth anniversary of the man of the Terror, the inexhaustible provider of living material for the "national razor," as he and his followers called it—the guillotine under which, in the end, his head would be placed as well.

CHAPTER 13

THE LADY OF THE PYRENEES

IN THE PRECEDING CHAPTER, we attempted to scrutinize the enigma behind the "calendar" of the Marian apparitions. Now we shall try to shed some light on the geography of those events. After the *times* of the mystery, we turn to the *places* of the mystery.

Lourdes is once again the exemplary case from which we must inevitably begin. No wonder: to the objective importance and authority of the facts that took place there, one must add the beneficial findings of studies that have been carried out on it. To the question "Why did this happen in nineteenth-century France?" one answer is to refer to the cultural tradition of that country, especially in the century in which "Gallic intelligence" seemed to have world dominance.

In 1858, both the United States and Russia lived in an isolated half-light; England was set apart on its island, more concerned with overseas commerce and conquests than with Europe; Germany and Italy were still only "geographical expressions"; Spain was ingloriously surviving on its past greatness amid misery and revolutions equal to that of South American republics. If they had occurred anywhere else, the events of the Pyrenees would not have found such lively opposition, stimulated by presumed "luminaries" of modernity; but certainly they would not have also enjoyed such passionate and competent defense and study.

Lourdes signified, from the very beginning, the participation of history, theology, medicine, psychology; and France was at that time the one country in the world that could put into action every sector of knowledge, the best energies and the most up-to-date learning. It could also disseminate throughout the world its thought, thanks to a language that every educated person, in any country, had to know. French had the role then that English has today. There was the natural vivacity of the people, supported by adequate intellectual structures and driven by religious fervor, that of Catholicism. It was a situation which, at least in part, has extended to our own times and continues, allowing for the construction and continual enlargement of a dossier of studies, reflections, certainties, and hypothesis around that grotto that have no comparison in any other Marian event.

Here, then, is a first possible response to the *why* of a place: the Christian God who, remaining in the chiaroscuro, entrusts to the work of men the task of making the *chiaro* (light) increase and the *scuro* (darkness) decrease. Nineteenth-century France was a fitting place for this to be carried out. The cause of the gospel needs the ignorance of Bernadette, but also the precision of the professor; the intuition of the mystic, but also the scientific method of the historian or the clinician.

So we stand before what seems an application of the Gospel parable: Some of the seed fell on good soil and yielded abundant fruit. Not forgetting, of course, that the French intellectual supremacy, often proceeding in a direction contrary to the Faith, needed more than elsewhere an extraordinary intervention that would counter the rationalism and positivism of the new culture.

Proceeding in this study, however, we happen upon another question: If, for the reasons given, France appeared to be the most "opportune" place for a great Marian apparition, why in that country was a little town of the ancient county of Bigorre chosen — a place rebaptized at the end of the 1700s as "Department of the High Pyrenees" in the obsession of the revolutionaries to subdivide the national territory into equal parts, giving them abstract names that had nothing to do with millenary history and traditions? If it had to be France, then why Lourdes? Why not any one of the twenty-five thousand other townships in the country over which the dazzling Napoleon III was then reigning?

Naturally, the same considerations can be applied here that we made about the "times": the choice of these, as with the places, belongs to the secret of God and it would be rash to try to penetrate it. But it is not presumption (nor a vain effort) to advance conjecture. I have been attempting to do so over the course of years of reflection.

But before speaking about my hypotheses, I would like to point out to the reader what was discovered (or better, rediscovered, rummaging through old books in old archives) by Émile Brejon, a lawyer in Bordeaux who became a historian through owing a debt of gratitude toward the Virgin Mary: his mother had been miraculously cured in the grotto. This *bâtonnier* (president) of the Order of Attorneys of his city (where, moreover, Bernadette had stopped during the only journey she ever made, on her way to the convent of Nevers) collected the fruit of his research in a little book printed by a publisher in Avignon in 1926.

The title is significant: *Notre-Dame de Lourdes avant les apparitions de 1858* (*Our Lady of Lourdes before the apparitions of 1858*). The subtitle reads, "A chapter of forgotten history." In 1983, the booklet was republished by a little provincial publisher, but it has continued to circulate only in a limited way, to the point that not even a trace of it can be found in many specialized bibliographies. This silence is surprising, considering that Brejon brings to light for everyone what had been formerly known only to a few local scholars, in his discovery in those archives of documents to which he applied his discernment as an expert in law, including feudal law.

We anticipate immediately the core of the book that seeks to respond to the question the author placed on the cover and on the title page: "Why Lourdes in France?" Because, he responds, here the Virgin is "*chez Elle*"; she is "in her own home" and "in no other place in the world would she have been so at home as she is here."

In fact, according to an ancient tradition (and confirmed by equally ancient customs supported by contemporaneous documents), the castle and the City of Lourdes were given as a fiefdom at the time of Charlemagne to the Virgin Mary venerated in the large, famous shrine of Le Puy-en-Velay, the Marian site that had been the most prestigious in all of France for centuries. Thus, Our Lady of Puy ("knoll," in the local French dialect) was declared "Lady and Sovereign" of Lourdes, with the right of an annual tribute, which the authorities acknowledged, according to feudal custom, and which, in this case, consisted of grass and clods of earth taken from the lawn in front of the castle. As Brejon demonstrates, even in 1829, for the feast of the Assumption (in other words, only twenty-nine years before the apparitions to Bernadette), a delegation of young women from Lourdes embarked for the last time, after more than a millennium of carrying out this tradition, on the long journey to Le Puy in the Massif Central, almost one hundred kilometers to the west of Lyon, to take to Mary, "Lady and Countess of the City," their ancient tribute.

It seems that a detail escapes Brejon at this point: the grass and the dirt given to Mary as a sign of her authority over Lourdes had to be taken, as custom required, from the "lawn of the Count" that runs down from the castle. Well, this is the place that, in Bernadette's time, was known as the "estate of Savy" and is the current esplanade in front of the basilicas, where the Eucharistic procession takes place every evening. And more than that: once the county of Bigorre disappeared, the ownership of this place, which from time immemorial symbolized in its very soil the dominion of Mary over the city, passed (until the sixteenth century) to the "Confraternity of the Most Holy Sacrament." *Ab immemorabili*, therefore, this place has been the "land of the Virgin" and also the "land of the Eucharist." As we can see, the evocative bonds are intertwined, if we look for them.

According to a document which some consider fictitious (but which, as demonstrated with passion and competency by our lawyer from Bordeaux, takes inspiration from realities confirmed by usages and customs rooted in centuries — history would be impossible if it had to be done only with pieces of paper!), the erection of Lourdes and its castle as a "fiefdom of Mary" must have taken place in a manner both poetic and dramatic. On his return from Spain, Charlemagne besieged in vain the fortress which sat atop the rock, which at the time was held by Muslims. Because the defenders would not surrender, and Charlemagne was already considering breaking the siege, the bishop of Le Puy, who was in his entourage, went to parley with the Saracen leader, telling him, "Since you do not want to concede to any man, concede to a Lady: the Mother of God venerated in Le Puy."

Touched by grace, the Muslim leader accepted the agreement and, accompanied by his men, rode to that famous place of worship. All the Saracen leaders carried, tied to their lances, bundles of grass and flowers cut from the lawn under the rock where the fortress rose. They placed those bundles, as a sign of submission, on the altar of Mary. The Muslim leader asked to be baptized and changed his name from "Mirat" to "Lordus." Lourdes took its name from this, whereas it had previously been called "Mirambel."

Although written documents are scarce (and among those we do have it is difficult to distinguish between authentic and fictional), one fact is certain and attested without a shadow of a doubt: as far back as one can go in time, all who took power in Lourdes repeated the act of homage to the faraway shrine in the Massif Central, taking bundles of grass tied to their lances. Confirming the ancient feudal right which Notre Dame du Puy exercised over Lourdes is the fact that the coats of arms of both cities are composed of an eagle. That of Lourdes shows its wings stretched open and carries a fish in its beak — was this perhaps to symbolize that it comes from the mountains of the center of France, bringing Christ, whose ancient symbol was in fact the fish?

This, however, is only the first act of a long story. From the realm of traditions (and written sources often tell us the same, if not more, whatever some Enlightenment historiographers might say), we enter here into the domain of secure and unassailable documents. The most important of them testify with clarity to what our scholar Brejon synthesizes in this way: "Our Lady of Le Puy, after having been recognized as 'Lady and Countess' of Lourdes and of her town from the time of Charlemagne, became the 'Lady and Countess' of the entire County of Bigorre, by an act of spontaneous and voluntary submission that Count Bernard I conceded at the Chapter of Le Puy, for himself and for all his successors, in the year 1062."

It was in 1062 that Count Bernard departed from Bigorre with his wife to visit the distant shrine in central Gaul, to deposit the annual sixty scudi on the altar of the Virgin "as a tax." More exactly, according to feudal law, it was a sign of vassalage to Mary, who, from "Lady" of Lourdes became "Lady" of the entire region of Bigorre. At the same time, Bernard declared anathema any of his descendants who did not recognize this vassalage by paying her the proper annuity. The document has come down to us intact and is still preserved in the archive of ancient Bigorre, in Pau.

These ancient documents enshrine an obligation which should stir those of us who know what would later take place: on pre-established days every year, from the highest tower of the castle of Lourdes, the count's banner (and later, that of the king of France who replaced him) was to be lowered and, in the place of the noble's standard, that of Our Lady of Le Puy was to be raised, to show that earthly authorities were only "administrators" of a land over which the Queen of Heaven exercised her rights.

In the shrine of Le Puy, Mary was venerated under the title of the "Annunciation" by all the peoples of Europe. The faithful flocked there in great numbers, especially when March 25 coincided with Good Friday and it was possible to enjoy the Great Pardon, the plenary indulgence granted by the popes.

The prestige of the place was so great that, according to the tradition followed by St. Bernard as well, it was here that the Salve Regina (Hail, Holy Queen) was composed, the most recited Marian prayer after the Hail Mary and which was in the medieval period called "the antiphon of Le Puy." Here, in 1449, the custom of reciting the Angelus not only at dawn and dusk but also at midday was established, which soon took hold throughout all Christendom. This was not merely a place of local worship, but rather universal, to the point that the Black Madonna on the altar (burned in 1794 by revolutionary vandalism on a bonfire fueled with the papers from the archive, after having been taken to where criminals were hanged using the wheelbarrow of the town sewer cleaner) was called by saints and popes the *Mater omnium,* the Mother of All.

This universality, this "catholicity," seems to confirm the thesis, supported by a peculiar historical intertwining highlighted by the believer Brejon: Could the Lady who appeared at Lourdes not be precisely the "Countess and Sovereign" of the city and the region, come to retake possession of her fiefdom, returning to "her home" to receive the people of the Gave, as was her custom on Mount Anis, where the shrine of Le Puy rises?

In fact, the coincidences (if that's what they are) are accumulating. The Lady in Le Puy was the Virgin of the Annunciation, and as we know, the apparition of Lourdes awaited precisely the twenty-fifth of March, the feast of the Annunciation, to show herself and reveal to us her name, as if to leave a sort of "sign of identification." It was the day of the greatest feast in her shrine, as confirmed four years before the apparitions in the Apostolic Letter *Ineffabilis Deus,* in which Pius IX summarized the reasons for the dogma he had promulgated and stated that the main foundation of faith in the Immaculate Conception is found precisely in the words of the archangel Gabriel at the Annunciation: "Hail, *full of grace*" (Luke 1:28, emphasis added).

Furthermore, if Christianity flocked to Le Puy as to no other Marian shrine, it was not only to implore of her the health of their souls but also the health of their bodies. They sought miraculous healing of incurable ailments in the waters of a spring which still exists and is still marked by a Latin inscription which says, "By the grace of the power of God, this spring serves as medicine to the sick and comes to their aid freely, when doctors can do nothing else for them" — a passage that could just as well be placed on the fountains and pools in Lourdes.

There is more still. We have spoken of the obligation, respected for centuries, of flying the Marian flag on certain days on the highest tower of the castle in Lourdes (protected by an honor guard from the shrine of Le Puy, symbolizing its authority over Lourdes). Now, whoever has been to Lourdes on pilgrimage knows that this castle faces the façade of the three superimposed basilicas, separated without obstacle to sight by a bend in the river and the "lawn of the Count," which is now the esplanade used for the eucharistic processions, from which the tribute to the feudal Virgin was taken, and which (by this singular chain of coincidences, if such they are) passed to the Confraternity of the Most Holy Sacrament. So, the "flag of the Madonna" fluttered for centuries in the wind right above the place where, beginning in 1862, perhaps the greatest shrine in the world would rise, but which already for over a thousand years was the "land of Mary" as attested in official documents.

For this reason, we can understand our old lawyer from Bordeaux who (while warning the reader to move from the level of history to that of faith) advanced an elegant hypothesis, not only concerning the "why" of Lourdes, but also "why" precisely in that place the eighteen apparitions took place, among them, one in which the Lady said to Bernadette, "Go and tell the priests to come *here* in procession and that a chapel should be built *here*."

Here, perhaps because, as Brejon writes, "the hill of Massabielle is situated in front of the rock of the fortress where the banner of Mary waved, which kept the city of Lourdes as a *fief et domaine*, a 'fiefdom and dominion.' The revolution stripped her of her ancient castle, and she built another, right in front of the previous one, another whose spire rises almost to the same height as the tower of the old fortress." And when the Lady said she wanted the faithful "to come here in procession," it was because "like every good sovereign, mother of her subjects, she wants her children to come to visit her in her abode and to present their needs to her there."

We realize that the desire to jump to such evocative conclusions has led us to suspend the historical synthesis at 1062, the moment of the voluntary donation of the castle, of the city, and of the entire county of Bigorre, to the Madonna of Le Puy, made by Count Bernard I and his wife, Clémence, motivated only by religious devotion. What happened next is that the tribute due to the "Countess and Lady" was paid every year on the altar of Le Puy for as long as the county of Bigorre existed. In fact, in 1303, due to a dispute between the king of England and the canons of the shrine in Le Puy, the Parlement de Paris reexamined the legal titles and solemnly reiterated that Lourdes and Bigorre were "domains of Mary." In 1307, Le Puy conceded its county in the Pyrenees to the king of France (who was Phillip the Fair, the one who suppressed the Templars), but the new sovereign had to recognize as well, according to the treaty that was signed, that he would only be a "vassal," the "administrator" of that *Terra Virginis* that was Bigorre. As a proof of this subjection, the king committed himself and his successors to pay the shrine of Le Puy a tax, quite high in fact, of three hundred *lire tornesi* per year. After that, those who took the throne maintained the tribute, paying for the right to administer what belonged to the Madonna. It was only with the bloody end of the monarchy in the decapitation of the king and queen and the declaration of the republic, the persecution of the clergy, the abolition of the diocese of Le Puy, the stripping of the shrine, the burning of that most venerated image — in other words, only with the drama of the Great Revolution — that it seemed that the rights of the Virgin over Lourdes and her entire region of Bigorre had come to an end.

So it *seemed*, we say, because there was a recovery, brief as it was, with the Restoration. In fact, in 1827, Charles X, the successor of Louis XVIII, reestablished the diocese of Le Puy and began once more to pay the tribute. And the youth of Lourdes returned to the distant shrine bringing the tribute of its subjects, the grass and flowers gathered in front of the castle. But this lasted a very short time: it seems that August 15, 1829, was the last time ancient Bigorre presented its offering on Mount Anis, reiterating its bond with Le Puy. The following year, another revolution placed Louis Philippe on the throne, the "bourgeois king" we have discussed, who in his youth had sided with the Jacobins who had burned the Black Madonna, hauling it to the bonfire on a sewage cart. He was certainly not a personality who had any intention of respecting the obligations assumed by preceding sovereigns. Thus, in 1830, the authorities ceased for the first time (besides the years of the revolutionary torment, obviously) to recognize Marian authority over Lourdes and Bigorre, an authority that had been recognized since the Carolingian period perhaps, but certainly since 1062 with the certificate of Bernard I.

Having reached this point, we hesitate to push further, delving into the hypothesis proposed by Brejon, whom we have been following thus far. This is a fascinating hypothesis, no doubt, but equally disconcerting.

Brejon, the legal scholar, observes that the rights of a liege lord over a plot of land are extinguished after thirty years of failed execution of the tributary obligations (the payment of the annuities, in other words) and of the honors due the lord. The terms of the provision, in our case, began in 1829 when for the last time the representatives of Bigorre brought their dutiful tribute to Le Puy. Thus, in 1859 the rights of Mary over her lands in Lourdes would have been interrupted. In 1858, behold the "Lady" (the name by which Bernadette very significantly addressed her) appeared in a cave in the hillside in front of the castle where for centuries her banner had waved by right.

Brejon notes,

> There is no doubt that statutes on earth do not apply in Heaven and that the Virgin Mary had no need to defend certain rights, which men had recognized to be hers, to remain the most noble of ladies and to be at home everywhere. Certainly, the crown of the Countess of Bigorre on her head added nothing to her greatness. Yet, we hold dear the thought that the Virgin Mary loved this terrestrial bond which might have gone back to the devotion of Charlemagne, but certainly to that of Sir Bernard. It was at the last minute (only a year before the expiry of the prescription in 1859, though with time to spare) that she herself appeared in Bigorre to ask, through the tribute of her dear old vassals, the homage of the entire world. The homage of the world? Well yes, was this not what took place in Le Puy throughout the Christian centuries, in the place where she was invoked as "the Mother of All"?

Our author adds that it was the instinct of faith that drove the faithful to venerate the Immaculate in the grottoes and to call her by a name that seemed to echo her ancient dominion: *Notre Dame*, "Our Lady" of Lourdes.

This, in summary, was the unique story of the "Lady of Bigorre." Much more could be added and observed, perhaps even something a reader pointed out: precisely that a "proletarian" named *Marie Bernarde* at her baptism would be summoned to restore the rights of Mary which had been recognized a thousand years earlier by a Count *Bernard*. But what we have said is sufficient, I believe, to make us ever more thoughtful in the face of the enigmas we find everywhere on the banks of the river that descends impetuously from the Pyrenees.

CHAPTER 14

Crumbs Gathered in Cana

Here we start another chapter not dedicated to just one theme, but rather annotations, drafts, and fragments that one would expect to find in a notebook or a diary. At times they are simple points in a more complex discussion needing to be elaborated. One might say they are crumbs collected below the banquet table at the wedding of Cana.

We begin by noting that the superficiality of post-Christian ideologies has sought to make us believe that the most profound divisions among men are those of a social, economic, or political nature. Thus, humanity is seen as marked by the division between masters on one side and workers on the other; between capitalists and the proletariat; between progressives and conservatives.

These are important separations, certainly. But equally certain, the lines that really divide men are quite different: the healthy from the sick, the content (at least reasonably so) from the desperate. It is *infirmity,* that of the *spirit* and that of the *body,* that creates barriers between men that precede all others.

In this sense, shrines carry out a "social" role of the greatest kind. Not by accident are almost all shrines Marian: the houses and in some ways the clinics of the common Mother, assisting those suffering in the flesh and in the soul, which is the first cause of all inequality.

Léon Bloy observed that those most devoted to Mary are either the great sinners or the innocent, the simple. Those who love her with a more intense love can be found either among those who have known sin in the depths or among those who have hardly known it at all.

Bernadette Soubirous and Paul Verlaine were born not only in the same country, France, but in the same year, 1844. The innocent shepherd girl of Bartrès and then the suffering, exemplary religious sister in Nevers, next to the "damned" poet, the alcoholic, cocaine addict, homosexual, attempted murderer, convicted felon?

The comparison will shock only those who do not know that we owe to Verlaine some of the most touching and heartrending verses in honor of the Virgin Mary. Here is one confirmation among so many of what we are trying to say: the most good-natured children or the most misbehaved, the innocent or the sinners, are the ones who most love such a Mother, and who seem most beloved by her.

According to the entire Catholic tradition, the devil is the personification of the "no." *Non serviam*, "I will not serve," is his motto, the very origin of his rebellion. But according to the same tradition, Mary is the "yes" par excellence: *Fiat mihi secundum verbum tuum*, Let it be done to me according to your word. To the diabolical *non serviam*, she contrasts her obedient *Ecce ancilla Domini*, Behold the handmaid of the Lord.

On one side, not only the refusal but also the revolt (modern revolutions have rediscovered, in their flags, the red which since ancient times has symbolized struggle and aggression, the "demonic" color par excellence). On the other side, not only assent but, as its immediate effect, obedience (and here too, the Marian blue has something to say, as we have mentioned, tied symbolically as it is to peace and quiet). Again, on one side pride, on the other humility.

In the light of reflections on Mary, the divine words placed at the beginning of history acquire all their prophetic significance: "I will put enmity between you and the woman; … he shall bruise your head, and you shall bruise his heel" (Gen. 3:15).

These things have been well meditated on throughout Christian history. We do well not to forget them now, when they are more than ever necessary. Has not all modernity presented rebellion as a positive reality always and in whatever form — the negation and refusal to serve, pride itself, understood as a decision of man to "go it alone," to be the sole judge of his destiny?

Thus, if we wish to continue to grant Mary the place that God Himself desired for her in the history of salvation, we must not forget her example.

Which is, in extreme synthesis, the *serviam* that opposes the *non serviam*. The "yes" opposing the "no" that is the measure of modernity born of a revolution that proposed to extirpate Christianity from man's memory. A revolution that piled on its massive bonfires the statues, paintings, and altarpieces stolen from the cathedrals dedicated to the Virgin Mary.

John Henry Newman (to whom we shall dedicate three chapters) was not only an Anglican pastor but one of the greatest theologians of the Church of England that arose out of the dynastic (and erotic) frenzy of the horrid, homicidal Henry VIII, who had two of his six wives decapitated. This king martyred thousands of Catholics who refused to join his church, in which he placed himself in the role of pope and where everything was reinvented for his benefit and for that of the aristocracy who took possession of ecclesial property. If England was not to return to Catholicism (which it seemed it might for a time), it was precisely because the new owners feared they would be forced to restitute the stolen property. At any rate, all branches of Protestantism enjoy as one of the reasons for their success the eager and avaricious divvying up of churches and abbeys among the powerful. This story would repeat itself during the French Revolution and then again with Napoleon, in the distribution of Catholic properties among new owners. Nevertheless, the great Newman came from this singular Anglican community that has now come to the end of its lifespan: around 2 percent attending Sunday services, and declining; ordaining practicing homosexual bishops and many others who are divorced and remarried; and still today depending on a vote of Parliament for its theological and liturgical decisions.

These are their problems, but what interests us here is to recall that the considered and convinced, though anguished, passage of Newman to the Catholic Church which later made him a cardinal was marked by a typically Protestant scrupulosity: the myopia, namely, of thinking that space given to Mary must be taken from Jesus. We cannot forget the contemptuous and horrified definition of Mariology given by Karl Barth: "a tumoral excrescence of Catholicism."

Returning to our Anglican theologian, we point out one of the considerations thanks to which he was able not only to overcome his Reform taboo but even to become the author of some of the most penetrating pages on Our Lady and on the veneration granted her by Catholics. Newman observed, with typical Anglo-Saxon realism, "If Christ had not truly desired that his Mother occupy in the Church the place she would occupy, that she would not exercise the influence that she would exercise, I dare say He would be the one who perverted us; or at least, who abandoned us to perversion, without assisting us, without warning us in some way."

This is an apparently paradoxical consideration in its pragmatism, though it has a profound truth. In fact, beyond theory and the theological pronouncements on the Virgin Mary, one must consider the concreteness of life, and the adventure of sanctity, which in no century has been lacking in the Church. If there is a constant in the innumerable saints whom Catholicism has inserted into its canon to be examples for believers, this constant is constituted by the ardor of their Marian devotion. It is unthinkable to find a saint who did not give to Mary the veneration which is her due according to doctrine, but also their fervent love. So Newman is right: paraphrasing a saying of Padre Pio, "If this is a mistake, it is God Himself who has deceived us."

To give just one example among thousands, Pius IX was deceived and deceived us in deciding, after having consulted the entire world episcopate, to teach in a definitive and solemn manner the Immaculate Conception of Mary, which had already been defended by saints and theologians for centuries; and four years later, the visionary of Lourdes was deceived and deceived us by saying that the Virgin Mary herself had ratified that infallible decision. If this were possible, one would be forced to draw some logical conclusions. What type of God would this be who, becoming man among men, presented himself as the "Truth" itself and who then allows those for whom he died to run after errors, misunderstandings, and even diabolical perversions?

Among the celebrations invented *ex novo* in recent decades, there are "Women's Day" and "Mother's Day." Both come from countries rooted in the Protestant tradition. For many centuries, Catholicism did not feel the need to celebrate "mothers" and "women" on a specific day. Might this be due to the hint of a void darkly perceived by the Reformation that (often going well beyond its founding fathers) expelled from its worldview the presence of the Woman and the Mother par excellence? Was not the inclusion of those commemorations in the modern calendar an attempt (at least unconscious) to resolve an absence which the Catholic liturgical cycle filled for centuries with its Marian feasts?

Nothing is by chance; nothing has not been premeditated or is not the fruit of experience in the liturgy: the law of prayer is the same law of faith. *Lex orandi, lex credendi*. We must therefore remember that the name of Mary is never pronounced in Catholic liturgy during the administration of the sacraments.

This is one response among many to those who suspect Catholicism for having placed the Virgin Mary almost within the Trinity, surrendering to the worst of sins according to Sacred Scripture: idolatry, the divinization of a human creature. The role of Mary, as relevant as it is, is entirely "within": within the mystery of the Son. Her power is indirect: she can do nothing on her own, but acts solely thanks to the power of intercession, based on love, that every son recognizes in a mother.

In this regard, we turn to the words of a convert with a taste for provocation and challenge: André Frossard, whom I knew well. "During the years of the Council," he wrote,

> when it was proposed to proclaim the truth of "Mary mediatrix," great protests arose from the theological world. To my great astonishment. In fact, for women, for every woman, mediation is a natural, daily thing. They are the ones who place themselves between fathers and sons, between one child and another, between their husband and the neighbors. They place themselves between nothingness and life, because they are the ones who give birth. And also, they mediate between all men and God, because they are the ones who have always represented the majority of those praying in Church. And they are by far more numerous than men behind the cloister, whose "work" is intercessory prayer on behalf of all humanity. Thus, forcing a bit the logic of the theologians hostile to the new dogma, one arrives at the surprising conclusion that all women are mediatrices; all, except that Woman of Nazareth to whom the angel Gabriel appeared!

As always, also in the doctrine on the Virgin Mary, the Catholic position appears as the one "in the center," far from the opposing extremes. It is the omnipresent *et-et* of Rome.

Expressing ourselves in comprehensible terms (though still entirely inappropriate since taken from politics): to the "left" is Protestant minimalism, which states that Mary was only a humble believer, a sister who fulfilled her task after being used as a sort of "surrogate uterus" by God, who thought it would be great to have a son, entrusting his gestation to a woman. After the delivery, she stepped back into line; no privileges, no special place. To the "right" lies a type of maximalism of the Eastern Church, where she seems to establish a sort of dualism with Christ, arriving at the extreme of the Ethiopian Church that teaches the "pre-existence" of Mary, her "eternity" which truly seems to add a fourth Person within the divine Mystery.

Some Protestants make of the Virgin of Nazareth a common person about whom they maintain silence, fittingly. In the super-abundant theological output of the Reformation, at least in modern times, there is scarcely a trace of her, as if Jesus grew up without a mother. Meanwhile, some Orthodox thinkers turn her into a celestial being, a *Theotokos* without any relationship to the humble Jewish woman of history; almost a goddess, inhabiting vertiginous heights, absorbed in the Heart of God.

The following is not facile apologetics but an obvious observation, almost a given, for those who know: as in many other aspects of doctrine or liturgical life, so too for Mariology, the Catholic perspective is "in the center," equidistant from both excesses. Is not this equilibrium a sign of truth?

Because the divine strategy has always been that of the chiaroscuro — of appearing and of hiding — in order to safeguard man's freedom, the Mother of the Word must share in this dynamic as well.

In fact, the "power of God" hides itself within creation. The "divinity of Jesus" hides itself in the river of history. The "sanctity of the Church" is hidden behind the sins and the limits of her children. The "role of Mary" hides itself in the whole of Scripture. It is hidden behind the prophetic proto-gospels of the Old Testament, where it can be perceived, but only post-factum, by the reflection of theologians and mystics. But it is hidden also in the New Testament, where the hints concerning her are few and meager, to the point of leading many to say that the constructs of Mariology are inappropriate because they rest on inadequate scriptural foundations.

In reality, those meager hints are like seeds: in order to bear fruit and reveal all their hidden potential, they require the heat of reflection guided by love. In any case, there is indeed a scarcity of words. Paul, for example, makes but one reference to her, without even citing her name, "But when the time had fully come, God sent forth his Son, *born of woman*" (Gal. 4:4, emphasis added). This scarcity, however, is not a sign of irrelevance, as if it were unworthy to speak of her too much. It is, rather, the inclusion of the Mother as well in the strategy of chiaroscuro that characterizes the entire action and manifestation of the Christian God.

In Jesus, faith sees God who stoops toward man. In Mary, it detects the human creature raised up toward God. The humility of the Creator and the dignity of the creature. This is the dynamic of the "double movement" (high and low) on which all Christianity is founded. Authentic faith is born of the synthesis of these two realities.

"**Pray for us sinners**, *nunc et in hora mortis nostrae*." On this final invocation of the Hail Mary, Jean Guitton has made a comment that is worth meditating on: "If Mary has a direct relationship with the hour of death of each man, it is not only because that hour is more difficult and anguishing than every other. It is also because death is the hour of our birth into eternity. And she was given to us as a mother both in time and in eternity."

Luke is the "evangelist of Mary." To him we owe the infancy narratives of Jesus, lacking in the three other Gospels. But also on other points, the third evangelist is noted for his particular attention to the Mother of Christ.

As is known, according to ancient tradition, Luke was a painter, to the extent that various images of the Virgin Mary are attributed to him. Is it by chance that it was an artist who was able to be so sensitive to the presence and fascination of her who would become over millennia the greatest inspiration of art?

CHAPTER 15

The Devoted and Devotions

I once worked (it was my first job after graduating) in the press office of the Salesian publishing house, whose origins date back to Don Bosco himself. At that time, one of the most well-known and caustic French journalists and writers, André Frossard, raised an outcry, first in Paris and then throughout the world, with his account of the mystery into which he had suddenly plunged thirty years before. When the translation of his disturbing *Dieu existe, je l'ai rencontré* (*God Exists, I Have Met Him*) came out, I was chosen to accompany the author on a publicity tour around Italy.

I later encountered Frossard various times at his house in Neuilly-sur-Seine. And it was there, one day, that I understood one of his many trenchant paradoxes. He spoke of the contempt of many intellectuals around the world for popular religion, and in particular, for what has characterized, and in part still does, Marian devotion: the environment surrounding shrines and pilgrimages to them.

The elderly André told me, winking with his ironic eyes and lighting his umpteenth cigarette after having attached to it a mouthpiece in a sort of ritual I knew well ("only an explicit order of the pope could force him to stop smoking," sighed his wife):

> The afterlife, believe me, will be quite a surprise for sophisticated savants. They will not only discover that another world truly exists, but they will find themselves the target of the benevolent, splendid irony of the Christian God. I truly believe that those fussy sirs will find in their paradise all that so horrified them in life: the plastic bottles shaped like the Virgin Mary, the glass orbs with the shrine

> inside that snows when you shake it, the images of Mary and popular saints to stick on the dashboard of your car, the kitschy paintings and holy cards. And the best part will be that all that bazaar will please them immensely, because God will have given them back the spiritual and intellectual childhood they had lost and so despised. They will live happily forever, blessed amidst the trinkets of shrine vendors' stands.

Frossard intended this as a provocation, one must understand. But not without truth; and a provocation made with the freedom and the irony that characterize those who have come to the Faith "from the outside," knowing secular culture well because they grew up in it (speaking from my own experience) and are not in the least intimidated by it — an intimidation that happens in the ecclesial world that imagines "secular intellectuals" to be some sort of omniscient oracles.

As I have already mentioned, the phenomenon of all that is tied to popular devotion and, in particular, to the veneration of the Virgin Mary, does not seem to "create culture," at least understanding this according to academic and Enlightenment categories. Referring to those pages in chapter 10, I now take my cue from the words of the late French journalist to try to clarify the ideas about what he called "the trinkets of shrine vendors' stands." If we think about it, it is not in the least a secondary topic but a theme to be faced squarely as experience would suggest.

In fact, those "trinkets" (setting aside for now their undeniable aesthetic mediocrity) constitute the constant point of departure for moralistic jeremiads on a "commerce" that seems intolerable to those who seek a Christianity of the "pure" and the "perfect." Our thoughts run immediately to the infinite number of comments expressing scandal over the jungle of shops, bazaars, and stands that besiege, and always have, the grounds of the shrine in Lourdes. There is always someone ready to cite Jesus' cleansing of the temple, using cords as whips, recorded in all four Gospels.

Let us reflect then, far from the demagogy that threatens even the world of believers and basing our reflection on a Gospel passage often called into account in an emotional rather than rational manner.

First, some cite the famous cleansing of the temple to condemn generally every instance of commerce in relation to the sacred, forgetting that even Mary and Joseph were, like all Jews, clients at those same markets and stands.

"And when the time came for their purification according to the law of Moses, they brought him up to Jerusalem to present him to the Lord ... and to offer a sacrifice according to what is said in the law of the Lord, 'a pair of turtle-doves, or two young pigeons'" (Luke 2:22, 24). Those birds were not brought from home: they were bought outside the temple, in the courtyard of the specialized market stalls.

Every year, then, Jesus Himself would return, in the company of His extended family or with the disciples, for the obligatory paschal pilgrimage to Jerusalem which He loved so dearly. And there, like everyone else, He made use of those indispensable merchants who provided the animals for the sacrifices that marked Jewish life and frequented the money changers whose tables he would one day overturn. Those changers supplied an essential service: to pay the tithe and to make the freewill offerings, the temple treasury accepted only the special coins, minted in Tyre, which were without human images, as the Law required.

Why, then, the famous "scene" on the Temple Mount? What unleashed the violent reaction of Jesus was not the economic activity being carried out in the service of the great temple, which was an indispensable complementary activity. What made Jesus indignant was that the priests, profiteering by it, allowed the merchants to perform their business in an illicit place. Reconsider the episode in John: "*In the temple* he found those who were selling oxen and sheep and pigeons, and the money-changers at their business. And making a whip of cords, he drove them all, with their sheep and oxen, *out of the temple*.... And he told those who sold the pigeons, 'Take these things away; you shall not make my Father's house a house of trade'" (John 2:14–16).

The italics are ours, of course, and serve to place in relief what we have said: what is being contested is the placement of the market stalls, not their existence, which, for a pious Jew, was entirely legitimate, even indispensable. Jesus has it out with the clergy who permitted this abuse, more than with the merchants and money changers who were providing a service. He did not say to destroy those things, but to take them elsewhere. In fact, those who know the Jerusalem of that period and its habits and customs know that not only the religious sensibility but even the rules of the temple prescribed that all economic activity was to be exercised outside the walls in the center of which was the Holy of Holies.

Instead, the same priests who had written those rules and were called to enforce them (and who had for this reason their own police force that would participate in Jesus' arrest) had reached an agreement as lucrative as it was scandalous with the merchants, which allowed them to set up their activities within the walls, in the so-called "Courtyard of the Gentiles," of the uncircumcised. It is this violation of the Law on the part of the priests of the Sanhedrin that explains, among other things, why Jesus was not arrested after this violent cleanup. The authorities knew they were in the wrong, that they had violated their own regulations, and so, instead of arresting and throwing this aggressor into jail, they limited themselves to confronting him verbally, asking him, "What sign have you to show us for doing this?" (John 2:18). As if to say, "We know very well that we are wrong. But what authority do you have to remind us in this fashion? Who has authorized you to act like this?"

Do not forget that most of Jerusalem's economy depended on its role as the Holy City, the destination of throngs of pilgrims who spent their money on an annual journey commanded by the God of Israel. The economic "trickle-down" effect of the great temple was the main source of subsistence for a capital without any industry and surrounded by a sterile region.

Coming now to the Christian shrines, in light of what we have just said, it would be better to inform oneself on the foundations of the Faith and reflect upon them before judging the economy that surrounds them. As for Lourdes, which we cited as a paradigmatic case: in the light of faith, the shrine, here on a par with Jerusalem, was desired by Heaven itself, following the recommendations that the Lady entrusted to Bernadette to be given to "the priests." And in Lourdes, if we are not deceiving ourselves, Jesus' whips do not seem to be necessary.

In fact, after the recognition of the supernatural character of the events, the bishops of Tarbes were keen on gradually acquiring the largest extension of land possible around the grotto (and who knows whether, in the enigmatic plans of Providence, the place had not been chosen from above to be able to isolate it more easily in the future: the plot of Massabielle, it so happens, belonged to the city). Everyone knows that, once entering the gates of this vast domain, all commerce is forbidden. The only selling (besides books, CDs, and DVDs in the official bookshop of the shrine) is of candles. But for many decades now, the administration has carried out a sort of self-service: those who wish can make use of containers of candles of various dimensions and can even do so for free (or pay less than the suggested offering stated on each container), given that, intentionally, no form of control is exercised. Regarding the candles, too, a meritorious self-limitation was decided long ago: it was left to the merchants of Lourdes to sell (many millions per year) the *flambeaux*, the torches with the characteristic cup to shield the flame from the wind, on which is printed in various languages the "Ave Maria of Lourdes," the song intoned every evening in the evocative procession along the *esplanade*.

What is true of the complex in the Pyrenees is true as well for the other great Marian shrines found throughout the world. For example, the exclusion of commerce within a wide radius around the sacred zone is practiced in Fatima, too. And we repeat, following the Gospel, it is not a question of the sale itself, but the place where the selling is exercised, that the believer must consider.

But if someone were to be scandalized by the commerce as such, by the "economic spillover" around these pilgrimage destinations, they would do well to remember that here too the universal law of supply and demand applies. There are vendors only where there are possible buyers. Those who hold in contempt the pilgrims who fill their bags with souvenirs and trinkets, or the believer busily choosing, writing, and mailing postcards, do not reflect on the motivations behind those activities. Precisely the size of that business, of that postal flow (Lourdes is second in France, immediately behind Paris, for postcards sent; and the same holds for Fatima, on the heels of Lisbon), demonstrates to what extent the faithful take pilgrimage seriously and appreciate the importance of a spiritual journey. And how, therefore, those people perceive the need to take home a souvenir not only for themselves but also for relatives, friends, colleagues, or neighbors. Just as they feel the need to entrust to the postal system a sign, under the form of a postcard, of their spiritual remembrance of those who could not come with them.

In this perspective, "sacred" commerce (so unbecoming for the spiritualists, always tempted to disincarnate Christianity, making of it a sort of arid, unhuman religious ideology), far from scandalizing the faithful, has the meaning of a confirmation of the love which the simple souls have for shrines, for the Mother of Christ venerated in them.

As a journalist, I felt the duty to go and see what was happening in Medjugorje from the very beginning of events there. I reached that village when nothing had yet been constructed and on the plain under the mountain there was only the white church with two bell towers, one on each side of the façade. In defiance of the police still under Communist rule (and perhaps attempting to mollify the agents with an appropriate bribe), only a few stands offered their products. And these were only foodstuffs, or the crude objects of local artisans. The "supply" was not able to get organized yet, there as elsewhere, to respond to the inevitable "demand" of the still scarce pilgrims. The latter wandered about lost, unable to find even a few postcards for sale (and those only of the city of Mostar), in a ground-floor shop of the building in which the Franciscans who ran the parish lived. Too little for devoted pilgrims! My intuitions were thus confirmed: the importance given to pilgrimage arouses the desire, the profound and instinctive need in fact, to share that important experience with the pilgrim's dear ones who are not present, who cannot participate in that celebration of the soul.

At any rate, why should the faithful (the authentic ones, not the imitators) be denied that which is granted to the devotees of the new, disturbing "alternative forms of worship," such as sports fans? Does not the sale of flags, shirts, scarves, badges, stickers, pictures of the players, and all the other gadgets at the service of the fan clubs respond to the same need, though at a lower level of compensation, which the pilgrim seeks to satisfy as well?

These things are worth repeating, even for the sake of reacting to the dangerous form of spiritualism that threatens Christianity — that presumed "purity" of faith which, rejecting the very human aspects which have always characterized it, risks disincarnating it. And it risks making it, moreover, an elite affair, marked by that dark austerity of the Calvinist or Jansenist stamp which, in the light of history, has obtained one result: detaching people not only from devotion but from religion altogether. This is who in the statistics (as well as the lifestyles) in the regions of Europe where a Christianity "purified of all superstition" was imposed — the category of "superstitious" including every coexistence of "reasons of the heart" with the "reasons of reason."

Thus, Marian devotion must not fear that which might scandalize an "adult, intellectual faith." On the contrary, it must react to the attempts to suffocate the human aspects of worship (or even merely to tolerate it as a deviation to be suffered while awaiting something better) in the name of a moralism that is contrary to the gospel.

It must also be mentioned, while we are at it, that sentimentalism is the opposite of sentiment. This is ground in need of being reclaimed. If we are not scandalized by the so-called "merchants around the temple," seeing in them rather the signs of enthusiasm with which the Faith is lived, we are bothered nonetheless by a somewhat vapid, saccharine, affected air that marks some of the Marian world. I mentioned this in the introductory chapter.

It was not always this way. Here too, one must return to the lessons of history. History reminds us that, perhaps from the beginning of the eighteenth century, but certainly from the nineteenth, Marian devotion had suffered a process of "feminization." To avoid alarming the guardians of the good name of the category of women — those conformists always ready to shout, "Discrimination!" and "Politically incorrect!" — we must clarify that, for a series of reasons known to historians and which cannot be listed here, from a certain point in time the Church witnessed the gradual abandonment of males. The numerical prevalence of females that has characterized religious practice in the West does not reflect in the least the constant reality but is a phenomenon of recent centuries. According to the law of supply and demand, popular pastoral practice has had to adapt itself (remaining profoundly affected) to feminine requests, tastes, and sensibilities, often in a shoddy sense. From this there has arisen the vapidity, sentimentalism, and rhetoric of some aspects of Marian devotion.

This would have been unthinkable in more "Christian" centuries (despite the limits of all things human): in medieval Christendom, in other words, when the veneration of Mary typified the virile world of knighthood. We recall that the great "doctor of the Virgin Mary," St. Bernard of Clairvaux, was also an intrepid and passionate preacher of the Crusades. In fact, he was even the one who wrote the Rule for the warrior monks who became the Knights Templar, the legendary Templars who, before growing lazy in their wealth at the end of the epic events in the Holy Land, performed acts of valor, preferring on oath to immolate themselves to the last man rather than concede anything to the enemy. Well, those armed monks fought under the banner of Mary — not a scandalous matter to those who reflect on that canticle not in the least "pacifist," at least in the whining modern sense, which is the Magnificat.

For good reason did liberation theology rediscover that song, as well as the Woman to whom Luke attributes it, as an example of strength, not of soppy submissiveness. Certainly, there have been illegitimate readings of the Magnificat, as when it was seen as a "battle hymn" by the medieval crusaders, or as when it was (and in part still is) interpreted as a "song of political-economic liberation" by religious enchanted by the provisional success of Marxism.

Beyond the stretching due to the changing spirit of the times and to ideological deformation, the fact remains that the Virgin of the Magnificat who says "*deposuit potentes de sede*" (He has put down the mighty from their thrones) has little to do with the enervated devotion to be found in the preaching, veneration, and pastoral practice of the past few centuries.

For the believer, the radical femininity of Mary, the Woman par excellence who recapitulates within herself the double vocation of virgin and mother, has nothing to do with the caricatural effeminacy that has often surrounded devotion to her. To see the difference, it suffices to compare some of the nineteenth-century hymns, some of the "Maytime sermons" (often collected in manuals), to the Canto in the climax of the *Paradiso* which Dante Alighieri dedicated to her, choosing precisely St. Bernard as his guide. As it would also suffice to return to the great Fathers of the Church, with their pages wherein the love for Mary is accompanied by language and concepts far from all rhetoric. And what about the saints? All of them Marian, and all (or most, at least) with so little affectation.

I point out this problem not for reasons of personal taste or because I'm tempted by some form of aestheticism. This is a question that impacts the renewal of evangelization, which the Church has insistently asked of us. This renewal cannot and must not omit giving to Mary the place that is her due, the rightful fruit of twenty centuries of meditation on the logic of the Faith. Today, more than ever, the kerygma, the proclamation of the Gospel of Christ, cannot keep silent about the Mother of Christ. But how can the importance of that Marian role be made clear, at least among the common people, buried as they are under the saccharine banalities that lead those on the "outside" to think that the Madonna is merely a matter of devotionalism?

The challenge is certainly not easy, as shown by the confusion on both sides, manifested throughout the centuries. The "strong Woman" of the

Gospels must be reproposed while safeguarding at the same time the tenderness of her maternal role. The meek girl of Nazareth must coexist with the "enemy of all heresies" ("terrible as an army fanned out on the battlefield," according to the verse of Manzoni, who speaks just before that, however, of her "gentle tutelage"). Yes, a recalibration that leads to a synthesis is not easy, but it is the usual task for a Catholic, called by vocation to unite the opposites, to bring contraries into coexistence.

We must at least become aware of the problem. The role of Mary is too decisive for the Faith to risk having people believe that everything can be reduced to a bit of sugary sentimentalism. Although one must not forget what has been said here about respect for charisms and sensibilities: space for different tastes must be safeguarded as well.

CHAPTER 16

A Fatima for Islam

MEDIA THROUGHOUT THE WORLD spoke about it, though with the usual imprecision and habitual inaccuracies with which they report religious news.

It was a sort of repossession by Islam of the shrine of Fatima, especially by Shiite Muslims who have their stronghold in Iran.

Those who follow these problems know that this reclamation is nothing new. It seems they have now gotten the masses involved, after the television transmission in Tehran of a documentary, produced by the Iranians themselves, on the famous site of Marian devotion in Portugal. A similar news story was presented in the West as something a bit odd, classified as Khomeinian folklore. "Muslim presumptions over a Catholic shrine! The Persians land in Portugal!" According to the headlines, this was the stuff of geopolitical humor.

But as for us, we are not laughing at all. In fact, we were not waiting for this type of journalistic information (or disinformation, if you wish) to meditate on a mystery to which we would like to give some coordinates, beginning in this chapter: the mystery of the presence of Mary in Islam, a presence that (enigma within enigma) seems to have to do with Fatima in an explicit manner.

Fatima, in fact, was the name of Mohammed's favorite daughter.

The prophet of Islam had, it seems, fifteen wives and a number of concubines, but his heart remained always bound to the first wife, the wealthy Khadija, whom he married despite her being much older than him, and with whom he had time to have three sons and four daughters. Almost all of them died at birth or very young. Fatima, his favorite, not only survived but assured the prophet posterity. She was given to her father's cousin in marriage, Ali, who is at the origin of the dynasty of the Fatimids, appropriately.

As we recalled, the daughter of Mohammed and Khadija played a decisive role especially for the Shiites: the term derives from *Shi'a,* namely, the "party" of Ali and Fatima. In contrast to the Sunni "party," they hold that the Prophet had designated his cousin (and son-in-law) as his successor; therefore, those men could be an *imàm,* or "leader of believers," only if they descended from the two relatives of the one to whom the Quran was dictated, whose original is kept in Heaven.

But Fatima is a decisive figure venerated by every Muslim, whatever party they belong to. The pious believer invokes her as "the glorious, the beautiful, the generous, the noble," exclaiming every time, after having spoken her name, "That above her be the honors and the greeting of Allah!" No other woman occupies such a place, in a universe that is not only as male but often as harshly chauvinist as is the *umma,* the community of believers in the Quran. No other woman, that is, with one other exception: Màryam, Mary, the Mother of Jesus.

All Islam, regardless of its school, remembers one hadith of Mohammed, a saying that is transmitted by oral tradition from the early disciples and considered a source of revelation next to the Quran. That hadith has preserved a word of the prophet of Islam addressed to Fatima: "You shall be the patroness of the women in Paradise, *after* Màryam." Thus a superiority in the Muslim Heaven for the one whom Christians call *Reginal Coeli.* And at the same time, a direct connection with Fatima. The two exercise together (although Mary is at the apex) a sort of dominion in Paradise.

It is no surprise that Louis Massignon, the great Christian Near East scholar and mystic of the encounter among the faiths born of Abraham, saw in this not an accidental coincidence but an eloquent sign of the fact that Mary, "Mistress of women" in the Muslim Paradise, chose to appear in a locality until then unknown even to many Portuguese, but which bore the name of the one who, according to Mohammed, is directly under her in the Heaven of the blessed.

Remember that the village of Fatima, with just a few thousand inhabitants until 1917, draws its name from the Arabs, according to scholars of toponymy. This etymology is attested independently by ancient tradition (long before the apparitions), according to which, in the twelfth century, when the region was still contested between Muslims and Christians, a noble Saracen girl, daughter of the governor of the Castle of Alcacer do Sal and named Fatima in honor of the Prophet's daughter, was involved in a clash between knights of both sides. A famous commander of the *Reconquista*, Don Gonçalo Hermingués, fell in love with her, and married her after she had agreed to be baptized. The tender love between them was prematurely interrupted by the death of the young lady.

Don Gonçalo, unconsolable in his pain, abandoned the army and became a monk in the Cistercian Abbey of Alcobaça (still a tourist destination today), where he obtained permission to bury the body of his beloved spouse. After some years, the abbey founded a little monastery several kilometers away and sent Gonçalo as its superior. Once more, the former paladin was allowed to stay united to the remains of Fatima, who was interred in the new church of the locale that had been uninhabited to that time and that ended up taking the name of her who had been born a Muslim but became an exemplary Christian wife. The monastery has long since disappeared, but the little church which received the body of Fatima still exists, and is dedicated to the Virgin Mary.

In a previous chapter, we tried to reconstruct the surprising, and too often ignored, "Marian vocation" of Lourdes, where the Lady who would appear in 1858 had been proclaimed "Lady and Sovereign" for at least a millennium already, such that whoever held power in those parts had to make an act of vassalage and commit to govern in her name.

We now discover that there is a precise "Marian vocation" also in Fatima. The place entered into history with the construction of a church dedicated to the Virgin Mary, at the service of the Divine Liturgy celebrated by the monks of St. Bernard, the great poet of the Madonna.

But historians have recalled many other episodes which only a vision far from that of faith would define unhesitatingly as "mere coincidence." For example, on the plateau of Fatima, on the eve of the feast of the Assumption in 1385, King John I and Blessed Fr. Nuno Álvares Pereira, "national hero and saint" of Portugal along the lines of Joan of Arc for France, won a prodigious victory against the invading Spaniards, after having made a public vow to Mary. Precisely in that spot sacred to the Portuguese nation, 532 years later, she appeared, preceded by the triple apparition of the mysterious creature who identified himself as "the angel of Portugal."

Much more could be said. Peculiar, for example, is the fact that Pope Boniface IX, at the request of the same King John I, victorious over the Spanish, decreed that all the cathedrals of Portugal be dedicated to the Virgin Mary. And he did so with a document promulgated on May 13, the date on which the first apparitions occurred in Fatima.

Besides these signs of possible "predestination," we stand here before a truly unique enigma. We have seen how there is a direct relationship between the name of the locality and the name of the venerated daughter of Mohammed, "prophetess" of Islam.

Among Muslims, Fatima is a type of Marian figure, seen as the one who offers her suffering, her prayer, her compassion for all men. The famous American preacher and writer, Archbishop Fulton Sheen, observed, "Just like Esther (before the first coming of Christ) was a figure of Mary for Israel, so Fatima (before the second coming of Christ) could be a figure of Mary for Islam."

This concordance of names is a "coincidence" (the quotation marks are necessary) that has not yet been fully understood by Christians, except in some cases, like that of the mystic and erudite scholar and lover of Islam (but a Catholic with a sincere and orthodox faith), Louis Massignon. Some Muslims have understood this, on the other hand — even if the masses are only now beginning to become interested (we began by speaking of the breaking news in Tehran) — such that Muslim pilgrims, though not in an organized manner, have never been wanting in Fatima and now are growing in number.

Judaism, as has been said, is the religion of hope; Christianity of charity; Islam of faith. The function of the apparitions of 1917 (the year in which the first regime in history based explicitly on "scientific" atheism was established) seems precisely that of placing believers on guard against the dangers that threaten the Faith in the age of ideologies. Was this the reason for the divine choice of a place like Fatima, whose name is a reference to those "sons of Ishmael, the son of Abraham," whose faith is such that atheism is considered inconceivable?

It seems, nevertheless, that the enigmatic case of the two "Fatimas" — the Arab woman and the Portuguese village — could at least stimulate us to rediscover that other, extraordinary enigma of the presence of Mary in Islam. The fulfillment of the Gospel prophecy ("All generations will call me blessed") seems truly to have involved even the Muslim people who, according to the projections of demographers, seem destined to overtake Christians numerically due to their elevated birth rates, as well as Islam's continual expansion.

It is remarkable that, for all the talk of ecumenism, the fact is often overlooked that precisely Mary is the "place" where Muslims and Christians (at least Catholics and Orthodox) are nearer than anywhere else. To the point of reaching a paradox: while today there is a continual "rereading," both reductive and ambiguous, of some Marian dogmas, beginning with the virginity of Mary, Islam tolerates neither doubts nor hesitations in this regard. In fact, it is ready to stone on the spot any who dare to offend the honor of her who is "the Virgin who preserved intact her womb." The Quran itself, confirmed in clear letters by the canonical tradition of the hadiths, teaches a truth about Mary that approaches to an amazing degree that of the Immaculate Conception, which struggled to be declared a dogma among Catholics.

Muslim commentators affirm that the Quran also proclaims the Assumption into Heaven of the Mother, together with that of her Son, in verse 50 of Sura 23, which we quote for the echoes that it sets off in Christians: "And We made the son of Mary and his mother a sign and sheltered them within a high ground, a place of flocks and springs of water."

"A sign": a meaningful word, so often applied to Mary by Christian tradition. And this cannot but spark a connection with "springs of water," considering that this was precisely the "sign" that characterized many apparitions.

But let us progress in an orderly manner (and limit ourselves only to the load-bearing structures of Muslim "Mariology"). First, in the Quran, Maryam is the only woman mentioned by name, which is repeated some forty times. Jesus is always indicated with reference to her: "the Son of Mary." Her Hebrew name is read by Arab exegetes with etymologies that are imaginative but seek to emphasize predestination: "the pious," "the devoted," "the servant of God."

We must immediately clear the table of any facile polemical motivation, used throughout the centuries by innumerable Christian polemicists and which can be found even in current publications. In fact, in Sura 19 (which in the canonical editions of the Quran is given the title "Sura of Mary"), when the young girl presents herself to her parents with the baby Jesus in her arms, she is so reproached by them that they ignore the fact that His conception was miraculous, preserving His mother's virginity: "Mary, thou hast committed a monstruous thing! *Sister of Aaron,* thy father was not a wicked man, nor was thy mother a woman unchaste."

Italics were added to the incriminating expression. In fact, Aaron and Moses had a sister whom the book of Exodus calls "Mary the prophetess" (15:20). This led to the accusation that the Quran had fallen into an unbelievable anachronism, mistaking Mary, the sister of the two who lived at least thirteen centuries earlier, for Mary, the Mother of Jesus.

In reality, the matter must be given greater attention, without falling into polemical temptations that would be unmerited, especially on the part of Christians, who should not forget the role the Quran has played in the glorification of Mary. The Quran concedes to her all that its incomplete perspective on Jesus will allow it: man of God, though not Son of God; among the greatest prophets, but the penultimate one; not the definitive and complete revealer of the will of God, the role that would be given only to Mohammed.

Believers in the gospel should not forget the dark side, of course, often violent, of that enigma of history which is Islam; but neither should they forget that, in contrast with what happens in Christian lands, it is unthinkable for a Muslim to take her name in vain, or to allow the least lack of respect and honor in her regard, even lighthearted irony toward her who, besides "Mother of Jesus," is called by the Quran "the daughter of Imran." (Arab commentators will say that the "true name" of Mary's father is Joachim, in harmony with Christian tradition based on an ancient apocryphal work.) Neither should Christians forget that the entire Islamic tradition, from the very text of the Quran, is a passionate defense of the honor of a Virgin who remained such although she became a mother, against accusations, defamations, and at times obscenities on the part of a Jewish tradition that continued for centuries, even to our own times to some extent. This is an important aspect we shall consider later: it is worthy of attention, given that there is something here that is often kept in embarrassed silence, considered as it is politically (and theologically) incorrect to reveal what is true but thought better kept silent.

But we return to the presumed exchange, in Sura 19, between "Mary, the Mother of Jesus" and "Mary, the sister of Aaron." One of the more renowned

Italian scholars of Islam, Cherubino M. Guzzetti, to whom we owe the most recent Italian translation of the Quran, said,

> It is difficult to imagine that Mohammed, in general quite accurate in his biblical chronology, would have made such a confusion. Probably, in the case of Mary, Mother of Jesus, for "sister of Aaron" one must understand "descendant of Aaron." This is not an absurd explanation, given that analogous expressions are frequent in Semitic languages: consider the "brothers" and "sisters" of Jesus, which the Catholic Church considers to have been cousins.

Or could it be possible that behind this contested quotation ("Oh, sister of Aaron!") lies not a grotesque misunderstanding but an additional praise of Mary. This is the thesis of Louis Massignon and, among his disciples, the Franciscan Giulio Basetti-Sani — he too a well-known scholar of Islam — who writes, "Aaron is the priestly figure of Christ. For the Jews of Arabia who heard Muhammed's preaching, the expression 'sister of Aaron' recalled the dignity of Mary. Over the centuries, Aaron had become the symbol of the Levitical priesthood, the class that was totally consecrated to the service of God." Nor must we forget the first chapter of the Gospel of Luke, where the "priest named Zechari'ah, of the division of Abi'jah, . . . had a wife of the daughters of Aaron, and her name was Elizabeth" (Luke 1:5). According to the same evangelist (1:36) Elizabeth was a "kinswoman" of Mary, probably a cousin. Given this kinship of the Virgin with a "daughter of Aaron" such as the mother of John the Baptist, Fr. Basetti-Sani concludes, in agreement with Massignon and other scholars, "In the contested expression, the Quran seeks to recall the dignity of the origin of Mary: if on one side she belonged to the royal house of David, she was also offspring of Aaron and of the family of Levi."

If that is truly the case, it would not be the only time in which the Quran seems to go beyond even the Gospels in its exaltation of the Mother of Jesus, although denying the Son His communion with God — which is, of course, a decisive aspect, never to be forgotten, given that it denies Mary her main role, the lofty role of the woman called to give flesh to the Creator Himself come down to His creatures. But this discussion deserves to be continued in a future chapter.

CHAPTER 17

Between Portugal and La Salette

HERE IS ANOTHER MEANDERING chapter along the paths of the simple, luminous, and unfathomable Marian mystery. We take up again that enigma within the enigma which is Fatima. After having spoken about the likely connection between the Portuguese town and Mohammed's beloved daughter, why not point out the singular coincidence of the dates?

In fact, there is a strange repetition of that May 13 which, in 1917, marked the first apparition of the Lady to the three Portuguese shepherd children, two of whom have already been inscribed in the lists of the Blessed. Precisely on that same day, and in fact, in the same hour that the events were happening on that remote Portuguese meadow, in St. Peter's Basilica in Rome, Eugenio Pacelli was consecrated bishop by Pope Benedict XV. While, in Fatima, the Madonna was speaking of war and peace and exhorting us to pray, the forty-one-year-old monsignor, descendant of a noble family of Rome, entered the episcopate, only to be sent immediately as nuncio to Bavaria (the only German state that maintained diplomatic relations with the Holy See during World War I) and there, in Munich, to work in every way in favor of peace.

This was a particularly significant coincidence, yet one which did not strike Pacelli, so it seems, until over a decade after he had become Pope Pius XII, when he decided to proclaim the new Marian dogma of the Assumption. The great event was planned for November 1, 1950. The two days before that, October 30 and 31, while strolling in the Vatican gardens, the pope saw the miracle of the sun of Fatima renewed in the sky before his eyes. An indiscretion by one of his collaborators (harshly reprimanded for this) brought the news to the attention of newspapers, who seized upon it and romanticized it to the point of arousing suspicion that the whole thing had been invented.

In reality, the definitive confirmation came at the start of the 1980s, when, just before her death, Pascalina Lehnert published her memoirs. The legendary "Sr. Pasqualina" was the Bavarian nun who had served Eugenio Pacelli from the time he was nuncio in Munich until his death and who thus witnessed his private life for forty-one years. Sr. Pasqualina confirmed the event which had taken place on two successive evenings, adding that the pope had asked for news of unusual reports from the *Specola Vaticana* and other scientific institutes — but as had happened in 1917 at the astronomical observatory of Lisbon, so too in Castel Gandolfo, the instruments registered nothing unusual. Nevertheless, from that day on, Pius XII sought to understand the events of Fatima more profoundly, on numerous occasions sending trusted people to Coimbra, to the monastery where the only survivor, Sr. Lucia, lived.

John Paul II would also confess to having known about and venerated the apparitions of Fatima but of not having given them particular attention until that fateful May 13, 1981, when the Muslim Ali Agca fired his pistol at him in St. Peter's Square. The following year, as is known, on the anniversary of the first apparition as well as of the miraculously failed assassination attempt (at least in its extreme consequences), Pope Wojtyla said to the million pilgrims gathered on the plain next to the *Capelinha* (Chapel of the Apparitions), "The assassination attempt mysteriously coincided with the anniversary of the first apparition. These dates intersected in such a way that I was moved to recognize a special call to come here." And to the Virgin Mary who had "guided with a maternal hand the bullet making it pass a few millimeters from vital organs" (as he later said to André Frossard, "One hand shot, another hand acted as a shield"), he offered the bullet, which was placed in the diadem on the head of Our Lady's statue used for solemn processions.

Some have noted that the name of the terrorist, Ali, is the same as that of the husband of Fatima. And some others have gone so far (and maybe too far) as to remark that the exact hour of the shots fired (17:19) seems to hide 1917, the year of the prodigies. The fact is that in the jubilee year, Pope John Paul revealed the "third secret" that had become mythical, in which he read a direct reference to the assassination attempt of which he had been the victim.

Pius XII, John Paul II: two popes who, according to the prophecies of 1917, were to "suffer much," even at the hands of totalitarian ideologies to which Fatima had made dramatic reference. The first pontiff to go to Fatima on pilgrimage was Paul VI (on May 13, 1967), a pope of suffering as well, above all due to the devastating effects of contemporary ideologies, especially a Marxism that had penetrated clerical environments and whose errors had been denounced by the Virgin herself.

The episodes we have recounted to this point are all well known. Known to very few, on the other hand, is another coincidence that is truly peculiar. On that May 13, 1981, the day of the assassination attempt, among the officially invited guests who awaited to pay the pope their homage there was an unusual group that had brought with it an even more unusual "object." These were scientists (almost all of them Americans, and a few Protestants, Jews, and agnostics among them) who had created the Shroud of Turin Research Project (STURP). This research group had long been subjecting the Shroud of Turin to examinations with the most sophisticated electronic instruments, obtaining results that pointed to the authenticity of the tradition that sees in that sheet the shroud of Jesus.

Moreover, with their computers they were able to extrapolate a sort of 3D model that reproduced to scale the three-dimensional relief of the mysterious image. Together with the volumes collecting the results of their studies, the scientists of STURP wanted to offer the pope, always a great devotee of the shroud, the 3D image of the ancient cloth. They did not have the chance to do so: having arrived just a few meters from the group, John Paul II was stopped by the shots.

"We had the impression," said one of the researchers on the team, a positive scientist far from any temptation to mysticism, "that the forces of evil that the visionaries of Fatima had glimpsed, and which had frightened them and made them suffer, wanted to prohibit the pope from seeing the fruit of our work that reproduced the traits of the one who for us and for millions of the faithful is the face and the body of Christ."

But there is more. In 1988, there arrived the radiocarbon dating results that dated the shroud to the medieval period. Later studies have shed radical and justified doubts on the reliability of those tests and on the seriousness of the laboratories that performed them. Nevertheless, the "custodian" of the shroud in the name of the Church, the archbishop of Turin, convoked journalists from around the world to communicate the results himself (indulging in lighthearted comments and assuring that, in his opinion, there was no pastoral problem, though he had other concerns), results that were passed off as "scientific" and to which, in that case, all must give their obedience. As if intimidated after all these centuries by the shadow of Galileo, the bishop seemed ready to convert to a scientism by now out of date. At any rate, a very sad day, though not so much for the "devotees" as perhaps for the truth. Well, that bitter day in the autumn of 1988 was October 13: the anniversary of the "Miracle of the Sun" in Fatima.

And that is not all. The archbishop of Turin, Cardinal Giovanni Saldarini, the new custodian, decided in agreement with the Holy See to remember in 1998 the centenary of the first photograph of the shroud. It was that famous negative by the brilliant amateur, the attorney Secondo Pia, which revealed the perfect photographic negative characteristic of the image. Therefore, it was decided to proceed with a new exposition in the cathedral of Turin. The official announcement was given by the cardinal archbishop at the plenary meeting of the Italian Episcopal Conference. Only at the end of the meeting did someone remember that it was no ordinary day; in fact it was May 13. Once more, the date of the beginning of the Portuguese events that seem tied to the Shroud of Turin.

Chance? Coincidence? Or enigmatic signs? There is obviously no humanly possible answer. We limit ourselves to registering a few facts—for some, they might be cause for curiosity; for others, of meditation. At any rate, long before 1917, the thirteenth of October was a well-recognized date among Church historians. On that date in 1307, the king of France, Philip the Fair, executed the dramatic suppression of the Templars, with the great roundup of knights, who were imprisoned and whose houses were confiscated. Meditate on what, then? What is certain is that we must never forget that all Christianity is supported by the "economy of signs"; thus even these coincidences can have their significance, however far from being convincing for everyone.

It is permissible to make an observation. There does not exist one institution in the Catholic Church, although it is the most organized religious community in the world (it can count more than six hundred universities and institutes of higher learning), that takes into consideration the impressive phenomenon that crosses the entire history of the Church: the apparitions and the extraordinary events related to them.

Several years ago there appeared the Italian translation of an imposing work by two German scholars, Gottfried Hierzenberger and Otto Nedomansky. The volume of more than five hundred pages was titled *All the Apparitions of the Madonna in Two Thousand Years of History*. The subtitle read, *Her Messages, Documents, Testimonies.* It provides a sort of mine containing all that one could possibly find of the nearly thousand events, around which devotion was often sparked, a place of worship built, pilgrimage initiated, while other cases fell into silence and forgetfulness. The two courageous authors remark in the introduction the extreme difficulty of their work: no one in the "official" Church seems concerned with these events. On the contrary, often those wanting to study them are even discouraged, almost as if they were visionaries or anachronistic cultivators of alienating devotions. Perhaps even outright enemies of ecumenism . . .

It seems to us — and we say this with all the humility and prudence owed to this matter — that there is a sort of contradiction here. In fact, on one side, the Church has always approved worship and favored the building of shrines, exhorting the faithful to make pilgrimage to places that it has proclaimed (even solemnly) to be privileged by a mysterious manifestation of the sacred. On the other side (today, above all), the Church seems at times even to refuse to examine the credentials of such places and events. This has two negative consequences. The first is that in this way it risks neglecting authentic signs (to be carefully separated from inauthentic ones) that Heaven has sent and continues to send. The second negative consequence is that the general disinterest (testified by the two German authors mentioned above) leaves room for visionaries, maniacs, suspect mystics, members of sects, and so on.

Here is a question that might sound naïve to many "adult Catholics" (as we have already said, we do not want to be one of them, considering it to be a contradiction in terms): In a Church where words and structures are multiplied, why has no one, even some enthusiastic amateur, some isolated devotee, been placed (in some way) in charge of verifying what has come of the "predictions," of the "prophetic proclamations" almost always tied to those apparitions, almost always Marian?

One day, in a column I wrote for a Catholic daily, I tried to carry out a little "test," even if isolated. Perhaps some readers remember that distant article, which was gathered, along with others, into a book. For those who do not recall it, one apparition was chosen, perhaps among the less appreciated to those caught in the spreading rationalistic spirit. Yet, many forget that it was officially approved by the hierarchy, which promotes and approves of pilgrimage there, having even recognized a religious community founded from that event and which bears its name. We are alluding to the apparition of the Virgin on the mountains of La Salette, in the Diocese of Grenoble. On that occasion, Mary announced calamities due to the rapid spread of irreligious attitudes. Among other things, she said, "They shall do penance with famine. The walnuts will grow moldy and *the grapes will rot*."

While attempting to discover what came of that prediction, I leafed through a number of unusual books in the library: manuals for viticulture and histories of agriculture. I discovered that the following year a devastating disease arrived in France from North America, wiping out vineyards. It was 1847 when this Phomopsis came (called "powdery mildew"), a parasitic fungus which causes the grapes to rot. This was only the beginning: from France, in 1868, there appeared suddenly that phylloxera (a microscopic lice), which, as observes the *Grand Larousse* encyclopedia, "took hold throughout all of France with the dimensions of a national disaster: over half the vineyards had to be destroyed and wine production was reduced by two-thirds, and the scourge could not be remedied for a long time." And it did not end there: in 1878, the late blight (or powdery mildew), until then unknown in France, arrived. The *Larousse* recounts, "This disease, also originating in America, reached the European continent, precisely in France, and spread throughout all the countryside where grapevines were cultivated, provoking terrible damage."

Paul Claudel was one of the famous devotees of Our Lady of La Salette, who, despite much contestation and an itinerary certainly much more troubled than that of Lourdes, includes among her faithful adherents many famous men of culture such as Léon Bloy, Jacques Maritain, and Joris-Karl Huysmans. Claudel wrote, "Grapes will rot. This was easy to attest: the prophecy was fulfilled to the letter. How many diseases have attacked the poor grapevines since that day of Mary's apparition!" In fact, the damage caused in the second half of the nineteenth century by the invasion of parasites until that time unknown was so great that in Europe today (and especially in France), there are no species of vines that predate 1847. And the announcement of what would happen comes from the previous year.

When I recalled these results of my little test in that Catholic newspaper, however insufficient and summary it was, I asked myself, "Would it be an injurious sin against science, even for men of faith, to propose an investigation in a systematic way into the fulfillment (or lack thereof) of 'predictions' given in the course of Marian apparitions which the Church herself has approved? Beyond being a devotional question, is this not a problem of integrity?"

These are questions we repeat here, although aware that there will be no answer, and the verification of the truth will be based on "volunteer" researchers more gifted with enthusiasm than with discernment and knowledge.

Too bad. Another pastoral problem, and not lesser in degree, that seems to be ignored while it seems urgent to compare (in a postmodern, and thus post-rational, environment) to realities that increasingly attract people's attention. And which seem to multiply to the point that René Laurentin observed,

> We must abandon the framework which comes to us from decades long past, of the "great" apparition, with the accompanying emergence of a "great" shrine and a "great" tradition of pilgrimage. The example, therefore, of Lourdes and of Fatima. It seems that the intervention of Mary in human affairs is becoming more "democratic" and "decentralized," if it is permissible to use such terms. A series, therefore, of supernatural (or at least humanly inexplicable) phenomena that are widespread, less spectacular, destined to foster local devotion and veneration.

Returning to La Salette: among the great pilgrimages, this was certainly among the most contested. Here, the visionaries were not characterized by their obvious and solid Gospel innocence like Bernadette. Melania and Massimino bore the cross of an event not only infinitely greater than they were ("How can the man live on whom God has set his eyes?" asked a mystic), but also the weight of fanaticism of some and the instrumentalization by others. Perhaps for the first time in events of this sort, politics wormed its way in, from the right and the left, monarchists and republicans, legitimists and revolutionaries, with its capacity to poison everything.

If, in Bernadette, the predictions of the Lady to "not make you happy in this life" were fulfilled above all through the calvary of illness, for the two children of La Salette it was fulfilled through the calvary of drifting lives, lived with good will but in a confusion that led them to wander aimlessly, the victims of others but also of themselves, with their personalities of poor, ignorant highlanders caught up in an extraordinary story where Heaven and earth clashed.

Even an extraordinarily charismatic personality such as the Curé d'Ars, in light of their testimony, went from acceptance to perplexity, if not outright rejection (although one tends to forget how the matter unfolded: Fr. Jean-Marie Vianney returned to accept entirely the truth of La Salette). Meanwhile, the cause for the beatification of Servant of God Giuseppe Zola seems to be proceeding, the bishop of Lecce who was the confessor of Melania and who received her paternally in his diocese and granted the imprimatur for the publication of the contested "secret." From this cause (promoted by the Postulation of the Canons Regular of St. Augustine, to which Zola belonged) the drama of the visionary emerged with fuller truth, she who was mistaken for a prophetess, unstable, a pseudo-mystic, while she seemed to have a spiritual life that was complex and unusual, but equally marked by an authentic gospel perspective. In the end, obscurity seemed to wrap around her, such that very few know that her body lies in Altamura, Apulia, in the Church of the Immaculate.

The fact is that not even La Salette was able to escape the logic we have so often mentioned: light and shadows, reasons for credibility and reasons for unbelief. The typical style, in other words, of the *Deus absconditus* who wishes to propose and not to impose.

Precisely the year celebrating the 150th anniversary of that September day on the mysterious mountain, I too returned there, finding the usual steady flow of pilgrims, which rarely becomes a crowd. As someone has said, "In Lourdes, Our Lady receives her children in a public audience; in La Salette, in a private audience." Seeing those people, recognizing the good fruit this tree has born over the past century and a half (here began the reawakening of French Catholicism, which would have such great importance for the history of all the contemporary Church), knowing that in this place the spectacular nature of the physical graces has more often given way to the spiritual, invisible prodigy which eye cannot see; seeing and knowing all this, I could not help thinking of the Curé d'Ars. When gripped by doubts regarding the truth of the apparitions, he associated himself with St. Paul's teacher, the wise Gamaliel: "If this is of men, it shall perish; if it comes from God, it will not perish whatever the obstacles." After a century and a half of religious vitality that continues and seems to grow, those words are to be considered with particular attention.

But in these difficult times, we ought to meditate as well on the words of the disturbing, tempestuous, fiery minstrel of this extraordinary "Marian city in the mountains," Léon Bloy:

> La Salette signifies, above all, the *serious side* of Christianity, the tragic nature of the choice placed before each of us. *Non irridetur Deus,* one cannot mock God without consequences. Here, we find ourselves in the heart of the Christian drama, at a vertiginous distance from every compromise with the spirit of the world. For this reason, the words of the Lady on that mountain will always be unpleasant to every Christian perspective that seeks to curry favor with the fashions of the moment.

CHAPTER 18

SUB TUUM PRAESIDIUM

IN THE TWO BOOKS I have written on the Paschal Mystery (Christ's Passion, death, and Resurrection), I mentioned of course the words Jesus spoke upon entering Jerusalem for the last time. To the Pharisees who invited him to silence the crowd acclaiming him, the Nazarene replied, "I tell you, if these were silent, the very stones would cry out" (Luke 19:40).

I noted then how peculiar it was that this expression directly preceded, in the same Gospel, the lament for the city in which the Romans would not leave "one stone upon another" (Luke 19:44). In fact, what little remains of Jerusalem where the Passion and Resurrection took place is almost solely what is called significantly the "Wailing Wall." In the vision of faith, those few stones shout out confirmation of the truth of the prophecies.

I also mentioned other "talking" (or "shouting") stones in those books. I spoke of the enigma of the five lines of five letters each scratched on one of the pillars of the gymnasium in front of the great theater of Pompey. It was that "magical square" (*Sator / Arepo / Tenet / Opera / Rotas*) in which Christians hid two *Pater nosters* that formed a cross and that revealed many things through the strength of the "stones" that the theories of the experts excluded with certainty, beginning with the precocious worship of the cross and the likewise precocious translation into Latin of the prayer Jesus taught his followers: all this certainly before A.D. 79, the fatal year of the eruption of Vesuvius.

We also saw that not only do the stones "shout," but at times even the papyri. In fact, one chapter of one of those books was dedicated to fragments discovered in cave 7 of Qumran and which seem to demonstrate (even though the fierce controversy is still raging) that at least one Gospel and several letters of

Paul already existed, and in their definitive forms, before 66–68, when the place was abandoned by the Essenes. If that is truly the case, the hegemonic biblical exegesis constructed on a foundational premise beyond discussion will have to be reconsidered: no Gospel before A.D. 70, in other words, before the catastrophe that devastated ancient Israel, with the subsequent disappearance of those who might have contradicted the evangelists had they strayed from what truly happened. In this light, one can see the importance of a "late" dating of the New Testament books to support their truth claims.

Well, there is an eloquent papyrus that directly concerns the Mother of Jesus as well, testifying (here too, against many other theories) how precocious her veneration really was among Christians. It is a text which seems to contain the seeds to be later developed in the much contested "Mariology." This archaeological find reveals what the faithful in the Roman and Ambrosian Rites recognize as the antiphon *Sub tuum praesidium*. It is still present in the Liturgy of the Hours of the Catholic Church and is even included in the repertoires of songs for the faithful.

In this regard, readers will allow me to make a brief and not irrelevant parenthesis, to recount a personal experience. I was finishing the documentation for this chapter when, during Sunday Mass, I checked the official hymnal of the Diocese of Verona, diligently distributed to every pew of my local parish, to see if that *Sub tuum praesidium* was among the 461 titles. Satisfied in finding it, I was surprised to discover something that satisfied me much less and for which I would not mind having clarifications from the luminaries of the "Commission for Sacred Music" that edited the hymnal. In it I found a warning that said, "Every hymn has been given an evaluation that takes into account the quality of the text and the expressiveness of its melody." Judgment was expressed in the following way: one bullet point for sufficient, two for good, three for distinguished.

Well, among the Marian hymns next to the one that interested me was the marvelous, moving, austere Stabat Mater, which tradition attributes to Jacopone da Todi, which the greatest artists have set to music, and which is used even in the liturgy. The experts of the Diocese of Verona assigned the three bullet points of "distinguished" to certain modern compositions by unknown musicians, but to the Stabat Mater (which was the classic version, given in the

Latin text, though with the Italian translation next to it) only two dots! Simply "good." Cause for amazement. Our hope is that it was a mistake, a typographical error. We await clarification from the monsignors and professors.

While we wait confidently, let us continue our discussion.

That antiphon of the *Sub tuum praesidium* was not given particular attention by liturgists, because the earliest testimonies they had dated it to the ninth century, at least in the West, and it was thought that it was one of the many other antiphons of the Carolingian Age. In 1917, the John Rylands Library in Manchester, perhaps the richest library in the world in terms of codices of the New Testament, acquired a batch of papyri in Egypt. One of these, approximately nine by nineteen centimeters, with ten lines, the right margin mutilated and a tear in the upper left, was published only twenty years later in 1938. According to some, perhaps with a bit of malice, the delay in publication was due to a sort of confessional embarrassment. The fact is that C. H. Roberts, the eminent papyrus scholar who oversaw the publication, was a convinced Protestant and that little, battered piece of material written in Greek letters contradicted everything the Reformation theologians had affirmed: namely, that the invocation and veneration of the Virgin Mary were late phenomena, constructs for the most part illegitimate that appeared as incrustations on an evangelical faith that looked only to Christ, and certainly not to His Mother.

Whatever one makes of the delay, more or less intentional, in publication, the fact is that Professor Roberts sought to shield himself, saying that he was certain that the papyrus was late, that it must date to a period in which what to Protestants was "Mariolatry" had already begun. In reality, it was his own colleagues who refuted him, and today there is unanimity in the recognition that the text cannot be later than the third century, and the most probable date is around 250. We find ourselves, then, in the presence of the most ancient Marian prayer (if we are to exclude the graffiti found recently on the walls of the shrine of the Annunciation in Nazareth, which we shall discuss later).

In our attempts to demonstrate the importance of those most ancient words, we shall provide here the translation which was made possible by integrating the text where it was mutilated, thanks to the liturgy of the Coptic Church which, in the same land of Egypt where the text originates, has used the prayer in its worship uninterruptedly and without variation.

"Under your mercy we take refuge, O Mother of God (*Theotóke*): do not despise our prayers in our troubles, but free us from danger: you, the only pure one and the only blessed one."

The handwriting of the letters is very clear, with but a few ornamental elements or traces of decorative symbols, as if it were one of those prayer cards still used today by the faithful when reciting certain prayers. According to some, it was a "model for engravers," a text to propose to an artisan for an inscription, perhaps onto metal or marble.

All this increases its importance, beyond its already extraordinary level, as an archaeological find. It is not a random, isolated matter, but rather "official," namely, something used in worship and in devotion not merely in private but also in public, ecclesial (in fact, the text is in the plural: "we" and not "I"). It is not a liturgical prayer in the strict sense, however; in fact, as can be seen in the text, Mary is directly addressed. And we know that every liturgical prayer, in all the Churches in the East as in the West, is directed exclusively to the Father, through the Son, in the Holy Spirit. It is a *troparion*, well-known even now in Orthodox communities: a brief hymn added to the liturgical part of the Office.

In any case, the external characteristics of the papyrus contribute to pushing back its date, demonstrating how the prayer on it had already been in use for some time, such that it had become traditional. Yet, the type of handwriting, as well as the ink found on the papyrus, leads the majority of experts to date it to around 250, as we have mentioned.

Well, before 1938, scholars had decidedly excluded the possibility of an "official" veneration of the Virgin Mary antecedent to the first ecumenical council, that of Nicaea in the year 325. As for the term *Theotokos*, later *Dei Genetrix*, Mother of God, the usual pedants deny that the term could have been in use before the celebrated definition at the Council of Ephesus in 431. And even if that demanding title appeared in some works of previous Christian writers, they state that it was a matter of private theological opinion, and certainly not approved (and not even tolerated) by the Church. And thus, the humble Egyptian scrap moves back nearly two centuries the date of Ephesus as the inauguration of this title, a date that had been cited as if it were a dogmatic terminus.

One must comprehend the "theological" embarrassment not only of the papyrus scholar Roberts, but also of all the Protestant world, with its theories on the late and illegitimate construction of Marian devotion and veneration.

In fact, there is not only that *Theotóke* (which, moreover, preserved all its letters, having escaped the tear that damaged some of the other words); there are also present in the text what we called the "seeds" of a further development that would be protracted throughout the centuries.

As is known, there are four Marian dogmas solemnly defined by the Church: the divine maternity, Mary's perpetual Virginity, the Immaculate Conception, and the Assumption into Heaven. As concerns the first, we have just explained that it appears in the papyrus. As for the second and the third, the last lines seem truly significant: "you, the only pure one and the only blessed one." The "only" suggests an exclusivity; a "purity," a "virginity," and a "blessing" that have no comparison with others, which distance the "Mother of God" from every other creature. We find here the category of "Marian privilege" that has always aroused reactions outside Catholicism (and, for some time now, also within it) as if it were a category elaborated according to an illicit theological vision, late, and detached from the sobriety of primitive Christianity.

And yet, once again we find here a *factum* against which *non valet argumentum*. The fact, namely, of the recognition of the absolute "singularity" of Mary many decades before Constantine. It has further been discovered that it is a perspective not isolated or tied only to settings of Egyptian Christianity, seeing that entirely analogous texts of this invocation have been found, also quite ancient, in every Eastern church, from the Jacobite Church to the Ethiopian Church.

As we have observed, this troparion ended up becoming an antiphon in the Western Church as well, though not without some variations that render less meaningful this extraordinary text.

The text is of course known by its initial words in Latin: *Sub tuum praesidium*. Now, the Greek term translated as *praesidium* in Latin literally indicates the quality of one who "has good viscera." It is the same term the Gospel uses to indicate the deep feelings "unto his viscera" of Jesus in seeing the crowds reduced to being a flock of sheep without a shepherd; to describe the emotion of the Good Samaritan before the wounded man on the road to Jericho; to speak of the agitation of the father upon the return of the Prodigal Son. Thus, the Latin term which most approximates it is *misericordia*, which, etymologically, means "the heart [the viscera par excellence] that feels pity." Thus, not *sub tuum praesidium configimus*, but *sub tuam misericordiam* (as the Ambrosian liturgy correctly preserves it, as distinct from the Roman liturgy). This is not a question, obviously, of a philological digression: from the very beginnings (the mid-third century!), the instinct of believers has recognized in Mary the one who is closest to divine mercy—a "privilege" to which the devout make their appeal to find assistance. And not, moreover, seeing in her only a means, an instrument, but rather acknowledging her unique abilities: "but from danger liberate us," says the papyrus. She is directly called to come to our help.

We are, in this way, well beyond the second part of the Hail Mary, a part added late and following a long and complicated itinerary. In this conclusion to the Marian prayer par excellence, repeated so many times in the Rosary, one appeals to her intercession: "*ora pro nobis peccatoribus*." The invocation which the desert sands have regurgitated in our times goes much further. And this applies too to those who take for granted that veneration of the Virgin Mary was a progressive increase of Marian prerogatives, a "something more" continuously added to a "something less." The *Sub tuum praesidium* (or better still, *sub tuam misericordiam*) shows the opposite: that the request of the faithful for a "direct intervention" of Mary preceded the prayer of mere intercession.

We have here, then, an exceptional text, a confirmation of many of the truths of the Faith that merits much greater diffusion and esteem than the pastoral practice and catechesis of the Church has given it. Even Vatican II cited it in the famous eighth chapter concluding the Dogmatic Constitution on the Church, *Lumen Gentium*—the part of the document titled "The Blessed Virgin Mary, Mother of God in the Mystery of Christ and the Church."

At the beginning of the paragraph on the "Foundations of Marian cult" we read: "From the earliest times the Blessed Virgin is honored under the title of Mother of God, under whose protection the faithful took refuge in all their dangers and necessities" (LG, no. 66). The Council Fathers thus employed the words taken directly from the traditional Latin version of the *Sub tuum praesidium* to which they refer in a footnote.

It would be a wholesome endeavor to return this to its rightful place in prayer, perhaps even a daily invocation of the faithful, preceded obviously by an adequate catechesis that explains to the faithful its inestimable value, which today is but an antiphon rarely employed or a brief composition for festive hymns (and probably seldom sung). Among many precious and indispensable Hail Marys, this invocation would also be fitting, which comes down to us from the earliest centuries and unites us with our brothers in the primitive Church, besides those of the current Eastern Churches. It would nevertheless be opportune if the work of rediscovery of such a venerated text could pass through a prior rectification of the traditional Latin, which was used in the translations into modern languages. In fact, there is not only that *praesidium* which appears inadequate, but other parts as well that should be retraced from the original Greek to preserve its density.

But in recent decades, other "stones" have "shouted" to deny theories born either of intellectual abstraction or of theological deformation. And this time not papyri, but actual stones: those that support the walls of the shrine that arose from earliest times to enclose the humble home (or grotto) of Nazareth, where it all began.

Every pilgrim to the Holy Land knows that, as distinct from the Church of the Nativity in Bethlehem or that of the Holy Sepulcher in Jerusalem, the Basilica of the Annunciation in Nazareth appears as a modern church: the work of a notable Italian architect of the twentieth century, Giovanni Muzio, it was consecrated only in 1969. The large building was created by demolishing a structure raised by the Franciscans in the eighteenth century. Fr. Bellarmino Bagatti, one of the leading biblical archaeologists, took advantage of the demolition to reconstruct the history of that place of worship.

First, he was able to establish the falsehood (to the contrary of what many held) that there were Roman tombs in that area and that for reasons of ritual purity there could not have been Jewish homes. In reality, it was discovered that there were not sepulchers, but rather quite visible traces of houses of the ancient people of that place. At any rate, the building from the 1700s showed, as was already known, that it had been erected above a church from the age of the Crusades. This in turn rested on a Byzantine church. But here they found a surprise: below even that they discovered the remains of a synagogue — a synagogue, however, not of Jews but of Jewish Christians. In fact, until about the fifth century, the countrymen of Jesus (and of Mary) either remained orthodox Jews or crossed over to Christianity while maintaining Jewish traditions insofar as possible. And in Nazareth, as in many other places throughout

Palestine, there flourished among Jews that important Judeo-Christian Church of which Fr. Bagatti was a great historian.

At any rate, it was this Franciscan archaeologist who experienced what he told me (when I went to meet him in Jerusalem) had been the greatest emotion of his life. On the plaster at the base of a large wall which sustained the roof of the church/synagogue, there was an inscription in Greek letters: a *Kaire Maria*, or the greeting of the archangel Gabriel in the Gospel, the first *Ave Maria* in history. On a column, a pilgrim had left another sign of devotion: "In this holy place of Mary I wrote." On another column, there was a word in ancient Armenian: "Beautiful Virgin."

It has been proved that all that was found in that place is certainly antecedent to the "Mariological" Council of Ephesus. Therefore, after the papyrus with the *Sub tuum*, here the stones of the shrine erected by the same countrymen of Mary proving that her cult, the invocation to her power of intercession, was much earlier than observers previously believed, or wanted to believe.

As is perhaps occurring for the Gospels, if the new discoveries in Qumran are confirmed, so for the Mother of Jesus "the pickaxe has demonstrated, as always, to be a gentleman with respect to tradition and merciless with respect to theories," to use the words of Fr. Bagatti at our encounter, evoking the excavations he directed in Nazareth. He added, during that rigidly cold winter evening as we walked (he an eighty-year-old, wrapped in a friar's mantle but with only sandals on his feet) along the alleyways near the Jaffa Gate:

> We now have proof that the invocation of Mary began with Christianity itself and in the same place where that young girl lived. Thanks to that excavation, Catholics know that, reciting the Rosary, they are reconnecting with a reality that began in Nazareth itself. A reality begun perhaps by someone who, on those wretched streets, among those caves, half house and half stable, had known the Mother of Jesus when to everyone around her she was but one girl among many, then the wife and then the widow of the carpenter Joseph.

CHAPTER 19

MARIAN, THEREFORE PAGAN?

In the second half of the nineteenth century, first the learned professors at German universities, and then, gradually, their colleagues in other countries, were smitten by the discovery of the ancient, non-Christian religions, especially from Asia, until that moment little known in Europe, or not at all.

This sort of intrusion of an exotic world was accompanied by the enormous interest in deepening knowledge of the Greco-Roman world, especially by German professors. By a sort of paradox, the descendants of the ancient German tribes, always tempted to rebel against Rome (even the Lutheran Reformation was an episode of impatience toward all that is Latin; so too National Socialism and even German Romanticism, born of the allergy for classicism, which could be contrasted to the Germanic Middle Ages), became in just a few decades the recognized masters of Mediterranean antiquity, erecting authentic monuments of paper with critical editions, manuals, and encyclopedias that are still consulted today.

From such a cocktail of erudition (and often of ideological sectarianism: it was the age of rationalism and positivism) "comparativist" schools emerged. One of these "compared" Christianity to the Asian religions and to the Hellenistic and Middle Eastern "cultural stew" where it took its first steps. Thus, they sought to demonstrate that the supposed "revelation" of the gospel was merely a jumble of religious elements and heterogeneous superstitions.

Thus, the roots of Christianity (but also of Judaism) were certainly not to be found in a mysterious divine initiative, but rather in the enormous religious patrimony of the ancient world which modern research was bringing increasingly to light.

Naturally, one of the preferred targets of those professors was Marian veneration, especially among Catholics and Orthodox. But even Protestants were called to task: as is well-known, the Reformation decided to accept the first ecumenical councils and thus to accept with them the dogmatic decisions the Fathers had made with regard to the divine maternity and the virginity of Mary. Everything about this figure of a woman, according to the "comparativists," was an obscure, foreign infiltration — nothing more than an echo of the myth of the eternal virgins and mothers found in many ancient religions and which appear as a constant in the symbolisms and mythologies of the human race.

The height of this type of attack on Christianity (and in particular on its hidden but decisive "heart" which is "Mariology") was reached over a century ago. Since then, the problem has had ample time to cool off, and many of the old works of "comparative history of religions," though at times remaining impressive monuments of erudition, have lost their aggressive charge and no longer seem to be a threat to Christian faith and worship, at least for those who resist being awed by them.

Here too, however, the usual drift has taken place. Once the "mythological hypotheses" about Jesus and Mary were abandoned or heavily mitigated by the most serious and active scholars, they entered into the realm of common knowledge for the man on street. The latter is often convinced that behind the devotion of Catholics to Our Lady, there is the anachronistic continuation of the cults of some legendary Great Mother, of some pagan Athena.

Thus the savant is never lacking, ready to look with pity on those who, for example, might believe in the truth of the apparitions of Lourdes: the grotto, the spring, the Virgin, the shepherdess.... But come now, must they use the entire arsenal of the pagan "*Athenophanies*"! Unfortunately, even some Christian scholars seem to be affected by this "cultural delay" which has too often characterized the ecclesial milieu (were they not priests and friars who admiringly discovered Marxism, when Marxists, the true ones, were already speaking of his "truths" and "historical laws" with a snide grin?). One happens upon books today that are quite reticent, if not openly demythologizing, as concerns the Annunciation, the visit to Elizabeth, the Magnificat, and above all, those "Infancy Narratives" in Matthew and Luke, on which the Christian doctrine on Mary is based.

These studies (although their authors fashion them to be modern and critical) make use of many of the theses of the comparativists from the *Belle Époque*, which are often no longer taken seriously outside of ecclesiastical circles.

Before reflecting on this topic, we can summarize the question as follows: Is the Marian presence in Christianity derived from Near Eastern and pagan cults already existing in the ancient world? There are two aspects to be examined in answer to this.

The first aspect is the origin of that presence, of Mary, Virgin and Mother, as a person in the Gospels. The second aspect is to establish whether, and to what extent, the Marian cult that developed especially in the Catholic Church had suffered pagan influences; whether the progression of Mariology and devotion toward her corresponds to non-biblical, or even non-Christian, categories.

The problem was studied in depth by Jean Daniélou, the great theologian who later became a cardinal. In the opinion of unbiased experts, in some schools his work remains fundamental; it must be remembered that this specialist of religions had professorial chairs not only in Catholic universities but also in the secular state universities of France.

Anticipating the conclusions of his research conducted on all the sources available, we turn to the words of Daniélou himself:

> What is the relationship, therefore, between the structure of Marian dogma in Christian revelation and the structure of feminine cults in mythology and pagan mystery cults? Examining the matter attentively, one perceives that the analogies (that have always struck people) concern the exterior circumstances: in the two cases, in fact, it is a question of an extraordinary birth and of a cult that have as their object a woman. It is honest objectivity to recognize that there is total opposition between the two structures — Christian and pagan — in their foundation and their nature.

In fact, continues Daniélou, "the pagan cults are all, without exception, the expression of a religion of biological life, of fecundity, where the woman is the symbol." If one observes the role of Mary, on the other hand, "one stands before a historical reference to a precise intervention of God in human affairs. An intervention, moreover, quite distant from any exaltation of fecundity; it removes this occurrence from the ordinary laws of life and does so to highlight its spiritual significance."

Thus, what we must understand clearly is the structure of Christianity and, therefore, of the figure of the Mother of Jesus: a fact, not a philosophy; a historical event, not a myth or a legend.

This does not involve speculation on the symbolism of fecundity or the rhythm of the seasons but rather examination of a narrative that, very significantly as far as Mary is concerned, is quite extensive in Luke, the evangelist who from the very beginning of his text specifies that he has set out to collect a dossier of the events, gathered from the most reliable eyewitnesses.

To understand better, here is Daniélou's synthesis: "Revelation is the historical action of God which carries out in time the plan of salvation, and where each event has a unique value and has as its instrument the Holy Spirit. It is in this biblical perspective that the Marian cult is situated. It is founded solely on the role attributed to a concrete woman, Mary of Nazareth, in the divine plan of salvation."

Contrary to revelation, mythology is "the transposition into the sphere of fundamental ideas the main realities of the life of the cosmos. It is the sublimation of the most profound instincts of man. The mythological cult of the Mother is based solely on her role in the order of the transmission of life, of the fecundity of the living species."

Charles Guignebert, one of the most important critics trying to destabilize the historical foundations of Christianity using the instrument of comparative religious history, wrote, "It is in the Greco-Roman world that we find the most evident analogies with the story of the miraculous conception of Jesus. It is in that world that we see, among other things, the legend of Perseus, born of Danae, a virgin whom Zeus impregnates under the form of a shower of gold."

Daniélou, and many specialists with him, easily demonstrated first of all that in this pagan myth (as in the others that the comparativists cite) it was not a matter of a virgin birth. Contrary to what Guignebert writes, none of the versions we possess state that Danae, impregnated by the monarch of Olympus, had not yet known man. At any rate, "the legend of Zeus and Danae appears as an anthropomorphic representation, quite mundane if not trivial, of the divinity, to which human customs are attributed. This, as elsewhere, is a case of a simple sublimation of sexuality, whereas the virginal conception of

Mary is situated in the perspective of the works carried out by the Holy Spirit throughout all Scripture and which here reaches its apex."

Everywhere, in fact, whether in Asian religions or in those of ancient Hellenism, one finds *theo-gamy*; in other words, sexual unions of a god with a woman. There is nothing similar to this in the Annunciation in Luke, where there is no apparition of a god (whether under the form of a shower of gold, a swan, or some other animal), and it is far from the climate of eroticism that accompanies all the other mythologies where the protagonist is a woman.

In this erudite study of "antecedents," Daniélou also shows that somewhat grotesque mishaps were not lacking. For example, some scholars fell into a trap regarding Buddha, of whom a miraculous birth is narrated through a theogamy common in myths not only in the West but also in the East. Naturally, there was no lack of scholars who established a comparison between the Mother of Jesus and that of Siddhartha Gautama, called the "Reawakened One," or *Buddha* in Sanskrit. The thesis pointed to an influence over the Gospel narration through complex cultural exchanges with Asia, seeing how Palestine was an opening onto the Mediterranean for one of the "silk roads" that ran from China through India. In reality, as was verified in a definitive manner, the texts that attribute to the Buddha a divine birth are a posteriori to the writing of the Gospels. Thus, the problem must be turned on its head: a possible Christian influence on the Asian beliefs, and not vice versa!

More generally, Daniélou comments,

> For those who know the period and the climate in which faith in the gospel arose, even the simple hypothesis of the influence of pagan myths on primitive Christianity appears to be impossible. The conflict between pagan polytheism and Christianity was too violent to hypothesize any influence. One might ask that question of the fourth century (when there was a mass influx of pagans into the Church), but certainly not of the first century, when the Gospels were set in a definitive manner.

In fact, specialists of comparative history of religions ended up realizing that the difficulty was insurmountable, finding themselves confronted by a nucleus of primitive Christianity that was impermeable to non-Judaic influences.

They then fell back upon a sort of emergency exit: they imagined that the pagan myth that must be at the origin of the Gospels' infancy narratives must have been assimilated into the new faith through pre-Christian Judaism. It was from this source that Christianity must have been "polluted." The most renowned exponent of the theory is a famous comparativist (professor in a German university, of course), Hugo Gressmann. In his famous work of 1914 (the very last year of the cultural *Belle Époque,* before the catastrophe of the Great War) Professor Gressmann held that the theme of the birth of the divine child found by some shepherds has parallels in Egyptian mythology, which was then introduced into Palestinian folklore — in particular (what a coincidence!), among shepherds of the region of Judea where Bethlehem lies. This source provided the pattern followed by the evangelists. The Christian response is all too easy: "All of this is based on a collection of unverified hypotheses of which one can preserve nothing." Just as the old Latin adage says: "*Quod gratis adfirmatur, gratis negatur*" (what is affirmed without proof, can be rejected in the same manner). Furthermore, the infancy cycle is developed by Luke, an evangelist who was not a Jew and who was of Hellenistic culture, certainly not conversant in Judaic folklore, even if we accept that this folklore actually existed.

If it is possible to establish the independence from pagan influences of the fundamental texts of the Gospels that concern Mary (above all, her maternity), there is another problem, as we said at the beginning. We know that the origins of Marian doctrine are biblical and respond to the historical laws of revelation, not to mythical and cosmic laws found in mythology, which focus on the feminine symbol of fecundity.

But what about its development? Even if it emanated from biblical data, was the construction of dogma, worship, and devotion marked by the influence of paganism? There is, in this question, not only the denial on the part of the incredulous of all the truth of faith, but also the Protestant suspicion of the "Mariolatry" of Catholics and of Christians of the East.

Albert Noyon, a specialist in this material, synthesizes the problem that was raised decades ago by the comparativists but which is still quite present in the common mindset and in the perspective of some sectors of Christian theology and exegesis:

> It is said that when, especially after the Edict of Constantine in the fourth century, pagans entered the Church in droves, they brought with them their mentality, only superficially impaired by the new faith. This influence was the price that Christianity had to pay. The pagan mentality remained attached to the feminine divinities, permeated to the depths by emotive cults, loaded with mysticism as well as eroticism. Those masses, often only Christian in name, were looking for an outlet: they found it in Mary. Unsatisfied by the austere, dry monotheism of the official Church, those aspirations were satisfied by inflating to no end the honor, the cult, the prayer, the requests for intervention by the Woman, Mother of Jesus. It might be the case that the Gospel figure of Mary has nothing to do with, in its origins, the mother goddesses, but that she later became their surrogate for the masses. In fact, without daring to admit it, she became a goddess herself.

This would be the origin of that "superstitious" or "unchristian" character which for Protestants typifies everything about the Marian doctrine and veneration in the Catholic and Orthodox Churches.

In the hope of taking up sooner or later this discussion (too important to be comprehended within the limits of just one chapter), we begin by proposing a couple of questions advanced by Albert Noyon.

The first can be summarized thus:

> If the cult and devotion toward the Virgin are pagan "products," why do they appear so weak, so reduced precisely in the third and fourth centuries in which pagans were entering the Church in droves? It was at that time that the paganization of Christianity ought to have occurred: Marian practices should have exploded. In reality, that was not the case at all. Mary was surely honored, but was above all scrutinized, not so much by the people but by theology, which sought to identify, with objectivity and almost "coldness" in the debates among the learned, the dimensions of the mystery that that Woman represents for the faith.

The second question, also without a plausible answer by those who suspect "pollution" and "infiltrations":

> If the cult of Mary had pagan origins, it would have certainly evolved toward practices of a mysterious, esoteric, and finally even erotic, if not obscene, nature that characterized all the cults of femininity. And this due not to the morbid tendencies of some perverted devotee but to the very nature of those cults, as has always occurred in similar cases. One remembers the excesses of immorality to which the cult of Astarte was drawn, the goddess of fertility so often cited as the inspiration for the cult of Mary. The latter, however, has never stopped following a trajectory that detached the Virgin of Nazareth from every "carnal" aspect. Devotion to her has in fact become synonymous with chastity preserved or rediscovered. Her devotees are those who strive to be "pure" of body, word, and thought. The exact opposite obtains for the devotees of Hellenistic feminine cults.

This offers an initial framework for the problem. We must not fail to remember, as mentioned earlier, that the Catholic perspective, faithful to its logic of the *et-et*, of the "fulfill and not destroy" announced by Jesus himself, would not have the least fear even if something had been assumed here from elsewhere — purified and Christianized, however. In the Catholic system there can, and there must, be room for whatever is good, opportune, and useful that has been intuited and lived by every other religion. As in architecture, Christianity in the early centuries did not create its own style but unhesitatingly adopted the structure of the Hellenistic temple and the Roman basilica as fitting places for celebrating its own worship — quite different from that of the pagans, just as its "architecture" of doctrine and devotion was. This adoption did not create a syncretistic heap, but a vital synthesis.

CHAPTER 20

WHY MARY?

WE HAVE ARRIVED AT the twentieth stage of our journey, and I realize that perhaps we need to start all over from the beginning . . . not in the sense of recanting all that has been said thus far: in fact, if my limits were not to allow me to go any further, it must be said, with humility equal to conviction, that there is no need to repent of what has been proposed herein.

The problem lies elsewhere. Let me explain. We began in the first chapter with our "soundings" of the Marian universe, continuing in many different directions. I was perhaps guided by an excessive optimism, writing as a Catholic and addressing Catholics above all.

I am convinced, in fact, that the presence of Mary is essential to faith but that, at the same time, it is "internal" to it. Mary cannot be the object of the kerygma, or part of the first proclamation. This concerns Jesus and the proclamation that, in Him, God Himself has been manifested. The function of the Mother of Jesus seems to be that of "staying in the home": one can know, love, and understand her essential function (Is there not a mother at the origin of every man? And is Jesus not also "true man"?) after having known and accepted the offer the Son makes of Himself to the believer. If the Son is the Word, the Mother is the silence.

This explains the possibility of speaking of her only within the realm of faith. This explains the intention also of this notebook: to help confirm in their conscious Marian devotion those who are "already believers." But precisely because of these latter, I have sinned through excessive optimism, as I said.

From indications that have arrived from readers, I have had confirmation of what I suspected. Namely, that many Catholics seem to have lost sight of the profound reasons for the presence of Mary in their faith. The insufficiency, if not complete lack of catechesis, seems to have removed Mary from the eminent place in the house and set her in the corner — honoring her still, certainly, but asking her not to take up too much space.

The following message is an example: "In a now long series of years, we have followed your encounters with believers and nonbelievers on the great issues of faith. Why limit yourself now to speaking about Mary? Certainly an honorable topic. But is it not something to be left to devotees or to enthusiasts of specific topics of spirituality or piety? Why not continue to dig, as you have done for so long, into the very roots of belief, counting on our benevolent interest? Are there not more urgent themes than Mariology?"

This, more or less, is the "signal" which some have sent my way. This has left me with the impression of needing to "start over from the beginning," in the sense of dedicating at least a brief introduction to our topic to justify its choice and its importance. I shall try to do what I should have done at the beginning.

They tell me, furthermore, that even the new programs in the seminaries where future priests are formed have introduced a novelty that aroused a few questions. From what I understand, whereas before, what concerned the Virgin Mary was to be found in various manuals, in support of and integrating the different aspects of theology, and above all Christology, now it has been united in one text — a book on "Mariology," precisely.

Some observe, however, that in this way one could reinforce a perspective that has little to do with the Catholic vision. A perspective according to which Mary can be present, but could also not be present. Precisely because it is compressed and isolated in one volume, without intertwining it with the rest of the contents of the Creed, Mariology could also be set aside, according to the time available, or personal interest, or devotion more or less intense. Some could think that the lack of knowledge of a book, of that book, would take nothing away, in the end, from what is essential to the perspective of faith.

Knowing nothing about the contents of ecclesiastical curricula, I do not know how serious such dangers might be. But if those dangers do exist, they are situated in a misunderstanding that is quite common among Catholics in general, and not only among seminarians. This misunderstanding considers to be "optional" the truths taught by the ecclesiastical tradition about the

Virgin Mary, the most important of which were defined in four explicit dogmas — yet not only these but the entire "Marian deposit" of the Church.

Fostering this orientation in many Catholics is a fear of giving to the Mother her traditional place, as if what is given to her has to be first taken from her Son; and in doing so to risk the sin of "injuring" ecumenism.

But in this way, one forgets that every step drawing nearer to the world of the Protestant Reformation means a parallel step away from the world of Greco-Slavic Orthodoxy. But as John Paul II repeatedly urged, Christianity must learn to breathe again with both lungs, and that "second lung" is precisely Eastern Orthodoxy.

It would be a strange ecumenism, then, which tried to mute Mary to please Protestantism, while digging a trench between us and our other Christian brethren, those in the East!

At any rate, to remain in the "feminine" dimension, it is the same problem that arises in the priestly ordination of women: if Rome were to accept this, she would be accepted by the Waldensians, but would create a grave wound in relations with Moscow and the other patriarchates of the glorious Churches of the East, where the figure of the "Christian priestess" is not a source of theological debate but rather of laughter both scandalized and incredulous.

Furthermore, we should of course welcome dialogue with what remains of the classic, historical Reformation, reduced now to a minimum in favor of the "uncivilized Protestantism" of the numerous sects that refuse all dialogue a priori. But many do not seem to have a clear idea that the problem does not lie in trying to rework some Catholic Marian assertion. As ecumenical experience has shown through many decades of meetings and debates, quite often sterile or bearing fruit only in documents that have had no concrete follow-up, the different ways of relating to the Virgin Mary derive from a different way of understanding ecclesiology, soteriology, eschatology, and even Christology. Precisely because it is not an accessory, an option, a marginal presence, the profound contents of the Faith are clustered around Mary, if in a way that escapes the superficial or inexpert. To preserve or remove the role she has in dogma and in Catholic Tradition means touching its very structure.

Not incidentally, the Second Vatican Council inserted the treatise on the Virgin Mary at the culmination of the Dogmatic Constitution on the Church: Mariology is tightly linked precisely to this reality, the Church in her directly

Roman conception. To modify our understanding of one means modifying the other as well.

Thus, confirming that the Virgin cannot be isolated in a separate manual, ecumenical dialogue sheds light on the ramifications of that which is not a "devotion" but rather a reality as discreet as it is pervasive and essential to all Catholic theology. Pulling up this "root" of the Incarnation (which is such because it passed through the womb of a woman, of *this* Woman) means risking drying up the tree of faith. In any case, it would deform the Catholic concept of Church.

Thus, to respond to those readers: this notebook, whatever its value or efficacy, is not the quiet corner where pious sentiments are cultivated, sentiments that the new spirit of dialogue and the new perspective of "adult" and "updated" Christianity would tolerate while awaiting their desired and inevitable disappearance. On the contrary, in these pages we intend to place ourselves more than ever in the heart of faith and not at its margins.

Let us now attempt to explain better and to finish what has been said thus far, and to do so in a brief and schematic form. We shall provide that prologue, then, which I failed to write before, thinking it was not necessary for those who are "already believers" and to whom these pages are addressed first and foremost.

This proposed scheme we shall develop in six points, without the pretense of being exhaustive, but which at least have the advantage of being up-to-date and authoritative. In fact, they come from the work of the custodian of Catholic Orthodoxy, Cardinal Joseph Ratzinger (some twenty years before becoming Pope Benedict XVI), during the days we closed ourselves into a sort of reclusion in the seminary of Brixen, for the meetings that led to the writing of a "report on the faith."[10]

Curiously, there was some background that seems private business but that had some consequences on the book that came out of those interviews, and which created an uproar wherever it was translated. In the summer of 1984, in the fresh air of a village in the mountains surrounding Lake Orta, I was busy with a book that I had titled *Hypotheses on Mary*. Much of that work later flowed into the archive from which I have drawn these pages.

[10] Editor's Note: Published in English as *The Ratzinger Report* (1985).

I was making good progress in the collection of material and in reflecting on it, when I was interrupted by an unexpected phone call. Cardinal Ratzinger invited me to meet him in South Tyrol, where he spent his brief and modest vacation, to follow up on a project which I had proposed to him and on which I had not received an answer from him for quite some time. The project concerned the breaking of silence by the head of what was formerly known as the feared *Sant'Uffizio* (Holy Office): a first in history, a series of conversations with a journalist that flowed into a book giving an overview of the situation in the Church two decades after the close of the council.

After having reflected at length, the prefect of the department now called the Congregation for the Doctrine of the Faith decided to accept. There were perhaps some risks in that unprecedented project. The historical silence of the Holy Office, its responses only in the form of *licet* or *non licet*, without explanations or justifications, the caution in accessing its archives, the anonymity of its functionaries — all this scandalizes the boisterous extroversion of the average man of today, but it had its reasons and its efficacy. There were thus some risks, but also possible advantages, for the cause which was close to hearts of both of us: a faith which seemed threatened from its very foundations. This was the motive for the telephone call that reached me, and for my departure for Brixen.

In a memo I had sent the cardinal, there was obviously a "Marian" excursus. By a curious coincidence, this happened just as I was working on those "hypotheses" I mentioned and which I had hoped to organize around some points. I spoke with Ratzinger about my outline; he said he could identify with them, and offering some clarifications and integrations, accepted them gladly as a sort of synthesis on the theme. In the book whose manuscript I had written on the basis of the interviews and which he later reread and approved, this outline was published under the subheading "Six Reasons Not to Forget Mary."

On the basis of those "reasons," we propose what follows. In them, there is not only the authority of the one who for twenty-one years was the custodian of Catholic doctrine; there is also his significant human experience, which merits comment.

The Marian testimony which my authoritative interlocutor gave me is rich in significance, in fact. He too had to pass through a personal journey of discovery, of investigation, and of deeper conversion to the Marian mystery, as he evolved from being an "avant-garde" theologian to becoming a bishop, then cardinal, and finally "prefect of the faith." He too, then, was involved in that minimizing perspective that has characterized so many Catholics of our day.

Joseph Ratzinger confided, "Before and during the council, as a young theologian, I mentioned my reservations about certain ancient formulas repeated by the Tradition, like the celebrated *de Maria numquam satis* [one can never have enough of Mary]. They seemed excessive and secondary, rather than authentic doctrine, devotional attitudes born in quite recent periods."

An exclamation by a Catholic theologian from northern Europe has been preserved in the chronicles of Vatican II. Thinking he was dealing with exaggerations intolerable to Protestants and even erroneous according to Roman doctrine, that professor turned the ancient motto upside down, saying *de Maria, et iam satis*: we have already said enough about Mary.

In fact, there was debate at the council between the "Latin" bishops (Italian, Spanish, Portuguese, South American, but also Polish and Irish and many from the Third World) and those of central Europe, the English, and some from North America.

The former not only wanted complete confirmation of the tradition, but also the proclamation of new "titles," above all that of "Mother of the Church," already widely used but never officially adopted. The latter, on the other hand, were either opposed or perplexed. In the end, a compromise was reached and *Lumen Gentium*, the Constitution on the Church in which the doctrine on Mary was inserted, says of the entire ecclesial community, "The Catholic Church [pastors and faithful], taught by the Holy Spirit, honors her with filial affection and piety as a most beloved mother" (*Lumen Gentium*, no. 53).

But on November 21, 1964, while signing that document (perhaps the most important, from the dogmatic point of view, of the entire council), Paul VI solemnly declared that an official postscript be added: "We proclaim the most holy Mary Mother of the Church, namely, of all the people of God, of the faithful as well as the pastors, who call her Mother most beloved." In this way, what was implicit in the conciliar text was rendered explicit by the pope, who would repeat this proclamation three years later in the document *Signum magnum*. And John Paul II would follow him with determination down this path from his very first encyclical, *Redemptor hominis*.

The choice of Paul VI required, however, a sort of show of force in the face of some theological schools. And in this theological current, the young professor Joseph Ratzinger participated to some degree. He was ready, however, to detach himself from it when it seemed to him to be going beyond what was permissible, considering Vatican II just a point of departure and ending up in open conflict with the Magisterium. In fact, when I asked him if his theological colleagues-turned-objectors, who accused him of having changed his opinion, were justified, the cardinal was quick to respond, "They were the ones who changed, not I."

But returning to his testimony, he told me, "If I was not fully capable of understanding the *de Maria nunquam satis*, it was equally difficult for me to comprehend the true sense of another famous expression which says that Mary is the enemy of all heresies." He immediately added, "Well, precisely now, in this confused period in which many ancient and modern heretical deviations seem to threaten orthodoxy, I comprehend that these were not the exaggerations of devotees, but truths that had never been more in need of being rediscovered. Yes, I confirm: we must make room for Mary once more that the faith might rediscover its authentic direction."

We shall see in the next chapter the scheme we elaborated together — the famous theologian, the "cardinal prefect of the faith," destined to become pope, and the poor journalist, self-educated in these matters — in that quiet Tyrolean summer.

CHAPTER 21

In the Name of the Lady All Pure

I made the observation that it needs to be explained even to many "good Catholics" that the role of Mary in the Christian system of faith is not in the least marginal, optional, or contrary to ecumenism. Therefore, we need to repeat what was once taken for granted by believers: that the presence of the Mother of Jesus not only does not obfuscate, but on the contrary, reinforces and guarantees faith in Jesus.

I said that I would reproduce "six reasons for not forgetting her," to use the expression which served as the title of one of the sections in *Report on the Faith*, written in the 1980s with Cardinal Joseph Ratzinger, then prefect of the Congregation for the Doctrine of the Faith. They are concise points and are only a few (although perhaps the most relevant) of the many possible. But this sort of chart, concentrated and compact, can contribute to understanding the reasons that inspired these "hypotheses about Mary," rendering them today more necessary than ever.

Let us consider, then, the first point. It is a misunderstanding into which, surprisingly, all Protestant theology has fallen, to think that giving to Mary means taking from Christ. On the contrary. In Cardinal Ratzinger's words, "To acknowledge the role that dogma, tradition, liturgy, and devotion have assigned to Mary means remaining firmly rooted in authentic Christology."

This is a reality that does not belong to old-time theology, but which finds secure footing in the documents of the Second Vatican Council. For example, number 65 of the Dogmatic Constitution on the Church, *Lumen*

Gentium, which places Mary at its apex: "Piously meditating on her and contemplating her in the light of the Word made man, the Church with reverence enters more intimately into the great mystery of the Incarnation and becomes more and more like her Spouse."

There are four Marian dogmas: the perpetual virginity and divine maternity; then, after nearly fifteen centuries of debate and investigation into the mystery, arrived confirmation of Mary's conception without the stain of original sin and her assumption into Heaven. These truths have been codified and solemnly safeguarded as dogmas, as basic, indisputable truths of faith, not so much for devotion to Mary as to defend faith in Jesus.

In fact, when we reflect on their content, we notice that they reiterate authentic faith in Christ as true God and true man: two natures in one person. They reaffirm the fundamental eschatological expectancy, pointing to Mary assumed into Heaven as the immortal destiny which awaits us all. And finally, they safeguard the faith, so threatened today, in a creator God (this is one of the meanings of the often misunderstood truth about Mary's perpetual virginity), a God who can freely intervene in the material world.

In the words once again of Vatican II, this brief but effective synthesis: "Mary, who since her entry into salvation history *unites in herself and re-echoes the greatest teachings of the faith*" (no. 65, emphasis added).

Again, this is only a brief summary, a simple reminder. Thus, the second point: in Mariology, the correct relationship is developed and lives in the necessary integration between the two sources of revelation, Scripture and Tradition. The four Marian dogmas defined over twenty centuries have their foundation in Scripture. But they are there in seed form, in such a discreet way, if not hidden, that they needed centuries to bear fruit, to be comprehended and defined. The rejection of Mariological development on the part of the communities arising from the Reformation comes from their previous no to the concept of Tradition, forgetting that even Scripture is part of Tradition, for it did not fall from Heaven as did the Quran, but is the fruit of the work of men, though under divine inspiration. And who, if not the Church, based on the authority granted her by her Founder, has established what is and what is not Scripture, distinguishing among canonical books and apocryphal books, establishing once and for all which texts are orthodox and which heretical, which historical and which mythological? I confess, though aware of how "ecumenically incorrect" it might sound, the contradictions (even naivete) of the foundations on which the Reformation was launched will never cease to amaze me.

Coming to the third point: in her identity as a Jewish girl who became mother of the Messiah, Mary ties together in a vital and inextricable way the synagogue and the Church. This Woman is like a point of intersection, without which the Faith risks losing its balance either toward the Old Testament, veiling redemption, or toward the New Testament, forgetting the root of Israel. Mary is the apex of Judaism and the beginning, in her very body, of the Faith that brings to fulfillment all that Judaism announced and awaited.

The fourth point: correct Marian devotion guarantees for the believer the coexistence of the indispensable "reasons of reason" with the equally indispensable "reasons of the heart," to use the famous words of Pascal. Man is neither only reason nor only sentiment, but is the inextricable union of these two dimensions. The head must reflect with lucidity, but the heart must be warmed: devotion to Mary ("without certain exaggerations, but also without meanness of mind which fails to consider the unique dignity of the Mother of God," as the council recommends) assures the Faith its complete human dimension.

Here is a fifth possible point: To use again the expressions of Vatican II, Mary is a "figure" or "image" of the Church. Both have maternity as their primary vocation. Thus, looking to her, this Church is safeguarded from a "male chauvinist" model that sees her as an instrument for carrying out a program of sociopolitical action. In Mary, her figure and icon, the Church rediscovers her maternal face and resists degenerating into an involution that transforms into a sort of political party, an organization, a lobbying group at the service of human interests. In Ratzinger's words, "If some theologies and ecclesiologies of today give no space to Mary, the reason is simple and dramatic: they have reduced faith to an abstraction. And an abstraction does not know what to do with a mother."

Finally, the sixth point: with her role of both virgin and mother, Mary continues to shed light on what the Creator intended for the woman of every age, ours included. Perhaps our age first and foremost, when the very essence of womanhood is being threatened. Her virginity and maternity root the mystery of woman in a destiny from which it cannot be eradicated without a high cost to womanhood, as has become evident in recent years. She is, at the same time, the creature of courage and obedience: she who sings the Magnificat and she who, in the isolated silence of the home, "kept all these things in her heart," as the Gospel says, all these truths of faith.

But from the principals, the cornerstones we have recalled, we descend immediately into several excursus; following the intentions and style of this notebook, sheets on which various and sundry things are jotted down. We take, in order of its proclamation, the penultimate of those dogmas which, more than "Marian," are "Christological," insofar as all are completely at the service of faith in Jesus.

We begin then with the Immaculate Conception, recalling the precise words of the bull *Ineffabilis Deus* of December 8, 1854: "The most Blessed Virgin Mary, in the first instance of her conception, by a singular grace and privilege granted by Almighty God, in view of the merits of Jesus Christ, the Savior of the human race, was preserved free from all stain of original sin."

This definition was not accepted of course by Protestants, but neither by the Orthodox Churches: to them, only the first two dogmas are valid (Mary's virginity and divine maternity), defined as they were when the Church was still undivided. In order to proclaim others, a council reuniting all the churches separated from Rome would have to be convoked. But in over one thousand years, they have never succeeded in convoking a general council among the Orthodox, due to quarrelsomeness among the communities and a certain indifference in delimiting with exactitude the contents of the faith. In fact, the true "book of theology" for the Orthodox Churches is the liturgy and the experience of the mystics.

Nevertheless, beyond the principled opposition that states that all things "papist" or "Roman" must be rejected a priori, the reasons for the refusal of the dogma of the Immaculate Conception on the part of the Eastern Churches are more or less the same as those held for centuries within the Catholic Church. The "privilege" of being exempt from the stain of original sin would remove Mary from the human condition, and in some way lessen her need for the salvation brought all men by Christ, no one excluded.

It is curious to observe, however, that whereas the Greco-Slavs accuse Catholics of unacceptable "novelty," the latter state that the true novelty lies in the negation, beginning in recent times, of the truth of the Immaculate Conception which ancient Orthodox theology had affirmed.

This is not the place to enter into the debate. It suffices here to observe that, denying the dogma or not, the attitude of Eastern Orthodoxy toward the Virgin Mary is not substantially different from that of Catholics.

Among the splendid, profound Marian titles of Eastern Christians, one of the most used is precisely that of *Panaghia*, "All Pure." Among the many possible authors to quote, this is from the patriarch of Alexandria in Egypt, Christopulos, who, after having repeated his rejection of the Catholic dogma of the Immaculate Conception, wrote, "This is what we think of her: Given that she was destined by God to perform a sublime task (what is greater, in fact, than being the Mother of God incarnate?) she received from Heaven the sublime gift of not sinning. And so we believe and profess that, thanks to this divine gift, she never committed personal sin."

A recent Russian theologian, Victor Ilija, went even farther:

> It is entirely unthinkable that the mystery of the Incarnation of the Divine Word had its origin in a creature wounded by sin. The mere suspicion seems nonsensical. We must recognize that the metaphysical language, the theological style, the liturgical formulae of the Churches of the East and West are very different, but in the depths speak of the same thing: the integral purity and impeccability of the Mother of God, new creature and Heart of the Church.

Thus, to simplify (and to realize how complex the question is): Catholics believe in the radical lack of fault, even minimal fault, in the Mother of Jesus, by a "singular grace and privilege" that preserved her from the consequences of the fall of Adam and Eve, "from the very first instant of her conception"; she was indeed redeemed by her Son, but "beforehand," "in light of his merits." The Orthodox believe in the same radical purity, but through a "sublime gift" of not sinning, granted her by God *after* her birth.

Whatever the origin, then, the consequence turns out to be the same: Mary never sinned; she is truly the Panaghia, the "All Pure."

It remains the case that the rejection of the dogma proclaimed by Pius IX in 1854 led the Orthodox world to believe they were "obliged" to deny the authenticity of the apparitions in Lourdes. These, along with the words spoken to Bernadette ("I am the Immaculate Conception"), seemed to the Orthodox an inadmissible confirmation of a papist deviation from the right faith. It must be clarified: in the Orthodox world, in contrast to what happens in the Protestant world, "theophanies," "Maryophanies," "hierophanies" — apparitions, in other words, of divine, Marian, or saintly nature — are certainly not foreign to their theology or devotion. One of the more recent examples occurred on April 29, 1951, in the village of Néa-Artaki, Greece, when the Panaghia (as she is venerated there) appeared to eight children. A large shrine was built on the site, attracting frequent pilgrimage.

In general, shrines and pilgrimages constitute common ground between the "two lungs of the Church," to use the words of the Slavic Pope John Paul II. In Constantinople, the Church of St. Mary of the Wellspring was even called "the Lourdes of Medieval Orthodoxy." There a Madonna was venerated in a posture of prayer before the Child Jesus. The group of statues appeared in the water of a pool. Pilgrims would come there from Asia and Russia to bathe in the waters, hoping to restore their health.

Yet, for the Lourdes of the Pyrenees, despite the instinctive attraction for that place among the Orthodox faithful, there reigned an a priori refusal, determined by the unacceptable confirmation of a Latin "error." No one doubted the Gospel innocence of the visionary or her good faith. But (often refusing a critical examination of the facts: the protest was based on "hearsay") some Vatican fraud was suspected in the desire to have Heaven confirm the dogma proclaimed by the pope.

There is good reason for the use of the past tense. In fact, beginning around the 1950s, there occurred a sort of acceptance of the truth of the events of Lourdes in the Orthodox world, including the words attributed to the Virgin Mary, justified thanks to a particular interpretation. It is worthwhile examining it, given that it is quite unknown, as far as I can see, even among many Mariologists and experts of apparitions, those of Lourdes in particular.

According to this perspective proposed by Orthodox theologians, Mary truly defined herself with the words "I am the Immaculate Conception." But, contrary to what Catholics think, it was not as a confirmation of the dogma debated for centuries and proclaimed just four years earlier. In other words, Mary did not mean to say, "I am the one who was conceived without original sin," but rather, "I am the one who conceived in an immaculate manner." Therefore, the expression of the Lady to Bernadette concerned not the original fall, but the virginal manner by which the Word became flesh. The phrase Bernadette heard should therefore be understood as follows: "I conceived immaculately." A Russian theologian, Antoni Merluskin, who translated into French a brief but dense booklet with several pages dedicated to Lourdes, *The Orthodox Point of View on the Conception of the Virgin Mary*, remarked, "The phrase that the Virgin entrusts to the visionary shows not the result (Mary herself) but the source (the Spirit who impregnated her). In these words, the nature, the very essence of the Blessed Virgin, is revealed, in relation to the virginal and immaculate conception of Our Lord. Is this not, perhaps, the supreme title of glory of the Mother without stain?"

Naturally, these Orthodox theologians do not fail to highlight the known fact that it was the day of the Annunciation, March 25, the day of Jesus' conception, immaculate because virginal, by the Holy Spirit who "descended upon her." It was on that highly significant recurrence that Mary responded to the repeated requests of Bernadette and defined herself in the words that are engraved on the pedestal of her statue in the Grotto of Massabielle. Taking this "rereading" as our starting point, there is in the Orthodox world an ongoing work of convincing the faithful no longer to see Lourdes as an unacceptable "papist exclusive," but as a gift of grace addressing all those who love Jesus and venerate His Mother. A work that seems positive, if it can lead our brothers in the faith to respond to the appeal of the Lady who invited all to "come in procession" to that place where waters flow.

It is interesting, then: this attempt to draw near to Lourdes those who had been distanced by prejudices that were more confessional than theological. As for the reliability of the Orthodox rereading of the famous, "I am the Immaculate Conception," we would not know what to say. Certainly, the recurrence of the liturgical feast of the Annunciation with the Lady's recalling the Immaculate Conception is striking. But we must not forget either that the "Catholic reading" allows for spiritual and theological investigations which many have made, with results both convincing and edifying.

Can one concede, from the perspective of faith, that Mary would have in some way deceived her devotees with an expression that would lead them into misunderstandings, making them think that a freshly defined dogma was being confirmed, when all the while it was a matter of something else? Certainly, one can think that, in the mystery of the divine plan, the expression was willfully "ambiguous" in the sense of allowing for two readings, thus allowing the message of Lourdes to be accepted by those who do not recognize the Holy See in Rome as the place for deciding questions of faith. Is a double interpretation possible, then, both a Catholic and an Orthodox one? We confess that this possibility is tempting, but we are ready to retract our openness to the idea if we are shown to be mistaken. It tempts us because the possible Greco-Slavic reading (understood not as an alternative but as a parallel) does not seem to mutilate the meaning of the message of Lourdes and also allows access to that place of grace to our brothers who are so admirable in their Marian devotion.

Given the dramatic times in which the papacy found itself at the time of the Lourdes apparitions, it is likely that certain sectors of "ultramontane" Catholics created an almost exclusive presentation of "Vatican apologetics." They risked, in other words, presenting the Virgin Mary as a sort of "notary" or "registrar" who came to authenticate the dogmatic declaration of Pius IX.

Let us be clear: I too, for what it is worth, am convinced of the good Catholic reasons, including the confirmation of the dogma, in reading the events of 1858. And I am also aware of the important effects provoked by Lourdes in the life of the Church, in decades in which the gravity of aggression, not only toward the papal institution but toward the Faith itself, seemed to require this extraordinary celestial assistance. I do not believe in the least, then, that there is anything to recant. But who knows if there is something that needs to be reexamined, next to and not against, the reading given by "others," if this can transform Bernadette and the message she communicated from being another ecumenical "stumbling stone" to a stimulus to coming together at the feet of the Panaghia, the "All Pure"?

Not only was the parish priest Fr. Peyramale surprised, but eventually everyone else, before the uniqueness of that self-definition: a person, Mary, cannot be a concept, the Immaculate Conception. This surprise for some became dismay: in some popular versions of the story of the apparitions, the phrase Bernadette reported has been "translated" in a way that has made it seem more correct and certainly more comprehensible at first. "I am the One Conceived Immaculate," "I am the One who was conceived without sin," and so forth.

Then, reflection and the *sensus fidei* led to the discovery of profound meanings in what had seemed only a unique expression, or at first some type of syntactical error. Those meanings remain; from the perspective of faith, it is certain that the Lady cannot but have approved of them. But what if, as I have said, in the mysterious divine plan the apparent obscurity of the expression was there by design to allow space for a reading such as that proposed by Orthodox Christians? Leo XIII, in his Marian encyclical *Adiutricem populi,* quotes a prayer of the Greek liturgy which had been used in one of the drafts of Vatican II for the document on ecumenism. In that prayer, Mary is invoked precisely as the "Immaculate," as the "All Pure," asking her to "inspire the same spirit into the whole Church." Was this a presage and an indication of a unity to be constructed also in places like Lourdes?

In any case, another enigma can be added to the list. One more confirmation of the fascinating complexity of this Marian world into which we have only made a few soundings to this point.

CHAPTER 22

The Power of the Assumption

> Also in the current crisis, in the confused situation after the council, one cannot speak of the Christian faith without, sooner or later, encountering the Virgin Mary. Her place in the mystery of God, in fact, does not derive from a late historical development, which would be accessory, artificial. She is not situated in a sort of lateral Christianity. On the contrary, all the currents and movements of renewal in the history of the Church, even those today, end up finding her along their paths. Because Mary is in Scripture. She is in the Church Fathers. She is in ecclesiology, simply because she is in the Church, of which she is the model and icon. Like it or not, the true fact, verifiable by anyone, is that in the history of salvation, the Virgin Mary occupies a key place.

This was the final synthesis of the report René Laurentin wrote, in the midst of the "Marian winter" which was the decade following Vatican II, to recall to the truth some of his fellow theologians and exegetes.

This is precisely what I tried to say by aligning, in the preceding chapters, some of the points that respond to the question, "But why Mary?"

But nothing in Christianity is abstract, nothing is an end in itself, everything is *pro nobis*, everything is *pro salute nostra*. We shall now make a few soundings into the concrete meaning of some truths that to many believers today might seem abstract. They probably do not contest them, but they ask, "What purpose do they have?" And we shall try to show that those truths respond to a demanding logic, they are part of a framework, and they establish relationships of cause and effect.

After the penultimate dogmatic point officially defined, the Immaculate Conception, which we discussed in the previous chapters, we now consider the last of them. We begin with what happened in Rome at midday on November 1, 1950, on the feast of All Saints. Right as the war was ending five years earlier, Pope Pius XII had asked by letter all the bishops throughout the world if "the bodily assumption of Mary into heaven could be a dogma of faith and if they, the bishops, with their clergy and their people, desired the definition."

Receiving the nearly unanimous affirmative response, the pope, using for the first and, until now, last time the charism of infallibility *ex cathedra* attributed to him by Vatican I, defined the dogma of the "bodily assumption of the Mother of Christ and therefore, of God." These were the official words of the decree: "We pronounce, declare, and define it to be a divinely revealed dogma: that the Immaculate Mother of God, the ever-Virgin Mary, having completed the course of her earthly life, was assumed body and soul into heavenly glory."

A novelty? Only in the fact that after the solemn definition, "proclaimed before Heaven and earth," according to the ancient formula, it was no longer licit for a Catholic to doubt the contents of the dogma. But this was present in the Church even in the times of the apocryphal Gospels. From the fourth century, the liturgy celebrated the "*transitus*" (or *dormitio*) and the *assumptio Mariae*. Thus, what the new dogma was saying was not at all new.

Just as what Pius IX decided to proclaim explicitly in 1854 was nothing new, what is called "Immaculate Conception" has been present practically from the beginning (even with imprecision, hesitation, opposition) in the "deposit of faith" and in the conviction of believers. We shall examine this in a later chapter dedicated to the history of the Immaculate Conception.

It took many centuries to explicate all the consequences already contained in the founding element of all Mariology, that solemn warning of the Council of Ephesus in the remote year 431: "If someone fails to profess that Christ is truly God and that for this reason the holy Virgin is Mother of God, who generated according to the flesh the Word of God made flesh, let him be anathema."

Returning to that autumn day in 1950 (the day which historians consider the highpoint of the "Marian movement" that began in the seventeenth century but which was also the beginning of its decline, at least in certain theological schools), can that feast of All Saints of 1950 signify for each one of us, for the Church, for all humanity, that the little Jewish girl, the hidden adolescent of Nazareth who was betrothed to the carpenter Joseph, was "assumed into Heaven in body and soul"? And how is this reality situated in the general Christian perspective?

First, it must be observed that this dogma is not an isolated truth, as is also the case of any other dogma. The Catholic "system of faith" is not similar to those mountain crags separated one from another in a haphazard mass of rocks fallen from above. That "system" should be compared rather to a mosaic where every tile has its function; none of them can hold on its own, and anyway, would have no meaning by itself.

When the one whom Catholics see as the Vicar of Christ proclaims that Mary was "assumed" ("seized" or "taken" by a divine power) to be placed in eternal glory, he adds a link to the chain that began in the fifth century in the ancient city of modern-day Turkey, Ephesus. The Assumption is thus a link that connects directly to the other, proclaimed ninety-six years earlier, that of the Immaculate Conception. It does not make of Mary a "goddess" but the contrary: it confirms her as a human creature like us, in need of salvation. And she was in fact saved, redeemed, although before being conceived by her parents. Such that, on earth, she was preserved from all sin, thanks to the power of the redemption by Christ, to whom she herself gave the flesh.

Well, in the Christian perspective death is tied to sin. In the energetic formula of St. Paul, one of the many Scripture passages that express the same concept: "Sin reigned in death" (Rom. 5:21).

According to the evangelist Luke (1:28), Mary was consulted by the Angel of the Annunciation in the famous words, "Hail, full of grace, the Lord is with you!" Words from which centuries of Christian reflection have gradually drawn the certainty of her "innocence," of her not being "stained by sin," to the point of arriving at the official proclamation of 1854.

Without sin, however, she must also lack the aspect of death which we recognize. In fact, according to the most widely held theological opinion, what is directly tied to sin is not so much death as a biological fact. It is likely that, in the unfathomable plan of God, even without the fatal fall in Eden, man would have undergone a form of "transit," a passage into some different form of life in another world.

Sin, therefore, bears with it, not so much the serene, natural end of a cycle or a quiet "transformation," but death as a drama, as a painful rupture, as an experience of loss and anguish. It is sin that gives death the sneering imprint that we know and fear.

Thus, if Mary was spared the consequence of the sin of Eve (and Adam), she was also spared (and it could only be this way) that "sneer." The end of her earthly life was a *dormitio* (as Western and Eastern tradition calls it), a serene falling asleep.

And not only that. According to the "system of faith" (which is not a fragmentary perspective, but a mosaic, a chain where *tout se tient*), it is moral corruption that leads to bodily corruption. The one who was "full of grace" had to be spared material dissolution. When chasing out of Eden the man who wanted to be God, Yahweh says, "You shall return to the ground, for out of it you were taken; you are dust, and to dust you shall return." But this is a destiny which cannot apply to one who, from conception, was pre-redeemed from that tragedy of initial disobedience, from that fall so remote and yet (according to faith) so tenaciously renewed in every man.

The "One conceived without sin" also comes "from dust," like every other creature of God. But she was not destined like all of us to return "to dust," awaiting the voice of Christ from there when he returns to lead us in resurrection. Her body could not disintegrate among the horrors of putrefaction. In her that sign reaches perfection which often occurs among the saints — those believers, in other words, who though wounded by original sin waged war against its consequences their entire lives. At one point in the long path to canonization (the insertion into the "canon," the list of those who have taken the gospel radically in earnest), the Church demands that the tomb be opened to proceed officially to the "recognition of the corpse," which not rarely reveals that it has resisted the corruption of time. For the reflecting believer, this does not come as a surprise: opposing sin means opposing its consequences, physical ones as well, even those verified by forensic medicine. In the following chapter we shall examine an exemplary case in this regard: that of Bernadette's corpse, a canonized saint intimately tied to Mary through the explicit promise given her by the Lady that she would be with her in eternity. "I do not promise to make you happy in this life, but only in the next."

If the struggle against sin leads to this victory over death, why should one not reach this extreme where there is no sin? The preservation from it, the pre-redemption which has come about only in Mary, signifies two things: ending the course of one's earthly life as a serene falling asleep; and not abandoning to corruption the body which was a pure temple of the Spirit.

But alone, the truths of faith in the Immaculate Conception do not signify the anticipated assumption of that body to heavenly glory and eternal life. Even while "full of grace," Mary could have gone to her dormition, and her mortal remains could have awaited the final resurrection lying incorrupt in some tomb.

That tomb, however, never existed. Or better, the presumed place is venerated in Gethsemani — and also in Ephesus, as we shall see in a chapter dedicated to this. But they are both empty. Just as, not far from the one in Jerusalem, the sepulcher of her Son is also empty.

We do well to recall that, despite all the searching throughout history, legend, and tradition, no one has ever been able to turn up any trace of Christian veneration around an "occupied" tomb of Mary.

This absence is also one (and not the least) of the historical reasons on which the dogma of the Assumption is based. Knowing how Christians of the early centuries venerated the corpses of the apostles and martyrs, the lack of a cult around the corpse of the Mother of their Lord is an unthinkable lacuna.

Where did that corpse go? Why did it not elicit around it an accumulation of an immense quantity of stone, marble, silver, and gold, like the tombs of Peter, Paul, or Santiago (James the Greater)? Did the leaders of the Church perhaps hide it? But why? Mary's assumption into Heaven was neither indispensable nor necessary to the faith of the community as it was becoming organized and when there had not yet developed any reflection around a "Mariology" as confirmation and defense of its "Christology."

Was the body, then, abducted by hostile authorities or notable Jews? If that had occurred, it would have been a case of self-inflicted harm. We recall Matthew (28:11–15), which fills us in on the "story" that spread "among the Jews," which said the tomb of Jesus was found empty because "his disciples came by night and stole him away," despite the guards, placed there precisely to keep the disciples from taking it and thus being able to say he had risen. And would the enemies of Christianity have taken away the body of the Mother of Jesus, providing a good pretext for the spreading of other "rumors" favorable to a miraculous event?

At any rate, we must not forget: no hiding of corpses by anyone could have stopped Christian piety, which is patient, tenacious, relentless. And it would have tried everything to identify a tomb, authentic or supposed, where free rein could be granted to its devotion. At the worst, the place could have been alleged, and it would not have been the first time.

Were not Peter and Paul martyred at the height of a persecution, when their fate could have attracted anyone who expressed religious interest in their corpses? And yet, for two and a half centuries, persecuted and often clandestine Christians insisted on passing down the memory of the places where the apostles had shed their blood for the Lord. When the moment finally came, they pointed with certainty to Constantine's architects the exact places where the bodies had been buried.

In the almost equally famous case of the brother of John the Evangelist, the apostle James the Elder, the veneration followed for centuries the peregrinations of the corpse throughout Palestine, North Africa, Spain, and then finally, to escape Muslim invaders, to Galicia, where a shrine was built that would set into movement a throng of medieval pilgrims.

The devout followers of Mary, in their desire to be near her in some way, and not being able to reach the place where she lived, were satisfied by seeing and touching the stones that surrounded her. Thus, they gave credence to the tale of the angels that transported the "Holy House" of Nazareth first to Dalmatia, then to the hills on the Adriatic, and finally to Loreto. Those same devotees surrounded it, through their impassioned love of true children, with phials of milk, tufts of hair, strips of clothing, and innumerable other Marian relics, all suspect. And yet were they capable of forgetting the place where Mary's remains had been interred, if they had remained on this earth? There is only one conclusion: if they did not insist on looking for those remains and if no tomb elicited their devout enthusiasm, it is only because they must have been quite certain of her assumption into Heaven, which took the Church many centuries to proclaim as dogma, but belief in which, in fact and in liturgy, it had always demonstrated.

Our digression on the lack of an "occupied" tomb to venerate does not seem a useless lecture, not in the least. This absence is entirely inexplicable according to the well-known laws that govern Christian piety, applied so often and for so many centuries. If Mary had not been believed to be "assumed," and immediately so, we would find ourselves before a uniquely improbable case.

In any event, for the *sensus fidei* of believers, for the liturgy, and then, since 1950, for the Magisterium of the Church, that tomb never existed for the simple reason that it could not have.

The exemption from sin is insufficient for comprehending why there could not have been a tomb for Mary. The Immaculate Conception is a necessary condition, but insufficient for explaining the assumption "in body and soul," this sort of anticipated resurrection.

If faith considers this to have been the final destiny of the Virgin Mary, if (after having been the first to be redeemed) she became the perfect redeemed person as well, saved beforehand also in her body, this took place because no human flesh had, as hers did, such real, intimate, complete contact, comingling, and union with the flesh of Christ. It was her body that nourished Him in her womb, it was her body that "formed" His; such that *caro Iesu, caro est etiam Mariae* (the flesh of Jesus is also the flesh of Mary), to use the ancient formula. Thus Jesus is, in the words of Elizabeth, "the fruit of [Mary's] womb" (Luke 1:42).

It is therefore by the power of this intensity of incorporation, in the full sense of the word, with Him who is "the resurrection and the life" (John 11:25) that the body of the Mother not only remained incorrupt (it was enough to be without sin for this) but entered immediately into eternal glory, preceding every other human being.

And this was because that intimate union which biological maternity gives was realized on the level of faith as well. An absolute union not only of the body, but also in spirit, as suggested in the Gospel of Luke, precisely in the two phrases of Jesus that might seem to belittle the role of the Mother when reading them superficially. Instead, they are situated within the logic of faith and emphasize the destiny of "radical" maternity.

The first passage reads, "Then his mother and his brethren came to him, but they could not reach him for the crowd. And he was told, 'Your mother and your brethren are standing outside, desiring to see you.' But he said to them, 'My mother and my brethren are those who hear the word of God and do it'" (Luke 8:19–21).

The second passage reads, "As he said this, a woman in the crowd raised her voice and said to him, 'Blessed is the womb that bore you, and the breasts that you sucked!' But he said, 'Blessed rather are those who hear the word of God and keep it!'" (Luke 11:27–28).

Luke is the evangelist who presented Mary from the beginning as the one who "listened to the word of God and observed it." Therefore, she is the Mother of Christ not only according to the flesh, but also according to faith. "Behold, I am the handmaid of the Lord; let it be to me according to your word" (1:38), as she answered the angel who announced the incredible news to her, that which human ear had never heard, the conception of Him who "will be called son of the Most High."

Again, "Blessed is she who believed that there would be a fulfillment of what was spoken to her from the Lord" (Luke 1:45). This was the greeting of Elizabeth, John's mother. In the grotto of Bethlehem, while the shepherds were honoring the newborn child, "Mary kept all these things, pondering them in her heart" (2:19).

For the evangelist, then, she is the one who believes, without hesitation and to her depths, even in the unthinkable; and who, meditating on faith, draws from it all the implications for her life. Thus, in the words of the Son Himself, she is the mother of Christ also on this spiritual level, and not only on the biological level. Her physical maternity is reinforced and heightened by this spiritual maternity. This double incorporation into the Risen One could not have failed to provoke her immediate entrance into eternal life "in body and soul," as if in a hurry.

It is fitting therefore that the Byzantine hymn of the liturgy of August 15 sings to the Virgin, "Neither the tomb nor death had sufficient strength to hold you. You passed into life, being mother of Life."

If we wish to continue along the lines of this logic of Faith, we can observe the following. If one believes in the "material" reality of the Eucharist and in the Presence that it effects, what happened in the body of the Virgin happens (in some mysterious manner) also in our own bodies: *caro Iesu, caro est etiam nostra,* the flesh of Jesus is also our own flesh.

We still live, however, in the economy of the Faith, in the hiddenness of the sacrament-sign, of the "obscure light." Salvation is already here, is already at work, but has not yet rendered visible and concrete all of its effects. And so, for us, the final victory of life over death remains hidden behind the apparent victory of death over life. There will be a tomb for us, however provisional; there will be a cemetery, a "dormitory." In our future, there lies the dissolution of the body. And only faith can ensure that that dissolution will not be our definitive future, but that an omnipotent power will be able to reassemble us and render us immortal.

But the adventure of the Virgin of Nazareth encourages the believer, testifying that the spiral of life which involved her to the full is already wrapping around us too — through the screen of the Eucharist, but in the end with the same power of resurrection.

CHAPTER 23

The Body in the Chapel of Nevers

Is there renewed interest in the secular world once again in the figure of Mary? Many think they have recognized this, based on a number of explicit signs.

Among these signs of a rediscovery of Mary, I am quite familiar with one in particular, given that I was directly involved in it. Recently, TV viewers were confronted with a peculiar novelty: Rai 3 — the television network assigned (during the breakup of public television and its parceling out to the various political parties) to what was then the Italian Communist Party and which had preserved its clear "left-leaning" orientation even after the painful (for its members, of course) metamorphosis of the party — seems to have discovered religion. And not a generic spirituality, which works for atheists as well, given that many of them seek it in Buddhism or New Age spirituality, where God is not an issue. No, the old apostles of "dialectical materialism" seem to have discovered something they had until recently ignored or mocked: popular devotion. And the "Virgin Mary" type, no less. Alienation par excellence ...

Thus, one Christmas Eve, in prime time, the above-mentioned channel Rai 3 aired a long documentary on the events of Lourdes. The directors of the channel insisted (another sign of the times) that I accept the role of consultant and author of the texts for the broadcast. Despite the many times I had refused collaborative roles in the past, for which I had little experience and little patience (*umbrae quae transeunt*: the scriptural expression has always seemed appropriate for describing the TV screen, where nothing and no one "leaves a lasting trace"), this time I felt a duty to agree to the adventure. But I confess, it was laborious. Amid snowstorms, pouring rain, and a truckers' strike in France that blocked the roads, I followed for many days a TV troupe led by a well-known and expert director, he too a (begrudgingly) repentant Communist.

Because I had full liberty in writing the script, I insisted on giving adequate space in the film to Nevers, which is often overlooked. It seems that in this beautiful, ancient town on the Loire River, to the south of Paris, the annual number of pilgrims is about five hundred thousand, which is only 10 percent of the five million that flock to Lourdes. Bernadette Soubirous reached Nevers in 1866 to begin the novitiate in the motherhouse of the Sisters of Charity and Christian Instruction, and did not leave there until her death on April 16, 1879.

Here she lived her passion to its depths, as Émile Zola said. Here are the words of the incredulous writer who called the visionary "an irregularity of hysteria," but who in the end was not indifferent (is that possible for anyone who has come to know her?) to the luminous, sweet figure of the little lady:

> She asked forgiveness of everyone. She said she would not forget anyone in Heaven. Her passion was by now consummated. She had, like her Savior, the nails and the crown of thorns, her flagellated limbs and pierced side. Like him, she raised her eyes heavenward, opened her arms in a cruciform and let out a shout, "I thirst." She wet her lips in a teaspoon they offered her, lowered her head, closed her eyelids, and entered death.

Bernadette's body has been exhibited in the convent in Nevers since 1925, in a large, artistic glass coffin. Previously, the corpse had been interred in a chapel in the garden that surrounds the building, where people are free to walk about. The cloister from the times of Sr. Marie-Bernard is now a distant memory, rejected by the surviving nuns, together with many other things, including their habit.

The mentality displayed by one of the nuns does not seem to me to be a sign of progress. She told me, a bit bothered, not only that pilgrimages and devotions in general are not among her tastes as an "adult Catholic" but also that the famous sister from the 1800s, well, she was a saint, but what is sainthood anyway? Aren't we all saints? Didn't the council remind us of that? And so on.

In what was then a convent closed off by a high, impenetrable wall, at the back of its gardens there was a corner which was dear to Bernadette. It is a sort of niche (which seemed to remind her of a grotto) where, among the evergreens, there stands the statue of Our Lady of the Waters, given this name thanks to the discovery of a spring, precious to the convent, which had previously been without.

Sr. Marie-Bernard took refuge here in her every free moment, because in that statue by an unknown artist she seemed to rediscover something of the beauty of the apparitions which she could not find in the marble of Fabisch placed in Massabielle. Perhaps what most moved her was the gesture of maternal welcome, the wide-open arms of that image.

As I tried to explain in the TV documentary, my suggestion to pilgrims not to forget Nevers where Bernadette was the first to live out to the bitter end the message of the grotto, was born of an obvious conviction. Getting to know better the messenger means knowing better the Lady who chose her. Mary's "tastes" (if they can be expressed as such) are witnessed in that little shepherdess whom she wanted as her ambassador, if not confidante.

Besides entrusting her with the three secrets that concerned only her — that concerned what she had to do (or avoid?) in the little more than twenty years of life that were granted her — the Lady also taught her a special prayer to recite every day (this fact is often forgotten). Of this as well we know nothing: on a par with the secrets, the "marvelously stubborn girl," as the novice mistress called her, took to the grave the words that Heaven had given her. What we know is that, as some have observed, it was the Blessed Virgin herself who assumed the "spiritual direction" of her darling, forging her with this prayer that was entirely hers. Thus, Bernadette, insofar as she was an image, a Marian icon, merits to be explored in depth in a notebook like this one.

Here, however, we want to investigate a reality that strikes everyone and moves many to tears. We observed it during the days of filming, watching the modest but constant flow of pilgrims. Entering the gates of the convent of Saint-Gildard and crossing the courtyard, to the right stands a reproduction of the Grotto of Massabielle, constructed after the death of the visionary. To keep her humble (a superfluous precaution, in her case) the superiors prohibited any mention of what had happened at Lourdes. Having crossed the courtyard, then, one enters what was the *Grande Chapelle* of the house by a simple lateral door.

Immediately to the right, not in the center but in a lateral niche, lies the large, decorated glass coffin: Bernadette, dressed in the austere black habit which was once that of the Sisters of Nevers, appears as if sleeping. Her face is reclined to the left, and wrapped around her hands is a rosary. The surprise and the emotion of the pilgrims are great. Immediately the questions begin: Is that truly her? Is she still incorrupt? Was she embalmed? Is that truly her face or is it a mask?

These are legitimate questions. To answer them, we shall follow a sure guide, the Jesuit Fr. André Ravier who, after having dedicated practically his entire life to studying the visionary, especially the period in which she was a religious, produced a special study on the body of Bernadette, reconstructing the events through documents preserved in the archives, both religious and civil.

We shall narrate that surprising sequence of events here in the hope of preparing a more informed pilgrimage along the Loire, after that we took along the Gave.

As soon as news of Bernadette's death began to spread, it seemed the whole town rushed to what was then a peripheral street, Rue de Saint-Gildard, to view and venerate the body exposed in the convent chapel. Not having been able to meet her while living, rendered inaccessible by the need to protect her from the crowds, often quite indiscreet, the townspeople wanted to meet at least in death the one who had become their fellow citizen. With the passage of hours, the trains began to pour in groups and pilgrims from afar who had received the news via telegraph. The town had to organize a service to keep the crowds in line, while four nuns remained uninterruptedly next to the open coffin to allow the faithful to touch the body of the deceased with objects of devotion they had brought. Thus, the exposition of the body had to be prolonged until Saturday, April 19, with the permission of civil authorities, although diffident and upset in that period of Masonic anticlericalism about such a manifestation of superstition. That Saturday, after closing the doors to halt the crowds that were still pushing to get in, Bernadette was enclosed in a oak casket covered with another made of zinc, and seals were placed on it, while a verbal report was written and signed not only by the religious and prelates, but also by a magistrate and two police officers who had witnessed the operation. The Third Republic watched on with its "religion of Progress" forged in the lodges.

Whereas all the nuns of Nevers, mothers general included, had been interred in the tomb of the congregation in the public cemetery of the city, for Sr. Marie-Bernard the isolated Chapel of St. Joseph was chosen, in the convent garden halfway between the great panoramic terrace and the garden wall. For this, however, special permission was required from the department prefect. The authorization arrived, reluctantly, only on May 30, 1879. On the same day, with a simple ceremony, the body of Bernadette enclosed in the double coffin was lowered into the underground crypt of the chapel. On the floor, a tombstone was placed which can still be seen today in the wall of the reconstructed chapel, the original having been bombed by the Americans after the Normandy invasion in 1944. The text reads: "*Ici repose / Dans la paix du Seigneur / Bernadette Soubirous / Honorée à Lourdes en 1858 / De plusieures apparitions / De la très Sainte Vierge*" (Here lies / In the peace of the Lord / Bernadette Soubirous / Honored at Lourdes in 1858 / By many apparitions / Of the Blessed Virgin).

Sr. Marie-Bernard remained untouched in that tomb for more than thirty years, venerated by a discreet flow of the faithful of every condition, age, and nationality. It was also this reputation of sanctity, this popular devotion (indispensable for initiating the process of beatification and canonization, where the Church limits herself to sifting through and sanctioning the *vox populi*) that accelerated matters. Accelerated, to be clear, according to the rhythms of a Church that uses as its unit for measuring time centuries, millennia, and in perspective, eternity. Three decades after her burial, however, in the autumn of 1909, the diocesan process "regarding the reputation for sanctity, virtues, and miracles" of Bernadette came to an end. As prescribed, the process had to proceed with what tradition calls "inspection of the body" — namely, its legal and canonical identification and the verification of its status.

This first exhumation took place on Wednesday, September 22 of the same year, 1909. The official accounts, preserved in the archives of the convent of Saint-Gildard, allow one to follow step-by-step the acts of the "inspection." We shall follow it. At 8:30 a.m., Bishop Gauthey of Nevers, followed by members of the ecclesiastical tribunal, entered the *Grande Chapelle* of the convent. At the entrance, a table was placed on which an open book of the Gospels was set. One after another, three witnesses (among them the mother general of the congregation), two doctors, two laborers, and two carpenters swore on the Good Book to speak the truth. The cortege walked through the garden toward the Chapel of St. Joseph. After raising the stone that closed the crypt, they beheld the coffin. This they transported to a pavilion next door, where they placed it on two sawhorses covered with a sheet. To the side, a table with a precious white altar cloth, embroidered by the sisters (Bernadette, patient and industrious, was quite capable in this art), waited to receive her mortal remains.

In an emotionally charged setting, in a great silence broken only by prayers murmured in a half voice by some of those present, the two carpenters cut the zinc covering and unscrewed the wood covering. There appeared the body of Bernadette: it was perfectly preserved. There was no unpleasant odor. There were also some elderly nuns present who, thirty years before, had participated in the burial. Their emotion was immense, almost frightened to see their sister just as they had laid her to rest, although they noticed just one thing different. The face and the hands were inclined to the left, conferring on her an even greater sense of being merely asleep and not dead. It is the posture that was found in the other exhumations, a position that she preserved and which every pilgrim can notice even today.

But now we turn to the two physicians, a surgeon and a doctor, reporting verbatim their sworn testimonies, equipped with seals of authenticity and preserved in the convent archives:

> The coffin was opened. We smelled no odor. The body was dressed in the habit of the Order, quite damp. Only her face, hands, and part of her forearms were exposed. The head was bent to the left, the face was a *blanc mat* (pallid white, opaque). The skin adhered to the muscles, and the muscles clung to the bones. The eyelids, sunken, covered the eyes. The nose was parchment-like and thin. The mouth, slightly open, allowed one to see the teeth still in place. The hands, crossed on the chest and perfectly preserved along with the fingernails, clutched a rosary devoured by rust. On the forearms the veins were visible. The feet, like the hands, had completely preserved the toenails.

The two physicians continued,

> After having removed the habit and the veils from the head, one could see the entire body *parcheminé* (parchment-like), rigid, sonorous in every part. One noticed that the hair, cut short, was still on her skull and adhered to her scalp; that the ears were in a perfect state of conservation; that the left side of the body, beginning from the hip, was higher than the right side. The lower parts of the corpse were a bit blackish. This seems due to the charcoal that was found in great quantities in the coffin.

The text ends with, "As witnesses to the above, we have drawn up the present certificate in conformity with the truth. Signed: Dr. Ch. David, surgeon, Dr. A. Jordan, medical doctor."

After this verification by the physicians, the nuns washed the body and placed it in a new coffin, made of wood, enclosed in zinc and decorated with white silk. During the hours in which it was exposed to the air, the skin darkened somewhat. The double casing was closed, welded, shut with screws, and sealed with seven seals. Finally, the workers took it back to the same site where it had been removed that morning. When it was all finished, it was 5:30 p.m. of that September 22.

Fr. André Ravier, whose study we are following, comments at this point that, even though there was no authorization to shout "Miracle!" for this perfect preservation after thirty years of burial, "One must notice however that, in the case of Bernadette, such a preservation was truly surprising. Her illness and the condition she was in when she died, the humidity of the place where she was interred (her wet habit, the rosary devoured by rust; the crucifix — also clutched in her hands — was copper-green), everything seemed to facilitate a dissolution of the remains which instead did not occur."

On August 13 of 1913, Pope Pius X, inspired by the positive decision of the Congregation of Rites, authorized the introduction of the cause for beatification and signed what in canon law is called the "Decree of Venerability." The First World War impeded the continuation of the cause. One had to wait until 1918, when the second "inspection of the body" was ordered. Two other physicians, Talon and Comte, were appointed to proceed with the examination. It took place on April 3, 1919, in the presence of the bishop of Nevers, the police commissioner, several representatives of the town council, and members of the ecclesiastical tribunal.

Starting with the oath sworn on the Gospels, everything was carried out like the first time, but with an important novelty: after the examination of the body, each of the two physicians was isolated in a separate room and wrote his report without being able to consult his colleague. As seen in the original documents, the two reports are completely in accord with each other, and also with the reports written ten years earlier by Drs. David and Jordan. The only difference in the body to be reported was the appearance of mold and salt, both of which the physicians attributed to the washing of the body performed by the nuns in 1909.

We quote here the first lines of Dr. Comte's report:

> When the double casket was opened, the corpse appeared absolutely intact, without odor. (Dr. Talon specified, "No smell of putrefaction was present, no one among those present *est incommode*.") The skeleton beneath the flesh is intact and the corpse was transferred without difficulty to a table to be examined. In some places the skin has disappeared, but it continues to adhere over most of the body. Some veins are still visible.

At 5 p.m. on the same day, the coffin was placed once more in the floor of the chapel.

Four years later, the pope declared the heroic character of the virtues of Sr. Marie-Bernard, formerly Bernadette Soubirous. The path to beatification was thus opened, and it now proceeded to the third and final inspection, during which relics were to be taken and sent to Rome, Lourdes, and some of the houses of the congregation. The doctors in charge were the same ones as in 1919, Talon and Comte.

The ceremony took place on April 18, 1925, forty-six years and two days after the death of Bernadette. The usual authorities and witnesses were present, including the bishop, the police commissioner, and even the mayor of Nevers. In fact, the tragedy of the war had softened a bit the hardline anticlericalism of the politicians who, terrified in August of 1914 when the

Germans were in sight of Paris, had set aside for a moment their incredulity, asking the Church for public prayers for the salvation of their political caste, as well as of France. At that time, the supplications seemed to have an effect, in the form of the "miracle" of the Marne. But their time had run out twenty-six years later when the Wehrmacht swept away forever the secular branch of the Masonic Lodge which had always been the Third Republic, with its religion of secularism, a new superstition exercised in continual, implacable persecution of the Church.

At any rate, returning to the spring of 1925, after the physicians and workers had sworn their oaths, after the usual procedures prescribed by canon as well as civil law, the coffin was transported and opened in the Chapel of St. Helen. The corpse was found in the now well-known condition of exceptional preservation. Here are some of the words from the report of Dr. Comte, the one in charge of extracting the relics, working with his scalpel, and uncovering some of the internal organs as well:

> The body of the Venerable was intact, the skeleton whole, the muscles atrophied but well preserved. The skin, *parcheminé,* seemed to have suffered only the effect of the humidity in the casket. For this reason, it has assumed a grayish aspect and is covered with some mold and calcium salts. But the cadaver has suffered neither the putrefaction nor the decomposition that is normal and habitual after such a long period underground.

Some time later, Dr. Comte published in a scientific journal an article addressing his colleagues, in which he wrote, "What really struck me in this examination is the perfect preservation of the skeleton, the ligaments, the skin, as well as the elasticity and tone of the muscles." But then he added,

> What surprised me above all is the condition of the liver, an absolutely unexpected state forty-six years after death. This essentially soft and friable organ should have decomposed very quickly, or calcified and become hard. Instead, cutting into it to take a piece for the relics, I found it to have an elastic consistency and to be almost normal. I brought this immediately to the attention of the assistants, telling them that this fact seemed beyond the normal order to me.

Besides a section of the liver and fragments of two ribs and several muscles, Bernadette's body was left intact. Above all, the heart remained, which (as the doctors wrote) "we suppose was intact, to the same extent as the other organs inspected." Fortunately, it must be said, the inclination to the left rendered difficult its removal and therefore they decided against it. Thus, the heart of the saint remained in the house in Nevers, where it had suffered so much but where she had loved so much, as the destination where Providence and the thoughtfulness of the Lady had placed her. I know all too well that the cult of relics, which seems to border on the macabre, is no longer part of our world, no longer in accord with our sensibilities. Yet, from the very beginning, and according to a centuries-long theory, the *sensus fidei* of believers led them to venerate the remains of the bodies destined to be glorified, called to be transfigured in the definitive resurrection. And the relics were also a healthy recall to Christian "materialism," an antidote to the heresy par excellence of which there is already a trace in the New Testament: the gnosis, which seeks to transform faith into a wisdom, a morality, an ideology, into something in any case intellectual, theoretical, sterile. Gnosticism says it loves the angels because it has a horror of matter — beginning with the matter that is venerated because it comes from the body of those who have witnessed to the gospel to the bitter end.

When the surgeons finished their task, the two wrapped the body in strips of cloth, leaving exposed only the face and the hands. The cadaver was then placed back in the coffin, though leaving it exposed.

The following account we draw from the words of Fr. Ravier:

> It was then that they took *par moulage* [a cast] of the precise form of the face, so that the House *Imans* in Paris might create a light wax mask. There was fear that, although intact, the face which had become blackish (through contact with the air and water during the washing), as well as the sunken eyes, might leave the faithful appalled. For the same reasons, they took the imprint of the hands, being quite careful not to modify in any way the demeanor that they had assumed in the coffin.

The body was left in the chapel, sealed to prevent any tampering before the official proclamation of beatification. This took place on June 14, 1925, by act of Pius XI. But because the artistic glass casket (created by Caillat-Cateland, a famous jeweler and engraver from Lyon) had not yet been finished, they had to wait until July 18 for the transfer. Bernadette, still wrapped in strips of cloth, was dressed in the habit of the congregation with its characteristic white apron, and the light wax mask was placed on her face and hands. The venerated body was transported on a white stretcher to the singing of the Little Office of Our Lady and placed in the glass sarcophagus in the same hall where the novice Bernadette, just after arriving from Lourdes still wearing her traditional Pyrenean dress, held her one and only conference on the apparitions before three hundred sisters. From that moment onward she never again said a word or even mentioned them.

It was August 3, 1925, when the coffin was transferred into the chapel to the right of the main altar, where pilgrims can still see it.

Fr. Ravier concludes, "Yes, it is her body, that of Bernadette, that we see behind the glass. It is intact, except for the relics removed in 1925. To contest this fact, as extraordinary as it might seem, one must place in doubt the oaths sworn by the physicians, magistrates, police commissioners, mayors, and ecclesiastical authorities. The official reports of a full three re-exhumations speak clearly."

Our scholar continues,

> Yes, this is precisely the body of the visionary in that countenance of recollection and prayer that she assumed in the first coffin; it is that face (under the mask) that looked upon the Lady; they are the hands that fingered the rosary beads before and during the apparitions; they are the fingers that dug into the dirt and found the miraculous spring; they are the ears that heard the message and the lips that spoke to the parish priest the name which the mysterious Lady gave herself. All around the sarcophagus are engraved the words of the Virgin, so simple and so precious and which she alone conveyed to us. From that little fragile body there seems to arise a mysterious voice. Here, Bernadette continues her mission; she is present, she prays, she bears witness, she reminds us that among her last words there was a reassurance addressed to each of us: "I will forget no one." She is, still and always, the instrument used by Heaven itself to tell us that God is Love and to exhort us to pass from the darkness of sin to the light of grace.

CHAPTER 24

Tiles of a Mosaic

Another chapter consisting of fragments, flashes, and crumbs collected under the table in Cana. We begin by observing that among the heresies of which Mary (according to the ancient antiphon) is the enemy, there are above all the modern ideologies. In particular, that psychoanalysis of which we do not wish to deny a possible Christian reading — a complex discussion which I have offered elsewhere and need not do so again here. Nor do I wish to repeat the facile jokes that might yet have some foundation in truth: psychoanalysis is beneficial, above all for the psychoanalyst's wallet; it is a sickness that is passed off as a cure; its is the remedy for all ailments of the spirit that no one — not even Woody Allen — believes in anymore (excepting only friars and nuns in the West); it is the "pseudoscience" par excellence (Karl Popper), for no one has ever been able to demonstrate its effectiveness, or even its ineffectiveness; perhaps it is merely chatter, hot air, cryptic words, and thus a waste of time as well as money.

No jokes or mockery here; we wish only to recall what is undeniable: in its most radical (or simply original, orthodox) form, psychoanalysis relegates all religions (and especially biblical religion) to the domain of evils that must be drawn up from the unconscious in order to dispel them. Whether his clerical followers like it or not, the "complex" from which Sigmund Freud was never able to liberate himself (and maybe did not want to liberate himself) was precisely his obsession against that "pernicious illusion" which Judeo-Christianity was to him. In a biography of Umberto Saba, the Jewish poet from Trieste, I read a passage from a letter written in 1949 to a psychoanalyst friend, Joachim Flescher, also a Jew: "I believe that the crux of all neuroses is to be found in religions; in all of them but, in particular, in Christianity. I know very well that everything in Christianity was not born in Jesus and that many elements, extraneous to Judaism, entered into its formation. But to me, it remains true that the original sin of the Jews was Jesus. And that from this sin they found deliverance only in another Jew: Freud."

These lines are the speculation of an artist, but born in concrete experience, given that Saba was among the first to subject himself to psychoanalysis, and for many years. In fact, a number of Freud's disciples entered the Jewish community of Trieste, having arrived directly from the Viennese doctor's school.

Why are we talking about this? Because it is obvious that what for believers is the "Holy Family" appears as an inextricable neurotic tangle to the cultivators of this "science." A woman and a man (young, moreover; it seems the myth of an elderly Joseph was the fantasy of an apocryphal work) who live together, officially married but in reality without having marital relations. To this is added (an even more defenseless pathology!) an only child who lives at home until he is thirty, without even a love life (as far as we know), without breaking the bond with those deviant parents — "was obedient to them" even, as the evangelist makes clear (Luke 2:51).

Before such a situation, radically pathological, what must a zealous analyst do but corral those three into his studio and try to convince them to talk about their neurotic problems and, naturally, to liberate themselves, beginning with a healthy practice of sex? There is here it seems yet another of the many confirmations of the Pauline observation: the gospel as the eternal "scandal" and continuous "folly" to the "wise of this world." And this world today is that in which psychoanalysis has become "wisdom" that gazes with a mixture of alarm and compassion on the unresolved knots of the family composed by Mary, Joseph, and Jesus.

But staying for a moment with modern ideologies. If psychoanalysis seeks to place Mary, along with her strange family members, in therapy, then feminism criticizes her because she did not rebel against the traditional role of women, that of the homemaker. And Marxism objects because, despite her good intentions expressed in the Magnificat, she did not put them into practice, accepting (politically passive, without a choice for the working class and subsequent militancy) the unjust condemnation of her son by Roman imperialists through the collaborating aristocracy and bourgeois elite of the Sanhedrin.

Not to mention the ideologies of the health fanatics, the prohibitionists, the apostles of the "healthy lifestyle," so numerous and petulant today. Was she not the woman who asked her son to procure more wine for people who had already drunk too much? And what can be said about Jesus, who should have gone on a diet to control obesity, another obsession of our time, given that the Pharisees defined him as "an eater and a drinker"?

The Orthodox Church tends to see in Mary above all the Mother of God; the Catholic Church above all as the Mother of men.

Different accents, confirmed in the different liturgies and artistic representations. On one side, icons of such transcendence as to make one think more of one who dwells in the celestial empyrean than of a human being. On the other side, paintings and statues (prohibited in the East, moreover, where only painters and not sculptors are permitted) marked at times by an excessive "realism," by a "humanity" perhaps suspect. No one ignores that there have been Catholic painters who had their lovers, or at least women of stained reputation, pose as models for their Madonnas.

This occurs in popular devotion as well: transcendence on one side, earthiness on the other, to the very limit of banality. History's first Slavic pope was decidedly correct in saying, "Christianity must breathe once again with both lungs," that of the West and that of the East. Only in this way can we safeguard that "law of *et-et*" that presides over authentic faith, even in all that concerns Mary.

Discreet but precise traces of a figure in the penumbra.

Luke 2:16: "And [the shepherds] went with haste, and found Mary and Joseph, and the babe lying in a manger."

As attentive biblical scholars point out, there is here a sort of "silent revolution": it is the first time in Scripture that the name of the mother is placed before that of the father. Not only is it a break with harsh Semitic male chauvinism; it is also a sign of the importance which that Woman had to the evangelist.

Mark 10:14–15, with its corresponding parallels in Matthew and Luke: "Let the children come to me, do not hinder them; for to such belongs the kingdom of God. Truly, I say to you, whoever does not receive the kingdom of God like a child shall not enter it."

Becoming like little children, however, means turning toward the mother and entrusting oneself to her. Is there here, perhaps (as some mystics have intuited), a sort of "hidden" exhortation to encounter her who, as Mother of the Son of Man, is proposed as Mother of all men?

Whatever the case, in the perspective of the Gospels, progressing in the spiritual life means "turning around" toward infancy. And that means toward a mother. The law of the spirit is not that of evolution but, if anything, that of a sort of involution: "innocence regained," to use the words of Henri Bergson, the convert from Judaism.

We saw in a previous installment that the series of Marian apparitions of the nineteenth century began in 1830, in Rue du Bac in Paris, when the future saint, Catherine Labouré, was tasked with minting the so-called "Miraculous Medal." The writing to be engraved was, "O Mary, conceived without sin, pray for us who have recourse to Thee." It was a powerful catalyst for the eventual 1854 definition (after centuries of bitter dispute) of the dogma of the Immaculate Conception of Mary. And under that name, Mary presented herself to Bernadette just four years later.

There seems to be a reason for this choice. In fact, if Mary (and only her among all human beings) was preserved "from the very first instant of her conception" from the stain of sin, it was obviously because that sin exists, because it is not an anachronistic myth, because it is a disturbing reality that demands redemption.

All modernity (which began right in those years, as we have explained) is characterized by this: by the negation of sin, by the conviction that science, culture, education, and technology will be able to make the world a sort of earthly paradise. There is no sin, and certainly no original sin, and progress will show the material results and moral perfection of which man is capable once he is liberated from the suffocating superstition of Christianity. A Redeemer come down from Heaven? Get real: there's no redemption, no salvation except for what man and his progress has won.

History demonstrated not only that this was not the case, but that the great hopes of secular humanism twisted into their opposite. The world saw that the illusion of the self-redemption of humanity led to its self-destruction. But then, during those decades of the 1800s in which modernity was born, it was not so evident that the search for an entirely human paradise would lead to quite different outcomes, such as the terrible massacres of the bloodiest war in history — the quintessentially "great" war, which was the logical, direct outcome of the ideologies of the nineteenth century, beginning with nationalism, that took the place of the Christian perspective. In that period, even many Christians were convinced: enough with this ball and chain of "sin," enough with this ballast of unbearable obscurantism, no longer believable, the source only of delays in the march toward "tomorrow."

This, I believe, was the cause of this insistence on sin in the message of the apparitions of the nineteenth century: the liberation from sin, but only as an outcome of faith in Christ, not trust in men. At any rate, is not the function of Marian apparitions that of reminding the faithful of one particularly topical aspect of the Faith, an aspect to highlight with urgency in a particular historical period? Those decades of the 1800s were those of the Immaculate Conception.

Verlaine, the wretched poet with an intense religious torment that in the end gained the upper hand, speaking of love for Mary said, "All other loves are by command." In such words he sought to underline the "free" character of Marian devotion that the Church has always safeguarded. Only a few dogmas regarding her have been proclaimed in twenty centuries, all of them to protect her Son more than to protect her. Only to these defined truths do Catholics owe their obedience. All the rest concerning Mary is left to the free sensibility and initiative of the believer.

The pope, the hierarchy, the masters of spirituality can recommend that we venerate her and pray to her, practice devotions, pilgrimages to her shrines, processions, and novenas. They can recommend, basing their counsel on the millenary experience of the positive fruit of these practices; but they do not dare mandate. Never has the Church transformed the apparitions into a dogma of faith, even those officially recognized and where the popes themselves have visited. Never will the Church impose as necessary for salvation practices such as the recitation of the Rosary, though it is recommended by countless encyclicals and even honored by its own liturgical feast. Never will someone have to confess as a sin not having participated in a procession of the Our Lady, not having gone on a pilgrimage to a shrine, or not having venerated a particular image.

Furthermore, the Catholic Church does not deny, nor has it ever, the eternal salvation of those who in good faith and integrity live their Christian life in the communities born of the Reformation. Communities which, according to their official creeds, recognize the first two Marian dogmas (perpetual virginity and divine maternity), defined when Christianity was undivided, but do not recognize the other Catholic dogmas and, above all, reject not only the necessity but the very legitimacy of every devotion to her whose demanding title of "Our Lady" they indignantly reject.

Thus, the entire imposing affair of Marian devotion and spirituality (one of the most widespread and profound phenomena in history) is characterized not by impositions but by freedom; not by law, but by love. Because, as Verlaine intuited, "every obligation harms love, every command kills it."

The spiritual fruit as well as the fascination of the veneration for Our Mother is precisely in this "gratitude," which is proposed in discretion, not imposed as a disciplinary edict.

Discretion, as I said. One of the fruits of this virtue is silence. In fact, there are innumerable reflections by the mystics and spiritual masters on the "silence of Mary." For this reason as well, meditating on her example is particularly topical today, at a time when even within the Church many are convinced that the more Christian one is the more one must multiply words. Hence the incredible "*documentitis*" of the postconciliar decades. And yet, it was in the decisive moment that Jesus kept silent (Matt. 26:63; Mark 14:61). Above all, Mary kept silent: before the words of others, she silently "kept all these things in her heart," as Luke repeats twice in the same chapter.

In our day, besieged as we are by the logorrhea that everyone has contracted, we perceive that her aid to the Faith passes through her silence, more than through her few and simple words.

She speaks so little. And, at least apparently, the Scriptures speak little about her. But then, if one looks closely, it is she who inspires Scripture. Always, to be clear, in her discreet manner, with her hidden style. There is agreement among many biblical scholars on the fact that the first two fundamental chapters of Luke, the so-called "infancy narratives," were inspired by her.

She was the one who told the story, almost certainly after the Resurrection, in the nascent Church, in Jerusalem, which only she could know. She lies "behind" as always: and her fundamental presence is noticed only by those who know how to see and listen.

Concerning her connection with the Faith: The strongest and most passionate Marian devotion is found in countries like those of the Iberian Peninsula, once famous for their orthodoxy; or countries on the periphery, such as Poland and Ireland, which had to safeguard their Catholicism from heterodox faiths threatening them. Mary was for them either confirmation or defense of their faith.

Certain slogans, which in recent years have gained ground even in the Church, need to be modified. Behind certain perspectives that seem edifying there can be errors in vision, or at least a danger of partiality.

I am thinking in particular of the emphasis given by some on Mary as a "sister" in faith. Or on Mary as "model," as an "example" for believers. True, but partial, in light of the Catholic perspective. Mary is *also* "sister," but above all she is "Mother." She is also "model," but first of all she is "presence," solicitous and powerful. For good reason, theology acknowledges her veneration as decisively inferior to the worship due to Christ alone, but at the same time superior to that due the saints. They are indeed intercessors as well, but they are, above all, brothers and sisters, models and examples.

This discussion is quite vast, and I am embarrassed for giving it just a few lines. There is here, however, a slippage toward Protestant perspectives, so common in recent years: Mary is honored because she prays *with* us; silenced is the conviction that she prays *for* us. Luther shouted in his sermons that there was no blasphemy worse than reciting the Rosary, or sin against Christ graver than building shrines to the Virgin Mary and setting off on pilgrimage to them.

From the Cross, the agonizing Jesus did not give John a "sister"; He gave him a "mother." He did not give her a "brother" but a "son."

In Matthew 18:19–20 we read, "If two of you agree on earth about anything they ask, it will be done for them by my Father in heaven. For where two or three are gathered in my name, there I am in the midst of them." The intuition of St. Louis-Marie Grignion de Montfort regarding this passage is striking: "Never have recourse to Our Lord if not by means of Mary: thus, you will never find yourself alone in prayer; and this, the word of Jesus Himself, cannot but be granted." A sublime "trick" on the part of the great apostle of the Virgin Mary!

Mary prays *for* us, but this does not exclude the fact that she also prays *with* us: taking part in our "group," "agreeing" with us (according to the Gospel expression), that we might obtain what we ask in prayer.

CHAPTER 25

PRIVILEGES, AND MORE

HERE WE OFFER A few more crumbs, or fragments, beginning with the observation that there are Catholic theologians today who condemn their preconciliar colleagues for having constructed what they call the "Mariology of privileges." This Mariology underlines the unicity of Mary: the only "Mother of God"; the only person preserved from original sin; the only one assumed into Heaven body and soul; the only one with rights to a special veneration, for which an equally special name was created ("hyperdulia"), and so forth.

This objection is no surprise. In fact, theology, like every human activity, is influenced by what Germans call the *Zeitgeist*, the "spirit of the times." Yet, the entire spirit that characterizes modernity, at least in the West, is egalitarian, an enemy of every privilege. Was it not for this that revolutions were started?

Naturally, these revolutions, as their first and often only result, created new privileged castes, even more exclusive than the preceding ones, and cloaked in hypocrisy. Marxism was exemplary in this regard, with its hierarchy sheltered in their comfortable summer homes, with stores reserved for those who had Western money and exclusive services for the more influential members of the party.

It is nevertheless clear that the modern allergy is to every "privilege," and this has led some theologians (perhaps unconsciously) to impatience in the field of Mariology as well. And maybe even in Christology. Was modernity not marked by the attempt to substitute God with man? Well, then, how can we tolerate that just one man, Jesus of Nazareth, would be recognized as having divine status? An inacceptable privilege on a par with the "Assumption" and the "Immaculate Conception" for His Mother.

Thus, Jesus must return to the ranks of pure and simple humanity, and Mary must return to her place among her sisters and brothers equal to her in the Church. This too is "democracy" for goodness' sake! Enough with favoritism!

We do not want to put the matter in such caricatural terms. What seems important is not to lose the awareness that (in every age, but especially today, vulnerable as we are to the "spirit of the times") theological reflection pays tribute to majoritarian perspectives. And so, shots aimed at "Marian privileges" ought to be taken seriously, but not too seriously. Just as in all things human.

Regarding what we have said, we find yet another of the many confirmations, browsing through a magazine published by Catholics concerned to be seen as "informed" and "critical." But there seems to be very little critical spirit in a violent article against what they define as "supposed messages of Marian apparitions." Such messages, even those whose authenticity has been recognized by the Church, ought to be rejected, considered false, according to these "enlightened" Catholics, because they are incompatible with the Gospels. They are "blasphemous" messages for one reason above all: because (quoting verbatim) "they are decidedly *reactionary* or, at least, *ultraconservative*." There it is, the pollution of the Zeitgeist; the "primacy of politics" (placing culture and politics in the place of religion is the program of the enlightened) leads to using its categories for judging the religious dimension.

Thus, the completely worldly antithesis born of the French Revolution and then of the post- and anti-Christian ideologies of the following two centuries ("progressives" against "reactionaries"; "left" against "right"; "proletarians" against "capitalists" ...) becomes the distinguishing pseudo-theological element. In fact, in the article, the Catholic writer inveighs first against Fatima: the messages entrusted to the three shepherd children there are judged "reactionary" and therefore unacceptable to a "progressive" believer.

But beware: the contrary happens (in reading certain pamphlets and listening to certain discussions) for the apparitions, still occurring, which began years ago in Medjugorje. Here, it is traditionalists who reject the possibility of their authenticity because the messages of the Virgin Mary are considered too "ecumenical," if not outright "syncretic." The followers of Archbishop Lefebvre[11] are leading a polemical campaign to demonstrate the unreliability of those phenomena in Bosnia-Herzegovina. They are, it seems, too far "left."...

Pascal has a famous *pensee* called the three "orders": the order of culture, the order of politics, and the order of faith. To judge any reality, adequate categories must be used. To mix the political order with the religious order means confusing everything. They may even believe themselves astute and profound, who discern Gospel truths (of which the messages of the apparitions are confirmation and fulfillment) using the criteria of "right" and "left," which were created for distinguishing modern political alignments and are entirely illegitimate elsewhere.

Still regarding "privileges": many contemporaries, convinced that each must be given always and everywhere whatever has been given to everyone else, ask why, in places like Lourdes, some few are healed while the vast majority are not? Why is there this narrow elite of the "privileged"?

In trying to formulate a response, one must remember what is, in the Christian system, the objective of the physical miracle. It has as its final objective not the healing of corporal evils, but the bearing of the fruit of salvation. Its function is to reiterate the existence of God, the providential Creator, and to confirm the truth of the Gospels. In them, Jesus heals, often moved by pity for those suffering—always, however, "that God may be glorified," that the people believe in Him and in the truth of His mission. Sending out the disciples to preach, He announces that in His name they shall perform wonders: but these will occur out of pity for souls rather than for the body, that the gospel might be accepted. And physical miracles are, to Him, only a sign (rare, discontinuous, unforeseeable) of the true miracle proclaimed by the good news: the liberation from sin and eternal salvation offered to every man.

In this regard, I have found in that mine of information, the *Revue Pratique d'Apologétique*, some considerations that are worth reproducing. This journal was published in Paris in the first half of the previous century. We shall

[11] Editor's Note: Archbishop Marcel Lefebvre (1905–1991), founder of the traditionalist Society of St. Pius X.

translate some sections, given that the task of one who writes on such topics is not always and only to find new things, but also to recall and meditate on what has already been written and retains its validity.

> The physical miracle, that of healing above all, always has a religious aim, namely a pedagogy for the faith. God grants it in light of this higher utility: health is restored to *someone* to give salvation to *all*. It is evident that the moral effect of every miracle would be less if the phenomenon were more frequent. If the miracle were a suspension of the habitual laws of nature, a suspension that were to become habitual, or nearly so, it would soon be transformed by men into a new law. If the prodigy became frequent, it would lose its typical characteristic, that for which it is granted by God: the fact that it is extraordinary, its appearance as something entirely unusual. Taking on an aspect of habit and regularity, someone might soon imagine a "constant" (however unknown at present) that supports it, removing from it the acknowledgment of a God who can intervene in the world.

At this point, the old but still-compelling theologians of the apologetic *Revue* recalled Émile Zola. In the novel in which Zola gave an account as an apostle of scientific atheism of his desacralizing investigation into Lourdes, he wrote, "If I were capable of making a spring of water flow that could heal wounds and cure every sort of bodily ailment, I would heal the entire world and not just some rare privileged ones." Here, too, the very modern rejection of "privilege" returns. If he had had the power of God, Zola would have been more just and "democratic."

The Catholic response was as follows:

> Do you see continuous miracles, the sick flocking to Lourdes from every continent and all of them returning home healed? Who cannot see that wonders multiplied in this fashion would only be interesting phenomena for scientists, who would not hesitate to place them in relation to some physical cause present there, starting with the water at the spring? Instead of awakening our thoughts of God, such events would lead us to forget Him. They would only speak of the curative powers of nature or of manifestations until then unknown.

St. Thomas Aquinas had already stated, "The prodigious intervention of God in the world must always appear beyond the ordinary course of things. This places necessary limits on His intervention: *assueta vilescunt,* what is habitual loses value. His goodness urges God to help us, His wisdom draws Him mysteriously to limit that aid."

Furthermore, it was another great saint and theologian, St. Augustine, who observed, "The greatest wonders are those of each moment: seeds, flowers, fruit that all reproduce without cease. The miracle is life. But all this fails to strike us because we are inured to it."

This would also occur in the case of the physical miracle (understood as a suspension of the habitual laws), if it were not rare, reserved for but a few, chosen by the impenetrable judgment of God. If it were to become the norm, it would lose its function as a sign, as a stimulus for the fruits of faith, and therefore, of salvation.

Marian apparitions are often connected to water. In the symbolism of all peoples, water is connected to life and to fertility, but also to purity and purification. Furthermore, water rises heavenward in the form of vapor and descends in the form of rain, and it is therefore a bond between Heaven and earth, between high and low.

Remaining with the modern apparitions, at La Salette Mary made abundant a spring that had been a periodic trickle up to that time. In Lourdes, we know how she guided Bernadette to discover the wellspring.

In light of this, there seems to be a premonition in the prayer of the Virgin Mary (so splendid and profound that it has entered into the official liturgy of the Church, a unique case) which Dante attributes to St. Bernard in the last chapter of the *Paradiso*: "Here you are the noonday torch of Love to us, and down there, among mortal beings, you are a living spring of hope."

I mentioned La Salette. That apparition raises particular problems also for a reason highlighted by Gustave Thibon, one of the most spirited modern Christian writers, a peasant-theologian. We do well to reflect on it, because the issue goes beyond La Salette, involving the other recognized Marian epiphanies.

Thibon writes,

> Some spirits are struck by the "threats" contained in the words of the Virgin who appeared in September of 1846 on the Alpine pastures in the Diocese of Grenoble. They say: "We cannot believe in a cruel God." But in this manner, they forget that the supposed "threats" were only divine promises rejected. God is "cruel" only to the extent that men, closing their hearts to grace, prevent God from exercising His goodness. The rejection comes from us. The Christian God cannot save us without our desiring it. God does not wish to punish us actively: it is enough for us to push Him away and, abandoned to the weight of sin, we roll fatally toward the bottom of the abyss.

Similar to Lourdes (and perhaps even more so), La Salette has attracted many artists, writers, and scholars in an irresistible way. Among them were Jacques Maritain and the one who was his guide to conversion, the sulfurous Léon Bloy. The latter, struck by tears poured out in the place dedicated to Mary (*Celle qui pleure,* "she who cries," he called her), he put believers on guard: "La Salette is the serious side of Christianity. It is the drama of the choice between salvation and eternal perdition which we all must make. *Non irridetur Deus,* One must not mock God. For this reason, words like the ones of the crying Lady before Melania and Massimino will always be unacceptable for every Christian expectation that seeks the favor of the fashions of the moment."

Why are the Gospels silent about a specific apparition of the Risen Christ to His Mother? This topic is so profound that we will not dare even to touch it. If we ask the question here, it is only to point out a possible answer provided by some ancient authors and which seems appropriate to our times, after the Second Vatican Council shed abundant light on the connections between Mariology and ecclesiology.

If, as those authors say, Jesus truly did not appear to Mary, at least immediately after the Resurrection, it might have been to help her (and us) understand that He was now to be found in the Church, which is His body. The Mystical Body is a body, equally real, that returned from death. In fact, it might also not be accidental that the only mention of Mary after the Resurrection is situated within the community, that she had become part of the ecclesial body of the One she had generated.

In one of his Wednesday catecheses, John Paul II offered a number of reflections on the Week of Prayer for Christian Unity then taking place. After listing the comforting signs, the pope made the comment, "Among Christians there remains, unfortunately, not only doctrinal difficulties, but also asperity, reticence, and mistrust that at times take the form of gratuitous expressions of aggression."

These last words recall to mind what I read in *Riforma*, the official weekly magazine of the Waldensian and Methodist communities. In plain view, occupying nearly an entire page, without any distancing by the editors (who in fact, as a sign of approval had given the title: "Neither Shrines nor Other Objects of Worship Can Be Ddded to the Gospel"), a letter of one of the readers was published, which commented on an interview I gave for the *Corriere della Sera*. The topic was the robust renewal throughout the world of Marian devotion, still alive even among the many who are no longer practicing Catholics.

A priest and I were both interviewed. We both reiterated the reasons for this type of Catholic devotion, confirmed by the recent council which had been convoked by John XXIII and closed by Paul VI on dates that were explicitly Marian and with passionate invocations, in line with Tradition, of the patronage of the *Mater Ecclesiae*. Nothing new, then, in the veneration of the Virgin Mary! And no concessions to credulity, sentimentalism, or devotionalism.

Yet, repeating the age-old Catholic reasons was enough to merit these closing comments in the letter published with such great fanfare: "Speaking as the Reverend and Messori do is certainly legitimate, from their point of view. But if this is their way of believing, it has nothing to do with Christianity. It is pure paganism."

And so, those who insist, beware! Reciting a Hail Mary, going on pilgrimage, praying in a shrine, carrying a rosary, you are nothing but a pagan — the word of a Waldensian-Methodist, in the fullness of the current ecumenical climate!

For centuries, they have been remonstrating with Catholics, whereas the Orthodox seem to be spared such insults — the worst one can throw at a fellow Christian — perhaps because of their hostility toward Rome. It has gone on for centuries, but thanks be to God, the *sensus fidei* of believers has preferred to be despised as "pagan" rather than renounce being "Marian." And this is nothing other than an essential part of one's effort to be simply "Christian."

CHAPTER 26

MONOPOLY ON THE MIRACLES?

CATHOLICS HAVE FOR CENTURIES attributed many graces to the intercession of Mary, extraordinary and visible ones, obtained not from her but from God, through what has been called, in a sort of oxymoron, *omnipotentia supplex*, the omnipotence of supplication. Miracles, wonders, mysterious signs are indissolubly bound to Marian devotion and to her shrines. From instantaneous and inexplicable physical healing to the crying of statues, and on through a range of miracles (including cosmic ones, for example in Fatima). This too has characterized the veneration of saints, and in particular of the "Queen of Saints," who despite this has no right to the "adoration" which is reserved jealously to God alone, but receives a veneration superior to every other saint (*hyperdulia*, according to the traditional term). For centuries, theological currents have affirmed that, in the divine plan, Mary is even "mediatrix of all graces" — spiritual graces, certainly, beginning with conversions, but also corporal, material graces.

Yet, the miracles that the Christian faithful recognize and perceive do not seem to characterize only Catholicism; it is said that such miracles have been verified in other Christian confessions as well (especially the Orthodox) and even among other religions.

We read in a publication of Adhémar d'Alès, the very learned Jesuit considered among the greatest and most effective Christian apologists at the beginning of the nineteenth century, of miracles that were observed outside of the Catholic Church. To many of the faithful this can seem disturbing, and we can already hear their objection: "But isn't a miracle a sign of divine truth?" Here arises an imperious dilemma: either the supposed miracles reported outside the Catholic Church are not "true" miracles; or the Church does not have a monopoly on divine truth.

Fr. Alès pointed out this problem many decades ago, long before Vatican II. Since then, the question has become increasingly topical due to ecumenical interest and also simply to daily contact of Catholics with people belonging to other religions. It seems important to confront this problem here. Let us not forget the close connections between similar extraordinary realities and the "function" attributed to Mary in the divine plan and perceived immediately by the *sensus fidei* of the people who, in need, turn spontaneously to "their" Blessed Lady.

To propose a solution to what Fr. Alès (along with other defenders of the Faith) called "an imperious dilemma," classical theology invites us to make a rigorous discernment, a careful criticism. It is not the case that every voice that shouts "miracle" is credible. One often fails to consider that the Catholic Church is the only religious institution in the world that long ago created a scrupulous organization for sifting through the "marvels" attributed to the Divine.

The veneration of the saints has always been overseen by the hierarchy, so that it does not degenerate and to avoid superstition. Beginning with the Council of Trent, increasingly precise and severe norms have been established for evaluating allegedly holy men and women before they are presented as examples worthy of veneration and intercession by the faithful. To cross the threshold of the title of blessed and then saint, the Church presumes that type of imprimatur, that divine "visa" consisting in one or two miracles that can be verified by human science. Thus, the archives of the Congregation for the Causes of Saints constitute the largest (and really the only) deposit of the "marvels" that have been sifted through commissions constituted not only by men of faith but obligatorily also by men of science. There is no "sacred place" in the world outside of Lourdes that has a structure, inspired by the most up-to-date, impartial scientific research as the *Bureau de constatations médicales*. But this supervision extends as well to every other miraculous phenomenon tied to Catholic worship. For example, the tears of an image of the Madonna which appeared in Syracuse, Sicily, in 1953 underwent a long examination before the Sicilian bishops would authorize its veneration, which then led to the construction of a magnificent shrine.

It is fair to note that nothing of this sort occurs in any other religion, nor in any other Christian confession. To Protestants, all "miracles" are not only irrelevant but even harmful, in obedience to the framework of the Reformers, according to which faith must remain pure "scandal and folly," without any supports. Protestant theology imposed a sort of "program" on the God witnessed by the New Testament (which in fact has a few miracles of its own), a God who never stops admonishing men who seek to confine his action: "My ways are not your ways." Nevertheless, any eventual prodigious "sign" is rejected by Protestants (that is, the "historical" confessions, whereas the sects and charismatic communities often go to the opposite extreme of unbounded miracle-seeking) before even examining it, which they refuse to do, and throwing it into the obscurity of the Gehenna of superstition.

As for the Eastern churches — Greeks, Slavs, Copts, and so forth — they lack the ecclesial institutions and related codified procedures for establishing the objective truth of facts that are "out of the ordinary," in which they too believe, however, and to which they foster popular devotion. For the Orthodox as well, the ratification of the church is required before a saint can be venerated, but that ratification is not based on rational, objective methods (or at least, only in a limited way) as demanded by the Catholic Church. What counts most of all to the Orthodox is not the objective verification of miracles but the conviction of the faithful that those miracles were obtained by invoking the Virgin Mary or men and women of God.

Thus, it is a fact and not a suspect opinion of the old "Roman triumphalism": outside the Catholic structure there is a lack of instruments for discerning truth from legend, real fact from hallucination, the "this is what really happened" from the "they say," reality from illusion and fanaticism.

We add that, in the vision of faith, one must take into account the possibility that extraordinary, amazing, inexplicable facts, which are also beyond deniability, may be ascribable to superhuman powers that are not divine. The devil, in other words. It is quite peculiar what is happening in Black Africa: there, Christians, priests, bishops, who have come to Christianity from indigenous cults, do not hesitate to believe in this dark diabolical reality and in its intervention in the form of miracles performed by witches and other leaders of indigenous beliefs. It is instead the Western clergy, sensible to the rationalism of the dominant cultures in the supposedly developed nations, who tend to minimize if not repress and deny altogether such "satanic" hypotheses.

It is difficult not to agree then with the early missionaries who came into contact with priests of the terrible religions of pre-Columbian America. Only ingenuity or sectarianism or disinformation can lead one to regret Christianity's fight against those frightening beliefs. In those cults based on mass human sacrifice, on the terror of deformed bloodthirsty divinities (as witnessed by the sculptures and paintings of the Maya and Aztecs), Christians perceived demonic power that often led even to impressive "miracles."

In the discernment, then, of apparently inexplicable facts, it must not be forgotten that, in their millenary effort at self-redemption, non-Christian religions, especially Asian ones, have developed ascetic and ecstatic techniques that often seem beyond human possibilities. One thinks of the set of amazing phenomena that make up "Fakirs." It seems a good Fakir can stand still for the longest time in impossible positions; or stop his heartbeat; or fast for months; or bury himself only to reemerge alive; or resist feeling pain even when touching sharp or incandescent objects; or make water boil from a distance; or bend cutlery with his intense gaze; or keep a cord suspended in a vertical position. These are a few items in a repertoire that only with difficulty can be classified as "miraculous" and which (according to scholars who are above any suspicion of Christian apologetics) find their explanation in the illusionist techniques. Often, this collection of the unusual belongs more to parapsychology or prestidigitation than to religion.

Yet, while giving due space to cautious criticism and attempting a variety of explanations, it seems appropriate to recognize that outside the confines of Catholicism, there have indeed been "true" miracles.

How can this be explained, then? The question is not at all new, given that the problem was already faced eight hundred years ago by none other than the greatest of theologians, whom the Church has officially adopted as its privileged scholar, while not excluding exponents of other schools of Catholic thought.

The response was given by St. Thomas Aquinas who has the merit of immediately warning "exclusivist" believers, worried about the Catholic "monopoly" on miraculous signs, that the situation which so embarrasses them should not shock them, if they read the New Testament properly. In fact, it is the Scriptures which announce things upon which we must reflect attentively.

Let us see, then. First, according to the good, clarifying habits of Scholastic theology, St. Thomas takes care to make distinctions. There are "physical" miracles, but there are also "moral" miracles which consist in prophecy. These can be authentic, although they come from people so morally disqualified as even to merit eternal damnation. Speaking of the Final Judgment, Jesus said, "On that day many will say to me, 'Lord, Lord, did we not prophesy in your name…?' And then will I declare to them, 'I never knew you; depart from me, you evildoers'" (Matt. 7:22–23). One could add to this the text in John (11:51) where Caiaphas, the high priest who according to the evangelist was among those bearing the greatest responsibility for the death of Jesus, was said to have "prophesied" truthfully because "he did not say this of his own accord." He was then, inspired from on high.

Therefore, the moral miracle of prophecy is independent of the virtues of the prophet; in fact, this gift, observes St. Thomas, is *gratis datum*, that is, granted as a pure grace and *propter utilitatem aliorum*, for the usefulness of others. The prophet is only an instrument. He can announce truths independently of his virtues. There could be, for example, cases of apparitions of the Virgin Mary or other charismatic Marian phenomena (they fall under the category of "prophetism") in which the moral character of the visionaries is suspect. This too has happened. But a prophet who announces authentic realities might not even belong to the Catholic Church, but simply be an instrument chosen by God, according to his unfathomable judgment, to bring about the good of all.

Coming now to "physical" miracles, St. Thomas proposes an answer to the question of whether *utrum mali possint miracula facere* (evil people can perform miracles). Remember that, in medieval Scholastic language, the category of *mali* included heretics, schismatics, infidels, idolators, and pagans — the entire world of non-Catholics, in other words. Here as well, the answer does not come from philosophy or theology but from Scripture itself.

Let us return now to the quotation from Matthew above, where candidates for perdition, "on that day" of the final judgment, will not only say, "Lord, Lord, did we not prophesy in your name," but also, "cast out demons in your name, and do many mighty works in your name?" (Matt. 7:22). St. Thomas recalls Paul's First Letter to the Corinthians as well (13:2), where the apostle supposes that one can have faith to perform the most spectacular miracles, "to remove mountains," and yet not have love — therefore, not be truly a Christian, despite that strong faith. (Don't forget that the devil is neither an atheist nor an agnostic: he is a profound believer!)

The Gospel of Matthew reminds us of another important sign at the end of the Gospel: "For false Christs and false prophets will arise and show great signs and wonders, so as to lead astray, if possible, even the elect" (Matt. 24:24). Pre-announced by the Scriptures themselves and confirmed by the experience of two millennia, why does this possibility of a miracle outside the Catholic Church exist? A nineteenth-century theologian and biblical scholar, the famous Fr. Léonce de Grandmaison, also recalled the dramatic and mysterious episode of the Canaanite woman who implores Jesus for a cure for her demon-tormented daughter: "And he answered, 'It is not fair to take the children's bread and throw it to the dogs.' She said, 'Yes, Lord, yet even the dogs eat the crumbs that fall from their master's table' " (Matt. 15:26–27).

Grandmaison, perhaps anticipating the opening of the council, recalls how the Catholic believes indeed that in his Church the fullness of truth subsists and that she alone is "the fully legitimate Bride, at whose disposition all the possessions of the Bridegroom have been placed." But this does not allow us to impede or limit the liberality, the condescension, the generosity of the Bridegroom. The question of the Master in the parable is true for everyone, even for Catholics (precisely because they are secure of their unmerited privilege): "Am I not allowed to do what I choose with what belongs to me? Or do you begrudge my generosity?" (Matt. 20:15).

Having recognized this, we must remember a limitation set by theologians (and derived from the divine essence, of which truth is a constitutive element), beginning with St. Thomas: "To non-Catholics, and non-Christians, it can be granted to perform miracles, but God cannot permit that they do so to demonstrate that their doctrines, if false, are true."

God is love and therefore can assist beyond the confines of what, for Catholics, is His Church. But God is also truth and, therefore, He cannot without denying Himself grant signs destined to validate what is not truth or does not enjoy the fullness of truth.

Taking the example of the miraculous healings outside the ecclesial setting, admitting they are authentic (which as we have seen is not easy to verify), they address the person in need and their religious fervor, and not the truth of the doctrine which that person professes.

In Matthew 24:24 we read that there will be "great signs and wonders." But although these are "true," not only will they not validate the "false Christs and false prophets," but they will be a cause of leading people astray. Jesus is warning us of a possible trap.

Because this point is essential and must be repeated, we quote the observations of a specialist, Fabio Fabbi, professor of dogmatic theology:

> The miracle is the most certain criterion of revelation and has an intimate connection to it. The miracle, in fact, is a divine work: man can only implore it. If therefore, the miracle-worker asks for it to confirm doctrine, it is God Himself who confirms it; if a person states he is speaking in the name of the Most High and is proclaiming to men a revealed religion and performs miracles, the latter are like a seal stamped by God to authenticate the affirmations of the ambassador.

At this point, our theologian draws the conclusions which we have already anticipated in part: "God is free, but not to do evil. If, under the circumstances mentioned, He were to grant miracles without the intention of approving the doctrine of the miracle-worker, they would become witnesses of falsehood and lead those beholding them into an insuperable error. The latter, in fact, based on common sense, would take the prodigies as divine confirmation and would accept as revealed a doctrine which is not revealed."

We have attempted to summarize here what we have understood to be the position of classical theology. This is only a suggestion, a proposed response which each can integrate, in the light of new theological perspectives on inter-religious dialogue.

What we hoped to do here was simply to recall that the problem, though not new to Catholic reflection, was however anticipated in the New Testament. We also sought to show that it is possible to avoid that dilemma we cited at the beginning: "Either the presumed miracles *extra Ecclesiam* are not true, or the Church does not have the fullness of divine truth."

No. They might be "true," but not for this reason is it legitimate to deduce that all doctrines have been approved by God wherever wonders have occurred, and that all religions are equally acceptable to Him.

CHAPTER 27

The Sign of Flowers

It is nothing new when, as recently, a national TV channel shows a rerun, a golden oldie: *The Song of Bernadette,* in this case, directed by Henry King, starring the still young Jennifer Jones in the role of the visionary. The film was made in 1943, during the war, and reached Europe only after the end of the conflict, enjoying great success, as demonstrated by its continual reruns on television.

The American screenwriters took their inspiration from the book of the same name (the German original was *Das Lied von Bernadette*), written by a Jewish author from Prague, Franz Werfel. With the arrival of National Socialism, Werfel was forced to abandon his home in Austria. Fleeing to Paris, he had to escape once more when France was overrun by the German blitzkrieg. From there he went to Spain. Among the many historical facts that have been repressed is the reality that the regime of Francisco Franco (whose origins, as the name hints at, were Jewish) did not align itself with the other totalitarian regimes, including the Soviets, in their anti-Semitic laws. Spain actually welcomed a great number of Jewish refugees from German-occupied Europe.

While awaiting the journey across the Pyrenees, Werfel and his wife (also elderly) found hospitality with the Chaplains of the Grotto of Lourdes. For months, those tender religious hid the couple and guaranteed them the best hospitality which the exceptional circumstances could allow. One isolated fact is certain: during the years of the German occupation, the population of Lourdes doubled. Many of the new arrivals were Jews and found here, as in so many other places, every form of assistance possible, provided by the clergy and Catholic faithful, both to keep them in hiding as well as to help them cross the mountains, thanks to an extraordinary network of *passeurs*, local people who offered themselves as guides. It is truly a shame that this too (like everything that concerned the help given by the Church to the Jews in those difficult years) was then forgotten amid the tendentious propaganda over the "silence" or even complicity of Catholics during the persecution, beginning with the saintly Pope Pius XII.

Returning to Lourdes, very few know that the enormous painting in the parish church depicting Bernadette in the grotto was painted by an escaped Jew. Welcomed fraternally by Catholics, he converted, and when the danger had passed decided to place his paintbrush at the service of the cause of the apparitions and of their protagonist. Some of the Jewish refugees remained there after the war and, I am told, some are even involved in the sale of religious goods for pilgrims.

As for Werfel, who was already in profound harmony with Christianity, although he did not go so far as to ask for Baptism, he made a vow to Miryam, the most beautiful of the daughters of Israel, who appeared in the grotto. If he and his wife were able to take refuge safely in the United States, he would dedicate a "song" (hence the term *Lied* in German) to the little ambassador chosen for that encounter. Arriving happily in America (where he remained for the five years he had left to live), he lost no time in fulfilling the promise he had made in the foothills of the Pyrenees and wrote the poem wherein the historical data, though quite accurate, are transformed and in some ways (though in good faith) deformed.

Nevertheless, there remains some ambiguity, given that Werfel did not clarify whether at Lourdes we find a miracle—a supernatural mystery—or rather a manifestation of "spirituality," in the contrast between the instinctive religiosity of Bernadette and the skepticism, and at times materialism, of the environment around her. He also dramatized the relationship between the future saint and the superior of the congregation of Nevers. He took aim, in particular, at the figure of Mother Marie-Thérèse Vauzou, who was the novice mistress in the motherhouse of Saint-Gildard, and therefore mistress also of the little novice who arrived in the convent on the Loire in her traditional Pyrenean dress.

But as René Laurentin says, Werfel's work was "a good novel," understood with the necessary caution and clarifications, from which was created "a bad film, which provoked even worse ones." "Bad" because, despite the final repentance (Americans love the happy ending, as we all know), Mother Vauzou and the other superiors are represented as inhumane slave drivers, obsessed with inflicting more suffering on that poor ailing girl. In reality, there were problems for the aspirant who became Sr. Marie-Bernard, but not to the extent or for the reasons depicted by the clever director, Henry King, and his Hollywood screenwriters, who wished to render their subject more spectacular.

Counting on the opportunity to examine the question later, I would like to pause for a moment on a phrase that, according to the testimony during Bernadette's beatification process, was pronounced precisely by the novice mistress — the "true" one and not the one in the novel or film. To one of the sisters who spoke to her about the supernatural truth of the apparitions, Mother Vauzou said, "All the same, still the rose bush didn't bloom."

I have already mentioned in this notebook the failure of this "miracle." I recounted what happened, in the rigorously historical reconstruction given by Laurentin:

> On the evening of March 3, Bernadette called at the rectory: "Reverend Father, the Lady still wants the chapel." "Did you ask her name?" "Yes, but she only smiles." "She is making fun of you." But at this point, it came to Fr. Peyramale's mind to ask for a sign. In Guadalupe, Mexico, in the sixteenth century, the Virgin Mary made the mountainside bloom with roses in the thick of winter. "Okay, if she really wants the chapel, she must tell you her name and make the roses blossom in the grotto." The next day after the apparition: "So, what did that Lady tell you?" "I asked her name. She smiled. I asked her to make the roses blossom. She smiled again. But she still wants the chapel."

I explained in that chapter what might have been, in the light of faith, her reasons for refusing that sign. It would have been, to some extent, too "visible"; it would have convinced everyone and would have taken away the freedom to believe or not to believe. Faith is not and can never be an ascertainment: it has good reasons on its side, certainly, but in the end, a "wager" is always necessary.

But if the roses did not blossom in Lourdes, flowers have blossomed and still do, elsewhere (more precisely, in a thorn garden). It is a fascinating story that merits being told, although it is hardly known outside of Piedmont. The document mentioned earlier, originally in German and translated as *All the Apparitions of the Virgin Mary in Two Thousand Years of History*, makes no mention of what took place in Bra, now in the Province of Cuneo, in the diocese of Turin, on December 29, 1336.

On the evening of that distant day, a young bride, soon to become a mother, walked past a votive pillar on the outskirts of the town. Behind the little structure were stationed two mercenaries of an armed gang that roved the countryside in that period. Egidia Mathis (the young lady), seeing she was about to be attacked by the two wanting to rape her despite the advanced state of her pregnancy, desperately clung to the image of the Virgin Mary painted on the pillar, invoking her aid. From the niche, a bolt of light was suddenly unleashed, blinding the two bandits, terrifying them, and setting them running for their lives. Next to Egidia, Our Lady appeared and comforted her for several minutes, assuring her that the danger had passed. The vision disappeared, but perhaps due to the fright and the emotions, she went into labor and delivered her child there next to the pillar. After wrapping the newborn in her shawl, the young lady was able to reach the nearest house.

Word of the miraculous event soon reached the town, and despite the late hour, a stream of people ran to the place of the attack and apparition. There, an extraordinary scene awaited them: the little pillar was surrounded by many, thick bushes of wild plum which were suddenly covered with white flowers, despite the bitterly cold weather of late December. Ever since then, the blossoming of these shrubs has always repeated itself and on the same days.

Around the place of the miracle, devotion naturally developed, which led throughout the centuries to the construction of a first shrine, and then another next to it. Here, moreover, the vocation of the most famous citizen of Bra matured, St. Giuseppe Benedetto Cottolengo. Also, the mother of Bl. James Alberione, founder of the Pauline congregations, would come here on foot to implore the help of the Virgin Mary when her son was going through a spiritually difficult moment as an adolescent. He became a fervent devotee of the shrine of Bra from that moment. It can be said that there is hardly a saint in Piedmont that did not frequent that shrine on pilgrimage.

Quoting the writer Franz Werfel, "For one who believes, every miracle is superfluous; for one who does not believe, no miracle is sufficient." Aware of this, it must nevertheless be said that the "Madonna of the Flowers" of Bra, with its blossoming that has continued for over 650 years, constitutes an authentic scientific enigma. The bushes, which are still luxuriant behind the fence, are composed of *prunus spinosa,* known commonly as blackthorn or "scrub plum." They belong to the same family as the rose (our thoughts go to Lourdes . . .). They usually flower beginning in March if the season is mild, or April if the weather is still cold.

Since the 1700s, scientists in Piedmont (including those of the Agriculture Department at the University of Turin) have carried out in-depth studies that have established that the miraculous "thornbushes" are the same in all respects as those that grow wild pretty much everywhere. Likewise, they are the same as all the others that grow in the territory around Bra. The terrain is the same as well. There are no geophysical reasons or subterranean electromagnetic or water currents that might explain their extraordinary winter blossoming, which does not occur anywhere else. Moreover, those bushes are exposed to the north, and so make use of very limited sunlight and heat — a disadvantageous microclimate.

Naturally, as often happens in these cases, coincidences have been observed which faith leads one to consider as not merely fortuitous. For example, only in the winter of 1877–1878 did the bushes fail to blossom at the end of December. The first white flowers appeared only on February 20. The next day, news reached Bra that in that very hour, the successor of Pius IX had been elected, Vincenzo Gioacchino Pecci, who took the name Leo XIII.

Even more remarkable is the relationship to the Shroud of Turin, preserved in the cathedral of the same diocese in Turin. In the winter of 1898–1899, the blossoming extended for more than three months (usually it lasts about ten days; I myself have witnessed this), in conjunction with the solemn exposition of the shroud, during which it was photographed for the first time, revealing its mysterious nature as a negative image. On November 23, 1973, the shroud was displayed for the first time on TV, at the behest of Paul VI. That year, the blackthorn bushes around the shrine were blossoming long before the usual date and continued to do so well into the following spring. Other exceptional phenomena took place during the exposition of 1978, when three million pilgrims visited the shroud, among them a certain archbishop of Krakow, soon to be pope, taking the name John Paul II.

In this unique connection in Bra between childbirth and blossoming, the words of the poet Tagore seem to find confirmation: "Like every child that is born, so every flower that blossoms is a sign that God is not yet weary of this world." The believer knows that Mary is a descendant of the king and prophet David and that, according to tradition, one of his symbols is "the tree of Jesse," David's father. Thus, the Fathers of the Church were able to see in the prophecy of Isaiah an anticipation of Mary: "There shall come forth a shoot from the stump of Jesse, and a branch shall grow out of his roots" (Isa. 11:1). In fact, in medieval iconography, taken up for example on the portals of great Gothic cathedrals like Notre Dame in Paris or Chartres, "the Tree of Jesse" covered with flowers is always present. And this was the inspiration for a mosaic found in the two shrines of Bra: *In flore Mater*. The symbolism that links the flowers to Mary is thus profound.

What we have sought to emphasize is that in Lourdes, the sign of the flowers was not given (while the wellspring flowed with water), whereas elsewhere and for centuries, that sign was already recalling a Presence, a blessed and unexpected visit.

We return now to Mother Vauzou, the novice mistress who for Werfel, and especially for the director King, acted pitilessly toward Bernadette, but also doubted the truth of the apparitions because the roses in the grotto did not bloom. We must now reestablish the historical truth in this matter as well, as a question of justice. Those nuns were certainly not sadistic. They were well-intentioned women of God who found themselves forced to manage the case of that extraordinary novice with unimaginable delicacy. Bernadette literally had to flee Lourdes to escape from the exaltation of the crowds (among them, even princes, nobility, and bishops), who saw in her not the humble instrument but the privileged darling of Heaven, the creature capable of performing wonders. An exaltation that had devastating effects on poor Melania, the visionary of La Salette, whose spiritual and (perhaps) psychological equilibrium was altered by the intemperance of the faithful devotees.

Mother Vauzou, in agreement with the superior general of the congregation of Nevers, Joséphine Imbert, thought it was her strict duty to help Bernadette remain humble, not only by refusing her any privileges but even by bringing upon her all the austerity of that religious rule. Even if Bernadette undoubtedly suffered (though she certainly did not need to be humiliated to remain humble), she never returned a harsh word to her mother superior. She understood all too well her good intentions, her sincere conscience, aware of having to give account to God.

As for the "skepticism" of Mother Vauzou, a learned and capable woman, René Laurentin, who studied the entire dossier, summarizes the matter this way: "Her reservations about the apparitions (in general, not only for those of Lourdes) were tied to her spiritual classicism, her distrust of new devotions and charisms. Her vigorous Christocentric mindset led her to be suspicious of Marian propagations, to the point of seeing in them only popular forms of devotion."

The fact is that after advancing from novice mistress to superior general of the congregation (in 1881, two years after the death of the saint), after being reelected five times and forced in the end to resign the post due to age and health issues, among the many houses of the congregation where she could have chosen to spend her last years, Mother Vauzou chose the one in Lourdes. She passed away at eighty-two on February 15, 1907. As testified by the sisters who witnessed it, her last words were: "Our Lady of Lourdes, protect my agony." For some time, moreover, she had been in the habit of praying, and counseling others to pray, to her Sr. Marie-Bernard, with whom her relationship was surely not easy.

One day, she even went so far as to say, in the presence of those who proposed that she promote the opening of the process of beatification of the visionary, "Wait until I'm dead."

This phrase was often manipulated to insinuate doubts and suspicion about Lourdes and its human protagonist. But remaining within the perspective of faith, those words can find a sort of illuminating unraveling in a little-known episode. This is the testimony given at the first process, the one in the diocese of Nevers, by Mother Joséphine Forestier, the new superior general, who had arrived in Lourdes for the funeral of her predecessor: "On February 16, 1907, before the mortal remains of Mother Vauzou, I said in our house in Lourdes the following prayer: 'My good Mother, in Heaven one sees things differently than on earth. Now that you are, as I hope, illuminated by God's light, take up the cause of Bernadette. I leave you the initiative in this affair. I shall not act: I shall await a sign from Heaven.' "

Mother Forestier's deposition continued,

> I entrusted the content of this prayer to my two travel companions, the assistant and secretary general, and we prayed together. Little more than fifteen days later, on March 5, I received a letter from Msgr. Bishop of Nevers, written from Rome, where I hoped to find the requested sign. The bishop ignored my prayer to Mother Vauzou and wrote me, "Cardinal Vives has solicited me imploringly to begin the cause of Bernadette. He says that we must begin to gather witnesses without delay of all the people who knew her. I believe, in fact, that this is our duty." I considered the words of this saintly cardinal as an invitation of Providence.

One of the best historians of these matters, François Trochu, comments, "One is allowed to believe that this was more than mere coincidence and that the deceased Mother Vauzou, liberated from her incomprehension on earth, was in haste to make reparation for it with God Himself."

To us as well it is granted to imagine in those "heavenly meadows" the embrace (half laughing and half crying, full of affectionate sentiment) between the two religious, so different in temperament but united in the seriousness, to the point of heroism, with which they had lived day by day the message of the gospel.

CHAPTER 28

FRAGMENTS OF A FRESCO

THIS IS YET ANOTHER chapter in which I draw from the bloated folders in which I have accumulated over the years the pages of my notepads, allowing myself to be guided by chance and the curiosity of the moment.

We begin with something obvious: the visionaries, by definition, "see." And so, it is quite rare that beyond beholding Mary, they might also touch her. It is an experience that occurred in Medjugorje (according to the visionaries' account), but Medjugorje is among the apparitions that have not been recognized by the Church, or not yet at least. Among the "official" ones, the body of Mary was touched only by the hands of St. Catherine Labouré in the chapel on Rue du Bac, during the apparition in which Our Lady gave her the task of minting the Miraculous Medal.

In Lourdes, Bernadette did not have this opportunity, even though (something that is not widely known) only a few times and only at the beginning of the apparition did the Lady remain in the niche high up where the statue of Fabisch stands today. In order to converse with her messenger, the Immaculate descended through an internal opening of the grotto, placing herself next to the girl, on the ground covered with the detritus left by the water of the torrent. In this way, it was possible for Bernadette to say, every time she was interrogated, that the Lady was "tall" (or rather "short"), like her. In fact, she found her right in front of her, at close quarters, and was able to estimate well her proportions. Perhaps this was another act of tenderness by the visitor who addressed the poor little girl in her own language, in the *bigourdan* dialect; that she addressed her formally; that she preceded her request to come to the grotto with a "Would you be so kind as to...?"; and finally, that she did not want to belittle her appearance, given that Bernadette's deficient physical development was due to malnutrition, misery, and the illness that was already afflicting her. Not incidentally for believers, this is the queen par excellence: her regality includes the most exquisite courtesy as well.

In the grotto, however, the distance between the two women was never eliminated to the point of having physical contact. The contact, instead, came in 1830, in the apparitions which, as we have said, opened a series of modern appearances of the Virgin Mary.

As always happens in processes of beatification and then canonization, after several decades of burial the cause of Sr. Labouré proceeded to the exhumation of the body. This inspection, as we have already described in Bernadette's case, was carried out with all the legal guarantees stipulated by the canonical procedure, beginning with the presence of authoritative witnesses. They were the ones who confirmed what was observed when the coffin was opened: time had accomplished its process of dissolution of the nun's body, except for the eyes which had seen and the hands which had touched. These were well-preserved, as if the Lady who, already assumed into Heaven and living for eternity, had communicated her life to the flesh of the messenger she had chosen.

Rue du Bac means "Ferry Street." In fact, in the Middle Ages, one passed through that street to cross the Seine on a raft. Travelers, merchants, and above all pilgrims passed through there, especially those who were en route to Santiago de Compostela, the most popular path to which passes right through there. Could it be coincidence or yet another of the many, enigmatic signs that precisely in that ancient street, traveled throughout the centuries by innumerable caravans of penitents, Mary appeared in order to propose a medal that seems to mirror, for modern times alienated from faith, the seashell carried by pilgrims during the centuries of faith?

Kabbalah, numerology, and games with numbers can be interesting and even fascinating. But often they are no more than entertainment, an intellectual pastime.

Thus, it is only out of curiosity that I bring to light here the observation sent to me by a reader: the Immaculate Conception of Mary is celebrated on December 8, numerically 12/8. If we add these three numbers (1+2+8), we get 11. As we all know, the first apparition of the Lady who came to confirm that she was the "Immaculate Conception" took place precisely on the eleventh day of February.

I will please that reader by pointing out what he thinks he has discovered. If it really is the case of a discovery . . .

Every religious tradition, not only Christianity, has played with numbers. And also with the letters of the alphabet. I found in the *Hortus pastorum*, printed for the first time at the beginning of the seventeenth century and ascribed to Jacques Marchant, a priest born in 1585 in what is today Belgium: "Many spiritual people have noticed that the first word of the angel to Mary, '*Ave*,' has as its first letter *A* as in *Adam*, its last letter *E* as in *Eve*, and between them, as mediatrix, *V* as in *Virgin*."

Naturally, one should take into account the fact that the original language of the Gospels was not Latin but rather Greek; therefore, it would be *Kaire* and not *Ave*. Or *Shalom*, if we really want to return to what the angel actually said. The matter is curious, nonetheless. And it does no harm to mention it.

Rodrigo Borgia, elected pope (by committing simony, it seems) and taking the name Alexander VI, became a proverbial example of the degeneration of the papacy during the Renaissance. And not incorrectly: Ludwig von Pastor, the great Catholic historian who was the first to gain access to the Vatican's secret archives, judged him "indefensible" on a moral level. Yet, in what is essential to the papacy, its service as a teacher of the Faith and as a shepherd, Borgia was impeccable, often exemplary. His was one of the cases in which we must keep in mind the invitation of Jesus to "do what they say, but not what they do." A pope who lives what he teaches would certainly be the ideal. But the assistance of the Holy Spirit is not necessarily guaranteed to Peter in his moral life — only in his function as guarantor of the truth of the gospel and the orthodoxy of the Faith.

Well, the corrupt Alexander VI was exemplary also as concerns Marian doctrine and veneration. He fostered a special devotion to St. Anne. But above all, he wanted to reintroduce the ringing of the Angelus three times a day, beginning in August of the Holy Year 1500, to remind the faithful of the mystery of the Annunciation. That pious custom was until that time limited to specific places; and even there it was falling into disuse. It was this pontiff, then, who despite his corrupt private life, not only wanted it to be resumed but extended to all Christendom. And this custom, where possible (in Muslim countries the sounding of church bells is forbidden), continues still today, after five centuries.

Saints, mystics, spiritual men and women have always affirmed that Marian devotion is a sure sign of salvation: the Virgin will not permit, they affirm, that one of her devotees might be lost. Why not hope that this is the case for a pope whose name became nearly synonymous with scandalous moral turpitude? And would it not be precisely his clinging, despite it all, to Mary, the enemy of all heresy, that kept him from swerving from orthodox belief, to continue to preach well though he practiced ill?

Passing from a pontiff of dissolute life to one of saintly life: "The one who refuses to welcome the helping hand of the Mother of Jesus and our mother places in danger his salvation, blown about by the tempests of this world." This was John XXIII's message in his apostolic exhortation transmitted by radio stations around the world on April 27, 1959. Everyone knows how tender was the devotion to Mary of that pope who began his opening discourse of the council in October of 1962 by recalling that "it begins solemnly under the protection of the Most Holy Virgin, on the same day we celebrate her divine Maternity." The closing discourse of the first session, then, was pronounced on December 8 of the same year and began by remembering that the day was chosen expressly by him "so that from the Immaculate Conception an effulgence of glory might radiate."

We recall John XXIII here for the sake of a peculiar episode that is little known. The primate of Poland, Cardinal Stefan Wyszynski, revealed that immediately after his election, before appearing in the loggia for the *Urbi et Orbi* blessing, Angelo Roncalli addressed him privately. He asked him for a formal commitment: every day he was to celebrate a Mass for his pontificate at the main altar in the shrine of Czestochowa, before the Black Madonna. He revealed to the Polish cardinal that, since his days in the seminary in Bergamo, he had always carried with him an image of Mary.

This memory certainly returned to mind as one of Stefan Wyszynski's students, an ardent devotee of that image of the Virgin Mary, was called by surprise to be one of John XXIII's successors.

Poland and "its" Madonna are also mentioned in an intervention by Stefano De Fiores, one of the most important Mariologists. Fr. De Fiores writes,

> We need to open Marian piety to an ecclesial dimension which is also national in a healthy way, beginning by considering her as an element of the unity of a people, of Italians. This element is missing in Italy, whereas elsewhere it is heavily felt: the example of Poland comes to mind. Before unification, the various cities, regions, and towns of the Italian peninsula had Marian devotion as an element of cohesion. While avoiding a chauvinist spirit, we need to rediscover and display the ties of love that bind Mary to the Italian people, so present in the history of our country and its culture.

De Fiores continues, "It would be a pastoral mistake to overlook or minimize the solemn act of consecration of Italy to the Immaculate Heart of Mary (1959). Awareness of a personal consecration to the Virgin Mary, while contributing to the true and profound unification of Italy, would lead to a life coherent with one's baptismal promises." Because, he concludes, "with Mary, a baptized nation returns to its origins."

These considerations seem important and urgent for our times. For a series of reasons (one of which was the so-called "Roman Question"), Italian unity was carried out not only without the Church but against it. A unique case in Europe and perhaps in all the world: consider Latin America, the Philippines, and Black Africa. Yet, such a mosaic of different ethnic groups, histories, and cultures as there was (and still is, to some extent), this peninsula had faith as its only cement. Adoration of Christ and devotion to Mary and the saints, training in seminaries that were uniformly organized — these were the only things that pastors from the Alps or from Sicily or from Sardinia would have in common. It is also due to this struggle around its unifying element that this country was born and developed with such difficulty.

In our own times, the chickens have come home to roost. So many years after the violent occupation of Rome to make it the (reluctant) capital of a country mostly hostile toward it, now in many town squares one finds declarations of secession. It seems this is truly the moment for rediscovering (to repeat the words of De Fiores) "Marian piety as the unifying element of the Italian people." This occurs in Poland, certainly. But it also occurs in highly secular France, where the Virgin Mary venerated in Chartres has been for centuries one of the symbols of national unity. It happens in Spain, where Catalans and Castilians, Basques and Andalusians, Aragonese and Galicians — divided among themselves even more than we find in Italy and where there are many dialects but at least one common language — find in the great shrine of the *Virgen del Pilar* in Zaragoza what they so meaningfully call the *santuario de la Hispanidad,* the place where all Iberians can be recognized as children of the same Mother.

Here in Italy, perhaps Loreto could fulfill this function of unity for historical reasons and because of its geographical centrality. And this is not a political choice. On the contrary, politics, by definition, divides. Devotion and piety unite. Above all when they are directed toward the Woman who seems to love nothing more than to see her children gathered, in peace and concord, around her.

Returning to Fr. Marchant's word games, mentioned above, placing the *salutatio angelica* and Elizabeth's greeting together, believers composed what we recite still today as the first part of the Hail Mary. Archaeological discoveries and graffiti in the Near East, especially in Egypt and Palestine, show that since the fifth century, the repetition of those words taken directly from the Gospel have been in use.

But the Hail Mary as we know it in its complete form entered the Western liturgy only in 1568 with the Roman Breviary promulgated by St. Pius V. It was the result of a process that lasted centuries and that led slowly to the addition of an explicit prayer in the first part based entirely on Scripture: first came the *Sancta Maria, Mater Dei, ora pro nobis*; then the *peccatoribus,* and finally the *nunc et in hora mortis nostrae.* And this came about not through the initiative of theologians but through pressure from below.

The Benedictine liturgist Fr. Benoît Capelle, who dedicated a study to the history of this prayer, by far the most widely recited in the Church, writes,

> This gradual growth of the prayer is quite moving: the Christian people were urged in an irrepressible way to raise their cry toward that power of intercession which they felt by instinct to be that of the Mother of Christ. Not content to praise her through the words of the Gospel, they felt the need to ask for her intercession, both in

> life and in death. It is the Christian people that made the Hail Mary a cry of needy sinners.

And so, here too, the phenomenon we saw regarding the apparitions, shrines, and pilgrimages can be witnessed. It is the people who intuit, who take the initiative, who push and open the path: the Magisterium and theology follow, limited to receiving and monitoring the exigency that rises from below. Before making it official, then, the Magisterium proceeds to retouch it by completing and guaranteeing it. In this case, the theological intervention lies in that addition, immediately after the supplication *Sancta Maria*: the Church wanted *Mater Dei*, Mother of God, not Mother of Christ or of Jesus. This is the guarantee against the temptations that continuously arise from Arianism, the negation of the divine nature of the Son of Mary.

Regarding intuitions of the *sensus fidei* of the people, I am told that in Faenza, near Bologna, there is a fresco on a public wall which portrays a Madonna with a hunched back. To those who are scandalized by the image, the townspeople respond that she is the "Madonna of the desperate"; due to her constantly looking down to keep an eye on her children and to give them a hand, she ended up with a humpback.

A beautiful intuition which brings to mind another. The term in the Neapolitan dialect used to indicate the Virgin Mary by that most lovable man, St. Alphonsus Maria Ligouri, was "The Fixer of Paradise."

There was a poem by Giovanni Pascoli that remained hidden for over a hundred years and still escapes all the publishers of this famous poet. The peculiar fact is that it consists of six hendecasyllabic quatrains with alternating rhyme, dedicated to the life of Mary and in particular to the Purification (what we often call the Presentation of Jesus in the temple) narrated in the second chapter of Luke. In fact, the title given by the poet is "The Purification."

This is the story: from 1898, Giovanni Pascoli held the chair of Professor of Latin and Greek at the University of Messina. In 1901, in the guest book of a Sicilian noble family with whom he had become friends, he could not restrict himself to merely signing his name with a brief note — as was the custom — but instead wrote this poem. And that's where it stayed, buried in the book—and not only metaphorically, given that his hosts' house collapsed during the disastrous earthquake that struck Messina seven years later.

It was recently rediscovered in an eventful manner, by a professor in Bologna, Anna Maria Andreoli, and the poem has been published in *La rivista pascoliana,* a small academic journal. Only *La Stampa,* the Turin daily newspaper, has published it to the broader public, with a commentary by a critic and scholar of literature, my dearly departed friend Giorgio Calcagno. He wrote, "Simple poetry, intentionally unsophisticated. Yet, the mark of the master can be felt in its confident meter, in its musical countermelody, enriched by the phonic play so dear to him. One verse alone suffices to defend it: *E mosse, Elì, dicendo, Elì, pur ella* (And moved, Eli, saying, Eli, and she too) where the exchange between Eli (God) and "she" multiplies the refraction of the sound and creates a kaleidoscope of meanings."

Since very few besides the readers of the Turin newspaper are aware of this precious little discovery that adds a tile to the mosaic of the Marian presence in literature, I print "The Purification" here in its entirety. Although he had a foot in Masonic lodges, pacifist Tolstoyesque tendencies, and a sentimental Christianity, in these verses Giovanni Pascoli displays his sensibility before the fascination of the gospel in general and of Mary in particular.

The Purification

Odes. The days were fulfilled, and pure
Was she according to the rite of Moses.
She ascended with profound humility,
Virgin and mother, to the city of kings.

She had in her eyes the sweet ardor of a mother,
As she passed by the bushes in bloom:
But the two white turtledoves so graceful
Wept near her virginal heart.

When she entered the temple, a white ancient of days
Forgotten by death, heard . . .
There came the grinding of hinges to his ear
And moved, Eli, saying, Eli.

In the temple was an elderly lady too, born
Of Phanuel, of the tribe of Asher.
And she heard under the great arcade
The coming of those steps and a light rustle.

And moved, Eli, saying, Eli, and she too:
Now my life is to be taken by you!
And the two saw the virgin young
Carrying in her arms, Jesus, her young.

Who had in her eyes the sweet ardor of mother,
As she moved in the temple of the Lord,
And the two white turtledoves so graceful
Wept near her virginal heart.

CHAPTER 29

EXORCISING MARIOLATRY

RECENTLY, THE WEEKLY OF the Waldensian and Methodist communities in Italy placed in the limelight, with a many-column spread, the article of a pastor who is an important contributor to the journal. The piece recommended to readers the Italian translation of the book *Mary, the Handmaid of the Lord,* written by Henri Gras, a French Protestant, well-known for his activity as a freelance writer, conference speaker, and evangelical catechist. In that book review, the author observed how the Marian theme was "often avoided in dialogue between Catholics and Protestants." In fact, "the *Madonna*" (with all that this term signifies, especially in terms of devotion) is among the topics that one prefers to set aside without too much investigation, considering the ecumenical leitmotif of "seek what unites and not what divides."

These Protestants, however, denounced the fact that, over time, this sort of embarrassed concealment has not been compatible with the truth or even with realism; and therefore, rather than helping, it risks compromising a serious inter-Christian dialogue that tries to avoid being a sentimental exchange of good people trying to like each other. For these reasons, the Waldensian and Methodist journal exhorted its readers to buy Henri Gras's book, assuring them that it is "a secure and clear exposition of the Protestant perspective, presented as a friendly expression of honesty toward Catholics." Saying with candor what one believes and what one does not believe is the presupposition for all dialogue — an excellent resolution which I have always espoused.

Accepting this invitation, therefore, I immediately bought the book which, presented with such authority, promised not to be the usual pamphlet of an amateur or a visionary. It is well known, in fact, that the absence of a recognized Magisterium leaves one in the dark as to how to judge the publications that spring from the soil of the communities born of the Reformation. When it arrived in the mail, on the last page of the book (I always read the first page and the index immediately) I found these reassuring words: "Dear Catholic friend, having read these pages, know that they were not written to offend you or to judge you. My intention is to love, and love is the guiding thread of the book."

In the end, the book was a repetition of the usual Protestant biblicism, with all the usual accusations against Catholics for not having respected the letter of Scripture, especially in its "scandalous Mariology."

We shall dwell for a moment on one of its final paragraphs, with the heading "Reflections concerning Supernatural Manifestations." Professor Gras considers these and the "miracles tied to the Virgin Mary" as "phenomena of autosuggestion," or "simulation and fraud," but he immediately adds that they might also be cases of "undeniable phenomena, verified by eyewitnesses and trustworthy." Here he proclaims his certainty without hesitation: "Such manifestations, whether true or false, are certainly the effect of the activity and the power of Satan and his demons. The devil has always tried to seduce men and too often he has succeeded. His great ability consists in having people attribute to God that of which he himself is the author and instigator."

It is therefore the devil at work in the Marian devotion of Catholics (and, although he does not say it, of the Orthodox as well — but as I observed, the Protestant world "protests" only against Rome). It is the devil who acts, "imposing idolatry and making use of miracles." "Satan, the ape of God, excels in manifesting himself by means of the supernatural, the miraculous, to make people believe in his lies." According to this pastor, the entire edifice of Marian veneration lies under the sign of the diabolical: "the pious images and statues," "fingering through the beads of the rosary," "superstitions like wearing medals and scapulars or the use of holy water." Every simple prayer to Mary, being "addressed to one departed," gives rise to "a form of spiritualism with religious trappings" but which is in reality "satanic" once more. Satanic like the "paganism" at work in the dogmatic development of Mariology, as if it were "simony" in the "marketplace of piety." Thus, if there were need to repeat it, "the Virgin venerated by Catholics is an idol which the devil uses to mislead and bind souls, changing the truth into lies and drawing upon them the wrath of God." This leads Professor Gras to propose a suspicion: Catholic Marian devotion might well be "one of the essential causes of the evils afflicting our decadent civilization." Honoring Our Lady, making place for her in the liturgy and in life is therefore a sort of social wrongdoing, a temptation foreboding disaster for the whole of humanity.

What has taken place at Lourdes, Fatima, Loreto, Oropa, Czestochowa, Guadalupe, or Zaragoza, as in all the other places of veneration and shrines officially recognized by the Church — all these inexplicable phenomena are neither frauds nor illusions, but something much worse: "We can look for solutions in but one type of intervention, the demonic, while devotees await the intervention of the Virgin or her mediation; Marian veneration is one of the most sophisticated — one of the most cleverly disguised as Christian — instruments of the Adversary." Nevertheless, the author shakes his head, "How many fairy tales have we heard from La Salette, Lourdes, and Fatima, just to name three of the places where apparitions have supposedly taken place, and all this to the detriment of genuine biblical faith!"

Catholics have been warned, and not by one of the minions of the many apocalyptic sects that have germinated from "*sola scriptura*," but from a distinguished descendant of the French Huguenots, signed and sealed by the brand of "serious" Protestantism. If Catholics wish to break from their devil worship — even if it is in good faith and only because they are deceived by their shepherds, who are in league with the Evil One — then they must "seek liberation" and have themselves exorcised by a Protestant (a true Christian) "after a confession of their sins to God and after having abandoned every idolatrous practice." Namely, every privilege they grant to Mary, who is nothing other than a sister in the faith, a believer among believers. Otherwise, Catholics "shall not inherit the kingdom of God" and, as Scripture threatens, "they shall be cast out into the darkness." And as we know, "there is weeping and gnashing of teeth" out there.

We must remember that Protestantism oscillates between two extremes. On the "liberal" end, demons and the demonic (as with everything that transcends modern rationalism) are rejected as entirely unacceptable by the conscientious adult believer, as folklore of an archaic society. In "classical" Protestantism, on the contrary, belief in Satan becomes an obsession; one sees his tracks everywhere, and in fact, the true, ruthless witch hunt was characteristic until recent times of this part of the Reformed world, and not of the Catholic world.

For this reason as well, it was surprising that the Italian publisher of this *Mary, the Handmaid of the Lord*, in one of its previous notes, while highlighting the "objectivity" and the "serenity" (!) of the book, mentions his "personal reservations about references to Satan as a source of Catholic Mariology." Such references, the publisher said, would be "a drop in tone, which however does not undermine the value of the work."

This "reservation" is surprising in my estimation. In fact, the conviction of diabolical idolatry in Marian veneration is not in the least a "drop in tone": it is the logical point of arrival of the author's argumentation, according to the perspective, the principles, the framework of classical Protestantism, which seems to be united, at least on this issue. Every affirmation of this "evangelical summary on Mary," as it defines itself, is sustained by biblical verses giving them the well-known reading typical of the great authors of the Reformation.

Not incidentally, the distinguished director responsible for the presentation in the official weekly of the Waldensian-Methodists in Italy, a pastor with excellent academic credentials, not only did not express reservations but even recommended the entire text as an "optimal and clear summary, shared by the Protestant world."

For what it is worth: far from being scandalized, we do not doubt the good faith and the good intentions of those who wrote those pages. They are entirely similar to an infinite number of others that have accompanied Protestantism since its beginnings five hundred years ago. One perceives in Professor Gras (the most recent link in an uninterrupted chain) the anxiety of one who seeks to warn his Catholic brethren of the hidden traps that threaten them. Which, in fact, have already devoured them in their acceptance of that "cancer of theology" (Karl Barth's description) which is Mariology, not only in its dogmas but also in its devotion to the Virgin.

We have no problem with recognizing that this age-old controversy, this plaintive warning cry to us Marian "idolaters" is not motivated by hostility toward Mary. On the contrary, it stems from their conviction that respect for her and for her Son must pass through denunciation of the "superstitious incrustations" around her person. As Professor Gras says, "Protestants rarely make reference to Mary. They recognize her faith as exemplary, but they do not address prayers to her, nor do they offer her their devotion." And this, he explains, is "according to the Scriptures, and therefore, according to the truth."

Neither embarrassment nor scandal. Deep down, rather, a feeling of gratitude for the clarity with which he reminds us of the differences in perspectives, much more radical than current misrepresentations — objectively inaccurate (although their promoters are honest) and presented as "dialogue" — would have us believe.

What can we learn from such situations? It seems that for one thing, Catholics need to become aware once again that Mary is not a secondary element of their faith but rather an integral aspect. It is therefore not legitimate to set aside the Mother, because as the millenary theological and spiritual tradition knows, she is vitally, ontologically bound to her Son. Mariology is tightly united to Christology, so that abandoning or shrinking the former has inevitable effects on the latter. One rightly speaks today (though not without risks) of a "hierarchy of truths." The Virgin Mary is not, nor can she be or ever will be a "peripheral topic" to the system of faith, as John Paul II never tired of saying, even by means of the choice of that *Totus tuus* next to the letter *M* on his coat of arms. Ecumenism has its sacrosanct motivations; it is blasphemous to forget that Jesus prayed for the unity of his disciples. But we must also share the response that Protestants themselves have given various times throughout history, in reply to Catholic proposals: "What is truth for us cannot be sacrificed for a unity that, on such foundations, would only be hypocrisy."

One must thus take heed of the second reality: still today, what to Catholics is "devotion," to Protestants is "blasphemy"; what for us is a fruitful and appropriate veneration, for our separated brethren is a satanic deceit; what to one side is a "pious pilgrim," to the other is a poor demon-possessed person to be exorcised or a superstitious person in need of conversion. An unpleasant situation, certainly, for our impatient desire for unanimity which often risks degenerating into carelessness. But among Christian virtues is the realism of one who faces reality as it is, not as he would like it to be. And the first of the virtues which informs all the others is prudence, which evaluates each situation and acts accordingly.

On the other hand, decades of ecumenical contact have by now shown just how illusory is the conviction of many Catholics who think it would suffice to eliminate "abuses" and "exaggerations" to achieve meeting each other once again on common ground. That is not the case, though, and the book by Prof. Gras is yet another confirmation. The role of Mary in Catholicism, as we have just recalled, is not optional, because it derives closely from Catholicism's vision of God, Christ, the Church, and Scripture. It is right and proper to eliminate the abuses, as the Magisterium has always been keen to do — and not only after Vatican II, which stated, "Theologians and preachers of the divine word [should] abstain zealously both from all gross exaggerations as well as from petty narrow-mindedness in considering the singular dignity of the Mother of God." Confirming what we have said, the council (as indicated in the footnote in the official text) is saying nothing new here, but is referencing the texts of Pius XII, written at the beginning of the 1950s — texts which, according to the argument of some, were infected by a sort of "Marian delirium."

No, it is not only a question of exaggerations and abuses, but of the very hinges of the edifice of faith, wherein *tout se tient*. Right after Vatican II, a progressive Catholic theologian presented one of his treatises on Mariology, edited according to all the canons of "ecumenical correctness," to Karl Barth as a gift. The great Protestant scholar, being a polite person, thanked his colleague, but he also observed, "I gladly acknowledge that this treatise is the best, the most advanced that a Catholic attentive to the cause of Christian unity could write. But look, for us it is not a question of 'better' or 'worse': it is this Mariology of yours that must be pulled up from the roots."

For Protestantism, the incapacity and even impossibility of understanding the Marian role recognized by both Catholics and Orthodox derives also (if not above all) from that framework based on one adjective: *solus*. Thus, *sola fides, sola Scriptura, solus Deus, solus Christus*. It is the *aut-aut* (either-or) of "the one who chooses" (in Greek: *heretic*) that impedes them from making room for any other reality. It is a framework that was established immediately by Luther himself, and which, instead of weakening, has become ever more radical over time.

In that exemplary book *Mary, the Handmaid of the Lord* which we examined, the followers of historical Protestantism admit that, in the area of current evangelical fundamentalism, the controversy against "Mariolatry" assumes aspects "hysterically polemical with regard to papist superstitions." This renders the situation even more disturbing. In fact, the confessions that arose from the sixteenth-century Reformation have been continuously declining, to the point that, in Great Britain, for example, "practicing" Muslims are more numerous than practicing Anglicans. English mosques are much more crowded than the churches of the queen, guarantor of the system born of the caprice of Henry VIII. The only Protestant community in the world today that seems to have a future is the fundamentalist evangelical branch composed of innumerable storefront churches, sects, and movements. But with them it is often impossible even to begin dialogue, which they obstinately refuse with all, but especially with that "beast" of Revelation which is for them the Church of the pope-antichrist.

At any rate, the foundations for the "Marian" rejection were laid at the beginning and characterize the entire history of Protestantism. Already in 1528, Luther had written in his faulty Latin: "*Non maior blasphemia facta Mariae quam illi qui rosaria instituerunt.*" In other words, "The worst blasphemy against Mary was committed by those who invented the rosary." We see immediately an upheaval: what for the Catholic is "prayer" to the reformer is a "horrible blasphemy." It's peculiar then, that Luther was not satisfied with dethroning Mary, dethroning her by his novel theological schemas, from "mother" to "sister," from "queen" to "simple believer." It is little known that the former Augustinian friar sought to find fault and sin in her, so as to diminish her in this way as well, to dampen the veneration of many who wanted to remain faithful to her cult. The shrines of the Virgin Mary were the last to be extinguished, not only in Germany but also in Scandinavia; the people did not want to renounce them, and they often had to be closed by force and then razed to the ground to prevent the return of the faithful.

Since Luther was not able to find sufficient pretext in *sola scriptura,* which had become his measuring rod, for declaring that Mary was a sinner like everyone else, he gave his own interpretation of the episode narrated in the second chapter of Luke, in which the parents of Jesus lost sight of Him during their pilgrimage to Jerusalem and then found Him in the temple among the doctors of the law. In this way, the rebellious friar assured his listeners during a sermon, "Mary fell into the gravest of sins and, giving in to desperation shouted, 'I have committed a sin more unforgivable than that of any other woman!' Thus, before God, she fell to the level of Eve after her disobedience." For this reason as well, warned Luther, "all praise was taken from her," and God would be offended by those who believe her to be without sin and, worse still, invoke her mediation. As we see, the reformer's proclaimed rigorous adherence only to the words of the Bible suffered some exceptions according to convenience. If necessary, for the sake of confirming his a priori paradigm, even fictitious episodes might be preached.

Concerning mediation, and Marian mediation in particular, the very concept is abhorrent to Protestants, always on the basis of the principle of *solus*. Man can obtain nothing, therefore, if not by *solus Christus*. But does Scripture really support this concept? It would seem to be the contrary, observes Jean Guitton: "An invincible instinct urges us to commend our needs to others that they might pray and intercede for us (and we for them), following the example of the people in the Gospels."

Guitton recalls at least two episodes, outside the decisive role played by Mary at Cana. One of them, narrated by Matthew (15:21–28), is about the Canaanite woman whose daughter was liberated from a demon. This only happened, as the text says, because "his disciples came and begged him, saying, 'Send her away, for she is crying after us.'" The other episode is narrated by the evangelist Luke (7:1–10), where the servant of a centurion is also healed, but after mediation ("they besought him earnestly," states the Gospel) by some of the "elders of the Jews." At any rate, at the beginning and the end of each of his letters, does not Paul commend himself to the prayers of the brethren to whom he is writing?

Here, as elsewhere, one has the impression that the principle of *sola scriptura* is not in the least applied, however fundamental it might be for evangelicals. What lies outside the theological framework is considered nonexistent. Or, as we have seen Luther doing, one adds what is needed.

The Protestant denial of the Catholic understanding of mediation does not only concern Mary, obviously, but also those whom the Church has declared saints.

I have here in my archive the document generated in the spring of 1984 by the "Base Community of St. Paul" (the one founded near the basilica of the apostle, outside the walls of Rome, by the former Benedictine abbot Giovanni

Franzoni). The document was presented to the Waldensians as the basis for an encounter, not only personal but also theological. Point number seven of this "profession of faith" of a community that defined itself as adherents of "critical Catholicism" reads: "The cult of the saints and of the Virgin Mary has completely disappeared among us, although a certain Catholic Mariology remains in the cultural-religious background of some. In any case, we are no longer in the condition of a cult of the saints and of Mary as mediators of men before God."

Beyond any judgment of their orthodoxy, which is not ours to make, there is cause for mourning that they voluntarily impose upon themselves the abandonment of such consoling realities. Not only the beautiful reality of the "communion of saints," of the profound union among all believers with the possibility to intercede for all the living and the dead before the one God, but also the reality that sees in the canonized saints, and in the saint par excellence, the Mother of Jesus, the words of the Gospels made flesh and blood—that sees pages that are *in se* inert, as are those of any book, even a sacred one, come to life in the life of history. A scandal? On the contrary, fraternally, we pity brothers like these of the "base community," who forfeited a treasure (with a delay of many centuries) in exchange for an error and a burden.

The rejection of the inexhaustible mystery which the Church has discovered during these two millennia in the few verses that the New Testament reserves for Mary (without however forgetting the many preannouncements of her that the Fathers of the Church saw in the Old Testament) does not take into account the promise of Christ. The promise, that is, to send forth the Spirit who would help his followers to understand, deepen, and clarify His teaching. The solemn promise in the most decisive discourse, that according to John at the table of the Last Supper: "I have yet many things to say to you, but you cannot bear them now. When the Spirit of truth comes, he will guide you into all the truth" (16:12–13).

Because, at bottom, Mariology is simply this: slowly rendering explicit what is implicit, almost hidden, in the letter of Scripture.

Despite the refusal of Protestants to accept the (scriptural) principle of the deepening of our comprehension of the Word, of the possibility to bring into light what was previously hidden or at least not evident, the Reformation instead is based on what it officially rejects. One of the greatest Waldensian theologians of this century recognized this. In one of the most important books on Mary from the Protestant perspective, pastor Giovanni Miegge wrote, "There are effectively in the Scriptures truths that are discovered and appreciated quite late. For example, justification by faith, whose value the Reformation highlighted."

It is said, in fact, that it all began on that day when the tormented monk Luther, meditating in solitude in the corner of a tower (in a place that was, to say the least, not "theological": the latrine of the monastery), believed he understood what Paul meant to say with his "the just man shall live by faith." In the preceding fifteen centuries, no one had given to that statement the interpretation that the Augustinian believed he had suddenly understood in a sort of illumination. This is how the Reformation perspective was born. And it was born, lo and behold, by accepting the principle of "deepening," of "fuller comprehension," of "further penetration" which is at the foundation of the abhorred Catholic "Mariolatry."

CHAPTER 30

OPERATION HOLY OFFICE

FOR MANY CENTURIES, ONE of the most tenacious myths in the West was that of the archive of the "Supreme and Sacred Congregation of the Holy Office," now called the Congregation for the Doctrine of the Faith. Tales were spun of who knows what tenebrous secrets which lie hidden behind the walls of the palace next to the colonnade of St. Peter's Square.

Their opening to all scholars, a decision made by Cardinal Joseph Ratzinger, later Pope Benedict XVI, disappointed those who did not want to take into account what had often been repeated: the Napoleonic robbery and subsequent deportation to Paris (and the terrible damage that came from this), and then the plundering by the followers of Garibaldi and Mazzini during the ephemeral Roman Republic, fatally impoverished the archives through the disappearance of the most important sections. Curiously, every time "clerical obscurantism" was chased from the Vatican, the real loser was culture itself, due to vandalism, arson, robbery, and plundering.

Nor is it true that, before the complete opening by Ratzinger, the mythical archive was inaccessible. Yet, in the late 1990s, I read in *Tribunal of Conscience* by Adriano Prosperi, professor of history at the University of Pisa, "The doors of this archive remain locked in the face of scholars. The Roman Inquisition is perhaps the only historical institution in the world today that still hides its assets."

In reality, just months later, crossing the doorway that opens into the courtyard of the ancient edifice and penetrating into the halls on the ground floor where the legendary files are kept, I was immediately surprised: the hall dedicated to consultation was completely full of scholars from around the world who were consulting ancient files and transcribing dossiers like there was no tomorrow. Due to the lack of space, I had to settle for a nearby room set up as a library.

"Hidden documents"? From that first impression I could see just how false the tale really was. With a justifiable request in advance, the congregation grants free access to qualified scholars (essentially university professors) to consult the archives.

What was I doing there, I who possess only a bygone degree in "profane" subjects and am certainly not a professor? I was there in the guise of assistant to a professor teaching in universities in Europe and America, Professor (and Father) René Laurentin. Permission to enter with him was granted as an exception, with my sole task being to assist him in transcribing texts, thus sparing him the fatigue unfitting to his eighty years (though he was still vigorous).

Laurentin dedicated decades to exploring not only all the possible archives, but also private foundations, even basements, attics, and warehouses of used book dealers, in order to publish seven dense volumes of his *Documents authentiques* on the apparitions of Lourdes. To be able to describe the grotto and its natural secrets, he went so far as to don the wetsuit of a speleologist, facing the dangers and the disgust of the bats and rodents, entering the guts of Massabielle, discovering caverns with stalagmites and stalactites that created fabulous scenery.

With his scholarship as well as his detective work, Laurentin has given us practically everything. Yet with one exception: whatever was contained (or better, what one presumed to be contained) in the secret archives of the Holy Office. Long before the sleuthing of our French priest, the Sacred Congregation truly defended its deposit of files. Several scholars had requested access to research the events of 1858 and their consequences, but the cardinal prefects (still indicated at the time with the appellative "supreme") had refused. This happened to Laurentin as well, who thus in his writings had to limit himself to suppositions. For example, in the four years between the apparitions and the famous decree of 1862 ("The Immaculate Virgin truly appeared in the Grotto of Massabielle to the young girl Bernadette Soubirous"), was it conceivable that the bishop of Tarbes, the zealous and prudent Bertrand-Sevère Laurence, had not consulted with Rome? It is true that canon law of the time left to him the responsibility of judging the supernatural nature of such events, but these were so significant that one would think the "ultramontane" and "papist" bishop would have wanted the comfort and support of the Holy See. In this case, his correspondence would necessarily have been addressed to the Holy Office, and one would find there, if it actually existed, a letter with firsthand news about the early moments of Lourdes. But it could not be ruled out that there would be other unexpected material as well.

All suppositions, at any rate. As I said, the "supreme prefect" clutched his patrimony jealously.

Then the cords were loosened and permission to access the archives began to be granted to a growing number of scholars, at the behest of another scholar and former professor, Joseph Ratzinger. In the meantime, however, after having given decades of his research to Lourdes, Fr. Laurentin had moved on to other interests, though he still remained within the field of Mariology. And so, I was the one who reminded him of this matter, and encouraged him to try to obtain what had become possible to obtain. Thanks to the courtesy of those in charge at the congregation, and thanks to my cordial relationship with the cardinal prefect, which had grown through the book we produced together, the permission was finally granted. I confess that I was quite emotional that morning I flew to Rome, where Laurentin awaited me, having arrived from Paris.

Notified of our arrival, the archive had already carried out the search and extracted the material available in the depositories. So we found on the table where the worthy and amiable Father and I had sat down, the documentation about which many had concocted wild hypotheses and which for the first time was now placed before the eyes of external scholars. From the appearance of the binding, it was immediately clear, as it so often is, that expectations do not correspond with the reality. In fact, instead of great binders bulging with documents, what was placed before us was but a thin folder. Inside it was just one bit of paperwork, to which the archive functionaries at the time had given the title, dated 1873, "Concerning a complaint by Mr. Enrico Lasserre, author of the story of Notre Dame de Lourdes, in the Diocese of Tarbes in Gaul, against the *Missionaries of* the Shrine, claiming alterations of the facts and commercialization."

Naturally, both Fr. Laurentin and I already knew about this disturbing affair to which the title referred. In summary: Henri Lasserre, a young writer just turned thirty, was losing his eyesight. Curiously, upon the advice of a Protestant friend and colleague, in 1862 (the year the authenticity of the apparitions was officially recognized) he wrote to Lourdes and had the parish priest Peyramale send him a bottle of water from the spring that had gushed under the fingers of Bernadette. After a few washings, his sight returned as normal and for the rest of his life caused him no further trouble. As a sign of gratitude, Lasserre promised to put his pen at the service of the Lady of the Grotto, making her wonders known. In fact, he obtained from the bishop of Tarbes the role of writing the story of the apparitions. But, distracted by other commitments, he allowed the years to pass, putting off the moment he would take up the project.

But in Lourdes, people were becoming impatient. Therefore, the chaplains to whom the diocese had entrusted the nascent shrine, in the 1868 edition of their *Annales*, the journal for pilgrims, began to publish a *Petite histoire* in installments. In the meantime, Lasserre had also started, by installment as well, to write his history in the Parisian *Revue du monde catholique*. Unfortunately, this was to set in motion an embarrassing case that dragged on and whose echoes reached Rome, as demonstrated by the dossier that was placed before us.

The author began by accusing the priests of the grotto of imprecision and inaccuracies in their account of the events of which Bernadette had been the protagonist. Even the future saint herself was caught up in the war between the two parties against her will and in her naivete and good faith, causing her much suffering. Furthermore, Lasserre seemed to claim a monopoly over the events thanks to his mandate from the bishop. He succeeded in impeding the collection into one volume of the installments published by the chaplains in their journal.

The reaction of the religious caused the confrontation to widen and elicited accusations of "commercialization" toward the custodians of the grotto, of overcharging for the shipping of the bottled water, of speculation in the sale of the candles and other pious objects, of suspicious real estate operations, and so forth. Naturally, as the proverb warns, "what comes around goes around"; thus, the friars in turn meddled in the affairs of Lasserre. The latter not only became famous worldwide thanks to his book *Notre Dame de Lourdes*, but also made considerable profits: the book was a resounding bestseller in the nineteenth century, and not only in French. In light of his lavish earnings, the custodians of the grotto asked if he needed to have a monopoly as well, to do away with the competition.

At a certain point, the writer turned to Rome and sent the Holy Office precisely this "complaint … claiming alterations of the facts and commercialization" contained in the file presented to Laurentin and myself a good century later. Nevertheless, in the file preserved in the archives of the congregation, there was nothing really new, nothing not already known from other sources. Together with the documentation attached by Lasserre, we also found that of the defendants, as well as correspondence between Rome and the bishops of Tarbes and Nevers, where Bernadette was still living and suffering in the convent of Saint-Gildard. I confess that the only interesting aspect was to be holding the original manuscripts signed by people fundamental to the history of Lourdes and whom to that point I had only known through reading about them.

In any case, in the report of 1873 prepared by the congregation's staff so that the ecclesial hierarchy might have a clear understanding of the matter and could make a decision, the annoyance of the Holy See was evident. They immediately made clear that the issue did not concern questions of faith, which the supreme prefect was called to oversee. None of the litigants placed in doubt the truth of the facts of Lourdes. "It is only a question of authors squabbling among themselves over questions of details," wrote the pragmatic Vatican functionaries. Details such as the light in the niche where the Lady appeared: Was it manifested before or after the event? Or another: Crossing the stream, did Bernadette really describe the water as "tepid like the water we use to wash the dishes," or did she even use this expression at all? Did the visionary reproach or her companions for the use of expressions in themselves innocent but which she found unseemly, or did she not?

It is truly an odd case, as one can see, which in no way undermined the general course of events. Much more grievous, however, was the quarrel over economic questions. How much did Mr. Lasserre make? How much did the chaplains profit from the sale of water and candles? This too, notes the Roman report, is certainly not a matter for the Holy Office, which *de minimis non curat* (does not deal with trifles), but would be, if anything, a disciplinary matter left to the local bishop.

In the end, the writer was treated "like the watering can getting watered," to use the expression of Fr. René Laurentin. He had turned to Rome hoping to triumph, but Rome found him in the wrong, siding with the opinion of the bishop, who was not favorable toward him. Thus, in the sentence, the historical problems were left to historians, as they should be. The accusation of commercialization, if not outright "simony," hurled at the chaplains was not only rejected but defined as insulting; it declared that, after the inquest carried out by the local ecclesiastical authorities, "nothing was found that would merit condemnation or censure." In fact, this controversy had caused the Holy See "profound displeasure." Finally, the congregation imposed silence upon the two opponents: neither of them was to raise similar controversy in public ever again, so as to prevent scandal among the faithful who had already begun to arrive in throngs on pilgrimage and who were displaying extraordinary generosity for the construction of the new Marian city that was rising along the banks of the Gave.

With this verdict of the congregation, the documents of the archive of the supreme prefect regarding Lourdes came to an end as well. There was nothing else there — only the Lasserre affair.

Is there really nothing else in that archive? The director of the archive is sure that after the Napoleonic spoliation and the vandalism of Garibaldi's band in 1848–1849, the assets of the Holy Office have suffered no further losses. Meanwhile, it cannot be imagined that other documents on Lourdes exist in other archives in the Vatican, given that the delicate topic of apparitions was the exclusive competence of the congregation that safeguards the Faith. Thus, attentively overseeing its responsibilities, it would never have allowed other dicasteries to intervene here — other than the pope himself, of course, but in such complex cases, he too followed faithfully the decisions of his collaborators at the supreme prefecture.

And so, Laurentin and I asked, could one of the events that has most influenced the pastoral life of the Church have left such faint and marginal tracks in the central archives of the Church? A possible answer was provided by the Spanish priest in charge of the archive, Msgr. Alejandro Cifres. This answer not only alleviated our initial disappointment but helped us to see a positive side to this scarcity of documentation.

He had us notice that precisely the lack of interventions by Rome or appeals for such interventions seems to be a further confirmation of the "limpidity" of Lourdes, and thus of its truth. Other charismatic events, other Marian apparitions have provoked vast and complex files in the cross-examination of doubts, problems, requests for clarifications, disciplinary interventions, exhortations to prudence, investigation, the sending of "visitors" or whatever else. Even in the case of a final approval of cult, the decision was often preceded by a tortuous process with advocates and opposition, with bishops in difficulty or at least perplexed, and who for this reason turn to Rome for advice and support. In this regard one might recall La Salette.

Well, nothing of the sort for Lourdes. The meager spoils of those who had the privilege of investigating the Holy Office's archives for the first time are confirmation of what was already known. There has been much controversy stirred up outside, but not inside, the Church (and this external opposition is obviously a good sign, in the Gospel sense) regarding the events at Massabielle to which Bernadette testified. As the men of the Holy Office noticed in their reports back in the 1800s, in the lively dispute between Lasserre and the priests, what was at issue was certainly not the truth of an event that no one doubted. On the contrary, precisely the certainty that the Mystery of God had been manifested there led to such an impassioned confrontation.

Nevertheless, one can be tempted by bitterness in finding that, around a place that was born for the edification of believers and the conversion of the incredulous, a prestigious Catholic writer and the religious custodians of the shrine accused each other of economic profiteering and of altering the historical facts. This reciprocal invective of illicit enrichment and inaccuracy is a sad picture, as the Holy See did not fail to notice as well.

Yet there is perhaps a lesson to be drawn from this too. Lourdes is a metaphor of the gospel: its proclamation always provokes great enthusiasm and great betrayals; it brings to light the nobility and the misery of man. The entire Church, gathered in that place ("I want the faithful to come here in procession," said the Lady), is not a sect of "favorites," nor a Cathar church of those "without stain." It is the fishing net drawn up from the sea with all sorts of fish in it; it is the great field where the good grain is mixed with the tares, where saints coexist with the mediocre and the just with sinners.

The sign of sin (in the world and, therefore, in the Church, all are called to embrace, forgive, and redeem it) is manifested in those misunderstandings, perhaps in good faith; with that rigidity confused for defense of the truth; with those egoistic demands of exclusivism; with seeing the sliver in our neighbor's eye but missing the plank in our own; with all that seems to characterize the clash between Lasserre and Father Sempé, the rector of the chaplains of the grotto. This is life, this is humanity, and this is also the Church which Christ wanted to be holy in its essence and yet is sinful in its men. This too is Lourdes, which is fully integrated into the history of the Church — an extraordinary occasion of grace, certainly, but also a temptation for the fragility of men. A sign of salvation and a stumbling block. Just like the gospel, in fact.

I confess that on the plane home from Rome that evening, I did not have the impression of having wasted the day. There had been no sensational discovery from our incursion into the mythical archive — but maybe grist for the mill of reflection, an end more important than turning up who knows what document that had previously been ignored.

As for documents concerning Lourdes, I would like to speak now of a man who is not inaccessible but is surely known to few, at least outside the Salesian world. I am thinking of Don Bosco.

Everyone knows that the life of that great saint was inconceivable without the presence of Mary, who was to him more than a devotion: she was a concrete, daily experience. But I do not wish to explore this too far at the moment, given that the entire following chapter will be dedicated to the topic. For now, we recall merely that, before becoming the apostle of devotion to the Virgin Mary, whom he wanted to be invoked above all as *Auxilium christianorum* (Help of Christians; the Battle of Lepanto is the background, and this is the title inscribed on the basilica of Valdocco[12]), Don Bosco was a most tenacious advocate for the proclamation of the dogma of the Immaculate Conception, to the point of offering his life that the definition might be achieved. Possibly, the last hesitations of Pius IX, who esteemed him so greatly, were overcome precisely thanks to his exhortations to conclude that millennia-long journey.

[12] Editor's Note: The Basilica of Our Lady Help of Christians in Turin, built by St. John Bosco in the 1860s. Valdocco is a neighborhood in Turin.

As concerns Lourdes, one is left speechless: according to the vast *Biographical Memoirs* written by Don Bosco's secretary Giovanni Battista Lemoyne and still today considered the primary historical source on his life, the Novena of the Immaculate of 1858 already had as its theme the preaching to youth of those apparitions, the last of which had taken place in mid-July of that same year! If this is how matters stand (and there is no need to doubt it), it is highly likely that the institute of Valdocco was the first place, and not only the first in Italy, where devotion to Our Lady of Lourdes began.

Over the years, the saint would dedicate to her many writings and an infinite number of homilies and "good-night thoughts." As for the document we mentioned, found in the eighteenth volume of the *Biographical Memoirs,* we shall consider it in the following chapter.

CHAPTER 31

THE "ASSOCIATE" OF DON BOSCO

AT THE END OF the preceding chapter, we mentioned a truly peculiar episode, practically unknown, that involved the great names of the English aristocracy and that tie St. John Bosco to Lourdes even more closely. We write "even more" because, as we have already seen from the *Biographical Memoirs* by Fr. Lemoyne, from the Novena of the Immaculate in 1858, the saint's preaching had as its object the apparitions to the "pious Bernadette," as he called her. An extraordinarily early instance of the cult, given that only in 1862 did the Church officially recognize the veracity of the events of Massabielle. But the same occurred in 1846 as well, when the events of La Salette immediately found an echo in the catechesis of the thirty-year-old priest from Castelnuovo.

The Catholic environment in Turin was particularly receptive to what took place in nearby France. For example, concerning Lourdes and the haunts of Don Bosco: he was able to remain in the capital of Savoy (instead of being relegated as assistant parish priest in some village of the diocese at the foothills of the Alps, for which he had been earmarked) thanks to the intervention of his extraordinary spiritual director, Fr. Giuseppe Cafasso. That saintly man obtained for the young priest, whose abilities and extraordinary spiritual mettle he had intuited, a spot as chaplain in one of the institutions that had just been founded right in Valdocco by that great figure whom we shall soon see elevated to the altars, Juliette de Colbert, a Vendean noble lady given in marriage to the richest man in the Kingdom of Sardinia, the Marquis Carlo Tancredi Falletti di Barolo.

Remaining childless, the devoutly religious couple invested much of their wealth in a series of impressive charitable projects, such as a new cemetery in

Turin, which the city government did not have the money to construct. Among the works of the Barolo couple was the construction of the large, beautiful parish church for the new neighborhood in Turin, Vanchiglia, following the plans of Alessandro Antonelli, who also designed the Mole Antonelliana.

The church of Vanchiglia was dedicated, by unanimous consent, to St. Julia, in honor of the charitable marquis. In the chapel that opens next to the high altar, a copy of the famous statue of the Immaculate Conception from the Grotto of Lourdes is still honored. According to tradition, supported by the documents, this is the first image of Our Lady of Lourdes to arrive in Italy and to be displayed in a church for the veneration of the faithful.

Another privilege for Turin was added to this in 1958. During preparations for the centenary of the apparitions, the Grotto of Massabielle was purged of all extraneous elements, to return it insofar as possible to its primitive state. Among the things removed was the large iron grate constructed by local artisans just after pilgrimages to the grotto had begun, which closed off access to the inside of the cave. Millions of imploring hands had clung to those bars over many decades. That metal was a mute witness to the massive expression of faith and miracles.

The bishop at the time of the centenary, Pierre-Marie Théas, impressed by the great number and fervor of the annual pilgrimages of Fiat auto plant workers, decided to give to Turin that relic so full of meaning and sought after by dioceses around the world. Since 1960, the iron grate surrounds a statue of the Immaculate made expressly for the occasion, placed in the square in front of the ancient church of Santa Maria del Monte, which overlooks the Po River and which the Turinese call "Monte dei Cappucini" (Capuchin Mountain).

Returning to Don Bosco, we shall now tell the story concerning him in the eighteenth volume of the *Biographical Memoires,* the work continued by Eugenio Ceria after the death of Fr. Lemoyne.

The event was reported by Fr. Cyril Martindale, the son of a famous English lord, who converted to Catholicism and became a Jesuit. The Martindale family was connected in kinship with the Duke of Norfolk, one of the oldest and most famous families in England, and one that had always remained Catholic despite the threats and even violence throughout the centuries by the Anglican dynasty. Henry, the fifteenth duke of that dynastic family, married Lady Flora, the Baroness of Donington, in 1877. They had just one son, but he was born with a serious disability and unfortunately was completely blind. To obtain the grace of a cure or, at least, of resignation, the famous couple went on several occasions to Valdocco to visit Don Bosco, whom they admired and of whom they were munificent benefactors. All English Catholicism was anxious: if the only child of the Duke of Norfolk, the great protector of the Roman Church in the Anglican kingdom, were to die, and if the duke was not able to have any other heirs, both the wealth and the titles would pass to the Protestant branch of the family, which was hostile toward the despised "papists."

In the *Biographical Memoirs* Fr. Martindale testified to the following:

> The Duchess of Newcastle, a great English Dame, relative of my parents and intimate of the Duchess of Norfolk, went to Lourdes in 1877 to implore her for a cure of her friend's only child, so ill-fated. This woman, neither easily stirred to emotions nor endowed with a wild imagination, had the experience of a phenomenon which caused her to fear for her mental stability. While praying in the grotto, she seemed to hear a voice that told her, "Pray for the mother, do not pray for the son!" She turned around, but saw not a living soul. Soon those same words were repeated to her, wherefore she was quite moved, and this feeling accompanied her all the way back to Turin, where she went to meet with Don Bosco.

Fr. Martindale continues,

> Arriving in the Italian city, the Duchess of Newcastle obtained an audience with the saint. When she entered the room where he worked and received visitors, the priest was writing and continued to do so, without noticing his visitor, who did not know how to react to such an attitude in a man of God so highly esteemed for his exquisite courtesy toward all he met. Finally, Don Bosco set his pen down calmly, turned to the noblewoman and said suddenly, but in a serene tone, "Pray for the mother, not for the son." Exactly as in Lourdes! Amazed and concerned, the lady prayed in the adjacent church of Mary Help of Christians as she had been advised. She returned to London, and four days later her friend the Duchess of Norfolk died.

As a verification of the episode, Fr. Martindale simply presented himself and his vocation. News of the Norfolk case naturally spread and was discussed in English aristocratic circles, and it reached the ears of the Anglican Martindale family as well. The young Cyril was profoundly struck, and this began the spiritual turmoil that led him to leave the Anglican communion and not only become Catholic but even enter the Society of Jesus. There he was one of the most active and prestigious members, a religious who observed the Rule impeccably.

One owes Fr. Martindale a debt of gratitude for having preserved the memory of an event that seems much more than an edifying anecdote. In fact, it points to the emergence of a mystery of "correspondence" between the patron saint of youth and the Virgin Mary who appeared to the young Bernadette; between the shrine in the Pyrenees and that in the Alps at Valdocco. A correspondence which seems to have begun immediately: we saw how Don Bosco did not hesitate to recognize the truth of Lourdes, to the point of proposing it to his youth just four months after the end of the apparitions. This made Valdocco one of the first places not only in Italy, but in the whole world, where, preceding even the judgment of the Church, the cult of the Immaculate "according to Bernadette" began.

In any case, even episodes such as the "English" one confirm what was written by his biographer, Fr. Lemonye: "Between the Virgin and Don Bosco there was definitely a pact." A "pact" which led him to become an instrument for the renewal of a devotion that was embodied in stone and marble as well.

The great temple dedicated to Mary Help of Christians, whose domes rise from the infamously insalubrious lowlands of Valdocco, is not there by chance. On the band that circles one of the domes is written in legible letters the words *Hic domus mea, inde gloria mea,* "Here is my house, from here my glory goes out."

These were words that Don Bosco attributed to the Virgin Mary herself. In fact, beginning in 1844, a series of dreams told him that he was to build an "enormous and exceedingly tall" church in honor of Mary and for which he was even shown the design. But only later he began to have another dream, in which the Mother of Jesus pointed to the plot of land (which in fact Don Bosco had called "the field of dreams") and marked with her foot a precise spot, saying: "Here, where Saints Avventore, Ottavio, and Solutore shed their blood for the Faith, I want my name to be especially venerated." The saint would later say that he perceived (and this time not in a dream but awake) a luminous globe indicating a place, and from the ground he saw the future basilica rising with the dome that radiated light.

Don Bosco favored the etymology of Valdocco that posits its origin from the Latin *Vallis Occisorum*, or "valley of those killed." The killed were soldiers who had escaped the massacre of the Theban Legion (composed of Christians) by the assassins of the pagan emperor. The exact place of their martyrdom, indicated by Mary in the mysterious visions, is marked in the basilica with a golden cross on the floor of the reliquary crypt, to the right after entering the main door.

Here too, then, is a connection with Lourdes: Massabielle and Valdocco were not chosen by man but by Heaven itself. From a human point of view, both places were to be avoided for constructing anything, not to mention great shrines!

In Lourdes, the river had to be rerouted and the hillside dynamited to create a foundation in the rock on which to build the first church. But the others that followed—that of the Rosary and the underground church excavated for the centenary—also created serious challenges for the architects due to the water from the Gave that filtered deeply into the soil.

In Turin, the difficulties were no less challenging to overcome. The plot indicated by Our Lady was not owned by Don Bosco, and the owners had no intention of selling it. Furthermore, halfway through the planned building site ran a public road, which the hostile, Masonic city administration had no desire to move. In any case, technicians warned that the area, like Lourdes, was marshy, being a floodplain of the nearby Dora River. Thus, both the lack of stability of the terrain as well as the continual and massive infiltration of water would not allow them to build a structure as large as that desired by Don Bosco.

Even his disciples jumped into the fray, insisting on moving the project to an adjacent area where not only was the land more suitable but the basilica would have a greater impact and greater visibility. Furthermore, it would be more accessible for the inhabitants of the neighborhood being constructed nearby, which did not have a parish church to allow them to fulfill the Sunday obligation. But the saint was unmovable: that was the spot indicated by Mary, therefore that was the place where he had to build the *domus magna* that she wanted. And there, finally, they began digging, finding the aquifer immediately (as foreseen), which multiplied difficulty and costs, due to the doubling or tripling of the dimensions of the foundations. If this was not enough, they even employed a system of oak piles, as in Venice; they took advantage of this to create large underground spaces with vast halls.

A century later, this proved to be providential. It was there that the "Marian Documentation Center" established its headquarters, created and directed by the Salesian Fr. Pietro Ceresa, recently deceased. Through his passionate work, he was able to gather testimony of devotion to the Virgin Mary from all times and all nations. It is one of the largest public collections in the world, a way of showing the concrete fulfillment of the prophecy in the Magnificat: "All generations will call me blessed."

Naturally, as is always the modus operandi with the saints, work on the great church began without a dime (no, to be precise, they had forty cents, as Don Bosco recalled when all the work had been finished). Equally typical, and just as he expected, the money began to arrive as if by magic just as it was needed.

That "mad priest" (as many considered him, even within the Church, and there were even attempts to commit him to an insane asylum) had proclaimed from the very beginning, as the realist and visionary he was, "It is Our Lady who wants the church, she will take care of the expenses. I am only her treasurer who pays the workers and artists." His estimate, at the start, was a cost of 200,000 lire; the architect and foremen estimated the need for 500,000. In the end, the cost exceeded the astronomical sum (for that time) of a million lire. As he explained, at least 800,000 had come from the faithful, in gratitude for graces received from Our Lady Help of Christians. Well, he was right when he repeated that there was not one stone in that enormous, resplendent edifice that was not marked by some miracle.

On the façade of the basilica, one reads in large script: *Maria Auxilium Christianorum ora pro nobis.* The symbol of Our Lady Help of Christians is in the enormous painting (more than twenty-three feet tall) that dominates the high altar and that was painted following the instructions of the saint, who tormented the artist by insisting that he not only respect what he wanted but that he add more and more symbols. In the end, he burst out, "Don Bosco, to put everything you want it would take a painting as large as Piazza Castello!"[13]

On top of the main dome, 230 feet from the ground and double its natural size, stands the statue not of Mary Help of Christians, but rather of the Immaculate Conception. In fact, on December 8, 1841, the young priest encountered the little wandering mason Bartolomeo Garelli in the sacristy of St. Francis of Assisi, which was the beginning of all his work with youth.

For many years, the veneration of Mary as the Immaculate seemed to predominate in him. Then, almost abruptly, nearing the years in which he decided to set to work on the great basilica, the invocation of Mary as *Auxilium Christianorum* began to prevail. In fact, at a certain point, the saint revealed some of his mysterious interior life: he once let it slip that "no one will ever know most of the things I have done in my life." He revealed himself a bit, therefore, and confided first to his fellow Salesians and then to all the youth that "it is Mary herself who wants to be invoked under this title." In the vision of May 26, 1862, known as the "dream of the two columns," he saw the enemies of God engaged in a furious naval battle against the Church and the pope. In the midst of the melee, two columns arose miraculously from the waters to protect the boat whose helmsman was the Vicar of Christ. On the first column stood a large Host; on the other, the Immaculate Virgin Mary, with a large sign at her feet on which was written, "*Auxilium Christianorum*."

From that time on, and in an increasingly exclusive manner, he made himself the apostle of this devotion, which had ancient roots in the Church. Renewed enthusiastically by the pope of Lepanto, St. Pius V, it had already been used as a Marian invocation for centuries.

Why this predilection of Don Bosco for Mary as Help of Christians?

It must be pointed out first, from a perspective of faith and familiar with his extraordinary life, that we cannot speak of *his* choice, but rather the choice of Another, of whom he was only an instrument.

The question then becomes: Why was he "asked" to revive that Marian title and in that particular moment? As a Salesian scholar observed, "This title of Auxilium Christianorum directly emphasizes the public and social form of

[13] Editor's Note: A large and prominent city square in Turin.

mediation that the Holy Virgin exercises, not only for the good of this or that person, institution, or nation, but above all in favor of all the Catholic Church and its head the Pope, especially in its most dramatic moments and in the face of its most urgent needs and most insidious dangers."

This is not, then, a "private devotion," but a cult for the entire Church, which, during the times of Don Bosco, was in a dramatic confrontation with modernity, facing an assault not only on the ecclesiastical institution but on faith itself, through Masonic deism and through the freedom of religion and propaganda granted to anyone, especially if they were hostile to Catholicism. According to the saint, there were two forms of remedy and defense: the two columns he saw in the vision of 1862 — in other words, Eucharistic adoration and Marian devotion. But not a personal, intimate devotion, as it had been practiced in Christendom. As this dissolved, it was now necessary to invoke Our Lady who is both maternal and combative, a Mother in the most difficult moments: the Help of Christians deployed in battle.

For this reason as well, just before his death, the saint said, "We are heading toward times in which every good Catholic must not fail to discover why Mary wants to be invoked above all as *Auxilium*."

These words have not lost their pertinence, even today.

CHAPTER 32

The Rosary—and Not Only

Once again we draw a file from our archive. This one deals with the Rosary. Here are two "literary" quotes, among the many possible. One is from Lacordaire (1802–1861), a Dominican but also a writer and preacher so highly esteemed that he was received into the *Académie Française*. To those who objected to the repetition for fifty times of the same Hail Mary, Lacordaire replied, "Love knows but one word. Saying it continually, one never repeats it."

Then there is a quote from another immortal of the *Académie*, François Mauriac: "Clutching in one's fist the rosary is like taking one's mother by the hand as she guides us in crossing a road." Also worthy of the history of literature is the intuition of a spiritual man of the Middle Ages, for whom the beads of the Rosary were "the berries on a divine tree."

We come to two other pages, this time written by theologians. One was among the greatest of the twentieth century, Hans Urs von Balthasar, who, in some ways, completes Lacordaire. For von Balthasar as well, the value of the Rosary was found in the continuous return of the same words because, in that way, "the Hail Mary becomes a sort of breath of the earth and sigh of humanity toward Heaven."

For the great French poet Francis Jammes, the diabolical aversion to the Rosary (claimed by mystics) stems from this: "To complete such an easy action suitable to children and the elderly such as fingering through the rosary, one must completely vanquish human respect and pride, the children of Satan. If the latter harbors so much hatred toward this devotion, it is because he rightly sees an abyss of humility and the weapon of the poor of spirit according to the Gospel."

Here is something on the Rosary from the words of Paul VI, the pope to whom it befell to suffer over the presiding of the Church through what the German theologian Wolfgang Beinart called "the decade without Mary." The period that began in 1964 with the approval of *Lumen Gentium* and the subsequent "reaction of rejection" (although entirely unjustified, because the council certainly did not want it) on the part of some of the intelligentsia, not only toward devotion but at times toward Catholic Mariology in general.

That "Marian winter" ended in February of 1974 with the publication of *Marialis cultus,* the apostolic exhortation on the cult of Mary signed by Pope Montini. Confirming this eclipse of the Virgin Mary in the Church, some cited the meaningful example of the assembly of Latin American bishops at Medellín (1968) and Puebla (1978). In the minutes of the first meeting, which took place in the year that became a symbol of protest, and even clerical protest, the name of Mary never appears, for the first time in the history of the Church. Ten years later, at Puebla, those bishops (many were the same as in Medellín) showed that they had recovered, or were recovering, the Catholic tradition. And this was inevitable, for *sine Maria non est Ecclesia.* One phrase in the final document of the assembly in Puebla says, "By means of Mary, God became flesh. Without her, the Gospel is disincarnated, deformed, transformed into ideology, into spiritualist rationalism." And this is, it seems, an excellent synthesis (and quite pertinent to our times) of the necessity of safeguarding the "Marian principle." In a previous chapter, I sought to point out this synthesis.

But the shift had come four years earlier, in *Marialis cultus,* which "broke the ice." Its title is also that of one of the three parts in which it is organized. One is called, "Observations on Two Exercises of Piety: The Angelus and the Rosary." Paul VI says here that he is in full harmony with his predecessor Pius XII: "The rosary of the Blessed Virgin Mary is a compendium of the entire Gospel." Montini's text is quite beautiful and merits a rereading. Not only did it close the period of eclipse (in the course of which, for the first time since the Reformation, the Church lost a fourth of its clergy and even more religious) but it prepared the future as well. In fact, Pope John Paul II on many occasions recalled *Marialis cultus* with admiring conviction.

We would like to point out, however, an aspect that is little known. After pages in which, with experience united to love, this "pious exercise" is praised, reaffirmed, and reproposed, Paul VI concludes in this way: "The Rosary is an excellent prayer; but the faithful should feel serenely free in its regard. They should be drawn to calm recitation by its intrinsic appeal."

A few chapters earlier, I pointed out the observation of a sociologist that pilgrimage (directed for the most part toward shrines dedicated to Mary) is "*proposed* to everyone and not *imposed* on anyone." For good reason, the *sensus fidei* perceives those sacred places as free spaces. Paul VI reminds us that even regarding the Marian prayer par excellence, the glorious Rosary, the believer must feel "serenely free." It is not precept but rather the need of the heart which must lead the believer to place himself in an attitude of veneration ("in composed tranquility"), of praise, of colloquy, of prayer before our Mother. Does not every form of compulsion extinguish love? This is what the old, long-suffering pope wanted to remind us of through this delicate yet profound touch.

Putting aside for the moment the Rosary, we come to a file with the words of John Henry Newman, the great Anglican theologian whom we have already encountered, who was received into the Catholic Church and became a cardinal. On many occasions he sought to convince his brethren who remained Protestant that Catholic devotion to the Blessed Virgin not only is not superstition or betrayal of the purity of the gospel, but is the fitting development of the logic of faith. After many observations of lofty erudition, subtlety, and theological wisdom, in the end Newman allows the traditional British pragmatism to re-emerge: "Well, who is it who wrote not only with words but also in their lives, the most beautiful pages on the one who for us Catholics is the Blessed Virgin? Who, if not the saints (all of them without exception), namely, those Christians who abandoned everything to follow Christ, to imitate his life to the full?"

An appeal to experience, then, following the example of concrete life. Perhaps we too have need of this, today, as we are ever more tempted by the words of many documents, conventions, and "debates" that only lead to more words.

Newman, as we know, was received into the Catholic Church by Pius IX. This was the same pope who had the courage to terminate almost a thousand years of often heated debate in the Church by proclaiming the dogma of the Immaculate Conception.

On the morning of December 8, 1854, in St. Peter's before fifty thousand of the faithful (the full capacity of the largest church in the world), there were fifty-three cardinals, forty-three archbishops, and ninety-nine bishops. It was the largest assembly of bishops in the history of the Church since the conclusion of the Council of Trent, three hundred years earlier. A contemporary chronicle of that historical day reads, "The proclamation of the dogma lasted for over eight minutes. And the Holy Father, deeply moved by the great act he was carrying out, from time to time lost his voice and had to interrupt his speech due to sobs and tears. Sobs and tears which admirably communicated to all those present."

This gives clear testimony to how the Church, in all that concerns Mary, has experienced the austere dogmatic truths not as a bookish, abstract reality but with impassioned participation, to the point of tears — the appropriate "reasons of reason" but next to them, the "reasons of the heart."

The historian biographer of Pius IX, Giacomo Martina, wrote, "The Church responded to cold, introspective positivism with a vigorous affirmation of the supernatural, expressed in a warm devotion accessible to the masses. Not a little flock, not a group of elite intellectuals, but an immense people, the net thrown into the sea that gathers in every type of fish.... This was the Church envisioned and sustained by Pius IX!" A precise strategy carried out by the slandered Pope Mastai Ferretti, a plan which entrusted to the presence of the Virgin Mary a decisive role. Considering the extreme difficulty of the times, its results still amaze us today for their efficacy and duration. This is another lesson of history that is worthy of our reflection.

In the second chapter of the Acts of the Apostles, we read of the descent of the Holy Spirit and the discourse of the disciples to the gathered crowds. Peter, "standing with the eleven, lifted up his voice and addressed them," declaring that what the prophet Joel had foreseen was taking place in that very moment:

> And in the last days it shall be, God declares,
> that I will pour out my Spirit upon all flesh,
> and your sons and your daughters shall prophesy,
> and your young men shall see visions,
> and your old men shall dream dreams;
> yea, and on my menservants and my maidservants in those days
> I will pour out my Spirit; and they shall prophesy.
> And I will show wonders in the heaven above
> and signs on the earth beneath,
> blood, and fire, and vapor of smoke. (Acts 2:14, 16–19)

Why this quotation? Because Fr. René Laurentin reminded us of it. Since many in the Church criticize and look skeptically on his long efforts in this field of Marian apparitions —as fascinating as it is full of landmines — as well as on charismatic phenomena in general, the scholar recalls the attention of Christians to this passage. "These words are often forgotten," Laurentin said, "yet they are decisive words, because they constitute a sort of foundational discourse of the newly constituted Church. It is like a charter, the Constitution of eschatological times that began with the resurrection of Jesus."

How then can we not also think of the likes of Bernadette, or Melania, or Lucia and all the other visionary children or adolescents, rereading words like those prophesied by Joel already in the Old Testament and whose fulfillment Peter was announcing: "Your young shall see visions . . ."? And how can we not return to Fatima when we hear "And I will show wonders in the heaven above . . . fire and vapor of smoke"?

This then is the "self-defense" (as if he needed it!) of one who spent time, energy, and even underwent religious anxiety in his efforts to examine the "reasons of credibility" of mysterious signs which, instead of diminishing, seem to be multiplying throughout the world today.

In this regard, we need to make a clarification about the seers of the Marian apparitions, true or supposed, recognized by the Church or not.

Often, beginning with the most famous cases of the previous two centuries, one is convinced that those privileged to have an encounter with the Blessed Virgin are preferentially children or adolescents, girls rather than boys, poor or even extremely poor (often shepherds and shepherdesses). This is the conviction of writers of a mystical vein such as Joris Karl Huysmans who, after his conversion to Catholicism, published in 1906 *Les foules de Lourdes*, a sort of believer's response (although critical, often pungent, in the name of aestheticism) to the desecrating work by his old master Émile Zola, *Lourdes*. Huysmans wrote that, appearing in Paris in 1830 in Rue du Bac, unable to favor a little shepherdess in the great metropolis, the Virgin Mary, who was in the habit of "choosing beings who were entirely uncouth and limited, set her eyes upon a former country servant, who entered the novitiate for poor girls without dowries."

It seems, however, that the stereotype of the visionary as a female adolescent of very humble background, though not lacking in numerous examples, is just that: a stereotype that often does not correspond to reality. In fact, we have a study carried out years ago by Fr. Giuseppe M. Besutti, one of the greatest Italian Mariologists. That religious priest directed his systematic investigation toward the Marian apparitions behind the construction of 190 shrines in Italy, especially the oldest ones. The results show that the visionaries are almost equally distributed between male and female, that adults are in fact more numerous than children or adolescents, and that no single social class is privileged more than others, at least in an exclusive manner. Thus, next to servants he found aristocrats, next to peasants, the bourgeois — though the poor, in the material sense, do constitute the largest group.

Fr. Besutti's research was limited to Italy and the apparitions behind our shrines. But these results were essentially confirmed by an investigation carried out in the 1980s by an American institute of religious sociology directed by Michael P. Carrol. As a cross section, he took one hundred cases from the second Christian millennium from every country in Europe. The results show that the beneficiaries of those encounters with Our Lady were men in 58 percent of cases, above eighteen years old in 62 percent of cases, and were not able to be classified in any homogeneous social class.

Exemplary cases such as Bernadette (and of all the other poor and little ones) must not lead us to forget the sovereign freedom of the God of Jesus Christ, who is, on every occasion, beyond our mental paradigms. He also addressed the idea of the association in all cases of the visionaries with sanctity (or at least an exemplary life). According to Catholic theology, "charismatic" phenomena in general (apparitions, visions, and gifts of prophecy in particular) belong to the category of grace *gratis datae*. They are granted, in other words, not because the beneficiary has merited them by their virtue. They are not "confirmations of sanctity," and it is not even necessary to be in a state of grace to be favored by them. We have already examined this matter.

We should not be amazed then by the results of these studies that show how divine freedom is manifested even by choosing sinners, unbelievers, perhaps even "heretics" and "schismatics" in manifesting such signs. These, in fact, are not foremost aimed at the good of the recipient, but at that of the Church, of all humanity even. We must not forget, then, that the studies we have cited rob the usual objection of its value: that the "apparitions" are an illusory effect of hormonal imbalances of adolescents, the fruit of hysteria, the byproduct of misery and ignorance. We find confirmation that this is not the case in the fact that the encounter with the Mystery takes place for the most part among categories of people not typically suspected of those conditions.

One last bit, a thought by the well-known moral theologian Bernard Häring: "Whoever speaks of Mary and has a hard, closed heart is a liar. Because Mary is the Mother of mercy and attentiveness."

CHAPTER 33

THE ENIGMA OF BANNEUX

THE SERIES OF RECOGNIZED Marian apparitions in Europe that began in 1830 in Paris in Rue du Bac with the Miraculous Medal seems to have ended in 1933. In that year, the Virgin Mary appeared in Wallonia, part of French-speaking Belgium, in the village of Banneux Notre-Dame. Actually, in 2002, the bishop of Haarlem recognized the truth of the apparitions that occurred in Amsterdam from 1945 to 1959 but did not commit the Church to a judgment on the messages which the visionary supposedly received. Therefore, a unique "partial" recognition was given. Returning to Banneux, here the last of the supernatural events officially accepted by ecclesiastical authorities took place. One would have to wait fifty-four years for another recognition on the part of a local bishop, but outside of Europe: it was in 1987, concerning the apparitions that took place beginning in 1976 in Betania, Venezuela, and to which some fifteen thousand people were witnesses. Syracuse, Sicily (1953), and Akita, Japan (1973), received the imprimatur of the Church, but were not apparitions but rather lacrimations (crying) of images of the Madonna. Recently, recognition was obtained for the events of Kibeho, Rwanda, which announced the terrible ethnic massacres about to be unleashed.

One summer, following a sort of itinerary of inspections of the places of that "Marian epiphany," as some called it, which began in 1830 (and whose prologue can be traced to 1796 in the Papal States), it is precisely to that corner of Belgium that I went to investigate.

Banneux is located on the plateau of the Ardennes, in the Diocese of Liège, extending eastward toward the German border. A coincidence made me smile (or was it unrest?): to reach the shrine from the south along the highway from Luxemborg, one takes the Belgian *Route nationale* 666, a figure, as we all know, considered to be the "diabolical" number which in the book of Revelation indicates the beast, the antichrist. The Diocese of Liège, at any rate, borders that of Namur, extending westward toward France, where another recognized shrine stands, that of Beauraing, whose apparitions preceded those of Banneux by just a few months.

In fact, the series of Marian apparitions of Beauraing (twenty-six of them to five youth, just one male and four females between nine and fifteen years old) began on November 29, 1932, and ended on January 3 of the following year. Twelve days later, on January 15, 1933, in nearby Banneux, there occurred the first of the eight apparitions to a girl of little more than eleven, Mariette Béco. Both events were officially and definitively approved by the bishops of the respective dioceses in 1949.

The proximity in place and time of the two apparitions not only amazes but has also provoked skepticism: Was this not a case of a psychic contagion, like the ones that often take place when news of presumed supernatural events spreads? Naturally, this objection was taken into account in the lengthy and meticulous procedure that led to the recognition of Banneux, the only incident that the Church judged authentic in a sort of "visionary epidemic" provoked by the apparitions of Beauraing, which sent rumors running throughout Belgium.

The investigative commission, in the end, had to acknowledge the freedom of God that follows mysterious paths.

Few people know, for example, that at Nouilhan, a locality within the municipality of Montoussé in the French Pyrenees, in the Diocese of Tarbes, just thirty kilometers from Lourdes, the Blessed Virgin appeared many times between 1848 and 1849, to eleven people aged eight to fifty-seven. These events were recognized as authentic by the same bishop, Msgr. Laurence, who just a few years later had to deal with Bernadette.

In that solitary place (I've been there, for what it's worth) the ruins of a shrine were once visible, constructed in the fourteenth century and then destroyed by the Revolution. The statue of the Blessed Virgin, considered miraculous, was saved and preserved in the parish church of Montoussé. Mary appeared near those ruins of her shrine, next to a fountain, in the very form in which the statue had depicted her, without ever speaking. The faithful devotees interpreted the matter as an invitation to reconstruct the place of worship. It was inaugurated on the feast of the Immaculate Conception, 1856, but just over a year later, the events of Massabielle would overwhelm the reborn devotion. Forgotten over time, today it seems that the pilgrimage to Nouilhan is beginning to revive. I too was struck by the mystical beauty of the place, while historians of Lourdes wonder about that enigmatic "prelude" to the apparitions along the Gave.

If very few know about Nouilhan, an even greater number ignore the fact that on May 10 and 11, 1917, just two days before Fatima and only 350 kilometers from there, in a Portuguese village called Barral, Mary appeared to a child, Severino Alves. This event seems to be credible, even though the religious authorities were not able to investigate it, submerged as they were by the extraordinary events in the Cova da Iria.

Returning to Belgium in 1932 and 1933: this proximity both chronological and geographical between Beauraing and Banneux is neither new nor an a priori reason for the unacceptability of the apparitions there. On the contrary, this situation ended up revealing a further motive for its credibility.

On December 31, 1932, among the twelve thousand people present at one of the apparitions of Beauraing, there was also Abbé Louis Jamin, the chaplain in Banneux, with his brother, also a priest. The tiny village of Banneux, with only 325 inhabitants, did not even have a parish. Amazed by the events they had witnessed but still unsure about the truth of the facts, the two priests asked the cloistered monasteries of the region and several friends to begin a novena to the Blessed Virgin asking for the return to the Faith of at least one unbeliever in Banneux. Anticlericalism and atheism were already widespread there, in part due to the presence of miners, workers in the peat bogs, and loggers come from elsewhere to work the vast Ardennes forests.

The Jamin brothers thought that in that one conversion, should it be granted, they would have a sign of the truth of Beauraing. The novena was to finish the day before the apparitions in Banneux were to begin. Some days before the first apparition, Julien Béco confessed and received Communion. He was a laborer, an agnostic filled with an ardent socialist faith, and the father of the little visionary. Béco had not received the sacraments since the distant day of his First Communion (whereas his daughter had not yet received First

Communion, nor was it planned that she would, for she was not attending Father Jamin's catechism classes).

At any rate, we want to examine precisely this last recognized European apparition here and in the following chapter. There is in Banneux an additional mystery, in fact: more than an *apparition*, it seems to be a re-*apparition* — the follow-up and perhaps the conclusion of Lourdes.

In 1955, a book by Fr. Samuel Poyard was published under the title *Lourdes-Banneux: la suite magnifique,* with a convincing introduction and blessing by Louis-Joseph Kerkhofs, the bishop of Liège who had proclaimed the "supernatural character" of those events.

Its three hundred dense pages examine the relationship between the apparitions along the Gave and those in the Ardennes, to Bernadette and Mariette, united by their very young age, their ignorance, the misery of their social condition, and perhaps also by their lack of any particular religious fervor. One must recognize (as did the bishop who followed the entire case from the beginning) that the evidence confirming Fr. Poyard's theses (and the theses of those in agreement with him) are not lacking. In Banneux, the Blessed Virgin's dress was the same as that in Lourdes, and the decisive apparition occurred on February 11 (the little visionary had no idea of the significance of that date). Even more surprising, every time Our Lady arrived she came from a point which Mariette indicated precisely: toward the southwest, along a line which, if extended, arrives exactly at the town in the Pyrenees! We shall discuss this further below.

First, it seems helpful to recall what seems to have been a mysterious, prophetic announcement. It is a very peculiar story. In August of 1933, about six months after the eighth and final apparition to Mariette, a visitor arrived in Banneux to see Father Jamin. The chaplain was a priest of deep spirituality and culture, highly esteemed by the bishop, who had assigned him to that little chapel upon his request to seek to reestablish his health, compromised by an excess of study and work, in the clean air of the highland covered in forests. Fr. Jamin was for Banneux what Fr. Peyramale was to Lourdes. He too initially harbored an appropriate suspicion and prudence, yet, in the end, was completely convinced of the supernatural nature of the events. The priest in Wallonia not only became an organizer of pilgrimages but also the historian of all the events.

Fr. Jamin's visitor we mentioned was one of the most recognized and authoritative religious in Belgium, Fr. Liekens, prior of the Dominicans in Brussels. This friar told the chaplain of Banneux that he had read in a Marian journal, over twenty years earlier, a prediction that said, "Seventy-five years after the apparitions of Lourdes, the Blessed Virgin will reappear outside of France, near one of its borders." According to Fr. Liekens (who by the way testified to the matter under oath and repeated it on numerous occasions before the ecclesiastical tribunal), that prophecy was circulating around Belgium and he had discussed it various times with his confreres. In fact, the matter was confirmed by another highly esteemed and renowned religious, the Jesuit Fr. Scheuer, also a Belgian.

It is certain, therefore, that for decades there were many throughout Belgium who awaited with curiosity, if not trepidation, the arrival of 1933, the seventy-fifth anniversary of the events of Lourdes. In November 1932, news of the apparitions in Beauraing began to spread: "outside of France" and "near the border," namely, in the Diocese of Namur right next to France. The facts did not align perfectly, however, since the years that had passed since Lourdes were only seventy-four. In mid-January of 1933, behold Banneux: there in the silence and discretion of the tiny village in the forest that kept the secret hidden for so long, four apparitions took place, the last on Friday, January 20. To Mariette's question about what the *Belle Dame* would like her to do, the Lady replied, "I would like a little chapel." Then she disappeared along the road heading southwest, from which she had always come, the figure rising luminously into the sky as she grew smaller in the distance.

The next day she did not return, leading Fr. Jamin — though not the trusting Mariette — to think that the apparitions had ended. Three weeks later, however, the Lady reappeared in the garden behind the poor Béco home and, for the first time, said what the purpose of her visits was: "*Je viens soulager la souffrance,*" I come to comfort, to assist the suffering. It was 7 p.m. on a Saturday, February 11 of 1933. That day marked the seventy-fifth anniversary of the first apparition to Bernadette. And Banneux, just like Beauraing, is "next to the border": the diocese borders with Germany. Interrogated that evening by the chaplain (and later under oath by various episcopal commissions on numerous occasions), the visionary said she knew nothing about the significance of that date, about what exactly had happened three quarters of a century prior.

If the existence of the "prediction of the seventy-five years" is certain (given the number and especially the authority of the witnesses; among them two of the most highly esteemed religious in Belgium, as we have seen), nevertheless the journal in which the written testimony was found was never located. This was true as of 1955, at least, when the book *Lourdes-Banneux* came out, as mentioned above: the author confessed having been able to carry out only a bit of private, "homespun" research into the old issues of the religious publications, and was unable to find in print the things the witnesses had read.

As far as I am concerned, despite having visited the sites and consulted local historians about these matters, I could not find more up-to-date news on the issue. I take this occasion, then, to make an appeal to readers. It seems that this prediction was published not only in French (or Flemish) religious journals but also in many other countries, including Italy. If, while skimming through old issues (obviously prior to 1933), someone were to find mention of it, it would be greatly appreciated if we were advised of this. The matter is not without importance to the world of Marian apparitions, in which signs, clues, and traces contribute to testifying discreetly though firmly to the truth of the visits of the Mother of Christ and our Mother.

Remaining with the calendar, there is another circumstance that is cause for reflection. In one of the previous chapters of this little notebook, we spoke of the millenary relationship between the city of Lourdes and the Marian shrine of Le Puy, one of the most ancient and important not only in France but throughout all Christendom. We said that from time immemorial (perhaps even from the time of Charlemagne) the territory of Lourdes was a fiefdom of the Lady of Le Puy, and therefore processions would periodically leave from the Pyrenees taking as tribute to Mary in her great shrine in the center of France a plug of grass from the meadow under the castle of Lourdes — in other words, earth taken from the place that would much later be transformed into the esplanade for the great processions. Throughout the centuries, all those who governed, not only in Lourdes but in the entire county of Bigorre, considered themselves merely the administrators of that "Land of Mary" and paid the regular tribute to the shrine of Le Puy. But as we read in that chapter, there occurred a peculiar coincidence: after that official tribute was abolished by the Revolution and then briefly resumed during the Restoration, according to ancient feudal law Mary's ownership of those areas would have lapsed had it not been renewed by 1859.

Well, during the apparition the year before in 1858, and right in the Grotto of Massabielle in front of the old castle (the seat and symbol of sovereignty over Bigorre), someone detected a reaffirmation of the ancient sovereignty, just before the rights were to lapse according to feudal law. One notices, as confirmation, that the Lady (reluctant to say her name, despite Bernadette's insistence) said that she is the Immaculate Conception precisely on March 25, the feast of the Annunciation. Well, that feast was the greatest celebration of the year in Le Puy, where the Blessed Virgin Mary was venerated as "the Annunciata." The Lady of Bigorre, then, "presented" herself officially on the day on which she was celebrated in her shrine in central France.

Now we are drawing nearer to that strange case of Banneux. Ever since the High Middle Ages, the Church proclaimed a jubilee year at Le Puy every time March 25 fell on Good Friday, with extraordinary spiritual concessions (enormous throngs of pilgrims would set off for Le Puy from all over Christendom). In other words, this happened every time the Incarnation and the Redemption were united on the same day, a rare coincidence which occurs two or three times per century.

In the 1800s, for example, it happened in 1842, 1853 and 1864; in the 1900s in 1910, 1921, and 1932. In this century, the Annunciation and the Passion were united in 2005 and only once again in 2016. The visionary of Banneux, Mariette Béco, was born not only on March 25, but in a year, 1921, in which the Annunciation coincided with the Redemption. In Le Puy they celebrated one of the three most solemn jubilees of the twentieth century in the house of the Lady who was also the "sovereign of Lourdes"!

Though with all due prudence and fitting respect for the mystery, it seems such "coincidences" are worthy of reflection, if they really are that and not discreet though unassailable signs. Above all, one observes that the year 1933 of the apparition was an extraordinary Holy Year of the nineteen centuries of the Redemption. The year 1858 of Lourdes was as well: Pius IX had decided to make this spiritual gift to France because, due to political turmoil, it was not possible to celebrate the Holy Year planned eight years earlier in 1850.

But perhaps there are still more elements worthy of our reflection. Someone (recalling all that we said about its relationship with Le Puy) went so far as to say that, if Mary desired to appear anywhere, Lourdes was among the most recommended, given that she was "at home" there. Something similar can be said of the Belgian village, too: officially it has been called *Banneux-Notre-Dame* since 1914. During the tragic days of the German invasion at the beginning of the First World War, all the towns of the region were sacked and set ablaze. Seeing the flames on the horizon, the inhabitants of the little village gathered in the Church and made a solemn vow to consider their hometown the "Land of Mary" and to add the name *Notre-Dame* to that of Banneux if they were spared. In fact, the Germans passed through so quickly as they moved toward France that nothing unpleasant happened to the residents of Banneux — neither at that time nor during the following four years of the war. When the war was over, the request was made, and the state granted the town's new title. Thus, as at the feet of the Pyrenees, so in the Ardennes, Our Lady was truly "at home."

We shall see, as we continue our discussion in the next chapter, that the footprint of the Mystery is truly present in these encounters that took place in the dark and cold of a great, bleak forest, in the mud of a barren and poor soil, despite its picturesque appearance during the few days of summer sunshine it receives, as during our fortunate stay there. A witness defined it ironically as "*une apparitionette de rien du tout*," a little apparition out of nowhere. Perhaps here, more than elsewhere, we see at work that strategy of the little seed placed in the earth, the discretion and poverty of which constitute a mark of gospel authenticity.

On May 25, 1985, John Paul II arrived in Banneux and revealed that such places occupied a privileged place in his Marian piety. But this devotion had been preceded by two great men of the Church of the past century: St. Giovanni Calabria, who placed his "Poor Servants" under Mary's protection, the Lady who there in the Ardennes had said, "I am the Virgin of the Poor"; and also a great devotee from the very start, the archbishop of Milan, Blessed Idelfonso Schuster, who sent to his ailing friends bottles of water from the springs that the Lady had said were flowing "for all the nations." And it was Cardinal Schuster who, for the parish in one of Milan's poorest neighborhoods (interestingly called "that of the minimal houses"), wanted a church dedicated to the "Virgin of the Poor."

These are eloquent examples (if any were needed) of the opportunity to continue to investigate the enigma of Banneux, this perpetuation of that other enigma which was and is Lourdes.

CHAPTER 34

The Virgin of the Poor

We take up once more our discussion of the "mystery of Banneux," this last Marian apparition to be recognized in Europe and which seems a continuation of that of Lourdes.

We have already anticipated numerous elements, but now we shall reconstruct in the proper order how things went. The place, first of all, was the plateau of the Ardennes, deep in the forests of fir, one of the few species that can grow in that land which is one of the most infertile in Europe. Still today, the area has for good reason a very low population density, in a country that is among the most congested in the world.

In her third apparition on Thursday, January 19, 1933, the Lady said, "I am the Virgin of the poor." It is an entirely unprecedented title in the history of Marian piety, a history that has not been sparing of titles. Yet, among the signs of the apparition's credibility is the coincidence between this definition of herself as the "Virgin of the poor" and the misery of the place.

Poor in its very name, Banneux depended for centuries on the Benedictine monks who, to assist the indigent inhabitants, conceded them certain "rights of banality," a tradition continued later by the civil administrators who succeeded the Benedictines. This term, in feudal times, indicated the privilege of being able to use without charge some of the pastures and logging. Without such concessions, they would have died of cold and hunger in those areas where the peaty soil inhibited almost all types of cultivation. It suffices to say that the region was known as *La Fagne* (as it still is today), a dialectical deformation of the French word *fange*, or mud. "Banneux" was not only

"Notre-Dame" from the vow made in 1914 which we mentioned above, but also a "banal" place: poor by definition.

The setting was miserable, but so was the main character in the encounter. The Béco family lived in a little house about one kilometer from the chapel where Louis Jamin performed his role as chaplain. The latter had to admonish the little Mariette, who was to turn twelve on March 25 (we have already commented the peculiarity of that date), for her absence from catechism. In the end, he told her that she would not be admitted to receive First Communion with the other children of the village. The matter did not make the least impression on the Béco family: the head of the family was a blue-collar worker with socialist sympathies, perhaps not an atheist but agnostic nonetheless, not practicing, and anticlerical. He was yet an honest man and a hard worker who, on his days off, remained at home and did not frequent the local tavern.

The mother as well was a woman who knew hard labor, between one pregnancy and the next. Mariette was the firstborn, but there were six other children in the home and four more were yet to come in the following years. In that crude little dwelling, without elegance, built with the typical dark red bricks of northern Europe, there were neither sacred images nor crosses. What dominated in the few impoverished rooms was religious indifference and hostility toward ecclesial institutions.

It was into this setting, which did not in the least prepare for an intrusion of the Mystery, that on January 15, 1933, it arrived. It was a snowy, icy, windy Sunday on La Fagne. At seven in the evening, in the pitch darkness, Mariette was at the window in the kitchen on the second floor that looked out over the vegetable garden that her mother cultivated to supplement the meager salary of her unskilled husband who worked in the peat bogs. Next to the garden passed the road that connected the plateau to the capital city of the province, Liège. The ten-year-old Julien, the oldest of the boys, had gone out with a group of friends in the afternoon and had not yet returned. Mariette looked out into the darkness anxiously, while keeping an eye on the baby sleeping in its crib.

Suddenly, the girl saw, just several meters from her in the garden, a luminous "Lady," standing still, slightly bent to the left. Frightened, she ran to her mother who was preparing dinner in a corner of the kitchen, who then stepped over to the window. The woman would later testify during the inquiry that she did not see with the same clarity as her daughter, but was able to distinguish "a luminous white form, like a veiled person, with the head inclined and hands together, such that her elbows were raised a bit off her hips." She too was frightened and exclaimed, "It's a witch!" Mariette replied, "No, Mama! It must be the Blessed Virgin. She's smiling at me! She's so beautiful!" The girl later said that the intuition that she was the Virgin Mary came to her when she noticed the blue band that the "Lady" was wearing around her waist. In fact, as we have said, the apparition in Banneux seemed to continue that of Lourdes, beginning with her clothing and the blue of her sash, but also in the rosary hanging from her right arm and the golden rose on her bare foot exposed by her garment.

Logically, Fr. Jamin's immediate suspicion was apt, therefore: in his church there was a statue of the Virgin of Massabielle, according to the classical model set by the sculptor Fabisch following the indications (not exactly carried out, moreover) of Bernadette herself. During those weeks in the village of Banneux, as throughout all Belgium, rumors were flying about the apparitions of Beauraing. Mariette might have heard talk of it at school and for that reason her curiosity would have fixated on the statue in the chapel. Thus, she was speaking of a presumed vision, not describing what she had seen in the garden outside her window and then, as we shall see, along the road, but rather what was on the altar she knew about, despite her limited attendance of that sacred place.

Everything seemed logical and clearly pointing in the direction of infantile fantasy, at least until the Abbé came across one detail. When asked to repeat the posture of the "Lady," Mariette joined her hands but instead of remaining straight as was the statue, she inclined her head forward, moving it a bit to the left: not the gesture of contemplation and ecstasy sculpted by Fabisch for the grotto, but an attitude of attention and welcome toward her little interlocutor. During all the interrogations, never once contradicting herself, Mariette repeated the fact that every time she appeared, the Virgin was "bent over," "stooped," "inclined." Never would she admit that she resembled in this manner the Blessed Virgin of Lourdes, despite her being the same in all other respects. Only at the end of the apparition did her figure straighten and seem to return from where she came, holding herself erect. It was then, and only then, that she resembled the Immaculate of Massabielle.

An insignificant detail? Neither the chaplain of Banneux (whose skepticism was strained here for the first time) nor the members of the many commissions that investigated the affair were of that opinion, all the way to the canonical confirmation by the bishop of Liège of the supernatural nature of those events. In fact, the demeanor of the Virgin described by Mariette, and the inclination of her head over the suffering of the world which (as she herself said) she had come to console, were not considered something that could have been invented by a little girl whose main character trait was that she "had no imagination whatsoever." At least, this is what those who knew her and the physicians who examined her declared.

We return now to that evening of January 15. After the exclamation of her daughter, Mama Béco had to run to the crib where the baby had awakened and was crying desperately. Mariette took out a rosary, though there had never been any in the house; she had found this one by chance a few days earlier along the main road. She began to recite a series of Hail Marys, even though (in contrast with Bernadette, in this case) she did not know how to recite the Rosary exactly. Meanwhile, she gazed out the window, enraptured by the beauty of the Lady. At a certain point, the Lady made a gesture that she come out to her. But Mariette's mother, fearful, prevented her forcefully, locking the door and putting the key in her apron pocket. When Mariette returned to the window, the vision had disappeared.

Thus began a series of apparitions. There were eight altogether, divided into two groups of four, which were separated by a pause of some twenty days.

The second appearance of the Lady was three days after the first, on January 18. Once again (and this was the case until the end), it occurred in the darkness of evening. The apparition appeared among the fir trees of the forest and guided Mariette out of the garden, along the road, to a place where water trickled from the embankment. There was only a puddle left by the rains there. But from the next day on, a fountain began to flow there, which is the very one in which pilgrims bathe today. The beautiful Lady said, "Put your hands in the water." She addressed Mariette formally, just as in Massabielle, showing great courtesy to the little girl. Then she added, "This fountain is reserved for me." Finally, she took leave, always using the usual tone of gentle manners, saying, "*Bonsoir. Au revoir.*"

The next evening, Thursday, January 19, again around seven, Mariette was led along the road once more. Kneeling in the snow that had fallen the previous night, she asked the question she had been told to ask: "Who are you, beautiful Lady?" "I am the Virgin of the poor," was her reply. Arriving at the spring, she asked her a second question, "Beautiful Lady, why did you say yesterday that this fountain is reserved for you?" The apparition smiled, "This fountain is reserved for all the nations." She paused and then said, "To refresh, to relieve [*soulager*] the sick." Mariette replied, "Thank you, thank you." And the Lady said, "I shall pray for you, goodbye."

Then she rose over the firs and went off in the same direction from which she had come, becoming smaller and smaller as the distance grew, until she disappeared. The direction of the "coming" and "going" of the apparition was southwest with respect to the Béco home, as we mentioned earlier. Except for the first time, when she appeared immediately in the garden, the other seven times she arrived "traveling," appearing first as a luminous dot, until she gradually assumed normal dimensions when she was in front of the visionary. To do this, she passed through a sort of triangle left open by two large trees. As we noted previously, the exact trajectory was calculated and reached the stunning conclusion that the line it traces connects Banneux with Lourdes.

Some see in this a further connection between the apparitions of 1858 and those of 1933, especially since, in the preceding Marian events, the modality was different: in La Salette, the Virgin was already "there" awaiting the two shepherd children; in Lourdes, she appeared in the opening of the grotto, preceded by a halo of light; in Pontmain, the visionaries saw her suddenly in the night sky above the houses, and she disappeared after having remained still in the sky without coming down to earth. In Banneux, however, there was a mysterious arrival and an equally mysterious departure, always following the same route: a "sign" to be interpreted? Perhaps an eloquent and not so well concealed reference to the connection between the Ardennes of the twentieth century and the Pyrenees of the preceding one?

Continuing our story, it is interesting to note that, just like Bernadette who had to repeat the strange term along the road so as not to forget what was incomprehensible to her, the name "Immaculate Conception," Mariette also did not know the meaning of the word "nations" nor the French word "*soulager*." As she later said during the interrogations, she understood that it concerned consoling realities "only because the Lady smiled as she said it."

The fourth apparition took place the following day, Friday, January 20. When she asked what the Lady would like, the Lady replied, "I would like a little chapel." Just as in Lourdes, so too here.

One notes, however, that in the Pyrenees the enthusiasm of the faithful went far beyond the Virgin Mary's request, erecting not the "chapel" she desired, but in the end, four large basilicas. In Banneux, on the other hand, they limited themselves to building a little structure in the Béco family garden. For great liturgies accommodating the many pilgrims, a large, open mall was created, surrounded by a portico. Only recently was a large pavilion raised, for use in bad weather, which is the norm there. It is peculiar to note that only a series of "fortuitous" cases (allowing that such a term can be used in a faith perspective) prevented the realization here of a customary large shrine in marble, stone, and cement. First came the war and then other difficulties and unforeseeable events that have always blocked the architectural project that had already been planned in every detail. Perhaps this is nothing to regret: even in the modesty of the place of worship, in the almost provisional appearance of the anonymous buildings scattered throughout that forest, Banneux seems to have remained faithful to the spirit of poverty that its message conveys.

After the fourth apparition, there were no more. The chaplain Louis Jamin, who interrogated Mariette every time and wrote the minutes of these sessions, was convinced that the events had come to an end. But not the visionary who recited Rosary after Rosary every evening, often alone (skepticism in the village was widespread), with a sack under her knees to protect her to some extent from the snow, as she looked hopefully toward the opening in the trees, the gateway through which the Lady arrived. The priest shook his head, her parents yelled at her, the neighbors mocked her; but in the end her waiting paid off. It took place on a Saturday, and on a very special day: February 11 of 1933, the seventy-fifth anniversary of the first apparition in Lourdes. The Lady arrived in flight, as usual, after seven o'clock and while Mariette and a handful of others were reciting their fifth Rosary. Descending to the ground, the Lady guided her, retracing her steps along the road all the way to the spring, where she said, "I come to comfort the suffering." "*Merci, merci!*" responded the visionary. After an "*Au revoir,*" the luminous figure rose into the sky and disappeared slowly in the usual direction, to the southwest, toward France.

After being led that very evening to the house of the Abbé, the visionary was quite amazed to learn from the priest that not only was it the liturgical feast of Our Lady of Lourdes, but it was also the anniversary, three quarters of a century since the beginning of events in the Pyrenees. Since the good faith of Mariette was examined at length by all the many commissions of inquiry, the believer must surrender to the "coincidence," remembering what we recalled in the previous chapter: the prophecy ("seventy-five years after … outside of France … near the border") about the return of Mary was a prophecy verified in a convincing way by trustworthy religious.

The sixth apparition, four days later, was on February 15. As the parish priest in Lourdes had done, so too did the chaplain of Banneux charge the girl to ask the Lady for a "sign." This time, as well, the Lady smiled, but added, "Believe me, I believe in you." After having communicated to Mariette a secret only for her, she added before returning toward the dark horizon, "Pray much. Goodbye."

The next apparition occurred on February 20, in the deep snow. Once more, the girl was led by the Lady to the spring, where again she heard, "My dear daughter, pray much." There followed the "*Au revoir*" which seems to be one of the peculiarities of Banneux, one of its "distinguishing traits."

The series of apparitions ended definitively with the eighth appearance on March 2, a Thursday. We pointed out earlier that Thursday seems to be the privileged day, also for the events in Lourdes. That evening, a cold rain fell in torrents on the dark forest. At the third Rosary Mariette had recited, the sky suddenly grew calm and stars came out. The Virgin arrived through her usual gateway in the trees. In contrast with the other times, her face was serious with no smile on her lips. She said, "I am the Mother of the Savior, the Mother of God." While a certain sadness seemed to overtake her, she repeated her recommendation: "*Priez beaucoup.*" Then she blessed Mariette with the sign of the cross, saying "*Adieu.*"

As the Lady was departing, the little girl cried profusely: she understood that that *adieu* was the last and she would no longer see the beautiful Lady. As the faithful accompanied her home in tears, the sky grew overcast once more and the rain resumed.

This is a summary account. Many other things could have been said, of course, about what someone has called "an apparition out of nowhere." In reality, it was indeed the atmosphere of solitude, of modesty, of littleness (observed as well by Bishop Kerkhofs of Liège who approved the events) that seemed to stamp the gospel seal on Banneux. The connections with Lourdes are undoubtable, even more so if one considers that the apparitions of Beauraing began and were mostly carried out near a "Grotto of Massabielle" built in the garden of some local nuns. Also, the chaplain of Banneux was the one who connected, through his vow, the two Marian events.

Bernadette and Mariette share not only their very young age, their ignorance, and their misery, but also the fact that they were the sole witnesses — something which did not occur in the other apparitions of the last two centuries, except for the first, that of the Miraculous Medal in Paris in 1830. There is also a connection in the fact that, while along the Gave the Marian dogma of the Immaculate Conception was confirmed, in the Ardennes (in the "*I am the Mother of the Savior, the Mother of God*" of the final apparition) the much more ancient dogma of the *Theotokos*, the divine maternity, was confirmed.

Particular to Banneux was the fact that the apparitions took place entirely at night, or at least in the dark, and were almost entirely unobserved, in contrast with Lourdes and Fatima, which immediately aroused great crowds. In Lourdes, then, the Gospel-like preference for the poor was "implicit" in the choice of the visionary and in the miracles which seem to favor the most wretched. In Banneux, instead, the preference was explicit: "I am the Virgin of the poor." There were even some who made illegitimate reference to the political faith of Mariette's father and went so far as to speak of a "Madonna of the socialists."

Putting aside such absurdities, the few words that Mariette heard and reported have an extraordinary theological density, on par with those of Lourdes, that must still be entirely unpacked. Although the flow of pilgrims is impressive, Banneux has probably not yet fully revealed its potential to attract cosmopolitan crowds around its miraculous fountain.

One observation in conclusion: the diocese of Liège borders not only with Germany but also with Holland. Just some twenty kilometers from Banneux is Maastricht, right at the Belgian border. This was the city where the European nations completed the initial phase of the process of unification. Was it truly by chance that right next to this city, Mary dedicated a spring to "all the nations"?

We ask this question in confirmation of the many enigmas that surround this Belgian stage of the modern Marian epiphany. Not least among the enigmas was that of Hitler's taking power precisely in January of 1933. Mary proposed once again humility, service, poverty, hiddenness, just as the bloody rise of a regime born precisely from the rejection of all these was rising.

CHAPTER 35

THE SILENCE OF JOSEPH

FOR SOME TIME NOW, I have wanted to make room for several of the reflections I have made over the years on St. Joseph. Naturally, there is no need for me to justify something as obvious as including in a book like this a discussion of the husband, humanly speaking, of Mary. Treating this subject is not only required by logic but comes spontaneously: where she is, he is too, as the *sensus fidei* of believers has always intuited.

Nevertheless, I put off my intention of speaking about him, attracted by topics that seemed more urgent. *De Maria numquam satis,* as we know. As I have already remarked, the problem for those who confront this world of Mariology is abundance, not penury. In any case, I was sure that good St. Joseph would not hold the delay against me. Remaining hidden and emerging slowly over time seems to be part of the extraordinary role attributed to him in the history of salvation.

The New Testament, as we know, attributes not one word to him; two Gospels of the four do not even mention him (and only the apocryphal gospels try to remedy this, applying their often-suspect imagination). Moreover, for centuries there was only darkness and silence around him in the history of theology and spirituality. If the Protestant world speaks very little and probably reluctantly of Mary, imagine their attitude toward Joseph. Usually, after Jesus is born, he is given the function of any normal husband, including the subsequent arrival of many other children.

For now, it suffices to say that our putting off the topic is part of a long tradition. Perhaps I would have procrastinated even further had it not been for a peculiar circumstance. In my research into Lourdes (not only regarding the period of the apparitions, but on what happened before and after: the roots in Le Puy, the continuation in Banneux, and so forth), I happened to frequent the library of the House of the Chaplains. It is the building that sits atop the rock of Massabielle, where the international team lives that oversees the religious services of the shrine. In that library I met the director, Fr. André Doze, well known in those environs not only for his fervor in carrying out his duties, but also for his unique charism that has come to light over the years. His vocation is spreading, through all means, devotion to St. Joseph, based not so much on sentiment (though commendable) as on the recognition of the importance of his role in the dynamics of faith.

Fr. André gave me his most important book, reprinted in France in many editions, despite having been published by a press without means and without an adequate distribution network—a distribution based on word of mouth (*de bouche à Oreille*, as the French say), in silence, as has always been the style of our saint.

Opening the volume by Doze, I assumed it would be the usual material, oscillating between enthusiasm and naivete (in the positive sense of Gospel simplicity). Instead, as I read those pages, I realized immediately that they were as devout as they were original, profound and based on the solid theology of which the author was professor.

Upon returning to Italy, I presented his *Joseph, ombre du Père* (shadow of the Father) to a good editor, who published it in translation, changing only the title: *Giuseppe, una paternità discreta* (a discreet paternity). Naturally, I was asked to write an introduction to assist the Italian reader in understanding those pages. I wrote the text just a few days before turning my attention to this chapter in this notebook, and so the right moment arrived to pursue the path I had begun, jotting down some of the reflections I had postponed for so long.

First, remaining for a moment with the book. Fr. Doze, a priest with much pastoral experience in the diocese, asked to be placed at the service of the pilgrims in Lourdes, especially in the confessional. As he explains in one of the chapters, his commitment to reawakening the attention of believers to St. Joseph is in complete harmony with the spirituality of St. Bernadette. To her, the husband of Mary was not only the traditional "patron of a peaceful death"; after the death of François Soubirous, her defamed and persecuted father whom she loved so much, the little religious in the cloister in Nevers took Joseph as her father on earth.

Entering the monastery on the Loire, she had said, "I have come here to hide myself," and she tried in every way to use words sparingly, spoke only when interrogated, and so naturally felt in complete harmony with that saint of shadow and silence. There were even some who suspected that one of the three secrets entrusted to her by the Blessed Virgin might have something to do with the mystery of the Holy Family, if not with Joseph himself.

In support of such a hypothesis, there are several episodes, small but significant. To cite one of them, the superior of the convent asked Bernadette (who accepted with the usual, humble obedience) to make a special novena to Our Lady.

Once, one of these austere mothers found her praying to the Blessed Virgin but kneeling before an image of St. Joseph. "Sr. Marie-Bernard, you are distracted! That is not the statue!" the superior reproached her when the saint rose to her feet. And Bernadette, with her enigmatic smile, replied, "But Mother, the Blessed Virgin and her husband get along perfectly." As other episodes likewise testified, for her the family harmony in Heaven was so great that prayer to the wife was in some way interchangeable with that to the husband.

There were two places where she took refuge to pray in solitude whenever she could: before the statue of the Virgin Mary in the most remote corner of the garden, which reminded her of the beauty of the Lady; and, in the middle of the same garden, the chapel of St. Joseph where she would be buried for thirty years, from 1879 until 1909, when the first inspection of her corpse was carried out.

Fr. Doze, attentive to signs, did not allow the chronological coincidence to slip past him: "Thirty years in obscurity in that chapel! The length of the hidden life of Jesus in the shadow of St. Joseph." But the priest and writer added,

> What strikes me is that this chapel in the garden in Nevers, which is like the mysterious *pendant* of the house of Nazareth but also like the Grotto of Lourdes, was to disappear on the very day the latter did. As the place of the apparitions, Massabielle ended its function on July 16, 1858, the feast of Our Lady of Mount Carmel. And it

> was July 16, 1944, when the Chapel of St. Joseph was completely destroyed by an American bombardment. Left intact was only the tombstone of Bernadette, found under the debris without even a scratch.

Do we have here another of those discreet traces in which God desired to wrap His mystery, the God who loves the chiaroscuro and who desires to be sought out?

It is certain that St. Bernadette followed the tracks of another woman of God, though quite different in time and temperament, the great Teresa of Avila. In her spiritual autobiography she wrote, "The one who cannot find a teacher in prayer must take for his guide the glorious Joseph and he shall not risk losing his way." Well, in the acts of the process for her beatification, one of Bernadette's sisters in the monastery of Nevers declared, "I know that, among the saints, the Venerable had a special devotion to St. Joseph. She often repeated this invocation, 'St. Joseph, grant me the grace of loving Jesus and Mary as they wish to be loved. St. Joseph, pray for me; teach me to pray.' Once, the Venerable said, 'When you cannot pray, turn to St. Joseph.'" It is likely that Bernadette had not read the works of Teresa; if she came to the same certainties, it must be due to those intuitions of which the mystics alone have the secret.

It is not due to this devotion of the visionary, however, but for profound reasons of religious symbolism, that the two access gates to the sacred zone of Lourdes are dedicated, one to St. Michael the Archangel (the more massive one, though less frequented, in line with the façade of the basilicas) and the other to St. Joseph (the lateral one through which the pilgrims coming from the city center pass), whose statue with the Child Jesus in his arms stands next to the gate. Among all the many possibilities, why this choice? Because presiding over the zone set aside by Heaven, it was fitting to place the head of the angels of whom Mary is the queen and who, in Revelation, fights victoriously against "the dragon," "that ancient serpent, who is called the Devil and Satan, the deceiver of the whole world" (12:9). But it was also fitting that next to the other gate to the shrine would be the one who was for thirty years at the door of the house in Nazareth, carrying out his service of watching over his wife and Son.

The pope during Bernadette's life was Pius IX. The great pontiff made appeal in one of the most dramatic moments of the Church precisely to the role of custodian and defender, discreet and effective, which was the main task of the carpenter of Galilee. On December 8, 1870, on the first anniversary of the occasion that the Immaculate was celebrated in Rome occupied at that time for just under three months by the Italian army, Pope Pius IX proclaimed St. Joseph patron of the universal Church, entrusting to him the defense of the people of God, threatened not only by military aggression but also and above all by moral and cultural aggression.

One notes that this solemn act by Pius IX was the point of arrival of a movement that had lasted more than a century and in which all components of society had participated. From aristocrats to peasants, appeals, supplications, and prayers were raised to obtain that proclamation of patron of the Church. In this as well, Joseph participates in the destiny of Mary, whose cult and devotion are the fruit of the fervor of believers, the result of a true "democratic" movement, in the sense of a push from below toward the hierarchy that often had to do no more than filter, direct, define, and at times pronounce dogma.

After the aggression of the nineteenth-century bourgeoisie, with their secular anticlericalism and scientistic, positivist incredulity, there now arrived the menace of Marxist materialism. Once again, a pope had recourse to the protection of that extraordinary "Doorman of the House of God." Few will remember that, in 1937, in the powerful encyclical *Divini Redemptoris* on the criminal ideologies of the 1900s, Pius XI placed "under the protection of St. Joseph, powerful protector of the Church, the great action of Catholics against Communist atheism." To make his intention even clearer, the pope wanted the encyclical to be promulgated on March 19, the liturgical feast of the saint.

Even Vatican II, although not proposing defensive aims and even less aggressive ones, accepted an important challenge to the Church. Namely, to confront modernity in the most effective manner, which for better or worse, was already unifying the world. And so, once more on March 19, 1961, John XXIII placed the council in the hands of St. Joseph, at the climax of a discourse that summarized all the work of his predecessors, Pius IX first of all, in order to increase the cult of the foster father of Jesus. Furthermore, it was also Pope Roncalli who, just after his election, had ordained that the altar of St.

Joseph in St. Peter's Basilica should be embellished and adorned in such a way as to attract immediately the attention of visitors to the basilica.

But there was something even more surprising. In the homily delivered in May 1960 for the canonization of Gregorio Barbarigo, John XXIII expressed his acceptance (though speaking prudently of a "pious belief") of the ancient idea according to which both John the Baptist and Joseph had already been resurrected in body and soul and had entered Heaven with Jesus during the Ascension. The pope was referring, obviously, to the mysterious verse in Matthew, "the tombs also were opened, and many bodies of the saints who had fallen asleep were raised, and coming out of the tombs after his resurrection they went into the holy city and appeared to many" (Matt. 27:52–53).

It is understandable that Pope Roncalli shared this reading of the Gospel text, for it was shared by many theologians and great saints, among them St. Francis de Sales. One of St. Francis's sermons ended in these words: "We must not doubt in the least that this glorious saint has enormous credit in Heaven with the One who favored him to such an extent as to elevate him next to Him in body and soul. Something that is confirmed by the fact that we have no relics of his body on earth. So it seems that no one should doubt this truth. How could He have refused this grace to Joseph, He who was obedient to him throughout his earthly life?"

The holy bishop of Geneva (who is also a Doctor of the Church) continued,

> If it is true that we must believe, in virtue of the Most Blessed Sacrament we receive, that our bodies will rise again on the day of Judgment, how can we doubt that Our Lord allowed Joseph to rise into Heaven, who had the honor and the grace of carrying him so often in his arms? He is therefore in Heaven, in body and soul: as for me, I do not doubt it. How happy we shall be to merit a part in his holy intercession!

The faithful son (and custodian) of Catholic tradition, Pope John, did not hesitate to align himself with it in this matter as well, although it has never been officially defined. According to the dogma of 1950, only Mary was assumed into Heaven body and soul; as for other "bodies" that already live in eternity, the Church has never negated or affirmed this, although on the affirmative side is found the conviction of many saints and mystics. And now, also that of a pope who was beatified in the ancient manner, by "popular acclaim."

Returning to the Second Vatican Council which the pontiff had announced and placed under the protection of the "Just Man" of Nazareth: on November 12, 1962, in the initial phase of the council, a bishop from what was Yugoslavia stood up to intervene without warning and out of turn (he later said he was "moved by the Spirit") and fraternally yet passionately reprimanded his confreres, stating that in their teaching they did not give Joseph the space he deserves. The council was obliged to make amends!

The stenographers' reports lead one to intuit that this outburst provoked in many Council Fathers feelings ranging from disbelief to hilarity. Immediately, another bishop arose, declaring with a bit of irony that, for such proposals, it was not fitting to convoke anything less than an ecumenical council! At any rate, the Slavic bishop's words had no further consequences: they let it pass and the assembly immediately moved on to discuss questions considered "important."

The next day, however, there was a surprise. During the night, Pope John had prayed and reflected, and thus came to the conclusion that what was expressed in the council in that extemporaneous intervention, though received with great skepticism, was offering him a providential occasion to carry out a project he had been incubating for many years. Therefore, on November 13, 1962, before the morning session began, Cardinal Cicognani, speaking on behalf of the pontiff, announced to the amazed assembly that beginning on the coming December 8, the name of St. Joseph would be inserted into the Canon of the Mass.

This was no light matter. For centuries, since the time of St. Pius V, no one had dared to add anything to that "heart" of the Eucharistic sacrifice which is the Canon. There was surprise, in fact, and even some grumbling, though in hushed tones, above all from the sector that confused the veneration of Joseph with one of those "popular devotions" which they sought to downsize. John XXIII made it clear that his decision was irrevocable and that, as Supreme Pontiff, he had full power to make it without anyone's approval. Pope Roncalli, moreover, was certainly aware that men and women in the Church, especially in the nineteenth century, were enthusiastic to the point of offering their lives to God to obtain the insertion of the name of Joseph into the Mass. Furthermore, it was his good friend, Tarcisio Vincenzo Benedetti, the bishop of Lodi, who probably played an active role in the pope's decision on November 13, 1962.

At the end of this medley of reflections, so hasty and partial (but with the hope of recalling attention to this theme at least), some might ask the question: Has Joseph ever "appeared" like Mary has? Of course. Throughout the history of devotion, several of his apparitions have been recorded and have given rise to shrines and pilgrimages, some of which are still well frequented.

As far as we know, the most renowned place where the patriarch has appeared "alone" is Mount Bessillon in Provence, in the current Diocese of Fréjus. It is a beautiful place, but also quite arid. On June 6, 1660, a shepherd whose name history has preserved, Gaston Ricard, was wandering about in a desperate search for water, about to die of thirst. He later told how St. Joseph appeared to him and said, "Lift up that rock and you shall drink." Ricard hesitated as the rock appeared too heavy. The order was given again, and he was able to roll the rock over easily and water began to flow.

Thus began a lively devotion. What's more, after the French abandoned Algeria, the Benedictines expelled from Africa were assigned to this shrine.

Joseph, along with John and of course Mary, was a protagonist of the apparition on August 21, 1879, which lasted half an hour before fifteen witnesses of all ages and which is at the origin of the national shrine of Ireland in Knock. Also in Fatima, the entire Holy Family appeared, and therefore also the husband. So too in 1944, in the contested apparitions in Ghiaie di Bonate near Bergamo, Italy.

In conclusion at least for the moment, that old Christian philosopher Jean Guitton's oft-repeated line comes to mind: "I am under the impression that Joseph's moment has not yet come. He has not yet come out from the shadow: he's just beginning to do so. You will see that the future holds some nice surprises about him."

This is a prediction that gladdens those who, loving Mary, cannot but love her husband.

CHAPTER 36

The Adventure of Fiorano

The reader will understand if, just this once, I indulge in a bit of autobiography. I will try to make it clear that this is not an end in itself but is for the sake of supporting the general discussion which interests us here. Here we go.

Just like my parents and grandparents, I too was born in Sassuolo, where the Modenese plain meets the Apennines. But my paternal great-grandfather, like all of his ancestors, was an artisan and peasant farmer in Fiorano, a town near Sassuolo. Their proximity was such that, over the centuries, the two communities were united into one municipality, even though each claimed its own local identity. Some older folks still remember the reciprocal lampooning if not altercations among youth of the two towns.

My family's surname is among those that originated in Fiorano and is directly tied to the agriculture of the borderland between the plains and the mountains. From the Latin *messores* came the Italian "*mietitori*," or day laborers, who, following the various periods of the ripening of grains, performed their work, moving from the lowlands to the highlands.

Almost overshadowed by Sassuolo, which was initially a little capital of a dominion, then an elegant summer residence for the Este Duchy, and finally a center (of world renown) of construction ceramics, Fiorano would be just one more town lacking any particular attraction were it not for the quality and quantity of figs produced there (as Tassoni recalls in his *La secchia rapita*, The Stolen Bucket). It "would be," I say, were it not for one peculiarity: on the hill that dominates the town and which is the very first outcropping of the Apennines, rises one of the most famous and illustrious shrines in the Diocese of Modena, if not in the entire region of Emilia. It is known as the "Shrine of the Blessed Virgin of the Castle," since it was erected on the ruins of the ancient fortifications.

On the arch over the entrance gate to the medieval village that encircled the manor house appears an image of the Blessed Virgin holding the Child Jesus, painted in the fifteenth century by an unknown artist. The image is pleasant but also naïve and delicate. It was immediately venerated, of course, but not distinguishable from so many others in every medieval neighborhood of Christendom — that is, if Spanish soldiers had not burned down the neighborhood on February 8, 1558, to take revenge on Fiorano for having resisted being sacked. The flames destroyed everything except the Marian image, thanks to what was considered an obvious and amazing miracle, even by the soldiers, some of whom took to their heels in fright while others fell to their knees begging forgiveness. As the flames reached the fresco, they divided to either side, leaving it intact. For this reason, a soldier was added to the image; he can still be seen, with his helmet and armor, kneeling with joined hands in prayer before Mary and her Son.

Though always respected, this "Madonna of the Castle" became particularly beloved and venerated. Her cult was practiced with prayers, flowers, some ex votos, but always with a very local character. Certainly nothing to justify the construction of a chapel, let alone a shrine.

The great change occurred in 1630. In mid-January of that fatal year, a peasant girl died in Modena. She was the first, and for several months the only, victim in the duchy of the plague (brought by the Germans during the siege of Mantua) narrated at the heart of Manzoni's *The Betrothed*. This epidemic became the worst scourge of the century and raged with particular vehemence here, given that Modena is close to Mantua, which was the epicenter of the contagion. In the city of Modena, almost half the population of around ten thousand inhabitants died: 4,662 to be precise. In the entire little duchy, the macabre count reached thirty thousand deaths.

Around Fiorano, people died, as throughout all the Po Valley. In the adjacent parishes of Sassuolo and Formigine, the survivors sank to under half of the original population. Nor were people in the mountains able to escape: according to the tombstones in churches and cemeteries, only a third of the population survived. When the imperial troops finally succeeded in entering

Mantua and sacking it, they too were stricken and almost entirely wiped out, while the thirty thousand inhabitants of the city of the Gonzaga dynasty were reduced to little more than six thousand. A similar fate awaited Milan, where the epidemic took with it three-fourths of the population: 190,000 deaths out of 250,000 inhabitants before the contagion.

The little town of Fiorano (about a thousand inhabitants) was particularly exposed because the ancient, heavily traveled foot-of-the-mountains route, the Via Claudia, passed through it. It was therefore the point of departure and arrival for numerous journeys into the Apennines. Upon hearing of the plague, the entire population gathered under the arch on which the venerated Madonna was frescoed, which had been miraculously saved from the fire in 1558. The people took a vow that, if they were spared the scourge, they would build a chapel where the image, until that time exposed to the elements, could be welcomed and venerated.

In the 1930s, a distinguished historian of the region, Professor Guido Bucciardi, gave an account of his research carried out directly in the archives, including that of the parish in Fiorano. He found that in 1629, the year before the plague, when there was no suspicion of its arrival, among the thousands of souls in Fiorano thirty-two deaths were registered, among them thirteen children under a year old. The following year, during the general demographic cataclysm, deaths in Fiorano matched the average of any other normal period: thirty-four deaths, among which eight were infants.

The parish priest, one Domenico Borghini, marked down next to every name of the deceased their cause of death. The archive testifies to "falls," "seizures," "stomach illnesses," "phlegm," "burns," and naturally "old age." But no cases of the plague. Professor Bucciardi (like the other researchers before and after him) found just one case that might arouse suspicion, a man who died "of a malignant fever." But it seems that the plague must be excluded: it would have been indicated as such, given that the symptoms were obviously too well known. Furthermore, the man's illness lasted twenty-four days, while a characteristic of that malady was that it led to death in just a few hours — or in a few days in cases of exceptional resistance. Moreover, before expiring, this obscure Giovanni Battista Tagliatti who died of "a malignant fever" regularly received all the sacraments, including what was then called "extreme unction" and which no parish priest (obeying the bishop's orders) dared to administer to those infected with the plague, for it required a mortal contact with the patient's body. Given the summer period (his death was registered on August 25), the phrase "malignant fever" probably conceals either malaria, present at the time even in Modena Province, an intestinal infection, or a case of typhoid, given the terrible condition of the water, especially in 1630 when chroniclers recorded a great drought.

Quoting the book of Guido Bucciardi, "It is to be observed, among other things, that of the thirty-four people who died in Fiorano in 1630, twenty-five died in the first half of the year, when the plague was only in its initial phase (in Sassuolo, the first victim died in June), while in the second half of the year, when the plague was raging more violently, there were only nine deaths, among whom two were infants."

Our historian had more things to tell, even more amazing realities: "After the seventeen-year-old Maria Mosconi died on September 21 after falling from a tree, and after sixty-year-old Maria Barozzi died on September 24 of a stomach illness and fever after four months of suffering, no one died in Fiorano until March 21, 1631, when fifty-year-old Battista Cuoghi died of "phlegm," comforted by all the sacraments.

For this reason, the researcher concludes, "Over the space of six months, from September 24, 1630, to March 21, 1631, while in all the territories nearby the plague continued to harvest victims, no one in Fiorano above one year of age died, for any cause whatsoever." Just two kilometers away in Sassuolo, as a local historian Matteo Schenetti, reports, "a greater number of deaths due to the plague occurred in 1631. During the winter there was a standstill, but in the spring the epidemic returned with greater vehemence, and many deaths every day, counting in many hundreds." Precisely in that year 1631, so devastating elsewhere, mortality in Fiorano reached its lowest level: only six adults and four newborns, none of them due to the plague!

The historian speaks of an "inexplicable event," of "the preservation, without any plausible explanation, of a territory from an epidemic that lasted for nearly two years and which struck every other area, including those adjacent to it." Should we be amazed if the people of Fiorano drew the logical conclusions from this, realizing with marvel equal to their gratitude the great, miraculous, mysterious privilege granted them by the Madonna of the Castle?

Nor should anyone be amazed at the devotion of my ancestors, given that the "inexplicable event" according to science (and the miracle according to faith) was repeated 225 years later in 1855. In that year, the duchy, on a par with the rest of Italy, was struck by one of the worst outbreaks of cholera. In Modena, the disease claimed 6,700 lives in just four months. Bucciardi also probed the archives researching this outbreak. He writes, "In Sassuolo, the contagion broke out with homicidal force. The vast halls of the ground floor of the former ducal palace were transformed into hospitals.... In a no less frightening manner, the cholera spread to the neighboring parishes of Formigine, Spezzano, Braida, Nirano, Maranello, Torre, and Montagnana, placing Fiorano in a deadly noose."

There is no need to say that the people of Fiorano made immediate appeals to *their* Madonna. And she did not delay responding concretely to her devoted people. Once more, in a humanly inexplicable manner, the town was the only one preserved from the epidemic. With just one exception, that of an upholsterer and mattress maker, who "having committed the grave imprudence of working on a mattress on which a woman had died of typhoid, caught this disease, which very soon assumed the symptoms of cholera, doing away with him in just a few hours on August 30, 1855." A doubtful case, then, since other scholars doubt that it really was "true cholera." A case, moreover, which the historian described as a "grave imprudence." At any rate, the exceptional fact remains: only one "infected" (if he really was) in Fiorano, against the thousands in all the surrounding territory. By comparison, in neighboring Sassuolo, both the parish and civil archives testify to 112 stricken and seventy dead in only four months.

Naturally, in the face of events of this type, a question arises spontaneously. Namely, what sort of divine justice is this that spares one place but not others? Facing the menace of the seventeenth-century plague and the nineteenth-century cholera outbreak, there was no city or village that did not pray to "its own" patron saints or "its own" Madonna, that did not take vows or make promises. But all this neither slowed nor stopped the disastrous march of the scourges. In fact, as Manzoni reminds us, in the case of the plague of 1630, the great mass liturgies and mass processions actually contributed to the diffusion of the contagion. So why "no" to all the rest, or almost, and "yes" to the little, insignificant Fiorano?

As is obvious, the secret of God and the mystery of His providence must be respected. Nevertheless, at least in men's eyes, there seems to be a reason here. The miracle of salvation from the plague in 1630 led to the decision to construct for that miraculous image first a chapel and then a great and glorious shrine. It seems Mary loves those who erect in her honor places where the fruits of her intercession can be dispensed, settings where she can gather her children around her.

Protection from the cholera epidemic of 1855 renewed construction work, after a long pause during which (in the period of religious persecution under Napoleonic domination) what had already been erected, after having been closed for worship by the authorities, ran the risk of being completely demolished. In any case, after the revolutionary storm had passed, enthusiasm in Fiorano seemed exhausted and workers had finished only part of the project elaborated in 1633 by the famous Roman architect Bartolomeo Avanzini, the official architect of the Este dynasty and designer of the ducal palaces of Modena and Sassuolo. It was the renewed miracle during the cholera outbreak that reanimated energies, bringing the project to completion in 1888, more than two and a half centuries after work had begun and 330 years since the "miracle of fire" that had given rise to this devotion.

We recall the very explicit words of the Immaculate to Bernadette on that March 2, 1858: "Go tell the priests that people are to come here in procession and that a chapel should be built here." Words that confirmed with clarity what the *sensus fidei* of Christians has always believed and which we have just mentioned: there are places which, mysteriously, Heaven wants to reserve for itself; there are places where the Mother of Christ desires the followers of her Son to come on pilgrimage. Next to the usual churches, parishes, and indispensable places of the daily life of faith, there must be these other places "in addition," those extraordinary places that we call shrines or *sanctuaries*—a significant term in its reference to *holy* and *sacred* realities.

Examining the events of Fiorano, it truly seems that the divine will has led matters toward a goal through its patient, timeless action. The goal was to erect a place of particular Marian devotion precisely there, on that hill dominating the plains which was probably the site of a pagan cult and which for centuries was occupied by an instrument of war, the castle.

If, in the Christian perspective, everything is providential and nothing is by chance, then the constellation of shrines that one finds throughout the Catholic world, and in certain places rather than in others, is most certainly not an accident. There is a "geography of the sacred" whose maps were not made by human will.

This church with its two bell towers on either side of the façade, inspired by Trinità dei Monti above the Spanish Steps in Rome, stands out as a sign of the Mystery from the rest of Fiorano and creates an oasis of serene beauty in a landscape brutally devastated by the ceramics industry. So it appears, at least to the eyes of faith, which see the scourge of two terrible epidemics being transformed into the benefit of one of those "homes of the Mother" where healing of the spirit is offered to all, and to some, healing of the body, as a sign and guarantee of the *unum necessarium*.[14]

May I confess another reason for emotion, at least for me? Within the shrine is a memorial stone commemorating the fact that one of the bell towers was constructed in the 1800s by a certain Fr. Giuseppe Messori, a native of Fiorano and a priest in the cathedral of Modena who wanted to be buried under the tower he had paid to erect. My surname is quite common in those parts, although as far as I know, the generous priest was not a distant relative. Yet I am pleased that a Messori left a mark of such tangible devotion in a place that the Blessed Virgin chose for herself. If I may say so, it is only thanks to her protecting my ancestors from the plague and cholera that I am here today, alive and writing about her.

[14] Editor's Note: The "one thing necessary," a reference to Jesus' words to Martha in Luke 10:42.

CHAPTER 37

"They Shall Call Me Blessed"

Makària means "blessed" or "happy" in the Greek of the New Testament. "All generations will call" Mary *makària,* therefore. In the meager efforts in the chapters of this notebook, we have tried to display the mysterious fulfillment of the prophecy that Mary attributed to herself in the Gospel of Luke.

Every so often, some scholar attempts to draw conclusions, however provisional and incomplete, of that prophecy which, after two thousand years, has lost none of its power. For example, at the end of the 1940s, a French Jesuit, Herbert du Manoir, began coordinating and publishing with the famous Parisian publisher Beauchesne a series of large volumes under the title *Maria* and a subtitle that explained the content: *Studies on the Holy Virgin*. These massive tomes, dedicated to Marian devotion in all countries throughout the world, are a veritable mine of information.

Recently, a book of about 1,200 pages reached bookstores announcing on its cover the *First Marian Atlas*. Its general title was *Mother of the Church in the Five Continents*. The publisher was "Il Segno" and the author an already elderly Italian priest, Fr. Attilio Galli. Moved by his passion for the Mother of Jesus ever since his ordination over half a century ago, Fr. Galli sought out and coordinated information for this *Atlas* of his. This work seeks to confirm through that information that there is no corner of the world where Mary is not called *makària*. He also intends to show how (in the words of the author himself) "Mary was the first missionary of her Son among every people of the earth." For good reason, the title calls her "Mother of the Church."

Those who tackle the over thousand pages, written by Fr. Galli with so much effort, can sense an air of another age: here, the author's pen portrays bishops as always "zealous," missionaries as "intrepid," the popular cult "edifying," Catholic statistics "consoling," and so forth. Whatever the case, Marian devotion continues not only to persist but to advance among what remains of the people of God, often no longer frequenting their parishes but still visiting shrines dedicated to the Virgin Mary. Fr. Galli documents how, after the fall of the wall of the Communist persecutor, in places like Albania, Slovenia, Chechia, and the Baltic countries, shrines were reopened or, if they had been destroyed, reconstructed, and are frequented more than they were before the arrival of state atheism. New places of worship are added to the old ones — and not only in Medjugorje, but in dozens of places around the world, the results of those "apparitions," approved by ecclesiastical authorities or not, that characterize recent decades.

Mary is both sweet and tenacious; therefore, fragile and strong.

This vast *Atlas* demonstrates this by giving the history and the pertinence of the presence of the Virgin Mary in the countries of northern Europe that passed over to the Reformation. In those areas, in the sixteenth century, a violence was waged against those who wanted to remain Catholic about which it would be "ecumenically incorrect" to speak. It is worthwhile to mention this, as a fitting memorial. In Denmark, Sweden, Norway, and Iceland, the Faith was still young. The resistance of ancient forms of Nordic paganism was tenacious, but once they accepted Baptism, those populations embraced "Roman" Christianity with sincerity and seriousness. Here too, as everywhere, the Marian aspect of the pastoral work was decisive, and the shrines dedicated to the Virgin constituted outposts and fortifications for evangelization.

The situation of the Church there at the time of Luther was quite different than that of Latin countries or of certain Germanic areas: in northern Europe, ecclesial life was carried out, in general, in an orderly fashion, with dignity, often with sacrifice and without the decline or worse, degeneration, that might justify a revolution that would unhinge everything. The Scandinavian kings, however, were soon interested and their mouths were watering at the possibilities which the Lutheran upheaval in the Germanic countries was revealing, where the princes were confiscating the goods of the Church to their advantage and directing the tithing of the faithful to their own coffers.

Thus, in Scandinavia the separation from Rome was decided unemotionally, by sovereigns and aristocrats, for merely economic and political reasons. And it was imposed on a population that was not demanding it, and did not even want it. Above all, those peoples did not want to renounce Marian devotion, the statues, the shrines where they went on pilgrimage. The strategy chosen by the powerful was therefore a passage to the new confession in silence, slowly, so that the people would not even notice. In churches throughout Scandinavia, destined to become Lutheran temples, the altars to the Virgin remained for a long time, and the Marian places of worship were not immediately closed. There were even Catholic and Marian "signs," such as the Angelus, that remained for decades, at least until the generation that had known "another" Christianity had died off.

It is true that in some places such as Norway (then subject to the king of Denmark), they decided to act immediately and with brutality, not stopping at destroying monasteries, with the works of art and documents they contained, or at wiping out every image of Our Lady with knives or lime, nor did they hesitate to kill those who refused to submit. As in 1555, in the Norwegian town of Hamar, where two peasants were burned at the stake, accused of not wanting to renounce "their meditations on the Virgin Mary." By this phrase they meant the abhorrent recitation of the Rosary, the black beast of Luther.

Among the many interesting points offered by Fr. Galli's *Atlas* is this possibility of following the war on Marian devotion and the resistance it put up in order to reemerge at the end of the persecutions. Consider that in Sweden, only in 1952 were the restrictions on the religious practice of non-Protestants abolished. The case of the frigid and remote Iceland is significant: when the Danish Crown, on which the island depended, imposed the transition to Lutheranism, the inhabitants, though few, had constructed nearly two hundred churches and chapels, of which the Blessed Virgin was the main patroness of 92 and the secondary patroness of 104. Here too, the princes came down hard: of the two Catholic bishops on the island, one was decapitated by order of Copenhagen and the other was deported and died in prison. Freedom of religious practice was restored to Catholics only in 1874, and then only in a limited manner.

We learn from the work of Fr. Galli that in the capital of Iceland, Reykjavik, the statue of the Marian shrine that existed there at the time of the

Reformation was hidden in the home of some peasants. They handed it down secretly from generation to generation, until 1926 when it could be restored to the bishop of Catholics on the island (little more than two thousand in all) and placed in the little cathedral for their veneration. In any case, Marian devotion not only seems to be returning to those parts, but even growing: in 1985, in the suburbs of the Icelandic capital, the first shrine since the Reformation was constructed, dedicated to Mary, Star of the Sea.

We continue our soundings into the *Atlas*, where there is so much to choose from. For example, we have often dealt with Lourdes here. It is thanks to this volume that one perceives the importance of the role played by those apparitions in the missionary field, especially in the last decades of the nineteenth century and the early decades of the twentieth. It is amazing to see how Africa and Asia are studded with "Grottos of Massabielle," around which shrines quite often are built and become pilgrimage sites even for Muslims, animists, Hindus, and Buddhists. From the forests of Burma to those of equatorial Africa, from the hills of Nagasaki to those of New Zealand, the statue with the blue sash of the Immaculate, brought there originally by the powerful and fervent French missionary organizations, has been a vigorous stimulus to the life of faith. And not only in the Third World: the author of the *Marian Atlas* reminds us that the oldest shrine of Our Lady of Lourdes in the United States, constructed in 1875, opens its door every morning right near Broadway, the heart of New York's entertainment district. How many know that the films that have marked our times come from a city that is not named Los Angeles, but rather Nuestra Señora de los Angeles?

It is moving to hear how every nation has considered the Blessed Mary "its own" to the point of competing with other nations. It seems that in Mexico they sing an old hymn that proudly says, "Look, Mary / that I am Mexican / and, therefore, I am yours. / Look anywhere, then / but in vain: / who can love you more than me?" At any rate, it was John Paul II who, during his papal visit in 1979, observed, "Mexico is 96 percent Catholic, but is 100 percent *Guadalupano*." In fact, everything is allowed except lacking respect for their most beloved *Morenita*, the Virgin Mary who appeared in 1531 on Tepeyac, identified as "Our Lady of Guadalupe" and honored with a series of shrines that have arisen on that site, each one bigger than the previous to contain the continuously growing crowds. The final version, inaugurated in 1976 (when Europe was still suffering the effects of the "Marian winter"), can hold tens of thousands of the faithful within, and hundreds of thousands in the plaza outside.

The Marian pride of the Mexicans can find its equal in that of the Ethiopians. Perhaps no other Christian people has mobilized like this one its imaginative poetic vein to find titles as impassioned for the Mother of Christ as they have. As observed by a Jesuit who arrived in Abyssinia at the beginning of the 1600s, "The Ethiopians are convinced they are the only Christians who know the inestimable value of the Blessed Virgin and the only to render her the homage she deserves." We shall dedicate an entire chapter to this extraordinary devotion; it is well worth it!

From near the equator to near the North Pole; from Ethiopia to Canada, it is extraordinary and worthy of meditation for those involved in pastoral care and evangelization, how the love for Our Lady is perhaps the only one that has been able to unite cultures and ethnicities at the antipodes, like those of Ethiopia and Canada. Since the time of its discovery in the early days of French colonialism, the North American country was consecrated to the Virgin Mary, to whom missionaries dedicated their preaching and to whom numerous churches and localities were consecrated — beginning with the city of Montreal, founded under the beautiful name *Ville-Marie*.

An aside concerning city names: Who would suspect that the great Indian city of Madras (and the surrounding state) derived its name from *Madre de Deus* (Mother of God), given by the Portuguese, who vowed before embarking on their ocean voyages that they would spread Marian devotion wherever they landed?

In Canada, the role of Mary, given primacy from the beginning, was reinforced by the long resistance of Catholics in Quebec to the English Protestant dominion, such that, until the years of Vatican II, no one in the West could compete with the French Canadians in their fervor for the Blessed Virgin. They had the highest number of priests and religious per capita in the world. Then, after the council, there was a stunning plunge which seemed to destroy devotion, although in recent years there has been a renewal, once again mostly under the sign of the Blessed Virgin.

We continue to frolic through the *Atlas*. Which continent has never witnessed an officially approved Marian apparition? The answer is not difficult: Oceania. This does not mean that the Marian presence there has not been strong, ever since its cruel beginnings. In fact, after the rebellion of the American colonies that formed the United States, Great Britain was without any "concentration camps" that it once had beyond the Atlantic. And so, London decided to transport its hundreds and thousands of condemned criminals to the still virgin and deserted coasts of Australia, which had just been sighted by explorers such as Cook.

The first expedition of deported prisoners arrived at the end of the 1700s. On the galleons there were not only common delinquents but many Irish (and English, Scots, and Welsh as well) who were guilty of but one crime: insisting on remaining Catholic and refusing to enter the Anglican State Church, the only one allowed. Therefore, along with those convicts arrived rosaries, sacred images, and Marian statues, even though the Protestant authorities permitted priests to enter the established colony only decades later. The Irish diaspora often found itself in this situation, Galli reminds us: "In the distant regions without priests, the Rosary took the place of the Mass: calculating the hour of the solemn liturgy in their homeland, the Irish exiles gathered and, kneeling on the ground, recited the Rosary together." We cannot forget, of course, that in Dublin the Legion of Mary was founded in 1921 by an Irishman, Frank Duff. It spread throughout the world and did much to transfer devotion into life and to take veneration beyond sentimentalism, becoming action and service of neighbor.

We move on now to Latin America. Lacking space, we pass over Brazil, where the Virgin Mary is not only at the heart of Catholic worship but also central to the Afro-Christian faith created by the descendants of the indigenous people transported there in the colonial period. We go instead to Uruguay. This little country is characterized by an early and intense Masonic influence.

Is it perhaps for this reason that *la Virgen*, their official patroness, is called "*de los Treinta y Tres*"? The name comes from the fact that there were thirty-three *libertadores* who showed up in the shrine of the city of Florida in May 1825, vowing either to defeat the Spanish or to die in the attempt. It is also true, however, that "thirty-three" indicates the highest degree of Freemasonry, which (through the lodges in the United States) supported the fight for independence of South American nations. The young sailor Giuseppe Garibaldi was initiated into the Freemasons precisely in this region.[15]

So, behind that appellation for the Uruguayan Virgin Mary, is there a Masonic symbol? We confess, at the risk of scandalizing some, that the matter (if it is true) does not disturb us, just as it did not disturb John Paul II, who kneeled in this shrine, following in the footsteps of millions of pilgrims. In the end, it would offer further proof that everywhere, even among the "brother Masons," that Lady is called "blessed." As the Magnificat announced two thousand years ago.

[15] Editor's Note: Garibaldi (1807–1882) was a prominent figure in the *Risorgimento*, the unification of the Italian nation that followed on a series of conflicts, including the seizure of the Papal States from the pope.

CHAPTER 38

Incursion into the Mystery

Here is yet another chapter covering a variety of themes. We begin with the surprises one comes across when thumbing through the products of "Catholic" publishing today. The quotation marks are justified, unfortunately. There is a recent player on this publishing scene that deserves our attention, if not gratitude, above all for the great works that it places at the disposal of readers. We are referring to the three large, sumptuous volumes that comprise the *Great Illustrated Encyclopedia of the Bible*, which came out in Germany in the 1980s and is now available in its Italian edition. We wish it success, obviously, even though experience tells us that, despite the efforts and costs of production, such works end up having a very limited distribution and even more limited use. In fact, experts and specialists compile them, but they do not consult them, having very different instruments of information at their disposal. As for the wider public, it is hard to imagine that people would take on such a great expense and then dedicate themselves to reading only some of the entries. The few who read the Bible usually content themselves with the notes. But perhaps our convictions are "pessimistic" (the label for all realistic opinions today) and subsequently wrong.

Nevertheless, the Italian edition is not a mere translation but rather a complete revision, with the elimination and addition of various entries and the collaboration of a group of consultants who constitute the elite of biblical studies in Italy within the Catholic sphere. The renowned exegete who edited the entire operation is also a Catholic and a member of an ancient religious community. Moreover, the introduction was entrusted to a bishop, he too the author of important works in biblical studies. The bishop was not sparing in his compliments of the work, affirming that "the efforts of the publisher were commendable" and that the labors of the Italian editors "deserve our gratitude and our explicit thanks."

All reasons that should cause us to be even more surprised (to use a euphemism) when looking through what should be the fundamental entry, the one that should support everything: "Jesus Christ." It states,

> The fact that Joseph is no longer mentioned after the infancy narratives and that Jesus, in his hometown, is indicated as the "Son of Mary," is often interpreted as a clue pointing to Joseph's death during Jesus' youth, leaving him as an oldest son. He therefore had to assume the leadership of the family and take care of his four brothers and an unspecified number of sisters. Under such circumstances, Jesus could not think of having a higher education.

Disturbing statements, it goes without saying, which place this entry entirely outside of the Catholic perspective which has always been tenaciously and correctly defended by the Church: that Jesus was the only child of Mary, a teaching directly tied to several dogmas that support the entire structure of Faith. We were saying that it does not seem to be a mere oversight. In fact, if one follows the reference given by the *Encyclopedia*, one finds the entry "Brothers of Jesus," where it is written, "Concerning the relationship of kinship between the 'brothers' of Jesus and Jesus himself, various hypotheses have been held."

One of these hypotheses, "that became the prevailing doctrine in the Eastern Orthodox Churches," the contributor explains, holds that "the brothers were the children of a previous marriage of Joseph." But "this does not find support in the New Testament." Another hypothesis "corresponds to the official doctrine of the Roman Catholic Church" and affirms that "the 'brothers' were in reality Jesus' cousins." This hypothesis was "held by St. Jerome in favor of the dogma of the virginity of Mary." By him alone? This is astounding! Nevertheless, they take care to state that "Jerome's exegesis, in this case, is shrewd but not entirely convincing."

Well, the only hypothesis they do not criticize is the one they presented first, explaining that "beginning with the Reformation, this became the dominant one among Protestants." This is the conviction, in other words, that "the brothers were the younger children of Joseph and Mary." Obvious, given that (as far as can be deduced from the Gospels, writes our biblical scholar) "Joseph and Mary, after the birth of Jesus, lived as husband and wife."

The bishop we mentioned concluded his ardent introduction by stating that there is in this *Encyclopedia* "a great mine to be excavated, with a profound experience of joy." Well, we confess that, for us at least, it gives little joy that Catholics are proposing the always rehashed, always refuted readings of Mary as the mother of a large family, the "normal wife" of Joseph.

Naturally, we hope for a revision of this in a second edition, if there will be one. As for us, such an entry passed off as Catholic convinced us of the need to dedicate an entire chapter to this question — so ancient yet so obstinately reproposed — about the "brothers" and "sisters" of Jesus spoken of in the Gospels. This will be in chapter 50.

Staying with this *Great Illustrated Encyclopedia of the Bible*, and to introduce an element of balance after the criticism: among the entries that seemed sound and relevant to our topic is the one dedicated to Joseph.

First of all, the information concerning the trade he practiced is of great current relevance, because just recently, newspapers placed in the limelight the affirmations of an exegete, according to whom Jesus belonged not to the poor social class but to what we now call the "middle class." This is something I have always held, for what it's worth, convinced that the demagoguery of pauperism, of exalting the *Misérables,* had no foundation in the Gospels but only in the paradigms of those who want to read in them a manual for political revolution.

The Greek word used by Matthew (13:55) is *tékton* and is traditionally understood as "woodworker" or "carpenter" (as in the official translation of the Italian bishops' conference). In reality, observes the editor of the work we are examining, "the word in the original text, translated literally, means 'construction worker': Joseph built homes out of mud and stone; he made caves inhabitable, creating entry rooms, digging steps in the rock and enlarging the cavity. The term 'carpenter' dates from the Middle Ages, because it was in that period that houses were built with wood." Interesting (and unusual) is what follows: "Joseph's hometown, Bethlehem, was famous as a city of builders and stone cutters whose services were sought out in the entire region. Those who were unmarried were in the habit of spending long periods in other regions of

Palestine. This is the explanation for why Joseph, from Bethlehem, had moved to Nazareth for work and settled there."

These elements contribute to confirming the historicity of the "infancy narratives," of which Joseph and Mary are the protagonists and which today are suspected of being only a fabric of legends.

With regard to *tékton*, we observe that, whatever Joseph's (and later Jesus') trade might have been, it must have dealt with wood as well. St. Justin Martyr, born in Palestine and a distant relative of Jesus' family, writing around the year 150, said that in Joseph's business objects such as plows and yokes for oxen were made. Justin confirms as well that the social setting of the putative father of Jesus was not in the least poor: he was an artisan, an honorable condition and usually well off in the Israel of that time, with particular skills and therefore with a solid clientele. The poverty of Jesus during His public life was a choice, supported by the assistance of wealthy women who followed him. Nor should we forget that the community had a cashbox and a budget, with a treasurer: one Judas Iscariot. In any case, during His years in Nazareth, Jesus certainly did not live in misery (thanks to the well-off Joseph), as many paintings have depicted it.

We continue to quote the entry on Joseph in this encyclopedia. When he received news of Mary's pregnancy, "he could have denounced the girl and demanded she be punished. The punishment set by the law for the infidelity of a wife, or betrothed, was stoning. But as the descendant of a family of priests (Luke 1:36), Mary must have known that the punishment would have been increased: she would have been burned at the stake." Joseph had another option: a "letter of separation"; in other words, "a form of public repudiation of the woman as one's wife or of one's girlfriend as one's betrothed. A repudiated woman was marked for life. Her honor was compromised forever." Not physical death, then, but something worse in the Ancient Near East: social, public, civil death.

We quote these lines to call attention to something we risk forgetting today: the courage, if not temerity, of that young girl in saying yes to the invitation of the angel. As a "virgin betrothed" (Luke 1:27), she must have understood immediately that no one would have believed in a "supernatural" pregnancy and that the fate that awaited her according to human standards, therefore, was death — and death in the most atrocious way, being burned alive. Or, the worst of dishonors, from which she would never have recovered. In her "Behold, I am the handmaid of the Lord; let it be to me according to your word," which Luke reports (1:38), there is in essence the acceptance of martyrdom.

But after her show of courage, we see why Joseph merits the title *just* given him by Matthew, in all of its significance.

> Instead of denouncing her or calling for separation, the man found another way out. He did not bring Mary into a rabbinical court for the inevitable death sentence, nor did he want to dishonor her. He decided to send her away quietly ("in secret," Matt. 1:19). With this, he took upon himself the guilt. The private separation would have attracted the harshest judgment upon both Mary and Joseph. Jesus would be born the illegitimate child of an abandoned woman. Joseph, therefore, had in mind to renounce his own reputation for the sake of not delivering Mary to the judges. But God intervened and spoke to Joseph in a dream.

Thus, on one side, a very young woman who in obedience and trust in God consciously accepts the possibility of a terrible death, whether physical or social. On the other side, a young artisan who, out of respect and love toward his fiancée, agrees to renounce his honor, which was for ancient Semitic peoples more important than life itself.

These should be habitual reflections for Christians. But we have the impression that it merits repeating, for we all run the risk of forgetting it.

As concerns publications, we now pass from one recent book to a journal, also recent. I saw in that weekly one of the usual interviews with Hans Küng. When the journalist pointed out to him that "Marian shrines are packed today," the theologian, a dissident by profession, replied, "This is not important to me: I was recently in India, and the same things are happening there, the same phenomena. It's folklore." The interviewer did not give up: "Millions of the faithful go to Lourdes." And since Küng states that he's been there too to please some friends ("Many told me, Go to Lourdes. I have been there, too"), the journalist asked him, "What was your experience?" He replied, "I asked that she show me something objective, rather than emotive. I 'm a sincere man, capable of accepting things. Yet, what I saw in Lourdes was not convincing." He then concluded, "For my faith, neither Lourdes nor Fatima nor Padre Pio are important."

Küng has the right to be skeptical, of course, like every Catholic, even if in reality his title as "Catholic theologian" was revoked a long time ago by the German episcopal conference. Even when the Church recognizes an apparition, she requires of no one the assent of faith: it is not a matter of a new revelation but, if anything, an aid in persevering in faith in revelation; something "extra" granted freely by God, a pure grace, interestingly almost always entrusted to Mary, the Mother of Mercy who, having a human heart, knows well what is in our hearts. At any rate, sensibilities are legitimately varied; what is important for the devotion of one will not be for that of another. And blessed is he who does not need, or believes he does not need, these "tonics" for reinvigorating his faith, always threatened by the world. Catholic freedom exists for this as well.

No scandal, then. Only a perplexed question regarding Lourdes: Is Küng truly convinced that around that grotto there is only "emotivity" and nothing "objective"? Precisely in the only place of worship in the world, among all religions, where for over a century a meticulous "Office of Medical Verification" has been working—precisely there one finds only the unleashing of vague sentimentalism, the "folklore" of the masses like to what is seen along the banks of the Ganges?

Beyond the controversies over the "scientific" inexplicability of so many healings, is there nothing "objective" in the Gospel innocence of the young witness, Bernadette, whom the Church made a saint not because the Immaculate appeared to her but because she was the first to live fully, radically, the message of prayer, penance, and sacrifice that she said she heard in the grotto?

One could continue with these questions, but would they serve a purpose? Or are we once again here before the paradigm of a professor who has reduced the Faith to a liberal ideology, to the modernism of the 1970s, and who has therefore decided a priori that something "is not important" and therefore must necessarily be "inexistent"?

Seeing the attention (intentionally) dedicated in this notebook to events such as Marian apparitions, it behooves us to mention another of the responses of the former Catholic theologian in that interview. For Küng, the events of Fatima are merely "mental projections," pathological illusions of the three shepherd children. And everything that came of them was nothing more than manipulation of the ignorant and superstitious masses, "propaganda of clerical obscurantism."

It is truly sad to notice how the so-called "strong spirits" of nineteenth-century Freemasonry and socialism are by now outside the current secular horizon and survive almost exclusively, one could say, among these old priests. And they consider themselves, by the way, on the cutting edge! Except for, we hope, the charity and respect that are due, the temptation is strong to let them be, to "let the dead to bury the dead." Also, because all discussion leads to nothing: a theologian (like every other "intellectual") cannot be converted, at least by human power, without a particular divine intervention. In fact, his ideological paradigm is the fruit of his labor, his study and his life's work; his doctrine is his capital, even social capital, the thing that helps him find a publisher for his articles and his interviews. Therefore, he is prisoner to that cultural-religious image, and to change it would mean to lose everything, including his income and social status. Among scholars, especially those well on in years, who would ever have the courage to renounce his own bibliography, recognizing that he has been deceived and has deceived his readers?

At any rate, a word about Fatima. Some have asked, after the fall of the Iron Curtain: What became of the prediction expressed on July 13, 1917, which constitutes the supposed "second secret"? On that day, the Blessed Virgin said (according to Lucia), "The Holy Father will consecrate Russia to me. It will be converted."

An initial response came from John Paul II, commenting on the declarations of Mikhail Gorbachev in a famous article published in Italy in *La Stampa* on March 3, 1992: "Today we can say that everything that has happened in Eastern Europe during these years would not have been possible without the presence of this pope." A few days later, the Polish pontiff said, "We must not forget something important: there was not only a crisis of Communism, there was also *perestroika*. This Russian word, among many things, also means conversion. It means that in the crisis and the rupture of atheistic Communism there has been a spiritual element, an interior struggle."

One of the most authoritative Mariologists, Stefano de Fiores, wrote in 1978 about that promise of Fatima, when the Soviet Union seemed more solid than ever and its Marxist-Leninism seemed to hold the future in its hands: "Regarding the word 'conversion,' it demands as a minimum that the Russian state stop fighting religion and stop employing tactics of revolution and war." A "minimum" hypothesized before its time and which actually came about; even if, in our haste, we might have wanted more. But history has its rhythms, and patience is one of the Christian virtues.

François Furet, the famous (and agnostic) French historian, gives us further pause to meditate in his *The Past of an Illusion,* over six hundred dense pages that make up the best and most insightful synthesis that has yet appeared on the completely unforeseen collapse of the powerfully united bloc of the Warsaw Pact: "The decomposition of the Soviet Union and the subsequent fall of its empire remains mysterious for the manner in which it occurred."

The believer is capable of giving a name to this "mystery." I was reading recently the memoirs of Markus Wolf, the legendary head for thirty-four years of the East German secret services and the protagonist of many films and spy novels. When the regime collapsed in Germany as well (and he too was taken by surprise, though he should have known and foreseen everything), General Wolf, a German Jew raised in Russia where he had been taken as a child by his Communist father, sought help from his "Soviet brothers" in Moscow to escape arrest. But there too, everything was disintegrating. He was received by the last, lost head of the KGB, who (quoting literally from Wolf's memoirs) "raised the palms of his hands high, in the gesture that means impotence to Russians, and told me, 'Do you see what is happening? We can no longer help you. Who could have imagined that it would end like this? May God help us.' "

Thus, the last act of the regime that had tried to challenge God concluded with the invocation of God by the very leaders of the once omnipotent secret services. In this drama as well, in this confirmation of the biblical word (*Nisi Dominus aedificaverit domum* ...),[16] here too, in some enigmatic way, Fatima shows that it has something to say.

[16] Editor's Note: The opening words of Psalm 127: "Unless the Lord builds the house, those who build it labor in vain."

CHAPTER 39

The Knights of the Immaculate

Should we insist on explaining or resign ourselves? In fact, not a day passes that does not see us falling into the usual confusion, not only in newspapers, but much worse, even in books considered to be serious. I am speaking about the dogma of the Immaculate Conception, confused with that of the Virginity of Mary, in other words, with "conception without the intervention of man, by the work of the Holy Spirit." We examined in chapter 21 the reflections of several Greco-Slavic theologians. Here we shall speak of the Catholic world, or what once was the Catholic world, where the issue is not only the religious ignorance of our contemporaries, though that is undeniably increasing. It seems that those two words, Immaculate Conception, lead instinctively to think not about Mary but about Jesus; the virginity of the Mother, not her preservation from original sin in light of the redemption effected by her Son.

The confusion is so universal and stubborn as to lead one to lay the blame on that expression: perhaps a less ambiguous formula might help comprehend its meaning better? A change, then? The dogma of 1854 speaks, as we know, of a "singular grace and privilege" by which Mary "was preserved." Therefore, it seems that it would not be lacking in fidelity to the dogma to substitute "Immaculate Conception" with something like "Marian Privilege" or "Preservation of Mary."

If the problem were placed before the Church's attention, I am sure that theologians would not be at a loss for finding alternative expressions. But a problem arises, and not a minor one in the light of Faith. The dogma proclaimed solemnly by Pius IX was the only one to be in some way "certified" by

Heaven, four years later during the apparitions in Lourdes. The theological formula seemed to have been approved to such an extent that, on March 25, 1858, the Lady defined herself as the "Immaculate Conception." How could we intervene then, however praiseworthy our intentions in clarifying the idea a bit for the people, including those who write books and newspaper articles, who think of Mary's "virginity," whereas it is "original sin" that is at issue?

So, is it better just to leave it at that? For now, we will content ourselves with clarifying if necessary, knowing from experience that this is a labor of Sisyphus.

Remaining on this topic, as readers know, I published a book (*The Miracle*) that recounts the extraordinary story that took place in seventeenth-century Spain. The region of Aragon in which the unprecedented miracle occurred was under the control of the Order of Calatrava. This was one of those monk-warrior orders, the most famous of which (too many imaginative books and films have dwelt upon it) was the Knights Templar.

While researching that book, I examined many documents, one of which was the Blood Pact in Favor of the Immaculate, solemnly promulgated by the Knights of Calatrava on December 23, 1652. Spain had made of the question of Mary's Immaculate Conception a point of honor, a national issue. When that truth (not yet made dogma) was denied from the pulpit by some preachers, such popular disorder followed that the king prohibited such denials and put pressure on Rome to reach a definition. It is such a fascinating story that we shall dedicate a chapter to it.

Well, the *Caballeros de Calatrava*, the monk-warriors who had fought on the front lines of the *Reconquista*, even added to their three traditional vows of the religious life another peculiar one. In the original document from the seventeenth century, it reads like this: "We make an oath always to defend, affirm, and advocate that the most glorious Virgin Mary, Our Lady, was conceived without stain of original sin and did not sin in Adam. To defend this most certain truth that redounds to the honor of the sublime Virgin, we shall fight with the help of God *hasta la muerte* (unto death)."

Other equally demanding statements follow, such as, "We take a vow and an oath not to admit anyone into this noble Order if he refuses to pronounce this vow and special oath before assuming the other obligations of religion."

With that typical Spanish gravity which knows how to push to the point of exaggeration (the *Todo o nada,* all or nothing, of which consists their greatness and nobility, but also quite often their tragedy), two centuries before Rome proclaimed the dogma, those knights were ready to die rather than renounce the Immaculate Conception! Was it perhaps for this reason that the Lady wished to appear in the Pyrenees, which divide France and Spain?

A rhetorical question, obviously. But it leads me to reveal a peculiar coincidence that I discovered during my research for the writing of *The Miracle*: Fr. Jeronimo Mascarennas, the commander and superior general of the Order of Calatrava who imposed the "pact of blood" in 1652, was also the "bishop elect of Leiria." This is the little Portuguese diocese in whose territory the village of Fatima is located.

So, the threads of the enigma of coincidences, of "random cases," run underground wherever one digs into the Marian mystery.

John Henry Newman also thought about Spain and its fervor for *La Virgen,* and so responded to his Protestant brethren who accused him of having passed over to the ranks of "Mariolaters":

> If we take a look at Europe, we find that the people who have stopped worshipping her Divine Son, and have moved on to a mundane humanism, are not the people who distinguished themselves for their devotion to Mary, but precisely those who rejected such devotion. The zeal for the glory of the Son has gone extinct where it was no longer joined to the ardor for exalting the Mother. Catholics who were unjustly accused of worshipping a creature rather than the Creator, still adore Him. While the accusers who had claimed to adore God with greater "purity" have ceased worshipping Him.

This is the usual truth, which we have recalled numerous times: as continuous historical experience demonstrates, the presence of Mary is a powerful element in the stability of the creed. Mariology is a type of guarantee of orthodoxy for Christology, at the service of which it exists entirely and exclusively.

We continue to fish around in the files of notes. Take this, for example: at the start of the twentieth century, a great German engineer and industrial leader,

Daimler, decided to produce automobiles that would offer the highest quality and performance in all Europe.

Before undertaking the construction of the car, he had to come up with a name. Daimler, a Catholic, chose that of his daughter who, despite being German, had been given a Spanish name from one of the titles of the Virgin Mary invoked in Spain — in this case, *Mercedes,* from *Nuestra Señora de las Mercedes,* Our Lady of Graces. It is a name which, as we all know, enjoyed such success that even the popes have traditionally used the cars named after the daughter of the German engineer.

A little anecdote, certainly. But not without its usefulness in confirming the often-unexpected Marian presence. Be honest: How many of us make the connection with Mary when we see a Mercedes pass by?

Another curious annotation. One definition of *shrine* which I wrote down when I found it somewhere runs: "A place where one can speak with the Blessed Virgin and, through her, with Christ, with the entire Trinity, without having to dial the area code first."

I found the comment of a Protestant, scandalized by that type of Catholic midrash which is customary in the dear old Marian devotion. Namely, Jesus shakes His head and complains smilingly, "What can I say? Even those to whom St. Peter closes the gates here in Heaven enter nonetheless: my Mother lets them in through the window."

A scandal, I said, to that serious Protestant whom I was reading and according to whom we thus grant to Mary the power of forgiveness, of welcome, of mercy superior even to that of Christ. It is true, we need to be attentive. But we also need to be attentive to the *sensus fidei* of believers who have always turned instinctively to the Mother when, in some way, they feel (how should I say?) "intimidated" before the Son. Why do they have this movement of the heart that urges them to seek maternal mediation?

There is here a mystery whose shape we can only catch a glimpse of. Judgment at the tribunal of Christ is characterized, certainly, by mercy, but this necessarily coexists with justice. Charity is not that if it ignores or overrides truth; namely, the truth of our sin, whose oppressive reality must still have some weight if divine justice is to be such.

But then, perhaps Mary, in the divine plan, was figured as only and entirely "mercy," to make the scales of her Son tip toward forgiveness? Perhaps, in her, Christ seeks some sort of alibi (let this inadequate term slide) to get beyond the demands of justice along the path of mercy? Is this perhaps the secret that believers, century after century, perceive instinctively, that throws them to their knees before the image of the Blessed Virgin and leads them to clutch their rosary instinctively in moments of greatest need?

Difficult questions, and risky, and necessarily imprecise, but perhaps worthy of further investigation.

Further investigation, as we said, for the sake of intuiting something of the Marian enigma.

Let us turn to Jean Guitton in this matter:

> The Virgin, who in the Gospel does nothing but reflect ("Mary pondered all these things in her heart"), has drawn upon herself the reflection of believers for over twenty centuries. In St. John, the entire essence of Mariology is already present, but time was needed to perceive her nature and her role in the divine plan. In order to be understood, Mary needs a long period of time, the millenary life of the Church. She, the Virgin "who ponders," calls upon her being the slowness of thought.

In his Second Letter to the Corinthians (4:3–4), Paul speaks of a gospel that is "veiled" from those who do not see "the glory of Christ" in it. Considering what Guitton said above, is there perhaps an enigmatic reference by the apostle here to that "Gospel of Mary" which, to be perceived, requires centuries of reflection?

Since men seem to have need of a Mother, with a capital *M*, besides the one who gave birth to them, when they have set aside the heavenly Mother, they go in search of another.

In fact, when in the late eighteenth century the French Revolution broke out (and above all the nationalisms of the nineteenth and twentieth centuries), behold the *Patria*, with a capital *P*, that becomes the Great Mother. The new military monks dedicate themselves to her as once the consecrated religious did to another Mother. Officers, like the clergy once, seek honor in the service of the Mother *Patria*. But the latter, unlike that of the Gospels, demands human sacrifice, the "immolation" of those "fallen on the fields of honor." The *Patria*, not incidentally, is represented as a young virgin: the anthropomorphism of Italy comes to mind, or that of France, or that of so many other nations on their stamps or currency. Or if one should recite the Litany of Loreto after the Rosary, applying it to the *Patria*, one would see that it actually "works" for the most part — that this substitution of the nation for the Mother has in fact come about.

I was recently in Spain, where they have begun a disturbing trend, parting ways with their tradition. In all the military barracks I read the motto, "*Todo per la Patria*." I could not resist thinking of that *Totus tuus* which John Paul II borrowed from St. Louis Marie Grignon de Montfort and which he placed on his papal crest. In this case, one must certainly "beware of imitations."

Another note that seemed illuminating and which I draw once more from Guitton reads: "Mary is the synthesis of time, this segment between two eternities. In her Immaculate Conception there is the state preceding Adam's catastrophe. In her Assumption into Heaven, there is humanity's terminal state, the return of the Son whom she anticipates. She is the creature of the *beginning* and the *end*."

It is clear that part of theology and of exegesis is silent and embarrassed in the face of the topic of the virginal birth of Jesus. For some time now, liberal Protestants have denied it, considering the marriage between Mary and Joseph to be a human relationship like any other, with many blood brothers and sisters of the firstborn named Jesus. But also among Catholics, there is no lack of stratagems, silence, and verbal tricks to affirm or not to affirm, as if we stood before a myth that was no longer acceptable. We saw this in the example of a recent encyclopedia, edited by Catholics and recommended by a bishop.

Perhaps Charles Guignebert was right. This priest, who was excommunicated for his exegetical positions, was the leader of Modernism and ended up losing his faith in the gospel. Following a typical route from *agape* to philanthropy, from the Church to the Freemasons' Lodge with their "humanism," he became in the end nothing less than a sort of apostle of the League of Nations, that hypocritical and impotent muddle, in which the former priest of Christ saw the realization of a sort of messianic kingdom on earth. Guignebert, nevertheless, warned his fellow theologians and biblical scholars to remain in the Church, however full of reservations and doubts they might be: "Seeing a Virgin give birth to a child is no less unlikely than seeing a dead man rise from his tomb."

It is not logical, therefore, to deny the virginal birth and then insist that one still believes in the Resurrection, as some theologians do. Whoever does not accept the beginning of the Gospel cannot guarantee the end. As the words of the schoolmaster of old Modernism remind us.

Another note to explore: Mary has only the smallest part to play in the words of Jesus. She is not part of his *teaching*. But she is part of his *body*: from her uterus, the Messiah came into the world, after being formed within her for nine long months. The bond between the two is not *flatus vocis* (merely a word), but much more: it is one of flesh and blood.

But isn't Christianity Jesus himself, his person, his flesh and blood in the Eucharist? So, is not "being part" of the body of Jesus more decisive than "being part" of his words?

Keeping myself beyond any presumption of being "illuminated," though ironic about my maniacal fixations, I confess that I am attracted to reflections on dates.[17] Time is a mystery whose definition neither science nor philosophy has been able to agree upon (and perhaps never will).

But there is a mystery also in the articulation of time which we call "date." From this perspective, I find significant that St. Louis Marie Grignon de Montfort was ordained a priest in the year 1700 (on June 5, to be exact). This saint, as we all know, was the apostle of consecration to Mary, the one who reinvigorated love for the Mother so as to rediscover the Son, traveling throughout the northwest of France and gathering immense crowds in town squares.

He journeyed through Normandy, Poitou, and Vendée. These places offered heroic resistance to the wickedness imposed by the Jacobins of Paris, to

[17] Editor's Note: A reference to the "Illuminati," a secret society known for its interest in numerology.

their bloody de-Christianization. In this heroic resistance, historians also notice the inheritance of de Montfort's preaching, centered entirely on the Virgin. The date of his priestly ordination seems truly symbolic, then, precisely in the year in which the century of the Enlightenment began, the eighteenth century of the Christian era, which would forge the anti-Christian weapons that have come down to our times. Just as modernity with its ideologies was beginning, the Spirit raised up a sort of "Marian" antidote to the evils caused by the errors into which men would fall.

Almost equally significant seems the year of St. Maximilian Kolbe's ordination, 1918, that other great herald of the necessity of not ignoring the Blessed Virgin. The "Great War" was drawing to a close, the bloodiest in history, caused by nationalism, while other post-Christian ideologies that had begun in the nineteenth century, fascism and communism, were about to explode onto the scene. The *red* and the *black* were preparing to give the world an infernal season.

Once again, precisely in that year, the Marian antidote seemed indispensable: as once it was Louis, so now it was Maximilian.

CHAPTER 40

THAT NAME

IN THIS CHAPTER I shall linger on the name of our heroine. After various peregrinations around the calendar, the Catholic liturgy has set September 12 as the specific feast of the Holy Name of Mary. As in many other forms of devotion to the Blessed Virgin, here too the Spanish took the initiative, going so far as to take a "pact of blood" in defense of Marian privileges, beginning with the Immaculate Conception. In the Iberian diocese of Cuenca, a specific liturgy has been dedicated to the Name of Mary ever since medieval times.

After extensions to other dioceses that requested permission, and even after suppressions (by the reform of Pius V), the feast ended up being fixed on the calendar on September 12, as mentioned. Most of the texts of the Office were taken from the writings of St. Bernard. An interesting point, because the great Cistercian was not only a minstrel of the Virgin Mary but also the writer of the Rule for the *Nova Militia*, the Order of the Knights Templar, vowed to wage war against the Muslims.

In fact, the date of September 12 was definitively chosen by the Church to recall how on one day in 1683, thanks to that Name, the Turks were defeated (and definitively halted) in their attack on Europe under the walls of Vienna. This connection to war in defense against the Islamic tide recalls the connection already inaugurated between the Rosary and Lepanto.

The liturgical itinerary of this anniversary, moreover, had the effect of following and disciplining the spontaneous movement of the devotion of the Christian people. And that is how it has always been in all that concerns Our Lady: the initiative has always come from the faithful; the hierarchy observes, monitors, regulates, and if it is appropriate, intervenes to officialize.

What does "Mary" mean? In the words of Elio Campana, the author of a weighty and now classic work, *Mary in Catholic Worship*, "Christian piety has always loved to think that the name of the Virgin had been preordained expressly by God and suggested by Him or by means of an angelic revelation to her parents or, at least, by means of supernatural inspiration. It is a name to which many theologians, and not the least among them, gladly append some sort of sanctifying virtue, as if there were in it something of the supernatural."

In fact, the Magisterium of the Church had to intervene against authors and preachers who, in their excessive devotion, gave to the mere repetition of that name an efficacy that bordered dangerously on the magical. It was a brilliant saint, Peter Canisius, who held (and many other Christian authors agreed with him) that "the name of the Mother of Christ contains a peculiar energy and a fragrance of the divine."

Veneration and respect, almost to the threshold of holy fear and trembling, had such an effect in many parts of the Christian world that no one dared name their daughter Mary. This is still the case today with the name "Jesus." Only the Sardinians go so far as to use the name "*Gesuino*," and in southern Italy they fall back on "*Salvatore*," while the Spanish-speaking peoples do not hesitate to baptize newborns with the resounding *Jesús*.

In Poland, it was formalized into a law issued by King Casimir I that prohibited all women from taking the name Mary. Over time, however, things began to turn around throughout the Christian world: not only did Mary become the most common female name, but (a unique case) it was also given as a middle name to many males.

The change came about throughout the entire Christian world — almost. There still exists a place where respect impedes the use of Mary even to indicate the Blessed Virgin herself, where she is always and only called Our Lady. That place is Ethiopia, where fervor for the Blessed Virgin reaches such heights as to fall into heresy: according to Ethiopian theologians, Mary seems in some ways to participate in the power proper to the Trinity, and is therefore deserving of worship. For the Ethiopians, the prohibition on using the name Mary for children has led them to find expedients such as the baptismal names "Plant of Mary," "Flower of Mary," "Virtue of Mary," "Servant of Mary," and so forth. In this way, devotion is preserved without breaching the traditional respect. But the Abyssinian case is so unique that we hope to dedicate an entire chapter to it.

And so, to come back to the question I asked before: What does that most venerated and mysteriously inspired name mean?

Modern studies have ascertained that there exist almost eighty etymologies, more or less well founded, proposed over the course of Christian history. At the beginning of the 1930s, the famous biblical scholar and Ancient Near East specialist Giuseppe Ricciotti attempted to sort it out. These were his first, significant words:

> Let us begin by shedding light on one point. The name of Mary, at the time of Christ, was widespread among the Jews, as we can verify both in the New Testament and in Flavius Josephus. Furthermore, it was not new to the Jewish people: we find its use around thirteen centuries before Christ in the sister of the one who was Judaism's leader and lawgiver, Moses. True, it seems that in later centuries it fell almost into disuse, but it is certain that in New Testament times it was very common, perhaps through the influence of the family of the Herodians, reigning at the time, in which there were several famous Marys.

Then, Abbot Ricciotti draws some conclusions which are interesting to consider: "It seems clear that the interpretations of 'Mary' that are based solely on the singular privilege of she who was the Mother of Jesus are without foundation. In this too, perhaps, one can see the fine example of the humility given to us by the Blessed Virgin: the docile wife of the carpenter of Nazareth bore a most common name that did not distinguish her from other women." This consideration could also be made about her Son: "Jesus," likewise, was quite a normal name among Jews of that time.

Having clarified this, let us make a survey of the crowd of interpretations of the name which, in Hebrew, does not use vowels and is written *Mrym,* pronounced *Miryam.*

Beginning with the Hebrew verb that means "to conceive," some have proposed "the Lord (comes from) my generation." But grammarians exclude its reliability. They give the same judgment to the etymologies based on the verb "to illuminate," which read *Mrym* as "the luminous one." Our scholar

Ricciotti comments, with his fittingly ruthless criticism, "Such an interpretation adapted well, in the light of pious devotion, to the Mother of the One who said of Himself, 'I am the light of the world.' But it does not fit with the many other Marys who bore the name of the Virgin: above all, it does not fit in with the rules of Hebrew syntax." Similar reasoning led to the rejection of "the gentle one" and "the exalted one."

The etymology of *Lady* became widespread in the Middle Ages, thanks to the encounter of the Crusaders with the languages of the Near East. This was based on the Syriac word *marj*, which means "lord" in its male version. But for the female version, in the same language, one says *martha* and not *miryam*.

A separate case, thanks to the good fortune it had in devotion and even in the liturgy, is the reading of Mary as *Stella Maris*, the star of the sea. The vast, authoritative acceptance of this evocative interpretation (the light that guides navigators through the night) can be explained by the fact that it was attributed to St. Jerome, the translator of the Bible, whose knowledge of Hebrew was considered unparalleled. In reality, it has long been shown that this great saint and philologist, spoke of *stilla maris*, a drop of the sea. It was the copyists who transformed an *i* into an *e*, and thus passed on the expression that became traditional.

Once again, Ricciotti guides us in this journey: "The authentic interpretation of Jerome surely does not clash as do others against the most elementary principles of Hebrew. The saint interprets, in fact, the name of Mary as Marjam and obtains the literally exact translation of 'drop of the sea.' Nevertheless, considered under historical light, this explanation as well seems unlikely and has in fact been abandoned by most scholars."

Continuing our exploration of the most curious etymologies, we find one that refers to the Hebrew verb *mara*, which literally means "to fatten." It is known that among Near Eastern populations plumpness is considered an essential element of feminine beauty. Therefore, "Mary" would mean "the plump one," a great compliment for ancient Semitic women — as it still is today among Arabs, who look upon Western women as being almost anorexic.

We put this eccentric reading aside as well, and find another that might sound nice to certain "revolutionary" theologies in fashion not so long ago: *Mrym* derives from another Hebrew verb that means "to rebel." Thus, Our Lady would be "the rebel." Today we would call this a demagogical reading in light of the banality of the modern political deformation that has polluted much of the clergy as well. The ancients, on the other hand, made of this a religious reading: "She who rebelled," yes, but against the devil, against the kingdom of evil, giving birth to the Vanquisher of Satan. Too bad if here, too, insurmountable grammatical problems arise.

Leaving aside other possibilities that are even less credible, we arrive at the one that, at the time of Giuseppe Ricciotti, was considered the most current and credible. A Jesuit and highly esteemed Semitic scholar, Fr. Zorrell, was its author. He was also an Egyptologist, interestingly.

He wrote,

> There is reason to believe that the name *Miryam*, given the fact that Moses' sister bore this name when the Hebrews sojourned in Egypt, might have Egyptian origins. We find that many proper names preserved in hieroglyphs are formed by two parts: the first is *myr*, which means "beloved"; and the second consists in the name of some divinity of the Nile. In the case of *Miryam*, the *yam* in the second part would be an abbreviation of the name of God among the Hebrews, according to an acceptable interpretation.

Therefore, from the sands of Egypt and the banks of the Nile comes the name Mary as the "beloved of God," referring to Israel's YHWH. At the start of the 1930s, when our Giuseppe Ricciotti attempted the summary which we used as our guide, a similar interpretation was taken by many as the definitive one. In fact, on the philological and historical level it seemed acceptable. Devotion as well was entirely satisfied: What more could be desired than this beautiful "beloved of God"?

But from the excavations of Ugarit, the ancient Phoenician city on the Syrian coast, another trail emerged, which in recent decades seems to be gaining support. The Ugarit language is written with a cuneiform alphabet, although it is quite similar in structure and vocabulary to Hebrew. In fact, its discovery and deciphering has permitted scholars to resolve several problems of interpretation in the Bible. Thus, they established that the phoneme *Mrym*, also present in Ugaritic, is the equivalent of the Hebrew term *marom*, which means "height." And so, Miryam should be understood to mean "the exalted, sublime." Here too, all are happy among both etymologists and devotees: Is not the Blessed Virgin "the most exalted" among creatures? Furthermore, it seems that this reading finds confirmation as well in certain hidden "word games" imbedded by Luke in verses where he narrates what happened before the birth of Jesus.

Could this Ugaritic etymology truly be the definitive one? I wouldn't bet on it. Research and interpretations continue. In the end, this too might be a confirmation of the old conviction of devotees: *de Maria, numquam satis*. If the mystery of her person is inexhaustible, why should the enigma surrounding her name not be?

CHAPTER 41

THE BATTLE OVER "LA PURÍSIMA"

THAT UNIQUE REALITY IN the world of Marian prodigies I have investigated extensively, *el Milagro de la pierna,* the miracle of the leg in Calanda, took place in seventeenth-century Spain. My research led me into the libraries and archives of the nation and the century in which the most incredible of battles raged: that between the *maculatists* and the *immaculatists.*

I would like to discuss this battle here in this chapter. It confirms what I have repeatedly mentioned: the progressive emergence of the truth about Mary, implicit and almost hidden in revelation; and then, the extraordinary role played by the people of God in stimulating the hierarchy to an investigation that led, in the end, to a dogmatic definition.

In speaking of *maculatists* and *immaculatists,* we are referring to one of these truths: the Immaculate Conception. When Pius IX proclaimed the dogma on December 8, 1854, he put an end to an extraordinary matter in Catholic history. This affair saw Spain as its greatest protagonist. Not incidentally, the commemorative monument of the dogma, the famous ancient column topped with the statue (we will speak of it in depth in another chapter), would be erected three years later in 1857, in front of the Roman palace which since 1647 has been the home of the Spanish embassy to the Holy See. It was the symbolic recognition of how much the entire Iberian Peninsula had done through the enduring and passionate activity of its people, including kings, theologians, and clergy.

Until recent times, schoolchildren upon entering class would address their teacher with an "*Ave Maria Purísima,*" and the teacher would respond, "*Sin pecado concebida,*" conceived without sin. This was (and still is in some areas) the habitual greeting the Spanish would exchange. And if the Spanish faithful remained immune to deviations from orthodoxy, as some historians have observed, it is due to this inflamed love for Mary which is the best safeguard against straying from the right path.

Various explanations have been proposed for this entirely Iberian ardor for the assertion and defense of that Marian privilege: namely, that she was exempted from original sin. Except, of course, for supernatural reasons (there was truly a providential aspect to this struggle), on the human level one can perhaps see an influence from the old, profound, knightly attitude that characterizes the soul of the peninsula. Don Quixote comes to mind, who in his delirium, with his jealous defense of the honor of Dulcinea, displays the true sentiments of the old Spain. If every knight had been ready to die for the honor of his beloved lady (a peasant girl, moreover, in the case of the *hidalgo* of Cervantes), all the more for the honor of the lady par excellence, the *Señora de las señoras*! The assertion of the Immaculate Conception of that Lady was seen by the Spanish as an inalienable part of her "honor."

It is therefore entirely logical that the orders of monk-knights that arose in the peninsula at the service of the *Reconquista* (the Orders of Calatrava, of Alcantara, of Santiago, of Montesa, etc.) would take, besides the three usual ones, a solemn fourth religious vow, to defend at the cost of their lives the truth of the Immaculate Conception of Mary. This was the famous "blood pact" which would be criticized in the 1700s by Ludovico Antonio Muratori. This erudite man, already under the sway of the Enlightenment, observed that, while it is meritorious to give one's life for the Faith, it is not meritorious to do so for a "theological opinion" such as the Immaculate Conception was at that time.

These are rational considerations that had to take into account however a particular culture and temperament. We should not forget that St. Ignatius of Loyola would confess to having felt the instinctive temptation (moved as he was by his recent conversion) to attack and even kill a random travel companion who expressed an irreverent opinion regarding the absolute and primordial purity of Mary!

In their fervor for the Immaculate Conception, besides the usual knightly defense of the honor of the most exalted *Señora,* there was at work as well a reaction to the Jewish issues that had troubled the Iberian Peninsula for centuries: first the presence of Jewish communities and then the problem of Marranos, the "false converts." It is known that the Talmud and other texts of diaspora Judaism defame the Mother of Jesus (and in particular, her virginal innocence), to the point of provoking even the reaction of Mohammed: the Quran inveighs against the Israelites precisely because they make this insinuation. This might explain the Spanish reaction: reasserting that Mary was so "pure" as to be the *Purísima* by definition, from her conception.

Whatever the case, the eternal Iberian struggle set two camps against each other, even within the religious world: the side of the *immaculatists* was supported by the Franciscans and the Jesuits, and that of the *maculatists* above all by the Dominicans. The latter found themselves to be almost entirely isolated: against them were aligned not only the other orders but also the people and the monarchy as well.

But the sons of St. Dominic wielded a formidable weapon in the fact that they controlled the Inquisition, which oversaw the matter, assuring that what was being discussed as theological opinion was not to be considered dogma to be imposed on believers. The "white friars" were not against Marian devotion; on the contrary, we all know how much they worked to spread the practice of the Rosary which, tied to their belts, is an integral part of their habit. And every friar takes Mary as a second name.

But as advocates of reason applied to theology, the Dominicans turned to their St. Thomas, who confessed he could not harmonize the redemption of Christ, indispensable for every human being, with the fact that it seemed to escape one human being, however supereminent she might be as the Mother of Christ. These difficulties, as we discussed earlier, were overcome by the recognition that Mary as well was redeemed, but "in advance," "in the foreknowledge of the merits of her Son," *ante praevisa merita*. For Mary, therefore, only the way and the time of the indispensable redemption were different.

This solution had already been imagined by the Franciscan *Doctor subtilis*, Duns Scotus, but it would take half a millennium to establish itself. It was during those centuries that the Spanish went to work, starting with the extensive practice of baptizing their daughters (and the cities in the American countries they were colonizing) with the name Concepción, implying naturally the *Inmaculada*. Already in the second half of the fourteenth century, King Juan I of Aragon had established by edict that in his territories liberated from the Muslim yoke there should be an annual celebration "with great solemnity" of the feast of the Immaculate Conception.

In 1489, the princess of royal blood, Beatrice de Silva, later proclaimed saint, founded the first convent of the Conceptionists: important not only because they were the first religious founded under the name of the *Purísima*, but also for their religious habit. According to St. Beatrice, this habit — a white cowl with a blue mantle — had been suggested to her by the Blessed Virgin herself during an apparition. These were the same colors that the Immaculate of Lourdes would wear (and they are the same as the Argentinian flag: General Manuel Belgrano, the national hero, wanted it this way in honor of the "All-Pure One"). After the completion of the *Reconquista* and the unification of all Spain (from which Portugal would withdraw, though it too was aligned with the enthusiasm for the Immaculate), the kings sent ambassadors on numerous occasions to obtain from the Holy See the proclamation of the dogma. It became a real affair of state, not only due to the sincere devotion of the sovereigns themselves, but also for reasons of public order. In fact, all sorts of turmoil broke out every time some imprudent preacher (usually a Dominican) stated that Mary, like every other human being, was born with original sin. Seville was shaken by unrest when a friar provokingly proposed a paradoxical thesis: namely, that Mary would have gone to Hell had she died before the redeeming death of Jesus on the cross.

The kings of Spain (especially in the 1600s), through their ordinary and extraordinary ambassadors, informed the popes of the reality that ferment was growing: town councils united in taking their "pact of blood" on behalf of their entire city, as did likewise the universities and professional associations. To teach in school or to hold public office, it was obligatory to swear to one's belief in the Immaculate Conception.

The popes knew about the situation but refused, under popular pressure, to resolve the theological question that was not yet entirely clear. Thus, at the beginning of the seventeenth century, Phillip III's delegation was given only the minimum of what could be granted: Pope Paul V issued a decree that prohibited the public denial of the Immaculate Conception, while authorizing the continuation of study and debate among the schools of the religious orders.

The Spanish people rejoiced, but immediately made it clear that this was not enough — especially because the Inquisition (under Dominican control) seemed to interpret this papal concession as favoring one of the two sides of the debate. Other official delegations were then sent from Spain to Rome, until in 1661 they obtained from Alexander VII the imposition of silence on the detractors of the *Purísima,* even in private discussions. Furthermore, in Spain and in all its colonial possessions, December 8 was recognized as an obligatory feast. Later, the Immaculate Conception, along with St. James (Santiago), became the official patroness of the nation. Every further concession was perceived by the people as a victory: great celebrations with corridas were organized as soon as the couriers from Rome brought good news for the cause of the *Immaculada.*

The decades passed until finally the year 1854 arrived. After so many struggles, the proclamation of the dogma, for which kings and campesinos, intellectuals and illiterate had fought for centuries, arrived at time when Spain was dominated by an anticlerical government controlled by Generals O'Donnell and Espartero and relations with the Holy See had been interrupted.

As a sort of supreme insult, perceived by the people as an offense, they went so far as to prohibit the publication of the papal bull on the Immaculate Conception — in Spain of all places! Nor did the threats and supplications of Queen Isabel II have any effect on the government: officially, the Spanish people were not to know that Rome had crowned the ideal that had energized generations for centuries precisely there, beyond the Pyrenees.

Today, we witness another sad contradiction: the socialists of the post-Franco era established that every year throughout all Spain, eight holidays are to be celebrated, with the corresponding day off work. Missing from among those holidays is December 8, which is left to the decision of the autonomous local governments. Thus, in some regions, the Immaculate Conception is (according to the law of the state) just one day like any other.

These are the paradoxes and mysteries of history, particularly evident in a country that seems to love extremes and which, enjoying primacy in missionary expansion throughout the world, is also that which has carried out the bloodiest persecution of the Church, during the civil war. And still today, despite aggressive secularization, the Church leaves no one indifferent but stokes the passions either to exalt her or to execrate her. A good sign, after all, according to Scripture, which sees the "lukewarm" as being the least acceptable to the Lord.

Postscript

I purposely left the final paragraph as it stood in the magazine. This allows me to remind the reader that bad news can at times be proved wrong. In fact, after the publication in *Jesus*, several Spanish readers wrote me to confirm the truth that, in 1988, socialists passed a law regarding national holidays that foresaw the abolition of the Immaculate. To take such a drastic decision in light of Spanish history, they had recourse to a clever trick: they set December 6 as the "Day of the Constitution." It would not be possible, they declared with feigned regret (they were not yet socialists with the secular arrogance exhibited as a virtue by Zapatero), to keep the festivity of December 8 as well. It would have created too long of a weekend and would have damaged the economy.

At this point, from the depths of history, the Iberian DNA reemerged with its instinctive and passionate devotion to the *Purísima*. There was a risk that the popular revolts of the past might return, as the streets were invaded by vociferous crowds, and it was organized so that the bells of all the churches in Spain would ring freely. The government was buried by protests that arrived from everywhere. But the winning move came from Andalusia, despite being a socialist stronghold in Spain and the homeland of their leader, Felipe Gonzalez. All the confraternities of Seville laid down an ultimatum that left no way out: if the feast of the Immaculate were to be suppressed, they would not turn out for the ancient, extraordinary Holy Week celebrations, considered to be the most impressive in the world. The example given by Seville was a signal to be followed throughout Spain: everywhere the confraternities decided to leave the floats, candles, crosses, and hooded costumes in their warehouses and began a sort of "Good Friday Strike."

It was a mortal threat to the socialists. Those processions were not only a cultural (as well as religious) heirloom tied indissolubly to the image of Spain in the world, but were also an enormous stimulus to tourism. Their suppression would mean an incalculable loss and a negative international image.

Thus, my Iberian friends inform me, the *Fiesta de la Purísima* remained on the national calendar among the bank holidays. As if vindictively, the socialists succeeded in passing the option, left to the decision of the autonomous communities, to insert as a holiday or not that other great Spanish feast of Santiago. One reader, a religious with the Trinitarians of Castile, wrote me, "Perhaps Santiago, accustomed to making heroic gestures, had to sacrifice himself for the honor of the Immaculate. A sacrifice he did not complain about, we his devoted followers are convinced, knowing the bonds that unite him indissolubly to the Virgin Mary and are at the origins of the national shrine, that of the *Pilar* in Zaragoza."

CHAPTER 42

The Perfumes of Laus

The world of Mary of Nazareth is truly inexhaustible and full of surprises small and great, though always comforting!

I thought of this during the blazing days of August, driving along the highway from Turin to the Tunnel of Frejus into France. Before reaching Bardonecchia, before the entrance to the great tunnel, there is an exit for Oulx that leads along the state highway toward the pass of Monginevro. There, one crosses the border (or former border: the police and customs agents are long gone) and continues along the French *route nationale* that arrives in Briançon, and from there to Gap. Before reaching the latter, about ninety kilometers from the Italian border, a series of road signs lead one up a steep road onto a pleasant mountain at an altitude of nine hundred meters above sea level. There, one finds a glorious panorama, very well preserved, and a tonic air. This department called the *Hautes Alpes* is famous for its climate, uniting alpine qualities with marine virtues from the nearby Provence.

There we reached *Notre Dame du Laus,* Our Lady of the Lake (this is the meaning of *laus* in the local Occitan dialect). An extraordinary place, and not only because of the lovely position, but above all due to the spiritual message that it has transmitted for over three centuries. It remains to be discovered by the French (as well as all the Church), either because they have never heard of it or have heard only the vaguest mention of its name thanks to what is called the "perfumes of Laus."

This is what happened, in fact: the woman at the origin of the shrine, and the pilgrimage to it, was guided to this solitary alpine plain by the Virgin herself, who told her that the exact place where she wanted her Son to be adored would be revealed to her by its "pleasant perfume." And this indeed was the case, and every time the visionary came out of her encounter with the Mother of God she was entirely imbued with mysterious and intense perfumes.

The phenomenon continued without interruption until recently. It can happen in the church (where the custom of offering flowers is not practiced, so as not to lead to confusion with the perfumes); but it can also happen in the hospitality dormitories for pilgrims that surround the church; or on the trails thereabout; or even, and this has often happened, in the large parking lot. During my stays there, I have spoken with many guests — solid, reliable people, definitely not visionaries — who have smelled these scents, whose effect seems to be that of giving great joy and an equally great spiritual consolation.

A university professor who has conducted research into this phenomenon, François de Muizon, has recently written,

> Several observations impose themselves. First, there is no possible fraud that one can hypothesize: no one could produce such perfumes in such diverse circumstances and places. This is not an event derived from natural odoriferous sources, given that the scents are smelled indiscriminately in all seasons, day and night, inside as well as outside. Before being suddenly immersed, many witnesses knew nothing about these "perfumes of Laus." This renders untenable the usual explanations which come to mind instinctively, such as autosuggestion, delirium, or hysteria. The mystery has grown not only due to the great number of witnesses, but due to their permanence throughout the centuries, throughout various times and cultures.

Naturally, the believer will not be surprised by these events, given that perfumes often accompany life in communion with the gospel. "In the odor of sanctity," says the stereotypical expression: not only after death, but even while living, as was told about Padre Pio of Pietrelcina, for example.

Perfumes are often connected to Marian miracles. I had one of many confirmations of this while reconstructing the events of *El Gran Milagro* of Calanda, to which I dedicated a book. When the parents of the young Miguel Juan Pellicer entered the room where the miraculously healed boy was sleeping, dreaming of the *Virgen del Pilar*, before they even realized that their son's leg, amputated two and a half years earlier, had been reimplanted, they were surprised by a very intense perfume they had never smelled before, indescribable, filling the room. This mysterious odor persisted for a long time in the room and in their clothing, as the mother testified at the canonical trial. A sign of the "Marian presence" which, in the French shrine has seems to have become permanent and so frequent that many visitors to this place consider it quite normal.

A Marian presence, we said. Well, if this is the reality that characterizes every place where the Virgin Mary has appeared, such a presence reaches a world record in Laus. In fact, the visionary enjoyed the visits of the Mother for some fifty-four years! Between one encounter and another with her, there were some with Christ himself, with the saints, and with the angels. For this reason, Notre Dame du Laus has been associated in recent years with Medjugorje, where the "apparitions" on which the Church has not yet made a pronouncement have been judged by many as untenable due to the duration of the phenomena and the consequent number of messages entrusted to the young visionaries. In reality, there has been at least one precedent, and it is that of which we are speaking.

The Lady who came to these Maritime Alps (where she is called *Dame Marie*) appeared and spoke to the same person for over half a century. This is not to be considered the usual unfounded popular belief, given that a long series of bishops have recognized and encouraged pilgrimage to the site — and given that the visionary has long been a "venerable" and her cause has recently been reactivated, with good prospects for reaching beatification.

The moment has come, though, to talk about this woman who was singularly privileged by Heaven, this "venerable servant of God" (this is the official title recognized by the Church), Benoîte Rencurel. She was born in this corner of what was then called the Dauphiné, on September 17, 1647. Benoîte's infancy was the typical kind for peasants of that time: misery, illiteracy, a widowed mother, and work as a shepherdess for the neighbors.

The mountains that surround her native village (then Saint-Etienne d'Avançon, now called Saint-Etienne Le Laus, in honor of the shrine) are rich in chalky earth which, when fired in the ovens dug in the form of caves, produces a good lime. It was in one of these ovens in May of 1664, while she was busy watching the sheep and goats and reciting her Rosary, that Benoîte saw the "Beautiful Lady" whom Bernadette would see over two centuries later, and who here as in Lourdes, during that first visit, limited herself to smiling radiantly. Other silent apparitions followed. Then, little by little, the Lady began to speak, to respond to questions, to ask some herself, and to give advice and indications to the young visionary. So began a sort of "pedagogical journey" which would continue until Benoîte's death.

This, in fact, is the extraordinary originality of Laus: *Dame Marie* took into her own hands, as would a mother or a teacher, the religious but also the human education of the girl who was only a coarse and ignorant mountain shepherdess. And then, once she had educated her, she entrusted her with the construction of a shrine, the organization of pilgrimage, welcoming, guiding, and preparing the pilgrims for the sacraments of Confession and Communion. When some nuns from Savoy proposed to take up residence in Laus, hoping to convince Benoîte to join them, the testimony of the visionary reported that "the Mother of God said that she was not to do that, that those religious were too secluded, that she wanted Benoîte to see the pilgrims, to speak with them when they asked, to give them needed advice, as God inspired her. And this she could not have done in a monastery, where she would have been too closed in."

From this peculiarity there derived another: from the very beginning, going up to Laus was not understood to be just a quick visit and then a quick return to where one came from, as with other shrines. This mountain was a place of "celestial pedagogy," of prolonged sojourn with the Mother. For this reason, it was necessary to build structures for hospitality, a kitchen, and dormitories to be able to meet the needs, religious and earthly, of fellow Christians. This has not only continued but has grown and has become well organized with great care, respecting the tradition of simplicity. Arriving at this alpine plain, one finds an efficient "Marian city" with *hôtelleries* open year round, hosting hundreds of people and placing at their disposal large meeting halls.

For us, this recalls a parallel in Italy, the shrine of Oropa. Here too, the shrine is surrounded by hospitality structures. *Ecclesia et domus*, church and home, according to the motto of Oropa. Its directors in the early nineteenth century conceded to Napoleon's troops without discussion when they demanded the rich treasury of the shrine; but they rebelled when they demanded the beds and mattresses too. The Madonna could live without her gold, but she could not be without her children who, at least for a few days and nights, lived next to her.

But we return now to Benoîte, whom we left at the start of her extraordinary adventure. After several months of familiarity, Dame Marie commanded her to go to the other part of the valley, to the plateau called "the Lake," *le Laus* in Occitan, where there were very few houses and one little, miserable chapel which Benoîte would recognize "by its pleasant perfume." With a nonsensical instruction in human terms — to an ignorant girl, without means, without social prestige — the Lady entrusted precisely to her the construction of a shrine.

Naturally, due to a series of providential circumstances, with unforeseeable twists in the plot, the impossible was realized. In just a few years, where there had been only sheep and goats, there arose a place of worship that would endure through time. Still today, the basilica constructed by the visionary contains within it the primitive chapel, called *La Bonne Rencontre,* the name given by the people of the Alps to the Annunciation. In the apse of the chapel stands the high altar and the tabernacle with its sanctuary lamp burning. The rite which all the pilgrims who come here carry out is unusual: after kneeling to adore the Blessed Sacrament, they dip their fingers in the oil of the tabernacle lamp and make the sign of the cross with it.

Little phials of the oil are sent throughout France and to many countries where this devotion has spread. In fact, according to a promise of the *Dame Marie* to her darling, contact with that liquid, with an attitude of faith in the omnipotent Son, would bring about miracles of spiritual healing as well as physical cures.

Therefore, along with the mysterious perfumes (and together with the sojourn: *ecclesia et domus*), anointing with the oil of the tabernacle lamp characterizes this Marian site. It was a healthily "material" way of living the devotion that won over a people, but which could not fail to repulse the Jansenism which beset much of the clergy, especially in France, in that second half of the seventeenth century. This caused skepticism and persecution toward the visionary after the initial positive though prudent welcome by the local Church, represented by the Diocese of Embrun (suppressed by the Revolution and then united definitively with that of Gap). As always, the opposition showed itself fruitful, confirming the spiritual solidity of the woman, formed in her faith by the Blessed Virgin herself, as the bishops recognized after long, exhausting interrogations.

In the end, the persecutions stopped and the pilgrimages were able to continue, though with occasional interruptions due to the passage of armies through the area.

Thus, the contact between Benoîte and Heaven continued until the end. She would die at the age of seventy-one, in 1718, surrounded by the veneration and gratitude of all. She was buried in front of the high altar, where she still lies today, right under the tabernacle lamp whose oil serves every day for the anointing of the devout.

Upon the death of the visionary, devotion for that place of worship was not in the least extinguished. On the contrary, it was so solid that it even survived the fury of the Revolution at the end of that century and took up its march even more steadily than before.

Nor did the veneration of pilgrims toward Benoîte, this human instrument chosen by Mary herself, burn out. But the suppression of the Diocese of Embrun, and the succession of various religious communities in managing the shrine, made it the case that only in 1872 could Pope Pius IX officially proclaim the visionary a "venerable servant of God."

The cause for her beatification met with obstacles from certain dour historians and not by any means from the popes (Leo XIII would grant Laus the title of "minor basilica") nor even the bishops of Gap, who unanimously visited the shrine and recommended their faithful to do likewise.

The problems for the cause arose, it seems, because it had been set up in a problematic way, with insufficient investigation of the sources. Yet Yves Chiron, currently one of the leading specialists, described the events at Laus as "among the best documented apparitions ever." We have at our disposal, in fact, written reports of four eyewitnesses of the life of Benoîte, totaling hundreds and hundreds of pages. Recently published in critical editions, these texts have allowed the cause to be reopened by the Congregation of Saints in the Vatican and a positive result seems imminent. The Church might soon have a new blessed and, after that, a new saint. The passage from venerable to blessed is a logical exigency. In fact, in 2008, the Church officially declared the events that occurred in Laus to be "supernatural."

Furthermore, the modern appeal of this laywoman must not be overlooked (Benoîte became a Third Order Dominican), for she assumed a precise and demanding spiritual leadership and showed that gifts of courage, decisiveness, and wisdom can emerge from faith. This was even more peculiar in that dark epoch of Jansenism and asceticism, often exaggerated, with her call (inspired by all that her "Mistress" taught her) to moderation even in penance. As she said, "If one eats too little and mistreats one's body, one cannot pray well."

Thus, we see even more figures and stories in the many-colored, fascinating world of Our Lady, quite unknown to so many Christians today. A world that a sojourn in Laus, this "perfumed" oasis of peace for the soul and relaxation for the body, can contribute to discovering.

CHAPTER 43

A JEW AND A MEDAL

IT MIGHT BE HELPFUL to bring to light one of the Marian interventions that had the most influence on the Church in the 1800s and that seems today not only forgotten but almost repressed out of embarrassment.

We are speaking about the lightning-strike conversion to Catholicism of the young Jew Alphonse Ratisbonne in the papal Rome of 1842. In the current ecclesial climate, it appears "ecumenically incorrect" to speak of conversions; and even more so if they concern Jews. According to some, each person should live and die in the religious (or irreligious) tradition he finds himself in. In many countries, there are even members of the clergy who would discourage those knocking on the door from entering the Catholic Church.

Evidently, however, divine categories are different and do not await the approval of men. It was the Jew Ratisbonne who became a priest and lived a full Christian commitment for more than forty years until his death, witnessing the solidity, and therefore the truth, of the mysterious event which in one instant changed his entire existence. Furthermore, immediately after that conversion, the pope ordered his cardinal vicar to instigate a canonical investigation into it, which concluded with the recognition of the miraculous character of that conversion, obtained by the Blessed Virgin who appeared under the guise found on the Miraculous Medal.

In fact, this mysterious episode is directly tied to the equally mysterious apparitions to the novice Catherine Labouré in the Parisian Rue du Bac. From those events (of which we have already spoken) it seems a sort of chain was set in motion, which involved Lourdes as well, where the Virgin Mary defined herself as the "Immaculate Conception." We know, in fact, that on the model of the medal that Mary "commissioned" of Catherine was written the statement that only in 1854 would be defined as dogma: "Oh Mary, *conceived without sin,* pray for us who have recourse to thee."

At any rate, the first link in the chain after the apparitions in Rue du Bac (which took place between July and November 1830) seems to be found in the inspiration of the parish priest of the Parisian church of Our Lady of Victories, Charles Dufriche-Desgenettes.

This pastor was aggrieved because, in the Paris of the early decades of the 1800s, his church had been deserted by the people. On December 3, 1836, while celebrating Mass at the altar of the Virgin, he heard an interior voice that enjoined him: "Consecrate your parish to the Holy and Immaculate Heart of Mary." The good priest thought he was suffering a hallucination, but the voice repeated the message when he returned to the sacristy. He immediately decided to establish an association dedicated to the Heart of Mary Immaculate, which enjoyed an immediate and inexplicable diffusion throughout the world, exceeding twenty million members in just a few years. According to its statutes, each of them took upon themselves the task of always wearing a Miraculous Medal, and of repeating at least once a day the prayer inscribed on it, with the invocation, "conceived without sin."

A further stage in this mysterious journey, where truly *tout se tient,* with a thousand connections, at times obvious and at other times discreet, is the one that we announced at the beginning of this chapter and that took place in Rome on January 20, 1842, in the Church of Sant'Andrea delle Fratte (run by the Minims of St. Francis da Paola), near the Spanish Steps, in the place where the famous column would be erected in honor of the Immaculate Conception in remembrance of the dogma proclaimed by Pius IX. It was at Sant'Andrea that the stunning conversion of the twenty-year-old Alphonse Ratisbonne took place. The Blessed Virgin appeared to him with lowered arms and open hands, in the exact gesture of the famous medal which the young Jew, as a derisive challenge, had agreed to wear around his neck.

Ratisbonne belonged to one of the richest and most influential families of the large Jewish community in Strasbourg. His older brother, Théodore, a convert to Christianity, was ordained a priest in 1830, the same year as the apparitions to Catherine Labouré. Fr. Théodore would become one of the main collaborators with the parish priest of Our Lady of Victories and, as such, an enthusiastic and tireless mouthpiece of devotion to the Immaculate Heart, to whom he recommended his brother Alphonse every day. This prayer would be resoundingly accepted in the apparition of the Blessed Virgin herself, as we shall see.

The young Alphonse, faithful to Judaism more for its ritual and tradition than through faith, felt the need to fight for the aid and liberation of his brethren in Israel. His hostility toward Christianity in general, and Catholicism in particular, was not only not concealed but was publicly manifested. In love with a cousin, Flore, he established the date of their marriage, one that would bring advantages on the social level, though desired above all for the sake of their mutual love. Before getting married, he decided to go on a journey that would take him to Jerusalem to see the land of his fathers. In a sudden change of plans, he decided to visit Rome as well. Arriving on the Epiphany in 1842, one of his first visits was to the Ghetto, where more than four thousand Roman Jews lived. This too reinforced his hostility, already alive and militant, toward Catholicism and papal governance.

In Rome, Ratisbonne, although unwillingly, came into contact with a group of fervent French Catholics (many of them converts), who were nourished by Roman spirituality and of whom one was the Baron Théodore de Bussières, a former Lutheran and a friend of his brother, Fr. Théodore. Bussières not only had his believing friends pray for the young Jew, but almost as a wager, was able to convince him to wear the famous medal. Moreover, he obtained from him the promise of copying the text of that famous prayer attributed to St. Bernard that begins with *Memorare* and runs, “Remember, O most gracious Virgin Mary, that never was it known that anyone who fled to your protection, implored your help, or sought your intercession, was left unaided.” We would like to recall that invocation in its entirety, because it has played a part in the depths of so many consciences and so many hearts and has been the harbinger of graces of which only God knows: “Inspired by this confidence, we fly unto you, O Virgin of Virgins our Mother. To you we come, before you we stand, sinful and sorrowful. O Mother of the Word Incarnate, despise not our petitions, but in your mercy hear and answer us!”

Despite the fact that he had already booked his departure in a coach bound for Naples (then to continue by freighter to Istanbul and from there to Palestine),

Alphonse, urged by a mysterious power, decided to remain a few days in Rome. In the late morning of January 20 of that 1842, he accompanied Baron de Bussières to the Church of Sant'Andrea delle Fratte, telling him he would wait in the carriage while his companion (not "friend," due to his animosity toward Catholics) spoke with the friars about arrangements for a funeral. He was alone with the coachman, but the curiosity to see the interior of the church led him to enter it. And there, entirely unexpectedly, arrived the "lightning strike" that radically upended his life, changing it forever.

We hear in the protagonist's own words, translating the text which the untiring René Laurentin (he dedicated himself for years to the critical reconstruction of this case as well) reconstructed from sure sources:

> Suddenly, I felt overcome by a strange disturbance and saw a veil descend before me. The church seemed dark, except for one chapel, as if the light had been concentrated there. I do not understand how I then found myself kneeling before the rail of that chapel: in fact, I was on the other side of the church and between me and the chapel, blocking the way, was the furniture that had been arranged for the funeral. I raised my eyes toward the light that shone so brightly and saw, standing on the altar, alive, great, majestic, utterly beautiful and with a mysterious air, the Blessed Virgin Mary, similar in attitude and structure to the image on the Medal that I had been given to wear. I tried repeatedly to raise my eyes toward her, but her splendor and due respect made me lower them, without preventing me from feeling the presence of the apparition. I fixed my gaze, then, on her hands and saw in them the expression of forgiveness and mercy. With those same hands, she gestured to me to remain kneeling. But an irresistible force pushed me toward her. In her presence, although she had said no word, I comprehended instantly the horror of the state I was in, the deformity of sin, the beauty of faith in the Gospel: in a word, I understood everything, in an instant.

The handwritten testimony of Alphonse continues,

> I could not realize the modality with which, in just one moment, I had acquired knowledge of the faith. All I can say is that, in the brief moment of the gesture of her hands, a blindfold fell from my eyes; and not only one, but many blindfolds that I had wrapped around myself, disappeared after that like snow, ice, mud under the action of

> the brightest sunlight. I could see, at the bottom of the abyss, the extreme misery from which I had been taken by an act of infinite mercy.

The dramatic testimony of Ratisbonne ends with a phrase that, for the rest of his life, he loved repeating: "*Elle ne m'a rien dit, mais j'ai tout compris*" (She said nothing to me, but I understood everything). Almost a century later, another Frenchman, he too an agnostic, if not atheist, and at least in part Jewish, André Frossard, had the experience that he recognized as being similar, of a radical, instantaneous conversion that came out of nowhere and had lasting effects for the rest of his life. For Frossard as well, the mystical phenomenon was exclusively "visible," without words; he too often said he "had understood everything, suddenly, without having heard anything." Both of these Frenchmen, one in the nineteenth and the other in the twentieth century, had no precise idea about Catholicism until the moment of the "encounter" (they detested it without knowing it), but when the catechism was explained to them, they said that its teaching only confirmed what they had already learned from the mystical vision.

Returning to the story of Ratisbonne: devoured by the desire to receive Baptism (the importance of which was revealed to him in the flash of his conversion), eleven days later he was admitted to the sacrament, taking the simple name "Marie," which he would keep even after entering the Society of Jesus. Ordained priest in 1848, he remained in the Jesuits for several years to the satisfaction of his superiors. But in agreement with Pius IX, he abandoned the society to unite with his brother in founding a congregation, that of Notre Dame de Sion, which still exists today, working for the conversion of the Jews to the gospel.[18] Alphonse described in this way his initial encounter with his brother, who, trusting in the intervention of the Virgin Mary, did not doubt his conversion: "We remained kneeling on the same kneeler for more than half an hour, without being able to say a word, only sobbing with joy and gratitude." Among the initiatives they took together was the foundation of a house for catechumens in Paris. (Among the throng of Jews arriving from the great settlements in the East were many who wanted a Christian education for themselves and for their children.) Alphonse died in 1884 at age seventy, in Ain Karin in the Holy Land, the traditional site of the Visitation of

[18] Editor's note: Following the promulgation of *Nostra Aetate*, the congregation works to improve Christian and Jewish relations.

Mary to her cousin Elizabeth. Among his last words were, "My confidence in Mary has reached what in human terms would be called audacity. I have only sought to be a sort of signal that points our brethren toward the Virgin, whose intercession is omnipotent."

I found a curious annotation in the *Diary* of Paul Claudel, under the date March 14, 1950: "Providence has reserved to a Jewish convert, Fr. Alphonse Ratisbonne, the honor of rediscovering under the mass of ruins and detritus he had bought in Jerusalem, an authentic paving stone of the *Lithostrotos,* the place of the *Ecce Homo,* where the Jews had shouted, 'May his blood be upon us and our children!'"

In fact, this was the case: the plot of land which the two Ratisbonne brothers bought in Jerusalem in 1856 turned out to be one of the most famous in the Gospel narrative, the place where Pilate had established his tribunal on that fateful Friday morning before the Passover feast. In the Holy Land, nevertheless, the work of the two convert brothers was incessant: preaching, apostolic activities, and assistance to orphans and other needy youth (Muslims, Jews and Christians).

Calumny would be the lot, especially of Alphonse (but also for Théodore). According to René Laurentin, the archive of the Holy Office preserves (in the part that is still reserved) a file with the testimonies of the defamation that accompanied the life of this "uncomfortable" convert. The opposition of members of their large family and of their Jewish coreligionists throughout Europe was violent and implacable. The break with Flore was quite harsh as well, his beloved fiancée who was preparing for their wedding while awaiting his return. Nevertheless, this heroic renunciation of human love was a guarantee of the reality and the strength of his conversion, which was even subjected to a trial before a court in the Chancery of Rome. Many theses were examined, and after months of investigation, Cardinal Costantino Patrizi signed the decree (bearing the date June 3, 1842) that concluded thus: "We fully verify the truth of the celebrated miracle worked by God Almighty through the intercession of the Blessed Virgin Mary, namely the instantaneous and perfect conversion of Alphonse Ratisbonne from Judaism."

To the defamation (not only from Jewish settings) that accompanied the life of "Fr. Marie," as he always wanted to be called, the usual prosaic psychological and psychoanalytic excursions were added, to reduce to a pathological phenomenon the vision that caused his conversion. This is not the place to discuss the matter. It suffices to remember the energy of the event that was unleashed in those few moments on January 20, 1842, and that, according to Guitton, seemed to repeat what had occurred to Paul of Tarsus at the gates of Damascus. For forty-two years until his death (which overtook him, as he desired, in the Marian month of May; on his tomb he wanted written only *Père Marie*), Alphonse Ratisbonne never placed in doubt the truth of what had happened to him and was faithful to his life of sacrifice and prayer, as a religious committed to both contemplation and action. At the mere name of the Mother of Christ, his eyes grew moist with emotion and gratitude.

Shortly before dying, he would utter expressions such as, "Why do you torment me with your care? The Most Holy Virgin is calling me and I need her. I desire only Mary! For me she is all!" As the end approached, while repeating the fact that he was a sinner, he confided to those who were caring for him that he did not fear the separation but rather desired it, so as to finally see once more the Lady who had appeared to him, radiant with light, for just a few moments, during that distant Roman winter. A nostalgia that recalls the equally heart-wrenching experience of Bernadette: "The grotto was my Heaven." Was this an "illusion," a "pathological manifestation" of Alphonse, a case for a psychiatrist or a psychoanalyst, when its effects plunged so deep and lasted so long? All those decades of fidelity to that flash in the chapel of Sant'Andrea are by far the best rebuttal.

Dispelling further suspicion regarding this conversion (even though not beloved by all even within the Church, and about which they would rather we kept silent today) and confirming the mystery that hovers around what happened in Sant'Andrea delle Fratte, many other elements can be added. Fr. Laurentin has highlighted many of them in his reconstructions, carried out despite the many obstacles and indifference that hindered him.

It suffices to remember this: the testimony of Alphonse spoke of furniture arranged for a funeral occupying the central nave of the church that would have impeded him from arriving suddenly at the chapel of the apparition. It was precisely for the sake of making final arrangements for that funeral that his companion Théodore de Bussières had gone to that church in Rome. Alphonse knew nothing about this, nor did he even know the name of the deceased. Yet, when overcome, he began kissing the medal around his neck and saying phrases full of emotion, on the love of God and the mercy of the Virgin Mary; and when he was led to the exit, he turned toward the bier and exclaimed in a loud voice: "How much that man prayed for me!" This was testified under oath at the process. That "man" was the Count August-Pierre de La Ferronays, former minister of the last of the Bourbons, the king of France Charles X, a fervent Catholic who had died several days before of a sudden heart attack. His friends had spoken to him about the young Jew from Strasbourg. Only after his death was it discovered that he had asked permission from his confessor that he might offer his life for the conversion of that Israelite, whom he did not know personally but whose salvation was very important to him.

Evidently, among "all" the things that Alphonse immediately comprehended in an instant was the revelation that the funeral being prepared in that church had some mysterious role to play in his mystical experience. God had accepted the heroic offer of Count de La Ferronays, just as he had granted the prayer of the group of Catholics to which the illustrious deceased belonged and that of the confraternity in Paris, at Our Lady of Victories. Jean Guitton seems to be right when he speaks (in a dense book of theological and philosophical reflections he dedicated to this conversion) of a "miracle of the Communion of Saints." In the perspective of faith, it was the network of prayers and vows created around Alphonse that provoked the divine intervention, effected as on many other occasions through the intercession of the Virgin Mary.

CHAPTER 44

THE HOUSE ABOVE EPHESUS

SHORTLY BEFORE THE YEAR 2000, a newspaper asked me (for one of the usual showpieces full of empty opinions) who in my opinion was "the most important personality of the past ten centuries that are drawing to a close."

An impossible question, of course. But it did at least give me the opportunity of reiterating the perspective of faith, of which we seem to have lost even the slightest awareness. Christian categories for judging history are different from, if not opposed (the word used in the Gospels) to those of the world. The believer, therefore, must ask who is "important" not in the eyes of men, but in the eyes of God, "whose ways are not our ways."

Jesus Himself, as we know, was not noticed by ancient historians. They did not perceive that human reality had undergone a decisive shift in that obscure provincial man who was executed and whose name was not even registered. For this reason, we need to rediscover the "evangelically correct" point of view: the history that really counts is written with one of those special inks that, if we wish to read it, requires equally special glasses, the glasses of faith.

I said to a colleague who had asked me (and who at that point listened to me with even greater perplexity),

> For the Christian God, the ignorant, the little ones, the simple, the humble are the ones who comprehend and do what really matters. For this reason, in my library, I have no portraits of the "wise" or the "powerful" according to the world, but I have before my desk the faded daguerreotype of a frowning adolescent, wrapped in a poor shawl and illiterate at that time: Bernadette Soubirous. I have her as my example and symbol of the many like her. Wanting to pass on a

> message for all humanity, Heaven did not choose professors, politicians, soldiers, writers, journalists, or even a bishop or the pope himself. Limited to repeating (maybe without even understanding) the words she had heard from the Lady, she provoked a silent, invisible revolution whose depths only God fathoms.

Thus, I concluded, this obscure, ignorant girl has a place reserved in the group of those who have been "important," even though one needs faith to perceive this. And who, if not the believer, can perceive that in the great capitals of political, economic, and cultural power, the people "who matter" are those whom no one knows or perhaps even sees: those who pray, those who offer their suffering, those who love silently to the bitter end?

There is, then, a "parallel" history which, as believers, we are called to notice and to interpret. Mary is one protagonist of this history; and in an especially adequate way, given that her style (beginning with the New Testament itself) is that of the chiaroscuro, of the discreet penumbra. Through her apparitions — and not only through their verbal content, which is nothing other than the gospel reiterated, but also through the choice of her human intermediaries — she comes to remind us, every once in a while, about what is the only history important in the eyes of God.

Those believers who seem to have had the vocation of helping us in our desire to "know more" about Christ and his followers, to go beyond the terseness of the Gospels, to fill the gaps (so to speak) of Scripture, belong to this alternative world. We are thinking of those people that secular culture ignores or qualifies hastily as "visionaries" or "hysterics" and who often fail to find a better reception even in certain ecclesial settings.

In the contemporary age, Maria Valtorta comes to mind. A movement of spirituality arose around her charisms, first of all her mystical visions collected in the many volumes of *The Poem of the Man-God*, a movement which has many little-known though impressive branches. I have had continuous confirmation of them from the correspondence of readers and from personal encounters. I know that the Church has suspended its judgment on her and her works and I confess that, due to my temperament, this type of spirituality is not for me. But being Catholic means making space for and respecting different sensibilities, so that the Faith rests secure and clear in its doctrine. And if, for the sake of supporting this faith, "pious reflections" and "devout conjectures" can be of use, why not?

It is impossible to ignore Anne Catherine Emmerich in this context. For this German woman, Mary was the *magna pars* of the "visions" which have been handed down to us.

We should immediately note that the canonical cause for Emmerich's beatification has recently been reactivated (and with good hopes for success), a cause that was blocked in 1927 at the decision of the Holy Office. This occurred due to the content of the visions attributed to the Servant of God, which has come down to us only in its edited version, most certainly embellished if not fictionalized by the German writer and poet Clemens von Brentano. Regarding the sanctity of her life, her sincerity, and her rectitude, the Church has no doubt. She was, moreover, the inspiration (according to its director, Mel Gibson) for the celebrated film reconstructing the Passion of Christ with crude realism.

Anne Catherine, who was born in Westphalia in 1774 and died in 1824, spent most of her fifty years of life on earth confined to bed, in the throes of unspeakable pain, which she not only accepted but desired, offering herself as a victim for sinners. The truth of the stigmata (which she received in 1812), as well as the fact that she lived for decades on water alone for her nourishment, was confirmed without a shadow of a doubt by innumerable investigations by religious and civil authorities. The room of her sickness became one of the settings of the most sublime spirituality in Europe at that time, and the list of miracles attributed to her, both in life and after death, is long.

From her infancy she was known for phenomena such as clairvoyance, telepathy, farsightedness, ecstatic journeys, and visions. What she saw was, as we said, gathered by Brentano, without clarity as to what was ascribable to the writer and what was in fact said by the mystic herself. At any rate, her life of suffering and superabundant faith inspires one to read with respect the words attributed to her, although it does not constitute an absolute guarantee: we know that the Church does not authenticate any "private revelations," even if the person who receives them has been raised to the altars, as will probably happen soon enough in this case.

Here, however, we would like to highlight that the name of this mystic with the stigmata who never left her homeland of Westphalia is cited in every publication (even those claiming to be secular and scientific) that speaks of the archaeological excavations in Ephesus. In her visions, in fact, the Servant of God says,

> After the Ascension of Our Lord Jesus Christ, Mary lived for three years in Jerusalem, three in Bethany, and finally, nine in Ephesus. Not in the city: her house was located three and a half leagues from it, on a mountain which one sees to the left when approaching from Jerusalem and which descends gradually toward the city. From the mountain, one can see Ephesus on one side and the sea on the other.... The summit opens onto a rolling, fertile plain of half a league in circumference: it was here that the Blessed Virgin settled.

Her narrative continues, giving many other minute details about the setting and the abode which the apostle John built for her: "It was a stone house, square, with two rooms, only the back side was rounded, the roof was flat. The hearth was divided in two, placed in the center." In contrast with the opinion then prevalent among scholars, the visionary stated that Mary's stay in Ephesus with the disciple to whom Jesus had entrusted her from the cross was certain. There she concluded her earthly life and was laid to rest in a tomb next to the house, before being assumed into Heaven.

At the beginning of the 1880s, a priest from Paris, Fr. Gouyet, read the "revelations" of Emmerich as Brentano had collected and published them. At first quite skeptical, in the end the priest decided to go to the Middle East, with her book in hand, to verify whether the places were as she described in her mysterious visions or (as he thought more likely) were illusions, though in good faith and edifying. His journey began in 1881 in Egypt, and there he had his first surprise: the places where the Holy Family in flight had stayed, according to the "visions," not only existed but were in conformity with how the mystic had described them. And then other disturbing confirmations followed in Palestine, from Capernaum to Tabor to Carmel.

But the most incredible concurrences were found precisely in Ephesus, which, despite having been one of the most important cities in the ancient world, was now reduced to a heap of half-buried ruins. Climbing the mountain (called *Alagad*, the ancient *Solmissos*) three and a half leagues from the city, as described by Emmerich, Fr. Gouyet not only found the site corresponding exactly, but also identified a house, ancient and isolated, still the object of veneration by the local surviving Christians as well as by Muslims. Without means for continuing his research and without connections in high places, the priest was not able to arouse the Church's interest in his discovery. He therefore returned to Paris.

Ten years later, things got moving again. The best way to recount summarily the outcome of this discovery is to turn to an authoritative source: the report written in 1951 (after the conclusion of new excavations) by the archbishop of Smyrna (Turkish Izmir), the territory where Ephesus lies. The archbishop at the time was Joseph Descuffi, who wrote,

> In 1891, Fr. Poulin, the superior of the French Lazarists in Turkey, having read with his confreres the *Life of the Blessed Virgin* attributed to Emmerich, decided to investigate the places described in that account to verify or disprove it. The learned and not in the least devout French official François Young, an archaeologist, was placed in charge of the expedition. After several days of their exhausting hunt in the mountains of Ephesus, they had, thanks to the directions of the peasants of the area, the surprise of discovering a site and a house in ruins [the one Fr. Gouyet had discovered ten years earlier, which had gone unheeded], which corresponded perfectly to the instructions of the visionary who, pinned to her bed, had never left her native Prussia. That place was called by the locals *Panaya Kapuli,* which in Turkish means "Chapel of the Panaghia (All-Pure), Mary." Others called it *Meryem Ana Evi,* or "House of our Mother Mary." The members of the expedition knew that the Orthodox Christians had always gone there every August 15 together with their pastor, to celebrate the Dormition of the Virgin. Moreover, despite the fact that their liturgical books indicated Jerusalem as the place of the end of the earthly life of the *Panaghia,* they were convinced that this was the holy place of the Assumption.

As it turned out, the more than four thousand Christians living in the villages of that region were the descendants of the ancient Ephesians who had taken refuge in those mountains at the time of the Islamic invasion, and there they had preserved faithfully their traditions, first among them that of the *Panaya Kapuli.*

Later excavations would demonstrate that the dilapidated edifice they saw was a chapel converted from a stone house, most certainly dating to Roman times, whose structure in two rooms (with a rounded back wall) coincided with that depicted by Emmerich. Particularly moving was the discovery of the hearth which the mystic had described and which stood between one room and the other, in the exact center. It was found under the altar which had been raised precisely in that spot, where the fire which the Mother of Christ kept lit had burned. It had been taken down but, out of respect, the stones it was made of were preserved in the hole under the altar: on one side they were white, on the other blackened with a thick layer of soot from the fire. Even half-consumed wood was found.

Emmerich had also explained, "The windows of the house were placed high in the walls and the second room was darker than the first." In fact, the openings of the house were situated at an uncommon height, almost three meters from the ground. And the second room had only a slit high up, making it very dim.

It must be said, however, that according to the mystic, Mary was laid to rest by the apostles, who had hastened to Ephesus, in a grotto "set about half a league from the house." That tomb has never been found, although there is no lack of archaeologists hoping to find it, given that efforts have been intermittent and that all the possibilities have not been exhausted.

It is nevertheless striking that, at the end of 1892, little more than a year after the discovery, or rediscovery, of *Panaya Kapuli,* the new archbishop of Smyrna (the only surviving city of the Seven Churches mentioned in the book of Revelation) desired to visit the site and celebrate Mass there, making a long, official declaration after having examined the places and spoken with historians and archaeologists.

That bishop, Andrea Policarpo Timoni, after having listed what had been discovered, concluded his document with the following words:

> Having good reasons, given the homage rendered to the good faith and the virtues of Anne Catherine Emmerich by her spiritual directors, to think that her revelations merit at least a certain amount of credit; verifying at the same time, book in hand and with our own eyes, the perfect conformity that exists between the place and the ruins we visited and what the visionary says about the house of the Blessed Virgin in Ephesus; knowing furthermore that the local traditions, still lately and especially consulted in this matter, affirm in the clearest way that the Blessed Virgin lived in *Panaya Kapuli,* where she is presumed to have died and where lies her tomb; having

> said and considered all this, we are strongly inclined to believe that these ruins are truly the remains of the house inhabited by the Blessed Virgin and we pray this good Mother to help us bring to full light a question that so interests not only the Church of Smyrna, but the entire Christian world.

There remains the problem of the equally ancient tradition, in some ways "official," that posits the place for the *Dormitio* in Jerusalem, in the Valley of Gethsemani. The excavations carried out there in 1972 confirmed, in the words of summary by one of the archaeologists, that "the current niche of the so-called 'tomb of Mary' testifies to the existence of a Judeo-Christian cultural center that surely dates from the pre-Nicene period, of a Marian character, connected to the memory of the end of the earthly life of the Mother of Jesus." Confirmation in Jerusalem as well, then.

But one notes that the tradition (and even texts such as that of Tertullian) establishes Ephesus as the place where John, to whom Mary had been entrusted, spent his final years and died. Is it possible that if the apostle had still been alive, the Woman would not be with him? Furthermore, the very message that the Fathers at the Council of Ephesus sent to the Christian people cites the stay of the two in that city. And the liturgical tradition of Jerusalem could be contrasted with the equally ancient one of the Jacobite Church, which places in the current Turkish locality the Dormition of Mary. This view was shared by the great Islamist Louis Massignon, according to whose research Mary could not have stayed in Jerusalem, as the mother of a "cursed wretch," according to the Law, because he was "hung on a cross"; nor could she have returned to Nazareth, because not only her Son but she herself had been erased with infamy from the registers of the local synagogue. Therefore, her exile from Ephesus was necessary. Massignon, moreover, did not hesitate to judge as authentic the extraordinary gifts of Emmerich, whom he venerated as a saint.

These questions affect not only faith but also devotion and therefore must be left open to debate among specialists; we sought here only to draw attention to the unique case of the visionary from Westphalia.

CHAPTER 45

Believing without Seeing

"Jesus said to him, 'Have you believed because you have seen me? Blessed are those who have not seen and yet believe'" (John 20:29). This striking reprimand which the Risen Christ gave to Thomas is often cited as a warning to the disciples of Christ who would give credit to things like miracles and apparitions, beginning with those that involve Mary.

It has happened to me many times: "called to order" because I have surrendered to the Mystery in my research, when necessary, after having weighed and discerned. Thus, almost five centuries after the Reformation, one of the most abstract and dehumanizing postulates of Protestantism seems to have prevailed: the true faith is only that which totally excludes visible signs and terrestrial support. Rudolf Bultmann, one of the leading Lutheran theologians and exegetes of the twentieth century, said that in this phrase from the Fourth Gospel, there was "a radical criticism of signs — among them even the Easter apparitions [of Jesus to the apostles] — and an apology of the faith fittingly deprived of every external aid."

The other big name of twentieth-century Protestantism, Karl Barth, considered all of Mariology a "tumoral excrescence of Catholicism." He clarified this in a phrase from his monumental *Dogmatics,* the work that occupied him for over thirty years: "The Catholic discourse on Mary is a malignant excrescence, a parasitic plant on theology: well, parasitic plants must be pulled up from the roots." Also to be eradicated decisively and impetuously is the waste of time on "superstitions" like Marian apparitions and the wonders obtained through her intercession. This verminous rubbish lies under the explicit prohibition of the Word of God, moreover. As we have just recalled, "Blessed are those who have not seen and yet believe!"

The translation we give to Jesus' warning to Thomas is the official one offered by the Italian bishops' conference (*Conferenza Episcopale Italiana*, CEI), used in the liturgy and approved in 1971, with a second edition revised (though not the verse that interests us) and published in 1974.[19] With Bible in hand, then, those who insist on wanting "to see," those who are looking for "signs" of the free and merciful divine attention to man's concrete history should amend their ways and return here "to the pure faith of the adult Christian."

A severe warning. Too bad, however, that it is not in the least valid: it is based, in fact, on a translation that is not only imprecise, but even backwards with respect to the Greek original. According to the biblical scholars of the Italian bishops, Jesus said, "who will believe;" if, instead, one looks at the text, we find that the verb tense used (*pisteúsantes*) is not the future, but on the contrary, an aorist participle; therefore, a past tense. The Vulgate, the Latin edition used for fifteen centuries by the Church and attributed to St. Jerome, also translated it correctly: *crediderunt*, "they believed." Likewise, the New Version of the Original Texts published by the Paulines: "You believe because you have seen me? Blessed are they who believed without seeing!"

In the past quarter of a century in which the CEI version has been in use, some have raised their voice to cite this error in translation, the consequences of which are certainly not irrelevant, as demonstrated by the enduring skepticism toward aspects of Christian life, of Catholic life in particular, that are not at all secondary.

Finally, in 1997, the Italian bishops presented a new edition of the Bible, but once again the original text was not respected. It reads thus: "Blessed are they who *believe*, without having seen." From the future (they *will believe*), they moved to the present (they *believe*), but still refusing to translate the Greek aorist: they *have believed* or they *believed*. This was not an oversight but a precise theological choice, as confirmed by the note we shall examine, which the CEI's biblical scholars added to the verse.

[19] Editor's Note: For this English edition, we are using the *Revised Standard Version Catholic Edition* of the Bible. The Italian version referred to in the text is given thus: *Perché tu hai veduto, hai creduto: beati quelli che, pur non avendo visto, crederanno!* (Gv. 20, 29).

It was precisely the ideological perspective guiding the "deformation" of the text that elicited the alarmed intervention of Fr. Ignace de la Potterie, the Jesuit professor emeritus at the Pontifical Biblical Institute and undisputed specialist on the Gospel of John. The prestigious scholar called attention to the note added by the Italian bishops to the revised text, which reads: "Thomas was reprimanded because he presumed to see and touch. The goodness of the Lord gives him confirmation, but blessed are they who believe based on the witness of those who have seen, without demanding a personal vision. The normality of faith rests on listening, not seeing. In the time of Jesus, vision and faith were paired, but now, in the time of the Church, vision must no longer be demanded."

"Fortunately," observes Fr. de la Potterie, with some bitter irony, "in the preface of the Italian bishops' edition, they clarify that the notes have no official character! In fact, the perspective advanced here is not Catholic, but is consonant with that of Protestants, who have always accused Catholicism of being 'a religion of seeing,' whereas the faith should be based only on naked 'listening.'"

In any case, the professor of the Pontifical Biblical Institute continues, stating that this note presupposes an erroneous translation:

> The imprecision in the version (first a future, now a present, contrasting with the past tense of the original Greek) is used by the exegetes of the CEI to confirm, with the authority of the Gospel, a paradigm that seems prevalent in the Church today and which derives precisely from the Reformers. This is the framework according to which the true faith is only that which seeks no confirmation, that excludes visible signs, that rejects them in fact.

Given the authority of Ignace de la Potterie (his weighty volumes on *The Truth in St. John* are now classics), we do well to let him speak. The Jesuit professor states,

> Translating first in the future tense and then in the present, the words of Jesus are transformed into a rule that is valid for all who live in times following the resurrection of Christ. And in fact, the CEI's note explains that only for Jesus' contemporaries "are vision and faith united," but that this is not the "normality of faith." According to this illegitimate interpretation, it seems that Jesus is opposed to the natural need to *see*, asking us to base our faith only on *hearing*.

A vagueness, as we said, that has something of the inhumane in it and that works well only for the doctrinaires who teach theology at university.

In the original, however, the verb is in the past tense: "Blessed are those who have believed without having seen" (me, in person, living again). "Therefore," continues de la Potterie,

> Jesus' allusion is not to the faithful who would come later, not to us who must "believe without seeing," but rather to the apostles and disciples who were the first to recognize that Jesus had risen, through the performance of the visible signs that testified to him. In particular, the reference alludes precisely to the evangelist who is conveying to us these words of Jesus; John, who with Peter had run to the tomb and reached it first, after the women had told of their encounter with the angels and their proclamation that Jesus was risen; John, who entered after Peter, *had seen* the signs, *had seen* the empty tomb and the funeral linens lying there without even having been undone and, even in the limitedness of those clues, believed.

Thus, our biblical scholar says, "the phrase of Jesus, 'blessed are those who without having seen (me) *have believed*' refers precisely to the *vidit et credidit* of John at the moment he entered the empty tomb." From this it derives that

> reproposing the example of John and Thomas, Christ wants to indicate that it is reasonable to believe in the testimony of those who *have seen* the signs of his living presence. It is not in the least the request for a blind, naked, gratuitous faith—as the Protestants demand and now, with a delay of half a millennium, so too Catholic exegetes—but is rather the blessing promise to those who in humility recognize His presence, starting with small traces, and give credit to the word of credible (eye!)witnesses.

Therefore, "the inexactness introduced by the Italian translators concerning the verb tenses used by Jesus served the purpose of changing the meaning of His words and making them refer no longer to John and the other disciples but to future believers." This was indeed the case, as is confirmed by the disturbing clarity of the note. Fr. de la Potterie continues:

> The interpretation of the Reformation from Luther to Calvin all the way to Bultmann: all of them, in fact, changed the Greek text and

> translated it in the present tense. Instead, the opposite is correct: what Thomas is reprimanded for is not that he saw Jesus, but that he immediately closed himself off and did not give credit to the testimony of those who told him they *had seen* the Lord God. It would have been better for him to give credence to his brethren, while awaiting his own personal experience as the others had; instead, he, in a sense, insisted on dictating the terms of belief.

As a relevant confirmation of what exactly the theological perspective behind the "manipulation" of the translation is, there is also the version produced by the Jehovah's Witnesses: "Happy are those who do not see and *believe*." A present tense here as well, and yet here too, illegitimate with respect to the original (though, in the case of the Jehovah's Witnesses, one should consider that neither their founder nor his disciples knew the Greek but only the English, and for this reason reused the Anglican translations, touched up like all the others by the communities detached from Rome).

Fr. de la Potterie gladly concedes, "It is true, as explained in the note by the experts of the CEI, that in the present time 'vision cannot be demanded.' Nothing in Christian experience can ever be the object of insistence." But he immediately adds, "Nevertheless, by construing as alternatives seeing and listening, and holding that 'the normality of faith rests on listening and not on sight' (namely, that it suffices to listen to the 'tale' of Christianity to become Christians), they contradict everything that Scripture and Tradition teach us." In fact, "the apparitions to Mary Magdalen, to the disciples, and to Thomas are the image of an experience that every believer is supposed to have in the Church. As for the apostle John, so too for us, seeing can be a point of entry to belief. One thinks of the contemplation of the Gospel scenes and of the application of the senses to them, according to the ancient and noble spiritual tradition." Here, the Jesuit de la Potterie is doubtless thinking of those extraordinary "Spiritual Exercises" of St. Ignatius of Loyola that have had such an impact on the life of the Church.

The Gospel of Mark concludes by testifying that the preaching of the apostles was not only a simple narration (thus, something only to be listened to), but was accompanied by events, by miracles, so that the truth of the words would be confirmed thanks to concrete signs "to be seen": "And they went forth and preached everywhere, while the Lord worked with them and confirmed the message by the signs that attended it" (Mark 16:20).

As the Fathers of the Church acknowledged on many occasions, those visible signs are not a useless "extra," a concession to human weakness; they are instead directly connected with the reality of the Incarnation. Now, we cannot "see" (except for some with extremely rare and unique charisms) the glorious body of the Risen One, but we can and we must see the works he carries out. As St. Augustine says, "*in minibus codices, in oculis facta,*" in our hands the books of the Gospel, in our eyes the facts.

At any rate, even the *Catechism of the Catholic Church* reconfirms the tradition (to the contrary of the Bible of the same Church!) according to which faith is not based only on hearing but also on the experience of exterior proof. The *Catechism* cites the dogmatic definition of Vatican I:

> Nevertheless, that the obedience of our faith might be in conformity to reason, God willed that the interior assistance of the Holy Spirit be accompanied also by exterior proofs of his revelation. Thus, the miracles of Christ and the Saints, the prophecies, the diffusion throughout the world and the sanctity of the Church, her fecundity and stability, are most sure signs of Divine Revelation, reasons for credibility that show that the assent of faith is in no way a blind movement of the spirit.

Fr. de la Potterie recalls one saint above all, Francis: "When he spoke, for those who were present it was clear that the Gospels were not a tale out of the past, to be read and heard. In that moment, it was obvious that in this man, Jesus was living and acting."

The preceding considerations are important and necessary to oppose an anachronistic theological deviation which seems to lead out of Catholicism, condemning, moreover, the long chain of devout generations thankful to God in Christ who has allowed them to "see" signs which sustain their belief.

But, I must confess, I have had to make use of similar considerations *pro domo mea*, when I was publishing my book *The Miracle*, where, for the first time in Italy, I reconstructed in a critical manner the most amazing Marian prodigy. I foresaw (knowing well the current climate) that its sympathetic reading by "normal" interested Christians and the interest of many non-Christians in good faith would be met by skepticism if not outright hostility in certain clerical circles. There was no lack of Catholic reviewers who, to condemn as "useless, even harmful, for a truly biblical and adult faith" this investigation of mine into the signs that God, in his generous freedom, decides at times to grant us, cited yet again (as if I didn't know it!) Jesus' admonition to Thomas.

This was thus a great reminder, from friars and priests, of the CEI Bible: "Blessed those who, though they have not seen, will believe!" (or for the more up-to-date, the 1997 version: "Blessed are they who believe, though without seeing!"). The wretch who is writing this (accused of "anti-evangelical bulimia of the miraculous") was left with no other option than to oppose them with a simple argument: fidelity to the "true" Word. Not to the one retouched to make it fit the theological perspective of ecumenism — an ecumenism that is necessary but should not distort what Jesus truly wanted to tell us.

CHAPTER 46

Between Texas and Castile

One of the most famous, most beloved, most discussed "Lives of Mary" is a strange, large book that since the day of its appearance has not lacked for enthusiastic readers and hardened detractors within the same Church. I say a "strange" book because it was approved after the most severe scrutiny by the most suspicious and zealous of the Inquisitions, that in Spain. But the Roman Inquisition (considered more tolerant) prohibited it, although with qualifications and reconsiderations. At the same time, saints, blesseds, and men of God in great numbers have sung its praises and recommended it to the devout, whereas theologians and biblical scholars still today turn their noses up in indignation.

It's a sort of one-off for the author of the work — a woman, in fact, whose cause for canonization was halted at the first step, that of venerable. Yet still today, after centuries, there exist groups of devoted Catholics fighting to get the cause reopened, a possibility ever more likely.

The book is in Spanish and its title is *Mística Ciudád de Diós* (Mystical City of God); the "Mystical City" it alludes to is precisely Mary, seen from her predestination before her birth until her Assumption and Coronation in Heaven as its Queen. The author was a Conceptionist nun, a cloistered branch of the Second Order Franciscans, similar to the Poor Clares. Maria Coronel of Jesus, the name of the religious, was born in 1602 in a town in the mountains of Old Castile, near Soria, Agreda. The name of her birthplace serves to identify her: for the Spanish, she was always and only *Sor Maria de Jesús de Ágreda*. From that hamlet with an austere and desolate appearance (I know that area, and the irremediable damage done by centuries of occupation by Muslims, enemies of trees and destroyers of vineyards, with their total deforestation and the subsequent erosion of the soil), she never departed until her death, on the feast of Pentecost in 1665 at age sixty-three.

The words of a biographer describe what Spain was like in the seventeenth century:

> At the age of eight, on Christmas Day, Maria consecrated her virginity to the Lord, and at twelve she asked to become a religious. Her mother, favored like her daughter with heavenly gifts, received the approval of her confessor to transform their home into a monastery in which they could retire with Mary and the other daughter, she too desiring to enter the religious life. All this was made possible by the entrance of the husband into the Franciscan Order, where he joined their two sons.

The entire family ended up in the convent or the monastery! This was the country that was involved in the greatest missionary effort ever sustained by a Christian nation, with results worthy of their efforts: besides Latin America, the authentic historical miracle of the Philippines, the only Asiatic nation Europeans succeeded in converting almost entirely to Christianity.

The charismatic phenomena, from ecstasies to visions, that Maria enjoyed from her infancy were so great that she had to ask the Lord to free her of them, or at least to temper them, so as not to be the object of curiosity and even veneration that went well beyond the walls of the house transformed into a monastery. Her prayer seemed to have been granted, but as was observed, "Christ continued to communicate to her and to work through her more secretly, elevating her to a higher state of contemplation, without corporal manifestations." Her gifts of wisdom and clairvoyance showed themselves to be so great that even the king of Spain, Philip IV, became one of her spiritual sons. We still have hundreds of the letters exchanged between the monarch of the world's largest empire and this Conceptionist nun, walled in her remote village yet with a vision that took in the whole universe.

It was in 1637 when the thirty-five-year-old María de Jesús began writing, by order of her confessor, what had been mysteriously revealed to her, or what she had intuited in a mystical way, about the life of the Virgin. An enormous manuscript was produced, of which Philip IV wanted a copy, subjecting it to the examination of theologians, who were left in admiration, judging it "a heavenly gift." But another confessor ordered his penitent, in 1645, to burn the manuscript along with all her other writings. Maria followed his order immediately, with no hesitation, confirming her obedience to the Church. But then yet another spiritual director was of the opposite opinion and ordered the religious to write it all over again. Thus was born the *Mística Ciudád de Diós* which, published five years after the death of the author, immediately translated, reprinted continuously until modern times, provoked a passionate controversy pitting the enthusiastic *agredistas* against the tenacious *antiagredistas.*

This is not the place to enter into this duel in which the most implacable enemies of the influence those pages had over the people, renewing their Marian devotion, were the usual Jansenists, those intellectuals (abstract and dangerous like all intellectuals) always averse to feeling and sentiment in living out the Faith.

Among the infinite number of things one could say about the work, I shall choose but one, which was the reason for my desire to investigate this extraordinary figure, though so little known in Italy. Namely, I would like to point out that in this work which she said was "revealed from Heaven," María de Jesús de Ágreda confirmed the tradition that lies at the origin of the cult of the Shrine of the *Pilar*: that the Virgin Mary, while still living in Jerusalem, truly came to Zaragoza to comfort James (and on a precise date: January 2, A.D. 40) and left a column as a sign of the power that Spanish Christianity would have. Since *el Milagro de Calanda* is directly tied to the shrine in Zaragoza, this is what led me to get to know better this mysterious figure who was a contemporary to the events that I narrated in the book and about which she certainly knew, informed by the king who had kneeled before the miraculously healed peasant while receiving him in Madrid.

Here then, a cloistered nun in Castile who resembled in some ways her fellow nun in France, Thérèse of Lisieux, proclaimed patroness of Catholic missions although she never left to convert non-Christians in distant lands. María de Jesús de Ágreda was a missionary out in the field, in remote New Mexico, at least five hundred times. Yet, like Thérèse, she never left her monastery.

This is one of the most incredible, yet historically verified, stories of the entire Christian adventure. It is one of those cases of "bilocation" (being miraculously present in two places at the same time) which is frequent in the tradition of sanctity, but which here seems to assume a shocking systematic nature.

Let us consider the facts in synthesis, as they have been reconstructed (with archival scrupulosity and not based on vague hearsay) by North American historians, often Protestants or Jews, nonetheless ready to admit the enigmatic character of the events.

At the beginning of the seventeenth century, the Franciscans, moved by their inexhaustible missionary zeal, began traveling from Central America toward the territory of modern-day New Mexico, Texas, and Arizona. They immediately had to deal with the bellicose, often bloody Native American tribes whose names were made famous by Western films: Apache, Navajo, Comanche.

The first friars were massacred, but surrender is not part of the Franciscan tradition. In 1622, a new expedition departed, consisting of twenty-two missionaries and guided by Fr. Alonso de Bonavides, the custodian of the missionary province of New Mexico. Arriving there and organizing as best they could several missionary compounds, the religious began receiving strange visits. They were the Caciques, prominent members of the great tribe of the Jumana, considered one of the most dangerous and intractable. This time, however, they were not coming with hostile intent. On the contrary, they came to beg the Franciscans to send among them some priests to administer Baptism and the other sacraments.

Up to that point, the friars had received only ferocious hostility, and so now were rightly stunned. The Jumana told them they had been convinced by the arrival of a "Lady dressed in blue," who for some time was with them and spoke of God, Christ, and Mary, exhorting them to accept the Faith. The Spanish religious had brought with them the portrait of a famous Poor Clare, Mother Luisa Carrión. They showed it to the natives, but they said that their "Lady" was younger, though her clothes were similar, not black and brown (like that of the Franciscans) but blue. This described the habit of the Conceptionists, to which Maria of Ágreda belonged. If there, in remote New Mexico, the friars thought of her, it was because some of them had heard the archbishop of Mexico City, Francisco Manso de Zuñiga, talking about strange stories that had reached him from Spain, where it was said that a Castilian cloistered nun knew America better than those living there.

That was the summer of 1629. Some of the friars accompanied the ambassadors sent by the Jumana back to their territory, as they had requested. Those friars left us precise reports that permit a reconstruction of what happened. When they reached the borders of the tribal lands, a multitude of men, women, elderly, and children came to meet them, preceded by large crosses adorned with flowers from their pastures.

They were walking as if in a procession, because (as they said) they had been taught to do so by the *Dama en azul*, the "Lady in Blue," who had so often preached the Christian faith there. The Franciscans, with ever greater amazement, attested to the fact that thanks to the Dama, the teaching of the catechism was already almost finished. What those people wanted was Baptism and the Eucharist: for this reason, the Lady had advised them to form a delegation to go and call the religious from the distant mission that had just been established.

This event in the summer of 1629 was only the first episode. In many other places (not only in New Mexico, but in modern-day Texas, Arizona, and California) the religious found "savages" who had never had contact with Europeans yet were already catechized by the mysterious missionary—namely, the nun whom North American historians call "the Lady in Blue" (they have also proposed the sister from Agreda as the protectress of Texas). The memory of her mysterious presence lives on in the Christian traditions of those areas of the United States, despite the arrival in the mid-1800s of Protestant American colonists and the subsequent marginalization of Catholics.

Returning to our story, in 1631, Fr. Alonso de Bonavides (who led the missionary expedition to New Mexico) was recalled to Spain. From Madrid he went to Agreda and was allowed to speak with Sr. María de Jesús in the convent parlor of the Conceptionists. His report to his Mexican confreres has been preserved. With great simplicity, the nun confided to the priest her profound desire for the salvation of souls and that perhaps for this reason the Lord gave her the possibility of being a missionary even while remaining in her convent. At the end of her life, she would confide that "at least fifty times" she had been to America, while not being able to say "whether she was in her body or not." Nevertheless, to the amazed and emotional Fr. Alonso, she described his confreres in the mission, recalled episodes that he himself had forgotten, confirmed having catechized not only the Jumana but also other tribes and having insisted on them going to look for the Franciscans. In the words this Franciscan used in the report for his confreres in America, "Asking her why we were not able to see her, whereas the Indians could, she answered that they needed to see her and we did not, and that, at any rate, it was all ordained by God according to His will."

Besides the evangelization of the Jumana (which is the most well-known episode, though it was only the first "discovery" by the missionaries), the presence of Venerable Maria is documented throughout the immense territory to the north of Mexico. In fact, it is in memory of her that generations of Iberian missionaries found the energy and the courage to face the dangers of nature and men. This was the case, for example, in the eighteenth-century evangelization of Upper California (the current state of California, the richest in the United States), the work of Junípero Serra, the founder of San Diego and San Francisco. In the dramatic moments of his apostolate, it was precisely the "Lady in Blue" whom he invoked as protectress of those missions.

At any rate, the concrete traces, and not only the spiritual ones, left by her more than fifty mysterious "raids" into the New World were found in the field by the religious even after the death of the nun whom the Church would later declare venerable. For example, the Spanish Captain Juan Mateo Mange, accompanied by the omnipresent and tireless Franciscans, guided an expedition up the Colorado River. Sometime before that, the caravan of another Iberian soldier, Juan de Oñate, had departed without returning. Captain Mange asked the indigenous populations they met along the way if they had any news about the passage of other Europeans through those lands. The elderly leaders responded that, when they were little boys, a Lady dressed in blue, "with a veil over her head," had appeared among them, showing them a cross and inviting them to kiss it. Frightened, they had her *flechada*, shot through with arrows, believing she was dead twice. But the "Dama" not only did not die, but every time started preaching again. Convinced they were in the presence of a religious mystery, they decided to listen to her.

Of course, for those who might be skeptical (and it is their right!), they too could consult, as we have, the vast bibliographical sources on these episodes, on which we have based our reflections, as well as historians in the United States, particularly beyond suspicion given their traditional diffidence toward the Spanish *Conquista*.

Thus, we have confirmation that the matter of the Lady in Blue is solidly based on abundant, firsthand documentation.

But the best guarantee comes from the investigation carried out by the Spanish Inquisition for nearly fifteen years and with the usual, fearsome severity. They interrogated the nun from Agreda for six hours per day, for six months, asking her hundreds of questions repeatedly. The intervention of the *Suprema* was provoked above all by rumors that were circulating back and forth across the Atlantic concerning those enigmatic "bilocations." The inquisitors, we must remember, were interested in repressing not so much heresy but rather superstitions, visions, false miracles, and suspect prophecies.

Despite the Spanish king's friendship and even veneration of her, the charismatic gifts of the nun had to be investigated to discover their veracity as well as their origin, to rule out the possibility of diabolic inspiration. After years of investigation, in January of 1649, the decisive turn came: in the Castilian monastery, religious and notaries sent from Toledo by the Grand Inquisitor subjected the suspect to an unrelenting interrogation subdivided into eighty chapters. "Most of which," her biographers clarify, "refer to the conversion of the natives of New Mexico." In the end a verdict was reached: the inquisitors declared they were "admiring of and satisfied with the virtue, veracity and constancy of the Servant of God." It also added that those judges "remained in correspondence with her until their death."

For those who are familiar with the suspicious severity and meticulousness of the Spanish Inquisition, such a verdict is the most solid guarantee of the historical reliability of accounts that might seem legendary.

Who knows? Perhaps in the perspective of faith, such events help us to get beyond the often one-sided, sectarian readings of the evangelization of America in a merely political, economic, or sociological light. We take the liberty to recommend the extraordinary text of a South American philosopher and historian, Alberto Caturelli, *The New World Rediscovered*. There one can find confirmation that the Spanish missionary heroism was entirely inspired by Mary. And that, not incidentally, the coast of the land that was later called America was sighted for the first time at dawn on October 12, 1492, the feast of Our Lady of the *Pilar* of Zaragoza, whose tradition was confirmed as well by Venerable Maria of Jesus of Ágreda.

Just before the hour of discovery, on the flagship which Columbus had christened the *Santa Maria,* all the mariners had just sung the Salve Regina, probably composed in the tenth century precisely by a Spaniard, St. Pedro de Mezonzo, bishop of Compostela. With such Marian beginnings, it is not surprising that mysterious missionary gestures were to follow, at the hands of one who had written a mystical "Life" of Mary inspired by Our Lady herself.

CHAPTER 47

NUMQUAM SATIS

I SHALL DRAW FOR the last time from my bulging binders wherein lie the files collected over the years concerning the Marian Mystery. These files bear witness to an excavation for which the joy (or *suavitas,* as the ancients said in all that referred to Our Lady) far outweighs the slight burden of creating them.

Piazza di Spagna. In 1777, during construction work to reinforce the foundations of a religious house in the Roman Campo Marzo, the heart of the ancient city, an enormous column made of precious *cipollino* marble was found. "Fifty-three palms high, and with a diameter of six and a half palms," as the sources say, it had never been used and had been abandoned for an unknown reason. With great difficulty, given its dimensions, it was pulled out and transported to the courtyard of the Palace of Montecitorio, exactly where the new hall for the Italian Parliament would be built. There were many proposals for its use, but nothing was done with it.

In 1854, as we know, Pius IX proclaimed the dogma of the Immaculate Conception after centuries of waiting and appeals from many parts of the Christian world. Someone remembered the ancient column that was lying on the ground and proposed to create the base of a monument to the perpetual memory of the dogma. The pope liked the idea and solicited its underwriting by the whole Catholic world.

The offerings were so abundant that, at the end of the work, a considerable surplus was left over and given to charity. The column was transported to Piazza di Spagna (the Spanish Steps), and it was raised there for at least two reasons. Spain was the country that had fought for centuries in favor of the

Immaculate and it seemed right that the monument be erected there in front of its historic embassy. But another palace façade shares that piazza: that of *Propaganda Fides* where, as an author of the time said, "those who must take the light of the Gospel among the infidels as heralds of the true doctrine of Jesus Christ are educated and raised in the theological disciplines." Therefore, "it seems fitting that, as they head to the most remote lands, they take as their polar star, as their infallible guide in their journey, the Immaculate Virgin."

On September 8, 1857, Pius IX, emotional and exultant as always when it concerned the Virgin Mary, was able to inaugurate the great monument which we can still admire today. Moses, Isaiah, Ezekiel, and David surround the base that supports the column, while mounted on the top is her statue, modeled on that by the sculptor Giuseppe Obici.

Why speak of this here? Because it seems a meaningful symbol of the fact (apparently random, due to an archaeological find) that the image of Mary be raised on an ancient, pre-Christian column. We have already dedicated several chapters of this notebook to the fact that the Marian cult is the point of arrival of a religious enthusiasm often dark and confused, in search of a Mother. It is the gospel that gives a name, a face, a story, a full meaning to this hope.

The Mother of Jesus has the role of uniting: the New to the Old Testament, certainly; but also Christianity to paganism. Let us not forget that Ephesus was home to the great cult of Artemis and was the site of the council that proclaimed Mary the Mother of God, with a continuity which, if it seems suspicious to the incredulous, reveals its symbolic wealth to believers who not only do not fear but rather venerate the *et-et* by which Christ did not wish to destroy but rather complete. Rome, Athens, and Jerusalem — the synthesis of which gave birth to and nourished the Faith — united in a column and a statue, in Piazza di Spagna.

Cesare Borgia. As we know, he was one of the most disturbing figures of the Renaissance. Called "*il Valentino*" (for having been archbishop at age seventeen of Valencia, in Spain, or for having been the Duke of Valentinois), he was the biological son of Rodrigo, who became pope under the name Alexander VI and transformed into the prototype of the papal dissoluteness of that period. We have already mentioned him. Machiavelli saw in Cesare Borgia an incarnation of the "Prince" for whom he longed, precisely for his brutal determination to chase after aspirations to human power.

An evil person? And yet, perhaps here too Mary placed her maternal, benevolent touch. Still today, at the gates of Imola, Romagna, the beautiful shrine called *Il Piratello* draws a constant flow of pilgrims. In 1483, a pilgrim who had stopped to pray before a Marian altar under a pear tree (*pir* in the local dialect, hence the name of the shrine) heard an invitation to go into the city and announce the Blessed Virgin's desire to be venerated in that place. The people of Imola set off immediately. It might seem curious today, but the people of the surrounding region of Emilia Romagna were for centuries some of the most devout Italians; in that region there were the most courageous "insurgencies" or popular revolts against the Jacobins of Napoleon, detested for their impiety. The people of Imola set off, therefore, but their misery was great, and construction was costly. Thus, the shrine was still unfinished sixteen years later, in 1499, when on November 23, *il Valentino* settled in those parts. His father, Alexander VI, had put him in charge of the reconquest of the Papal States that had fallen prey to feudal lords and foreigners who deemed those lands their own. Imola was the first city that the young Cesare set about reconquering.

Having set up camp, the warlord entered the church under construction and came across a future Blessed, Jeremiah, of the noble family of the Lambertenghi of Como, who had become a Franciscan for the sake of penance. The pious religious had dedicated his life to the construction of the shrine, and even joined the laborers in their work with shovel and trowel. But despite the alms he collected, the money was not enough. Well, learning of this need, the terrible Valentino kneeled in prayer before the image and promised the Madonna that, if he were successful in taking Imola without shedding blood, he would provide for the completion of the shrine, and also erect a special chapel dedicated to the Immaculate, providing it with artistic furnishings as well as rich benefices.

The following day, unexpectedly, the people of Imola, tired of the domination of their tyrannical overlords, opened the city gates to the son of Alexander VI. Thus, Borgia entered at the head of his troops, acclaimed by all as a liberator. A happy, if rare event, seeing how afterward he had to conquer the other cities of the region of Romagna through blood and ferocious ransacking.

The warlord, usually accustomed to every sort of deceit, this time kept his promises: one year after the peaceful taking of Imola, with a fervent decree, he consigned the promised money as well as exemption from taxes, asking in exchange only prayers for himself and for his family. In addition, his father the pope added to the *Piratello* spiritual favors along with the material ones, writing with his own hand a bull in which (as a good Spaniard) he rejoiced in the dedication of the chapel to the Immaculate Virgin.

And so, this terrible duo was united in Marian devotion. A political move? Superstition? An attempt to ingratiate themselves with the unruly population of Romagna? Understandable questions, but ones which we must reject. Why not consider their sentiments genuine, not incompatible with the many shadows in their lives? Is not Mary the *refugium peccatorum*, the refuge of sinners? And, according to the testimony of many mystics, is not Christ ready to forgive many things for just one gesture of veneration toward his Mother?

Revelation. "And a great portent appeared in heaven, a woman clothed with the sun, with the moon under her feet, and on her head a crown of twelve stars." This is the famous beginning of chapter 12 of the last book of the New Testament. These are verses that have not only heavily influenced iconography, spirituality, and liturgy (and now, even the flag of Europe!), but have also caused rivers of ink to flow.

Who or what is represented behind the striking and majestic symbol of the "Woman"? From the Fathers of the Church until our day, essentially two solutions have been offered: some see in that figure the Church; others, Mary, the Mother of Christ. In recent decades, official, academic theology seems to be tightening around the former interpretation: what the author of the book of Revelation was thinking about was the ecclesial community, and only that. The "Marian" interpretation is either silenced as "unacceptable for an adult biblical scholar" (the usual refrain) or is rejected with a bit of irony, if not disdain, because it would be "entirely preposterous," "devotional."

And yet, as in the case of other theological or biblical themes, strange things happen here as well. Like what was noted in an issue of *Marianum*, the journal of the Pontifical Marian Theological Faculty (vol. 59, no. 151, 1997). In that journal, a well-known and respected scholar recalls our attention to an article of nearly twenty years earlier, which also appeared in *Marianum* (vol. 40, no. 121,

1978), signed by Bellarmino Bagatti, the great specialist in biblical archaeology, on the origins of the Faith, especially that of Judeo-Christians.

Fr. Bagatti gave an account of the work carried out by his *Studium Biblicum Franciscanum,* for a critical edition on an apocryphal work of the New Testament known by experts under the Latin title *Historia Josephi Fabri Lignarii.* This text has come down to us in several Arabic copies; though it has been proven that the most ancient version, which we also have, is in Coptic. The Franciscan scholar showed, by means of serious reasons of internal and external criticism, that the apocryphal work is indeed ancient, dating back to no later than the late second century and that it was drawn directly from the circle of the apostle John, the traditional author of Revelation.

In the *Historia Josephi,* the "Woman" in chapter 12 of the book of Revelation is interpreted in a clearly Marian hermeneutic. Thus, we find ourselves in the presence of a stunning fact, at least for the current prevailing criticism: in antiquity, and moreover in the settings in which Revelation was written, there was no hesitation to seeing in the "Woman dressed in the sun" Mary herself!

In the later issue of *Marianum* we mentioned, the silence and indifference that accompanied these revelations of Fr. Bagatti were denounced. The journal writes, "This news, given twenty years ago, did not seem to find an echo among scholars, as one would have expected and as the argument would have merited. The question, in our view, merits further investigation. If the data were to be confirmed (a document from the second century and within the Johannine tradition!), then the interpretation of Revelation 12 should truly be reconsidered. In any case, the Mariological interpretation seems anything but secondary." Whereas now, according to the words of this article, seeing the Mother of Christ behind the apocalyptic symbol "is often considered as something arranged and devotional."

As in all human activities, so too theology and exegesis are not set apart from the "spirit of the times." The latter, for decades now and even in Catholic settings, is oriented toward "demythologizing" the Marian presence, toward considering it a sort of late product, not original, characterized more by popular devotion (always a bit malodorous to the delicate nostrils of some professors) than by authentic tradition. It is in line with these premises that one should discard a priori, in the name of a "theologically and ecumenically correct" paradigm, the possibility that the book of Revelation was thinking of Mary.

And instead, it seems that what the *sensus fidei* of Christians and artists has always comprehended needs to be rediscovered, for it never hesitated to see the Blessed Virgin in the striking Johannine symbolism. In any case, we the "devout" can rest assured: we have no reason to be ashamed as ignorant, anachronistic believers for reading those eighteen verses in our own way. It might be the case that this "way" is not at all "ours" but instead that which the biblical author had in mind. Words which a biblical scholar of the scientific caliber of Fr. Bellarmino Bagatti understood well.

Apparitions. Marian apparitions, as we know, arouse suspicion or indifference today in many circles. At best they are relegated to the private sphere, considered a marginal phenomenon. And yet, if we wish to call ourselves Christians, we must admit that Christian faith is entirely based on two "apparitions": one at the beginning, when the angel Gabriel appeared to a maiden in Nazareth named Mary; the other at the end, with the apparition of the Risen Christ.

Experience. In 1974, Paul VI published the apostolic exhortation *Marialis cultus*, a decisive document insofar as it was the first sign of thawing after what was called the "Marian winter" that followed the council, despite the fact that the latter had reiterated all the traditional doctrine. We have already mentioned this. Rereading that worthy reflection by Pope Montini, I pause on paragraph 57: "The Church, taught by the Holy Spirit and *benefiting from centuries of experience*, recognizes that devotion to the Blessed Virgin, subordinate to worship of the divine Savior and in connection with it, also has a great pastoral effectiveness and constitutes a force for renewing Christian living."

In the face of the protests (entirely theoretical and ideological) of theologians of his time, Paul VI makes an appeal to experience: the voice of history is unanimous, not referring to paradigms but to events. The Christian people bear witness to this: the maternal and beneficial presence of Mary is an *experience*, made obvious in an infinite number of cases. This people might well respond to skeptics just as the man born blind and healed by Jesus responded to the intellectuals of that time, the scribes and the Pharisees, "What I can tell you is that before I could not see, and now I can see."

CHAPTER 48

THE QUEEN OF THE ETHIOPIANS

THERE IS ONE CURIOSITY among the many to which we would like to give at least the outline of a response. We wonder if there has ever been a place where the praise prophesied by the Blessed Virgin reached its apex.

Obviously, this is a hypothetical question. Marian devotion is a phenomenon that has involved to the depths all peoples that have been reached by the Christian message and has done all it can to survive tenaciously, even where the violence of pastors and princes united has tried to suffocate it. All these peoples have competed in multiplying their homage, claiming that theirs merited to be called "the Land of Mary" par excellence. The first land (in Europe) to become a Christian kingdom, Armenia, laid claim to this title, as did the most recent to convert to the gospel, Lithuania. One must not forget that what only God sees is hidden from men's eyes, for God "probes the heart and the mind," and He alone knows what lies beneath so many moving expressions of faith.

Having clarified this, it must also be said that it is possible (according to many) to hazard a response, though with the necessary caution. The nation where the presence and the praise of Mary seem to reach their summit is the same one that gave the Church the first baptism of a non-Jew, the eunuch treasurer to Queen Candace, led to faith in Jesus by the deacon Phillip (Acts 8:26–39).

Yes, we are speaking of Ethiopia. For over a millennium and a half now (the region was evangelized quite early), the problem seems to have been excess. The highest place given her by the other Eastern churches has been given to Mary here; they have also recognized the "Catholic" privileges of Mary, including the Immaculate Conception and the Assumption — and much earlier than did Rome. But the Ethiopians go further: they go so far as the belief, held by authoritative theological schools though never officialized, that the Mother is worthy of the adoration that all other Christians reserve only for the Son.

It is the case that in Ethiopia, even more so than elsewhere, the Marian presence has shown itself a powerful means for preserving the faith. Isolated from Christendom by the Muslim wall, invaded twice by Muslims, subjected to fierce pressures from pagan Black Africa, the Ethiopians have always stubbornly preserved their Christianity. And so faithfully that (aside from the Marian "excesses") in the sixteenth and seventeenth centuries, a Jesuit mission succeeded in reestablishing union with Rome, finding that even the creed had been handed down intact. If the entrance of the Ethiopians into communion with the Catholic Church ended in failure, it was not due to theological issues but to both human and ecclesiastical politics.

This is a case that merits in-depth study, confirming what experience has so often shown, as I have often pointed out: where Mary is venerated, the Son is believed in, and in an orthodox way; Mariology is the guarantee of authentic Christology. This is what the ancient antiphon of the Liturgy of the Hours sang: "You alone have destroyed all the heresies in the entire world."

The "Ethiopian Case" could be confirmation of something else: first of all, of the fact that devotion to the Ever-Virgin Mary can nourish and sustain a strong, virile, and if necessary combative faith, far from leading to a sentimental, enervated, cowardly religiosity. This has happened among other populations marked by a robust presence of the Blessed Virgin — the Spanish for example — or as was the case in the great medieval movement of knighthood, placed entirely under the insignia of Our Lady. Let us not forget that the rule for the knightly order par excellence, the Templars, was written by the greatest of Marian troubadours, the mystical and robust St. Bernard of Clairvaux.

The Abyssinians, though never satiated with multiplying poetic expressions and acts of homage for Maryam (as they call her), have been able to defend themselves from their enemies (religious as well), becoming the African nation that has maintained for the longest its political and cultural independence. In all their infinite struggles, the Mother of Christ has always been on their banners, invoked as the patroness of the people and leader of their armies. Although the fact might not be appreciated by some of my fellow Italians, at Adua the Abyssinian troops inflicted one of the bloodiest routs on the Italian army in all of its colonial history. With a particularly humiliating sequel, given that the anticlerical government in Rome at the time had to beg the pope to intervene as a mediator to negotiate the release of prisoners, even though they had forced him into the Vatican as a prisoner.

At this point, I cannot resist the temptation to tell an anecdote that very few know. At Adua, the Italians were surprised not only by the number of their attackers but also by the efficacy of their muskets. Behind this there is a story that could be seen as a case of what Vico called the "heterogeny of ends."[20] It once occurred that, in order to reinforce the papal troops threatened by Savoy, many Catholics in Europe gave their best sons, who enrolled as volunteers under the banner of Pius IX. Belgium, a land of great gunsmiths, organized an appeal among believers for the purchase of a thousand modern, breech-loading carbines. The best was yet to come. These guns were shouldered by the Papal Zouaves on September 20, 1870, for the little more than symbolic resistance at Porta Pia in Rome. After their surrender, the Italians sent the foreign volunteers home, after having disarmed them, of course. And since the Belgian rifles were not accepted by the Savoy army because they used different ammunition and would have created logistical problems, they ended up being sold to the Ethiopian government. And so, the firepower of the soldiers of the Negus who vanquished the Italians at Adua came from arms bought for the pope by fervent Catholics and ceded to an African emperor by Italian Freemasons.

Returning to Our Lady and the Abyssinians: the tradition of the country affirms that the Holy Family, in flight from Herod, passed into Ethiopia from Egypt. In light of the warm welcome reserved for His mother, Jesus supposedly gave her to the country as a "tithe of the universe." Moreover, Menelik I, the progenitor of the reigning dynasty in Ethiopia until 1974, was born of the Queen of Sheba and Solomon, the Son of David, of whom Mary was a descendent. Therefore, there would have been a sort of "blood bond" between the Virgin and these Africans among whom she lived.

[20] Editor's Note: Giambattista Vico (1688–1744) was an Italian philosopher, critical of much then-current Enlightenment thought.

But consoling to all, and not only to devout Ethiopians, is the basic principle of their belief. In the words of one Abyssinian, Fr. Mario da Abiy-Addì, a Capuchin priest and one of the leading scholars of his country's religiosity,

> More than anything else, what renders limitless, truly more unique than rare, the cult of the entire population toward the Virgin Mary, is that she is the *Kidane Mehret*, the "Pact of Mercy," by which the Redeemer supposedly promised to save all those who would commend themselves to her, invoking her name and honoring her memory. This pact is, in the Ethiopian mentality, like a "third" or "Newer" Testament of the divine economy for the salvation of the human race. The *Kidane Mehret* was supposedly stipulated on Calvary, where Mary, after the death of Jesus, went every day to pray. There, the Son supposedly appeared to her, granting her this privilege for those devoted to her.

In other Christian traditions as well, including Catholicism, the conviction that Mary is *refugium peccatorum* is cultivated: by placing oneself in the shadow of her mantle one finds sure refuge; and devotion to her is a clear sign of predestination of eternal salvation. But only among Ethiopians, so it seems, is this certainty so deeply rooted that it marks the entire life of believers. To them, the role of the Virgin Mary is only that of mercy: justice is not her concern.

In fact, making appeal to the pact can always hold back the hand of her Son, obliging him to "tear up the verdict" and to adjourn the celestial court, if a baptized person should appear before it who has invoked and venerated her. The connection between this "third Testament" and Mary is so great that the *Kidane Mehret* is synonymous with Maryam. In fact, the latter name is used less frequently than the former, both out of respect and to remind the Mother of the power of Mercy granted to her and to induce her in this way to exercise it.

The liturgy has such a truly stunning superabundance of names that it represents, moreover, the most important part of the entire Ethiopian culture. Take a random hymn sung during the thirty-two annual Marian festivals, as well as during the other liturgical days, in which Mary is called: "permanent temple," "polished temple," "grain depository," "the Son's garden," "lightning of the King," "lamp of the world," "light of the stars," "thin linen veil," "mine of gems," "fiancée of heaven," "golden thurible of the Seraphim," "compensation for the years of famine," "inextinguishable torch."

This could go on for page after page, in amazement not only at the luxuriant poetic spirit but also at the theological profundity revealed by these titles taken from the Bible as well as from the experiences of life, and never at random. Whatever the case, the enchanting beauty attributed to the "Queen of Heaven" has a concrete reflection on earth as well. In fact, among the tasks that the people of God in Abyssinia attribute to Mary, there is that of creating every child in its mother's womb. Thus, no one would ever consider anyone else ugly: all are "beautiful" because each is the work of the hands of the Virgin Mary.

Beauty, though, is also tied to the name given each newborn at Baptism, and almost always with reference to the Blessed Virgin. As in the West where, out of respect and humility the name of Jesus is not given to children, the same occurs in Ethiopia for Maryam, a name too sublime to be granted to a mortal. And so, the remedy is found in connecting it to a noun. In this way, they can use that name for males, too. Thus, one finds "Grain Ear of Mary," "Servant of Mary," "Gift of Mary," "Beloved of Mary," and so forth.

All travelers in Ethiopia have noted how, in proximity to numerous churches, little mountains of stones are created. And this too is a sign of devotion to the Blessed Virgin. In fact, whoever walks in front of a place of worship dedicated to Mary (nearly all places of worship) throws a flower in her direction. If the season does not allow this, the passerby finds a stone, kisses it, and throws it on the others on the little hill, to which they give the name "heights of *salàm*," or "greetings," obviously to Our Lady.

Returning to the Ethiopian Capuchin we quoted earlier, he writes, "Among the main particularities of Abyssinian Mariology, the very close relationship between Maryam and the Eucharist stands out. This theological concept is highlighted in the liturgy with surprising insight. Our Lady is the Mother who generated the Eucharist, she is the Wellspring from which it came forth, she is the Tabernacle of flesh in which He was kept safe."

It is precisely the presence of Mary that safeguards the concreteness of the Incarnation, the healthy "materiality" of faith. Whereas, on the contrary, where the Mother is forgotten, the Son as well ends up disappearing in the fog of culture, morality, and Gnosticism, becoming an "ethics teacher" more than the Word incarnate.

We do not know exactly what the religious condition of Ethiopia is today, after decades of coups d'etat, dictatorships, Marxist propaganda, and wars. Here too, the Muslim minority has become ever more aggressive and seems to be pursuing the objective of Islamizing the country, no longer by means of arms but by taking over political and economic power. In light of their more than millenary history, however, one would hope that the Christian faith of this people, inspiring and proud, might overcome this harsh trial as well. And one can expect that it will, given the incomparable love for Mary that, as a theologian says, "has more than satisfied the famous adage of a great lover of the Mother of God: *De Maria numquam satis*."

In conclusion, I draw one of my favorites from the "Miracles of Mary," an ancient collection to which the Abyssinian people turn for nourishment and which, even if illiterate, they listen to avidly as priests read:

> While some women were at the well with Our Lady Maryam, a thirsty dog came wanting to drink some water and those women chased it away. But Our Lady, the twice Virgin Holy One, the Mother of God, saw the dog, had pity on its thirst and cried. The women then said to her, "You would have pity on it? Is that really like you who gave birth to Christ the Messiah?" [For the Ethiopians, who have preserved many things from Judaism, dogs are impure animals to be avoided.] But when Mary heard this discourse, a great joy entered her, and taking her jar she left. Removing a sandal, then, she poured water into it and offered it to the thirsty dog to drink. One of the women then said to her, "See, the water from your jar is finished and the pail in the well is broken, so you will find no more water." Maryam answered them, "Water does not flow from below but comes from heaven. And God, who made this dog drink, will give me water from on high."

CHAPTER 49

A Stumbling Block

IN THIS BOOK WE have already spoken of the presence of Mary in the Quran (in chapters 16 and 17) and in general in the Islamic tradition. This is an important and highly honored presence, and in shrines in the East dedicated to the Virgin Mary, Christians and Muslims can be found together — for example, in Ephesus where, based on the mystical visions of Anne Catherine Emmerich, the Church discovered what according to many is the "house of John" where the mystery of Mary's final days on earth was fulfilled. Every August 15, that little plateau looking out over two seas is full of pilgrims: Catholics celebrating the Assumption, Orthodox celebrating the Transit, and Muslims celebrating the return to Allah of the "Lady Mary," the only woman worthy to stand next to Fatima, the Prophet's daughter.

By a sort of paradox, the Islamic world (at least the people and many theologians) has peacefully accepted the apparitions that provoked the indignation of Protestants and the diffidence of many Catholics who consider themselves "adult," all the while forgetting that it is to "those who become like a child" that the comprehension of what really counts is promised.

So, it is a true throng of Muslims that daily visits the Coptic church dedicated to the Virgin in Zeitoun, on the outskirts of Cairo. Here, starting on April 2, Easter Day in 1968, the fateful year of pseudo-revolutionary tantrums by the opulent Euro-American youth (could this be a sign as well of the mysterious "Marian calendar"?), thousands of people, both Muslims and Christians, saw the Blessed Virgin accompanied by angels on the dome of the sacred edifice. Only later was the connection made that it was no ordinary place, but the place where ancient tradition venerated one of the stages of the flight of the Holy Family into Egypt. Nor does the name seem random: Zeitoun means olive, the tree that is a symbol of peace. The apparition, furthermore, was surrounded not only by angels but also by white doves, to the scale of the female figure, which was quite large. A Coptic bishop wrote, reflecting on the meaning of the events:

> The coming of Mary truly saved peace, preserving Egypt from a bloody civil war like the one that exploded in Lebanon. In fact, President Nasser, looking for a scapegoat for the Egyptian debacle in the war of 1967, had organized a propaganda campaign against Christians, accusing them of having betrayed the country and therefore of being responsible for the disaster. The apparitions created a climate of concord between the faiths, and the Egyptian Copts were once again accepted, without suspicion, into the national community.

An incalculable number of miraculous healings flowed from those apparitions, such that little more than a month later (the events were to last for another thirteen months) the Coptic patriarch issued an edict: "In full faith, with fervent joy and profound gratitude toward Heaven, I declare that Mary, Mother of the Light, has appeared clearly visible for many nights." The Catholic patriarch, Stephen I, united himself to his Coptic confrere, declaring he was persuaded by the truth of the facts. "I have no reason to doubt," he always said and wrote.

Since the two Christian prelates were immediately joined by the Muslim leaders, the apparitions of Zeitoun are perhaps the most ecumenical in history. Not only did Mary appear on top of a "schismatic" church (according to Catholic categories), but the first to see her were five laborers, all Muslims, working in a mechanic's garage in the nearby square. Despite her impressive size, they mistook her for a nun dressed in white and started shouting at her to stop walking on top of the dome. Seeing that the figure did not listen to them and was greeting them with her hand, they called the police, thinking she was about to commit suicide, and they ran to knock at the parish priest's door to warn him, while the crowd began to gather, doing instinctively what it would do at every successive apparition: Catholics sang Marian hymns, Muslims recited aloud verses of the Quran dedicated to the Mother of Jesus, and the Orthodox intoned their litanies in liturgical Greek, while some who had converted to Protestant sects recited the Magnificat and the verses of Luke on the Annunciation. Ecumenism was in this way immediately and instinctively being practiced in that miserable suburb of Cairo.

As one priest wrote after investigating the scene,

> The Virgin of Zeitoun did not speak, but her silence is eloquent. The hour had not yet come in which she could present herself as the Mother of God, for the Muslims do not believe in the divinity of Jesus. Nor could she call herself the Immaculate Conception because the Orthodox, while admitting it in practice, in theory do not accept the official proclamation of this privilege. In order to be accepted by all without reservation, as their common heavenly Mother, she could manifest herself only under the form of protective Mercy. In fact, according to all the testimonies, she never spoke but rather used the language of gestures: outstretched arms, gestures of greeting, bowing, smiling, moving around the dome of the church to see everyone and to make herself be seen by all, and at times she waved an olive branch in her hand.

Zeitoun merits greater recognition in the West than it has received, especially because there is not the least doubt about the reality of those hundreds of apparitions, given the thousands of witnesses. There are also many photographs of the event and even videos. A sort of Fatima, then, with its dancing sun before the stunned crowd, immortalized by several famous images.

Returning to the Islamic perspective on Mary, one of the bulwarks is the purity, innocence, and virginity of the Mother of Jesus. This stands in regrettable contrast with some Jewish traditions, which must be mentioned in the name of a dialogue that demands clarity and truth for it to be authentic.

We open the Quran to the fourth Sura, verse 155. In a series of invectives against the Jews, it is stated harshly that they have been punished by God "for their incredulity and for having pronounced a monstruous calumny against Mary." The calumny, namely, of having conceived her Son in sin, breaking her fidelity promised to her fiancé and, moreover, getting pregnant by a foreigner. And this during her menstrual period, when according to Semites a woman must not be approached because she is impure, rendering even more monstrous the calumny. This, the Quran reminds us, comes from the Jews. And it comes from the very beginning: there is a trace of this even in the Gospels, as we shall see, and down through the centuries to our own day.

Take, for example, *Brother Jesus*, whose subtitle is *A Jewish Point of View on the Nazarene* and which, appearing in German in 1967, is famous as a significant testimony to a new, Jewish attitude of solidarity toward Christianity. This is a "dialogical" work, a little classic of ecumenism. On page 54 of the Italian translation of this essay by the Israelite Shalom Ben-Chorin, with an affirming introduction by a priest and well-known theologian, we read:

> This obscurity [regarding the origins of Jesus] has led adversaries to the obvious conclusion of an illegitimate birth. In the Talmud, we have the so-called tradition of Pandera or Pantera. A Roman official by that name supposedly seduced a certain Myriam and left her pregnant, though she was the fiancée of Joseph, and the fruit of this sin would be Jesus. In the cold, alienated relationship of Jesus with his mother, whom he never refers to if not as "woman," there might be a reflection of the painful awareness of his illegitimate origins. Jesus does not honor his mother and rejects his biological father, given that he evidently knew of his illegitimate and non-Jewish provenance.

One notes in these words of Ben-Chorin that final "evidently" by which the hypothetical tone maintained up to that point is dissolved. His disturbing surety is confirmed as well by the pages devoted to the wedding at Cana, where the words of Jesus to His Mother were supposedly "frightful" and his attitude "injurious." And this, according to Ben-Chorin, is due to the same reason: the "complex" of that "young wandering preacher," obsessed with his illegitimate and even shameful birth.

As can be seen, even on this Israeli writer of our day, presented as one of the foremost experts of the "new Jewish opening" toward Christianity, there lies the shadow that we find behind John's words (8:41): "They said to him, 'We were not born of fornication.'" According to many exegetes, this would be an explicit and malicious reference to defamatory voices that were circulating in settings hostile to Jesus. Voices that arose immediately and characterized the Jewish polemic against nascent Christianity.

The Jewish communities of the Diaspora provided for the widespread diffusion of this controversy, as Celsus tells us already around the year 180.

Debating with the "Nazarenes" in the name of classical civilization and its Olympus, the Roman philosopher placed similar words in the mouth of a Jew who accused Jesus of having a mother who, pregnant by a soldier named Panthera, was supposedly chased out by her husband and after having roamed about, gave birth in hiding and shame. Tertullian, writing a little later in 197 (informed by Israelites in Roman Africa), confirms the calumny as well, with the aggravating claim that Mary was supposedly not only an adulteress but also, not mincing words, a prostitute, a *quaestuaria*.

This calumny flowed into what Charles Guignebert, the famous radical critic of the historicity of the Gospels, described with embarrassment, despite his professed incredulity and harsh anticlericalism, as "the injurious malice against Mary found in the Talmud." Here too, in this collection that is fundamental to post-biblical Judaism, Jesus is called *ben Pantheras,* the son of Panthera. As explained by the Jew Joseph Klausner, professor at the University of Jerusalem and writer (in Hebrew) of a famous study on the origins of Christianity, there was an additional mockery behind the invention of the name of that supposed soldier. Since Christians stated that Jesus was the "Son of the *Parthénos,*" the Virgin, by means of a play on words, the Jews began to call him the "son of Pantheras." A malicious assonance with which the slanderers were particularly satisfied, given that the name was plausible (as has been proven), being quite widespread among the Roman troops. Furthermore, in Greek *panther* has the same meaning as in English, which like all other wild animals arouses in the Jews a mixture of fear and revulsion; the hated Jesus then was the son of a horrible beast. In other lines of the Talmud, the negative traits of Mary are embellished with the identification of her trade: a hairdresser. Thus, she was tied to a profession whose morality was at that time quite dubious and which many considered impure. In other words, an untouchable.

From the eighth century onward, there began to form, based on the previous rabbinical writings, what would become an outright "Jewish anti-Gospel." It would be continuously enriched with details until the end of the nineteenth century and circulated mostly among the people of the circumcision. It was read according to tradition on the day that Christians celebrated Christmas, as if to exorcise that solemnity. It was called the *Toledòth Jéshu,* the *Stories of Jesus.* The rabbi of the Roman synagogue, Riccardo Segni, recently published a critical edition of it under the title, *The Gospel of the Ghetto*. Those "stories" are not the work of just one author but are a kind of collective work. As a contemporary biblical scholar, Armando Rolla, says, "Here, Jesus is presented in an even more negative light than in rabbinical literature. When he learned of his illegitimate birth, he fled to northern Galilee. He later passed himself off as the Messiah and Son of God, until he was condemned to death, accused of various crimes. In fact, besides being the son of an adulterous and menstrual woman (conception during menstruation is prohibited by the Law and thus considered to increase fault), would make him a parricide, sodomite, insurgent, magician, and corruptor." The worst of the worst, in other words.

These *Toledòth Jéshu* have come down to us in various versions. In some, Mary was supposedly raped, it being assumed that the rapist was the usual, horrid foreign soldier, so that the pregnancy fell under the condemnation of the Law. And Jesus was (as He is called in various Jewish sources, in fact) a *Mamzer*, a "bastard."

Mohammed came into contact, then, with denigrations of this sort, having known well communities of Arab Jews. It was this that led to the Quranic verses we quoted above: the Jews merit to be punished by Allah "for having pronounced against Mary a monstruous calumny." The matter seemed so intolerable to the Prophet that he not only claimed the miraculously virginal character of the conception and delivery of Mary but portrayed Jesus in the crib defending Mary's honor. It was the newborn who spoke while still wrapped in his swaddling clothes, confirming to all that, far from being a "woman of sin," his mother was Virginity and Purity itself. Islamic commentators are amazed that this episode in the Quran is not found in the Gospels as well: they ask how Christians could resign themselves to God allowing such shameful libel concerning the honor of Mary without immediately intervening to defend her?

We find something here which in the West we are practically unaware of. For a dozen centuries, unanimous Muslim tradition repeats its indignation against the Jews (and this is one of the reasons for the aversion between the two faiths), not only for having slandered Mary from the beginning but for never having repented of this intolerable defamation or never making fitting retractions and amends. In fact, as we have seen when speaking about the contemporary book by Shalom Ben-Chorin, even today "the illegitimate and non-Jewish provenance" of Jesus is given as one of the possible hypotheses, if not the most historically probable.

Louis Massignon — perhaps the greatest Catholic scholar of Islam in the twentieth century, the man who dedicated not only his studies but his whole life to mutual understanding between Christians and Muslims while remaining firm in his orthodox Catholicism — shared the Quran's scorn, wondering as well why believers in the gospel are silent about such calumnies. And when, after World War II, the State of Israel was constituted in violence, Massignon was shocked also, and above all "by the shame, because the Jewish troops dared to surround and bomb Nazareth, the city of the Annunciation, the secret well-spring of the salvation of all, without the least respect for Mary, for the Virgin who is the glory of Israel, for this Flower of flowers of the Torah."

Then, Massignon addressed all Judaism, writing,

> As long as the Jewish people doubts the honor of Mary, we Nazarene Christians cannot believe their diplomatic, tactical assurances of respect for our faith, because they lack filial veneration. I make my appeal to all the children of adoption whom Jesus gave to His Mother on Calvary! Before the crypt of the Annunciation, Zionism crashes against the Fourth Commandment of the Decalogue: "Honor your father and your mother."

Uniting himself here with Muslims, and more passionately so as a Christian, the venerable Islamologist asked Judaism (in its own interest, as well as for its honor and the honor of the other Abrahamic faiths) for a public and solemn retraction of the calumny against the purity and honesty of the Mother of Jesus.

To those who pointed out to him that this slander had come from a sort of legitimate defense by the Jews in reaction to persecution by Christians, Massignon replied that this was not true. It is true, he said, that the *Toledòth Jéshu* appeared when Christianity had at its disposal the power of the state and, as the majority confession, had Judaism at its mercy. But, he observed, that libel merely resumes the infamies against Mary that arose immediately among Jews, while Jesus was still preaching. In any case, testimony like that of Celsus and Tertullian are from the second century, when Christians were still persecuted and had no way of vindicating themselves. And then, adds

Massignon, it is certain that still in the nineteenth century, and even in the twentieth (when the emancipation of the Jews was an accomplished fact), the *Toledòth* were widely diffused among Judaic communities. And their content has never been retracted by anyone.

A Franciscan Near East scholar and student of Massignon, Fr. Giulio Basetti-Sani, wrote, "For us Christians, the efforts made by some Jews of our day to accept Jesus as a moralist, as a great figure of Israel, cannot be convincing as long as the legitimacy of His birth continues to be contested and, therefore, the honor of His Mother is defamed."

Delicate problems, as can be seen. But the time to confront them with fraternal candor has perhaps arrived, as today revisions and requests for pardon have multiplied. No form of dialogue is tenable if not on the presupposition of that truth which is the only one that "will make us free," in the words of Jesus himself.

Episodes like that reported by newspapers around the world on July 8, 1997, are certainly disturbing. The previous day (after more than two months of silence, despite pressure and protests), the Israeli premier at the time, Benjamin Netanyahu decided to make public apologies to Arabs and Christians for the cover of the most widely read scientific monthly, *Galileo*, published in Tel Aviv. To highlight a story on genetic engineering and the possibility of creating hybrids of humans and animals, the journal had chosen the portrait of a woman with a child in her arms, the woman having been digitally altered to have the head of a cow. The original painting, however, was Christian, and the feminine figure with child was the Virgin Mary.

It must be observed that the tumult that exploded immediately in Israel was spearheaded above all by Muslims, who saw therein the latest version of the "monstruous calumny" denounced in the Quran. Was Mary not always presented in Jewish tradition as a prostitute? And is not the cow connected to this disgraceful concept? In the end, after several months, the Israeli government apologized, as did the editors of the magazine, saying that the choice of Mary of Nazareth rather than any other woman was "random." As we said, those who say there is still a long way to go along the path of dialogue are not wrong, and certainly not only for Christians. This is only possible on the basis of reciprocal respect. This respect has been lacking, unfortunately, even on the eve of the Christian Jubilee of the year 2000. To "celebrate" it, the Israeli government of the same Netanyahu supported a group of Islamist fanatics who wanted to construct (on state land!) a mosque next to the Basilica of the Annunciation, with five minarets one hundred meters high to disturb Christian worship with their powerful loudspeakers and to conceal from view the church where the Annunciation of the angel resounded. Seeing that the inhabitants of Nazareth are Arabs, both Muslim and Christian, the aim of the Israelis was to divide the two communities and rake in votes for the Likud, the party in power. After the bombing in 1948, here was another attempt to suffocate pilgrimage to one of the holiest places in the Christian world. Mary, the Flower of Israel, continues to be rejected by her own people.

CHAPTER 50

"Your Mother and Your Brethren Are Outside, Asking for You."

I ANNOUNCED IT IN a preceding chapter, the thirty-eighth, expressing bewilderment (a euphemism) about a new biblical encyclopedia, edited by Catholic exegetes, printed by a publisher with a long ecclesiastical tradition and bearing the introduction of a bishop assuring readers that the work "merits our gratitude."[21] I announced that I would return to this topic, for what is at stake here is too important for us to limit our reflections to a brief comment, however energetic.

In fact, those reverends, monsignors, and editors have written and allowed to be printed statements such as this: "Joseph died when Jesus was a youth, leaving him as his oldest child. Thus, he had to assume the guidance of the family and take care of his four younger brothers and an unknown number of sisters." In another entry of that unique encyclopedia which claims to be in line with the Tradition of the Church, three hypotheses are given concerning the "brothers and sisters of Jesus" of which the New Testament speaks: they were children of a previous marriage of Joseph, the prevalent opinion among the Eastern churches; they were cousins or other relations or members of the family clan, as affirmed by the Catholic Church; and finally, they were children of the young Joseph and Mary, seeing that the two, according to the biblical scholar, "after the birth of Jesus lived as husband and wife — thus having regular and fertile sexual relations. And this is the only hypothesis that the

[21] Mark 3:32.

encyclopedia does not criticize, accepting it as its own. We owe it our gratitude, as the bishop who wrote the preface counsels us!

But there is even worse now. The levee seems to have collapsed, and everyone, even in the Church, thinks he can give his own "in my opinion." In the 1990s, perhaps the greatest work of historical Christology, immediately hailed as a classic and translated into the main languages, was a colossal work in various volumes under the title *Jesus: A Marginal Jew*. Beware: the author can certainly not be said to be "marginal." These are the biographical notes copied from the inside of the dust jacket: "John P. Meier, Catholic priest, former professor of the New Testament at Catholic University of America in Washington D.C., is currently professor of the New Testament at the University of Notre Dame in Indiana. He was president of the Catholic Biblical Association and editor of the journal *Catholic Biblical Quarterly*. He is probably the most eminent biblical scholar of his generation."

Could there be anyone or anything more "Catholic" and more authoritative than this Professor Msgr. John P. Meier? On the same flap of the dust jacket, one reads the concise judgments of other luminaries of universities and institutes officially aligned with Rome, offering their enthusiasm. In the author's acknowledgments there is a long list of names that represent the elite of biblical studies, not only in the United States. The Italian version was edited by a publisher managed by a religious order and its introduction is obviously wholehearted.

For this reason, it dismayed me to see how this illustrious tenured professor at the University of Notre Dame, this leading intellectual of the American Church, ended the twenty dense pages he dedicated to the topic we are dealing with here: "If, regardless of the faith and the subsequent teaching of the Church, the historian or the exegete is called to express a judgment on the New Testament and on the Patristic texts we have examined, considered simply as historical sources, the most probable opinion is that the brothers and sisters of Jesus are true brothers." Over the course of the chapters of this massive work, "the most probable opinion" has been transformed into a certainty: Meier takes for granted that, in the home of Nazareth, together with his parents, there were at least seven children if not more, the fruit of normal conjugal relations between the two. The cherry on top of the disturbing cake: the ecclesial imprimatur was granted on June 25, 1991, by Msgr. Patrick Sheridan, the vicar general of the Archdiocese of New York.

This then seems to have become the thesis of the clerical intelligentsia which, despite it all, insists on calling itself Catholic (and obtains from the bishops the "have seen, can print" or at least, encomiums in their introductions), aligning themselves with their Protestant colleagues. Let us not omit recalling, however, that it is not true that, as the biblical encyclopedia says, "after the Reformation, the acceptance that the relatives of Jesus as true, uterine 'brothers and sisters' became dominant in Protestantism." The statement is correct insofar as they are referring to recent decades, but it is entirely erroneous as regards the early centuries of Protestantism: both Luther and Calvin accepted and defended fiercely the truth of faith, taught since antiquity, of the perpetual virginity of Mary. And Friar Martin, in his usual caustic language (the cultivators of dialogue do well not to place him on their reading lists!), defined as "mad and uncouth" the few heretics who denied this belief. More than a century later, in the mid-1600s, the Calvinist confession of faith, the more rigid Protestant branch, confirmed that according to the reformers themselves, it continued to be true that "Jesus was born of the Virgin Mary who remained a virgin before and after his birth."

Therefore, even the Fathers of the Reformation drastically deny these distant descendants of theirs, the great majority of whom today have no hesitation in putting aside as wreckage of past sexual phobia the perpetual virginity of Mary; and in affirming with a certainty which is not in the least established that, since it is a duty of the usual "adult belief" to take Scripture seriously, it is inevitable that one admits that Mary was nothing but the usual Palestinian wife, loaded down with children — at least four sons and two daughters, if not more.

That's their problem, that of modern-day Lutherans and Calvinists, followers of the infinite denominations born in the rebellion of the sixteenth century, as well as the Jehovah's Witnesses, they too aligned in this at least with current liberal Protestantism. Their problem, had they not infected Catholic professors as well, always intimidated by their German-speaking colleagues, who dedicate just a few lines of every page to text and all the rest to footnotes (where, in reality, they quote one another constantly, in a suffocating academic circle wherein it is the guild that decides who is authoritative and who is not) and who declare themselves "free from confessional biases." This belated acquiescence of the Catholic intelligentsia is strange indeed, as Pope Ratzinger noticed (as a good German, he knows well the current situation in the home of the Reformation), because the historical Protestant communities are now dying — supplied with university chairs thanks to the state and having grown fat from "church taxes" but almost entirely deprived of believers, with indecipherable convictions because they are subjective and mutable, being continuously deformed to adapt them to the fashions that the "world" elaborates and adopts. There is no modern ideology (from communism to National Socialism, from anarchism to authoritarianism, from feminism to sexual libertinism, from pacifism to ecologism) that Protestants have not agreed to baptize, isolating from Scripture ad hoc quotes adapted to the political or cultural conformity that dominates at the moment and "demonstrating" its alleged conformity to the divine will.

What remains of the Reformation born five hundred years ago is heading toward its destiny, which has not been given to men to know. But what disturbs and surprises is this current feigning to ignore, by Catholic biblical scholars and theologians, an evident truth: mistaking the family of Nazareth for any normal family where people mate and reproduce, is not in the least a secondary or irrelevant matter, as if it were a marginal reality that might interest only some elderly devotees, clinging to their cheap reproductions of the Holy Family. This is disturbing, I emphasize, and surprising because if those mentioned in the New Testament were really brothers, born of the same uterus from which Jesus emerged, not only would the entire Tradition be obstructed, but it would remove one of the foundation stones of the edifice of Catholic faith. No, of Christian faith, given that the Orthodox consider one of the "Western aberrations," which they cannot comprehend and which horrifies them, the negation of the immaculate and eternal purity of the *Theotokos*; and as I have said, such a denial would unleash the wrath of the Reformation fathers. It would even provoke the indignation of Muslims as we have seen, to the point of urging them to pick up stones and execute the blasphemer who would deny the perpetual and absolute purity of the Mother of Jesus, the penultimate of the great prophets, the Blessed One who opened the path to Muhammed.

As a short and appropriate reminder and in order to stay within the bounds of official pronouncements: the statement according to which "Mary lived as a virgin even after the birth of Jesus" is a truth *de fide* that appears in the earliest statements of faith, in the Apostles' Creed, and was proclaimed by Pope Siricius in 391. In 553, the Fifth Ecumenical Council of Constantinople attributed to the Virgin Mary the title of *aeiparthenos*, Ever-Virgin, by which she had already been invoked for centuries in the liturgy. The Lateran Council of 649 and that of Lyon in 1274 placed anathemas on those who should deny that "the Holy Mother of God and ever Virgin Immaculate Mary conceived without seed by the work of the Holy Spirit and gave birth without corruption, her virginity remaining intact and constant even after the delivery." Pius XII defined in 1950 the dogma of the Assumption and placed the perpetual virginity of Mary among the reasons for her "anticipated" elevation, body and soul, to the glory of Heaven. Pope Paul VI solemnly reiterated that "a constitutive part of Catholic dogma" is the conviction that "Mary always remained in virginal integrity, before giving birth, during the delivery, *et perpetuo post partum*." This statement was repeated by Vatican II (no less than twice it cited the *semper virgo*), is part of the "Credo of the People of God" which Pope Montini composed when the Faith was being attacked by protests against the Church, and is so well-rooted and beyond discussion that it had to be defended energetically even by the rash Dutch Catechism, published in that fateful year, 1968. In the face of that heavy-handed move by which the episcopate of the Low Countries proceeded to the publication of this manual, whose fruit, as we can now ascertain, was the rapid and almost total dissolution of the hitherto fervent and exemplary Catholic Church in Holland, the Holy See demanded that in the following editions an appendix should be added with clarifications, additions, and corrections. The cardinals of the commission summoned by Paul VI intervened in many parts of the catechism, but not here, demanding only one clarification: "The perpetual virginity of Mary is confirmed by the Tradition of the Church and the Magisterium proposes it to be believed by the faithful."

We must add to this the impressive parade of Church Fathers, Doctors, and all the saints who never had the least hesitation and never expressed the least doubt about this. This should be enough to convince those priests and professors at universities and seminaries within the Church who, with glaring inconsistency, have dared to leave the confines of the Faith which, in this matter, has been defined without hesitation throughout the centuries.

But let us be careful, however, not to fall into the misunderstanding fostered by the current champions of Mary and Joseph's numerous offspring. The great German exegete Josef Blinzler exhorts us not to fall into the trap. This university professor of the New Testament published a dense, impeccably academic work on the "brothers and sisters of Jesus." He warns in the introductory chapter of his study,

> What clearly defines the attitude of Protestant scholars is the conviction that the Catholic thesis ("cousins" or, at least, members of the family clan) is not the fruit of a rigorous study of the historical documents but rather the obligatory consequence of the doctrine of the perpetual virginity of Mary that every Catholic is bound to believe. The reformed rationalist Maurice Goguel wrote, "For history, the problem of the Lord's siblings does not exist; it exists only for Catholic dogmatics." Or the Lutheran Joseph Bornkamm, "Only Catholic (or Orthodox) doctrinal convictions and not the documents at hand, have transformed these brothers into stepbrothers or cousins to defend the perpetual virginity of Mary."

This is also the thesis of the famous Catholic Fr. Meier (of the Jesus as a marginal Jew), who says with unbearable ambiguity that he does not want to discuss faith, but rather demolish the historical and exegetical reasons that support it and justify it. And so he falls into the usual, contradictory distinction that had previously been that of the most radical critics but not of Catholic priests on prestigious university faculties: the Jesus of history might be different, and often in contrast, with the Christ of faith. And the same for Mary: the *Virgo Immaculata* can stay on the altars if we want, while ignorant devotees finger through their rosary beads, but let it be clear that she has nothing to do with the woman of Nazareth, the subject of a long series of pregnancies and births.

The following is the challenge of Professor Blinzler, whose conviction, thank God, is not yet an isolated voice even in the often disturbing milieu of theology and exegesis: "We can demonstrate that we have here a prejudice and that the Catholic interpretation of the expression 'the Lord's brothers' is not *a priori*, it is not an abstract defense of dogma, but rather takes seriously into consideration the testimony of history, in other words the New Testament and the most ancient Tradition."

This challenge has remained once more unheeded. As Blinzler noted with disappointment, "If there is a difference in the way Protestant and Catholic exegesis present their positions, it consists in the fact that the Catholic side takes into account the arguments of its counterpart so as to respond to them; while Protestant authors as a rule consider it a superfluous waste of time and go straight to the confrontation." A sort of contemptuous superiority complex, not limited to this topic, by which the stern specialists who take their inspiration from the Reformation (whose founders as we have seen were not actually on their side, but this they try to hide) look to those late-coming, miracle-chasing, superstitious Catholics for whom certain mundane questions might be important, such as the gynecological triviality of the perpetual virginity of the Mother of Jesus. And this nonchalance is a further proof of how so much of biblical exegesis and theology have wandered far from the religious perspective, from spiritual reflection, from mystical investigation which, bowing to that mystery of purity, go far beyond that bodily sign and reach a dimension of unfathomable wealth.

Furthermore (and this is just one of an infinite number of possible reflections), the truth of the perpetual virginity of Mary safeguards that "law of the *et-et*" that presides over Catholicism: beginning with Christ, God and man, one person in a double nature, divine and human. The Fathers of the Church argued bitterly against the Docetists and the Gnostics who, not believing in the humanity of the Messiah, "despise his dirty swaddling cloths." "We," said those Fathers, "believe in a God become flesh, who wrapped himself in the filth of human nature." Perhaps to draw attention to this scandal, Luke reminds us that after giving birth, Mary "wrapped him in swaddling cloths" (2:7). And right after that, in the same Gospel, the angel said to the shepherds, "And this will be a sign for you: you will find a babe wrapped in swaddling cloths and lying in a manger" (2:12).

Not a word of Scripture is random: that double reference to swaddling cloths, apparently redundant (every infant was wrapped in them, so why remind us?) is a reminder of the complete humanity of Jesus. Jesus is also, however, the Christ, the Anointed One, the Awaited of Days: he is born "in filth" like some of us, but also comes from a mother not inseminated by man, safeguarding a virginity that she would preserve until the end. Thus, the normal and the miraculous, the quotidian and the prodigious. In a profound homily, St. Ambrose said,

> You shall find many things in Christ, some in conformity with nature, some transcending nature itself. In fact, in conformity with corporal nature, He was in the womb of a woman, was born, was placed in a manger, was nourished with maternal milk. But at the same time, He transcended nature by His being conceived and generated by a Virgin, so that you might believe that He is God who renews nature and was also man that, according to nature, was given birth by a daughter of man.

The *et-et*, as usual, which presides over every aspect of faith and which is guaranteed by the mystery of the perpetual virginity that the Faith attributes to Mary.

Much more could be added concerning the investigation into the symbolic and spiritual aspects: how much more we feel sorry for those who renounce without much regret such vast riches, all the while declaring they are followers of the gospel and members of the Church.

We come now to the data of the issue. All four Gospels, the Acts of the Apostles, the First Letter to the Corinthians, and the Letter to the Galatians all mention the "brothers of Jesus." They also cite in passing his "sisters." According to two Gospels, the brothers' names were James, Joseph, Simon, and Jude, while we know nothing about the name or the number of the sisters.

In the early years of the Church, these expressions did not raise problems or discussion. Everyone knew that, according to the Eastern usage (and common, in general, to all traditional communities), the terms "brothers" and "sisters" indicated not only those of the same parents, but also other relatives, and in general, members of the clan, as we shall see in detail. According to an apocryphal work, the Protoevangelium of James, those relatives of the Lord were the children of a previous marriage of Joseph, a widower remarried at a ripe age — stepbrothers, then, and such they have been considered by the Eastern churches. The first mention in non-apocryphal, Christian texts, we find in verse 160 in Hegesippus, who knew Palestine well (he came from there and had known even some of the descendants of Jesus' family) and who recalls that at least one of the "brothers" was, in reality, a cousin; and so the others might have been as well. Hegesippus explains this in an aside, without any reference to an ongoing discussion or dispute, with the air of one who is simply repeating what everyone already knows.

In fact, there was no problem for another two centuries and more, when toward 380 the pamphlet of a certain Helvidius appeared, an obscure layman who entered the debate that was raging at the time over the superiority of celibate religious life over matrimony. The explosion of the phenomenon of monasticism (as a sort of substitute for martyrdom), after the tolerant measures of Constantine, led to such an overestimation of virginity and such a strong skepticism toward conjugal relations as to provoke a lively reaction. The pamphlet by Helvidius had a part in this controversy and was "based not on the ancient Tradition but on a certainly erroneous and amateurish exegesis of the New Testament." This was Blinzler's estimation of it. What the obscure polemicist wanted was to reply to those advocating the superiority of monasticism, to show that even Joseph and Mary had established a family that, beyond the Firstborn, had many other children. His point of departure was not an investigation of the texts of the Faith, but rather a pre-established thesis which he sought to justify.

The greatest biblical scholar at that time was St. Jerome, who would probably not have deigned to respond to such a polemicist, so much his inferior. But implored by distinguished people (he was in Rome at the time and not in Palestine where he had lived for many years), he wrote a treatise: *De perpetua viginitate Mariae*. The fiery saint tore Helvidius to pieces thanks to his knowledge of every hidden nuance in Scripture and the Greek and Hebrew languages in which it was written. For Jerome, the "brothers" and the "sisters" of Jesus were cousins and not the children of Joseph, and he demonstrated this with arguments whose substantial validity is still recognized today.

All the great Christian writers, then as now, praised this work, which has become a classic. As one ancient historian said, the great biblical scholar "was praised and confirmed by all that the world of believers considered learned, illustrious, holy," in the West as in the East. From that time on, there were practically no more debates over Jesus as the only son, born by the work of the Holy Spirit; not even during the Reformation, as we discussed. The thesis that Mary was the mother of numerous children arose again only in the eighteenth and nineteenth centuries, in the context of liberal Protestantism and Enlightenment rationalism. Although it has held sway for some time now among Evangelicals, and is now threatening Catholics plagued by an inferiority complex, we must remember that despite the "scientific" certainty with which it is proposed, it is a recent theory, limited to a few professors, and conflicts with the certainty of faith unanimously expressed for many centuries.

I want to reveal immediately that modern biblical scholarship has been adding other arguments to the classical ones such as those of St. Jerome (to which we shall return). Only recently, in fact, scholars have begun to take into account the fact that at least three of the Gospels are likely Greek translations of an Aramaic text, and therefore, behind the Hellenistic expressions lies a Semitic substratum, not infrequently translated in an imprecise manner. Moreover, these investigations that turn up surprising results are contributing to rendering less solid the so-called "historical-critical" exegesis, which for so long was dominant among biblical scholars, who presented it as a sort of new dogma. This dogma claims that in Scripture only the commentary of professors is beyond reproach and criticism. This exegesis is based on the certainty that the Gospels are late constructions and therefore thoroughly manipulated. If, instead, their original redaction was in a Semitic language, this would mean that they were written before the great catastrophe of the year 70, when the society that spoke Aramaic and Hebrew was massacred or dispersed to the slave markets throughout the Mediterranean.

As far as we are concerned here, we can take for example the wedding at Cana, of which John says, "The mother of Jesus was there; Jesus also was invited to the marriage, with his disciples" (2:1). There is no trace of his "brothers," who do however appear at the end of the episode: "After this he went down to Capernaum, with his mother and his brethren and his disciples; and there they stayed for a few days" (2:12).

José Miguel Garcia, one of the biblical scholars opening new paths by investigating what lies behind the language we read in the Gospels, says the following: "The Greek particle *kai* translates literally an Aramaic *waw*, which often corresponds to the copulative conjunction *and*. But in this case, the *waw* is explicative and the modern equivalent is '*namely, that is to say, or rather*.' In the Greek of the Gospels, the cases in which this Greek conjunction takes on this meaning are not rare." For example, in Mark 15:1 we read, "the chief priests, with the elders and scribes, and (*kai*) the whole council." Incomprehensible, since those three categories already represented "the whole council." In reality, the original Aramaic has here a *waw* that was not translated correctly as an explicative, but rather incorrectly as a copulative. The phrase, therefore, should be read as "the chief priests, with the elders and scribes, *namely* the whole council": the evangelist, before alluding to the whole tribunal, specifies its components with historical precision.

Returning to Cana and the Spanish biblical scholar, he states, "Also the context of the narrative of this marriage requires that the Greek *kai* be attributed the sense of *namely*." In fact,

> At the beginning, John mentions the disciples as accompanying Jesus and his Mother. And so why, in the end, would he say that he went down to Capernaum with his mother, brothers and disciples? The narrative congruence between the beginning and the end of the account would require that in the final part as well, only two groups of accompaniers be mentioned: his mother and his disciples. And this becomes perfectly possible reading the Greek conjunction as an explicative particle.

And so, the text should be correctly read in this way: "After this he went down to Capernaum, with his mother and his brethren, *in other words* his disciples; and there they stayed for a few days."

But Professor Garcia adds another remark that seems to give confirmation of this:

> If this were the case of actual brothers, it would be obvious to suppose a return to Nazareth, where they were all at home. The fact that they head to Capernaum, the city chosen by Jesus as his base of action in Galilee, is simply because those accompanying him are not brothers or other relatives, but rather disciples. Consequently, this verse in John specifies with clarity who these "brothers" really are.

One notices that this modern biblical scholar, as a Catholic without quotation marks, excludes the possibility that the group might be composed of blood brothers, and therefore other sons of Mary; but he also excludes that they were cousins or, in general, other family members. In fact, here is another result of modern scholarship, a result that surpasses the two classical hypotheses that posit the "brothers" as either the children of Joseph (apocryphal gospels) or cousins (St. Jerome). To be clear, even if it should be obvious, there is among Catholics complete freedom of discussion about the degree of kinship or at least proximity which united Jesus with those who are called by the New Testament his "brothers and sisters." The truth of the perpetual virginity of Mary has nothing to do with these clarifications which, in the end, are secondary.

Gianfranco Ravasi, whose authority as a biblical scholar who is both forthright and orthodox is widely recognized, summarizes the current prospect in this way:

> In the New Testament, "brothers" actually designates a well-defined group: the disciples bound to the Nazareth clan of Jesus. They constitute a type of community in themselves, furnished with authority such that they can propose their own candidate as the first Bishop of Jerusalem. In the passage in Mark 3:33 ("'Who are my mother and my brethren?' And looking around on those who sat about him, he said, 'Here are my mother and my brethren! Whoever does the will of God is my brother, and sister, and mother.'"), Jesus seems to scale down their privileges and reduce them to the horizon of fidelity to the word of God. They are never called "sons of Mary": this is a designation reserved only for the Christ. In this light, more than a genealogical distinction, the phrase "brothers and sisters of Jesus" aims at indicating a pressure group.

Thus, a sort of distinctive title, a label, a society — so it appeared as well to early Christian writers — to which even relatives and cousins belonged.

The *Catechism of the Catholic Church* (no. 499) clarifies the matter thus: "Against this doctrine the objection is sometimes raised that the Bible mentions brothers and sisters of Jesus. The Church has always understood these passages as not referring to other children of the Virgin Mary. In fact James and Joseph, 'brothers of Jesus' (Matt. 13:55) are the sons of another Mary, a disciple of Christ (Matt. 27:56), whom St. Matthew significantly calls 'the other Mary' (Matt. 28:1)."

But the Gospels give two other names of "brothers": Simon and Jude. And so, in order not to add even more pages to this chapter that is already longer than the others, I will not get into this complicated question of names and kinship, although the result seems clear and has been summarized by Josef Blinzler in the conclusion to his solid volume, to which I refer the reader seeking further investigation and which remains faithful to the ancient thesis that considers them cousins:

> The so-called brothers and sisters of Jesus were his cousins. The kinship of Simon and Jude came through their father Cleophas, who was the brother of St. Joseph and like him, a descendant of David. Their mother's name is not known. The mother of James and Joses (Joseph), on the other hand, was a Mary, different from the Mother of Jesus. She, or her husband, was related to the family of the Lord, but what exactly their kinship was cannot be ascertained. There is some evidence that points to the father of James and Joses (Joseph) as being of priestly or Levitical origin and that he was a brother of Mary.

The Gospels are quite clear when they speak of "the other Mary" at the foot of the cross and thus exclude that the one who is for us Holy Mary could be the mother of at least two others who are called the "brothers of the Lord." But as we have repeatedly said, quite often those who claim they seek to base their conclusions only on Scripture avoid confronting positions that contradict their own — in this case, their position being that the one who for Catholics is the Woman par excellence (the Madonna), having gotten through the first pregnancy as a sort of task assigned to her by Heaven, requiring a female Jew, was only a mother like any other, and thus, the opposite of a virgin. Behind this clearly lies the Protestant demythologization of Mary, the desire to take from her what they consider to be "absurd and non-biblical privileges," and maybe even the eternal Arian temptation: Jesus as a "man of God" but not the "son of God," as the "great Initiate," but not the "Redeemer and Lord."

It is certainly difficult to understand how specialists in the Ancient Near East refuse to accept such an obvious fact, one which can be verified by those who travel in those areas today. Behind the Greek *adelfòs* (brother) of the Gospels stands the Aramaic *aha*, or the Hebrew *'ah*, which can mean blood brother, stepbrother, cousin, or nephew, but also disciple, ally, member of the same clan, or even "neighbor" in general, belonging to the same city or nation.

Still today, there does not exist in modern Hebrew a term to distinguish brother from cousin, and one must have recourse to expressions such as "son of the same mother (or same father)." In the Old Testament, there are hundreds of passages where the word *brother* is used to indicate various types of kinship or relationship. To give a few examples: Abraham calls his nephew Lot "brother," and Laban does the same with Jacob.

In the New Testament, Paul uses the term *brother* almost 120 times to indicate a spiritual commonality or a bond that is not uterine and, often, not even one of kinship. Precisely for this reason, the evangelists (or the translators from Aramaic to Greek) do not hesitate to use the phrase "brother of Jesus," in general usage at the time, certain that no one would misunderstand them. This still holds true in the East (neither modern Arabic nor modern Hebrew have a term to distinguish brothers from cousins), as in Africa and in all traditional cultures. A missionary once told me that what seems a problem for European and North American biblical scholars, often incredibly convinced that their categories are universal and thus apply to biblical times as well, is not at all a problem for his African seminarians, whose languages and dialects have only the term *brother* to indicate a vast diversity of kinship or tribal belonging. To indicate without ambiguity provenance from the same seed and uterus, Africans say, "same father, same mother." Scripture comes down to us from a Semitic, Eastern, Mediterranean universe where brotherhood is not the narrow sort of our mononuclear families, each one closed inside its metropolitan apartment. Not incidentally, in the early centuries there was no ambiguity; for the one hearing or reading the Gospel *kerygma*, when they heard talk of "brothers and sisters" there was no thought of a large family gathered around Mary the Mother of Jesus. At any rate, even in Italian there exists a similar linguistic lacuna: it distinguishes blood brothers from cousins, but uses the same term *nipote* to indicate both the children of one's children (that is, grandchildren) as well as the children of one's siblings (nephews and nieces).

In our case, a particular promiscuity was added to the general usage. Blinzler writes,

> As can be deduced by the silence of the Gospels with respect to Joseph, he must have died early. After his death, Mary along with her son must have gone to live with the family of his closest relative(s?). The children of this family (or families?), growing up

> with Jesus, were called by the local population his brothers and sisters, because Semitic languages do not have a more precise term to indicate such kinship.

Thus, continues the German biblical scholar, "the primitive Church took up the term, and maintained it in the Greek as well, to honor in this way the relatives of the Lord who in the meantime had become eminent members of the community. And it maintained the term because it also offered an excellent means for clearly and comfortably distinguishing them from the many who shared the same names within the primitive Church." In fact, as everyone who reads Scripture realizes, Hebrew names are not numerous; they reoccur continuously (James alone has quite a number). So, by adding a "brother of Jesus," it clarified unambiguously who was meant.

There exists in Greek a word that indicates cousin. But the Greek version of the Hebrew Scriptures, the Septuagint, completed little more than a century before Christ, almost never uses it, preferring to translate it as *adelphòs*. In the Gospels, then, there must have been an additional reason: better the generic term "brothers," given that it probably had to do not only with cousins but with a heterogeneous clan, a "pressure group," as Ravasi says — and therefore a term was needed that would include all of these.

As an objective realist, and not as an apologist, this does not seem to me to be stretching the issue. Just as the other arguments placed on the table by Catholics, from St. Jerome in the fourth century to our own day, seem acceptable. Let us review them in quick summary, not with the intention of compiling a treatise, but to indicate some of the elements that can justify those who are convinced that the Catholic reading of these terms from Scripture is not guided by necessity, fanatic and fearful, to protect the dogma of the perpetual virginity of Mary.

We recall, then, the famous episode, so full of significance, that ended up penetrating even the impenetrable criticism of Ernest Renan. In the first edition of his famous and rationalist *Life of Jesus*, he accepted the hypothesis of the carnal brothers and sisters that was beginning to spread among liberal Protestants. But with the tenth edition of that *Life of Jesus*, and in his subsequent studies, Renan changed his mind: it was probably the first and only time he retracted a position that stood in contrast with the Catholic view. He changed his mind above all due to reflection on the dramatic and pathetic episode in John 19:25–27, where the dying Jesus entrusts his Mother to “the disciple whom he loved”: “ ‘Woman, behold your son!’ Then he said to the disciple, ‘Behold your mother!’ And from that hour the disciple took her to his own home.”

For my own convenience (and the reader’s as well, I hope) I entrust myself to the pen of Josef Blinzler again:

> If Mary had had other children, it would have been exceptionally peculiar that the dying Jesus would entrust his mother to the disciple. Despite everything that has been written to explain this peculiarity, the only interpretation of the event that satisfies and that imposes itself on whoever is not biased is the one given by the Fathers of the Church. Jesus must leave his mother truly alone, in other words, without actual children who could take care of her; for this reason he commits his most trusted of disciples to take care of her as if she were his own mother.... Why did he consider it necessary to make such a decision *in extremis*? This is comprehensible only if Jesus was the only son of Mary, but would have seemed quite strange if she had had four other sons with whom her relationship would have continued after (Acts 1:14) as before. With this act of entrustment, Jesus would have taken from adult men, who like him were true sons of Mary and they too quite close to her, the right to continue to see in her their mother.

This somewhat indignant conclusion by this German biblical scholar is comprehensible: “What a terrible attitude to attribute to the dying Jesus!”

Perhaps, if Jesus had broken into tears seeing a funeral and even intervening to resurrect the deceased at Naim, it is because, as the Gospel explains, the young man was “the only son of a widowed mother” — the same situation in which His mother as well would soon find herself and which He wanted to rectify in His last moments of life, for it was unthinkable that a woman should live alone.

But Renan’s exemplary change of mind, this persuasive teacher (“a marron glacé with needles inside,” as Mauriac described him) of all nineteenth-century rationalists, was brought about by the observation that, whereas the “brothers” and “sisters” are never considered “the children of Mary,” Jesus is invariably called "the Son of Mary." *The* and not *a*, as if to specify that He was the only one. But there is more: in the Hebrew world, and the Semitic world in general, the son is never indicated with the name of the mother, unless the father has died and the widow has no other children. Therefore, to say "the son of Mary" and not "of Joseph" was another clear indication of the official status of Christ. It was Renan who observed how the usage has continued even in the Western world, citing the example of the painter Piero della Francesca, also the only son of a widowed mother.

Continuing with the clues (the Gospels often invite one to a sort of "treasure hunt," or if you will, into a mystery novel, where one is forced to interpret the tracks: this is the logic of the *Deus absconditus*, the God who wants to be sought out), all those who believe in numerous offspring for Mary recognize that, as the Gospels make clear, Jesus was the first to be born. But while they accept this chronological preeminence, they display once more how little they know about ancient civilizations, especially of the Near East. In fact, these "brothers" criticize, advise, and even try to get their hands on Jesus to render him powerless, considering him "out of his mind." Unthinkable attitudes for younger brothers, scandalous and intolerable in societies of those times and places. The rigid family hierarchies established quite different, much more respectful ways of behaving before the male firstborn, whom only the father had the right to reprimand and above all to strike! Thus, the book of Genesis instructs the eldest child: "May you be the master of your brothers, may they bow before you, the sons of your mother." Blinzler writes, "The idea that the oldest has the right to a position of privilege with respect to those who came after him is foreign to our modern Western way of thinking, but is deeply anchored in Eastern thought. Consequently, the brother of Jesus in Mark 3 or John 7 must have necessarily been older than him. And this too must exclude that they were sons of Mary."

But concerning the oldest among sons, behold Luke 2:7: "[Mary] gave birth to her first-born." The objection of the "experts," whether misinformed or tendentious, runs thus: if we say firstborn, it is because others followed. Is it possible they do not know, or do not want to know that among the Jews every first son, even if an only son, was designated as the "firstborn," because to this primogeniture the Old Testament tied privileges and precise religious rites to fulfill? That "primogeniture" had a juridical-religious significance, as Luke himself testifies a few verses later (2:3) when he narrates the presentation of the child in the temple and quotes the ancient Scripture passage: “Every male that opens the womb shall be called holy to the Lord.” We have tombstones and Aramaic papyri from the first century that recall mothers who died in childbirth as they delivered their “firstborn,” after whom, obviously, no others would follow.

In conclusion (we must conclude, though so much more could be said), we turn once more to Professor Blinzler:

> Mary also participated in the Passover pilgrimage to Jerusalem (Luke 2:41–52), although she was under no obligation to do so. This concerned only male Israelites, in fact. According to Luke, Joseph and Mary made the pilgrimage not only that once, when Jesus was twelve years old; they “went to Jerusalem every year at the feast of the Passover” (2:41). One might ask if Mary were actually in good enough physical condition to make this annual trip, had she given birth, after Jesus, to at least another half dozen children. Anna, Samuel’s mother, would go every year as an act of special piety with her husband to Shiloh; but after the birth of her son, she stayed home until he was weaned (1 Sam 1:7, 21ff.); in other words, until he was four years old. The Passover pilgrimage to Jerusalem required at least two weeks away from home. As we learn from Luke again, when Jesus was twelve, his parents remained in the Holy City for the entire feast, seven days long. Nor was this obligatory. One must logically deduce that Mary could not have had a multitude of children at home, the oldest of which could only have been eleven.

But among the many tracks and clues, there are some that bear witness to the truth through their silence. Important here too is what Josef Blinzler seems to have been the first to sleuth out, because no one had previously discovered it. As we know, precisely the inexhaustibility of the gospel, its capacity to allow us to discover hidden folds, even after two thousand years of analysis and tireless reflection, is the proof of its mystery and therefore of its truth. We end then with the German biblical scholar sharing with the reader in an observation not found elsewhere: “There is something which until now, I believe, has never been considered in the discussion about the brothers of the Lord. As the modification of Mark 3:20 in the parallel passages in the other Gospels and their subsequent variations of the text show, the accounts of the incomprehension which Jesus encountered among his relatives were already in the ancient Church found difficult, if not scandalous."

And yet, "There would have been a very simple means not only to assuage the discomfort caused by those accounts, but to use them in a positive fashion, as a proof of the messianic prophecies."

In fact, in Psalm 69:8, one who was zealous for the cause of God and persecuted for it, laments, "I have become a stranger to my brethren, an alien to my mother's sons."

Blinzler observes,

> It has been verified that this Psalm, from the very beginning, has had an important role in the Church and was applied to the Messiah, Jesus. In the New Testament, reference is made to it no less than eighteen times. It is amazing therefore, that recourse was never made to this verse 9 in the New Testament to explain the incomprehension of the Lord's brothers. How obvious it would have been for Matthew to conclude the pericope of 12:46ff. with an allusion to the fulfillment of these prophetic words! Only one convincing explanation for this silence exists: the application of Psalm 68 [i.e., 69] to Jesus and to his relatives was impossible because the brothers the Gospel mentions were not "sons of his mother."

And yet another tile is added to the mosaic of what the Gospels truly desire to tell us.

A little moral can be drawn from this: we should not allow ourselves to be awed by the great stars, the fawned-over university chair, the tenured professors of New Testament criticism in some Catholic university, furnished with episcopal imprimaturs no less. Once more, the faith of the Church, accepted constantly and spontaneously by us simple people (what "normal" Catholic has ever imagined Our Lady in a house in Nazareth full of children, the fruit of a prolific husband?), will not be swept away by an erudition that wants to make us feel backward, still tied to myths and fairy tales that Science has dispelled. Devotion toward the *Aeipàrthenos*, the Ever-Virgin, can still convince today, and maybe more than ever, with the awareness that there are good reasons in support of a Tradition that demands faith but without renouncing history, and with it, renouncing our reason.

CHAPTER 51

The Surprise of John

The Belgian Jesuit Fr. Ignace de la Potterie long occupied the chair of New Testament studies, considered (and rightly so) the most important of the institute which in turn was considered (again, rightly so) the most distinguished in the Church in biblical studies. We are speaking about the Pontifical Biblical Institute, an outgrowth of the Gregorian University, whose rector is nominated by the pope himself, as confirmation of its importance. The "*Biblicum*," as it is called, was founded in 1909 by St. Pius X to respond, using the same weapons of scientific precision, to attacks on the foundations of the Faith by the so-called "higher criticism." Higher criticism dissected the texts of the Old and especially the New Testaments, concluding (as an a priori framework) that they are not historical but rather myths, symbols, and legends, and that the "Jesus of history," the one who actually lived, was an obscure person with an uncertain biography, who had little or nothing to do with the "Christ of faith." And so, the creed was based on illegitimate and historically untenable foundations and Christianity was nothing but a late construct born among Hellenists and marginal elements of an obscure Judaism. Despite the name it gave itself (in Italian, it goes by "*critica independente*" or "independent criticism"), this was not an "independent" criticism, but rather one that was rigidly ideological: the Gospels were not history but myth — this is the initial certainty — and so it was only a matter of generating justifications with a "scientific" appearance in support of this preconceived concept.

In the face of such an assault, the Church realized that it was not enough to become indignant and hurl invective against the "unbelievers," but that she needed to respond with the same instruments, with the same scholarship. To this objective the Pontifical Biblical Institute was dedicated, and with fine results which, above all, freed Catholics of the fear that the bases of their faith were no longer defendable in the face of Science (with the capital *S* as the professors of secular universities wanted) and removed their suspicion that the Incarnation of God in history was improbable when placed before the meticulous and implacable jury of modern history.

Professor de la Potterie, who died a few years ago, was an eminent and worthy figure in the long line of scholars who have made the Biblicum famous for over a century, among whom could also be counted Carlo Maria Martini as professor and director. Obviously quite learned, the master of many languages both modern and ancient, Fr. Ignace honored me with his friendship and shared my objective (obviously on my own level, nonacademic though knowledgeable about the subject matter) of finding confirmation of the historicity of the Gospels. And when he was already quite old, and had retired to his native Belgium, he occasionally surprised me with a telephone call that delighted but also saddened me. In fact, he would vent to me about the "modernism" and "rationalism" that had infected even Catholic biblical scholars, often out of imitation of the overly venerated professors in German theological faculties at their public universities, and not infrequently causing great harm to the cause of the Faith. Immediately after the unification of Italy in 1861, the anticlerical Freemasons in power hastened to suppress the theology departments of all the universities that had been turned over to the state. They had hoped to damage the Church in this way, but experience has shown that in reality, that suppression was providential, for it has allowed theology, and the *depositum fidei* therefore, to remain under the control of the hierarchy. This has spared us rancor, vindictiveness, complexes, cults of personality, careerism, and the exhibitionism of a throng of supposed "experts" perched on their prestigious university chairs — often former seminarians or laicized priests, formed in their polemical outlook directly by the Masonic lodges.

As for the emeritus professor de la Potterie letting off steam, I could only agree with him, for the excellent Jesuit was anything but a narrow traditionalist; on the contrary, he was knowledgeable of all the methods and modern theories, of which he accepted whatever did not transform the historical realism of the Gospels into a credal formula of obscure origins. In contrast to these modern-day professors of biblical studies, for whom nothing in Scripture must be taken as it is written and the only matters not up for discussion are their "demythologizing" footnotes and introductions.

Though he was an authority in all aspects of Scripture and in particular of the New Testament, Fr. Ignace was known above all as the leading specialist on John: his Gospel, of course, but also the three letters attributed to him. In the fourth evangelist he identified, clarified, and highlighted with a certainty hitherto unknown, an aspect as important as it was little recognized. In the famous prologue ("In the beginning was the Word, and the Word was with God, and the Word was God . . ."), John gives us explicit testimony of the triple virginity of Mary: before, during, and after giving birth. Fr. Ignace told me, and had written in articles, that biblical scholars today, even Catholic ones, prefer to pass over this aspect of the history of redemption, despite its importance. In some environments, those who speak of the *Semper Virgo* with convinced faith arouse suspicion, as if they were "fundamentalists"; or they provoke the irony due an old retrograde, ignorant of the progress in academic research. But behold, here comes this illustrious professor of the most illustrious pontifical university, scrutinizing "his" John, and right at the start of the Gospel discovers (or rediscovers, as we shall see) that the text had been manipulated already in ancient times, hiding in this way a simple passage of a verb from the singular to the plural.

While still active, our scholar had expounded his very well-documented thesis in two articles of some fifty pages each in *Marianum* —the journal of the aforementioned pontifical theological faculty of the same name — the first in 1978 and then picking up the argument again in 1983 and enriching it with new studies. Those one hundred pages, dense in footnotes and citations in Latin, Greek, and Hebrew, were widely read by specialists, although in response he received only silence. As often happens in the world of biblical scholarship, what might upset the paradigms and frameworks of the moment is repressed if it is not possible to remove it altogether, given (in this case) the critical seriousness of the research and the authority of the author. I remember how in one of his last phone calls, the old religious lamented this silence concerning such an important topic. It seems he was offering me an unexpressed yet courteous invitation to help him make known this "discovery," so relevant to the

Faith and offering the support of the authority of the fourth evangelist to the dogma of the perpetual virginity of Mary. In this chapter, then, I shall seek to respond to this desire of the good father who has since passed on to Heaven, giving news of that research of which he was the instrument, although this does not concern his academic prestige but rather the faith of us all. For the sake of making his ideas better known, I shall attempt to give a summary of them — a faithful one (I hope), given the attention I have given to those hundred pages. It would be good, however, for those who wish to read those two articles by de la Potterie, to request them by e-mail from the journal itself (marianum@marianum.it): I assure you it would be worth your efforts. This is not a matter of curiosity, but a way of reinforcing a truth about Mary, based on Scripture, that the Church has always believed and proclaimed, and that seems under threat today.

Let us examine, then, where the matter stands, reproducing the short verse of the fourth Gospel on which it is entirely based: the thirteenth verse of the first chapter in the Johannine prologue we mentioned above. In order to comprehend it, we must give the two preceding verses as well, the eleventh and the twelfth: "He came to his own home, and his own people received him not. But to all who received him, who believed in his name, he gave power to become children of God; who were born, not of blood nor of the will of the flesh nor of the will of man, but of God."

This, then, is the official Catholic version, whereas the following is the authentic version according to the professor from the Biblicum: "Not of blood, nor of the will of the flesh, nor of the will of man, but of God was he [Jesus] generated."

As we can see, the verb "generated" is in the singular and not the plural as given by the translations in our editions of the Scriptures. In fact, there is but one subject, Jesus, whereas in the conventional version it is in the plural, the subject being "those who believed in his name." Therefore, to repeat this decisive point: put in the singular, the verse is speaking of the divine generation of Christ; put in the plural, it is speaking about the transformation by grace of those who believe in Him. It should immediately be acknowledged that, in all the manuscripts we have, "blood" is in the plural in Greek, and while in the Latin Vulgate the plural was respected (*ex sanguinibus*), in modern languages it is translated in the singular. Yet, the plural "bloods" is rare in modern languages, since it is usually deemed uncountable. But if it was not used in the translations of this verse, it is not because it does not exist, but because its importance in Johannine thought was not comprehended. We shall examine this in a moment.

The first question to ask is this: Do the ancient documents of the New Testament at our disposal allow for the use of the third person singular of the verb "generate" (attributable to Jesus) instead of the third person plural, attributable to all Christians? It must be acknowledged: all, or almost all, of the Greek manuscripts that we have use the plural. But the oldest of these date only to the fourth century, excluding some isolated fragments on papyrus. However, we have texts of Christian writers as well as Church Fathers, as far back as the second century, which quote the verse in the singular. The very oldest, St. Irenaeus of Lyon around 190, uses the singular. The ever-polemical Tertullian, even, around the year 220, puts together a disputation over this passage and accuses a sect of heretics of having falsified the words of John, putting them, precisely, in the plural. The same plural, namely, that has entered the Catholic text of the Gospel and that our official editions still use. Besides the Latin, we have witnesses of the singular in the oldest Syriac, Coptic, and Ethiopian texts.

It must be clarified for those not familiar with biblical criticism: the reconstruction of the original text of Scripture using only the surviving ancient documents is called "external criticism." But this must be complemented by "internal criticism" (as all modern scholars agree), which goes deeper and which, in our case, tends to prefer "he was generated" rather than "they are generated." Thus, the situation is such that Fr. de la Potterie could already write in 1978, and then repeat in 1983 in his second article, that research not only on the ancient Gospel manuscripts but also on the citations of the earliest Christian writers seems to render necessary a return to the "was generated by God," having Jesus as its subject. Let us reread the verse in what seems to be the original version restored by our biblical scholar according to the intentions of the evangelist, for we realize that we have a most important testimony of the triple virginity of Mary. We were convinced that John had made no reference to her who, in his Gospel, is never referred to by name but instead as the "Mother of Jesus," and whom he cites only in the episode of Cana and at the foot of the cross. Yet behold, a third Marian testimony, one of primary importance, emerges from the text.

Let us now ask the question: Why, as early as the fourth century, did that reference to the divine origin of Jesus disappear and was the plural imposed, as a sort of foreign body, on the text that has come down? The entire prologue of John is a solemn hymn to the Incarnation of the Word and yet, there appears in a surprising and unjustified way "those who believe in his name," who are the members of the Church. And in what way would these baptized believers, of flesh and bone and certainly not angels, be generated "not by blood, nor by the will of the flesh, nor by the will of man"?

It seems the following occurred: in the primitive Church, the ideas of the sect known as the Docetists were raging; they negated the human nature of Jesus and, consequently, His conception by Mary. She was supposedly not the mother who nourished the creature in her womb for nine months, but a sort of conduit through which Christ, whose human image was only apparent, had passed. Docetism (whose "spiritualism" was particularly dangerous, rendering Jesus not a person, but a sort of super-archangel) relied precisely on that verse 13 of the prologue which we are examining. Christ came among us in a virginal manner, as attested by the phrases "nor by will of the flesh" and "nor by the will of man." But above all, the Docetic thesis would be proved by that "*nec ex sanguinibus*." But what was this "bloods"? As I said above, the fact that this plural is part of the original text is beyond debate: all the witnesses give the plural, whether they see the subject as Jesus or his disciples. But if (as John must have written in his prologue) the subject was the Messiah, this expression could easily have been used by Docetists: if He had not been "generated by bloods," it was because he did not have a body as human beings do, and thus there was no delivery, always accompanied by an effusion of blood from the woman. For this reason, in the words of our scholar de la Potterie, "to radically resolve the question and to remove a weapon from the heretics, probably at the beginning of the third century, ecclesial writers began to change the verb to the plural, placing the subject entirely on Christians but interrupting in this way the unity of the Johannine Prologue, which is entirely focused on the mystery of the Word made flesh." The touch-up made by churchmen ended up involving even the original of the Gospel, and that is what has come down to us today.

But let us reflect for a moment on that "bloods," turning to the summary supplied by Fr. Domenico Marcucci, one of the scholars who has had the courage to break with the conformity of his colleagues, taking utterly seriously the study of his colleague at the Gregorian.

> In the Greek texts, *aima*, blood, is only found in the singular. But John uses it in the plural. Why? To understand this, de la Potterie turned to Hebrew, given that the fourth evangelist is profoundly imbued with his native culture, Judaism. In the Hebrew Torah, the word "bloods" (*damim*) means the blood that flows from a woman during menstruation and while giving birth. It rendered her impure, and for that reason she had to go to the temple for her purification.

Therefore, "The 'not of bloods' means that the birth of Jesus took place, different from all other births, without an effusion of blood, and therefore in a virginal manner."

Let us attempt to reconsider verse 13 in what would be the original version and observe the consequences: Jesus "was generated by God" and therefore, "not by the will of the flesh, nor by the will of man" (*virginitas ante partum*). Furthermore, the delivery took place "not by bloods," that is, without the usual bodily damage, and this presumes the *virginitas in partu* as well as postpartum, not having had the passage of the body of her son to provoke bleeding and thus leaving the mother intact.

As we can see, this is a result of extraordinary importance, and was attained only by replacing a verb in the singular, as seems to have been John's intention. Furthermore, this immediately clarifies that it does not place in doubt the bodily materiality, the human reality of Jesus. And, in fact, the prologue continues with the words, "And the Word became flesh and dwelt among us." As de la Potterie rightly notes, if the early Church Fathers already saw in Matthew and Luke evidence for the virginal birth, it is precisely in the first chapter of John that they found not only its confirmation but also a direct reference to a virginal delivery, without the loss of blood that Judaism considered impure in the case of all deliveries.

Why then is there so much disregard, so much silence surrounding this rediscovery of the precise scriptural foundation of a truth such as the *semper*

Virgo, already present in Christian Tradition in the second century and which became dogma in the Church? This is a point of faith considered so important that in the East, among the inflexible rules prescribed for iconographers is one of never representing the *Theotokos* without three stars — one on her head and two on her shoulders — as a sign of her triple virginity. Fr. Ignace was not wrong in lamenting the conformity of so many of his colleagues to whom such a topic is a cause for embarrassment, such that, as Fr. Marcucci says, "in many manuals of Mariology used in Catholic seminaries, the virginity *ante, in,* and *post partum* is an object of silent embarrassment more than a subject that is taken seriously."

But beware! In one of his last books, Fr. Stefano De Fiores, perhaps the greatest Italian Mariologist (recently deceased, regrettably) and a former professor at the Gregorian as well, cited de la Potterie's studies and was convinced of his conclusions, judging them well-founded not only in the documents but also in terms of John's logic. This was a very important acknowledgment. And others have followed, and the path now seems open to recognition of the true intentions of John.

But the last article regarding Fr. Ignace is, as I said, from 1983. Why, in the translation of the Bible, revised and updated by the CEI twenty-four years later, did they not point out in a footnote to John 1:13 at least the possibility, which seems to be approaching certitude, that the primitive text had Jesus and not believers as its subject?

One thing was confirmed yet again: Scripture is still capable of revealing surprises, some of which, as in this case, concern the Mother of God, whose mystery is both discreet and inexhaustible.

CHAPTER 52

Newman, Part 1: From Anglican to Cardinal

On September 19, 2010, Benedict XVI traveled to Birmingham, Great Britain's second largest city by population and industrial importance. The reason for his trip was a beatification. This was an exceptional case: it was Pope Ratzinger himself who had established that only the pontiff could preside over canonizations (to be held in Rome), while for the "first degree" of sanctity, beatification, the local bishop should preside.[22]

The exception was justified. The man to be glorified was Cardinal John Henry Newman, not only a personality of great importance for the entire Church (and not only for that of nineteenth-century England), but also quite dear to Joseph Ratzinger, who on numerous occasions expressed his debt to the thought of Newman. John Paul II confessed his homage to him as well, and in 2001 celebrated the second centenary of his birth, writing to the Catholic bishops of Great Britain: "He arrived at an exceptional synthesis between faith and reason, which for him, were like two wings on which the human spirit reaches the contemplation of the truth." This synthesis of faith and reason is particularly topical and urgent, according to both Pope John Paul II and Pope Benedict.

In these thoughts and reflections on Mary, it seems a duty to turn to Newman, and not only for a few insights as we have done thus far, because we are indebted to him for his authoritative, powerful, and reasonable research

[22] Editor's Note: John Henry Newman was canonized as a saint by Pope Francis in 2019.

showing that the doctrines of the Roman Church on the Virgin, including the dogmas proclaimed over time, are entirely legitimate and in conformity with gospel faith. And also that the devotion offered to her by the people of God is fully justified, despite exaggerations and perhaps abuses due to the temperaments of individual countries. The work of this saint is extraordinarily important because it comes from one who was first a prestigious Anglican theologian and pastor, converted to Catholicism at forty-four, was ordained a Catholic priest two years later, and at seventy-eight was created cardinal.

It is essential for understanding the value of Newman's testimony that we recognize the salient traits of his life of nearly ninety years. He too was aware of this and wrote a famous autobiography which he called *Apologia pro vita sua*, in which thoughts and events are closely intertwined. Thus, to understand what Newman thought, we must understand what he lived. For this reason, the reader must resign himself (or rejoice ...): I have decided to dedicate this chapter to a summary of his biography and two additional chapters to his Marian thought. If I might make a confession, I am delighted to talk at length about him, having consulted with gratitude his thought and admired his Christian way of living. First, pastor of an Anglican community; then, after detaching himself from it, a religious of the Oratory of St. Phillip Neri; and finally a cardinal of the Holy Roman Church; the tall, thin figure that photos show us almost always smiling has nothing clerical about it, but is that of an elegant gentleman by upbringing and education. And his granitic faith, expressed in splendid sermons and homilies, is not that of a theologian, but that of a modern man seeking to be understood by all, with a high-quality didactic style. The day of his beatification was very joyful for me, as I considered it the recognition of how much all Catholics owe him. And I would add: interest in him was raised by another believing thinker to whom I owe so much, Jean Guitton, whose reflections on the English theologian are, as always, illuminating for understanding how modern his thinking was. The Church lost so much when it lost Great Britain: an inscrutable mystery of Providence!

We come now to his biographical features. John Henry Newman was born in London in 1801, his father a rich banker of the city, and his mother a descendant of French Protestants, the Huguenots, expelled by Louis XVI in the seventeenth century. It was thus a setting of fervent Protestantism in which he was raised, as he himself says, "in the adoration of the Scriptures and in hatred of papism." As a member of the upper bourgeoisie of imperial Great Britain, he had the best education at Oxford, where he immediately won the admiration of his companions and the esteem of his professors for his intelligence, his moral seriousness, and his faith. At the end of his university studies, he chose to enter the career track of his ecclesial community, the Anglican Church, and to dedicate himself entirely to theological studies and the exercise of intellectual charity, deciding as well to follow the Pauline counsel to renounce marriage and a family of his own. This was quite rare in the Church of England at that time, when even bishops and the primate himself were married men, often with numerous offspring. Nor was the choice motivated by a sort of sentimental aridity or distance from the passions: on the contrary, he was sensible to the affections and he cultivated friendships throughout his life. His correspondence, courteous and often intimate with all types of people, fills some thirty volumes. The long, meticulous process that led to his beatification even had to deal with rumors of his supposed homosexuality; in reality, the gay lobby is often incapable of comprehending the depth of spiritual friendships between true believers and tends to judge impossible close bonds without sexual implications. Let us not forget that that lobby is on the continuous search for "icons," not infrequently manipulated in order to make them fit, whether the subjects like it or not, into the homosexual display case. Newman, at any rate, cultivated poetry, and in his verses religion intertwines delicately with earthly loves. Not incidentally, when Leo XIII nominated him a cardinal, Newman chose as his motto *Cor ad cor loquitur*, "heart speaks to heart."

A brilliant pastor and admired chaplain of students at his alma mater, with a group of other pastors and students he dedicated himself to publications in defense of Anglicanism, seen by him as the "true Church" insofar as it was an intermediary between "papal superstitions" and the "excesses of the reformers." Attracted above all by his studies of the Church Fathers of the early centuries, both Greek and Latin (he read them all, in chronological order and in the original languages — a formidable undertaking), this is what set off his dramatic interior struggle. A man of great honesty and precision, and a preacher of the need to obey always and everywhere the voice of one's conscience, the more he studied and meditated on those authors he so venerated, the more he discovered that what was born of the Reformation, the Church of England included, was no more than the recrudescence of ancient heresies. At the same time, there was growing in him the awareness of the "substantial identity, beyond certain exterior appearances, of primitive Christianity with current Roman Catholicism," which has developed dogma in a legitimate manner, ever more deeply plumbing the depths of Scripture. It was with dismay, as an Anglican teacher, that he had little by little to accept such a discovery. Moreover, as a young man of just over thirty, he had traveled throughout Italy, going all the way to Sicily, and wrote upon his return home, "The superstitions and religious ways of the Latins disgusted me." In his family and in his ecclesial community, everything was characterized by repugnance for "papism," leading them to identify the pontiff of Rome without hesitation as the antichrist.

It was in 1839 that he had a first intuition that would shake him profoundly and that led him into years of doubt, though this too dissolved gradually by the progress of his studies and research, to the point of full acceptance of the Catholicism he had hitherto execrated and despised. Almost frightened by it, there grew within him the awareness that the Anglican Church was not the true Church and therefore, by defending its doctrine and prestige, he was fighting a lost cause. He was bowled over by this evidence, which he did not expect in the least, while studying the history of the Council of Chalcedon. He perceived that the Monophysites of those distant centuries were the predecessors of the Anglicans, and the followers of Eutyches were the ancestors of Protestants, but the truth was on the Catholic side, that of the pope, then St. Leo the Great, who defended the true gospel doctrine. This caused him torment, torn between his reason, which leaned ever more in favor of Rome, and his sentiment, which rendered too painful his break with the Anglican Church. He felt at home there, English to the depths as he was, while among Catholics he intuited the truth but saw them surrounded by a popular religiosity which seemed mere illegitimate superstition to him, while the clergy did not intervene energetically to crush such deviations.

What seemed to him most worthy of condemnation were the "Marian exaggerations" (certain statues, processions, invocations, tales of miracles!) that not only offended his tastes as a British gentleman but seemed to him downright offensive toward the Virgin Mary, who, he was convinced, did not appreciate that type of veneration and devotion. It was thus love for Mary, the "true" Mary, the Gospel Mary, that led him to want to stomp out those devotions which seemed intolerable, those Catholic absurdities. The Virgin Mary was to him doubly defaced: through the abuses of devotion and through the theology which had created an illegitimate "Mariology," a sort of excrescence of the primitive faith, because it lacked adequate biblical foundations.

Lacerated by doubt, he attempted a solution: he tried to show to himself and to others that, on the doctrinal level, Anglicanism and Catholicism professed the same faith, although with different emphases. He published a tract which proposed to demonstrate that the Anglican creed, expressed by the famous "Thirty-Nine Articles" elaborated at the end of the 1500s, coincided in all counts with the Catholic creed as it was expressed by the Council of Trent. But this was too much, even for the tolerant High Church of England, the branch that was closest to Catholicism, and some forty-two bishops condemned his attempt. Thus, it was not possible to have the two perspectives coexist as if they were but one; a radical choice was necessary.

A man of precise and demanding conscience, incapable by that time of continuing in the Anglican ministry, yet still reluctant to knock on the doors of Rome, Newman decided to resign from all ecclesial and academic roles and retreated to a little village near Oxford. There, for four years, he lived a sort of hermit's life, visited only by some friends who shared his search, praying, studying, and entrusting himself to Christ that He might show him the community in which He was best recognized and adored in truth and fidelity. Finally, after much prayer and meditation, he was convinced unequivocally that the true Church was the Catholic Church and that its doctrinal development (beginning with its Marian doctrine) was legitimate, necessary even, since Rome had descended to the depths of the revealed Truth and had elaborated a greater comprehension of doctrine over time, though always in coherence with the gospel.

His honesty then led him to face a painful separation, cutting ties with his beloved Anglican Church, with his beloved students at Oxford, and with many friends who looked upon his passage to "papism" with indignation. On October 9, 1845, he officially entered the Catholic Church, which, at that time, did not even enjoy full civil and political rights in England and was a very small reality, composed mostly of impoverished Irish immigrants. It was, at any rate, surrounded by suspicion and disdain, which certainly did not attract a refined gentleman, an esteemed pastor, a celebrated theologian, and an acclaimed writer like John Henry Newman.

Furthermore, he had the fortune of being welcomed into Catholicism by a saint, the Passionist priest Domenico della Madre di Dio, who, following a mystical experience that had led him to work for the return of England to Catholicism, followed Newman in his preparations for this great step. It is significant that this future saint, giving the news to Rome of Newman's conversion, described him as "the pope of the Anglicans, the great oracle of this Nation, the most learned man in all Great Britain."

After his conversion, painful yet happy, dolorous as well as liberating, he continued to deepen the truth that he had rediscovered, and strove as well to live out concretely the principles of the new faith. *Ancient* faith, rather, given that his discovery was precisely this: Catholicism, and only it, was the legitimate descendant and custodian of the creed of the Apostles. To be close to the tombs of Peter and Paul, he went to Rome, where he frequented the university of the Propaganda Fide and would be ordained priest in May of 1847. He had already received Anglican ordination many years before that, but Rome did not consider this valid. After much prayer and reflection, as was his custom, he decided to become a religious with the Oratory of St. Philip Neri, finding in it the joy and freedom he had always sought. With the approval and the blessing of Pius IX, he transplanted the oratory into England, beginning in Birmingham, since it was the city most in need of charity due to the spiritual and material misery that had accompanied intense industrialization. He was not to move from that house for nearly forty years, living as a monk, studying, writing, and supervising the oratory's school for the children of factory workers.

His only considerable absence was when he went to Dublin to establish a Catholic university. He had in mind an authentic athenaeum, where orthodoxy would coexist with freedom, and devotion with academic precision, whereas the local episcopate wanted, in the end, only a large seminary.

The deep serenity that he drew from the Faith and that was favored by his temperament (never lacking the typical British humor) was continuously threatened by two opposing fronts. The Anglicans, as was foreseeable, did not resign themselves to the fact that their most prestigious theologian had crossed over to the disagreeable "papists." Not only did they doubt his conversion, but they attributed it to the most sordid reasons. As for Catholics, not all were happy to have among them that unexpected brother; and the most suspicious (among them several bishops in the United Kingdom) considered him dangerous, a sort of infiltrator who had come to inject into the Church well-disguised Protestant errors. It was to respond to both sides, with charity as well as clarity and passion, that he wrote *Apologia pro vita sua* which was appreciated by non-Catholics as well, transforming suspicion and invective at least into respectful silence. As for Catholics, the decision of Leo XIII to make him a cardinal arrived when he was already approaching eighty, although he still had ten years to live. The pope recognized in him "genius and doctrine," besides orthodoxy, and conceded to him all that the new cardinal requested: namely, not to move him from his beloved and peaceful oratory of Birmingham so as to continue to pray, study, and give spiritual direction. The Latin inscription he wanted inscribed on his simple tomb is well known: *Ex umbris et imaginibus in veritatem*; Out of shadows and images, into the truth.

We have now finally come to what interests us here; namely, reflection on Mary. In 1865, twenty years after becoming a Catholic, an old friend of his, the pastor Edward B. Pusey, published a book in which, on behalf of the ecumenical encounter he welcomed between the Anglican Church and Catholicism, he attacked what according to him was the greatest obstacle: Marian theology and devotion to the Virgin. Pusey denounced as illegitimate and contrary to dialogue among Christians the definition of the dogma of the Immaculate Conception by Pius IX eleven years previous. These matters cut Newman to the quick, having lived, suffered, and in the end resolved them personally. He spontaneously wrote his *Letter to the Rev. Pusey,* which remains one of the best apologies Mary has ever been given in the Church. In the following chapter we shall discuss it.

CHAPTER 53

Newman, Part 2: His Discovery of Our Lady

We have seen who John Henry Newman was and the importance his unforeseen conversion had on Catholicism — a conversion that cost him greatly on an emotional level as well as in terms of his social respectability in Victorian England, but which was imposed on him by his own conscience. In fact, his studies on the early centuries of the Church, his systematic reading of the Greek and Latin Church Fathers, and his investigation into the ancient liturgy all revealed to him an unequivocal reality. Namely, that the Catholic faith of his period was the legitimate development of the apostolic faith and not (as horrified Anglicans and Protestants piously affirmed) a jumble of elements extraneous to revelation and tending toward paganism. The fact is that one who believes that the Christian is called to the *aut-aut* cannot understand the richness of the *et-et,* of that synthesis of opposites which is the formula of Catholicism and which enables it to embrace all that is good and true. Gradually, as he advanced in his studies and reflections, the pastor John Henry, up to that point a convinced apologist of the Anglican Church as a via media between Catholic superstitions and the exaggerated Protestant reaction, discovered with dismay what at the beginning of his search he would never have imagined. Namely, that the authentic Roman creed was the legitimate and harmonious result of a centuries-long deepening of the gospel "deposit."

And this was also true of Catholic "Mariology," that progressive expansion of the presence of the Virgin Mary in theology and devotion which was the greatest scandal to the Reformers who saw in it only Mediterranean myths. We have already recalled how a hundred years later, the most famous and influential

Protestant theologian of the twentieth century, Karl Barth, whom John XXIII invited as an observer to the Second Vatican Council, described Marian doctrine as "a cancer that must be eradicated to liberate the true Gospel." It was, according to Barth, a metastasis that the hierarchy permitted, even fostered, and thus, as with the early reformers Luther and Calvin, he believed that the Roman pontiff tragically deserved the label "antichrist." It was precisely the pope who was the guarantor of a religion that had become idolatrous, with the adoration of the Grand Mother of pre-Christian paganism.

The young Newman, a very gentlemanly Englishman, was perhaps less brutal but substantially in agreement. After his journey through Italy in 1832 (he was thirty-one at the time) he wrote, as we have already quoted, that "the Italian devotions" disgusted him. Again in 1841, in the thick of his tormented search, just four years before his conversion which would later lead to his becoming a cardinal and eventually to the honors of the altar as a saint, he wrote: "I could never go over to Rome as long as it tolerates that Marian cult which, in conscience, I consider incompatible with the honor of Christ and the glory of God."

He knew well what he was saying when, more than twenty years later, he recounted his experience to the Rev. Edward Pusey, who had published a book whose complete title was *The Anglican Church, Part of the Church of Christ, One, Holy, Catholic, and Means for Reestablishing Visible Unity*. Pusey was an old confrere and friend of Newman's, both of them active in the "Oxford Movement" which, while respecting Anglican traditions, advocated a rapprochement with the Catholic Church. This commitment was not peacefully tolerated in England, and Pusey was censured by the authorities at the University of Oxford, where he taught, for a sermon in which he defended the thesis of the Real Presence in the Eucharist. He then had other problems when he asked for the return of Anglicans to the Catholic practice of individual confession.

Rev. Pusey respected and venerated the Virgin Mary. And he desired the reopening of talks between Rome and Canterbury, considering them two equally legitimate branches of the same Christian trunk. But along the path to reunion, there lay the Roman abuses, especially in the fields of doctrine and Marian devotion. These abuses were not only tolerated but often provoked by the hierarchy which, in 1854, eleven years earlier, had proclaimed a third, unacceptable dogma, that of the Immaculate Conception. The book which he published in 1865 sought to be a gesture of ecumenical goodwill, an exhortation to Rome that it might remove from the path to the desired unity this obstacle of the growing superstition, century after century, around the Virgin Mary, for whom a sober veneration was to be reserved, as in the primitive Church. The exaggerations of Catholicism were certainly cause for affliction and not pleasure to Mary in Heaven.

As soon as Newman received Pusey's publication, Newman reacted, setting to work with age-old respect for his former confrere in the Anglican communion and faculty colleague at Oxford. Respect and friendship, but also clarity and theological precision. For him, ecumenism (which he practiced in substance, even though the name was not yet in use) did not mean an impoverishment of Catholicism, but the proposal to the brethren separated in the sixteenth century of an inalienable wealth that is the Catholic understanding of the Mother of God. What was needed, according to him, was not divesting one interlocutor of his doctrinal patrimony to please the other, but to share what the *sensus fidei* of believers and the reflection of Catholic theologians have drawn from the depths of the Word of God. From Newman's work there emerged in just a few weeks the *Letter to Reverend Edward Pusey*, which summarizes the results of decades of research as well as his personal struggle.

The fundamental question that needed to be answered was this: If, as is evident, the Mariology of the early centuries is certainly not that of the nineteenth century, is it an illegitimate extension of revelation or a deepening of it that is not only legitimate but appropriate, which has led to an organic development of doctrine?

To try and understand the background to the problem, we begin by saying, for love of the truth, that the Reformation affirms that it takes inspiration only from Scripture and from all of Scripture; but in reality, it created a theological filter that accepts whatever confirms its perspective and excludes all that contradicts it. Luther began by basing his reflections on a pair of verses from St. Paul (taken out of context no less), constructing his novel form of Christianity around justification by faith alone and hurling anathemas against the works of charity which supposedly do not save but rather present a danger insofar as they create the illusion of being able to save ourselves by our own human strength. The motto attributed to him, *Pecca fortiter sed crede fortius,* Sin boldly but believe even more firmly, reflects in a harsh but accurate light his perspective.

But in Scripture, matters are always more complex than those would believe who wish to read and interpret it basing their understanding only on one aspect and rejecting the Magisterium of the Church. Thus, Friar Martin excluded from his theological construction, formulated in proud seclusion, the many passages of the Old and New Testaments that affirm precisely the necessity of works inspired by faith for obtaining eternal salvation. One of the most embarrassing passages is found in the letter of the apostle James who, in the second chapter, says the exact opposite of what Luther was preaching: "What does it profit, my brethren, if a man says he has faith but has not works? Can his faith save him? . . . So faith by itself, if it has no works, is dead. . . . Do you want to be shown, you foolish fellow, that faith apart from works is barren? . . . For as the body apart from the spirit is dead, so faith apart from works is dead" (2:14, 17, 20, 26). We could continue with other quotes. But this suffices for understanding why Luther (and, after him, Calvin and all the innumerable founders of Protestant communities) attempted to escape this embarrassment by declaring that the Letter of James was "a letter of straw," that it should not be taken seriously, and that it was "apocryphal." An exclusion made of his own initiative, given that no one prior to him had shared this view.

Returning to our topic. The filter of the Reformation, often more ideological than theological, blocked and repressed even a statement by Jesus in his solemn farewell discourse to his disciples during the Last Supper. This decisive discourse is a sort of spiritual testament and gives valuable guidance for the future of the community. Jesus, who was to rise again in three days after dying on the cross, states, "I have yet many things to say to you, but you cannot bear them now. When the Spirit of truth comes, he will guide you into all the truth; for he will not speak on his own authority, but whatever he hears he will speak, and he will declare to you the things that are to come. He will glorify me, for he will take what is mine and declare it to you" (John 16:12–14). If those who, in the 1500s, had discovered "authentic Christianity" and who bound themselves to basing their doctrine entirely on Scripture, nothing excluded, censured this passage as well, the reason for this is clear: this is the foundation of the Catholic view that there are two sources of the Faith: the written Bible, of course; but also Tradition, which is nothing but the deepening reflection on the words of Jesus, the discovery of the density of His statements, under the guidance of the Spirit, announced by Christ himself. In the Gospels lies the truth, but this is not only what appears on first view. Those texts of inestimable depth do not exhaust their significance in a reading, however attentive it might be, but hide riches that the apostles, when the Master was still physically among them, "were not able to bear." Thus, after so many centuries, after so much deepening offered by Tradition through the evaluation of the Church, we possess a more complete and profound vision of revelation than that which was granted to the apostles. An often-repeated phrase claims that we modern Catholics are only "dwarves standing on the shoulders of giants." Perhaps on the moral level, but not in terms of doctrine.

Many things in Scripture are only in an embryonic state, destined to grow in an organic manner — beginning with the truths about Mary. She is the icon of the Church because the Church is also mother, because in her mystery the Church is also immaculate, and because she generates Jesus anew in the Eucharist every day. The Gospel of Luke (2:19) says that "Mary kept all these things, pondering them in her heart." This is what the Church has done throughout time: it has meditated on the Marian mystery and has drawn what was implicit from what is written in revelation. This has required much time: four centuries before arriving at the definition in Ephesus of the divine maternity; and only in Newman's time did the Magisterium arrive at clarifying and proclaiming as dogma the Immaculate Conception.

This is the dynamic which Protestantism has not understood and has refused to accept.

Rev. Pusey hoped, through his book, that the Church would halt and would not proclaim any further Marian dogmas after those of her perpetual virginity, her divine maternity (these two were, at least formally, accepted by the Reformation as well), and the very recent and contested Immaculate Conception. But Newman responded that it is not for us to place limits on the Spirit who, according to the promise of Jesus, would continue until the Parousia to guide believers to the full truth. And in fact, in 1950, the official proclamation was made by Pius XII of Mary's Assumption into Heaven. And no one can say what will come in the future, and whether other truths will be brought to light. As the future cardinal, and now saint, wrote, "Those who at least intuited what the divine maternity is, know that limits cannot be placed on the sanctity of the Mother, neither in praising her nor in venerating her. Our duty is only the awareness, ever vigilant, that this creature is merely that, she is one of the many whom her Son has redeemed, she is not a goddess nor a demi-goddess." The slight mention that Paul makes of Mary in the Letter to the Galatians is full of significance (another example of the scriptural word that must be excavated to the depths): Jesus, says Paul, was "born of a woman." A woman, precisely, and not a celestial being.

The case of Mary is the issue in the *Letter to Pusey*, but Newman perceives that the deepening and development of gospel truth concerns not only her.

He writes,

> If Marian doctrine and the consequent devotion had been the only ones to develop throughout the centuries, we would have a deformed and perhaps monstruous doctrine. But the Faith is an organic, balanced whole and the Spirit continues his work, inspiring and assisting believers as they meditate on these things. Thus, the entire Catholic understanding of the creed has grown, such that the proportions of the parts of the whole have remained the same and all support each other and illuminate each other reciprocally.

Newman adds that this balance has not been preserved at all in the Protestant world of his origins and to which he adhered in his youth with conviction and passion. The Reformation does not accept Tradition (judging it hypertrophy, a metastasis, a return to idolatry) and remains firm to the letter of the Gospel when it concerns her of whom the Sacred Book speaks so little (apparently). And yet, with one of its many contradictions, the Reformation admits the legitimacy of the development of dogma in the very foundations of the Faith: the Divine Trinity. Newman writes,

> The oldest Christian creeds mention the Father, the Son, and the Holy Spirit but without specifying that they are One and Equal, entirely uncreated and eternal without making clear the internal relations within the Trinity. To comprehend better the

> unfathomable mystery, centuries of reflection, investigation, and theological battles were necessary, digging into the words of the New Testament. Regarding God, the growth is recognized and approved, whereas this growth was rejected with indignation when it concerned the Mother of God.

There is here, at any rate, a profound connection: the Council of Ephesus, in 431, proclaimed Mary the *Theotokos*, the Mother of God, which opened the path to the deeper and surprising discovery of the glories of Our Lady. But at the same time, meditation on her role helped to distinguish better the mysterious reality of the Trinity itself. The Virgin Mary is not at the margins of the Faith; she is not an accessory, an option for old sentimentalists. On the contrary, she is at the heart of the creed. Do the Gospels speak very little of her? Only those who read them superficially can say that. Not many verses concern her, but what counts is not the quantity but the quality. From the very beginning of it all —namely, from the Annunciation — until the foundation of the Church at Pentecost, the Virgin Mary was present at all the fundamental turning points in the life and teaching of her Son. Those few words by and about her have not yet finished revealing their astonishing substance. Newman explains,

> The Bible is a narrative; therefore, it speaks above all of those who exercised a visible role. Thus, the New Testament says much about Paul, although he was not a follower of the Master in life, yet it speaks more about him than about John who was the "beloved disciple." It is as if Christ wanted to preserve in the intimacy of the chiaroscuro His most sacred sentiments, like the love towards His mother and the affection towards the preferred disciple.

But another love, that of Christians for Him, slowly penetrated that discretion, revealing at least something of the truth hidden in the apparent half-light.

Precisely because he realized that Mary was not marginal but central, Newman invited Pusey to reflect first of all on *Turris davidica*, the Marian invocation in the Litany of Loreto. It recalls the defensive tower that King David built and on which the shields of the valorous men ready to defend the Holy City were hung. The progressive discovery of the importance of the Mother was, especially in the early centuries (though all throughout history) the best defense of her Son. Every dogma about her is, in essence, a defense of Him. Here are some of the words of our English saint:

> Among her many titles, we call Mary "Tower of David" because she has carried out in an admirable way her task as defender of her Divine Son against the assaults of His enemies, the heretics, with their heterodox pseudo-truths. For Protestants, it is a habit to think that the honors which we Catholics offer to her whom we call Our Lady would harm the supreme worship due to Jesus Christ, worship that is supposedly eclipsed by the veneration of the Virgin Mary. But this is entirely contrary to the truth, as shown by doctrine as well as the experience of the Roman Church.

For this reason, Newman could write his friend who remained an Anglican and who was asking for a reshaping of the Virgin's presence, the following words that are worth quoting directly from the *Letter*:

> One continues to affirm that the honors which Catholics bestow on the Virgin Mary, which have their origin in the devotion to her Son and omnipotent Lord, end up weakening this devotion. And it is said that it is not possible to exalt a creature in such a way without distancing one's heart and mind from the Creator. But I observe that those who admit the authority of the Council of Ephesus (and Anglicans and the Reformed confessions admit it, at least officially) ought to know that the definition of *Theotokos*, Mother of God, given by the Council Fathers to the Virgin, has the aim of defending the reality and the truth of the Incarnation of the Word and of preventing the Faith from becoming a form of humanism. If she is "Mother of God," it is because the One she gave birth to is not only man. To state that God had a Mother is the best way to save the faith in Christ in His entirety as true God and true man.

In the manner of a good pragmatic Englishman, Newman continues on the level of experience:

> If we take a look at Europe in this second half of the nineteenth century, we see that those who are abandoning the adoration of Jesus as God are not the Christians who have always distinguished themselves for their devotion to Mary, but precisely those who have

> abandoned and rejected with indignation this devotion. Zeal for the glory of the Son is being extinguished where zeal for exalting the Mother is extinct. In this way, those who were accused of adoring a creature in place of the Creator still adore Him. And those who claimed to adore Him with greater purity, removing if not despising the veneration for the Mother, have ceased adoring Him.

To understand Newman's alarm at the weakening of the Faith, one must remember that this man was not a "liberal Catholic" in the least, as some who only know him through hearsay often believe. He was "liberal," certainly in his appropriate refusal of all religious coercion and in his awareness that the gospel can and must be proposed and never imposed. If God is love and desires to be loved, we all must realize that to love on command is not to love at all. We see here his "pastoral liberalism," accompanied by his lifelong struggle, first as an Anglican and then as a Catholic, against "dogmatic liberalism." Namely, that which in Protestant countries especially was transforming Christianity into a sort of Masonic deism and sought to "demythologize" prophecies, miracles, and even the Trinity. For this reason, he venerated Mary as the "Tower of David," but also as the "Morning Star": the one who indicates the right course for following Jesus, who is not "an illustrious man," or a "great initiate," nor "a sublime moralist," but the Savior of men.

We shall need another chapter, the third, to understand better that this gentleman of the old yet always modern England is a truly valuable guide for walking knowingly and joyously next to the Virgin Mary.

CHAPTER 54

Newman, Part 3: In Conclusion

We return to Newman for the third time: his historical role was important in the nineteenth century, but today is more relevant than ever. Benedict XVI wanted to travel to Birmingham for a brief stay, simply to have the joy of proclaiming him Blessed. We have already mentioned how the Anglican community had perceived the conversion of Newman to Catholicism as a harsh blow, losing their most esteemed and prestigious pastor and theologian. But the bitterness extended to the civil and political sector as well: remember that Anglicanism was founded as a "state church" in which the king (by violent imposition of Henry VIII, through his Act of Supremacy) also became pope, where the pastors are state functionaries and where Parliament is called to deliberate and vote on theological and ecclesial decisions. These things seem to us either ridiculous or blasphemous, but for centuries they made the English proud, knowing they were subject to no one, not even to Rome.

Thus William Gladstone, the renowned British statesman (aged twenty-three when he entered Parliament, where he stayed for over sixty years), stated publicly on the floor his displeasure for the "apostasy" of Rev. Newman. Even the prime minister, John Russell at the time, as soon as the conversion was made public, turned to his fellow members of Parliament with a saddened air at the start of the session: "I must communicate to the honorable members of this Parliament that a man of great talent and profound culture, one of the greatest in our country, has abandoned the Church of England." For his part, the future cardinal did not assume a polemical attitude toward the community he was leaving, following as always his conscience and explaining serenely the reasons for his choice, without wanting to condemn the reasons of those who thought it better to remain in the Church of England.

Thus, the historical role of Newman gave the Catholic Church such prestige in the proud and often arrogant United Kingdom that many of the conversions to Rome in Britain have found in him their origin and guide. But his role is more important today than ever, above all regarding Mariology. We spoke of this in the two preceding chapters and here we shall conclude our summary. He was the one who showed how superficial and often clearly ideologically driven were the arguments of the Protestants against the doctrinal development on Mary (acting out of the necessity of not contradicting the theological cage the Reformers had constructed). Yet, today, in some circles of Catholic theology, the theses of Protestantism are being reclaimed (five hundred years later!) and the radical downgrading of the Woman of Nazareth is presented as "respect for Mary" and "a return to primitive simplicity." From the Madonna to a sweet, pious Jewess, married with children. From Queen of Heaven to housewife, to make an apparent joke — though, in reality, this is precisely what the works of many contemporary scholars teach, even in pontifical universities. Many keep silent on the Marian dogmas of the Church, especially the last two, the Immaculate Conception and the Assumption into Heaven, proclaimed by two popes, by the way, both named Pius (IX and XII), who are viewed with great suspicion.

All of this is presented as "purification of the faith": Mary can stay with us, but certainly not as the Mother of the Church (to safeguard her reputation above all); instead, as daughter and member of this Church. And we renounce the excessive and unfounded Mariology and popular devotion, superstitious and unacceptable for an "adult Catholic." Better, much better for her and her historical reality. This theology is quite persuasive and at times eloquent: give her great lip service but please, show her the respect of not calling her Our Lady, leave the rosaries in the back of our desk drawers with their intolerable litanies, let us look with skepticism on the medieval practice of pilgrimage. And perhaps, with great respect for her, let us transform into centers for social causes or something useful the innumerable shrines erected for her by popular credulity, sustained and promoted by the preconciliar Church.

And so, we must comprehend (on the heels of the popes) just how important John Henry Newman is today. As a prestigious theologian — and hailing from the Anglican community that razed to the ground the shrines and mandated prison sentences for anyone caught reciting the Rosary or practicing any of the other "superstitious papist practices" — Newman has demonstrated once and for all that what Catholicism says about the Virgin Mary was already contained in the primitive faith and is the legitimate fruit of a progressive fathoming of the depths of the New Testament. As the great expert in patrology, both Greek and Latin, that he was, he reached a conclusion based on the sources that refutes the claim of every Protestant or "adult Catholic":

> It is not possible, as concerns Mary, to establish contradictions between the dogmatic teaching of modern Catholicism and that of the Church Fathers who, we must not forget, lived and were active when the Church was not yet divided. In a period that even the Reformed accept, recognizing, at least officially, the dogmatic conclusions of the first ecumenical Councils. By calling Mary the "New Eve," the "Mother of the Living," the "Mother of God," those Fathers laid the foundations for the royal pedestal on which the research of theologians and the love of the devout have placed her in the Catholic Church as in the Orthodox as well, both Greek and Slavic.

The New Eve, therefore. Here is one of the keys of what our English theologian has helped us discover (or rediscover). In his *Letter to Pusey*, he dedicates dense pages to textual quotations taken from the ancient Fathers of the Church, both from the East and the West, in any case when the schism between Rome and Constantinople was still far off and both professed the same faith and recognized the same hierarchy.

In these quotations it becomes quite clear that from the beginning Mary was the "second Eve," the woman from whom would come ransom from the sin committed by the "first Eve" in Eden. Eve received from God the highest dignity of being the "mother of all men," but made terrible use of this privilege and, with Adam, caused the fall. But then, at the time chosen by God, Mary arrived, and it was from her, by means of her faith, her consent, her very body, that salvation came: "Well then, is not this clear parallel sufficient reason to see in the Virgin of Nazareth not a simple 'instrument' with which to give flesh to the Word, as it seems in certain Protestant perspectives, but one of the pillars of the divine strategy?" This is what the Fathers thought, and on that basis Christian reflection throughout the centuries has elaborated a Mariology that is not an illegitimate accessory but rather a central part of Christology.

Edward B. Pusey published his work in 1865, in other words eleven years after the proclamation by Pius IX of the dogma of the Immaculate Conception. A dogma on which this Oxford professor expressed a severe judgment, equal to that of all other theologians not only in the Anglican communion but throughout the Protestant world. For Pusey, the decision of the pope to break the ice and reach a definition of faith that had for centuries been requested by the Catholic faithful was another obstacle to the encounter with Rome, continuing on a path that created distance instead of unity.

Newman's precise response to Pusey is worth quoting verbatim:

> For the unanimous ancient Church, Mary was the second Eve. But Eve, at the moment of creation, did not bear the stain of original sin. Are we to think that the second Eve, the *Theotokos* (Council of Ephesus, accepted by the Reformation as well) would be inferior to the remote progenitrix? If Eve had been privileged from the very beginning by Grace, is there any temerity in stating that in Mary Grace acted in an even more elevated manner? Is this not the sense of the greeting of the Archangel to her whom he called "full of Grace"? If Eve received a supernatural gift from the moment of her conception, it is not possible to deny Mary this. I do not see how such a conclusion can be refuted. It seems inevitable.

The theologian continues,

> Well, this is simply the conviction of faith attested by the dogma of the Immaculate Conception. This, nothing more and nothing less: equal to Eve, Adam's companion, the second Eve, the Mother of Jesus, was free of sin from birth. It is quite strange to me, and nearly incomprehensible, that this doctrine creates problems for our Christian brethren whom I know to be educated and pious. I can only suppose that their rejection is derived from a simple reason: they have not understood what the Catholic Church means when it speaks of the Immaculate Conception.

Analogous considerations were made by Newman regarding the Assumption into Heaven, which had not yet been officially proclaimed dogma (only in 1950), but in which the Church had believed ever since the period before the divisions. "Eve would not have become ashes and dust had she not sinned. And would Mary not have inherited this gift? Would she, the Woman of Salvation, have been inferior in this way to the woman of the Fall?"

Our theologian recalls that some of the ancient texts attribute to Mary some faults that sinlessness would exclude: the gravest would be having doubted the glorious destiny of her Son at the moment of the Passion. Nothing in the New Testament allows one to affirm this, nor does another supposed fault have any perceptible foundation: namely, that of having committed the sin of vainglory if not pride when the crowds followed enthusiastically and acclaimed her Son. Newman finds in these authors (rare moreover) confirmation of his conviction: he claims that they are texts under the influence of Arianism. He deduces, "If you do not believe in the divinity of Christ, and therefore in His perfection, even less will you believe in the impeccability of his Mother. Here we have confirmation that only the decisive, unhesitating assertion of the divine nature of Jesus justifies and requires Catholic Mariology." Including the Immaculate Conception.

Newman then summarizes his thought in remarkable words which we must not forget: "History has shown that she has not been the rival, but the servant of her Son; not the one who hid Him, but She who manifests Him in all His grandeur and truth. She is the one who protected Him during His infancy, and continues to protect Him until the end of history." God, in His mysterious plan, has desired that the maiden of Nazareth should have forever one role among all: that of Mother.

For good reason therefore, and not out of devotional sentimentalism, the theologian who was formerly the glory of the Anglicans writes at the end of the reply to his friend and colleague Pusey, "If we take seriously from the very beginning, the implicit content that only over time becomes explicit, we must conclude the following: we cannot assign limits to the sanctity of the Mother of God, except for the limit of being a creature, not a goddess or a demigoddess. There can be no excesses in praising her in whose body the Eternal Creator chose to dwell, her from whom the Word made flesh has come to us." And again, "She is the All-Beautiful and All-Pure, because God is her son.

According to the laws of nature that the Creator willed to respect, the son resembles the mother, takes from her body but also from her spirit: this happened between Mary and Jesus as well."

Pusey's book took umbrage not only with Catholic Marian theology but also with the popular devotion of the Catholic unwashed, with great bitterness and at times with haughty disdain. Newman was certainly not indifferent to this criticism, given that he too as a young Anglican pastor was taken aback to the point of being scandalized by seeing the ways in which veneration of the Virgin Mary was manifested in Mediterranean countries, in Italy in particular. That the problem is not secondary for him (at least on the practical level of concrete experience) is demonstrated also by the fact that he deals with it in three of the five chapters of the reply to his fellow theologian. The titles of those chapters are significant: "The Belief of Catholics concerning the Blessed Virgin, as Distinct from Their Devotion to Her"; then "Belief of Catholics concerning the Blessed Virgin, as Colored by Their Devotion to Her"; and finally, "Anglican Misconceptions and Catholic Excesses in Devotion to the Blessed Virgin."

Important for understanding his position are the initial lines of the first of the three chapters just cited:

> I begin by making a distinction which will go far to remove a good part of the difficulty of my undertaking, as it presents itself to ordinary inquirers, the distinction between faith and devotion. I fully grant that *devotion* towards the Blessed Virgin has increased among Catholics with the progress of centuries; I do not allow that the *doctrine* concerning her has undergone a growth, for I believe that it has been in substance one and the same from the beginning.

And then, to clarify even more, "By 'faith' I mean the Creed and assent to the Creed; by 'devotion' I mean such religious honors as belong to the objects of our faith, and the repayment of those honors. Faith and devotion are as distinct in fact, as they are in idea. We cannot, indeed, be devout without faith, but we may believe without feeling devotion."

In the many pages that follow, Newman admits that an Englishman or in general a Northern European might be surprised and even bothered by certain Catholic devotions, but what matters is the doctrine professed by the

Church. The indisputable excesses in pastoral practice are to be purified, but this must not lead to a rejection of Marian dogma, which is perfectly legitimate, being the organic explication, the "vital development" of what lies implicit in the Faith from the beginning. Furthermore, Newman adds, a theologian must have above all comprehension for the diversity of cultures and temperaments that "color" in various ways their forms of expressing love for the Mother of God. And does not love necessarily lead to excesses? "Matters that do not lead to excesses, or even abuses, are those which have little life in them. And where else is there greater life than in the truth of the divine maternity? Among all the passions, is not love the most difficult to govern? Do not lovers exchange words that, if written down, would seem absurd or at least ridiculous?"

In any case, Newman shows how the scandalous expressions of excessive Marian devotion mentioned by Pusey should not be taken out of context (whether literary or cultural), which explains them and often justifies them — without forgetting that they have often been condemned by the Church herself. At any rate, it must never be forgotten that these expressions do not touch on dogma and its living expression in Catholic liturgy. Which seems to be the case, on the other hand, in the Orthodox churches, to whom Anglicans have always looked with interest and sympathy, contrary to what they have done with Catholics. In Byzantine liturgy, the name of Mary substitutes that of Jesus in the invocation at the end of prayers: "Hear us O God, in the name of the *Theotokos*." Something that is unthinkable for Catholics who do not name Mary in the formulas for imparting the sacraments, for example, and who always direct their prayers only to God, "in the name of Jesus Christ."

Thus, undeniable excesses if not outright abuses should be (when necessary) corrected and even suppressed, but they do not undermine what truly counts: the doctrine that the Catholic Church defines, proclaims, and professes in her teaching and in her liturgy. After his long resistance to this doctrine, the Oxford theologian had to succumb to it, for his benefit and ours.

CHAPTER 55

When Stalin Obeyed the Virgin Mary

There will be plenty of work for historians, for who knows how many decades, in the archives that preserve the memory, always obscure and nearly always tragic, of the seventy-four years of the Union of Soviet Socialist Republics. As in the monstruous archives of the *Stasi* (the secret police of "democratic" Germany, with one spy for every twelve inhabitants, the highest percentage of informants in all times and places) in East Berlin, so too for those in Moscow, the most compromising documents were destroyed as the fall was approaching, by politicians, military officers, and bureaucrats implicated in the many crimes committed. But there remains an immense amount of material still to explore. And there will be further innumerable confirmations of the truth of the paradox stated by the Catholic philosopher Augusto Del Noce, "They say in justifying themselves, those who took part in Communist Parties in the West (we had the largest one in Italy, unfortunately) that Communism was a good ideal that was poorly executed. In reality, the opposite is the case: it was a bad idea, well executed." In other words, it had all the time and power it needed to be fully put into effect, realizing to the full its negative potential, but instead of creating the promised New Man, it created dehumanized man.

After so many decades of "socialist education," as soon as the state and police coercion collapsed, the same human vices as always immediately reemerged more virulent than ever. They said they were building the kingdom on earth, on which the sun of justice and peace would shine without end, and instead it was only a temporary parenthesis of history which the "saved" were glad to leave behind, rejoicing even. It is a shame that so few among the "ex" seem to reflect on the warning, in light of that disastrous experience, valid for all times, given in Psalm 127, this precious reminder for those who might still be attracted to earthly utopias offered by politicians, or gurus or false prophets: "Unless the Lord builds the house, those who build it labor in vain. Unless the Lord watches over the city, the watchman stays awake in vain. It is in vain that you rise up early and go late to rest, eating the bread of anxious toil." And it is surprising, grievous even, to see that many Christians have forgotten over the past decades (following Marx and Lenin and others of their school, as if they were wise and beneficent teachers) that the message throughout all Scripture is the rejection of all human idols, whether political, cultural, or economic. We are forgetting that at the end of the 1970s, to cite one example among many, the topic of the annual meeting of the French episcopal conference in Lourdes (there, right next to the grotto!) was the discussion over and approval of a document entitled "The Socialist Shift of the Church." As if it were a positive presupposition, a positive reality to be verified, without the least discernment.

But we are off track here. Returning to the archives of Moscow, we would have expected to find anything except for testimony of a Marian apparition that concerned no less than a former seminarian of the Georgian Orthodox Church, a certain Joseph Vissaroniovich Dzhugashvili, a.k.a. Stalin. We shall go immediately to the facts and save the comments for later. As far as I know, this episode is little known outside of Russia.

In 1997, six years after the end of the USSR, there appeared in Moscow a biography of the terrible despot whom Communists throughout the world, Italians front and center, acclaimed as the "Great Father," "Pride of the World," "Unconquered Hero." The author of the biography, published by Vagrius, was Edvard Radzinski, a Russian publicist, quite well known and who, in turn, knew well the defunct regime, having been part of the cultural *nomenklatura* as a dramatist staging historical subjects. Radzinski was known to the public and to scholars as the author of important studies on Nicholas II (the czar whom Lenin had shot in 1918 along with his entire family), as well as a work on Rasputin. The importance of this biography on Stalin, written "from within" — that is, by a man who knew him and frequented his circle — is confirmed by the fact that the book was immediately published in English by the prestigious Sceptre Editions of London which, in a promotional blurb, called it the "best biography of the dictator yet." And they added that it was the first study made after the opening of the state archives, previously impenetrable. Translations into French, German, and other languages soon followed.

A serious source, then, which makes reliable what the author says in chapter 21, citing the document sources. To avoid any misunderstandings in the English edition, I had this chapter translated directly from Russian, by a reader whom I did not know personally but who wrote me some years ago. This gentleman brought my attention to the matter and, being a professor of Slavic languages, kindly sent me his literal translation of what Radzinski had written. We shall examine the matter now.

In June of 1941, Germany attacked the Soviet Union with all the force it had, taking it by surprise and disappointing Stalin bitterly. In 1939, Stalin had allowed Nazi Germany to unleash the Second World War by signing a pact of nonaggression with Hitler. Fighting as a corporal in the previous war (and courageously it must be said — he was awarded two crosses of valor which he always wore as the only ornamentation on his military coat) — the young Führer had lived in person the truth of an axiom of Teutonic military strategy: Germany is capable of conquering France in the west and Russia in the east, but only one after another and not at the same time. The Prussian commander-in-chief, the celebrated Marshall Alfred Count von Schlieffen, had perfected over the course of decades the plan that bears his name: in case of war, an immediate hammer blow to France, storming it in four weeks, and then transport all men and vehicles to the east to beat Russia before it can mobilize its masses. We know that this plan did not work in World War I (though only by a hair, when the Germans were approaching Paris and the French government had fled to Bordeaux), and the war was lost after four years of fighting to the last man.

Hitler, preparing his revenge, was careful to reach an accord with Russia, which had become the Soviet Union in the meantime: Stalin was to have eastern Poland and Germany would take the western half in exchange. Not only that: the Communists would supply the fuel needed by the Nazi tanks and airplanes and would obtain in return great quantities of Marks, a valuable currency which the USSR badly needed, given that beyond the borders of the Soviet Union the ruble was not accepted anywhere. The plan worked this time: having its back covered, the German Blitzkrieg defeated France in the planned four weeks, and chased the English off the continent as well, and so Hitler and Stalin were able to divide their Polish booty. The Soviet dictator trusted his German colleague, but instead was attacked by surprise, falling immediately into a sort of catalepsy, closing himself into a secret bunker, without giving any signs of life to his armed forces or his countrymen while the *Wehrmacht* advanced triumphantly. Only on July 3 did he deliver a speech on the radio, denouncing the betrayal of his ally and inciting his people to resistance. This was a famous appeal also because he did not address the people of the USSR with the canonical, obligatory "comrades," but instead as "brothers and sisters," which he had previously never used.

This Christian language amazed the Russians as well as governments around the world, who knew the implacable and bloody persecution of the Church and of all Christians carried out by this former Georgian seminarian with truly satanic constancy and cruelty. In 1938, Stalin had launched his "Five-Year Plan for Atheism" that forecast for 1943 the closure of the last churches and the elimination of the last priest. But in that 1941 something even more shocking occurred: army officials were given orders to return to the old practice of sending the troops into battle with the cry "Forward, with God!" The army was assigned a good number of chaplains, who had obviously ceased operating since the days of Lenin. Other stunning measures followed, such as the order to reopen twenty thousand churches for worship and, with particular solemnity, two of the most venerated shrines: the monastery of the Trinity of St. Sergio and that of the "Three Grottoes" in Kiev. The regime had never allowed the role of the patriarch of Russia to be filled, and now *Pravda* was giving news for the first time that Stalin had received an ecclesiastical delegation and (in the exact words of the official newspaper of the Party), "The Supreme Commandant of the Armed Forces and Head of the Government has expressed his comprehension for the proposal of religious to elect a Patriarch and has declared that the government shall place no obstacle to this."

Even more amazing, for a people used to suffering the implacable battle against "superstitions": in Leningrad, under siege by German troops, there reappeared from the warehouse it had been thrown into along with many other sacred images, the most venerated icon of the Mother of God of Kazan, protectress of Russia and, under fire from German artillery and from the *Luftwaffe,* authorities organized a devout procession with it. Not only that, but the icon so dear to all believers was transported to Moscow, as well, also under fire, and another procession was announced with the collaboration of the atheist Communist Party. But these wonders reached their apex when the Mother of God of Kazan, after a long and troubled journey, arrived in another besieged city, a city bearing the name of the Supreme Leader himself, giving it great symbolic value: Stalingrad. The ruler of the Soviet Union wanted to go even further: as the icon of Kazan was on pilgrimage between Leningrad, Moscow, and Stalingrad, he wanted another of the most sacred images to the Russian people, the Vladimir Icon, to be taken from a museum. He ordered it to be placed on a military plane and flown over the capital, at that moment surrounded by the Nazis, to bless the city from above. On his first visit to the Vatican, President Putin gave Pope Francis a copy of this sacred image.

What had caused this entirely unforeseeable change? Why, in the midst of the "Five-Year Plan for Atheism," did the oppressive regime become not only tolerant but even a promoter and protagonist of the religious rebirth of the Communist Soviet Union? Until the publication of Radzinski's book, historians had cited Stalin's *Realpolitik*: seeing that he was on the brink of the abyss, he made an appeal to the resistance of the Russian people in the name of Christianity to which the Russians had adhered late, but in a most passionate way. Already with Napoleon and then with the kaiser's German divisions in 1914, the masses of peasants, however poorly armed or unarmed they might be, had gone to their slaughter fearlessly because in their lead were the priests who raised the sacred icons of Mary and the saints. The war of the USSR had to become the war for the Fatherland, but the religious spirit was indelibly part of this and so it had to be resurrected. There is truth, of course, in this reading of the instrumental use of religion.

But there is more—something that, before Radzinski's consultation of the secret documents, was only the subject of confused theories and conjecture. Now it was clear: behind all this was no less than an apparition of the Virgin Mary.

This is how it went: in that crucible of religions and confessions which is Lebanon, Orthodox Christians (the second most numerous religious group after Catholics) had as their metropolitan an ascetic venerated by the people by the name of Fr. Elijah. Seeing the disaster that was looming over Russia as a result of the German invasion, this priest decided to close himself into the crypt of his cathedral, on his knees for three days and three nights, without eating, drinking, or sleeping, praying to the Mother of God. Fr. Elijah had no sympathy for the Soviets, knowing how they had persecuted believers, and yet that country remained for him an Orthodox, Holy Russia, and Moscow remained the Third Rome that must not be violated by unbelieving foreigners and pagans like the Nazis. In the last of his three days of penance, he had a miraculous vision: in a column of fire there appeared the Queen of Heaven whom he had invoked with such ardor and who communicated to him Heaven's bidding: "Churches and monasteries throughout Russia must be reopened. Priests must be liberated from their prisons. They will not surrender in Leningrad if they carry the venerated icon of Kazan in procession. It must then be honored in Moscow and Stalingrad." We shall speak in the next chapter about this Marian image of Kazan and the most important role it had in Russian history (and therefore in all European history, by extension). For now, let us merely say that this icon had already displayed its prodigious effects, having liberated Moscow in the fourteenth century, when it was occupied by Tamerlane at the head of his Mongols.

After this vision, the patriarch Elijah did not hesitate: he immediately wrote a letter to his Russian confreres and sent it through the Soviet ambassador in Beirut. We know that this letter was certainly read by the dictator, because the commander of the Red Army, General Boris Shaposhnikov, said it should not be underestimated. He had been a valiant colonel in the czar's army and enjoyed Stalin's favor for his military talent, and so had escaped the terrible purges carried out by the despot among the upper echelons of the army, despite not hiding the fact that he still considered himself a believing Orthodox (though no longer practicing). But the dictator was willing to "pardon" him, needing his extraordinary abilities. According to the historian Radzinski, behind the amazing "religious about-face" between 1941 and 1942 (lasting until the end of the war) there was this prophetic letter and not merely political calculation, the pseudo-devout fiction to enlist the people in the defense of the regime. This change, in fact, was not entirely repudiated by the regime after the victory was won. The repression continued, but the persecution was alleviated, and the Five-Year Plan aimed at uprooting the faith was never again mentioned. In fact, in 1947, the Lebanese metropolitan was given the Stalin Prize, the Soviet Nobel, granted every year not only to artists and scientists, but also to those who carried out "important service to the Soviet Union and to the cause of socialism," as its statute says. Everyone asked, obviously ignoring the Marian background to the story, why such a prestigious award went to that foreign priest, unknown in Russia. Fr. Elijah, however, though expressing his courteous gratitude, refused the prize (we mentioned how he was hostile to Communism), but requested that the large sum of prize money should be spent to help Russian orphans of war. He also promoted a collection among his faithful for the same purpose and sent it to Moscow. Our own Pietro Nenni was not as generous, if we may say in passing, when in 1951, he was awarded the Stalin Prize for Peace.[23] He accepted it in person from the hands of the despot and spent the large sum of money building himself a villa on the beach in Campania. But that is a story for another time ...

Returning to Fr. Elijah: this was certainly a mysterious affair, though well documented, and it places before Christians some serious questions. As Pius XI wrote in his encyclicals against all forms of totalitarianism: Communism and National Socialism were twin brothers; or, rather like "the plague and cholera," one could not say which was worse. Why then did Heaven choose to favor Stalin over Hitler? Was he perhaps the lesser evil at that moment? Was it a way of alleviating the suffering of Christians, at least in the USSR, interrupting the genocide planned for making the faith, the faithful, priests, and churches disappear entirely? Would the eventuality of the subjugation of Russia to Germany (this was Hitler's plan: the Slavs, an ethnicity of "slaves," were to be forcibly placed under the dominion of the Aryan *Herrenvolk*, the "people of lords") have been worse than the expansion of Communism westward, as happened after the war? In such cases, one finds a voice in the Islamic expression in the face of the enigmas of life: "God knows more!" We must not forget that His plans are not our plans, His ways are not our ways. It is our lot to accept the facts, certain that Providence (and Mary is His spokeswoman, here as in so many other cases) knows what is best for the good of man, especially amid so much suffering provoked by men, as during war.

[23] Editor's Note: Pietro Nenni (1891–1980) was an Italian political figure and longtime secretary of the Italian Socialist Party.

CHAPTER 56

Mary and the Russians

We saw how Stalin, previously committed to carrying out a genocide of Christians, did not hesitate to take seriously a Marian apparition *ad personam* in order to save himself and his regime threatened by the Germans, going even beyond the instructions sent from above. A message from Heaven just for him!

The former seminarian from the devout region of Georgia (with five crosses on its flag!), the aspiring priest who passed over from the Gospel of Christ to that of Marx and Lenin, knew well how Christianity had permeated every fiber of Russia for a thousand years, uniting itself to the people's love for their homeland; and so, to try to arrest the Nazi onslaught, an appeal had to be made not to "comrades" but to "brothers and sisters." Only in this way could he hope for an energetic reaction to the point of heroism from the great majority of Russians whose faith he had persecuted. "The Russian people," it has been observed, "are on God's side but can also be against God: at any rate, they are never without God." In this omnipresence of the Divine (to be venerated or combated) that has led to miracles of sanctity or to massacres of believers, the two extremes of Europe, Russia to the east and Spain to the west, seem to resemble each other. It has also been said of the Iberians that they are always following a priest, whether grasping a candle for a procession or a rifle to kill him. Russian history shows that when they try to cut their bond with the transcendent, they end up in a ferocious nihilism that can even take on the traits of satanism — and no one is as obsessed with God as Satan is.

It is mysteriously significant that precisely Russia and its destiny play an important role in the message of Fatima. Mary prophesied (it was 1917, and Lenin was taking power) an ominous role for that country that "would spread its errors throughout the world" and "would destroy various nations." But there were positive consequences to the prophecy: "In the end, the Holy Father will consecrate Russia to me, and it will convert." In fact, as we all know, John Paul II was wounded in the abdomen in such a manner that only "through the intervention of Mary who deflected the bullet" (his words) was he able to survive, precisely on the seventy-fourth anniversary of the first apparition of Fatima, May 13, 1981.

In passing, we should point out a peculiar coincidence of dates with another, decisive Marian apparition, that of April 16, 1917, recalled solemnly every year in the USSR because on that day, Lenin returned from his long exile in Switzerland, disembarking at the Finnish train station near St. Petersburg and beginning in those very hours his domination over all Russia. Well, the sixteenth of April is the *dies natalis*, the birthday into Heaven of St. Bernadette, the date on which the promise of the Immaculate was fulfilled: "I cannot promise you happiness in this life, but only in Heaven."

Returning to John Paul II and the assassination attempt of 1981: on the feast of the Annunciation, March 25, four years later, with the participation of bishops from every continent, the pope proceeded with the consecration of the world, making clear reference to Russia. Five years later, behold, to everyone's amazement, including that of secret services from around the world, the mortal, definitive collapse of the Soviet Union and its satellites took place. Let us leave aside all debate over the "conversion" of Russia: this, in effect, has already occurred, given its immediate passage from a state that persecuted the faith to one that, in the name of the same faith, has reconstructed at its own expense cathedrals, churches, and monasteries destroyed by the preceding regime. A nation whose leader, Vladimir Putin, took a copy of the Mother of God of Vladimir in homage to Pope Francis in 2014, the icon which, as we said in the preceding chapter, is one of the symbols of the faith of the entire nation of Russia.

A peculiar fact: the video of the meeting circulating on the Internet shows that the pope admired the icon, but not enough, as if distracted, and moved on immediately. Such that Putin immediately got his attention and, trying to stimulate greater interest in the precious gift, said to the pontiff, "Beautiful, is it not?" Francis nodded and then the political leader reiterated his own personal devotion, to which he wanted to witness in public, and so raised the icon from the table where he had set it, brought it close to his face, and kissed it delicately.

Francis then understood, and he too decided to kiss the sacred image. Thus, a former officer of the KGB, the dark secret police of Soviet Russia, seemed to impart a lesson on Marian devotion to a pope. The fact is, it is not inconsistent to speak of "conversion" before a leader of Russia who did not bring as a gift for the Roman Church a "secular" object but a devotional object, seen as such by him as well — the former spy and Party enforcer, who for that reason should be averse to all symbols of religiosity. Furthermore, it became known from an intimate of the president that during the Soviet years, the icons of the Putin family lay hidden under the flooring in his grandmother's house (and all the family members knew this, including Vladimir), and were recovered and hung once more on the walls immediately after the first thawing of atheistic policies under Gorbachev.

Returning to Fatima: in the light of that prophecy, other facts seem to suggest mysterious signs, besides those we have already recalled. The agreement for the dissolution of the USSR was signed on December 8, 1991, and on December 25 of that same year, the flag with the hammer and sickle that had flown over the dome of the Kremlin was furled and replaced by the old flag with the czarist eagle. One might say "Catholic" dates: the dogma of the Immaculate Conception, celebrated since 1854 on that fateful December 8, is not accepted by the Russian Church, although more for polemical reasons than for theological ones, and perhaps also due to misunderstanding about what that dogma truly means. In fact, in the liturgy, as in the hearts of the Orthodox faithful, there clearly appears a faith in the Mother of God without sin from the moment of her conception. But Eastern theologians have closed themselves into their obstinacy, as if there were a millenary need to oppose out of principle the one whom they consider at the very most the patriarch of Rome, lacking authority to proclaim dogma, which is a right that belongs to an ecumenical council reuniting East and West and giving each bishop an equal vote. Again, for reasons of controversy with Rome, Russian Orthodoxy did not want to accept in the liturgical calendar the Gregorian reform, remaining bound to the computation called Julian, that of imperial Rome rather than papal Rome, such that the date of Christmas does not coincide with the Catholic date.

Is there in these "signs" that are not merely Christian but clearly Catholic and that characterize the destiny of Russia some sort of meaning? One can meditate on this, but we cannot presume to penetrate the enigma: once again, God alone knows.

But we do well to say something to help us understand the Russian faith with which we will have increasing contact: due to immigration after the fall of Communism, this contact has become quite frequent, even in daily life. Moreover, for the first time, just several years ago, a church was financed and built in Rome not by the Patriarchate of Moscow, but (notice again the "conversion" of the public structures) directly by the Russian state, which granted, as a prominent plot of land for building the place of worship, the garden of the embassy that was formerly owned by the USSR. Never would a Soviet diplomat have suspected such an outcome from the atheism of dialectical materialism! I am told that this lovely church with onion domes and innumerable icons is always packed not only with Orthodox, but also Catholics attracted by the splendid liturgies, however long and requiring attendees to stand or kneel on the naked pavement.

It must be said first (and rarely is a thought given to this) that what we call Russia today, and what we call Ukraine and Belarus, once historically united, became part of Christendom when it was still undivided. In fact, for a long time, relations between Rome and the patriarch of Constantinople were increasingly troubled and at times quite turbulent. But the schism between Catholics and those who called themselves "Orthodox" (because they considered themselves to be the only ones following the ancient doctrine of the earliest ecumenical councils) occurred in 1054. On July 16 of that year, pontifical legates arrived in Constantinople, seeing the impossibility of overcoming the intransigence of Patriarch Michael I Cerularius, fiercely anti-Roman, and laid upon the altar of Hagia Sophia the papal decree of excommunication. Naturally, the Byzantine patriarch responded to this with a counter-decree of excommunication. Since then, there has been no further bond, at least canonical, between Byzantium and Rome. But the "conversion" of Vladimir, prince of what would become Russia, Ukraine, and Belarus, dates to sixty-six years prior to that mutual excommunication: thus, the entrance of those Slavic people was into a Christianity that was still entirely "Catholic," at least formally.

The history of this Christianization is peculiar: Vladimir (whom the Orthodox Church venerates as a saint) decided that his people, to carry weight in Europe, had to leave behind their pagan cults and embrace one of the three great monotheisms.

Therefore, according to ancient accounts, he sent several wise men to investigate and find the faith that best suited the temperament and spiritual needs of his people. Judaism was immediately discarded as the faith of a defeated people, without a homeland, with a creed that was not universal but rather tied to a particular ethnic group. Islam as well was rejected, because it too was closely tied to one people, the Arabs; but also because, according to the chroniclers, its holy book, the Quran, prohibited alcoholic beverages. "I cannot deny my people what is so important to them: drinking," Vladimir supposedly exclaimed. Only Christianity was left. If they chose it, it was only because those Slavs, still a bit barbarian, arrived in Constantinople and were charmed by the grandeur of the liturgies in the marvelous basilicas of the capital of the Roman Empire of the East. "Here," wrote Vladimir, "we knew not if we were in Heaven or on earth. We experienced how God truly converses with this people." And so, the prince had priests and Greek theologians sent that they might instruct them in the faith they had chosen, and in 988 he was baptized.

A unique story, not only in its beginnings but also in its millenary outcome: the Russians as well as the Ukrainians and the Belarussians became Catholic, though in the Byzantine Rite, and just a few decades before the schism — not by free choice, not because they had been catechized and convinced by missionaries, but because, according to their laws, they were obliged to follow the religion of the prince. *Cuius regio, eius religio*... They were baptized en masse, according to the order of Vladimir, before they even knew anything about this new faith to which they had adhered by royal command. Only afterward, hosts of missionaries sent by the emperor from Constantinople introduced them to the mysteries of Christianity, built churches, and began to celebrate those liturgies that had led Vladimir to make his choice. To us moderns, all of this seems unacceptable if not outright scandalous. And yet, that foreign and unknown faith, imposed by law before even knowing what it was, gave rise to one of the most profoundly Christian peoples, most radically imbued with the gospel, most heroically willing to die rather than to renounce their beliefs. Our ways are not God's ways. Not by accident did Slavic theologians proclaim, when Constantinople had fallen to the Turks (1453), that now, following both the fall of the first Rome (to the barbarians in 476) and the fall of the second Rome (Constantinople), it was Moscow as the "third Rome" that would guide all Christianity.

This Eastern Christianity was characterized above all by one element: the place of absolute prominence it gave the Mother of Jesus, always next to Him in icons. This prominence is obvious at first glance when one enters any Russian house: the place of honor has once more been given to that icon resplendent with gold leaf of "Mary All-Holy" that had been hidden for seventy years but reemerged with the fall of the enemies of religion. In their private dwellings as well as in public places, there are no crosses, as there are in Catholic settings: the latter are sacred objects placed on the altars in churches which only priests may touch, presenting them to the veneration of the kneeling faithful. Everywhere else, one finds only icons of the saints and above all of the Mother of God, indicated on the canvas (as a canonical requirement) with the initials of her exalted role: her divine maternity.

The famous theologian Sergey Bulgakov once wrote, "A Christianity with Christ but without the Mother, according to us is another Christian confession: for Russian Orthodoxy it is, in essence, another religion, and with this the faithful want nothing to do." Over the centuries, European Protestants have tried to ally themselves with Moscow to fight Roman Catholicism in a united manner. But every proposal has been rejected, and this, it must be said, has not been out of love for a papacy which it distrusts (Russia is perhaps the only country the popes have never been invited to visit, due to a stubborn and perhaps discourteous refusal by the patriarchate). Not for love of the pope, therefore, has this alliance been rejected by Russia. Rather it has been for love of Mary, downgraded by the Reformers from Queen of Heaven to a member of the primitive Church, a woman who provisionally loaned her uterus to a God who decided to become incarnate in a female human being. Having fulfilled her mission, she consummated her marriage with Joseph (he too just an artisan like many others) and along came the house full of children, returning to the shadows from which she had come, to perform her service of giving birth. Even more so than Catholics, the Orthodox, especially the Russians, do not agree with this perspective. A resounding confirmation of this, with international impact, occurred in 1927 at the first meeting of the World Council of Churches in Switzerland, an organization desired by the League of Nations, that creation of the hypocritical utopianism of President Wilson. The representatives of the Russian Orthodox Church — temporarily free from Communist persecution thanks to the ruling Party's acceptance of the nomination of the surviving bishops — immediately declared they would not participate in the work if all the participants, Protestants first and foremost, did not first agree to place the meetings under the protection of the Mother of God and did not pray to her at length, as is fitting for true Christians. The Reformed churches refused, amid embarrassment and scorn, and the Russian delegation returned home, even though what awaited them there was an uncertain future that turned out to be ever more tragic.

St. Dimitry of Rostov (eighteenth century) was another of the innumerable voices: "After Our Lord, no one is more powerful than our Sovereign and Mother of the Lord, the Ever-Virgin Mary. She touches the very heart of God with her intercession. She who wrapped the Word in swaddling clothes wraps him now and in eternity with prayers of mercy on behalf of men." Other holy Russian mystics have even held that her power of intercession can go so far as to change divine judgment and obtain the liberation of the damned in Hell.

Yet, despite this total trust in her merciful intervention toward the needy, the Russian liturgy has a disinterested, gratuitous character. Praise for praise's sake, and for nothing else. For those of us who are children of the Western Church, prayer to the Mother always ends invoking her aid. The Hail Mary itself, after the first Gospel-based part, with the salutation of the archangel, expresses an intercession: Pray for us sinners, now and at the hour of our death. The Rosary often ends with the litany where, after every proclamation of one of Mary's glories, those praying reply with an *ora pro nobis*. In Russian ecclesial prayer, instead of asking for something, God is glorified, praised, and thanked for the gift He has given us in such a Woman. Instead of the *ora pro nobis* there is the Greek *kaire,* which is translated into Latin either as *Ave* (Hail!) or *Gaude* (Rejoice!).

This liturgical orientation derives from the fact that, whereas for Catholics Mary is above all our Mother (according to Jesus' words from the cross to John, present as humanity's representative), for Russian, Ukrainian, and Belarussian Orthodoxy one never forgets that this is derived from the fact that an ecumenical council proclaimed her not only Mother of Jesus but Mother of God. This gives rise to a sort of bewilderment, the solemn aura of the icons, the gratitude repeated unceasingly for having elevated a human being to such a height. As her most glorious title, we call her the "Blessed Virgin." For the Russian Orthodox, the triple virginity (before, during, and after childbirth) raises neither problems nor discussion because it is a given: in the icons, Mary is surrounded by three stars, symbols of the three phases in which she remained physically intact. The hypothesis, unfortunately adumbrated today by some theologians of "Catholic" universities and not only by Hans Küng and his followers, that Jesus was only the first of many siblings provokes among the Russian people not scandal but amazement, followed by irony over the state of mental health of those who dare to propose such impieties. They have no doubt about the perpetual and total purity of Mary. Being an obvious reality, they focus on the title from which it all derives: *Theotokos*, Mother of God. This majesty shines through the icons, which are not "painted" but "written," and not by artists, but by ascetics who, between fasts and penances, even work on their knees. Nothing is farther from this devotion than certain Italian Madonnas of the Renaissance and of the eighteenth century, whose artists painted them using as their model of beauty a peasant girl or at times even a prostitute.

At any rate, we must never forget our indebtedness toward those Greco-Byzantine Christians, at times mistreated, who profoundly formed the Slavic peoples. It is from there, from the east, that all the great Marian festivities come to us, with their liturgies that inspired the Latin imitations: the Nativity, the Presentation in the Temple, the Annunciation, the Assumption (Dormition), and all the others that followed. It is an inestimable patrimony that we have inherited from our brethren in the East and that merits the gratitude of every believing Catholic.

CHAPTER 57

The Theologian She Saved

"SHE WHO SAVES HER own," says a verse in Manzoni's *Hymn to Mary*. Many saints, mystics, and seers have repeated the idea that devotion to her is a sign of predilection and, therefore, of salvation. And not only that: being the "enemy of every heresy" and having vanquished them all (as an ancient antiphon proclaims, unfortunately excluded from the new liturgy), Our Lady prevents every error and deviation from the Faith for those who let themselves be guided by her. Her name is synonymous with orthodoxy, and her voice repeats to us as at Cana: "Do whatever He tells you." If her role is recognized, the right path will not be lost, as displayed by the history of heretics and heresies that often began by expelling her, even if accompanied by great displays of respect. As we have already observed, she is the *Stella Maris* for navigating the ocean of life. Or the *Thurris Davidica,* the fortress that repels every error.

If that is the case, how is it possible that the priest who (in the words of Pius IX himself), through his work as a learned and untiring theologian, did more to bring about the definition of the dogma of the Immaculate Conception after centuries of debate, could leave communion with the Church and be suspended *a divinis* (removing priestly faculties)? Why was he the one who went off the tracks? And how does this fit with what we have just said? The Jesuit priest Fr. Carlo Passaglia is the protagonist of this story, forgotten by most but worth being told. The struggle that united the Italian peninsula was also a factor in this matter. And in the midst of it, above all is the sure protection of the Lady for those who love and honor her. Where she is involved, the story always has a happy ending, even after dramatic vicissitudes.

Carlo Passaglia was born near Lucca in Tuscany, in 1812, and entered the Society of Jesus (just reconstituted after their dissolution) at a young age, responding to a well-considered and sincere vocation. A vivacious intelligence, a great scholar and worker, he was also one of the founders, in 1850, of *Civiltà Cattolica,* along with Fr. Curci and Fr. Tapparelli D'Azeglio. A professor of theology in the best Roman universities, in 1851 Pius IX put him in charge of collecting the documents that proved how over the centuries the Immaculate Conception of Mary had always been concealed, welcomed, and confessed. Passaglia was given permission by the pope to leave the Jesuits and become part of the diocesan clergy, to be free to dedicate himself entirely to his research, liberated from the order's rules. In three years of great effort, working with just one other collaborator, he published the three volumes which were given the title *De immaculate Deiparae semper viginis conceptu.* These were the weighty tomes that set the solid theological foundation for establishing the dogma of 1854.

But these were the years in which patriotic excitement was spreading and the aspiration of uniting the peninsula had reached the clergy as well. Patriotism was then the dominant ideology, as Marxism would be after Vatican II, when priests and friars were bewitched not long before its inglorious collapse. Sacred ordination does not always preserve one from conformity to the spirit of the times. Passaglia himself was caught up in the Zeitgeist and convinced himself that the papacy ought to renounce its temporal power, though with every guarantee to ensure its total freedom of governance over the Church. It was also the aspiration of a Catholic like Manzoni, who agreed to be elected senator in the first Parliament, even though he never sat in the Senate in Turin.

The former Jesuit met Cavour and was fascinated by his program. So enthusiastic was he that he wrote a manifesto that became famous, titled *Pro causa italica ad episcopos catholicos* (For the Italian cause, to the Catholic bishops), campaigning to obtain the participation of the clergy. In fact, some nine thousand priests signed the petition from every region in Italy. The matter not only grieved Pius IX but also alarmed him, for he had not imagined there could have been so much sympathy in the Church for the ideal of unity.

Passaglia had written the document anonymously, but as one could imagine, he was soon discovered and took refuge in Turin, where his friend Cavour immediately arranged a professorship in moral philosophy for him at the university. Rome then suspended him *a divinis,* and as the Holy See ordered, he set aside his priestly cassock, but substituted it with clothes that were always and only black, such as today's priestly garb. Furthermore, he continued to respect with perfect fidelity his priestly duty of chastity which he had assumed as a religious, never seeking the company of a woman, and of poverty, giving to the needy nearly all his wages as a professor. What was lacking was obedience to ecclesiastical authority and to the pope, but his dissent was entirely political and did not in the least regard the Faith. As he repeated continuously in pamphlets, in the newspapers which he founded, and in conferences, his conscience was convinced that the renunciation of the Papal States in favor of the Kingdom of Italy would be greatly advantageous to the Christian cause. His apostolate, he said with conviction, was *pro bono fidei.* The future would show that in substance he was not wrong (Paul VI defined the breach of Porta Pia "providential"), but his demands were premature: the *Conciliazione* of 1929 could not have been realized at that time.[24] History has rhythms that must be respected; it does not heed the impatient. Thus, Pius IX and his successors did well to hold the line, despite threats and insults, because, without that resistance, they would never have obtained the result of the Church's full independence, becoming once again sovereign in her own house. Even though this "house" is the smallest state in the world, it is solid, such that even the Germans in their occupation of Rome halted at that symbolic yet impassable border.

Nevertheless, the hand of the Immaculate was on the head of "her" Carlo Passaglia. Despite the invitations to pass over to some Protestant community as its pastor, or even to found an Italian National Church dependent on the new state (the dream and the project of the *Risorgimento*), his fidelity to the Catholic Church remained ironclad, without the least concession. In a university

[24] Editor's Note: The Porta Pia is a gate in the ancient walls of Rome, breached during the decisive battle by which Italian troops captured Rome, ending the Papal States and uniting the nation of Italy. The *Conciliazione* or Reconciliation of 1929 refers to the Lateran Pacts between Italy and the Holy See, which normalized relations between the two and finally settled the disputed status of the Papal States by establishing the independent state of Vatican City.

such as the one in Turin, where Freemasons and anticlericals in general were in charge, the philosophy lessons of Passaglia were in full agreement with natural law and Christian doctrine. Despite no longer being able to administer the sacraments and to celebrate Mass, he remained the Catholic apologist he had always been. When, in 1863, Ernest Renan published his desecrating *Life of Jesus,* which did so much harm to faith, especially that of the middle classes, Passaglia put believers on their guard not with a pamphlet but with an entire book, into which he poured his vast erudition. The significant title was *Renan's Life of Jesus Discussed and Refuted.*

On Good Friday 1876, afflicted ever more by the dissidence between accepting the entire Catholic creed without exceptions and his political passion for the united *Patria,* Passaglia decided to write his beloved Pius IX, making an appeal to his heart to be readmitted to full communion with the Church in exchange for a mutually agreeable retraction. The old pope (he had only two years left to live) was comforted: among the many pains with which events involving and seemingly crushing the Church had afflicted him, the defection (though only political) of his Don Carlo was particularly vexing. Of all people, him! The theologian of the Immaculate, the priest of such enormous knowledge and ardent Marian devotion! Thus, Pius IX immediately arranged for him to speak with Francesco Faà di Bruno, a future Blessed, whose charitable efforts, knowledge, and prudence he greatly admired and who was a colleague of Passaglia at the University of Turin, which refused a professorship to Francesco despite his great merits, because he was "too Catholic" and moreover a "papist." Faà di Bruno approached the tormented priest suspended *a divinis,* and he too was struck by his good faith, his impeccable life, and his total orthodoxy. A practical man, as a former captain of the military command, possessing great delicacy as the son of ancient nobility, the future Blessed Francesco did his best to mediate and find a formula of retraction that would satisfy both the Holy See and Passaglia. But eleven years passed before, in March of 1887, a few weeks before his death, Passaglia made a full retraction for having distanced himself from obedience, asking pardon for any scandal he had given to good Catholics, and even requesting readmission to the Society of Jesus. An eyewitness described the scene as he kissed his stole, weeping, and began to celebrate Mass once again. Just four days later he died.

Thus, through this last-minute rescue, truly *in extremis,* the one who had worked more than anyone else to enable the dogma to be proclaimed on solid theological foundations proceeded toward the encounter with the Immaculate. Was Manzoni not correct in saying, "She saves her own," even if sometimes by complicated and painful means?

In this book I have dedicated an entire chapter to the age-old battle for the Immaculate Conception. As I recounted therein, an interminable struggle was needed to arrive at 1854, when Pius IX consulted by letter the entire world episcopate and cut the knot of the dispute and proceeded to proclaim the dogma.

One of the obstacles to the dogma (unique in the history of the Church, this one would receive a sort of celestial imprimatur in Lourdes) was the fact that some great theologians could not see how the Immaculate Conception could be reconciled with faith in the universal necessity of redemption achieved by Christ. Entire religious orders, beginning with the Dominicans and the Cistercians, were opposed to the dogma precisely out of respect toward the Virgin, whom they sincerely loved and honored. It was evident therefore that an influential part of the theological tradition stood against this Marian "privilege"; this is what caused centuries of delay in the definition of the dogma.

Well, investigating the other "modern" dogma, proclaimed ninety-six years later by Pius XII, that of the Assumption of Mary into Heaven body and soul, one fact strikes me: distinct from the Immaculate Conception, this conviction in the eternal destiny of the Virgin Mary, in her salvation in spirit as well as in her flesh, was never doubted, in any century, by any Church Father or Doctor of the Church. St. Thomas, who was reticent about the Immaculate Conception, did not treat explicitly the Assumption because he considered it an obvious truth, believed in universally. Furthermore, even the liturgy, the norm of faith, is explicit: the solemnity of August 15 is among the most ancient feasts, both in the East and in the West.

Consider then the words of Fr. Gabriele Roschini, one of the leading Mariologists of the twentieth century and one of the most aggressive supporters of the possibility of proclaiming the new dogma in the Holy Year 1950:

> In the dogmatic bull of Pope Pacelli, the close connection between the Immaculate Conception and the Assumption is discussed. The

> Most Holy Virgin was associated with the Son in His complete triumph over sin and death. That triumph of Our Lady over the corruption of the flesh and her immediate assumption into Heaven are indicated by the papal bull as a consequence of the triumph of Mary over sin. She was not subject like everyone else to the law of decomposition and decay in the tomb and for this reason did not have to await the end of time to be resurrected in body like everyone else. The Virgin Mary is granted victory over death in virtue of the victory granted her over sin. The Immaculate Conception excludes the stain of original guilt and excludes therefore the consequences of that fault. Christ vanquished death because He vanquished sin, but His Mother was preserved from this in anticipation of the merits of the Passion.

Thus, as usual in Catholicism, *tout se tient,* everything is connected in a coherent whole. The dogma of the Assumption is a logical, inevitable consequence of that of the Immaculate Conception. But since Tradition had nothing to say about belief concerning the end of Mary's earthly life, why did it have such difficulty (among many theologians) accepting belief regarding the immaculate beginnings of that same life? Were the beginning and the end not logically connected? I ask this question not as a theologian, which I certainly am not, but based on that simple common sense which is always needed, also when reflecting on faith. I am certain that the all-knowing (at least in these matters) Fr. Passaglia would have had in this case too a reasonable and convincing explanation.

CHAPTER 58

Abercius? Who Was He?

I am speaking from personal experience. Many well-educated Catholics, including members of the clergy, have little idea or have never even heard mention of what scholars call the "Epitaph of Abercius." This ignorance is disheartening, because that epitaph was defined "the queen of all Christian inscriptions" by Giovanni Battista De Rossi, Italy's greatest epigraphist, the man who rediscovered the Roman catacombs in the second half of the nineteenth century. He was the one who wanted the tombstone of Abercius to be placed at the center of the Pio Christian Museum in the Vatican. It is still there, given pride of place, although the rivers of tourists mostly ignore its extraordinary value, as is natural.

The fact that we are dealing with it here is due to its great historical and therefore apologetic value, but also because it gives us one of the first testimonies of the importance the primitive Church attributed to the Virgin Mary. The story of the discovery of that tombstone, moreover, has a scent of archaeological mystery about it — a case for Indiana Jones, to use an image from Hollywood. In fact, it was noticed by accident in 1882, by a great Scottish archaeologist, Sir William Ramsay, inserted in a pillar in front of a mosque in ancient Phrygia, modern-day Turkey, near the ruins of the city of Hierapolis. Though the Greek text was mutilated, the scholar realized its important immediately, and Turkish authorities of that region allowed him to extract it from the column and transcribe it, though, despite its Christian origins, they then confiscated it for their collections. Seven years later, however, for the birthday of Leo XIII, the sultan of Istanbul decided to give it as a gift to the Catholic Church, recognizing the value of that stone for Christian believers, whereas for Muslims it was religiously irrelevant. In those times, at any rate, Muslims knew how to be friendly to Christians....

The marble slab, destined for use on a tomb, was broken, and only the central part of the text is preserved. It was possible, however, to make an exact reconstruction of the entire inscription. Here is a literal, and therefore not elegant, translation of it:

> Citizen of an elect city, I made this while still in life to have here a burial for my body, I, Abercius by name, disciple of the chaste shepherd who leads his sheep to pasture on the mountainside and in the plain and whose great eyes see everywhere from on high. He taught me the Scriptures worthy of faith. He sent me to Rome to contemplate there the kingdom and to see there a queen with golden vestment and golden shoes. There, I saw the people that possesses the splendid seal. I saw as well the plains of Syria and Nisibis, beyond the Euphrates, and everywhere I found the brethren. I had Paul as my guide. The faith accompanied me everywhere and at table presented me with the food of a fish from the font, immense, pure that a pure virgin took hold of and she gave it to friends to eat always, having an excellent wine mixed with water that is usually given with bread. I, Abercius, have had these things inscribed, in my presence, at seventy-two years of age. Whoever comprehends what I am saying and thinks as I do, pray for Abercius. May no one place another in my tomb, otherwise he shall pay two thousand gold coins to the Roman treasury and a thousand to my dear homeland, Hierapolis.

Before discussing the rich and profound meaning of this text, let us try to see who its author was and how archaeologists were able to reconstruct the damaged part of the tombstone he had inscribed for his burial. Abercius was the bishop of Hierapolis at the end of the second century, the capital of what the Romans called *Frigia Salutaris*, near the center of what is now Turkey. Phrygia was one of the very first regions to be evangelized and to give its church a hierarchical structure. This rapid success of Christian preaching was unique, despite the fact that this region was home to Cybele, the Great Mother, the Queen of Heaven and Earth, a cult that spread throughout the entire empire, having as its sacred site par excellence the great shrine that was precisely in Phrygia. Devotion to Cybele was orgiastic and bloody: suffice it to say that every springtime the youth aspiring to be her priests castrated themselves in public, at the climax of a great festival where every sort of transgression, especially erotic ones, were allowed. Arriving in Rome, the cult of Cybele lost some of its more traumatic and gory characteristics, although it did not renounce its sexual promiscuity and the castration that the priests practiced on themselves with their own hands. And it is truly strange that among the admirers and devotees of the Phrygian goddess there was a man as culturally sophisticated and refined in his education as the emperor Julian, called "the Apostate" because he sought to purge the empire of Christianity and return to paganism. But that of Cybele seemed to be the worst, and certainly not the best, of the ancient religions.

And yet, as we said, it was precisely the central region of Asia Minor, famous for its veneration of these idols, that was first to open itself to the gospel with serious commitment. We possess an ancient *Life* of Bishop Abercius which narrates how, after the promulgation of a decree by Marcus Aurelius requiring everyone to offer sacrifice to the gods, he entered the temple of Apollo in Hierapolis during the night and shattered his image. This was around the year 170, when Christianity and paganism still coexisted in the region. When this sacrilege was discovered the next morning, the throng of Apollo's devotees gathered in the main square in tumult, but Abercius arrived and calmed the agitation by preaching the gospel, freeing the demon-possessed, and restoring the sight of the blind mother of Eussenian, a local nobleman and personal friend of the emperor. But to vindicate himself, the devil took possession of the soul of Marcus Aurelius's daughter, stating that only the Phrygian Bishop Abercius could rid her of him. The emperor then wrote to Eussenian in Hierapolis to have that Christian priest sent to the capital of the empire. When he arrived in Rome, after a long journey over land and sea, Abercius did not find Marcus Aurelius, who was then encamped in Germany fighting the barbarians. The bishop presented himself to the empress and implored her to lead him to their possessed daughter, who was at the hippodrome. There, before a great crowd (whom he wanted to be gathered there so as to perform in public his apostolate and impress the greatest number of pagans possible), with a solemn liturgy of exorcism, he liberated the possessed girl. Abercius then ordered the devil, as he came out of her, to pick up a heavy marble tombstone from the Roman hippodrome, transport it to Hierapolis, and place it at the southern gate of the city. He then asked the empress to tell her husband when he returned from his wars to have baths for the sick built near the city of Hierapolis, given that medicinal waters flowed there due to his prayers. On his return journey to Phrygia, he visited Syria and Mesopotamia, hosted by the local Christian communities, preaching the gospel and healing many of the sick. Once returned to Hierapolis and being now quite old, he dictated the epitaph for his tomb and had it inscribed on the tombstone which, by his own orders, the devil had brought there from Rome.

Naturally, this *Life*, so complex and adventurous, appears to modern scholars as entirely legendary, and only a few defended even its basic historicity. But then came a great surprise: In 1882, as we said, the archaeologist Ramsay discovered near Hierapolis the large stone plaque that, despite the damage it had suffered over so many centuries, reproduces the exact text just as it is narrated in the *Life* of Abercius, at least on the extant part of the epitaph. Everything corresponds, down to the letter, confirming that the author of that account had seen the text inscribed and had reproduced it faithfully. And so, it was easy to reconstruct the missing part of the text, simply integrating it with what was reported in the manuscript of the anonymous contemporary of Abercius.

But this is not all: the "mystery" had an antecedent. The Scottish archaeologist had discovered another tombstone the year before, also walled into a home and used as building material. In this prior inscription, an unknown Alexander, a worthy Christian of Hierapolis, had also dictated his epitaph, and for the beginning and end of it had copied verbatim the text of Abercius's. In the end, he even gave the date, the year 300 according to the Phrygian calendar, corresponding to 216 in the Christian one. Paleographers have established that the stone of Alexander is later with respect to that of the bishop, which must then be dated before 200, namely in the period in which Marcus Aurelius was emperor.

Thus, the pieces of the puzzle were slowly coming together, and the conclusion could only be that the epitaph is authentic and is as ancient as it needs to be to confirm the *Life* that had until then been considered only legendary. But the authenticity of the text and its antiquity had dramatic consequences, exhilarating not only for Christians in general but for Catholics in particular. Here, in fact, we have an extraordinary testimony to the Eucharist: the "fish from the font, immense, pure that a pure virgin took hold of and she gave it to friends to eat always, having an excellent wine mixed with water that is usually given with bread." This is nothing else than Christ under the consecrated species. We know that among the main proto-Christian symbols is the fish, whose name in Greek, *ichthys*, corresponds to the initials of "Jesus Christ, Son of God, Savior."

The entire epitaph is written in a symbolic manner so as not openly to challenge the pagans and provoke their reaction. This same author requests of the reader of the inscription, "Whoever comprehends what I am saying and thinks as I do, pray for Abercius." Thus, an allusive, mysterious language recognized by the baptized but not by those who adore other gods. It is significant that he indicates the amount of the fine (truly astronomical: two thousand gold coins, and slavery was the punishment for those who could not pay their debts), foreseen by Roman law, incredibly strict concerning the violation of tombs. The reminder is a severe warning to the pagan who dared destroy a Christian tomb or its epitaph. It speaks of Christ as well, by means of allusions and symbols, describing him as that "chaste shepherd who leads his sheep to pasture on the mountainside and in the plain and whose great eyes see everywhere from on high" who taught Abercius "the Scriptures worthy of faith." Jesus Himself "sent me to Rome to contemplate there the kingdom and to see there a queen with golden vestment and golden shoes." That queen is the Church, which in the Eternal City has its see; we read here, therefore, a significant and most ancient recognition of Roman primacy. Golden stole and footwear were among the symbols of royalty. "There I saw the people that possesses the splendid seal"; this is the people of believers, marked with that "splendid seal" which is Baptism. Who is the "Paul" whom Abercius says he had as "his guide"? It is Saul of Tarsus of course, called Paul in Latin, the apostle particularly venerated in Asia Minor, who exercised much of his preaching there and to whom some of the churches in that region owe their foundation.

This profession of faith given to us by Abercius has an entirely Catholic taste to it, in which already — at the end of the second century! — the see of the successor of Peter is the "queen" and in which the Eucharist is venerated in the dimension of the Sacred, far from the normality of a dinner among friends, as the Reformation more than a thousand years later would have us believe. In the face of the discovery of the truth of this text that was considered until that time legendary and apocryphal, the world of Protestant scholars reacted as it did in 1917 when a piece of papyrus emerged in Egypt that brought to light the first "complete" hymn or rather prayer to the Virgin Mary in our possession. This is the rightly famous *Sub tuum praesidium*. We reconstructed this affair in an earlier chapter, the eighteenth, and saw how universities in the Reformation tradition waited twenty years before publishing a critical edition, and the editor, the famous scholar and fervent Anglican C. H. Roberts, tried to minimize it by speaking of a more recent text. But it was his own colleagues who unanimously contradicted him: that invocation to Mary dates to no later than 250. And so, all that Protestant theologians had affirmed about the Catholic perspective, that the cult of the Virgin Mary and her presence in the liturgy were late and illegitimate phenomena, now collapsed. The invocation to the Mother as a decadent phenomenon, as a construction that slowly encrusted the austere gospel unity of *solus Christus*, was shown by that scrap of papyrus not to be the case, whether the pastors and professors liked it or not.

Against the epitaph of Abercius, at least part of the Reformed world, the more fundamentalist among them, attempted similar reactions. They stated in erudite publications that in reality the one who composed the text was not a Christian but rather a priest of the cult of Cybele. But the great archaeologist De Rossi swiftly and indignantly replied, "Such an extravagant paradox is of such manifest absurdity that I would consider it a waste of time if I were to set myself to contradict it." Then other experts went on the attack: according to some, the writing bore witness to pagan syncretism, and to others, the shepherd recalled by Abercius was to be identified not in Jesus but in Attis, the young and handsome lover of the goddess Cybele. Other learned eccentricities followed, but it is interesting what the great specialist Antonio Ferrua wrote: "All the attempts to deny the Christian character of the epitaph fell into the void and always will, because we have here, without a shadow of a doubt, the symbolism that developed among those faithful to Jesus." A text, therefore, that is not only Christian, but fully Catholic. Furthermore, we should not let that phrase escape us: "Whoever comprehends what I am saying and thinks as I do, pray for Abercius." This is the confirmation of what the Reformation has always denied: we can intercede for the dead, and therefore, there already existed the belief in Purgatory.

Was Abercius also Catholic in inserting the Mother of Christ, giving her a role of the greatest importance? Here we find a sort of mystery novel within the mystery novel. How should we read, how can we interpret those lines: "The faith accompanied me everywhere and at table presented me with the food of a fish from the font, immense, pure that a pure virgin took hold of and she gave it to friends to eat always, having an excellent wine mixed with water that is usually given with bread"? Who is that "pure virgin," in Greek *parthénos agné*? What is the subject of the sentence? Mary or the faith of the Church?

To clarify this, we reproduce here the preface of an article of some seventy dense pages that appeared in 1969 in the journal of the Angelicum, the prestigious Roman university of the Dominicans, written by an esteemed scholar and specialist in these matters, Fr. B. Emmi, also a son of St. Dominic. We see his way of framing the question so clearly: "In two recent, widely distributed works, the *Catholic Encyclopedia* and the *Bibliotheca Sanctorum*, containing articles written by two renowned archaeologists, it is asserted as certain and beyond discussion that the 'pure virgin' mentioned in the Epitaph of Abercius is not the Blessed Virgin Mary, but rather the Church."

Fr. Emmi responds, "Since the diffusion of these works risks making this opinion common, at least in Italy, a quite recent opinion at that, we would like to examine carefully and exhaustively its origin, the arguments it makes, and oppose them with arguments that validate the ancient and common opinion of the Marian reference." And then, "It seems necessary to us that nothing be omitted, so that the result we reach may not be considered a pious belief, but the most well-founded scientific conclusion, corroborated by an accurate examination of the text and of the consensus of the vast majority of scholars."

Fr. Emmi keeps his promise. In fact, the seventy pages filled with footnotes, exacting and complete in their documentation, were read and discussed by experts with the attention they deserved. And many scholars, after having examined this work, returned to the traditional reading: the "pure virgin" Abercius mentions is truly Mary who took the Word from Heaven and, with her own body, gave to Him a human body as well. Emmi says in the conclusion to his study, "The expression 'the pure virgin held' is so precise and strong that it cannot be attributed to the Church, of which it can be said that she is the genetrix of spiritual children but of which one cannot say that she made the Word descend to the earth, taking Him out of Heaven." Thus we are assured by the ancient bishop of Phrygia that every time the Eucharist is distributed, it is as if the fruit of the human womb of Mary were given as food. Mary who, despite her maternity, is "a pure virgin": a precious example of how, in the primitive Church as well (let us not forget that the Edict of Constantine was still 150 years away!), the virginity of the woman of Nazareth was already serenely and commonly believed and confessed by the Christian community.

The Dominican scholar concludes his study saying, "The foundation of Abercius's faith is salvation worked by Christ, God and man, continued in the Church through the sacraments of Baptism and the Eucharist. But in this faith, the Virgin Mary is already present and intrinsic, at the beginning of it all." She is not the accessory or random personality, whose remembrance one can do without, to which some theological currents have reduced her. On the contrary, every day, in every Eucharist, the Virgin is not only present but she is at the center, having been the one who gave us "fish from the font, immense, pure," in which faith believes. What the bishop of Hierapolis has left us is an important testimony—hence, the regret that it is not well enough known or that it has even been repressed in the name of a misunderstood ecumenism, as if authentic dialogue did not demand the full truth.

CHAPTER 59

LIVES "REVEALED" BY HEAVEN?

We find him here once again, the Abbé Laurentin, as he is called with both affection and suspicion within the Church in France and elsewhere. Having made it to ninety and nearly blind, his beloved sister passed away, who was his secretary throughout life and the custodian of his immense archives. But he has not given up. Following St. Paul's exhortation, Fr. René continues energetically to "fight the good fight."[25] He continues, not content with all that he has accomplished in the innumerable, important things written in the more than one hundred books published, but rather pushes forward into uncharted waters in a new work: *The Life of Mary according to the Revelation of the Mystics*, subtitled *What Should We Make of It?* Here he has investigated one more time, with surprising results, some true discoveries worthy of discussion. Laurentin has to his name many enduring bestsellers circulating around the world, above all in Italy, where he has more readers and friends than in France. There, a certain ecclesial intelligentsia has not forgiven him for being a promising progressive theologian (at the time of the council), only to become the leading specialist in topics *maudits et dérangeants*, insufferable and disturbing, as he himself calls them with irony: apparitions, miracles, exorcisms, prophecies ... horrifying stuff for every theologically correct modern scholar!

But every Catholic who has no desire to "revisit" the creed according to the ideologies in vogue at the moment owes our Abbé his gratitude precisely for this reason. And for many other things, beginning with the decades of labor in constructing an authentic monument to the truth of Lourdes, as we have seen.

[25] Editor's Note: The famous Mariologist Fr. René Laurentin died in September 2017, one month shy of his hundredth birthday.

The extraordinary seven-volume collection of his *Authentic Documents* on the apparitions, the six volumes of *Authentic History,* and the many others on what occurred in and around that grotto are a model of scientific historiography as well as a great gift to believers and to all those who love the truth.

And now this new book, where wisdom and experience accrued over seventy years of research and reflection are placed at the service of the faithful as well as unbiased scholars. Once again, he has set out into uncharted territory filled with hazards, putting at risk his academic reputation, already so compromised, for love of the truth.

The project which gave rise to this *The Life of Mary according to the Revelation of the Mystics* is quite innovative. It is surprising that almost no one in the Church has looked into this, despite its importance, especially on the pastoral level. This is one of those liminal zones where professors have preferred not to tread, and at times not even to mention, whether out of fear of compromising themselves or out of negligence if not contempt for the topic. In the meantime, however, crowds of believers were left to their own devices, without the least catechesis or guidance.

From the end of the seventeenth century to the end of the twentieth, at least four "Lives of Mary" appeared, presented as inspired by their authors (all women) and considered such by a great multitude of readers. These "Lives" supposedly reveal what the Gospels do not say, since they limit themselves to what is essential, especially concerning the Virgin Mary, but also concerning Jesus and the other Gospel figures. These four women wrote at a time when male chauvinism was still dominant, even in ecclesial circles, and so this feminine predominance was (and is) considered suspect and has contributed to discouraging research on similar works. We said a few things on this topic in chapter 44, "The House above Ephesus," where we reconstructed the discovery in Turkey of the ruins that, according to a tradition come down to us though forgotten in the West, are all that remain of the house in which Mary lived with the apostle John and from which she was assumed into Heaven. We mentioned how the research of that site was carried out based on instructions provided by a visionary, Anne Catherine Emmerich, proclaimed Blessed in 2004 by St. John Paul II.

Fr. Laurentin had thought about this for years and desired to set to work on it. Due to his advancing blindness, he sought a suitable partner to help him in this endeavor. Providence eventually led him to François-Michel Debroise, a lay political sociologist and economist and former member of the radical Left, who had his entire life sung the Communist anthem "The Internationale" with a closed fist. He then scandalized his companions when he ended up discovering an ardent and active faith, thanks to pilgrimages to Marian sites and to his personal reading of the same mystical literature that Fr. Laurentin wanted to investigate. Theirs was a fortunate encounter, as can be seen in the book that sprang from it: both realists, both believers, though different and complementary in their personal history and religious perspective — Fr. René's more theological; Debroise's more mystical, even though resistant to all visionary temptations, as confirmed by his concrete professional experience.

Let us examine these "holy women" (which they certainly were, if we consider their fervor as believers) whom the priest and the sociologist investigated.

The first author is María de Jesús de Ágreda (1602–1665), a Spanish abbess, honored by many of her contemporaries, not least the king of Spain, though looked on by others with suspicion. The Church declared her venerable just a few years after her death, although her process of beatification is still open (with good prospects for a positive outcome, it is said). She was the author of the celebrated *The Mystical City of God*, eight books on the "secret life" of the Holy Family, on Mary in particular, books supposedly inspired directly by Heaven.

The second woman, already cited in the chapter on Ephesus, is Anne Catherine Emmerich (1774–1824), a German nun chased by Napoleon from her monastery that had been confiscated by force, who became a poor domestic and then was bedridden by countless sufferings, including the stigmata, and who fasted perpetually the last fifteen years of her short life, all offered to Christ in expiation for the salvation of sinners. After a process that lasted more than a century and a half, she was beatified in 2004. Although she wrote nothing herself, the great German literary figure Clemens von Brentano wrote on her behalf. Amazed by her mystical gifts, he left everything and spent the last six years of her life at her bedside, often throughout the night. He took notes and wrote what she said, publishing it in *The Sorrowful Passion of Our Lord Jesus Christ*, which enjoyed (along with the text of Maria of Ágreda) enormous diffusion and inspired the actor and film director Mel Gibson in the production of his *The Passion of the Christ,* which aroused interest and controversy throughout the world.

After a Spaniard and a German, there is an Italian from Caserta, Maria Valtorta (1897–1961), also pinned to her bed of pain for nearly thirty years, offering herself as a victim as well. The Servants of Mary (in whose church in Florence her body lies buried) opened the cause for her beatification in 2002, although, as Laurentin observed, speaking with all due respect, "it seems premature still." In fact, the great work of Valtorta, the five thousand pages in many volumes of *The Poem of the Man-God,* has had extraordinary circulation in many languages and was verbally approved by Pope Pius XII. But immediately after this pontiff's death in 1959, the book was placed on the Index of Forbidden Books, just before that institution was abolished.

The quartet of mystics and visionaries is completed by another Spaniard, Consuelo, the pseudonym of a mother of a family who wanted to remain strictly anonymous and about whom we know only that she died toward the end of the previous century. Six books on the life of Mary are attributed to her.

After these four, Laurentin and his collaborator moved on to the works of three other women and a man (the only among seven women) who have left us only "fragmentary accounts," without claiming completeness, of what the Gospels do not say about Mary.

The first is Theresa Neumann (1898–1962), whose life was similar to that of Emmerich: she received the stigmata and practiced a complete fast as well as complete abstinence from water (her only food was daily Communion), to the point where the Nazi regime did not grant her a ration card during the war. A peculiar confirmation of a mysterious charism! Her cause of beatification is also underway and she has been declared venerable.

Next is Luz Amparo Cuevas, a Spaniard (1931–2012), known throughout the world by devotees for the apparitions she received for over twenty years in the town of El Escorial, near the famous palace of the kings of Spain.

The third person from whom they gathered "fragmentary accounts" on Mary is Rosa (the only name we know, and a pseudonym at that), mother of a family of Italian origin, married to a Frenchman and living in Brittany. She wrote a book of "visions" published several years ago.

Finally, our only male, another Italian name: Domenico. He was a civil servant at the post office in Rome who died in 1973 and who left a work of 1,300 pages, mostly dedicated to Mary.

This is the "catalogue" of authors and works which Laurentin and Debroise pored over for four years, compensating for the blindness of the priest by his intact memory and extraordinary knowledge of the topic, as well as the patient and affectionate help of his lay friend. Their aim was to verify the historical and theological value of those thousands of pages on the Virgin. Both were well aware that revelation transmitted to us through Scripture is one thing, whereas "private revelations" are another, and for this reason the hierarchy generally looks on the latter with suspicion. Believers, however, welcome these private revelations with sometimes premature and excessive favor and interest.

The great Mariologist confided,

> From a historical and also theological point of view, I was eager to know why these sincere people, in perfectly good faith, disinterested, orthodoxly Catholic, some already beatified and others on their way, had felt the impulse to write their "Life of Mary"? Why did they attribute, each in her (or his) own way, so much importance to it? Why did these "lives" present both convergences and differences, some incompatibilities and agreement, harmony and dissonance? Why have these works had in general a great, lasting diffusion? Why have they provoked so much controversy and at times even condemnation, like that of Maria of Agreda by Catholic universities of her time or that of Maria Valtorta by the defunct Holy Office, being put on the Index?

Laurentin and Debroise took into consideration seventy-seven episodes in which Mary was protagonist, examining the convergences and divergences in the accounts of the eight "seers." With great critical candor, ready for anything (here, in effect, the Faith is not under scrutiny, and so the believer's freedom of judgment is unlimited), they were not disturbed by the many initial dissonances that seemed difficult to reconcile. They also encountered numerous points of convergence that are cause for reflection, given that these were points in which the eight were not dependent on each other and went against venerable traditions, beginning with that of the apocryphal works and followed by popular devotion. For example: in many ancient works such as the Protoevangelium of James, which enjoyed great authority, St. Joseph is an old widower with a number of children, while according to Maria of Ágreda, Emmerich, Valtorta, Consuelo, and Neumann, he was between thirty-three and thirty-five years old. The unanimous convergence on the tragic technical aspects of the crucifixion of Jesus is amazing; the "lives" give similar accounts, which would require historical knowledge well beyond that of the authors of these "visions." There are other points in common that give one pause: the wedding at Cana connected to relatives of Mary; Jesus giving the bread and wine of the Last Supper to His Mother as well; the end of her earthly life (at least according to most of them) in Ephesus, against the ancient tradition placing it in Jerusalem; the city of Hierapolis as the place where the Holy Family sojourned in Egypt. And much more.

Let us draw some conclusions. The skeptical reader (and here this is permitted, while still being a practicing and fervent Catholic) will have to admit that in the pages of Laurentin and his assistant there are no desperate escapes or gimmicks for reconciling what seems to be beyond reconciliation. The devout reader who finds spiritual nourishment in these "lives" must acknowledge the spirit of openness and "Catholic" pluralism animating the two scholars. Their study of these works did not equate with reading a fifth Gospel, but with seeking to live the one gospel by entering into the daily reality and the confidences of its protagonists. For many believers, it constitutes a sort of pilgrimage in the steps of Jesus and Mary, mixing with the crowd of disciples in the dust on the roads of Galilee and Judea and in the shadows of the house of Nazareth. One must not forget that the eight authors remain always within orthodoxy, constantly in agreement with what the four Gospels narrate, simply enriching that which remains always the one source of revelation.

The undoubted dissonances among them are never doctrinal, and at any rate, many differences exist even among the four canonical Gospels and have created problems. And for that matter, has not art history depicted Mary, maybe even more than Jesus, in the same manner and yet quite different under the same brush or scalpel of every painter or sculptor throughout the centuries? Is the devotee not free to pray before the image most in harmony with his spirituality?

Some believers (I count myself among them, for what it's worth) love the *brevitas*, the dryness or essentiality of the canonical Gospels that concede nothing to our curiosity. Some have spoken not only of the evangelists' taste for summary, but also of their imperturbability: not one cry of grief during the Passion, not one cry of exultation at the Resurrection.

But other believers have different sensibilities. They love detailed stories, they appreciate anecdotes, and they seek out the chiaroscuro of sentiments, the definition of character. And why not? Is the Christian community not the great net that gathers in all kinds of fish, in the words of Jesus? And did he not say that "there are many rooms in my Father's house"? Does not the Catholic dynamic of the *et-et* give full rights of citizenship to all the baptized, making the Church "the largest zoological garden in the world, where there is and must always be place for every species of animal possible," as someone has said? As long as it remains clear (*repetita iuvant!*) that revelation is one and only one: that which the Church safeguards as it is in Sacred Scripture and Sacred Tradition. The mystics, often saints (Emmerich is Blessed, Maria de Ágreda is Venerable, as is Neumann) can help us to meditate, reflect, and maybe even deepen the meaning of that immutable revelation. Thus, they contribute to adapting the reception of the one gospel to the infinite variety of men willed by a Creator who is the enemy of uniformity. Infinite are the paths of God and many the roads that lead to His Son.

Let no one feel guilty (Laurentin and his collaborator reassure us, and this, it seems, is the ultimate meaning of their analysis) for being attracted to this path of "private visions and revelations," as long as they see its limits and understand it not as a universal path, but rather a personal one.

It is significant that the Church explained clearly at the moment of the beatification of Emmerich that the recognition was given to her exemplary evangelical virtues and to her extraordinary discipleship of Christ. This does not entail the approval of the writings that are attributed to her and on which the Church looks with respect, being entirely sound doctrinally, though without making a pronouncement on them, and much less imposing them on Catholics. The Faith depends on the Gospels, and only on that: all the rest, if it remains within the confines of the creed, can help some to reinforce their faith but cannot be spiritual nourishment for everyone.

CHAPTER 60

Those Two under the Cross

Part 1

Using the unsettling metaphor of the universe, the limitless and continually expanding space of the Internet allows us to find everything. Prayers and pornography, culture and ignorance, courtesy and brutality, information and disinformation, wisdom and idiocy. Not belonging to the latter is a website recently pointed out to me that seeks to construct what it calls "counter-apologetics." Using my three books on the historicity of the Gospels as its starting point (*Jesus Hypothesis, He Suffered under Pontius Pilate?, They Say He Is Risen*), it proposes to demonstrate the opposite — in other words, that the New Testament is historically unreliable.

I do not know the author, but considering his firm grasp of the subject, I would guess that he is one of the many priests (more than a third of the total number throughout the world) that the postconciliar hurricane stole from the priesthood and from the Faith as well. Behind the dense pages of the website, rich in quotes from authors known only to those in this field, there is no amateur. Not the usual quaint self-instructed scholar, bothersome as he shoots off uninformed stupidity, but most likely an old student of Sacred Scripture.

I read with great attention these studies that directly contradict what I wrote, with data that are questionable, certainly, but concrete and without insults or the sarcasm that is common. Showing that the Christian God left His creatures the freedom to accept Him or refuse Him, and thus, both manifests and reveals Himself, I am among those who consider refusal and nonbelief to be physiological, as my readers well know. And I am also among those who never forget that faith is a gift that demands gratitude and whose lack is not always a fault to be imputed, as in the case of so many fellow human beings who do not see the truth in the gospel. In any case, here more than ever, we leave judgment to the One who "searches hearts and minds."

I regret, however, that the author often accuses me (and all other Catholic apologists along with me) of trying to hide certain exegetical problems with embarrassment and discomfort because, incapable of explanation, they would have created problems for us in our attempt to defend the Faith. Yet, the one who wrote the material on this site knows, and admits, that in those three books of mine on Jesus I did not pretend to be comprehensive, but only intended to carry out "soundings," "probings" into the depths of Scripture. I am well aware, in fact, of the unfathomableness of the Gospels and of my own limits too, as a "poacher in the game reserve of the specialists," as I have defined myself at times. I speak of this online "counter-apologetics" in this book on Mary so as to respond to the accusation of voluntary and cunning repression of the facts.

Let us cut to the quick. Our online author claims that those who still take seriously John's account of the scene under Jesus' cross concerning His Mother and "the disciple whom Jesus loved" must be naïve or in bad faith or a victim of apologetic paradigms. The "beloved disciple" was John himself, according to the vast majority of exegetes. This man's intention is to show that the two were not there, and could not have been there, and so the famous words "Woman, behold your son, son behold your mother" were a pious fraud of the author of the fourth Gospel. We know how Catholic spirituality has given great importance to this last testament of Christ on the cross, seeing in the favorite disciple the symbol of all humanity entrusted to Mary. But if these words are an invention, it is clear that the consequences are serious not only for theology but for the very life of faith of the Catholic (and Orthodox) believer.

In reality, whatever the "counter-apologist" suspects, there is no unease to be confessed if, among the soundings I made in the terrain of the Gospels, this episode that only John recalls is not present. If I did not consider it, it was not due to any difficulty I saw in it; on the contrary, it is precisely because I saw none in it. And I am in good company, at any rate, seeing that Ernest Renan, who doubted everything (except himself) in matters of Sacred Scripture, here instead seems open to various possibilities. And another great "secular" critic,

Charles Guignebert, takes care of the matter in just a few lines. The account seems secondary to him. Among Catholics, the old but always authoritative Fr. Ricciotti and Fr. Lagrange do not even open the debate — and not for fear (no difficulty of the texts is overlooked by these paladins "without stain and without fear" among Catholic critics) but for a lack of interlocutors, seeing that even nonbelieving scholars were not available to take up this fight.

As for contemporary exegetes, Blinzler, a leading specialist on the trial and death of Christ, does not debate what seems to him entirely possible and plausible, such as the presence on Calvary of Mary and John. Within the Protestant world, one of the most respected biblical scholars of the twentieth century was the Anglican Charles Harold Dodd, his whole life a professor of the New Testament at Oxford. In his book on the historical tradition of the fourth Gospel, he deals with the matter in just a few words. This "novelty" of John, he declares, must be authentic, given that "it does not offer cause for theological reflection and the various attempts to find profound spiritual meanings there are not convincing." In a footnote, he explains that everything that Catholics and Orthodox have believed they have found in these words from the cross (Mary as a symbol of ancient Israel called to become the Mother of the Christian Church) is nothing other than "meandering interpretations that have no demonstrable connection with Johannine thought." Thus, he concludes that it can be true, though as a minor fact in the narration of events.

But despite the fact that the scene is not in the least central to non-Catholic scholars, and given that our anonymous interlocutor has raised the challenge, accumulating reasons for refuting the historicity of those few, pregnant lines, we accept the provocation and propose our reasons.

We note right away a contradiction. The Anglican Todd does not doubt the truth of the words of Jesus because he does not see in them any symbolic dimensions. If anything, he sees in them the concrete concern to "arrange" matters for His mother, a widow. Yet, along the lines of the Anglican scholar, all the Reformed tradition in the past few centuries holds that Jesus is the firstborn of many siblings, that the "brothers" and "sisters" spoken of in the Gospels are to be understood in the literal sense and not as cousins or, in general, extended relatives. We dedicated a lengthy chapter to this. But if this is the case, why is Jesus so concerned to entrust the woman to John? Were there not other sons and daughters ready to take her into their home, not only out of natural affection but also in obedience to the Mosaic command: "Honor your father and mother"?

Unthinkable, blasphemous in fact, to think that, with other adult offspring, a mother would have to turn for support to others who were not her natural children but only spiritual ones, like John. Not by accident, Catholics and Orthodox who hold that Jesus was the only son of one mother find here pertinent evidence in support of their thesis, which has been the same all throughout tradition. The great Church Fathers of old — Augustine, Jerome, Ambrose — all underlined this entrustment from the cross as additional proof of the one and only pregnancy of Mary. And they see in it, moreover, a confirmation of the death of Joseph before that of Jesus.

Let us consider now the questions to which, according to our "counter-apologist," there would be no possible answers from faith, at least from traditional faith which sustains the correspondence of what the Gospels say with what actually happened. First, could Mary and John have been there, right at the foot of the cross? The response is certainly in the affirmative. The four soldiers in charge of the execution guarded the site to prevent uprisings, possibly by "accomplices" in the crimes, or to deter relatives of the condemned who might try to remove the nails. Josephus narrates that in A.D. 70, among the innumerable crosses surrounding the walls of Jerusalem during the siege, he saw three of his dear friends. Hastening to the Roman authorities, he obtained their liberation: two died shortly after of tetanus, but one was able to survive and recover, despite his wounds. Therefore, a last-minute attempt at liberation was possible, and so it was necessary to guard the condemned with troops.

But that horrible execution had a double purpose: to punish the condemned in the most painful and drawn-out way possible (it could last as long as three days and three nights of agony), but also as a warning to all not to challenge the *lex romana,* with its implacable severity. For good reason the executed were put to death next to the main city gates, where they had maximum visibility. Therefore, as long as the crowds around the cross were peaceful, they were not only tolerated but encouraged, so that the greatest number of subjects possible could behold what happens to delinquents. Thus, I can see no reason why Mary and John could not stand near the dying man.

Turning to another question, what was the Mother of Jesus doing in Jerusalem? And if she was there, why did the Gospels not mention this before the tragic execution? Actually, as a devout Jew, Mary had to be in the Holy City. Luke 2:41 declares, "Now his parents went to Jerusalem every year at the feast of the Passover." That pilgrimage every spring was a religious obligation for every Jew, and even the Mother of Jesus, even as a widow, took part in the caravan of relatives and friends that went up from Galilee to the temple for the great Passover rites. But why do the Gospels not mention earlier her presence in the city? A counter-question: Why should there be such mention? Throughout the entire public life of Jesus, after Cana that is, Mary disappears, and just one fleeting and dramatic nod is made during a preaching tour of her son in Galilee, from which she did not move. Her participation in the life of her Jesus is only interior and thus escapes recording by the Gospel chroniclers. At any rate, did her Son not go about preaching that if one did not have the courage to abandon parents, relatives, and friends, fracturing the family to the point of not participating in the funeral of a father, that person was not worthy of Heaven? It is surprising to find those who ask why, if the woman had been in Jerusalem, she would not have participated in the Last Supper. The intricate Jewish issues regarding female presence at such banquets aside (almost all rabbis prohibited it), Jesus' farewell supper was reserved to His apostles, all men, who were charged with continuing His presence among men.

Therefore, Mary could have been, and certainly was, in the Holy City, even though the Gospels do not declare it. But neither do they say many other things, as the final words attest, written by John as well: "But there are also many other things which Jesus did; were every one of them to be written, I suppose that the world itself could not contain the books that would be written" (John 21:25). In Gospel exegesis, the silence of an event does not count as an argument for its ahistoricity.

Another question of my antagonist: Why is the youngest of the apostles present on Calvary? I respond by saying that it amazes me never to have found in any exegetical text the response suggested by the Gospel itself: John is there because his mother is there. Together with his brother James, he is the son of Zebedee and Salome. She was part of the group of women "who had followed Jesus from Galilee." Luke mentions them as present on Calvary but does not give their names, while Mark does name some of them, as does Matthew. In one, the woman's name is explicitly given, while in the other she is identified as "the mother of the sons of Zebedee." John knew how much his mother loved Jesus, he knew how pained she would be to see the horrible torture, and he knew that the group of women had decided to be there as a last gesture of love. Therefore, he considers it his filial duty to be there with her. And in that group, he also saw the mother of Jesus, to whom he drew close.

Possible responses to several other questions remain to be outlined. The first: Why do the Synoptics, the first three Gospels, mention the women at Calvary and (at least two of the Gospels) give their exact names, but they do not mention the presence of John and Mary?

Then: If all the apostles had fled at the moment of the arrest, how is it that only John dares to appear and in such a visible way, under the gaze of the Sanhedrin present at the execution?

Again: How can it be reconciled with Peter's primacy that, at the moment he was tested, he hid, while the younger apostle gave proof of his greater courage?

We shall need another chapter to do justice to these questions.

CHAPTER 61

THOSE TWO UNDER THE CROSS

PART 2

WE TAKE UP ONCE more our analysis of the verses in John's Gospel on the presence of Mary and the apostle under the cross. This is our response to those who hold that that presence could not have been historical and that the entrustment of His Mother to John by the dying Jesus is a pious fraud, a late manipulation of the text. In this way, the consequences of Mary's spiritual maternity of all men were built upon nothing, consequences derived from a millenary reflection by believers. This is obviously not merely the denial of a secondary, insignificant episode: on the contrary, at stake here is one of the foundations not only of devotion but also of Marian theology.

As I said in the previous chapter, similar to many other researchers, in my three books dedicated to the Jesus of history I did not posit the problem of the historicity of those Johannine verses, not because I feared I was incapable of resolving it but because it did not seem in the least problematic. And I have already mentioned the good company I keep; in fact, even secular-leaning authors and Protestants, though they obviously give a different meaning from the Catholic one to the words of Jesus from the cross, considering them only a "practical" entrustment that is necessary to provide for a widow without other children, they do not consider the presence of the two at Calvary an invention.

We saw, at any rate, that the presence of the relatives and friends near the execution site was not prohibited by Roman law and customs. In this regard, we add another detail we forgot to mention previously. It has been said that, in the wretched condition they were in, those crucified could not speak. This affirmation has been refuted by historians as well as doctors. Ancient historians, in fact, often quote not only the horrible and continuous cries of the wretched hanging there, but recount actual dialogues between the dying men and bystanders. The emperor Theodosius in the late fourth century abolished crucifixion as a punishment, out of respect for the Passion of Christ, and no more official cases were registered in the West. I say "official" because anarchists and Communists often nailed priests, religious, and nuns to the doors of their churches and convents during the Spanish Civil War that began in 1936. Several crucifixions occurred in Italy as well, unfortunately, carried out by "red" partisans on captured fascists during the days following the end of the war in 1945. Those Communists evidently wanted to imitate their Iberian companions. Apparently, too, some similarly terrible actions were performed in the Nazi concentration camps for supposed "scientific" aims, as well as in the horrible camps of the Soviets, Chinese, and Cambodians. In the East, the Muslim world often practiced this inhuman punishment, inflicted for certain crimes by "regular" tribunals. And we know not only from historians of antiquity but also from more recent chroniclers that the condemned man's ability to speak is not physically impeded, at least not until reaching the final stage of exhaustion. Doctors have confirmed that, even in the case (like Jesus') of crucifixion without a "seat" (the piece of wood sticking out that the condemned straddled), the one hanging could articulate words, though with terrible pain as he raised himself for the sake of breathing, pushing off of the one nail that pierced both feet.

Returning in summary to what we said in the preceding chapter: Mary must have been in Jerusalem, as every pious Jew would have, for the obligatory Passover pilgrimage. And there is no problem with the fact that the Synoptics do not record her presence in the city before Golgotha, since this reservation corresponds to their manner of writing. We saw how the presence of John in that place was in some sense obligatory, for the affectionate son he most certainly was. Together with his brother James, John was the son of Zebedee and Salome. And she was part of the group of women "who had followed Jesus from Galilee" and who, according to the Synoptics, were present at the Master's martyrdom. The evangelist, therefore, was present to comfort and assist her.

But let us move on now to new considerations. What was the reason for John's presence? The Synoptics say that after the capture of Jesus, the disciples had all fled out of fear of falling into the hands of the Jewish Sanhedrin and the Roman procurator. How is it possible that only John challenged the hostile powers and faced the dangers and that he appears in full view next to the cross, risking execution as a member of the "subversive band," an accomplice of the supposed Messiah?

But this is a question that does not take into account the fact that he who would become the last evangelist was in an entirely unique situation. In fact, he alone informs us that before being taken to Caiaphas, the High Priest in office, Jesus was brought before Annas. The latter, after having held religious leadership for many years in Israel, now old, had formally passed on the role to his daughter's husband, though he continued to call the shots as a "godfather," similar to a modern mafia boss. In fact, the Jewish sources themselves come down quite hard on this prominent figure, power hungry and avaricious, with little concern for worship of Yahweh. A certain Christian anti-Judaism should take into account the fact that Jews at that time were hostile to the dominant religious caste. The condemnation of Jesus was not requested by the "Jews," but by Israelites who were part of the ruling class despised by the people.

Let us reread the text in John where it is said that the prisoner was conducted to Annas's house: "Simon Peter followed Jesus, and so did another disciple. As this disciple was known to the high priest, he entered the court of the high priest along with Jesus, while Peter stood outside at the door. So the other disciple, who was known to the high priest, went out and spoke to the maid who kept the door, and brought Peter in" (18:15–16).

I examined this episode in minute detail in my book *He Suffered under Pontius Pilate?* and refer those wishing to investigate it to that work. Here I shall only report what is strictly necessary, beginning with the fact that, according to many "adult" biblical scholars, we find here ridiculous, inadmissible boasting, invented by the evangelist. They exclaim that there could no be plausibility in that phrase "the disciple known to the high priest," repeated twice no less! A young, obscure fisherman from Galilee on familiar terms with the most powerful Jew in Israel!

Well, as happens elsewhere, these hypercritical specialists display here too the superficiality of their acquaintance with the Semitic language. In Semitic languages, when a person is identified, his relatives and even slaves and servants are included as well. This is true above all in a case like this one, dealing with influential and renowned people. By saying "High Priest," therefore, his entire house is intended, with all those who live with and for him, including that door girl the evangelist mentions, who allows Peter into the courtyard. We obviously do not know how John came to know her, but a credible hypothesis is that she was from his hometown. And her Galilean origins (perhaps, like many others, attracted by the possibility of working in the capital) would explain why she did not overlook the fact that John followed the prophet who was from their homeland. Few consider the implications of verse 17: "Are not you also one of this man's disciples?" Why that "you also," if the girl had ignored John's situation, to whom she need ask nothing?

In *He Suffered under Pontius Pilate?* I advanced this hypothesis for explaining the personal acquaintance. But there could be other possibilities, like the one that starts with the observation that Zebedee and his sons were owners of a fishing business that supplied Jerusalem, like all the fishermen on Lake Tiberias. The Dead Sea is nearer the city, but as we know, it is called dead because the salinity of the water renders it sterile, lifeless. Thus, in the capital of Israel, the supply of fish was assured by the Sea of Galilee. Perhaps as supplier of that house, John made the acquaintance of the servants and in particular the door girl to whom he delivered fish for the kitchen. I did not speak of this hypothesis in my investigation of the Passion nor of another interesting hypothesis, also probable, held by a series of scholars. John's mother, Salome, according to some ancient authors and some modern biblical scholars, could be the sister of Mary, the mother of Jesus. Such that he and John were cousins, though as it seems, separated by age, given that the disciple would have been about eighteen to twenty years old. So Mary and also Salome were relatives of Elizabeth, the wife of Zechariah who was of priestly lineage and participated regularly when it was his turn, in the rites in the temple of Jerusalem. Therefore, the elderly Annas must have known Zechariah well and probably his family too, his wife in particular. This raises the possibility that the relationship of John with the house of the "godfather," still the High Priest behind the scenes, was not one of servitude but of much higher status. Might this be the cause for the fact that the "beloved disciple" — and not Peter and (it would seem) all the other disciples — was not afraid to move freely in Jerusalem and did not hesitate to go to Golgotha under the cross to comfort his mother and to be next to his aunt, Mary? The nocturnal episode in the house of Annas shows how John gets through smoothly, while Peter is certainly not able to do the same and is even led to a triple denial of the Master, with his desperate oath of not knowing him.

And here, the answer to another controversial question of the "counter-apologists" can be found. Why is it that next to the cross was John but not Simon, the one whom Jesus had renamed Peter to show that on that "rock" he would give secure foundation to the Church? Some, including our Internet protestor, even speak of the vanity of the younger disciple, of his desire to show off, as if to prove he was the more faithful one, or even to put himself forward as the leader of a "faction" in contrast with the Petrine one. For this reason, when writing his Gospel, he portrayed himself as the only courageous one under the cross, fearless about showing his face, not like that trembling traitor Simon!

Those who affirm this have not taken into consideration the full situation. First, Peter did not have the connections that John did, as we have just explained, no less in the house of Annas, who, together with his son-in-law Caiaphas, was the one who sought the death penalty. But even more: it is only the fourth Gospel that mentions Peter (and thus recognizes his courage) in telling what happened at Jesus' arrest: "Then Simon Peter, having a sword, drew it and struck the high priest's slave and cut off his right ear. The slave's name was Malchus" (John 18:10). The matter would not be without consequences, seeing that, around the fire in Annas's house, disturbing things would happen: "Now Simon Peter was standing and warming himself. They said to him, 'Are you also one of his disciples?' He denied it and said, 'I am not.' One of the servants of the high priest, a kinsman of the man whose ear Peter had cut off, asked, 'Did I not see you in the garden with him?' Peter again denied it" (18:25–27). The situation was most dangerous. Peter was guilty of what we call "resisting arrest" — armed resistance no less, wounding a servant of the house of the High Priest and potentially killing him. The apostle had aimed his sword at the fellow's head and only just missed splitting his skull: attempted homicide of a man of law who was only exercising his duties. Simon was risking a sentence alongside Jesus on a cross. Furthermore, he was the leader (or deputy) of the band, and his punishment might have served as a warning.

For these reasons, John was able to stand under the cross (protected by his status as a friend, or at least an acquaintance, of the clan of the High Priest), whereas Peter certainly could not have. This was not boasting, but rather the description of an entirely credible event.

Furthermore, reflecting yet again on the Johannine Passion texts, I noticed that no other biblical scholar seems to have lingered on some of the words that are only in that Gospel. We return, then, to Gethsemane, to the arrest scene and the Master's reply to the shouts of those trying to capture him: "'I told you that I am he; so if you seek me, let these men go.' This was to fulfill the word which he had spoken, 'Of those whom thou gavest me I lost not one'" (John 18:8–9). Jesus had made this promise just a few hours earlier at the Last Supper, where John was in a privileged position next to Jesus to hear all the words of his solemn farewell discourse. In fact, it seems he was the only one who remembered it. He showed his radical trust in the One whom he loved and of whom he was the beloved. Would not these words contribute in a decisive way to giving him the certainty that nothing bad could happen to him even if he showed himself openly to their enemies? There remains another question. Why do the Synoptics speak of the presence at Golgotha of some "women who had followed him from Galilee" and Mark and Matthew even give their names, whereas only John says that Mary was there, too? If we look closely, we realize that what the first three Gospels speak of is a compact, well-defined group, almost a sort of confraternity or the feminine equivalent of the college of apostles: that of the Galilean women who had followed His travels, had helped Him with their goods, and who had served Him. Even before the Passion accounts, the Gospels refer to this "category" of which Mary was not a part, having remained habitually in Nazareth, as evidence seems to support. Therefore, there is nothing strange about Mark and Matthew mentioning names but excluding that of the mother. She was a separate case, as demonstrated by the Acts of the Apostles which, giving us an organizational chart of the nascent Church, lists the names of the apostles and adds that they were "together with the women and Mary the mother of Jesus" (1:14). Here too, we see how she is distinct, not part of the group.

The observation of Charles H. Dodd, the Anglican biblical scholar whom we quoted and who is certainly not biased toward Catholicism, is very important: "According to the three Synoptics, the women were not part of the narrative of the crucifixion, but of what followed it." Namely, the taking of the body from the cross, the preparation of the body, the closing of the tomb, and then the accounts of Easter morning. Thus, it seems that to the first three evangelists it did not matter who was on Golgotha, but they simply make passing notice of the presence of the women around the cross for the important role they would carry out when it was all finished. But in those operations Mary did not carry out any role, perhaps because John had begun his mission of assisting her, taking her to some house where she could be alone with her pain. Thus, the evangelists do not consider it important to mention her.

We must also carefully examine the verse in Luke 23:49, "And all his acquaintances and the women who had followed him from Galilee stood at a distance and saw these things." Some women of the "confraternity," as we said. But who are "all his acquaintances" — in Greek *pàntes oi gnostòi*?

I consulted the highly authoritative *Kittel,* as those in the field call the *Great Lexicon of the New Testament.* The entry for *gnostòs* was written by no less than Rudolf Bultmann, the prince of demythologization, who states that "in Luke 23:49 the word *gnostòi,* together with friends, includes relatives as well." But who is more of a relative than the mother who, perhaps, was first "distant" and then was able to approach all the way to the foot of the cross, supported by her nephew John? Therefore, in the Synoptics as well, could there be an acknowledgment, however hidden, of Mary? It seems there is.

That should suffice, although other observations could be possible. But what has been said seems to confirm the calm and reassuring recommendations of Jean Guitton to believers confused by the denials of the historicity of the sources of the Faith: "Take everything seriously but nothing dramatically: do not forget that criticism is possible, but it is also always possible to criticize the criticism, knocking down the many castles of sand that present themselves as solid and therefore threatening."

CHAPTER 62

GLEANING

PART 1

IN THESE LAST TWO chapters I shall put together various notes and reflections, a sort of gleaning in the vast Marian wheatfield. Beginning with this: on several occasions I have recalled the ancient antiphon (eliminated by the questionable postconciliar liturgical reforms) that recites how Mary is "the enemy of all heresies." She continues to carry out this function, which is that of all mothers: to defend her child from those who would do him harm. I have also mentioned the historically inexplicable case of Catholic and Orthodox Christianity, which despite the thousand years of often hostile separation still have essentially the same creed. And under certain conditions, they can share Communion. The schism did not degenerate into heresy, as it did with the Reformation, thanks to the fact that both the faith of the Latins and that of the Greco-Slavs and Eastern Christians in general give a fundamental place to the figure of the *Theotokos*, the Mother of God. The "Morning Star," as their devotion and theology call her, indicates the correct route, to avoid taking errant paths.

I thought of this providential role of Mary while speaking with an Italian missionary in Brazil. As is unfortunately well-known, throughout Latin America, North American sects are spreading rapidly — a sort of "Protestantism gone crazy," where theology is replaced by emotions, obsessive songs, a closed-off group, apocalyptic doctrines, and perhaps the return of Old Testament taboos. For many of these communities (and not only for Jehovah's Witnesses or Seventh-day Adventists) one of the worst sins, practically unatonable, is drinking a glass of wine or lighting a cigarette or doing any sort of work, even intellectual, on Sunday. The wonderful freedom of the Gospel, which distinguished it from every other religious message, does not agree in the least with prescriptions of a Talmudic or even Islamic flavor. My old missionary friend told me that because these sects are quite well off, very active and well-prepared as efficient "schools in community," Latin America no longer has a Catholic majority but has already slid toward these spurious and deformed versions of what arose in Europe with the Reformation. Or at least it would have, had the love and devotion for Mary not gone so deep among Brazilians and, in general, among Latin Americans. When they baptize their children, they choose a relative as their godfather, but as godmother they name "Our Lady," and there's always a struggle to convince them they need to choose a woman still on earth and not already in Heaven.

The fanatics arriving from the United States, loaded with cash from their sponsors, fail to take into account this attachment and, as bitter enemies of all Catholic devotions (which they consider manifestations of the antichrist), in the early period they went so far as to destroy statues of Mary in public. Some even preached that she is in Hell because of her pride in having such a Son. But they soon realized the horror that these gestures and theories provoked among their South American listeners, and so they have become much more prudent. Now the tactic is not to talk about her, but to wrap her up in silence. And only when the candidate has entered the sect, when he has received the "true baptism" (not the diabolic one of Catholics), when the North American directors think they can trust the loyalty of the initiated, they show their cards and instill hatred for the Marian superstition. But even then, my priest friend told me, many draw back frightened and repudiate their newfound faith, despite the threats from leaders of these cults, and return to their parish priest, asking if they can pray as always before a statue of the Brazilian *Aparecida,* or the *Morenita* of Guadalupe, or any of the many Virgin Marys that accompanied the ancient Spanish and Portuguese colonization. Is Mary not, then, the "enemy of all heresies"?

But she is also the enemy, in another way that seems little explored, although it lies within Catholicism. In fact, in today's Church, respect for obedience seems to raise more problems and to be (perhaps) less practiced even than respect for the promise or vow of sexual continence. Many laws, precepts, and exhortations of the hierarchy and the pope himself are not observed by priests, friars, and religious, and the rejection of obedience is justified as "a right to personal autonomy." Even in religious orders where, besides poverty and chastity, one takes the vow of obedience as well, the authority of superiors quite often seems diminished by new ideologies that are more or less "libertine."

Well, Mary is the "Woman of the yes" par excellence. Ready to bow her head and obey the voice of Heaven that came to her through the archangel, she even obeys the shocking request (incomprehensible to her humility) to become the mother of the Messiah. In the words of Luke, "And Mary said, 'Behold, I am the handmaid of the Lord; let it be to me according to your word.'" Therefore, looking to her, cultivating devotion to her, and desiring to imitate her implies, as it always has, believing her to be the "Lady of Obedience," with important effects in the life of the individual, the community, and the entire Church.

But was not the Virgin of Nazareth always the one to whom hermits, anchorites, and cloistered nuns looked? Has she not also been the "Lady of Silence," in the years of which the Gospels say nothing because there was nothing to say about a life retired and hidden? Behold, the perspective of Luther in the words of Hartmann Grisar, one of his renowned biographers: "Retreat, examination of conscience, solitude, desert, were to him things accursed, works of the devil. Silence and being alone, he warned, can provoke the worst thoughts." Once more, the example of Mary can be the star that points the way, even by night, for avoiding heretical pitfalls.

I happened to return to the article from *Le Monde* of May 2000, when John Paul II revealed to the world what they call the "third secret" of Fatima. The piece in the French newspaper was written by Jean Cardonnel, a Dominican friar who died a few years ago and who was a lifelong, intractable leader of every clerical or political protest, one of the inconsolable widowers of the violent years of protest in the Church and Western society. To him, not only the usual Mao, Che Guevara, and Ho Chi Minh, but also the exterminator of the Cambodian people, Pol Pot, were to be venerated on the Olympus of sacred revolutions. Cardonnel is notorious for an innovative and dangerous juridical precedent. He was already quite old, going on ninety and unbearable to most of his confreres due to his obsession with protest and his cult of the a priori "no," but he continued to reside in the Dominican monastery in Montpellier.

In the end, the superior of that religious house could put up with his distemper no longer and took advantage of one of Cardonnel's journeys to empty out his cell, carefully pack his belongings, and find a place for him in a retirement home. Upon his return, Cardonnel's ire (like every self-respecting "adult" priest, he refused to be called "Father") exploded loudly; though he claimed he was a victim of intolerable violence, he did not avail himself of the law of the Church, canon law. Instead, he turned to the law of the secular French Republic, calling the police and denouncing his superior for the violation of his domicile. After a long controversy, the court sided with him and condemned the superior of the monastery who had carried out the vacating of his cell. Thus, for the first and not only time in France, a civil court had declared the cell of a religious to be a private habitation like any common accommodation. A partisan and dangerous decision, as I said, because it overrides and in some ways handcuffs ecclesiastical authority even within its own space.

But let us return to Cardonnel commenting on Fatima. He wrote in *Le Monde*,

> That supposed "secret" is a fake, as fake as the Constantinian donation by which a diabolical oxymoron was legitimized: a Christian empire. A great Italian theologian — don't forget his name: Enzo Bianchi, founder of a new monastic community — immediately realized that the Vatican had perpetrated superstition and fraud in Fatima. In the Roman daily *La Repubblica*, Brother Bianchi places his finger implacably in the wound. He wrote, "A God who, since 1917, thinks about revealing that Christians will be persecuted but does not talk about the Shoah and the six million Jews annihilated is not a credible God."

Cardonnel's article continues, "Yes, we must uncover the wound. How can one not see the blemish of the supposed secret of Fatima, the glaring proof that it is false, that it cannot have come from God? A fake that disqualifies and discredits the Eternal. A God, I repeat, who is not credible: the God of Catholic racism interested only in its own, in the Catholic race, to the oblivion of the people of Jesus."

There is much in this discussion that surprises us — especially, for us Italian Catholics, in the quote (not denied, but rather reaffirmed, by the interested party) by Br. Bianchi. A conviction has been circulating among some

Christians that sees the persecution of the Jews by the Nazis during the twelve years from 1933 to 1945 as supposedly, without any possible comparison, Absolute Evil, the Most Heinous Crime of all history, the Radical Example of human wickedness. Not incidentally, Nazi guilt is considered unredeemable, and still today they chase down to bring to trial and condemnation ninety- and one-hundred-year-olds considered in some way responsible for what is called, with a religious term, the "Holocaust" par excellence. For such a crime, and only for it, there is no statute of limitations. According to Cardonnel and Bianchi, God himself *must* first remember and obviously curse the Shoah if he wants to speak through Mary; otherwise, He is not a "credible" God. He is not truly the Lord if He does not explicitly execrate Auschwitz.

Let it be clear: we are not trying to diminish the gravity of the crime perpetrated under the shadow of the bent Nazi cross, which was the tragic inversion of the Christian cross. We must obviously unite ourselves to the universal condemnation of it. But it is truly paradoxical to see a Christian rejecting Fatima because in 1917 Our Lady did not foresee and condemn, on behalf of her Son and of the entire Trinity, those German concentration camps that were to follow twenty years later. In 1917, we repeat: the exact year in which Lenin took power, unleashing his Communist monster that would cause at least one hundred million deaths and would carry out the most violent and bloody religious repression in history, in the name of a state atheism proclaimed in the very constitutions of the Soviet Union and its satellites. Recent historical research, led by the famous German professor Ernst Nolte, shows with documentation that National Socialism arose as a reaction to Marxist-Leninism: without Lenin in 1917, there would have been no Hitler in 1933. Without the coup d'etat in St. Petersburg, the former dauber of Vienna would at most have become an ideologue for some obscure fanatical group, holding forth in some *Stube* in Munich. Fatima's warning about Communism, right when it was coming into its own, meant warning the world of other deadly ideologies that were to follow as a reaction to it, Nazism first of all.

Furthermore, Bianchi and Cardonnel are incomprehensible when they denounce the idea that at Fatima, "the God of Catholic racism" supposedly manifested Himself, "only interested in His own, in His Catholic race." Where is the logic to this? For Soviet atheism, nothing in the religious world was off-limits. Besides the fact that the vast majority of the victims, from Lenin through Stalin to Gorbachev (he too was a persecutor in his youth), were not Catholic but rather Orthodox, the two forget that all religions were present in the immense Soviet Union. Thus, Orthodox priests were massacred alongside Catholic priests, Jewish rabbis, Muslim imams, and Buddhist gurus.

The same thing occurred around the world wherever Communism came to power: no escape for anyone who did not accept materialism and refused to condemn religion as the "opium of the people." And this began precisely during the fatal year, 1917, when the Virgin Mary sounded the alarm about the perverse ideology, for it presented itself with a noble face, almost evangelical (justice, liberation, equality, fraternity), but it set about awaking all the devils, including that German regime that presented itself in its very name as the union of nationalism and socialism.

The apparitions of Fatima, like all the others that have been officially recognized, are not *de fide*: they can be criticized and even not accepted by the faithful. But one should do so on grounds more presentable than these.

Speaking of Fatima and Communism, we should recall what took place in Vienna during the decade between 1945 and 1955. While the English, expert and pragmatic, wanted to contain the USSR to the east, American ignorance halted its tanks within sight of Berlin to allow Stalin to steamroll through Eastern Europe, occupying Austria as well. The country was divided into four zones, following the German model, though the Russian zone, where the capital lies, was the largest and most important. The foreign minister Molotov, who had signed the treaty with Hitler, allowing him to unleash the war, said repeatedly that Moscow would never retreat from the lands it had occupied, and everyone waited for the Communists to organize a coup d'etat to take sole control of all Austria, as had happened in Prague and Budapest. Western diplomats seemed resigned to this fate. To oppose it would almost certainly have meant starting another war. But one Franciscan did not resign himself: Fr. Petrus, who, returning from prison in the USSR (and thus knowing firsthand the horrors of that regime), went on pilgrimage to the Austrian national shrine in Mariazell to ask inspiration regarding what his homeland should do. There he was surprised by an interior voice, a locution, that told him, "Pray the Rosary every day, all of you, and you will be saved." A good organizer, as well as an esteemed priest, Fr. Petrus promised a "National Rosary Crusade" in the explicit spirit of Fatima, and in a short time gathered the support of millions of Austrians, including the president of the republic, Leopold Figl. Day and night, large groups gathered, often in the open, in the cities and in the countryside, reciting the Rosary, and even Vienna saw impressive Marian processions in the streets, watched with hostility by the Red Army.

The years passed and the occupation did not come to an end, but the people never tired of praying to Our Lady of Fatima. Then, suddenly, in 1955 the Austrian chancellor was called to Moscow and received in the Supreme Soviet in the Kremlin. There it was communicated that the USSR had decided to withdraw its troops and give Austria full independence. In exchange, they set one condition that the Austrian authorities gladly accepted: a commitment to neutrality, which would be very advantageous to Vienna, creating there a third hub of the United Nations, after New York and Geneva. Western governments were taken by surprise by this entirely unexpected decision, unique in all the Cold War. Never, as Molotov had reminded them ten years earlier, had the USSR agreed spontaneously to withdraw from an occupied nation.

Politicians, diplomats, and military officers around the world were stunned—but not those who had been praying with the "Rosary Crusade" for years. In fact, the day Moscow announced the news of the withdrawal to the chancellor was May 13, the anniversary of the beginning of the apparitions in Fatima. To complete the picture, the total removal of what remained of the Red Army was set by the Communist government for October. Among the Russian generals (displeased to be leaving such a beautiful and strategically important country), no one, obviously, suspected that October, dating back in the Catholic tradition to the Battle of Lepanto, was the month of the Rosary.

I discovered that I jotted down a "Marian" note while reading the famous novel by Umberto Eco, *The Name of the Rose*. Eco was a fervent Catholic in his youth, and the national director of Catholic Action. He had even written his thesis on St. Thomas Aquinas, before, however, becoming one of the leading figures in the camp of liberal agnostics and atheists. Recently, in an interview for a German newspaper, Eco called Benedict XVI "a mediocre theologian." Catholic media rose up in arms, asking indignantly how he could dare give such a judgment, someone who is not even a theologian but only a professor of semiology and a writer of novels, albeit masquerading his essays as literature.

This was a weak response because it was entirely unjustified. Eco actually knew his theology, but he read it according to his own interpretation, according to the categories of the "apostate" believer he said he was. It was therefore obvious that he did not comprehend his fellow university professor Joseph Ratzinger.

But let us stay on target and quote the passage from one of his characters in *The Name of the Rose*: "In the glory of heaven, no man (no one who is only a man) shall be king in that eternal Homeland, while one woman shall be queen (one who is only a woman and whom they call Mary). Who then would dare to say that men exceed women? That will not be the case in blessed eternity." We dedicate this with a smile to those men and women who still stubbornly say that Catholicism reserves to women only a subordinate role.

CHAPTER 63

GLEANING

PART 2

WE CONTINUE AND DRAW to a close our fruitful gleaning in the field of Mary. I found a file on which I wrote down, I know not when, a phrase of St. Paul from the First Letter to the Corinthians: "There is one glory of the sun, and another glory of the moon" (15:41). I wonder if it is legitimate to suspect that Paul is making here a discreet reference to Mary, based on an enigmatic and perhaps unconscious intuition. As we know, from the beginning the Christian tradition has compared the Virgin Mary to the moon, and innumerable paintings and statues show her standing on a crescent moon. This symbol has nothing to do with the Islamic crescent moon, adopted only after the taking of Constantinople and derived from a pagan iconographer, something that enrages many fundamentalist Muslims who would have it removed from the flag of Islamic nations. In fact, Saudi Arabia, the guarantor of Sunnite orthodoxy and custodian of Mecca and the other sacred sites, has never adopted it.

The moon is not a star, but only a satellite that does not have its own light. The blazing star is the Son, not the Mother, who only reflects its rays. If the sun's light did not strike it, it would not exist for us but would be invisible. And more: just as the lunar influence works, so too does Mary's influence work, symbolically. It is a powerful influence and yet hidden and mysterious. The moon provokes day and night the incessant rise and fall of the tides, but does so with such discreet force that even Galileo had not yet intuited it and thought that their periodic movement was determined by the "emptying" of the earth as it spins on its axis. The influence of the moon determines what astronomers call the "nutation of the terrestrial axis" and the so-called "precession of the equinoxes." Additionally, I saw in the recent text of a specialist: "The moon produces less evident effects as well, on the climate and on animal and vegetable life, that have not yet been determined by scientists." Science has some surprises in store for us here.

Just as it has taken much time to discover the function of the moon, so too did it take centuries to discover those truths about Mary that the Church has enfolded, so far, in four dogmas. I say "so far" because, as we just heard, there are things we do not yet know about the moon and maybe also about her whose icon it is. The "glory of the sun," to use St. Paul's phrase, is evident to all, but the glory of our satellite is not. Besides the cycle of the tides, consider that other extraordinary cycle: the female menstrual cycle, connected as well to the power of the moon, whose times it respects, and mysterious in its direct connection to life. But here too, this intimate intervention in the bodies of billions of people (and animals) of the female sex is carried out discreetly, in secret even. Power and hiddenness — the chiaroscuro — as displayed in the reserve women have in speaking of that cycle which in former times could not even be explicitly named.

These are only notes, in need of deeper investigation; here we have only sought to mention the possible discoveries (symbolic, obviously) one might make looking into the Mary-moon relationship which the tradition was quick to understand and maybe even St. Paul intuited.

Staying with St. Paul, a well-known Protestant objection (now coopted with the usual delay of centuries by some in the Catholic intelligentsia who mistake the past for the cutting edge) states that in the epistles as well as in the many words attributed to him in Acts, the Apostle of the Gentiles never mentions Mary by name. It is supposedly a confirmation that she was not considered important by the nascent Church and that everything that has been constructed around her is only a late and illegitimate excrescence. Once more, Mariology as a "cancer of Catholicism that must be eradicated."

Does Paul really not mention Mary by name? First, no one ever observes, as far as I know, that when the great convert wrote his first epistles the Mother of Jesus could still have been among the living, at an age of around seventy or a little more, not at all rare even in ancient Israel, where

Psalm 90 reminds us: "The years of our life are threescore and ten, or even by reason of strength fourscore."

It is deceptive to think that few reached old age back then. Statistics take into account an extremely high infant mortality rate, which obviously drastically reduced life expectancy. In reality, it was probably due to this implacable natural selection, which cut short the life of the weaker ones, that the survivors were stronger and had more or less our same life expectancy. When Jesus was born, Mary was quite young, as was the norm at the time, perhaps around fifteen. St. Paul wrote his first letters around A.D. 60. For women especially (then as today, with greater longevity) to be still alive at that age was not the norm, yet was also not exceptional. As we see in the words of the psalmist…

The Church has never taken a position on this matter. It formalized the dogma of the Assumption into Heaven, though without clarifying when it happened, obviously. Nor did it establish where the event took place, as we have seen, whether in Jerusalem or in Ephesus, in the house of John. At any rate, if Mary had still been an active member of the Church Militant, still alive, her veneration, or even the beginnings of a theology around her person, would have been entirely unthinkable. This might also be the cause of Paul's silence about her — an apparent silence, as we shall see.

But let us presume that when Saul founded his communities, the Mother of Jesus had already been received into Heaven body and soul by her Son. And let it be noticed that the apostle does not really talk about a lot of things. The miracles of Christ, for example, he does not in the least mention, concentrating all his attention on *the* Miracle on which everything is founded: the Resurrection. In general, Paul does not seem interested in the earthly life of the Messiah, adding nothing to what we already know from the Gospels, with the sole exception of the Lord's words Paul quotes at Miletus to the elders of Ephesus: "Remembering the words of the Lord Jesus, how he said, 'It is more blessed to give than to receive.' " This is the only saying that Paul hands down that is not contained in the Gospels.

Furthermore, he explains the reason for this relative disinterest of his: "Even though we once regarded Christ from a human point of view, we regard him thus no longer" (2 Cor. 5:16). If, however, the apostle does not mention the Virgin by name, he recalls her function, and this is what really counts. In the Letter to the Galatians we read, "But when the time had fully come, God sent forth his Son, born of woman" (4:4). It seems a simple aside, but instead, according to one of the leading professors of Mariology, the German Georg Soell, who recently passed away, "From the dogmatic point of view, this is the most important text on the Ever-Virgin Mother in the New Testament. Here, in fact, Mariology attaches directly to Christology through the declaration of her maternity." Professor Soell sees here the clear premises of the fundamental Marian dogma which after four centuries was proclaimed in Ephesus: the divine maternity. The theologian says, "There is a cogent logic here: 1) In the fullness of times, the Son of God was sent by the Father into the world; 2) His entrance into the world occurred through the womb of a woman; 3) This woman, therefore, in the divine plan is not only Mother of Jesus, but also the mother of Christ God."

Not exactly Pauline silence, as those affirm who claim they base their beliefs on Scripture alone! But there is more that must not be overlooked: Paul does not say, "Mary," but speaks of "woman." But he must have known very well her name, not only as a member of the nascent Church but also because, in the Letters to Philemon and to the Colossians, the apostle speaks as a "collaborator" of Luke the evangelist, who was quite close to the Virgin Mary and had received information that only his Gospel reports. But Paul does not give the name of the "woman," because what counts is not so much her, not her personal story after giving birth. What counts is her role in God's plan. Even the Gospels do not tell Mary's story, but only recall her presence during key moments in the story of her Son: the Annunciation, His birth, the Epiphany, the beginning of His public life, His Passion and death, and the birth of the Church. It is only logical that the apostle does not give her historical name but rather recalls the task of that "woman" in the history of salvation.

In fact, those who wish to demythologize the role have not understood that, in her, it is not so much the historical individual that is of interest but rather the "theological type," her mysterious yet clear function. Some Christians count precisely how many words are dedicated to her in the New Testament and, given how few there are, deduce that neither should we say much about her. But this means forgetting that neither the Gospels nor Paul have the intention of presenting us a biography of a young maiden form Nazareth: they are interested in the Virgin Mother who could have been called something else and could have come from a different family, because what is important is that God decided to send us His Son not by having him descend from Heaven but by passing through a woman's body. She was chosen, and to her alone was given the privilege of an advance on the redemption (the Immaculate Conception), but beyond what she obtains directly in that redemption, it is not her daily affairs that are important to the Faith. In fact, after the mention made in the Acts of the Apostles of her presence at Pentecost, silence falls upon her, and no other mention is made in the New Testament of the years that separated her from the new, definitive encounter with the Son at the end of her earthly life. Therefore, to give to that "woman" the place she deserves does not mean elevating a human being illegitimately, transforming the historical Mary into a sort of goddess. Rather, it means giving space, along with her, to what in her, *ab aeterno*, God Himself wanted for His Son.

I found some notes of one of many conversations with the "usual suspect," René Laurentin. "You see," he told me,

> I have frequented on many occasions catechism for the children in French parishes today. It is almost always taught by men and young women of good will but quite often with insufficient knowledge (to use a euphemism) of the authentic perspective of the Faith in its entirety. These excellent people are saturated by the surrounding culture, and therefore also by the constant concern to appear at all costs "democratic." For this reason, speaking about Mary, they are reluctant to use the terms of French tradition such as *Notre Dame* or the *Sainte Vierge*, but speak of her always and only as the "mama of Jesus" or "the wife of Joseph." Above all, it seems they were never taught to say that she is also the Mother of God, the Ever-Virgin, the Immaculate, the Assumption. Things that are not only difficult to take seriously in a culture saturated by secularism, but which seem especially "privileges" that are at odds with the fitting equality of each and everyone. But no! Jesus has a mother and a father like the children who are listening to the catechist, a family like all others, a family where they love each other and behave properly. Mary is a good person, just like everyone else. If not, where would modern democracy end up, founded as it is above all on a sacred *égalité* which the Great Revolution obtained for everyone?

About the Author

After obtaining his degree in political science in Turin, Vittorio Messori worked as a journalist for *La Stampa, Avvenire,* and *Famiglia Cristiana* and as a columnist for *Corriere della Sera.* His twenty-four books on religious themes have been translated around the world. He was the first to write a book with John Paul II (*Crossing the Threshold of Hope*) and with Joseph Cardinal Ratzinger (*The Ratzinger Report*), who later became Pope Benedict XVI. Among his many recognitions are two Bancarella Awards and the International Award of Catholic Culture. Messori also wrote *A Wager on Death, Some Reasons for Belief* (with Michele Brambilla), and the great trilogy on the historical truth of Jesus of Nazareth: *Hypotheses about Jesus, He Suffered under Pontius Pilate?,* and *They Say He Is Risen.*

Sophia Institute

Sophia Institute is a nonprofit institution that seeks to nurture the spiritual, moral, and cultural life of souls and to spread the gospel of Christ in conformity with the authentic teachings of the Roman Catholic Church.

Sophia Institute Press fulfills this mission by offering translations, reprints, and new publications that afford readers a rich source of the enduring wisdom of mankind.

Sophia Institute also operates the popular online resource CatholicExchange.com. *Catholic Exchange* provides world news from a Catholic perspective as well as daily devotionals and articles that will help readers to grow in holiness and live a life consistent with the teachings of the Church.

In 2013, Sophia Institute launched Sophia Institute for Teachers to renew and rebuild Catholic culture through service to Catholic education. With the goal of nurturing the spiritual, moral, and cultural life of souls, and an abiding respect for the role and work of teachers, we strive to provide materials and programs that are at once enlightening to the mind and ennobling to the heart; faithful and complete, as well as useful and practical.

Sophia Institute gratefully recognizes the Solidarity Association for preserving and encouraging the growth of our apostolate over the course of many years. Without their generous and timely support, this book would not be in your hands.

www.SophiaInstitute.com
www.CatholicExchange.com
www.SophiaTeachers.org